The Sunday Telegraph

GOOD WINE GUIDE

1996

𝕿𝖍𝖊 𝕾𝖚𝖓𝖉𝖆𝖞 𝕿𝖊𝖑𝖊𝖌𝖗𝖆𝖕𝖍

GOOD

WINE

Guide

1996

ROBERT JOSEPH

MACMILLAN

Editor: Robert Joseph
Senior Editorial Assistant: Justin Howard-Sneyd
Editorial Assistants: Simon Clarke, Lucy Faulkner, Sarah Groves
Editorial Production/Coordination: Sheila Keating
Author Photograph: Patrick Mark

Published in Great Britain 1995
by *The Sunday Telegraph*
1 Canada Square, Canary Wharf
London E14 5DT
in association with Macmillan Reference Books,
a division of Macmillan Publishers Ltd, 25 Eccleston Place, London
SW1W 9NF and Basingstoke.

First edition published 1983

ISBN 0 333 638271

Designed by Peter Ward,
John Gowers and Paul Elmes
Typeset by RJ Publishing Services
Film produced by MPA Fingal
Printed and bound in Great Britain by
BPC Hazell Books Ltd
A member of
The British Printing Company Ltd.

CONTENTS

ACKNOWLEDGEMENTS

Winemakers and the editors of annual guides like this have one thing in common. Every year, for two months or so, harvest and publishing schedules, respectively, monopolise their lives.

Of course, much of the work has been done during the preceding 12 months – with the pruning shears in the vineyard and, in my case, with glass, notepad and spittoon at countless tastings throughout the world. But, ultimately, for a book like this to be up-to-date and accurate, most of the effort has to be made during the weeks before the press is set to work.

Just as winemakers rarely work completely alone, I could not have begun to produce this year's *Guide* without the dedicated effort of Justin Howard-Sneyd, Lucy Faulkner and Simon Clarke all of whom gave up normal existence for the sake of the book.

The final editing was, once again, the responsibility of Sheila Keating who patiently ironed out the wrinkles and inconsistencies, despite the efforts of various pieces of high tech equipment to foil us all. Francis Jago of MPA Fingal again converted the computer disks into film, while Judith Hannam of Macmillan Reference Books oversaw a journey from manuscript to bookshop more speedy than that of many a royal kiss-'n-tell.

Mark Hughes Morgan, who, after two years, ceased to be my editor at the Sunday Telegraph just before the *Guide* went to press, was as indulgent as ever, as were my colleagues at *WINE* and *Wine & Spirit* magazines – Casilda Grigg, Jonathan Goodall Peter Tromans, Barbara Cormie and Damian Riley Smith – and my partner at Vintage to Vintage Video, Paddy Mark.

I owe a special debt of thanks to Charles Metcalfe and Kathryn McWhirter for their advice on matching food and wine; their book on the subject is published this year by Sainsbury's and deserves a space on every food and wine lover's shelves.

As ever, I should also like to thank, for their various forms of help and support, Marilyn Warnick of Telegraph Books, Piers Russell-Cobb, Clare Anderson and John Clay, and for their patience, Tim and Liam White and Sue Pike. Similarly, I am of course indebted to the wine merchants of this country and winemakers worldwide without whose help and information, the writing of this book would never have been possible.

Finally, there is one person whose efforts were absolutely indispensable. Sarah Groves, my assistant, chief nappy-changer and all-round minder.

All of these people share any credit for this *Guide*. Any blame falls on my shoulders alone.

INTRODUCTION

This is not the only wine guide to be published this year. Since the first edition of the Sunday Telegraph Good Wine Guide appeared way back in 1983, a growing number of publishers and writers have paid it the compliment of producing comparable books, each of which aims to be an essential handbook for the wine drinker. So why buy this guide rather than one of the others?

Well, everything depends on the kind of person you are. If you are such a committed supermarket shopper that you never stray beyond your local supermarket and are happy to be led by the nose through its aisles from one $^{15}/_{20}$ wine to the next; if you have never wondered about the comparative attractions of Thresher, Oddbins, Victoria Wine and Majestic; if you have never been tempted to buy wine from a traditional merchant, to join a wine club or order a case by mail; if you are never sufficiently curious to want to know what the words on a label mean, or which vintage to look for, or what to eat with a particular wine, or how it is likely to taste...

If you are the person I have described above, one of the other guides should suffice. If, on the other hand, you believe that wine is like food and that it is the variety of flavours and styles that makes it interesting and if you like to shop around for great flavours and great value – whatever the price, then this *Guide* is for you.

Over the next 270 or so pages, you will find a controversial introductory review of the last year in the wine world, a section aimed at helping you to find the best glasses, corkscrews, wine courses and wine clubs, followed by appraisals of over 170 merchants ranging from Kwiksave to Justerini & Brooks, from the biggest merchants to the one-man-band operations, together with representative selections of their wines.

Finally there is a 2000-entry encyclopedia covering almost all of the wines and terms you are likely to encounter or read about, from the humblest Vin de Pays to the grandest Grand Cru and Newest Wave superstar. And for the majority of those wines, regions and grapes, there are recommended wines to give you the chance to discover what they taste like for yourself.

The result hopefully makes for a comprehensive, quirky and unashamedly personal *Guide*. I hope you enjoy it.

Robert Joseph, July 1995

HOW TO USE THIS BOOK

Over the years, as the *Guide* has evolved, it has become more comprehensive, more accurate and, hopefully, simpler to use. Two years ago, there were just 500 recommended wines; with this edition there are over three times as many – each accompanied by a brief description to give you an idea of how it tastes. Despite maintaining the pocket book format, there are still reviews of some 175 merchants, as well as a comprehensive encyclopedia covering just about every word you are likely to encounter on a label, or in this or any other wine book. To help you to use it easily, the *Guide* has been divided into six main sections:

THE WINE WORLD

In this section, I review the last 12 months both in Britain and throughout the world, and make a few predictions about the future of the wine world.

THE GRAPEVINE

This is the place to look for all those useful telephone numbers – for suppliers of corkscrews and information on wine cellars, courses, holidays and clubs, auction houses and specialist fine and rare merchants. This is also the section where I take a look at the question of wine and health and of the validity of buying wines in Calais.

THE MERCHANTS' CODES

The key to much of the rest of the *Guide*, these pages list the space-saving codes by which the 175 merchants are routinely referred in the other sections.

A PERSONAL SELECTION

If you are looking for bargains, there are plenty recommended throughout the Guide. Here, though, I have picked out a few personal favourites in various styles and prices.

THE MERCHANTS

From the biggest supermarket chains to the tiniest independent merchants – this is where to find them, their addresses, a profile of their style and a list of recommended wines rated for their value-for-money from *** (good value) to ***** (great value).

THE A-Z

The core of the *Guide*: a fully updated encyclopedia of wines, grapes, producers, regions and terms, which is unique in that, not only does it provide definitions and descriptions, but it also recommends over 1200 wines, graded from *** to ***** according to their value for money.

THIS YEAR

Three weeks after I sent last year's *Guide* to the printers and started work on this, the 1996 edition, the Italian delicatessen across the road closed. Last week, the butcher four doors along finally gave up the struggle; I wouldn't want to give odds on the off-licence surviving another six months. After all, he not only has to compete with the superstores who sell wine for less than he pays for it; he's also up against the growing wave of wine and beer that washes onto UK shores with every tide. It won't take many more VAT and Business Rate final demands to close his doors too.

It is a pattern reflected in letters I have had from dozens of independent wine merchants throughout the country who've sold up or taken early retirement over the last 12 months. Far more depressing, though, was the conversation I had with the manager of a branch of Bottoms Up which had recently opened in Grantham, birthplace of Lady Thatcher. 'Our problem, you see' I was told 'is that people don't know we belong to Thresher and they expect us to go bust in a year or so like all the other independent shops in the town. It's only when we tell them that we're part of Whitbreads that they feel confident enough to shop with us'.

So, if you're not a brewery or a multinational distillers and you fancy starting a small business selling good wine in 1996, think twice before opening up in Thatcherland – or just about anywhere else in Britain, for that matter.

Of course, you don't have to start your business in this country; you can follow the example of Sainsbury, the Wine Society, and – this year – Tesco, and Victoria Wine, and pitch your tent in Calais, attracting British customers with wine at least a pound a bottle cheaper than it would cost at home. And why not? After all, by July 1995, around one in seven of the bottles of wine we drank at home was crossing the Channel duty free – legally or illegally. In other words, we now buy more wine in Calais than in Sainsbury.

MARKET FARCES

Conversely, if you're big enough, and with sufficiently deep pockets – like, say, Somerfield supermarkets – you could simply compete with all those imports by selling wine on this side of the water at £1.39 a bottle – or at what a competitor with an intimate knowledge of the costs of wine, bottles, corks and shipping prosaically calls a 'thumping loss'.

Somerfield's motives are clear: to attract new customers to their stores; as a competitor wrily pointed out, Somerfield's management isn't in the wine business. Unlike Asda, whose new method of setting out its wines probably says more about the wine scene in Britain than anything else. Having watched their customers, Asda have decided that, when buying wine, most of them are only really concerned about three things: its colour, its sweetness or, in the case of a red, its fullness of body and, just as crucially, its price.

So, Asda shoppers are no longer challenged to choose between more than a handful of grape varieties, countries and regions. Wines here are all laid out by basic style and price. So, a £3.99 Frascati will rub shoulders with a similarly dry £3.99 New Zealand Sauvignon and a £3.99 Australian Chardonnay. The implication is clear: when the price of any of these goes up, the bottles will make way for a wine which *can* hit that all-important price point.

FUNNY MONEY

There is only one tiny drawback to this. Britain is not an ideal country in which to sell wine cheaply, thanks to its combination of a greedy Chancellor of the Exchequor and a feeble currency. Let me illustrate.

Buying wine is a little like buying that other highly taxed stuff, petrol. There are two kinds of motorists: the ones who fill their tank every time they visit a service station, grumbling at how much more it seems to cost every year – and the ones who carefully put in ten pounds' worth of unleaded, somehow ignoring the harsh logic of the fact that they get to travel fewer miles between top-ups. British wine drinkers are like those ten poundsworth motorists.

Despite rises in the cost of duty, the fall in the value of the pound and inflation here and elsewhere, the average retail price of a bottle of wine in Britain remains stuck at around three pounds – roughly the level it has been since 1987.

So what are you getting for your money? When you bought your £3.49 bottle of French wine in 1990, approximately £2.54 went towards the costs of duty, VAT, shipping, bottles, corks, labels and cartons and a reasonable margin of profit for the retailer. This left 95 pence which, at the prevailing rate of 9.9 francs to the pound, would have bought 9.38 francs' worth of wine.

Now let's look at 1995. Duty rates have gone up from 83p to £1.05 and VAT (which is cleverly levied on the duty, thus effectively taxing a tax) has risen from 15 to 17.5%. Even if you generously assume that the costs of basic wine, bottles, shipping, wages and so on, have remained immune from five years' inflation, all that's left to pay for the stuff you are going to drink is 58p. Which, at a current rate of 7.5 to the pound buys just 4.38 francs. So, don't be surprised that it, and most of the similarly priced bottles on the shelf, tastes so ordinary.

In fact, it is only thanks to modern winemaking, and the development of vineyards in climatically privileged regions like Languedoc Roussillon that wines are even drinkable. Cooler parts of France, where rainstorms arrive as predictably as London buses, have had a tougher time – as you can taste in the watery, weedy flavours of almost any bottle of cheap, own-label claret.

When Nick Dymoke Marr, buyer for Asda, stated this year that, if quality and value for money were his only criteria, he'd have delisted his basic Bordeaux ages ago, he was speaking for his colleagues almost throughout the trade. As Steve Clarke of Tesco told a roomful of disgruntled French producers, his stores can sell more bottles of a good Vin de Pays in a month-long promotion than they can of some appellation wines in a year. And at a higher price.

REGAINING CONTROLEE?

The French Appellation Contrôlée authorities initially paid as much respect to this kind of implicit criticism as President Chirac offered to the Antpodeans who disliked the idea of his letting off atom bombs in their back yard. Behind the scenes, however, they quietly acknowledged that Something Might Have to Be Done to improve the currently shaky system of quality control on which is built the words, 'appellation controlée'. Even some of the hardest-line apologists for the existing system admit that if France's traditional regions are to compete with their non-appellation neighbours in France, let alone vineyards across the rest of the world, there will have to be fewer bottles of some appellation wines in the future. In the words of the internationally respected consultant winemaker Michel Rolland, 'There'll be some corpses'.

All that is required is a solution which causes minimal offence to the kind of quality-unconscious farmers and winegrowers whose response to unwelcome competition usually involves lorry-roasted lamb and tarmac-flavoured Spanish wine.

Mind you, the Italians, Portuguese and Spaniards have all reviewed their appellation rules too, with the latter country following the Italian lead by creating two levels of denomination, the superior of which – the 'DOC' (currently restricted to Rioja) – confusingly has the same initials as the *inferior* one in Italy.

Whether these efforts at quality control will yield discernable differences remains to be seen. Everything depends on the willingness of the wine industry in each country to accept that, in the long term, it makes sense to sell fewer bottles of better wine. In the short term, however, it's very hard to argue with the power of the huge supermarkets on mainland Europe which will generally sell wine irrespective of its quality – provided that it has the right name on the label and a low enough price.

In the meantime, throughout the New World, from Tasmania to Chile, winemakers are busily emulating the French by creating their own appellation systems, potentially instituting precisely the kind of restrictive practises which have so handicapped the French in their fight against wines from countries like Australia and the US.

THE REIGN OF TERROIR

Europe in general – and France in particular – is so hidebound by appellations that, even if it were possible to make a brilliant wine by blending a Bordeaux with a Rhône, the resulting marriage could only be sold as a *vin de table*. The names of the regions and grapes involved could not appear on the label; nor could the vintage.

Hardly surprisingly, such wines are rare – though Dulong's 'Rebelle' (see page 136) shows how good they can be. In Australia, however, some of the most successful wines proudly declare themselves to have been produced in 'South-east Australia', a region covering every inch of the states of New South Wales, Victoria and South Australia – in other words, the parts of Australia where over 90% of the wine is made.

California now takes its own regional appellations seriously enough to have spawned a glossy promotional magazine called NAPA Appellation – but not so seriously as to stop one of its biggest wineries from labelling as 'Napa Ridge' a wine from various parts of the state which has as much to do with the region of Napa as 'Domaine Chardonnay' – another short-lived piece of California marketing genius – had to do with the grape of that name. In Europe, ironically, we have sufficient respect for Californian geography to rename it 'Coastal Ridge'.

The argument of the last few years of the century will not be between New and Old Worlds, but New and Old *Wave* wines. In one camp will be wines made from grapes grown across large regions; in the other, the stuff produced from specific regions and vineyards which have what the French would call a genuine *gout de terroir* – the recognisable 'taste of the earth', which comes from the unique combination of soil and climate of a particular vineyard. Good Coonawarra Cabernet, Marlborough Sauvignon and Santa Barbara Pinot Noir, like Nuits St Georges, Barolo and Pomerol have this characteristic. Regions like the Napa Valley bordered by county boundaries, do not. And places which cannot regularly produce wine of competitive quality – like the least well sited vineyards of Bordeaux and southern Burgundy – will inevitably lose out to competition from places like Languedoc Roussillon, which can.

GRAPE VICTIMS

This year, wine retailers began to realise that, by spurring producers from Bulgaria to the Barossa Valley to make bargain basement Chardonnay, they had begun to kill the goose which laid all those tasty golden eggs. When 'Chardonnays' – albeit flavourless dilute travesties of that grape – can be bought for less than four pounds, it is hardly surprising that wine merchants and supermarketeers are busily scouring the world for 'new' and 'unfamiliar' varieties for which they can charge a premium price. Suddenly, the shelves are filling with Viogniers and Vermentinos, Marsannes and Mauzacs. Some of these wines do precisely what they are intended to: broaden the range of flavours we can buy. Others, however, are dull fare which could just as easily be sold as basic Vin Rouge or Blanc.

The mania for new grapes is echoed in a spirit of wanderlust among professional wine buyers rarely seen since imperialism went out of fashion. This year, if the magic has gone out of your drinking life, you could spice it up with a bottle or two from Brazil, Canada or Uruguay – without straying beyond the shelves of Sainsbury and Tesco. Maltese wines are bound to find their place over the next few months following the success one enjoyed at the 1995 International Wine Challenge and the only reason you haven't yet been offered an Albanian white is that the first attempt by an Australian winemaker to produce one – in 1994 – did not quite work out.

By the time those Albanian efforts bear drinkable fruit, the vinous explorers will have to admit that – apart from newly independent former Soviet republics – they've more or less run out of novel countries with which to excite jaded palates.

If those buyers turn back to traditional sources of supply, however, they are going to face another problem which has nothing to do with exchange rates. In a number of countries, there is a worrying shortage of wine.

The 1995 Australian harvest was 25% lower than expected – and followed a disappointing crop in 1994. This lack of wine, coupled with a growing thirst among the Australians themselves, is going to make it increasingly difficult for anyone to offer cheap bottles of Aussie red and white. Early estimates were that prices were set to rise by at least 30p per bottle.

One country which might seem set to challenge Australia's place in wine drinkers' affections is South Africa, a country whose wine exports to Britain more than doubled over the last 12 months. In many ways reactions to the wines of the 'new' South Africa resembled those afforded to the 'new' Labour party. On the one hand, there were those who welcomed an old friend back into the fold, hastily declaring that Australia, like Michael Heseltine, had had its day and that they greatly preferred the subtler style of wines from the Cape. On the other, there were merchants and tasters – including this writer – who complained at the effort required to avoid reds which commit the old South African crime of being made from unripe grapes.

The South Africans can, however, be forgiven for ignoring those complaints; the world wants their wines and, for the first time in living memory they are faced with a shortage rather than a surfeit of them. So, prices here are rising too – indeed, in June 1995, producers of wines which had sold at £3.99 were brazenly asking for the following vintage to carry price tags of £5.29. These leaps will be exceptional, but, the cockiness which attended the South Africans' victory over New Zealand on the rugby pitch is far from absent among the winemakers.

Spain and Portugal, two relatively weak-currency countries, ought to be building on the growing success of their new wave wines, but a combination of drought and frost was set to cut the 1995 harvest in both, and to raise prices. The Portuguese crop in particular could be half its usual size.

So what's left? The one hope for inexpensive wine in western Europe is Italy. Stand by for a growing range of wines, especially from unfamiliar regions in the south, Sardinia and Sicily, including an even larger number of offerings from flying winemakers like Kym Milne, Geoff Merrill and Gaetane Caron.

Eastern Europe will come back into fashion, as people rediscover the value-for-money offered by Hungarian and Bulgarian reds. Elsewhere, the focus will be on the Americas, with a growing range of own-label Californians and wines from Washington State, and – wath this space – Argentina. Much more evidently, there will be a flood of increasingly impressive reds and whites from Chile – the country responsible for over a quarter of the wines Bottoms Up chose to show to the press in July.

As for France, the focus will increasingly be on the Rhône, the south and south west, as buyers look for the best, ripest flavours at the lowest possible prices.

ANCIENT AND MODERN

Wherever a wine is made, however, and whatever its price, the end of the decade will be marked by an increasing polarisation between what the Australians would call 'fruit-driven', oaky wines and more traditional styles. This will not set the New World against Old, but will divide regions within countries and producers within regions and appellations. In Bordeaux, for example, there are already two quite clearly defined styles of wine: 'Parkerised' clarets – made to please the all-powerful American guru Robert Parker – with lots of ripe fruit and new oak – and more tannic, less woody wines which get higher marks in France and among British traditionalists.

The same trend is just as evident among Chardonnays, with Australians and Americans increasingly rushing to make Chablis-style examples which have never seen a barrel while a fair few Burgundians do their damnedest to emulate the biggest, brashest blockbusters from the Barossa.

The only problem implicit in all this is the confusion it is beginning to cause. How is anyone to know whether the Sauvignon they have bought is full of tropical New Zealand-style fruit, Bordeaux steeliness or Californian Cream Soda? If you don't like the flavour of new oak, how will you know to avoid it – especially given the trick pulled by one big Australian winery whose so-called 'unoaked Chardonnay' tastes as though it was made from freshly sawn planks?

The ultimate winner though has to be you and me – the people who go out and buy and drink wine. After all, we're being offered a wider choice than ever before.

JUMPING INTO THE NET

But how are we going to exercise it? Inevitably, perhaps, while parts of the wine trade hesitantly began to discover that computers might provide a better means of book-keeping and the preparation of their price lists than pocket calculators and typewriters, a few more dynamic firms took a more dynamic leap – into the Internet. When I first began to edit the *Guide* a decade ago, there was no need to list fax as well as telephone numbers; with this edition, for the first time, we are including E Mail numbers and the means to order wine directly from your home computer via the Internet.

The highest profile merchants on the 'net were, predictably enough, Tesco and Sainsbury's, but customers of the somewhat less well known Allez Vins! a small mail order French specialist in Yorkshire can already place orders for their French wine by tapping into 100271.2711 @compuserve.com. So, it would be a brave or stubbornly Luddite observer who would expect it to take much longer than a year or so for a great many more of Britain's wine merchants to hitchhike their way onto the super-highway.

Ironically, all this high tech could rescue the surviving small merchants who will be able to inform the world – and I mean the world – of their existence, and of the particular wines they sell.

THE GRAPEVINE

WINE AND HEALTH – a little more of what you fancy...

Alcohol has a 'socio-psychologically' damaging effect...' Well, whatever else you can criticise, it's hard to fault the anti-alcohol lobby's mastery of jargon. The spokesman responsible for this gem was being interviewed on the BBC Radio 4 *Today Programme* following the anouncement of yet another survey – this time from Denmark – indicating that alcohol significantly reduces the risk of heart disease. If the latest paper was to be believed, the current BMA advisory figures of three units per day for men and two for women are overly cautious; indeed, for the alcohol to have its beneficial effect, a rather higher daily dose is prescribed.

Revealingly, the BMA hesitates to dismiss the results of what is now an impressive international body of research; on the other hand, they are not prepared to alter their advice to the populace because – my italics – *of the other risks to health associated with alcohol*. In other words, because drunks crash cars and get into fights, the rest of us are not to be told that an extra glass or so of wine per day might actually do us good.

It has already been proved that red wine raises the levels of (good) HDL cholesterol while reducing those of (bad) LDL cholesterol, making blood clots less likely. But that's not all it can do; research in the UK suggests that wine can deter the common cold, and according to the American Cancer Society, red wine drinkers are subject to 15-20% fewer deaths *from all causes...*

ORGANIC WINES

The organic wine lobby has not had a happy time over the last few years. With the very best will in the world, it is not easy to grow and pick healthy rot-free grapes in the kind of weather France, Germany and Italy and indeed New Zealand have had to endure. Commitment, ingenuity and skilled winemaking have achieved minor miracles but it is no coincidence that the red and white winners at this year's Safeway/ *WINE* Magazine Organic Wine Challenge were both from Australia. It is simply far more practicable to make organic wines there and in places like Chile, Argentina and Southern France.

Over the next year or so, thanks to new plantings and relaxed US regulations, I would predict that New World organic wines will become flavour of the month, with offerings from such names as Fetzer, Gallo, BRL Hardy, Mondavi and Penfolds. Whether we will all be prepared to pay the price for them is another question.

A selection of top class organic wines:
1994 Penfolds Organic Chardonnay-Sauvignon Blanc (see page 65)
1993 Penfolds Organic Cabernet-Merlot (see page 109)
1994 Millton Vineyard Barrel Fermented Chenin Blanc (see page 131)
1994 Millton Vineyard Barrel-Fermented Chardonnay (see page 109)
1992 Domaine Richeaume Syrah (see page 131)
1989 Ch. de Beaucastel, Châteauneuf-du-Pape (see page 112)

LEARNING ABOUT WINE

Teaching people about wine is clearly not a job to recommend to your son and daughter – or not in Britain, to judge by the paucity of decent commercial wine courses on offer. Compared with New York, for example, London is a vinous educational desert in which courses are launched and fail by the year. For the moment, the only accessible 'fun' courses we can recommend are the ones run by Leith's and the Scala Schools of Food and Wine.

For those who want more classical training, Michael Schuster, runs first class courses, while Christie's and Sotheby's hold emphatically serious tastings, usually hosted by Masters of Wine.

Out of London, Lay & Wheeler run Saturday Wine Trails which are educative bargains at £6.50 a time and Château Loudenne and Chateau Gratien's International Wine School both boast UK-trained lecturers. If you want to join the wine trade, you should make directly for the Wine & Spirit Education Trust, where you can take the basic (very basic) 'Certificate', the useful 'Higher Certificate' and the testing two-part 'Diploma'. Only after you have cleared all three hurdles may you try the real high jump, the Master of Wine written and tasting exams. But be warned: it's now a two-year course, and just over 200 people have earned this qualification in three decades.

> Recommended wine courses: Christie's Wine Course (0171- 839 9060; fax 0171-839 1611); Daventry Tertiary College (01327 300232); Ecole de Vin, Château Loudenne (00 33 56 73 17 80; fax 00 33 56 09 02 87); Grant's of St James (0181 542 5879; mobile 0850 995718); International Wine School (01582 713290); Kensington & Chelsea College (0181 964 1311); Lay & Wheeler (01206 764446; fax 01206 560002); Leicestershire Wine School (0116 2542702); Leith's School of Food and Wine (0171-229 0177 fax 0171-937 5257); Scala School of Wine (0171 637 9077); Michael Schuster (0171-254 9734; fax 0171 249 3663); North West Wine & Spirit Association (01244 678624); Sotheby's (0171-493 8080; fax 071-409 3100); Wine Education Service (0181 801 2229); Wine & Spirit Education Trust (0171-236 3551; fax 0171-329 8712).

TASTINGS

For many people, a course is quite unnecessary; much can be learned by attending tutored tastings given by wine merchants, writers or winemakers. The following people are especially worth travelling to hear:

> Tim Atkin, Liz Berry MW, Michael Broadbent MW, Tony Brown MW, Nick Clarke MW, Oz Clarke, Clive Coates MW, Nancy Gilchrist, David Gleave MW, Richard Harvey MW, Richard Hobson MW, Jane Hunt MW, Tony Keys Willie Lebus, Patrick McGrath MW, Richard Mayson, Maggie McNie MW, Charles Metcalfe, David Molyneux-Berry MW, Angela Muir MW, David Peppercorn MW, Jethro Probes, John Radford, Anthony Rose, Michael Schuster, Derek Smedley MW, Steven Spurrier; Serena Sutcliffe MW, Pamela Vandyke Price, John Vaughan Hughes MW, Roger Voss.

THE CASE FOR JOINING A WINE CLUB

Wine clubs are like any other groups of like-minded individuals; some are congenial; others serve as models for one of Alan Aykbourne's ghastlier plays. Still, all you have to lose is your £10-20 membership fee. The risk is potentially greater when you join a wine club run as a sideline by a wine merchant; it is all too easy to find yourself paying for the dubious privilege of overpaying for your wine – and receiving a few newsletters. Before joining any club, check carefully how much you are going to have to spend and what is being offered that you could not get for less from another merchant.

The Sunday Times Wine Club offers an enjoyable annual tasting in London, and good wine tours. The Wine Society, which genuinely belongs to its members, is worth joining for the quality of its wines – and its duty free depot in northern France. If, however, you want a club whose existence is not geared towards purchasing, try the ones listed below or read about new ones in the diary pages of both *WINE* and *Decanter* magazines. The following clubs and societies mostly meet monthly, charging £15-20 per year membership. The clubs whose names appear in italics are associated with wine merchants.

Amersham Wine Appreciation Society (01494 721961); Association of Wine Cellarmen (0181 871 3092); Ava Wine Circle (01247 465490); Bedford Fine Wine Club (01234 269519); Bramhope Wine Tasting Group (0113 2666322); Cambridge Food and Wine Society (01954 780438); Carlisle Wine Tasting Society (01228 576711); Chandlers Cross Wine Society (01923 264718); *Châteaux Wines* (01454 613959); Chiltern Wine Society (01582 414803); Chiswick Wine Society (01850 329111); Civil Service Wine Society (01634 848345); Cleveland Wine Society (01287 624111); Coopers Hill Wine Club (01628 25577); Eastbourne District Wine Society (01323 648919); Edinburgh Tasting Group (0131 332 5332); Essex Fine Wine Tasting Group (01787 477877); Evington Wine Appreciation Society (0116 2314760; fax 0116 2875332); Garforth Wine Group (0113 2666322); Guild of Sommeliers (0161 928 0852); Hatfield Wine Apreciation Society (01707 263129); Herefordshire Fine Wine Society (01432 275656); Hertfordshire Fine Wine Society (01582 794867); Hextable Wine Club (01732 823345); Hollingworth Wine Society (01706 374765); Horsham Wine Society (01403 253179); Leicester Grand Union Wine Society (01533 871662); Lincoln Wine Society (01522 680388); Lymington Wine Society (01590 674818); *Maidenhead Wine Circle* (01628 25577); *Moreno Spanish Wine Society* (0171 286 0678); Myster Wine Club (01633 893485); North Hampshire Wine Society (01734 815358); Opimian Wine School (01625 611542); *Penfolds Wine Club* (0181 940 1917); Petersham Wine Society (01932 348720); Rochester Wine Society (01634 848345); Scottish Wine Society (01368 864892); Sittingbourne Fine Wine Society (01795 478818); South African Wine Appreciation Society (01708 743808); *Vin de Garde /Vintage Expectations* (tel/fax 01372 463251); Welland Vale Wine and Food Society (01604 811993); West Country Wine Club (01726 63114); West Hampstead Wine Club (0171 794 3926); The Wine and Dine Society (0181 673 4439; fax 0181 675 5543); The Winetasters (0181-997 1252).

BUYING AT AUCTION

Over the last year or so, there has been a fascinating phenomenon in the wine world; money from the Far East has begun to flow into classic wines. Without the influx of Japanese yen and Hong Kong dollars, it is very questionable how busy the auction market for fine old wine would have been. But if 'fine wine' – essentially good vintages of big name Bordeaux and ports, plus selected high fliers from other regions – is fetching good prices, auctions can be great sources of slightly humbler fare. When restaurants and wine merchants go bust, for instance, their stock usually goes under the hammer somewhere – often at attractively low prices.

But don't get carried away. It's still worth keeping a check on what you end up paying per bottle. Auctions are not inevitably cheaper than wine merchants.

For details of the 'right' prices for top-flight wines, check *WINE* Magazine's Fine Wine section. Remember, too, that a 'bargain' £50 case of Chablis can be less of a snip by the time you have added the 10% buyer's premium, over £1 a bottle duty and 17.5% VAT – and driven to Edinburgh to collect it.

Among fine wines today, my tip would still be to go for the 1985s, the best 1986s which are beginning to soften, and the 1988s which have yet to do so. Fairly priced 1982s are worth buying, as are 1983s, provided they are for early drinking. Watch out too for 1986 and 1987 red Burgundies from good producers. These too are ready to drink but when well made, are well worth buying.

Auction Houses: Christie's Auction House, South Kensington (Wine Department) (0171-581 7611; fax 0171-321 3321; Christie's Auction House, King Street (Wine Department) (0171 839 9060; fax 0171 839 7869); Sotheby's (0171-924 3287; fax 0171-924 3287); Bigwood Auctioneers (01789 269 415; fax 01789 294168); Lacy Scott (01284 763531; fax 01284 704713); Lithgow Sons andPartners (01642 710158; fax 01642 712641); Phillips (01865 723524; fax 01865 791064).

BUYING EN PRIMEUR/INVESTING IN WINE

Just when you thought it was safe to go back to the doormat, they're back in force: offers for *en primeur* claret have reappeared in force for the first time since 1991. It seems only yesterday that the idea of buying wine in the barrel was declared dead and buried in the wake of a series of unspectacular vintages and the Hungerford Wine Co debacle which left a host of wine lovers with neither wine nor cash.

1994, however, despite the rainstorms which punctuated the harvest, has been given the seal of approval by no less a guru than Robert Parker who compared its wines to the reliably attractive 1985s. So, it's hardly surprising that a long list of merchants have entered the fray with offers.

Unlike 1992 and 1993 in which the wines were generally not worth even thinking about at buying *en primeur*, 1994 did produce some delicious wines which actually seemed fairly-priced when compared to the 1989s and 1990s. On the other hand, unlike 1985, there is no reason to suggest that 1994 was even a reasonable-quality vintage, taken as a whole. Many of the wines – especially the ones from less well-sited vineyards in the Médoc – taste of the rained-on, unripe grapes from which they were made.

People who bought good wines from St Emilion, Pomerol, the Graves and who chose carefully in the Médoc – Léoville Barton was a particularly good; the usually reliable Lynch Bages was not – will have little reason to complain. But nor, I suspect, will those who wait to pick these wines up when they arrive on the market in bottle.

WINE TOURS AND WINE BREAKS

You've bought the bottle and read the book – now take the tour. Over the last few years, a growing number of inventive holiday firms have discovered that many of the world's most interesting vineyards are conveniently situated in pleasant places in which to take a break. At first, they rarely offered much more than organised coach tours, but now, as you will discover from the small ads in *WINE* magazine, *Decanter* or the *Wine Spectator*, you can make your way between cellars on foot, by bicycle and even, if you have won the lottery, by hot air balloon. And, for those whose interests extend beyond wine, Arblaster and Clarke offer combined wine and opera tours of Italy.

If you are taking an organised tour, make sure you know the name of the 'expert' leading the trip and the producers to be visited. A quality-conscious tour operator will take the trouble to choose high-quality winemakers; travel agents who are playing at wine tours will often opt for 'big names' irrespective of their worth. Before booking, be sure to check that you are protected through some kind of bond. And if you fancy setting up your own tour, it's worth asking a wine merchant from whom you buy to help with letters of introduction.

From personal experience, we recommend **A**lternative Travel Group (comprising World Wine Tours) (01865 513333; fax 01865 310299), Arblaster & Clarke (01730 893344; fax 01730 892888) and The Sunday Times Wine Club (see The Stockists). Other companies and hotels include **A**ccompanied Cape Tours (tel/fax 01531 660210); Château Latuc, Cahors (00 33 65 36 58 63); California Wine Country (01425 655177); Château de Maklitourne (01440 730263); Chinon Loire Valley Cottages (01524 37676); Classic Wine Tours (tel/fax 01803 292008); Connoisseur Holidays (0171 3767966); Ian Dickson Travel (0131-556 6777; fax 0131 556 9065); Edwin Doran Travel (0181 744 1212); Facet Travel (01825 732266; fax 01825 733330); Francophiles (0117 9621975; fax 0117 9622642); Friendship Travel (01483 268621); Grenadier Travel (01206 549585); Moswin Tours Ltd (tel 0116 2714982; fax 0116 2716016); Reblaus (0171 413 9524); Specialised Travel (01225 315834; fax 01225 446093); Tanglewood Wine Tours (019323 48720; fax 01932 350861); The Cape Vine (01604 648768); Travel Club of Upminster (01708 229678); Tylney Hall Hotel (01256 76881); Vacances Cuisine (00 33 94 04 49 77); Vinescapes (01903 744279); Vinidoc (00 33 67 93 84 65); Walker's France (01734 402153); Walking with Wines (01432 840649); Wessex Continental Travel (tel/fax 01752 846880); Wink Lorch's Wine Holidays in the French Alps (0181 670 6885).

Hotels running wine weekends include Chewton Glen Hotel 01425 275341); Gleneagles (with Jancis Robinson, 01764 62231; fax 01764 62134); Hollington House Hotel (01635 255075); Hotel du Vin (01962 841414); Imperial Hotel (01493 851113); Millers House Hotel (01969 622630); Mynd House Hotel (Tel 01694 722212; fax 01694 724180); Norton House Hotel (0131-333 1275; fax 0131-333 5305); Porth Avallen Hotel (01726 812183); Studley Priory Hotel (01865 351203; fax 01865 351613).

STARTING A CELLAR

A few simple rules: avoid areas in which the temperature varies – constant warmth is better than the variations in, say, a kitchen. Avoid areas that are too dry; well-insulated cupboards and attics can make ideal cellars, but be sure to keep the humidity up with a sponge left in a bowl of water. Try to find a space where there is at least some air movement; cut air holes in cupboards if necessary. If the area you have chosen is damp, remember not to store wine in cardboard boxes. It sounds obvious, but even experienced wine buffs have lost wine by letting it fall from soggy boxes.

Spiral Cellars sell (and install, if you like) a purpose-built kit that can be sunk into the floor of your kitchen, garage or garden. Wine racks, custom-built to fit awkward areas, are available from Majestic Wine Warehouses and most other helpful wine merchants.

To buy direct, contact: RTA Wine Racks (01328 829666; fax 01328 829667); The Wine Rack Co. (tel/fax 01243 543253); A & W Moore (0115 9441434; fax 0115 9320735). Spiral Cellars Ltd (01372 372181; fax 01372 360142).

A simple exercise book can make a perfect cellar-book. Simply rule it up to allow space for you to indicate where and when you bought each wine; the price you paid; its position in your racks; when you open each bottle; tasting notes; and the guests to whom you served it. Most home computers will enable you to log the same information electronically; I can particularly recommend the database within Claris Works for a Macintosh, but any spreadsheet programme will perform the same task very effectively.

If you would prefer not to store your wine at home, there is always the option of cellaring it with the merchants from whom you bought it, provided you ensure your stock is clearly marked. Or you can rent space at the following specialist cellars:

Smith & Taylor (0171-627 5070; fax 0171-622 8235); Abacus (0181-991 9717; fax 0181-991 9611); or Octavian (0181-853 5551; fax 0181-858 4402).

GLASSES AND VINOUS GIFTS

The Austrian glass producer Georg Riedel has created a series of attractive tailor-made glasses which convincingly bring out the best in specific styles of wine – and cost a small fortune. For wine lovers who do not want to spend as much on glasses as on their wine cellar, however, my advice is simply to use any kind of clear glass whose rim has a smaller circumference than its bowl, and which is large enough to hold more than a few mouthfuls.

The Riedel range is available from the Conran Shop (0171-589 7401) or Bibendum (see The Stockists). Far more affordable and almost as pleasing are the Schott range (for local stockists contact Schott UK on 01785 223688), the Cristal d'Arques' wine taster-designed glasses (from Roberson, see The Stockists) and Royal Leerdam's bargain Bouquet range (from The Wine Glass Company (01234 721300; fax 01234 720759). For tasting, rather than drinking, Schott (see above) also produce the standard ISO glasses used by professionals.

> For vinous gifts, try Hugh Johnson's ultra-smart St James's shop (071-491 4912; fax 071-493 0602), Harrods or The Wine Society. Richard Stanford (071-836 1321) also stocks old wine books, while Richard Kihl (071-586 3838) is a good source of vinous antiques and curiosities; Birchgrove Accessories (048328 5369; fax 048328 5360).

CORKSCREWS

I still haven't found a corkscrew to better the Screwpull range, most particularly the 'Spin-handle' (from The Kitchenware Merchants: 01264 353912) If you cannot lay your hands on a Screwpull, the 'waiter's friend' is the next best bet. The corkscrews to avoid, however, are the ones which have a central shaft within the screw, rather than those which just look like a coil of wire.

WINE PRESERVATION DEVICES

An opened bottle of red or white wine keeps remarkably well for a few days in a fridge. To keep it that bit fresher, however, there are several devices on the market which work more or less well. The Vacuvin vacuum pump, for example, though economical, seems to suck fruit out of some wines. I prefer the same distributor's 'Winesaver' (01264 339821; fax 01264 356777) which keeps wine fresh in the same way as most modern wineries, by creating a layer of harmless, heavier-than-air inert gas which sits on the wine surface and prevents oxidation. It was once again used to great effect in the 1995 International Wine Challenge.

CHILL OUT

Ten minutes in a bucket full of water and ice will chill most bottles very efficiently. As an alternative, there is the widely-available 'Rapid Ice', a £5.99 foil jacket which lives in the freezer and cools bottles in six minutes, keeping them that way for up to three hours (it works better on table wines than fizz). (Rapid Ice 01264 339821; fax 01264 356777). Professionals who can spend £700 or so to chill bottles in two minutes, should also consider the Chilla (0850 264582) machine, commercial versions of which are becoming familiar in more go-ahead wine shops.

WINE IN PUBS

The search for good wine-pubs continues. Unfortunately, the problem is one of critical mass: until more of us demand good wine, there will be little reason for the brewers and landlords to bother about serving anything much better than three-day-old Liebfraumilch. And while that's what's on offer, most of us will stick to gin and tonic or beer.

Youngs, Eldridge Pope, Adnams and Greene King all encourage their publicans to stock and pour decent wine, so if you are in a smartish pub associated with any of these, it may be worth asking for a glass of house white. The list below includes the cream of the crop of wine pubs, but we'd be grateful to hear from readers and publicans about pubs we should include in the 1997 Guide.

> Beetle & Wedge, Moulsford, Oxfordshire; The Cornish Arms, Pendoggett, Cornwall; The Crown, Southwold, Suffolk; La Galoche, Tunbridge Wells, Dorset; The Green Man, Toot Hill, Essex; The New Inn, Cerne Abbas, Dorset; The Nobody Inn, Doddiscombsleigh, Devon; The Plough, Blackbrook, Surrey; The Red Lion, Steeple Aston, Oxfordshire; The Royal Oak, Yattendon, Cornwall; The Wykeham Arms, Winchester, Hampshire, The Chelsea Ram, London SW10.

BUYING ABROAD

With the opening of the Tunnel, it was perhaps inevitable that Tesco and Victoria Wine would join Sainsbury's and the Wine Society on the other side of the water. It can only be a matter of time before other major UK firms follow in their wake. Unless of course, pigs take wing and the duty-free rules change.

For a brief while, in 1995, an enterprising entrepreneur brought wine in using the same loophole as used by the manufacturers of Death Cigarettes, who shipped their product duty-free from the European mainland. As we go to press, the service has been halted pending the results of a UK court hearing, but, given the merchant's readiness to take his case to Europe, I'd recommend watching this space – and pondering the fact that while British merchants who deliver wine 'at cost' commonly charge £5-7 per dozen, French growers reckon they could ship their wines from southern France to your door for just £6.

Apart from The Wine Society, Tesco, Sainsbury and Victoria Wine, the following are all more recommendable than the supermarkets frequented by most by most cross-Channel shoppers.

> **Calais Beer & Wine Co** – Rue de Judée, Zone Marcel Doret (tel: 21 97 63 00). Also: Marco's UK (tel 0181 871 3233).
> **Le Chais** – 40 Rue de Phalfbourg, Centre Fradère, Calais. (tel: 21978856).
> **East Enders** – Rue Garenne, Zone Industrielle des Dunes ; Calais (tel 21 34 53 33).
> **Royal Champagne** – 9 Rue Andre Gerschell, Calais (Tel 21 96 51 62)
> **PG** – Ave Roger Salengro Calais 62100 (tel 21 34 17 34)/Rte St Honoré (tel 21 34 65 98).
> **Inter Caves** – 28 Rue Mollien, Calais 6210 (tel 21 96 63 82)

A PERSONAL SELECTION

Of all the wines listed in the *Guide*, here are some personal favourites. (Merchant codes are explained on page 32; country codes on page 271).

WHITE WINES UNDER £5

£2.95 (KS)
Pelican Bay Dry White, Aus. Juicily ripe tropical fruit flavours — a very simple easy-to-drink Aussie.

£2.99 (A)
1994 Bordeaux Sauvignon, Ch. le Desert, Fr. Light and grassy Sauvignon Blanc with a clean appley flavour.

£3.45 (JS)
1994 Bianco di Custoza, Geoff Merrill, Veneto, It. Nutty and greengagey with lots of fruit from the mad moustachio'd Merrill.

£3.49 (SMF)
1994 Dom. Bordeneuve VdP des Côtes de Gascogne, Yves Grassa, Fr. Lovely clean peary wine from the man who made this region's name.

£3.99 (BU)
1994 Kings Canyon Sauvignon Blanc, H Ryman/Arciero, California, US. Hugh Ryman's first effort in California, and a far fresher, tangier example of this grape than is usual from America.

£3.99 (D)
1994 Nuragus di Cagliari, Cantina Sociale di Dolianova, Sardinia, It. Pleasant, easy going, herby dry white wine. Perfect for a party.

£3.99 (VW)
1994 Deakin Estate Colombard Chardonnay, Victoria, Aus. Good value, easy-going party wine with a lime marmalade flavour.

£4.29 (WMK)
1994 Solana Torrontes & Treixadura, B&B & Mitchelton Wines, Sp. A joint venture between the Australians and Spanish. Appley dry white wine.

£4.75 (ALZ)
1993 Gaillac Blanc Sec, Dom. de Labarthe, South West, Fr. Fresh, dry, lemony wine with exotic fruit and crisp acidity. A good example of a classic from the south-west of France.

£4.99 (JS)
1994 Enate Blanco Maccabeo/Chardonnay, Somontano, Sp. From a new region of Spain, a richly fruity wine with flavours of melon and pineapple.

£4.99 (M&S)
1994 St Michael Mandeville Viognier, Midi, Fr. Great wine from a grape once restricted to the Northern Rhône. Peachy and deliciously perfumed.

£4.99 (M&S)
1994 Montana Kaituna Hills Sauvignon Blanc, NZ. Gooseberries galore; lovely, typical Kiwi Sauvignon with lots of juicy fruit flavours.

£4.99. (MOR)
1994 Casablanca Sauvignon Blanc, White Label, Curico, Chi. This has gooseberryish flavours too, plus a rich creamy texture. Top class wine.

£4.99 (SMF)
1994 Gewürztraminer, Caves de Turkheim, Alsace, Fr. Good, perfumed rich wine; full of typical lychee fruit.

£4.99 (AV)
1994 Nobilo White Cloud, Gisborne, NZ. Light, slightly citrussy, and very refreshing wine. Very moreish.

WHITE WINES UNDER £10

£5.45 **1994 Danie de Wet Grey Label Chardonnay, Robertson, SA.** Buttery and
(JS) chocolatey –like aged Champagne, with some minty oak.

£5.99 **1994 Primo Estate Colombard, S Australia, Aus.** Highly unusual, fruit
(AUC) salady example of a generally under-exploited grape variety.

£5.99 **1994 Dry Creek Chenin Blanc, California, US.** Honeyed, appley and full of
(BH) ripe fruit flavour.

£5.99 **1994 Neil Ellis, Elgin Vineyard Selection Sauvignon Blanc, SA.** Lemon
(DBY) and lime; quite a restrained wine from a newly developed region.

£6.49 **1988 Kiedricher Sandgrub Riesling Kabinett, Schloss Groenesteyn,**
(VW) **Rheingau, Ger.** Full of pineapple and apricot fruit. Floral and zesty.

£6.50 **1993 Chablis, Dom. des Manants, Jean Marc Brocard, Burgundy, Fr.**
(WIK) Serious Chablis; lean and just made for shellfish.

£6.75 **1994 Soave Classico, Nino Pieropan, Veneto, It.** Fresh, youthful fruit and
(PAV) cool acidity

£6.90 **1990 Sylvaner, Vieilles Vignes, Dom. Ostertag, Alsace, Fr.** Rich,
(HN) concentrated wine with peary perfumed fruit.

£6.99 **1993 Mitchelton Reserve Marsanne, Victoria, Aus.** Traditional in style and
(J&B) full of honeyed fruits – apricots and grapefruit.

£6.99 **1993 Asda Chablis, Burgundy, Fr.** A ripe and fruity wine – typical Chablis
(A) with good tangy acidity.

£6.99 **1994 Pewsey Vale Eden Valley Riesling, S Australia.** Ripe, appley, limey
(BEN) Riesling from a coolish high altitude vineyard

£7.49 **1989 Vouvray Sec Le Haut Lieu Gaston Huet, Loire, Fr.** Concentrated
(BU) Chenin with lingering flavours of apple and honey.

£7.72 **1994 Vernaccia di San Gimignano, Teruzzi e Puthod, Tuscany, It.** Bone
(CWI) dry, yet richly flavoured lemony, almondy wine.

£7.75 **1989 McWilliams Elizabeth Semillon, Hunter Valley, Aus.** Lovely rich
(ADN) texture with hints of peaches.

£7.99 **1993 Albariño Lagar de Cervera, Rias Baixas, Galicia, Sp.** Delightfully
(SHW) aromatic and beautifully balanced. One of Spain's best white wines.

£7.99 **1994 Pipers Brook Ninth Island Chardonnay, Tasmania, Aus.** Chablis-
(HOT) like, appley-pineappley Chardonnay. Unoaked and deliciously un-
Australian.

£9.75 **1990 Wehlener Sonnenuhr Riesling Spatlese, Dr Loosen, Mosel, Ger.**
(HN) Wonderfully rich, honeyed lemon flavours with fine balance. Late Harvest
German wine at its best.

WHITE WINES FOR SPECIAL OCCASIONS

£5.99 (¹/₂) **1987 Lindemans Botrytis Semillon, S. Australia, Aus.** Barley sugar, oak
(MWW) and ripe peaches. A great alternative to Sauternes, and pure hedonism

£5.99 (¹/₂) **1993 Kiona Late Harvest Gewürztraminer, Washington State, US.**
(OD) Unusual, raisiny, lycheeish dessert-wine from near-desert.country.

£6.59 (¹/₂) **1992 Katnook Botrytised Chardonnay, Coonawarra, S. Aus.** Distinctively
(VW) creamy, raisiny wine: Burgundy-meets-Sauternes.

£11.25 **1989 Piesporter Goldtröpfchen Auslese, Reichsgraf von Kesselstatt,**
(BBR) **Mosel, Ger.** Classic Mosel; clean and refreshing with lots of ripe apple
flavour.

£11.75 **1992 Sancerre le Chêne Marchand, Pascal Jolivet, Loire, Fr.** A perfumed,
(BND) herbaceous wine with delicious crisp acidity. Modern Sancerre at its best.

£12.99 **1992 Coldstream Hills Chardonnay, Yarra, Victoria, Aus.** Superb, ultra
(AUC) Burgundian-style wine made by lawyer-tuned-wine writer James Haliday.
Would blow away many a Puligny.

£13.45 **1991 Kumeu River Chardonnay, Auckland, NZ.** Wonderfully opulent and
(WHI) very convincingly Meursault-like Chardonnay from one of New Zealand's best.

£13.50 (¹/₂) **1985 Ch. de Fieuzal Blanc, Bordeaux, Fr.** Absolutely stunning white
(RD) Graves; peachy, rich and creamy with lingering oak.

£13.99 **1993 Condrieu, Dumazet, Rhône, Fr.** Classic, perfumed, apricotty Viognier
(BI) One of the most fascinating dry white wines in the world.

£14.49 **1993 Beringer Private Reserve Chardonnay, California, US.** A stunning
(MTL) combination of hot buttered toast and honey. New World white at its best.

£15.00 **1988 Riesling Cuvée Frederic Emile, Trimbach, Alsace, Fr.** Delicious apple
(WSO) and honey flavours. A classic Alsace Riesling.

£15.99 **1990 Gewürztraminer Clos Windsbuhl, Domaine Zind Humbrecht,**
(DBY) **Alsace, Fr.** Peaches, lychees and apricots – gorgeously spicy!

£16.99 **1991 Puligny Montrachet Dom. Louis Carillon, Burgundy, Fr.** Nutty,
(BU) buttery yet subtle. Built to last.

£20.25 **1991 Meursault, Dom. Comtes de Lafon, Burgundy, Fr.** Fabulous, rich,
(BRO) complex and nutty Burgundy to drink now or keep for a decade.

£16.49 **1991 Rosemount Roxburgh Chardonnay, NSW, Aus.** Ultra-rich, very oaky
(TH) flagship wine from the winery which turned so many of us into Aussophiles.

£16.99 **1986 Ch Lafaurie-Peyrauguey, Sauternes, Bordeaux Fr.** Honeyed, yet floral
(THP) Sauternes with delicious dried apricotty flavours.

£18.99 **1993 Chassagne-Montrachet 1er Cru Les Grandes Ruchottes, Pillot,**
(OD) **Burgundy, Fr.** Pure class; a biscuity young wine, built to last.

RED WINES UNDER £5

£2.69
(KS)
1994 Alta Mesa, Estremadura, Por. Refreshingly crisp with a dark berry character and flavours of tobacco and prunes.

£2.99
(TH)
1993 Côtes du Ventoux La Mission, Rhône, Fr. Good, peppery, inexpensive alternative to Côtes du Rhône.

£3.69
(KS)
1994 Cono Sur Cabernet, Chi. Rich cassis fruit and good vanilla oak: a very well-made bargain.

£3.79
(TH)
1993 Montepulciano d'Abruzzo, Umani Ronchi, It. Earthy tobacco and strawberries; a good spicy, old fashioned rustic wine.

£3.79
(VW)
1994 Victoria Wine Claret, Calvet, Bordeaux, Fr. Earthy, herbaceous and plummy. An unusually good example of this traditional style.

£3.99
(SAF)
1994 Galet Vineyards Syrah, Midi, Fr. A big, rich, jammy and smoky wine full of sweet, spicy fruit.

£3.99
(JS)
1990 Oriachovitza Special Reserve Cabernet Sauvignon, Bul. Eastern European red at its mature, plummy blackcurranty best.

£4.25
(ADN)
1991 Villa di Vetrice, Chianti Ruffina, It. Classy Italian wine, with flavours of berries and wild herbs. Very tasty.

£4.50
(DBY)
1993 L A Cetto Petite Sirah, Baja California, Mex. Excitingly fresh pepper and spice wine from Mexico – full of red fruit flavours.

£4.59
(FDL)
1991 Cosme Palaçio Tinto Rioja, Sp. Smooth, creamy oak with rich damson fruits. Classic woody Rioja.

£4.79
(W)
1995 Avontuur Pinotage, Stellenbosch, SA. Latest vintage of this commendably smoky, chewy wine. Lovely berry fruit.

£4.90
(HHC)
1992 Domaine de Limbardie, VdP de Côteaux de Murviel, H Boukandoura, Fr. Crisp red fruit flavours, full of Southern sunshine.

£4.90
(M&V)
1993 Douro Tinto, Quinta de la Rosa, Por. Australia meets Portugal: rich, concentrated berry fruits and spice with a touch of oak. Lovely with strong-flavoured dishes.

£4.99
(BU)
1994 Prosperity Red, Firestone Vineyards, California, U.S. Cooked fruits, herbs and just enough sweet vanilla oak.

£4.19
(OD)
1992 Peter Lehmann Vine Vale Shiraz, S. Australia, Aus. Big unashamedly vociferous, spicy red with loads of oak.

£4.99
(THP)
1989 Ch Haut-Sociondo, Premières Côtes de Blaye, Bordeaux, Fr. Serious, fairly priced claret with ripe plummy Merlot and enough tannin to make it worth keeping.

£4.99
(MWW)
1993 Les Jamelles Mourvèdre, VdP d'Oc , Fr. A good example of a characterful, spicy, leafy grape variety widely used in the Rhône.

RED WINES UNDER £10

£5.25
(AV)
1993 Chinon Les Violettes, Morin, Loire, Fr. Good, chunky, blackcurrant wine made from the Cabernet Franc. Delicious chilled.

£5.39
(SHJ)
1994 Ch. du Grand Moulas, Marc Ryckwaert, Rhône, Fr. Peppery, redcurranty and ripe Côtes du Rhône with real class.

£5.49
(EWC)
1991 Barbera d'Asti 'Ceppi Storici', Piedmont, It. A mouthful of wild young summer pudding flavours .

£5.59
(CHF)
1992 Carignanissime de Centeilles, Minervois, Fr. An extremely dense brambly red wine, full of herby, earthy flavours.

£5.80
(HN)
1993 Ch. de la Liquière, Cuvée des Amandiers, Faugères, Midi, Fr. Toffeeish, gamey wine with young mulberry fruit.

£5.95
(VDV)
1993 Hardy's Coonawarra Cabernet Sauvignon, S Australia, Aus. Classic Aussie Cabernet, full of blackcurrants, cassis, eucalyptus and spice.

£5.99
(OD)
1993 Pinot Meunier, Bonny Doon, California, U.S. Made from a grape variety normally used for Champagne; wonderful, creamy, raspberryish wine.

£5.99
(W)
1991 Fairview Shiraz Reserve, Paarl, SA. Quite a French-style, medium-bodied version of this grape – for those who find some of the Australian offerings too full of fruit flavour.

£6.59
(BTH)
1990 Parrina Riserva, Tuscany, It. Lovely chocolate, tobacco and black cherry fruit.

£7.08
(JAR)
1990 Bourgogne Rouge Mont Avril, Michel Goubard. Raspberry and plums. Good value young Burgundy with classic flavours.

£7.59
(JN)
1992 Laurel Glen Terra Rosa, Cal. Fabulous value —a really full, rich and fruity junior version of Patrick Campbell's Cabernet.

£7.99
(HOL)
1993 Stoniers Pinot Noir, Mornington Peninsula, Aus. Classy, oaky, mulberryish wine with lovely vanilla oak.

£7.99
(TH)
1990 Monte Alpha Cabernet Sauvignon, Curico, Chi. Soft, ripe, plummy wine with good, sweet oak.

£7.99
(VW)
1990 Pomino Rosso, Frescobaldi, It. Ripe cherries galore. A tasty mouthful from one of the best producers in Tuscany.

£8.99
(BU)
1991 Warwick Farm Trilogy, Stellenbosch, S.A. Fine, concentrated blend of Cab Sauvignon/Franc and Merlot. Chewy and flavoursome.

£9.25
(L&W)
1993 CJ Pask, Cabernet-Merlot, Hawkes Bay, NZ. One of the most successful red wine efforts from New Zealand, with rich, plummy fruit.

£9.69
(LUV)
1991 Cape Mentelle Zinfandel, W. Australia, Aus. Gutsy, spicy fruit. A very concentrated berryish wine to beat the best efforts from California.

RED WINES FOR SPECIAL OCCASIONS

£10.99 (BI) **1991 Duxoup Charbono, Dry Creek, Sonoma California, US** Made from a rare Italian grape variety. Like soft, Californian Barolo.

£11.00 (HN) **1991 Crozes-Hermitage "La Guiraude", Alain Graillot, Rhône, Fr.** Wonderful white pepper, blackberry, leather and fine new oak.

£11.35 (JN) **1993 Saintsbury Carneros Pinot Noir, Cal.** A raspberryish wine to match all but Burgundy's very best.

£5.99 (½) (MWW) **1988 Recioto della Valpolicella, Tedeschi, It.** Mouthfilling raisiny wine, which the Italians traditionally call 'the wine of meditation'.

£12.50 (ADN) **1992 Basket Press Shiraz, Rockford, S. Australia, Aus.** Made from grapes grown on century-old vines. Concentrated, brambley and delicious.

£13.90 (GB) **1990 Clos Mogador, Priorat, René Barbier, Sp.** Arguably Spain's most interesting red wine. Made in a very old fashioned region, this is packed with dark berry flavour. Worth keeping.

£14.99 (M&S) **1989 Ch. Gazin, Bordeaux, Fr.** Classy, honeyed, plummy Merlot-based Pomerol. Richly drinkable now but worth keeping.

£15.39 (MWW) **1991 Ridge Lytton Springs Zinfandel, Sonoma County, US.** One of the world's great wines, with delicious ripe berry fruit and sweet oak.

£16.55 (T&W) **1992 Umathum St Laurent, Austria.** Serve this blind and your guests will swear that it's a top class mulberryish Pinot Noir.

£16.94 (L&W) **1990 Cornas, Guy de Barjac, Rhône, Fr.** Ultra-concentrated wine with gorgeous smoky-spicy flavours. A wine to keep.

£16.99 (OD) **1990 Domaine Drouhin Oregon Pinot Noir, U.S.** Real Burgundy style, with cherry and raspberry fruit and oak.

£19.83 (ELL) **1989 Nuits Saint Georges Grandes Vignes, Daniel Rion, Burgundy, Fr.** Top class modern Burgundy with berry flavours and sweet oak.

£19.95 (RBS) **1982 Ch. Labégorce Zédé, Bordeaux, Fr.** Lovely mature claret with the gentle blackberry fruit of Margaux.

£19.99 (MWW) **1989 Berringer Cabernet Sauvignon Private Reserve, Napa Valley, US.** Tasty, blackcurranty Californian, with a touch of eucalyptus and sweet oak.

£24.95 (MFW) **1990 Barolo "Bussia Soprana", Aldo Conterno, Piedmont, It.** Top-class Barolo from a master producer: tobaccoey, plummy and intense.

£29.95 (SEB) **1989 Ch. de Beaucastel, Châteauneuf-du-Pape, Rhône, Fr.** Massively complex beast, with extraordinarily gamey, spicy, maturing flavours. Demands the sacrifice of a prize piece of game.

£33.40 (THP) **1986 Ch. Haut Bailly, Graves, Bordeaux, Fr.** A ripe, ready to drink wine with lovely blackberryish Graves flavours. Mature and very stylish.

SPARKLING & FORTIFIED WINES

£7.99 (OD) **Yalumba Cuvée One, Pinot-Chardonnay, Aus.** A real bargain to serve at the smartest event. Stylish dry fizz.

£8.99 (A) **NV Scharffenberger Brut, California, US.** A class act; rich ripe Champagne-style wine: long and nutty and yeasty.

£8.99 (TAN) **NV Pongracz Brut, Bergkelder, Coastal Region, S.A.** Classy, very rich, Champagne-like fizz in a very classy bottle.

£8.99 (WR) **NV Cuvée Napa Brut, Mumm, California, US.** Lots of fresh fruit and doughy, yeasty flavour. Great value fizz.

£11.49 (MWW) **NV Nautilus, NZ.** Creamy-rich fizz with ripe fruit flavour. Dry, but mouthfilling.

£11.75 (ADN) **1990 Recioto Spumante, Bertani, Veneto, It.** A stunning combination of black cherry and bitter chocolate – with bubbles.

£11.75 (BH) **NV Daniel le Brun, Marlborough, NZ.** Rich, buttery and toasty Champagne-like fizz made by a Frenchman born in Champagne.

£13.49 (OD) **NV Champagne Bonnet, Carte Blanche, Fr.** Rich in style, biscuity and toasty with luscious appley fruits.

£12.49 (OD) **1984 Seppelt Show Sparkling Shiraz, Aus.** A very distinctive example of this uniquely Australian style with bags of concentrated berry and damson fruit.

£37.50 (ADN) **Billecart-Salmon, Grande Cuvée, Fr.** From my favourite Champagne house, a bottle for a really special moment.

£7.99 (WR) **NV Don Zoilo Manzanilla, Jerez, Sp.** Classic salty, tangy dry sherry. Serve very cold – and generously.

£18.99 (OD) **NV Gonzalez Byass Mathusalem, Oloroso Jerez, Sp.** Liquid Christmas pudding! A mouthful of dried fruit and spice.

£6.89 (¹⁄₂) (TO) **NV Yalumba Museum Show Reserve Rutherglen Muscat, Victoria, Aus.** Dundee cake and crystalised ginger with lovely sweet spices.

£19.95 **Cossart Gordon 15-Year Old Malmsey, Mad.** Very concentrated **(L&W)** raisiny, marmeladey and moreish.

£11.99 (EWC) **1988 Quinta Do Crasto L B V, Oporto, Por.** Lovely stewed-fruit port from a small estate.

£19.99 (DBY) **1976 Fonseca Guimaraens Vintage Port, Oporto, Por.** Lovely rich, classic port with stewed fruit, chocolate and spice. Still fresh.

£20.99 (ES) **1985 Graham's Vintage Port, Grahams, Douro, Por.** Superbly rich and concentrated port. A wine to keep.

MERCHANTS BY REGION

The following will help you to find the nearest wine merchant in any part of the country. Companies marked in red are regional chains and the area they cover is indicated in brackets after the company name.

LONDON
EC1
Corney & Barrow
EC2
The Pavilion
Wine Co
N7
Le Nez Rouge
N13
Amathus
N21
Howard Ripley
NW1
Bibendum
Laytons
SE1
Le Pont de la Tour
Morris & Verdin
Waterloo Wine Co
Charles Taylor
O W Loeb
SE11
London Wine
Emporium Ltd
Mayor Sworder
SW1
Berry Brothers &
Rudd
Farr Vintners
Justerini & Brooks
Harrods
Harvey Nichols
Haynes Hanson &
Clarke
Heyman Barwell
& Jones.
SW3
Nicolas
La Réserve
SW7
La Vigneronne
SW8
Goedhuis & Co
Adam Bancroft
SW10
Lea & Sandeman
The Wine
Business
SW11
Philglas &
Swiggot

SW12
Fernlea Vintners
Georges Barbier
SW13
Barnes Wine Shop
SW18
Enotria
Winecellars
SW19
Findlater Mackie
Todd
W1
Fortnum & Mason
Selfridges
W2
Moreno
W4
Fullers (South
East)
W8
Lea & Sandeman
Bute Wines
W9
Les Amis du Vin
W11
John Armit Wines
Holland Park
Wine Co
W14
Roberson
WC1
Domaine Direct

AVON
Bath
Great Western
Bristol
Averys of Bristol
R S Wines
Reid Wines
The Vine Trail

BEDFORDSHIRE
Luton
Smedley Vintners

BERKSHIRE
Maidenhead
Helen Verdcourt
Reading
Bordeaux Direct

Slough
Australian Wine
Club
Wargrave
Vintage Roots

BUCKINGHAM-
SHIRE
Great Missenden
Turville Valley

CAMBRIDGE-
SHIRE
Cambridge
Noel Young
Ramsay
Anthony Byrne

CHESHIRE
Chester
Quellyn-Roberts
Knutsford
Hammonds of
Knutsford
Nantwich
Rodney Densem
Brookshaws of
Nantwich
Sale
Portland
Wine Co
Sandiway
Sandiway
Wine Co
Stockport
Booths of
Stockport
Warrington
Berkeley Wines

CORNWALL
Truro
Laymont & Shaw

CUMBRIA
Carlisle
Corkscrew
B H Wines
Penrith
The Cumbrian
Cellar

DEVON
Doddiscombsleigh
The Nobody Inn
Ivybridge
Brian Coad
Ottery St Mary
Christopher Piper
Bideford
Wickham & Co
DORSET
**Blandford St
Mary**
Hicks & Don
Bridport
Wessex Wines
Dorchester
Eldridge Pope
(South)
Woodhouse Wines

ESSEX
Colchester
Lay & Wheeler

GLOUCESTER-
SHIRE
Cheltenham
The Rose Tree
Wine Co
Chipping Norton
Bennetts
Stow on the Wold
Haynes, Hanson
and Clarke

HAMPSHIRE
Basingstoke
Berry Bros & Rudd
Bentworth
High Breck
Vintners
Bishops Waltham
Just in Case
Stockbridge
Trout Wines

HEREFORD &
WORCESTER
Bromsgrove
Noble Rot Wine
Warehouse

Malvern Wells
Croque en Bouche

HERTFORD-
SHIRE
Bishops Stortford
Hedley Wright
Harpenden
Le Fleming Wines
St Albans
Sherston Wine Co
Stevenage
The Wine Society
(Hesdin-France)

HUMBERSIDE
Hull
House of
Townend

KENT
Appledore
Vin du Van
Bexley
Village Wines
Dartford
Unwins
(South East)

LANCASHIRE
Bury
The Ramsbottom
Victuallers Co
Clitheroe
D Byrne & Co
Whitesides of
Clitheroe
Preston
E H Booth
(North West)

LEICESTERSHIRE
Leicester
Evingtons

NORFOLK
Norwich
Hall Batson & Co.
Thetford
T&W Wines

NORTHAMPTON-
SHIRE
Kettering
Ferrers Le
Mesurier
Northampton
Summerlee
Wines Ltd

NOTTINGHAM-
SHIRE
Nottingham
Gauntley's of
Nottingham

OXFORDSHIRE
Banbury
S H Jones
& Co
Blewbury
Sebastopol
Wines
Oxford
Grape Ideas

SHROPSHIRE
Shrewsbury
Tanners
(Central England
and Wales)
Ludlow
Halves

SUFFOLK
Bury St Edmunds
Thos Peatling
(E. Anglia)
Ipswich
Seckford Wines
The Rogers Wine
Company
Southwold
Adnams

SURREY
Brockham
Ben Ellis
Davisons
(South East)
Gomshall
Gallery Wines
Haslemere
The Haslemere
Cellar
Wallington
The Wine House

SUSSEX
(East)
Brighton
The Butlers Wine
Cellar
(West)
Arundel
Pallants
Chilgrove
The White Horse
Inn

WARWICKSHIRE
Coventry
Parfrements
Shipston on Stour
Edward Sheldon
Warwick
Waters Wine
Merchants

WEST
MIDLANDS
Birmingham
Connolly's
Stourbridge
Nickolls & Perks

WILTSHIRE
Mere
Yapp Brothers
Salisbury
Nadder
Wine Co

WORCESTER-
SHIRE
Tenbury Wells
Hopton Wines

YORKSHIRE
(North)
Skipton
Wright Wine Co
Harrogate
Allez Vin!
Martinez
Fine Wines
(South)
Sheffield
Barrels & Bottles
Eckington Wines
Mitchells
Penistone Court
Wine Schoppen
York
York Wines.
Otley
Chippendale
Leeds
Great Northern
Wine Co
Hoults
Vinceremos
Wakefield
Wm Morrison
(North)

N IRELAND
Co Down
James Nicholson

Belfast
Direct Wine
Shipments
Winemark
(N. Ireland)

SCOTLAND
Edinburgh
Peter Green
J E Hogg
Justerini & Brooks
Corney & Barrow
Raeburn Fine
Wines
Valvona & Crolla
Cockburns of
Leith
Glasgow
The Ubiquitous
Chip
Cupar
Luvians
Isle of Bute
Bute Wines
Moray
Gordon &
McPhail
Peebles
Villeneuve
Wines
Perth
Matthew Gloag &
Son
Lay & Wheeler

WALES
Dyfed
A Case
Of Wine
Llandudno
Terry Platt
Gwynedd
Shaws of
Beaumaris
South Glamorgan
Ballantynes of
Cowbridge
Swansea
CPA's Wine

ISLE OF WIGHT
Benedicts
Wine

CHANNEL
ISLANDS
Guernsey
Sommelier
Wine Co

MERCHANTS CODES

Merchants listed throughout this *Guide* are referred to using the following codes. Those who do not appear in The Merchants section (beginning on page 37) are listed with their telephone numbers.

WINE WITH FOOD

Who needs rules? Isn't all that stuff about the perfect wine for a particular dish outdated? Surely you just introduce your favourite food to a bottle of wine you like. Well, yes and no. Just as the notion of marrying off your best friends can end in tears, there are some combinations of wines and foods which will always clash – on the other hand some dishes and bottles were made to make music together. The key to happiness lies in understanding the character of each partner. Hefty dishes need flavoursome wines; that's obvious enough, but you should also take into account the character of the heftiness and the nature of the full flavour. Some partnerships you might expect to work splendidly, don't. For example young red Bordeaux and rare beef fail because of chemical reactions between the meat and tannin which make the wine seem tougher that it might with, say, lamb. By the same token, fresh white wine goes better with creamy cheese than most traditional reds. Don't treat these rules as gospel; just as a guide when you are experimenting with food and wine – and remember: you're preparing a *meal*, not contributing to a scientific paper.

APERITIFS & WINES TO DRINK WITHOUT FOOD

Wine apologists attempting to fight off the anti-alcohol lobby tend to bang on about wine and food having a horse-and-carriage and love-and-marriage relationship; you can't, they argue, enjoy wine *without* food. But that's tosh. Some wines, like horses – and love come to that - are fine and possibly even at their best on their own. And there's nothing wrong with that; German wines have traditionally been enjoyed in their homeland before and after meals, and in Italy, wines like Recioto are actually called *Vini da Meditazione* and are made for sipping while setting the world to rights and making bets on who's going to be the next prime minister.

LIGHT STARTERS

Delicately flavoured dishes such as vegetable terrines need the gentle touch of a soft white, such as a St Veran or a Soave, while patés are well suited to fruity reds. As a general rule, wilder New World concoctions of tropical fruits and oak are difficult to pair with light food, so go for something more delicate with good acidity such as the lighter style of Chardonnay or Muscadet or a subtle Sauvignon; play safe with sherry, or go a little frivolous with a glass of fizz.

SMOKED FISH AND MEAT

Smoked salmon and fizz might be a cliché – but as a partnership, they are hard to beat – and far better than the smoked-salmon-and-Gewürztraminer pairing often recommended in books. Due to the combination of oily food and oily wine, this never really works.
Light, lemony wines can't handle the distinctive tastes and textures of smoked fish and meat either. Foods like these need something more robust, like New World Chardonnays – the oak goes well with the smokiness – or good fino sherries. Smoked meats are well matched with light fruity reds or dry spicy rosés.

EGG DISHES

If your egg dish contains an assertive ingredient such as strong cheese, you'll need something fairly full bodied. Straight eggs like something crisp, such as a Sauvignon, Muscadet, a good English wine, or even a light north-east Italian red.

WHITE MEAT WITHOUT SAUCE

Grilled or roasted chicken, pork or veal will happily partner a range of wines from White Burgundy to Cabernet Sauvignon, but to bring out the best in a plainly cooked duck or goose, choose something fleshy, ripe and fruity, like a Merlot-based claret or a young Rioja.

FISH WITHOUT SAUCE

Delicate dishes are happiest with a light Chardonnay or a Soave with gentle acidity. Oily fish, such as sardines, need the refreshing bite of a good Muscadet or Vinho Verde. Fino sherry works here too, though.

WHITE MEAT OR FISH IN CREAMY SAUCE

Subtle dishes such as salmon in a cream sauce like a fairly soft wine such as an unoaked Chardonnay. Chicken can take on something firmer, perhaps a fresh gooseberryish Sauvignon, or a dry Vouvray.

SHELLFISH

There's no finer match for oysters than a steely Sancerre or Chablis. Richer shellfish enjoys the company of something fruitier. If you like to spice things up with a little aioli or garlic butter on the side, you might fancy a fino sherry or a retsina – provided you achieve the miracle of finding a fresh one.

WHITE FISH OR FISH IN A PROVENCALE-TYPE SAUCE

New World Chardonnays with strong acidity and freshness are the natural partners for forceful, tangy sauces – or choose a red with strong fruit and some tannin such as a red Loire.

PIZZA & PASTA

Obviously these Italian dishes are at home with flavoursome Italian wines, but they'd go just as well with all sorts of similarly herby and tasty non-Italians such as new wave young reds from Portugal, fresh youthful Rhônes or unambitious Shiraz from Australia.

LAMB AND BEEF

The French dogma gets it right for once; claret is far better with lamb than beef, though you'd be surprised at how a subtle dab of mustard on your rare steak seems to soften the tannins in the wine. Burgundy is great with stews, though the more rustic the dish, the more it makes sense to go for a rustic wine like a Corbières or a basic Spanish red.

GAME

The assertiveness of well hung game and venison needs the gutsiness of big Italian and Portuguese reds, Rhônes, Zinfandels or Shirazes; lighter game is better with a fruity red without too much wood: a *cru* Beaujolais, richly mature Burgundy or Merlot-based Bordeaux perhaps.

SPICY AND ORIENTAL FOOD

Why the distinction? Because there's a world of difference between the sweet-and-sour character of Chinese and Thai dishes and the fiery mouth-burners of Mexico and the hottest dishes from India. Spices have very varied effects on wine. Ginger, for instance, can be particularly uncongenial but can work with full flavoured New Zealand Sauvignons and crisper Gewürztraminers, while pepper has an affinity with Rhône reds made from the naturally peppery Grenache grape. Sweeter Chinese dishes can go well with off-dry Rieslings, with good demi-sec Loire whites and even well-chilled Asti Spumante. The only absolute no-nos with wine are dishes with enough chilli to numb the palate completely; confronted by one of these, order water, tea or the cheapest, coldest lager in the house.

FAST FOOD

So, what would you order to drink with your Big Mac, if McDonald's and company weren't so scared of spoiling their 'family' image by serving wine? (What's so anti-family about all those Italian trattoria and French bistros anyway?) Go for fun wines; Southern French Chardonnays, light Zinfandels and good Mosel or Aussie Riesling.

CHEESE

Think tradition: cheddar with claret and blue cheese with port are perfect combinations, as is the French favourite of serving blue cheeses with late harvest whites and goat's cheese with Sancerre (a wine from a region where shepherds and vignerons work as neighbours). On the other hand, if there's tannic claret or Barolo in your glass, steer clear of the creamier cheeses; they'll make the wine taste horrible. Save those for fresh dry whites or reds with more acidity than tannin, such as Burgundies and wines from the Loire.

CREAMY & OLD FASHIONED PUDDING

French tradition recommends dry Champagne with pudding; I'd rather drink Perrier than Perrier Jouët with my pud, as most decent sweet dishes strip flavour from the fizz. Good old-fashioned stodgy puddings are delicious with Sauternes or the stickier German wines – and positively sinful with Madeira or Rutherglen Muscat. Creamy desserts are trickier to partner. Try a sweet wine made from the Chenin Blanc or Sémillon, or go for a good-quality sweeter fizz.

FRESH FRUIT AND FRUIT PUDDINGS

Fresh and fruity dishes meet their match with Muscat (though not Australian fortified) or semi-sweet Riesling (Spätlese from Germany, for example). Fruity tarts and puddings can handle later-harvest Rieslings from the New or Old World.

CHOCOLATE

Surely the ultimate hedonistic dream: chocolate and wine. However, to make this partnership work, there is nothing for it but to throw caution to the winds and go way over the top. Forget soft, subtly flavoured wines, and revel in the strength and assertiveness of Brown Brothers Orange Muscat and Flora, or a Christmas pudding-style fortified Muscat from Australia, Portugal, Spain or France. Utterly decadent!

THE MERCHANTS

After the description of each merchant we select some of their most interesting wines. The letters following each wine indicate the kinds of food that go well with it (see also Wine with Food p. 34):

AP	aperitif	**G**	game	**SF**	smoked fish
B	beef	**LB**	lamb	**SM**	smoked meat
CC	cheese, creamy	**LS**	light starters	**SP**	spicy food (Chili)
CH	cheese, hard	**P**	pizza/pasta	**WFC**	white fish in creamy
CHO	chocolate	**PF**	pudding, fruit		sauce
CS	cheese, strong	**PS**	pudding, creamy	**WFP**	white fish in
D	drinking without	**PY**	party wines		Provencale sauce
	food	**O**	oriental	**WM**	white meat, no sauce
E	egg dishes	**RM**	red meat	**WMC**	white meat in
FD	delicate fish, no sauce	**RMS**	red meat in		creamy sauce
FO	oily fish, no sauce		rich sauce/stews	**WMP**	white meat in
FF	fast food	**S**	shellfish		Provencale sauce

For an explanation of the country abbreviations below (i.e. Chi. SA) see page 271

ADN   Adnams Wine Merchants   ★★★★★

The Crown, High Street, Southwold, Suffolk IP18 6DP. Tel 01502 727220. Fax 01502 727223. Independent Wine Merchant. 2 branches. **Opening Hours:** Mon-Fri 0900-1700, Sat 0900-1200. **Delivery:** free for 2 cases or more. **Tastings:** regular in-store; lectures and tutored tastings can be arranged. **Services:** cellarage, *en primeur*, mail order (cases only), gift mailing, wine search, glass hire, ice.

It is a little unnerving that one small company in out-of-the-way Southwold seems to have discovered the magic formula. How else can you explain the rise and rise of this once tiny brewery-owned merchant? Not content with winning a clutch of regional and national Wine Merchant of the Year awards, Adnams forges on with innovations. The company is driven by the boundless energy and enthusiasm of Simon Loftus and Alastair Marshall whose wilder excesses are tempered for the most part by sound commercial judgement and an unerring eye for the unusual. Who else would persuade customers to attend a 'speakeasy' weekend and watch Old and New World winemakers argue the toss over the importance of old vines? Southwold can not only boast Britain's best canned ale, a great wine merchant, kitchen store and a decent pair of hotels; but, thanks to six miles of optic cable coiled sinuously around the Crown it is also ready for the superhighway. So hungover customers who can't face the new dayglo list should be able to place their order using their black-and-white computer screens.

★★★★	1985 Seppelt Show Sparkling Shiraz, Aus. £12.49. *Ultra concentrated wine with all sorts of ripe hedgerow fruits.* ¶ **CH**
★★★★★	1988 Champagne Le Mesnil, Fr. £18.80. *A great example of Chardonnay-based Champagne, full of flavours of buttered toast. Classy.* ¶ **WFC, AP.**
★★★★	1990 Recioto Spumante, Bertani, Veneto, It. £11.75. *A stunning combination of black cherry and bitter chocolate – with bubbles.* ¶ **G, VMS**
★★★★	1993 Soave Classico, Tedeschi, Veneto, It. £5.20. *Proper Soave, with interesting almondy flavours.* ¶ **S, LS.**
★★★	1994 Quinta de Azevedo, Sogrape, Vinho Verde, Por. £5.15. *Just as proper Vinho Verde. Lemony and refreshing.* ¶ **SM, AP.**
★★★★	1994 Casablanca Sauvignon Blanc, White Label, Curico, Chi. £5.20. *Brilliant gooseberryish wine from Chile.* ¶ **WMC, WMP.**

38 Merchants

**** 1993 Martinborough Vineyard Sauvignon Blanc, NZ. £7.95. *Richer than many Kiwi Sauvignons: asparagus, gooseberry and lime.* ¶ **E, D.**

**** 1994 Neudorf Moutere Semillon, Nelson, NZ. £9.90. *More like ripe Sauvignon than Semillon: gooseberry and barely ripe peach.* ¶ **WM, CH.**

**** 1993 Chablis 1er Cru Montmains, Domaine des Manants, Jean-Marc Brocard, Burgundy, Fr. £10.75. *Classy, buttery Chablis.* ¶ **FD, S.**

**** 1991 Pouilly Fuissé, Domaine Corsin, Burgundy, Fr. £13.20. *Complex, fruity, succulent Burgundy.* ¶ **AP, WFP.**

**** 1991 Mountadam Chardonnay, Adam Wynn, Aus. £11.95. *Rich, buttery, complex and very attractively oaky.* ¶ **WM, CH.**

**** 1994 Viña Santa Rita Reserva Chardonnay, Maipo, Chi. £5.75. *Soft, ripe, quite easy going wine.* ¶ **S, D, WFC.**

*** 1992 Mitchell's Watervale Riesling, Aus. £6.70. *Spicy, juicy Riesling with citrus undertones.* ¶ **SP, S.**

**** 1992 Dr Loosen Riesling, Mosel, Ger. £6.50. *A ripe and grapey wine full of refreshingly simple citrus and honey flavours.* ¶ **SM, AP.**

**** 1989 McWilliams Elizabeth Semillon, Hunter Valley, Aus. £7.75. *Lovely rich texture with hints of peaches.* ¶ **SM, SF.**

**** 1991 Brown Bros Semillon, Milawa, Victoria, Aus. £7.20 *Mandarins, lime and old English marmalade plus sweet oak. Deliciously indulgent.* ¶ **O, WM.**

*** 1992 Gewürztraminer Hornstein, Cave Vinicole Pfaffenheim, Alsace, Fr. £5.85. *Richly textured palate with an attractive, bitter almond finish.* ¶ **S, O.**

**** 1995 Rose of Virginia, Charles Melton, Barossa Valley, Aus. £6.75. *Vibrantly refreshing pink wine to put Provence to shame.* ¶ **AP, SM.**

**** 1992 Domaine St Eulalie Minervois, Midi, Fr. £4.60. *Good value, flavoursome country red.* ¶ **SP, WFP.**

**** 1992 St. Hallett Cab Sauv/Franc/Merlot, Barossa Valley, Aus. £7.90. *A Bordeaux blend at Australian volume. Ripe, oaky, impressive.* ¶ **CH, G.**

**** 1992 Ridge Santa Cruz Mountains Cabernet Sauvignon, California, US. £16.45. *Intense but approachable wine with cassis and oak.* ¶ **BF, WMP.**

*** 1994 Terrasses de Landoc Grenache, Vignerons de Villeveyrac, Midi, Fr. £3.95. *Fresh young, peppery wine. Great party fare.* ¶ **LB.**

***** 1991 Morris of Rutherglen Durif, Morris Wines, Victoria, Aus. £9.95 *Tough knife and fork wine with loads of concentrated spice.* ¶ **G.**

***** 1992 Jasper Hill Georgia's Paddock Shiraz, Victoria, Aus. £12.20. *Marvellous intense, spicy red. Smokey aroma with hints of liquorice.* ¶ **G, SP.**

***** 1994 Chateau du Grand Moulas, Marc Ryckwaert, Rhône, Fr. £4.85 *Peppery, redcurranty and ripe.* ¶ **SP, WMP, FD.**

**** 1993 Fairview Shiraz Reserve, Paarl, SA. £6.95. *Refreshingly minty Shiraz – at once spicy and leafy.* ¶ **BF, RMS.**

*** 1994 Clos de Gilroy, Bonny Doon, California, US. £7.75. *Pepper galore – with damson jam and a touch of vanilla.* ¶ **LB.**

**** 1994 Meadowbank Vineyard Pinot Noir, Tasmania, Aus. £10.95. *Mint and plum aromas. Still youthful. Herbaceous quality.* ¶ **CC, WM.**

***** 1993 Saintsbury Carneros Pinot Noir, California, US. £11.95. *Burgundians, this raspberryish wine matches all but the very best. Burgundy* ¶ **BF, CC.**

**** 1994 Capezzana Barco Reale, Tuscany, It. £6.55. *Intense, herby, berryish and delicious.* ¶ **RM, P.**

**** 1989 Quinta de Camarate, Jose Maria Da Fonseca Succs, Setubal, Por. £6.65. *A tobaccoey, blackcurranty and very characterful blend of Portuguese and Bordeaux flavours.* ¶ **G, CH, RMS.**

**** 1991 Rioja Conde de Salceda Fourth Crianza, Vina Salceda, Sp. £5.90. *A rich, cocktail of mulberry and oak flavours. Deliciously Spanish.* ¶ **P, SP.**

**** 1993 Domaine Chanier Vouvray Moelleux, Loire, Fr. £5.30. *Rich, appley, sweetly honeyed wine, typical ultra-ripe Chenin Blanc.* ¶ **D, O, SM.**

**** 1993 Madrona Late Harvest Riesling, North Yuba, California, US. £4.08. *Over-ripe apples with a hint of spice.* ¶ **WMC, CC.**

***** 1990 Dow's Crusted Port, Douro, Por. £11.20. *A great alternative to vintage port. Plummy with a hint of ginger.* ¶ **CC, CH.**

ALZ   Allez Vins!   ★★★

Hillside, Nidd Lane/Clint Bank, Birstwith, Harrogate, N. Yorkshire HG3 3AL. Tel 01423 771 863. Fax 01423 771 863. Independent Wine Merchant. **Opening hours:** Sat 1200-1700. Call for other times. **Delivery:** free locally. **Services:** mail order, glass loan.

Congratulations to Ann and John Boutall for making a go of the kind of business of which countless Peter Mayle fans have idly dreamed – importing wine mostly from the lesser-known regions of France. Their evidently home-prepared list – complete with basic computer graphics of glasses and grapes – also includes such oddities as the new Loire Appellation of Cour-Cheverny which offers a rare opportunity to taste a wine made purely from the Romorantin grape. Wine may be bought from Vittles shop in Kings Court, Pateley Bridge or ordered by phone, mail, fax or, for more high-tech wine lovers, via their computer on their E-Mail number: 100271,2711 @COMPUSERVE.COM.

***   1993 Cour-Cheverny, Dom. des Huards, Loire, Fr. £5.50. *A rare white wine made from the Romorantin grape – it's fresh, limey and honeyed.* ⁋ *AP, SF.*

****   1993 Gaillac Blanc Sec, Dom. de Labarthe, South West, Fr. £4.75 *A fresh citrussy dry wine with exotic fruit and crisp lemony acidity.* ⁋ *CC, E.*

***   1992 Pacherenc-du-Vic-Bilh, Plaimont, South West, Fr. £5.25. *A highly traditional sweet white made in Gascony from the Gros and Petit Manseng. Lots of fruit.* ⁋ *O, PF.*

***   1989 Buzet Ch. De Padère, South West Fr. £5.65. *Nicely mature and classy red from one of the lesser known areas around Bordeaux.* ⁋ *BF, CH, RMS.*

AMA   Amathus Wines   ★★★

377 Green Lanes, Palmers Green, London N13 4JG. Tel 0181 886 3787/1864. Fax 0181 882 1273. Independent Wine Merchant. Also at 97 Muswell Hill Broadway N10 Tel 0181 444 8599. **Opening hours:** Mon-Sat 0930-2130, Sun 1200-1430. **Delivery:** free locally. **Services:** glass hire, ice.

The Amathus list begins frustratingly for anyone whose only alcoholic tipple is wine: page after page of mouthwatering whiskeys, ranging from Caol Ila and Springbank 21 year old to Middleton Rare from Ireland and Rebel Yell from the US. Equally serious gins, rums, brandies and liqueurs follow before one finally reaches the undistilled fruit of the grape. But the delicious journey is worthwhile, with a fascinating set of Italians including the unprepossessingly named Terre Arse Marsala, Torres's Milmanda Chardonnay, Alsaces from Zind Humbrecht and Schlumberger, Dr Loosen's Riesling and Leeuwin Chardonnay. Curiously, the only real weak area is red Burgundy, but doubtless this will be addressed before long. In the meantime, we'd recommend you spend your money on a bottle of 'Something Special' whisky.

****   Cloudy Bay Pelorus, Marlborough, NZ. £12.90. *Rich butter on toast. Aromatic and concentrated. Distinctive New World fizz.* ⁋ *D, WM.*

****   1993 Marc Brédif Vouvray, Loire, Fr. £8.49. *Dry, yet honeyed, appley wine. Ripe and good.* ⁋ *AP, E.*

****   1995 Santa Carolina Sauvignon Blanc, Lontue, Chi. £4.69. *Leafy Sauvignon with lovely ripe blackcurranty fruit.* ⁋ *BF, WMP.*

****   1985 Weinert Cabernet Sauvignon, Ar. £8.99. *Mature and cedary – almost Bordeaux-like Cabernet with baked fruit flavours.* ⁋ *CH, G.*

****   1990 Cumaro, Umano Ronchi, Marches, It. £9.60. *Ripe and tarry dark red fruit with hints of tobacco leaf and new oak.* ⁋ *SP, RM.*

*****   1990 Torcolato, Maculan, Veneto, It. £10.89 (half). *Stunning combination of creamy peach, apricot and butterscotch. A wonderful alternative to Sauternes.* ⁋ *PS.*

40 Merchants

JAR — John Armit ★★★★★

5 Royalty Studios, 105 Lancaster Road, London W11 1QF. Tel 0171 727 6846. Fax 0171 727 7133. Independent Wine Merchant. Wines by the case only. **Opening hours:** Mon-Fri 1000-1700. **Delivery:** free for three cases or more. **Services:** cellarage, *en primeur*, mail order, gift mailing.

This year marked a rare trip to Britain by Robert Parker, the American wine guru. On that visit, the only tasting and lunch he tutored was for John Armit's customers. Mr A's avowed intention is to give "the best service in the wine business", and an impressive list of restaurants – Bibendum, The Ivy and Le Manoir Aux Quat' Saisons – all benefit from Mr Armit's personal attention, as do a growing number of private customers prepared to buy fine wine in case quantities. And Fine Wine is the rule here, with not a lot for less than a fiver. The heart and soul of the list lies in Burgundy and Bordeaux with clarets from J P Moeix and wines from what Mr A calls the 'Mafia' of young Burgundian winemakers as well as a fair few old favourites. Elsewhere, there's an expanded range from Australia, the Loire, the Rhône and South Africa where Mulderbosch remains an especially bright star. Watch out also for the monthly 'Great Wine Offers'.

*** 1993 Muscadet Clos de Beauregard, Dom. Leroux, Loire, Fr. £5.92. *A fruity well-balanced Muscadet. An honourable exception to a dull rule.* ⅋ *AP, LS.*

**** 1993 Bourgogne Blanc les Sétilles, Olivier Leflaive, Burgundy, Fr. £7.42. *Well-made, clean, fruity white. Classy.* ⅋ *WFC, SF.*

***** 1994 Mulderbosch Chardonnay, Stellenbosch, SA. £8.33 *A wonderful Meursault-like Chardonnay made by the eccentric 'Mad Mike' Dobrovic.* ⅋ *LS.*

**** 1993 Tokay Pinot Gris, André Kientzler, Alsace, Fr. £8.33. *Concentrated, spicy full-flavoured wine.* ⅋ *AP, WM.*

**** 1992 Ch. Le Gay, Pomerol, Bordeaux, Fr. £11.92. *Flavoursome, finely balanced and fruity.* ⅋ *RM, LB.*

*** 1994 David Wynn Shiraz, S Australia, Aus. £7.58. *Medium-bodied, ripe berryish, peppery wine to drink with lamb.* ⅋ *LB.*

**** 1992 Eden Ridge Shiraz, S Australia, Aus. £8.83. *Very approachable, perfumed wine with mulberry fruit.* ⅋ *RM.*

*** 1991 Lirac les Queyrades, André Méjan, Rhône, Fr. £6.92. *Delicious, concentrated and ripe.* ⅋ *CH, SP.*

**** 1992 Ravenswood Old Vine Zinfandel, Sonoma County, California, US. £12.17. *Tropical, spicy, New World red.* ⅋ *BF, RMS.*

***** 1990 Santenay les Charrons, Dom. Lamy Pillot, Burgundy, Fr. £11.58. *Classy, complex red Burgundy at a very fair price.* ⅋ *BF, CC.*

A — Asda ★★★★

Asda House, Southbank, Great Wilson Street, Leeds LS11 5AD. Tel 0113 243 5435. Fax 0113 241 8146. Supermarket Chain. 206 branches. **Opening hours:** most stores: Mon-Sat 0900-2000, Sun 1000-1600. **Tastings:** regular in-store. **Services:** glass hire.

Asda's wine department comes straight out of a traditional French winemaker's worst nightmares. Mâcon Blancs, Frascatis and New Zealand Sauvignons all stand indiscrimately shoulder to shoulder irrespective of nationality and region, grouped only by their price and level of sweetness. For anyone wanting a £3.49 bottle of not-too-dry white or pretty-full-bodied red, the approach is ideal; for a Bordeaux fan wanting to choose from a range of clarets, it is a little more frustrating. This chain's modest view of its customers' vinous sophistication is reflected in a range whose prices rarely stray far beyond £5. Even so, given these constraints, Nick Dymoke Marr and his team have enthusiastically put together what is probably the most consistent selection in the high street. If you don't believe us, pop in and invest in a few of their 25cl taster bottles for an idea of what's on offer.

***** Scharffenberger Brut, California, US. £8.99. *A class act; rich ripe Champagne style, long and nutty and yeasty.* ¶ *AP.*

**** Champagne Nicolas Feuillate Blancs de Blancs, Fr. £14.99. *Rich and yeasty slightly off-dry – this is both ripe and mature.* ¶ *AP, LS.*

*** Coltiva Il Bianco, It. £2.69. *A light, clean and simple wine with hints of pears.* ¶ *P, FF.*

*** 1994 Lugana Sanroseda Boscaini, Valpolicella, It. £3.99. *Leafy and fresh with lots of flavour.* ¶ *CH,P.*

*** 1992 Rozzano Villa Pigna, Tuscany, It. £4.99. *An unusual wine; oaky, rich and rustic, but perfumed.* ¶ *LB, G.*

*** 1993 Muscadet de Sevre et Maine Sur Lie, Dom. Gautron, Loire, Fr. £4.49. *A light and lemony wine with some bready richness.* ¶ *O*

*** Asda VdP des Côtes de Gascogne, Fr. £2.99. *Light and peppery wine with some good plum fruit and a touch of spice.* ¶ *RMS.*

*** 1993 Ch. de Parenchère, Bordeaux, Fr. £5.25. *Light, grassy and simple with good soft fruit.* ¶ *LB.*

*** 1994 Bordeaux Sauvignon, Ch. le Desert, Fr. £2.99. *Light and grassy Sauvignon Blanc with a clean appley flavour.* ¶ *AP, PY.*

**** 1994 Stoneleigh Sauvignon Blanc, Marlborough, NZ. £5.99. *Brilliant asparagus and gooseberry flavours. Classic Kiwi Sauvignon.* ¶ *D, LS.*

**** 1993 Asda Chablis, Burgundy, Fr. £6.99. *A ripe and fruity wine – typical Chablis with good tangy acidity.* ¶ *AP, FD.*

*** 1994 Cono Sur Chardonnay, Chi. £3.99. *A light and simple creamy Chardonnay with a touch of oak.* ¶ *WFC, LS.*

**** 1994 Saint Veran, Dom. des Deux Roches, Burgundy, Fr. £6.49. *A good rich white Burgundy with toffee and pineapple hints.* ¶ *E, SF.*

**** 1994 Goundrey Langton Chardonnay, W. Australia, Aus. £5.25. *Serious oaky vanilla and pineapple fruit with good fresh acidity.* ¶ *WM, S.*

*** 1994 Graacher Himmelreich Riesling Kabinett, Von Kesselstat, Mosel, Ger. £5.99. *Lovely grapey summer fruit flavours. Very refreshing.* ¶ *CC.*

**** 1994 Penfolds Bin 21 Semillon-Chardonnay, S. Australia, Aus. £4.35. *A good oaky well-made wine full of toffeed vanilla and peach flavours.* ¶ *PY, WM.*

*** 1994 Asda Hungarian Muscat, Hun. £2.69. *A delightful easy-going grapey wine.* ¶ *P, PY.*

*** Asda Fitou, Midi, Fr. £3.29. *Earthy, gamey and rustic with good spice flavours. Excellent with stew.* ¶ *RMS.*

**** 1993 Cono Sur Cabernet Sauvignon, Chimbarongo, Chi. £3.79. *Good, creamy, ripe cassis and plum with minty flavours.* ¶ *PY, LB.*

**** 1992 Ch. d'Arcins Cru Bourgeois, Bordeaux, Fr. £5.99. *Good green pepper and cassis flavours; typical old-fashioned claret.* ¶ *LB.*

*** 1993 Penfolds Rawson's Retreat Bin 35, Ruby Cabernet/Shiraz, Aus. £4.45. *A good ripe and rich wine with tangy cherry fruit and tastily spicy oak. Proof of what the Ruby Cabernet can do outside California.* ¶ *SP, P.*

**** 1994 Terra Alta Cabernet-Garnacha, Catalonia, Sp. £2.99. *Pepper galore! Rich and spicy wine full of berries and classic Grenache pepper.* ¶ *LB.*

**** 1994 Dom. des Grangeneuve, Coteaux du Tricastin, Fr. £4.35. *Very pronounced pepper and redcurranty fruit.* ¶ *LB, RMS.*

**** 1994 Fairview Estate Shiraz, Paarl, SA. £4.49. *A real mouthful of wild bramble fruit; ripe and intense.* ¶ *PY, D.*

*** 1993 Arius Neuf, Arius Vineyard, California, US. £5.99. *Peppery Rhôney flavours, with lovely berry fruit. Beefy and ripe.* ¶ *LB.*

*** 1994 Asda Hungarian Kekfrankos, Hun. £2.69. *Simple, juicy berry fruit and a touch of spice – an alternative to Beaujolais* ¶ *FF, O.*

*** 1994 Beaujolais Villages, Dom. des Roches, Burgundy, Fr. £4.39. *Clean modern Beaujolais; boiled sweets and chocolate.* ¶ *AP, SM.*

**** Asda Valpolicella, Veneto, It. £2.79. *A lovely soft wine full of cherry fruit and nut flavours.* ¶ *P.*

**** 1988 Asda Late Bottled Vintage Port, Por. £6.75. *A good plummy wine, nutty and rich with lots of Christmas pudding flavour.* ¶ *CC, CH.*

42 Merchants

Emerging from his haunt down under South Australia House following the closure of the Australian Wine Centre shop, Craig Smith is clearly relishing life above ground as a purveyor of Aussie wine by mail. And who can blame him, given the time he can now take to frolic with the likes of Charlie Melton, Bob McLean and Joe Grilli, all of whose individualistic wines he proudly sells? Customers get the chance to frolic too – at the Club's annual May tasting, in their imaginations via the pages of its regular newsletter or as members of the new *Four Seasons Wine Plan* through which, for the specially low price of £75 they receive four mixed cases per year of Aussie wines, some of which are pretty well unfindable in Adelaide or Sydney.

★★★★ Taltarni Cuvée Brut, Victoria, Aus. £7.99. *Classy, quite subtle fizz made by a Frenchman from cool-climate grapes.* ¶ **WM, FO.**

★★★★ 1994 Allandale Chardonnay, New South Wales, Aus. £6.99. *Lovely, sunny Hunter Valley white, with comparitively subtle fruit.* ¶ **WM, FO.**

★★★★ 1994 St Hallett Chardonnay, S Australia, Aus. £7.49. *Big, rich, ripe, up-front... I'm sure you get the picture.* ¶ **D, LS**

★★★★★ 1994 Chapel Hill Winery Unwooded Chardonnay, S Australia, Aus. £7.99. *And the absolute opposite. Elegant lemony and peachy wine.* ¶ **LS, D, WM.**

★★★★ 1992 Coldstream Hills Chardonnay, Yarra, Victoria, Aus. £12.99. *Superb, ultra Burgundian wine to blow away many a Puligny.* ¶ **LS, FO.**

★★★ 1994 St Hallett Poachers Blend, S Australia, Aus. £4.99. *Well-balanced, fruity blend.* ¶ **WM, E.**

★★★★★ 1994 Primo Estate Colombard, S Australia, Aus. £5.99. *Highly unusual, fruit salady example of a generally under-exploited grape variety, produced by an eccentric Italian in the fruit growing country of the Adelaide Plains.* ¶ **LB**

★★★★★ 1993 The Willows Vineyard Semillon, S Australia, Aus. £6.99. *Dry Aussie Semillon at its ripe, buttery, peachy best.* ¶ **CH, SM.**

★★★★ 1992 Dead Man's Hill Gewürztraminer, Delatite Wines, Victoria, Aus. £6.99. *A rare satisfactory Aussie attempt at Gewürztraminer.* ¶ **LS, AP.**

★★★★ 1990 Henschke Riesling, S Australia, Aus. £10.99. *Gorgeous maturing, slightly petrolly Riesling from cool vineyards - and Australia's best red winemaker.* ¶ **BF, RMS.**

★★★★ 1994 Heritage Cabernet Franc, S Australia, Aus. *An unusual minty/ blackcurranty example of a grape rarely grown in Australia.* £7.49. ¶ **SP.**

★★★★★ 1993 Mitchelton 111 Shiraz/Grenache/Mourvedre, Victoria, Aus. £6.99. *Characterful, perfumed with pepper and blackberries.* ¶ **LB.**

★★★★ 1992 Chapel Hill Shiraz, McLaren Vale, Aus. £7.99. *Ultra-ripe, soft smoky Shiraz you could enjoyably spread on toast.* ¶ **D, RM.**

★★★★ 1992 St Hallett Old Block Shiraz, S Australia, Aus. £9.99. *Deep intense sweet fruit – pepper, chocolate and spice with hints of gamey leather.* ¶ **CH.**

★★★★ 1992 Wignalls Pinot Noir, W. Australia, Aus. £11.45. *Very Burgundian, raspberryish wine from a winery with a cult following down under.* ¶ **G, RMS.**

★★★★★ 1992 Mitchelton Print Label Shiraz, Victoria, Aus. £9.99. *Soft but concentrated berryish wine with good oak spice.* ¶ **G.**

★★★★★ 1993 Morris of Rutherglen Durif, Victoria, Aus. £9.99. *Stewed plum and blackcurrant jam. The Australian version of the Petite Sirah.* ¶ **G.**

★★★★★ 1993 Aberfeldy, Tim Adams Wines, S Australia, Aus. £11.99. *Plummy with spices and herbs. A mouthfilling wine that's built to last.* ¶ **RM, RMS.**

★★★★ Seppelt Show Muscat D.P. 63B, Victoria, Aus. £10.49. *Enormous raisin fruit and Oxford Marmalade flavours – pour it on your ice-cream.* ¶ **CHO, D.**

AV   Avery's   ★★★★

Orchard House, Southfield Road, Nailsea, Bristol, Avon BS1 5NG. Tel 01275 811 100
Fax: 01275 811 101. Mon-Sat 1000-1900. Wine Cellar (Culver Street) Mon-Sat 0900-
1900. **Delivery:** mail order sales – free nationally for 2 cases or more. **Tastings:** in-
store and Wine Cellar tutored events. **Services:** *en primeur*, mail-order, gift mailing,
storage, export, glass hire, ice.

Founded in 1793 as shippers of wine, sherry and slaves, Avery's recent history has
been almost as interesting. First it fell into of the hands of a Californian millionaire-
banker-cum-winery owner who (wrongly) believed he could persuade the firm's arch-
traditionalist customers to switch allegiance to a range of pricy-if-good wines from his
home state. Now, John Avery and his team find themselves indirectly working for
Pieroth, ultra-successful door-to-door purveyors of sometimes less-than-dazzling
German wine. So far the purchase seems merely to have allowed Avery's to
consolidate, converting one of their historic vaulted cellars into the Culver Street Wine
Cellar and to build on the success of Avery's Bin Club which offers members
discounts of 10%. Cynics watch with interest to see how the alliance will develop.

- ★★★★ Averys Special Cuvée Champagne, Fr. £14.75 *Intensely flavoursome, rich, biscuity fizz.* ⁋ *AP, PY.*
- ★★★★ 1989 Champagne Taittinger, Champagne, Fr £26.99. *Subtle, classic Champagne with good appley Chardonnay character.* ⁋ *AP, D.*
- ★★★★ 1994 Enate Blanco Maccabeo/Chardonnay, Somontano, Sp. £4.99. *Clean, new-wave wine with attractive peary fruit.* ⁋ *WMC.*
- ★★★ 1994 Nobilo White Cloud, Gisborne, NZ. £4.99 .*Light, slightly citrussy, and very refreshing wine. Very moreish.* ⁋ *PY, FF.*
- ★★★ 1994 Houghton Gold Reserve Verdelho, W Australia, Aus £7.49. *Unusual l lime marmalade flavours - a rich, tasty change from Chardonnay.* ⁋ *WM.*
- ★★★★ 1994 Tyrrells Private Bin Vat 47 Chardonnay, New South Wales, Aus £12.99 *Australia's first Chardonnay. Rich, ripe, mouthfilling.* ⁋ *WM, SM.*
- ★★★★ 1993 Klein Constantia Estate Chardonnay, Constantia, SA £6.75 *Classy lean, Chablis-like Chardonnay. Worth keeping.* ⁋ *WM, FD.*
- ★★★★★ 1992 Swanson Carneros Chardonnay, California, US £13.45 *Stunningly concentrated layers of toasty oak and biscuity nutty Burgundy flavour.* ⁋ *SM.*
- ★★★★ 1993 Clos l'Envège Côtes de Bergerac, Yvès Pagès, Bergerac, Fr. £4.59 *Well made, Bordeaux-style. Quite grassy.* ⁋ *PY, WMC.*
- ★★★★★ 1993 Chinon les Violettes, Morin, Loire, Fr, £5.25. *Good, chunky, blackcurranty wine. Refreshing if drunk chilled.* ⁋ *LS.*
- ★★★★ 1991 Rustenberg Estate Cabernet Sauvignon, Stellenbosch, SA £7.99. *Middleweight, very attractive old-fashioned claret style.* ⁋ *LB, RMS.*
- ★★★★ 1992 Swanson Vineyards Merlot, California, US £13.99. *Ripe, full-bodied but very approachable plummy wine.* ⁋ *BF, LB, CH.*
- ★★★★ 1992 Rouge Homme Shiraz Cabernet, S Australia, Aus £5.29 *A classic Aussie blend of ripe fruit, eucalyptus and oak. Delicious.* ⁋ *LB, RMS, G.*
- ★★★ 1991 Nobilo Pinotage, Huapai, NZ. £6.75 *The only serious Pinotage made outside South Africa, and it is more than just a curiosity. Plummy.* ⁋ *RMS, G*
- ★★★★ 1992 Nuits St Georges, Ch. Gris, Lupé Cholet, Burgundy, Fr. £18.00. *Typical, quite tough, berryish Nuits.* ⁋ *RMS.*
- ★★★ 1993 Marechal Foch, Inniskillin Wines, Niagara, Can £6.25 *Berryish Beaujolais-like wine from an unusual hybrid grape.* ⁋ *AP, D, O.*
- ★★★ 1994 Morgon Louis Genillon, Eventail, Beaujolais, Fr £6.29 *Fresh, soft, chocolatey. Will develop.* ⁋ *D, O, CH.*
- ★★★★ 1993 Hamilton Russell Pinot Noir, Walker Bay, SA £7.99 *Plummy, cherryish, lightly oaky wine from South Africa's top Pinot producer.* ⁋ *RM, CC.*
- ★★★★ 1992 Enate Tempranillo/Cabernet Crianza, Somontano, Sp. £6.25 . *Good, modern, oaky strawberryish-blackcurranty red.* ⁋ *WM, LB.*
- ★★★★★ 1989 Vin de Constance, Klein Constantia, SA. £3.50. *Wonderful, honeyed, raisiny wine. A taste of one of South Africa's classic styles.* ⁋ *PS.*

BH B H Wines ★★★★★

Bousted Hill House, Boustead Hill, Burgh-by-Sands, Carlisle CA5 6AA. Tel/Fax 01228 576711. Independent Wine Merchant. Wines by the case only. **Opening hours:** Mon, Tues, Wed, Fri, Sat 0900-1700, Sundays and evenings by appointment. **Delivery:** free locally. **Services:** mail order, glass hire. No credit cards.

Richard and Linda Neville continue to offer the same formula of 'wines of character, quality and value' combined with the flexible, knowledgeable service that won them the North of England Wine Merchant of the Year award in 1994/5. The Southern France section of their list alone shows classics like Chateau Simone alongside new stars Carignanissime de Centeilles from Minervois and oddballs such as Long Tall Cabernet Sauvignon from Corsica, and other areas of the world are covered with equal perspicacity.

★★★★★	Daniel le Brun, Marlborough, NZ. £11.75. *Rich, buttery and toasty Champagne like fizz.* ⁋ **S, P.**
★★★	1994 Chardonnay dei Sassi Cavi, Grave del Fruili, It. £5.85 *An attractive lemony alternative to New World Chardonnay.* ⁋ **LS.**
★★★	1994 Seppelt Moyston Semillon Chardonnay, Aus. £4.50. *Oaky, creamy wine with lovely peachy fruit.* ⁋ **O, WMC.**
★★★★	1990 Newton Unfiltered Chardonnay, Napa, California, US. £15. *A big wine, full of buttery fruit, and left unfiltered to preserve maximum flavour.* ⁋ **D, FO.**
★★★★	1994 Dry Creek Chenin Blanc, California, US. £6.45. *Honeyed, appley and full of ripe fruit flavour.* ⁋ **WM, FF.**
★★★★	1986 Château Sénéjac, Médoc, Bordeaux, Fr. £10.80. *Classy wine from a top vintage which is just beginning to show its promise.* ⁋ **LB, CH.**
★★★★★	1989 Vasse Felix Cabernet Sauvignon, Margaret River, Aus. £11.15. *Minty and cedary Cabernet with a great deal of concentration.* ⁋ **BF, G.**
★★★★	1991 Rosso Conero, San Lorenzo Single Vineyard, Umani Ronchi, It. £5.70 *Deep pruney fruit with nuances of tea and ripe figs.* ⁋ **G, P.**
★★★	1993 Passito Di Pantelleria, Carlo Pellegrino, It. £9. *Luscious Old English marmalade flavours with peachy freshness.* ⁋ **PS.**

BAL Ballantynes ★★★

3 Westgate, Cowbridge, South Glamorgan, CF7 7YW. Tel 01446 774840. Fax 01446 775253. Independent Wine Merchant. **Opening hours:** Mon-Sat 0900-1800. **Delivery:** free locally. **Tastings:** regular themed. **Services:** cellarage, *en primeur*, mail order, gift mailing, glass hire.

'There is always a member of the family available to offer advice' – quite possibly Richard Ballantyne who enjoys nothing better than expressing his enthusiasm for Burgundy, Italy and such stylish New World wines as those of Cullens in Western Australia and Kumeu River in New Zealand. Quite simply everything a small family wine merchant should be.

★★★★	1993 Vin Sec du Chateau Coutet, Graves, Bordeaux, Fr. £8.49. *Characterful nutty, gooseberryish Sauvignon.* ⁋ **LS, AP.**
★★★★★	1991 Kumeu River Chardonnay, Auckland, NZ. £14.67 *Wonderfully opulent and very convincingly Burgundian Chardonnay.* ⁋ **WFC.**
★★★★	1993 Anjou Rouge "Vieilles Vignes" Château de Fesles, Loire, Fr. £6.99. *Intense, black cherryish wine. Crunchy, freshly picked berries.* ⁋ **P, SM.**
★★★★	1993 Campbells Bobbie Burns Shiraz, Victoria, Aus. £7.49. *Soft, plummily rich wine from a very warm region of Australia.* ⁋ **BF, CH.**
★★★★★	1988 Pommard "1er Cru Epenots", André Mussy, Burgundy, Fr. £23.70 *Good, traditional, concentrated and mulberryish. Worth waiting for.* ⁋ **BF, CH.**
★★★★	1988 Amarone Classico della Valpolicella Speri, Casa Girelli, Veneto, It. £11.5 *Rich, concentrated wine – at once pruney and raisiny yet dry.* ⁋ **RMS.**

BAN   Adam Bancroft   ★★★★

The Mansion House, 57 South Lambeth Road, London SW8 1RJ. Tel 0171 793
1902. Fax 0171 793 1897. Independent Wine Merchant. Wines by the case only.
Delivery: free locally.

Three unusual wineries from Western Australia: Madfish Bay, Howard Park and
Devil's Lair should be enough to get the tastebuds going. But don't be misled into
expecting a New World Extravaganza; all the other wines on the list come from
France. You won't find a lot of classed growth Bordeaux either; Mr Bancroft is not
the sort of man to rely on Parker or Broadbent ratings to choose and promote his
wines, rather the reverse – every wine has been sourced direct from the growers that
he admires. As a result, you will rarely find a more carefully chosen, comprehensive
and excellent range of Burgundy, Rhône and Loire wines. If you need a further
carrot, the cachet of being the only U.K. source for the Cornas of Jean-Luc Colombo
(possibly the most exciting new name in the Rhône) should seal the matter.

- ★★★★   1993 Reuilly, Henri Beurdin, Loire, Fr. £6.46. *Berry fruits galore. Crisp,*
  clean Sauvignon. ¶ **WFC.**
- ★★★★   1992/3 Marsannay Blanc, Alain Guyard, Burgundy, Fr. £8.64. *Good ripe fruit*
  overlaid with oak – a worthy alternative to Chablis. ¶ **AP, LS.**
- ★★★★★ 1990 Saumur Champigny, Régis Neau, Loire, Fr. £6.99. *Gorgeous, crunchy*
  blackcurrant flavour with just a hint of earthiness. ¶ **WFP.**
- ★★★★★ 1992 Devil's Lair Cabernet Sauvignon, Aus. £9.69. *Hard to find in this*
  country – one of Western Australia's better small wineries. ¶ **RM, G.**
- ★★★★★ 1991 Cornas, Jean Luc Columbo, Rhône, Fr. £12.87. *This is wonderful*
  peppery stuff full of black fruit, smoke and a hint of leather. ¶ **SP, CH.**
- ★★★★   1990 Volnay, Bernard Glantenay, Burgundy, Fr. £12.63. *Old-fashioned*
  flavours, but seriously concentrated smoky black fruit. ¶ **CH, E.**

GB   Georges Barbier   ★★★★

267 Lee High Road, London, SE12 8RU. Tel 0181 852 5801. Fax 0181 463 0398.
Independent Wine Merchant. **Opening hours:** Mon-Fri 0900-1800. **Delivery:** free
locally. **Services:** mail order, cellarage. No credit cards.

Concentrating almost exclusively on the Old World (the ultra-traditional Chateau
Tahbilk almost counts as an honorary European) M Barbier offers classy Burgundies
from domaines like Ballot-Millot, a Bordeaux list which includes the ultra-rare
Château Guillot, a rising star of Pomerol, and distant cousin Rene Barbier's
impressive Clos Mogador from Spain. Wrily regrets that he has not been able to list
the entire Metté Alsace eaux de vies; customers will have to be content with such
run-of-the-mill fare as Holly Berry, Asparagus, Red Whortleberry, Medlar and Sloe.

- ★★★   1992 Mourvèdre, Vin de Pays d'Oc, Vignerons du Val d'Orbieu, Fr. *Dry, herby,*
  very distinctive, old fashioned red. £3.90. ¶ **BF, CH.**
- ★★★   1993 Faugères, Ch. de la Liquière "Vielles Vignes", Midi, Fr. £5.48. *Lovely,*
  gamey wine with rich meaty concentration. ¶ **PY, P.**
- ★★★★★ 1985 Ch. Guillot, Pomerol, Bordeaux, Fr. £16.95. *Classic maturing Pomerol:*
  plummily intense with a slightly 'stony' character. ¶ **LB.**
- ★★★★   1988 Ch. Lascombes, Margaux, Bordeaux, Fr. £18.50. *Elegant claret*
  beginning to mature; blackberry and violets. ¶ **RMS, BF.**
- ★★★★★ 1992 Chambolle-Musigny, Dom. Jacques-Frédéric Mugnier, Burgundy, Fr.
  £15.56. *Deep, richly concentrated cherryish wine with sweet oak.* ¶ **WFP, CC.**
- ★★★★   1992 St. Aubin 1er Cru 'La Chatenière', Dom. Gérard Thomas, Burgundy, Fr.
  £10.90. *Classy, raspberryish Pinot from a little-known village.* ¶ **LB, SM.**
- ★★★★★ 1990 Clos Mogador, Priorat, Dom. René Barbier, Sp. £13.90. *Arguably Spain's*
  most interesting red wine. Made in a very old fashioned region, this is
  packed with dark berry flavour. Worth keeping. ¶ **SP, CH.**

BWS   Barnes   ★★★★★

51 High Street, Barnes, London SW13 9LN. Tel 0181 878 8643. Fax 0181 878 6522. **Opening hours:** Mon-Sat 0930-2030, Sun 12-1400. Independent Wine Merchant. **Delivery:** free locally. **Tastings:** regular in-store. **Services:** cellarage, *en primeur*, mail order, gift mailing, glass hire, ice.

Barnes is so timelessly village-like that it easy to imagine ambling down the high street popping in at the butcher, the baker and the candlestick maker before arriving at former policeman Francis Murray's small but delightful establishment. A visit here – especially on a Saturday when bottles are open for tasting is a must, especially now that easier times have permitted him to expand his stocks of a range which whisks you from Argentina to South Africa via France, Italy and the Lebanon.

★★★★   1990 Champagne de Venoge Blanc de Blancs, Fr £23.95. *Stylish, appley, lemony Champagne which will improve with keeping.* ❙ **AP, LS.**

★★★   1994 Pinot Grigio, Le Veritière, It. £5.29. *Crisp, modern Italian wine. Lemony and slightly spicy – and very easy to drink.* ❙ **WFC, P.**

★★★★   1992 Sylvaner Vieilles Vignes, Ostertag, Alsace, Fr. £7.45. *A rare, perfumed dry example of the potentially dull Sylvaner.* ❙ **AP, LS.**

★★★★   1992 Wignalls Pinot Noir, W. Australia, Aus. £11.45. *Very Burgundian wine from a winery with a cult following down under.* ❙ **G, RMS.**

★★★★★ 1983 Côte Rôtie Brune et Blonde, Guigal, Rhône, Fr. £21.50. *Ultra-serious smoky Northern Rhône with all sorts of berry fruit. Made to last.* ❙ **LB, RM.**

★★★★   1988 Quinta de La Rosa Vintage Port, Douro, Por. £13.95. *Sweet and very well-balanced port from a small independently owned estate.* ❙ **CC, CS.**

B&B   Barrels & Bottles   ★★★

1 Walker Street, The Wicker, Sheffield, S3 8GZ. Tel 0114 276 9666. Fax 0114 279 9182. Independent Wine Merchant. **Opening hours:** Mon-Fri 0900-1800, Sat 0900-1400. **Delivery:** free locally. **Services:** cellarage, glass hire, ice.

B&B's 'Cellar Swap' scheme one of the most original we've seen in years. Just bring in any 'unloved or unwanted' bottle from your rack and part exchange it for 'the perfect wine of your choice' from B&B's list. Quite how many bottles of 1968 Liebfraumilch it would take to get a 50cl bottle of Kueling Gillot Laubenheimer Edelman Trockenbeerenauslese Scheurebe, we cannot imagine, but we'd be happy to hand over real folding stuff for most of this German enthusiast's range. If German wines – including an almost unique late harvest red Pinot Noir– are not your thing, turn straight to the regional French wines and the Bordeaux. But hurry, we're on our way right now with some really juicy old bottles of Bulls Blood and Anjou Rosé.

★★★★★ 1979 Champagne Pol Roger Cuvée Sir Winston Churchill, Fr. £52.58. *Truly great, nutty, mature Champagne, named after its greatest fan.* ❙ **AP, LS.**

★★★★★ 1992 Oppenheimer Kreuz Spätlese, Weingut Kühling Gillot, Rheinhessen, Ger. £5.99. *From one of the best producers in Germany. Concentrated wine with lovely perfumed, grapey flavour.* ❙ **WM, PF.**

★★★★   3 Year Old Vega Sicilia, Valbuena, Sp. £27.14. *Younger than the Spaniards like it. Good for us though: plummy, strawberrish wine.* ❙ **SP, LB.**

★★★★   1984 Beira Mar Garrafeira, Alentejo, Por. £6.40. *A great example of maturing gamey, slightly raisiny Portuguese red.* ❙ **SP, RMS.**

★★★★   1990 Crozes Hermitage, 'Comte de Raybois', Rhône, Fr. £6.56. *Concentrated smoky, brambley Syrah. Exciting wine.* ❙ **CH, RM.**

★★★★   1986 Ch. La Tour du Pin Figeac, Bordeaux, Fr. £16.44. *Nicely aged Merlot, with gentle dried fruit flavours coupled with a bit of tannin.* ❙ **LB.**

★★★★   1991 Waldulmer Pfarrberg, Baden, Ger. £7.40. *Extraordinary, berryish German red with susprising depth of flavour.* ❙ **RM, BF.**

BND   Benedicts Wine   ★★★

28 Holyrood Street, Newport, Isle of Wight PO30 5AU. Tel 01983 529596. Fax 01983 826868. Independent Wine Merchant. **Delivery:** by application. **Services:** wine glasses for sale, decanters, sundries, wine racks made to order.

'We are unique in selling all 16 wines made on the Isle of Wight'. Well, we're delighted someone is doing their bit for their local English vineyards – and happy to see wines such as the excellent Yarden Cabernet from Israel, Yarra Yering from Australia, Mâcon Clessé from the Domaine de Bon Gran, and an eclectic range from Italy and Spain. With luck, these, combined with Benedicts' delicatessen fare might deter the residents from filling up their yachts with bottles from Calais supermarkets where good white – let alone Wight – wines have yet to make their mark.

- ***** 1992 Sancerre le Chêne Marchand, Pascal Jolivet, Loire, Fr. £11.75. *A perfumed, herbaceous wine with delicious crisp acidity.* ¶ **FD, S, WFP.**
- **** 1991 Pinot Gris, Domaine Schlumberger, Alsace, Fr. £8.45. *A subtle wine reminiscent of apple strudel.* ¶ **O, AP, WM.**
- **** 1986 Château Caronne-Ste-Gemme, Cru Bourgeois, Bordeaux, Fr. £11.25. *Nicely maturing, quite cedary claret from a tough vintage.* ¶ **CH, G, RMS.**
- **** 1987 Coleraine Cabernet Sauvignon/Merlot/Cabernet Franc, NZ. £16.50. New Zealand's most famous red wine. *A delicious mixture of blackberries and green, appley fruit.* ¶ **D, SP, RM.**
- **** 1988 Meerlust Merlot, Stellenbosch, SA. £9.50. *Plums, damson jam and that distinctive South African earthiness which serves as a living reminder of the way many Bordeaux and Burgundy used to taste.* ¶ **FF, G, WMP.**

BEN   Bennetts   ★★★★

High Street, Chipping Campden, Glos GL55 6AG. Tel/Fax (24 hours) 01386 840392. Independent Wine Merchant. **Opening hours:** Mon-Fri 0900-1300, 1400-1730, Sat 0900-1730. **Delivery:** free locally. **Tastings:** tutored wine dinners. **Services:** mail order, glass hire.

Sounding like a market gardener, Charlie Bennett claims to have experienced 'enormous growth at the top end' over the last year, and remains convinced that the independent merchant must increasingly focus on the quality end of the market, leaving the supermarkets to supply our everyday drinking needs. This involves developing an encyclopedic product knowledge. To give customers an honest assessment of wines like Roederer Quartet from California, Engel red Burgundies, the Lafon Montrachet 1968, Sassicaia 1990 or Noval 1966, corks have to be pulled – a chore that, given your support, Mr and Mrs Bennett are prepared to undertake.

- ***** 1994 Thelema Sauvignon Blanc, Stellenbosch, SA. £6.99. *Is this South Africa's best Sauvignon? Crisp and concentrated.* ¶ **CC, WFC.**
- *** 1994 St Veran, J Drouhin, Burgundy, Fr. £6.99 *Fresh, lemony alternative to Pouilly Fuissé. Good, modern white Burgundy.* ¶ **WM, S.**
- ***** 1993 Calera Chardonnay Mount Harlan, California, US. £23.50. *Subtle young wine from a winery better known for its Pinot.* ¶ **CH, SM, WM.**
- **** 1994 Bonny Doon Ca' del Solo Malvasia Bianca, California, US. £8.75 *Perfumed, dry yet grapey blend of Californian and Italian flavours.* ¶ **P, D, WM.**
- ***** 1994 Pewsey Vale Eden Valley Riesling, S Australia, Aus. £6.99 *Ripe, appley, limey Riesling from a coolish high altitude vineyard* ¶ **O, D, S, AP.**
- **** 1992 Parrina Rosso, Tuscany, It. £5.95 *Tasty herby red wine to drink with almost anything Italian or an underdone piece of beef.* ¶ **RM, P.**
- **** 1982 Ch. d'Angludet, Bordeaux, Fr. £24.50 *Classic Margaux from one of the best years of this century. Gently mature but still packed with fruit.* ¶ **RM, P.**
- **** 1988 Chivite 125 Aniversario Gran Reserva, Navarra, Sp. £9.95. *First class, modern Spanish wine with spicy fruit and oak.* ¶ **LB.**

48 Merchants

BKW Berkeley Wines ★★

P.O. Box 476, Loushers Lane, Warrington, Cheshire WA4 6RT. Tel 01925 444555
Fax 01925 415474. Regional Chain. 140 branches. **Opening hours:** Mon-Sat 1000-
2200, Sun 12-1500 1900-2200. **Delivery:** free locally. **Tastings:** regular in store.
Services: glass hire, consumer wine fairs.

Once Cellar 5 in its Sunday Best, this chain is now steadily becoming the more
modest cousin of the same company's smart Wine Cellar (qv) shops and boasts much
of that chain's increasingly well chosen range. It will take time to raise staff
knowledge to the level of some of the wines but efforts are being made – by the man
responsible for creating Wine Rack and the current incarnation of Bottoms Up.

****	Cuvée Napa, Mumm, California, US. £8.99. *Ripe, quite serious Californian fizz with lovely appley, berryish flavours.* ⁊ *AP, D.*
***	1993 Montana Sauvignon Blanc, Marlborough, NZ. £4.99. *The original, and still among the best Kiwi Sauvignons. Deliciously gooseberryish.* ⁊ *CC, S.*
****	1992 Wolf Blass Yellow Label Cabernet Sauvignon, S Australia, Aus. £6.99. *Big, rich and unashamedly Australian. Soft, oaky and seductive.* ⁊ *RM, LB.*
***	1990 Chateau Monbousquet, St Emilion, Bordeaux, Fr. £9.99. *Young St Emilion with plummy, slightly earthy richness.* ⁊ *RMS>.*
***	1991 Côtes du Rhône Villages Cuvée des Toques, Co-op Beaumes de Venise, Rhône, Fr. £4.69. *Great value peppery, brambley wine.* ⁊ *LB, CH.*
***	1982 Marques de Villamagna Rioja Gran Reserva, Bodegas Campo Viejo, Sp. £11.29. *Serious Rioja with squashy strawberry fruit and sweet oak.* ⁊ *LB.*

BBR Berry Bros & Rudd ★★★★

3 St. James's Street, London SW1A 1EG. Tel 0171 396 9600. Orders: Tel 0171 396
9669. Fax 0171 396 9611. Independent Wine Merchant. **Opening hours:** Mon-Fri
0900-1730. Also at: The Wine Shop, Houndmills, Basingstoke, Hampshire RG21
2TB. Tel 01256 23566. Fax 01256 479558. New Fine Wine Warehouse at Hamilton
Close, Houndmills, Basingstoke, Hampshire, RG21 6YB. Warehouse **Opening
hours:** Tues-Weds 1000-1700, Thurs-Fri 1000-2000, Sat 1000-1600. **Delivery:**
free locally. **Tastings:** regular in-store, tutored on request. **Services:** cellarage, *en
primeur*, mail order, gift mailing, glass hire.

Holding Berry's reassuring list in your hand makes life seem simple and certain once
again. Here is a veritable catalogue of the familiar, tried and trusted. There's claret a-
plenty, starting with a range of Berry's own generic wines such as 'Good Ordinary
Claret', and Berry's Margaux, right up to 1982 Petrus at £800 a bottle. This St James
merchant remains one of the few companies that really undersands Mosel Riesling, and
offers some remarkably fine examples from Max Ferd Richter, Dr Loosen and
Reichsgraf von Kesselstadt. Port, Champagne and Rioja are predictably strong, and the
New World, though less evident, is increasingly well handled. Earlier this year,
Berry's opened a wine warehouse in Basingstoke, the latest of its recent innovations
which include a shop in Heathrow's Terminal 3, a wine-by-subscription service
called 'Like Clockwork' and the revamping of the wine broking department.

***	1994 Touraine Sauvignon, Domaine Joel Delaunay, Loire, Fr. £4.95. *A far better than usual wine from this appellation. Like ripe grapefruit.* ⁊ *O, AP, SM.*
****	1994 Forrest Estate Marlborough Sauvignon Blanc, NZ. £8.25. *Lovely, herbaceous wine with typical Marlborough gooseberry fruit.* ⁊ *D, S, WMC.*
***	1994 Maison Vergnes Chardonnay Domaine Lamoure, Aude, Fr. £5.50. *Fresh, melony, quite Californian-style Southern French Chardonnay.* ⁊ *WMC.*
****	1992 Petaluma Chardonnay, S Australia, Aus. £10.99. *Ripe, peachy very Australian-style fruit with Burgundian subtlety and richness.* ⁊ *SF, SM, WM D.*
*****	1989 Riesling Cuvée Frederic Emile, Trimbach, Alsace, Fr £17.40 *Ripe, spicy Riesling with a fresh lime marmalade character.* ⁊ *O, AP, S.*

**** 1989 Niersteiner Rehbach Riesling Auslese, Eugen Wehrheim, Rheinhessen, Ger. £11. *Hugely complex – orange rind, almonds and petrol.* ¶ *O, CC, SP.*

***** 1989 Piesporter Goldtröpfchen Auslese, Reichsgraf von Kesselstatt, Mosel, Ger. £11.25. *Clean and refreshing with lots of ripe apple flavour.* ¶ *O, CS, PF.*

**** 1990 Backsberg Klein Babylonstoren, Paarl, SA. £7.50. *Beefy, almost porty, Bordeaux blend from one of the Cape's most reliable Estates.* ¶ *LB, G, RM.*

*** 1991 Château La Tour St Bonnet, Médoc, Bordeaux, Fr. £6.25. *A well made, maturing claret with quite concentrated berry fruit.* ¶ *LB, CH, RM.*

***** 1990 Cornas, Domaine de Rochepertuis, J. Lionnet, Rhône, Fr. £14.80. *Serious, gamey Syrah with leathery spice from a top producer.* ¶ *WM, SP, RM.*

**** 1991 Kanonkop Pinotage, Stellenbosch, SA. £9.98. *Deep spicy red fruit, hints of ripe bananas and jammy fruit with great new oak.* ¶ *BF, P, RM, SP.*

**** 1991 Flynn Pinot Noir, Oregon, US. £11. *Sweet, ripe and alcoholic. Creamy with raspberries and fresh summer fruits.* ¶ *G, D, AP.*

***** 1993 Wignalls Pinot Noir, King River, W Australia, Aus. £12.45 *Youthful, berryish Pinot from a specialist producer in Western Australia.* ¶ *CC, WFP, RM.*

**** 1989 Chivite Reserva, Navarra, Sp. £5.25. *Softly ripe, but with impressively concentrated fruit and oak flavours.* ¶ *CH, SF, WM.*

***** 1990 Hermitage, Vin de Paille, M. Chapoutier, Rhône, Fr. £66. (half) *Highly unusual white wine made in the traditional way, by drying grapes on straw mats. Concentrated, rich and honeyed.* ¶ *LB, SP, G, RMS.*

**** 1991 Taylor's Terra Feita, Oporto, Por. £16.25. *Full of damson and plummy fruit, excellent now and will continue to improve.* ¶ *CH, AP.*

**** 1980 Gould Campbell Vintage Port, Douro, Por. £18.45 *Classy plummy port from an underrated producer and vintage.* ¶ *CC, CH, CS.*

***** Cossart Gordon 10 Year Old Special Reserve Malmsey, Mad. £19.65. *A complex mix of rich spice, chocolate and dundee cake.* ¶ *PS, AP, CHO, CS.*

BI Bibendum   ★★★★★

113 Regents Park Road, London NW1 8UR. Tel 0171 722 5577. Fax 0171 722 7354. Independent Wine Merchant. Wine by the case only. **Opening hours:** Mon-Thurs 1000-1830, Fri 1000-2000, Sat 0930-1700. **Delivery:** free to all mainland England addresses. **Tastings:** regular in-store, informal and tutored sessions. **Services:** cellarage, fine wine desk, mail order, gift mailing, glass hire, ice.

Simon Farr and his team have come a long way since the days when outsiders imagined them to be running a one-store competitor to Majestic. Today, having assimilated Yorkshire Fine Wines and become one of the most successful mail-order merchants in the country, they have also colonised substantial sections of top flight restaurant cellars, set up an international fine wine broking business and quietly pioneered widely available branded wines such as La Serre from Southern France, the Australian Deakin Estates wines and the Catena wines from Argentina. Back at base, however, the focus is on Burgundy, Bordeaux (how many other merchants run tastings of 1961 first growths and Super Seconds for their customers?), the Rhône and Italy. Bibendum's new designer list is boldly entitled 'The Great Crusade'. Stand by for caped wine merchants, quite possiby wearing their boxer shorts over their trousers, fervently defending the true vinous faith.

***** 1986 Champagne Dom Ruinart, Blanc de Blancs, Ruinart, Champagne, Fr. £38.99. *Lovely, buttery, honeyed wine. Deep, rich and long.* ¶ *AP, PY.*

**** 1988 Champagne Pommery Cuvée Louise Pommery Brut, Fr. £39.99. *Ripe raspberry and attractive yeasty/biscuity character. Long, fruity finish.* ¶ *PY.*

**** 1994 Orvieto Classico, Scambia, Umbria, It. £5.49. *Subtle, gently nutty, high quality modern Italian wine.* ¶ *FD, S.*

**** 1993 Condrieu, Dumazet, Rhône, Fr. £13.99. *Classic, perfumed, apricotty Viognier.* ¶ *SP, FD, WM.*

**** 1993 Dom d'Astros, Vin de Pays des Maures Blanc, Midi, Fr. £3.99. *Light, spicy, slightly gingery wine. Very unusual.* ¶ *PY, SP.*

50 Merchants

**** 1992 Valley Vineyards Fumé, Berks, Eng. £8.49. *Oaky English wine to compete with Sancerre. Dry, fruity, impressive.* ¶ **SM, SF, CC.**

**** 1993 Sauvignon Blanc. Konocti, California, US. £4.99. *Unusually good value appley Californian Sauvignon.* ¶ **PY, AP, D.**

**** 1994 Wildekrans Sauvignon Blanc, Walker Bay, SA. £5.99. *Very classy, grassy wine from a new wine region. Good enough to worry the New Zealanders – and the winemakers of the Loire.* ¶ **SP, D.**

***** 1993 Chablis Domaine des Marrenniers, Bernard Legland, Burgundy, Fr. £8.49. *Good modern Chablis with lovely pineapply fruit and complexity.* ¶ **S.**

**** 1993 Catena Estate Chardonnay, Mendoza, Arg. £7.99 *Very attractive ripe juicy Chardonnay. Peachy.* ¶ **WFC, WFP.**

*** 1992 Red Cliffs Estate Colombard Chardonnay, Victoria, Aus. £3.99. *Good value, easy-going party wine with a lime marmelade flavour.* ¶ **PY, AP.**

*** 1994 Te Koironga Mortinborough Chardonnay, NZ. £8.49. *Attractive melony, slightly tropical Chardonnay with spicy oak.* ¶ **SF, LS.**

**** 1993 Edna Valley Chardonnay, California, US. £9.99. *Oaky, buttery wine with pineappley fruit.* ¶ **WMP, CH.**

**** 1991 Pernand Vergelesses Blanc, Rollin, Burgundy, Fr. £13.49. *Classy, quite nutty alternative to Meursault.* ¶ **WM.**

**** 1994 Basedow Semillon, S Australia, Aus. £5.99. *Big, rich, with lovely tropical ripeness and sweet oak.* ¶ **WMP, FO.**

*** 1994 La Serre Rosé de Syrah, Midi, Fr. £3.99. *Brambley, peppery, refreshing, gulpable.* ¶ **AP, PY, SP.**

**** 1988 Recosind, Cellers Santamaria, Ampurdan Costa Brava, Sp. £3.45. *Concentrated, very old fashioned Spanish red, with intense earthy-plummy fruit and pepper.* ¶ **LB, BF, G.**

*** 1994 La Croix Rouge, Midi, Fr. £3.45. *Rich, berryish young wine. Good party fare.* ¶ **PY, LS.**

**** 1994 La Serre Cabernet Sauvignon, Midi, Fr. £3.99. *Ripe crunchy blackcurrants. Lovely modern stuff.* ¶ **PY, LB, D.**

**** 1991 Ch. Tour Haut Caussan, Bordeaux, Fr. £8.95. *Serious, quite oaky claret to drink over the next year or so.* ¶ **LB, RM, CH.**

***** 1991 Ch. Sociando Mallet, Bordeaux, Fr. £9.75. *Classy, ripe, quite cedary, Bargain Bordeaux.* ¶ **CH, LB.**

**** 1986 Vieux Chateau Certan, Pomerol, Bordeaux, Fr. £34.75. *Worth every penny. Intense, inky dark wine with complex dried fruit flavours.* ¶ **LB.**

***** 1992 Côte Rôtie, Jamet, Rhône, Fr. £17.49. *Very classy smoky Northern Rhone. Well worth keeping.* ¶ **G, RMS.**

**** 1992 Rosso di Montalcino, Talenti, Tuscany, It. £7.99. *Juicy, berryish wine with a hint of smoke. A surprisingly subtle, easy drink.* ¶ **RMS, BF.**

**** 1993 Grangehurst Pinotage, Stellenbosch, SA. £7.75. *Serious dense plummy – spicy Pinotage with sweet oak. Built to last.* ¶ **RM, G.**

**** 1993 Beaujolais Villages, Domaine Dalicieux, Fr. £5.99. *Rich, ripe summery wine – raspberries and spice.* ¶ **LS, WMP.**

**** 1993 Morgan Pinot Noir, California, US. £11.99. *Burgundian-style Pinot with lovely raspberry fruit.* ¶ **RMS, CC.**

**** 1990 Chalone Pinot Noir, California, US. £21.99. *Earthy, mature Pinot from a Californian pioneer of the variety.* ¶ **G, BF.**

***** 1992 Volnay, Michel Lafarge, Burgundy, Fr. £18.49. *Great, plummy, ripe redcurranty wine with subtle oak. Worth keeping.* ¶ **RMS, LB.**

***** 1988 Valpolicella, Quintarelli, Veneto, It. £9.99. *Great, concentrated wine with exciting cherry fruit. Made by a master of the style.* ¶ **LB.**

***** 1992 Zinfandel, Topolos Winery, Russian River, California, US. £12.75. *Classic, intense wild berryish wine. Original Zin!* ¶ **O, CH, RM.**

**** 1992 Cascina Castlet, Avie Moscato Passito, Piedmont, It. £12.49. *Delightful. Soft bananas, marmalade, citrus fruit and ginger.* ¶ **PS.**

***** 1990 Deidsheimer Hohenmorgen Rieling Auslese, Bassermann-Jordan, Rheinpfalz, Ger. £15.99. *Classic maturing late harvest Riesling from a great estate.* ¶ **PS.**

BTH   Booths (supermarkets)   ★★★★★

4-6 Fishergate, Preston, Lancs PR1 3LJ. Tel 01772 251701. Fax 01772 204316.
Supermarket Chain. 22 branches. **Opening hours:** vary from branch to branch.
Services: occasional *en primeur*, glass hire.

Booths, like Sainsbury's, is a family-run supermarket chain. Unlike its larger counterpart down south, however, the Preston-based firm is able to concentrate more of its efforts on buying small lots of really exceptional wines. Sadly, in a country where most of the media attention is focused on the region closest to the European mainland, merchants like Booths are often overlooked. Which is rather a pity for all those southerners who imagine that supermarkets are as interchangeable as High Street banks – and all the better news for the customers of these 22 stores who get Edwin Booth's first class selection to themselves. A supermarket chain whose range is second to none.

★★★★ Booths Brut, Champagne, Fr. £12.49. *Toasty fruit and a lemony tang. Good, clean fizz.* ¶ **AP, EN.**

★★★★ 1990 Seppelt Sparkling Shiraz, S Australia, Aus. £7.99. *Luscious fizzy blackberries and raspberries. Drink chilled.* ¶ **AP, D.**

★★★ 1994 Ch. Pierrail Blanc, Bordeaux, Fr. £4.75. *Crisp and fresh, melony fruit and a crisp acidity.* ¶ **WFC, PY.**

★★★ 1989 Meursault, H. Gaboureau, Burgundy, Fr. £9.99. *Softly toffeed oaky, richly honeyed but with balancing summer fruit and acidity.* ¶ **D, WMC, CH.**

★★★★ 1993 Sancerre Blanc, M. Brock, Loire, Fr. £6.99. *A crisp, steely sauvignon with clean gooseberry, pineapple fruit.* ¶ **SM, S.**

★★★★ 1994 Pinot Blanc d'Alsace, Cave de Turckheim, Alsace, Fr. £4.69. *Light, melony peachy fruit, soft and slightly spicy.* ¶ **O, WFP.**

★★★★ 1994 Chardonnay d'Oc, Hugh Ryman, Languedoc, Fr. £3.99. *Crisp, lemon-lime fruit with hints of honeyed oak.* ¶ **SM, D.**

★★★ Louis Chatel Sur Lie, Languedoc, Fr. £2.89. *Good glugging party wine. Made like Muscadet.* ¶ **FF, PY.**

★★★★★ 1994 Rothbury Estate Sauvignon Blanc, Marlborough, NZ. £6.99. *Gooseberry, peaches and ripe melon. Crisp and fresh.* ¶ **AP, S.**

★★★★ 1989 Ch. Pavie, St Emillion, Bordeaux, Fr. £18.95. *Earthy, jammy fruits and rich oak. Needs time.* ¶ **LB.**

★★★★ 1989 Ch. Kirwan, Margaux, Bordeaux, Fr. £12.59. *Luscious mossy fruits, herbaceous and jammy. Opening up.* ¶ **LB.**

★★★ 1993 Côtes-du-Rhône Villages, St Maurice, Rhône, Fr. £4.39. *Pepper and spice with damson fruit.* ¶ **SP, G.**

★★★★ 1990 Mas de Daumas Gassac, Languedoc, Fr. £10.99. *Complex, earthy berry flavours.* ¶ **D, G.**

★★★★ 1990 Parrina Riserva, Tuscany, It. £6.59. *Lovely chocolate, tobacco and black cherry fruit.* ¶ **P, BF.**

★★★ 1991 Ochoa Tempranillo, Navarra, Sp. £6.15. *Smooth caramelly oak and tobaccoey fruit.* ¶ **RMS.**

★★★★★ 1992 Penfolds Bin 28 Shiraz, S Australia, Aus. £6.49. *Spice galore, with chocolate, blackcurrant and black cherry. Worth keeping.* ¶ **SP, G.**

★★★ 1991 Zonnebloem Shiraz, Coastal Region, SA. £5.19. *Rich and beefy with a generous helping of plum fruits and pepper.* ¶ **SP, BF.**

★★★ 1988 Syrah, Luigi Bosca, Arg. £7.99. *Luscious berry fruit, peppery and herby.* ¶ **SP, G.**

★★★★ Lustau Oloroso Viejo Almacanista, Sp. £5.99 (half). *Rich and creamy. Nuts and old wood with grapey fruit.* ¶ **AP, CH.**

★★★★ 1978 Niepoort Colheita, Por. £23. *Rich, dark port with sweet damson and plum fruit, herbs and allspice. Lovely oak.* ¶ **CC, CH, CS.**

★★★★ 1983 Warre's Vintage Port, Oporto, Por. £13.99. *Woody and herbaceous. Peppery spices and sweet berry fruits.* ¶ **CC, CS, CH.**

52 Merchants

BOO   Booths of Stockport   ★★★★

62 Heaton Moor Road, Heaton Moor, Stockport SK4 4NZ. Tel/Fax 0161 432 3309. Independent Wine Merchant. **Opening hours:** Mon-Fri 0900-1900, Sat/Sun 0900-1730. **Delivery:** Free locally. **Tastings:** Monthly tutored sessions. **Services:** Glass hire.

One of the best merchants in the country, Booths continues to build up an enviable range of Australian wines from blue-chip producers such as Henschke and Yarra Yering while seeking out similarly tasty offerings from Spain – Artadi – Italy and France. California is also given unusually serious treatment with wines like Newton's unfiltered Merlot and Frog's Leap's brilliant Zinfandel.

★★★★   Champagne Veuve Clicquot White Label Demi-Sec, Fr. £22. *Very unfashionable, indulgent wine with the flavour of fresh apple-pie.* ¶ *CC.*

★★★   1992 Mont Marcal Cava Brut, Penedes, Sp. £5.99. *A lively wine, creamy and fresh.* ¶ *AP, D, LS.*

★★★★   1994 Le Voyager Blanc, Benoit and Valerie Calvet, Bordeaux, Fr. £5.50. *Dry, slightly lemony. Good modern white Bordeaux.* ¶ *FD, WM, WFC.*

★★★★   1994 Montana Sauvignon Blanc, Marlborough, NZ. £4.99. *Gooseberries galore. Lovely, typical Kiwi Sauvignon.* ¶ *D, WMC, AP, E.*

★★★★   1993 Pouilly Fuissé Les Vieux Murs, Ets Loron Et Fils, Burgundy, Fr. £8. *Very characterful tropical fruit with a rich texture.* ¶ *SF, SM, CH.*

★★★   1993 Kourtakis Mavrodaphne Of Patras, Gre. £3.50. *A complex mixture of nuts, dried fruits, sandalwood and anise.* ¶ *PF, PS, AP.*

★★★   Leziria, Almeirim Cooperative, Ribatejo, Por. £2.99. *Lovely, simple jammy fruit – very gluggable easy red.* ¶ *PY, D, FF, RM.*

★★★★   1991 Alianca Bairrada Reserva, Caves Alianca, Por. £3.99. *Rich, tobaccooey wine with a touch of spice. Could be worth keeping.* ¶ *CH, FF, RM.*

★★★★   1987 Lindemans Botrytis Semillon, S Australia, Aus. £5.99. *Barley sugar, oak and ripe peaches. Pure hedonism.* ¶ *CC, PF, PS.*

BD   Bordeaux Direct   ★★★

New Aquitaine House, Paddock Road, Reading, Berkshire RG4 5JY. Tel 01734 471144. Fax 01734 461953. A group of five shops selling the same range as the Sunday Times Wine Club (qv). **Opening hours:** Mon-Fri 1030-1900, (Thurs 1030-2000), Sat 0900-1800. **Delivery:** available free on orders of £50 or more within the UK area. **Services:** Mail order, glass loan, tasting, en primeur offers.

The retail arm of the Sunday Times Wine Club and the only UK merchant which offers its customers the chance to meet Hugh Johnson – at the annual tasting in the Royal Horticultural Hall in London. In the past, we have been very critical of the value-for-money offered by this company in both its guises, but there have been definite signs of improvement over the last year. It still pays to pick and choose carefully – some offers are a lot more attractive than others – but, as we have always said, Bordeaux Direct's tastings and trips are rightly popular with wine enthusiasts.

★★★   1994 Coteaux des Carbonnières Sauvignon Blanc, Bordeaux, Fr. £5.25. *Green and grassy, citrus fruits and good acidity.* ¶ *S.*

★★★★   1994 Chardonnay, Domaine de Régismont, Midi, Fr. £6.49. *Delicate and fruity with a refreshing crispness.* ¶ *PY, WM.*

★★★★★   1993 Château La Clarière Laithwaite, Bordeaux, Fr £9.99. *First class blackcurrant claret made by Bordeaux Direct's founder, Tony Laithwaite.* ¶ *LB, RM.*

★★★★★   1990 Château Lascombes, Margaux, Bordeaux, Fr. £18. *Classic Margaux which needs time to develop. Lovely blackberryish fruit.* ¶ *LB.*

★★★★   1994 Hacienda San Carlos Cab Sauv/Malbec, Colchagua Valley, Chi. £5.79. *Rich blackcurranty fruits with soft spices and smooth tannins.* ¶ *FF, WM.*

BU   Bottoms Up   ★★★★

Sefton House, 42 Church Road, Welwyn Garden City, Herts AL8 6RJ. Tel 01707 328244. Fax 01707 371398. National Chain. 72 branches. **Opening hours:** Mon-Sat 1000-2200, Sun various. **Delivery:** free locally. **Services:** gift vouchers, glass loan.

Still the most interesting and possibly least appreciated part of the Thresher empire. These shops are a cross between a slightly more sober Oddbins and a smarter Majestic; somehow, the big-company ambience of Wine Rack and Threshers is far less apparent here. The range is good, the shelves well stocked and the staff mostly enthusiastic and knowledgeable. The employee who, presumably talking about his knowledge, answered one query with 'I'm much better on lager than wine' was hopefully an exception; certainly, customers of other branches who have placed their trust in managers' selections have not been disappointed and there is a growing number of satisfied members of the Bottoms Up Imbibers Club.

★★★★ Champagne Hamm Premier Cru, Fr. £15.29. *Good, buttery, full-flavoured wine. A mouthfiller.* ¶ *AP, D, S.*

★★★★★ Champagne Pol Roger White Foil Extra Dry, Fr. £19.99. *Yeasty and creamy with soft fruit. Delicate and delicious.* ¶ *AP, D, S.*

★★★★ Moscato Spumante Frassino, Piedmont, It. £3.79. *Zesty and refreshing fizz with plenty of fruit.* ¶ *AP, PY.*

★★★★ 1994 Stoneleigh Sauvignon Blanc, Marlborough, NZ. £5.99. *A brilliant asparagus and gooseberry aroma; classic Kiwi Sauvignon.* ¶ *WMC.*

★★★★ 1994 Kings Canyon Sauvignon Blanc, H Ryman/Arciero, California, US. £3.99. *Hugh Ryman's first effort in California. Great drinking.* ¶ *AP, E.*

★★★ 1993 Moldova Chardonnay/ Sauvignon, Hugh Ryman/Penfolds, Komrat, Mol. £3.39 *Simple, melony, grassy wine. Party fare.* ¶ *PY.*

★★★★★ 1992 Dr Loosen Riesling QbA, Mosel, Germany. £5.99. *Lovely Mosel Riesling at its floral, grapey best.* ¶ *AP, LS.*

★★★★ 1994 Prosperity Red, Firestone Vineyards, California, US. £4.99. *Cooked fruits, herbs and a splash of oak.* ¶ *RM, P.*

★★★★★ 1991 Warwick Farm Trilogy, Stellenbosch, SA. £8.99. *Fine, concentrated blend of Cab Sauv/Franc and Merlot. Chewy and flavoursome.* ¶ *WM, BF.*

★★★★★ 1990 Nuits-Saint-Georges, Clos de l'Arlot, Côte d'Or, Fr. £27.99. *Berries, oak and allspice. Lovely modern Burgundy at its best.* ¶ *CH, RMS.*

★★★ 1994 Santara Dry Red, Conca de Barbera, Concavins/Hugh Ryman, Sp. £2.99 *Oaky, jammy black cherryish wine. Good modern Spanish.* ¶ *WFP.*

★★★★★ 1989 Gran Sangre de Toro Reserva, Miguel Torres, Penedes, Sp. £5.49. *Very seductive wine with vanilla oak, spice and ripe squashy strawberries.* ¶ *LB.*

★★★★★ 1989 Vouvray Sec Le Haut Lieu Gaston Huet, Loire, Fr. £7.49. *Concentrated Chenin with lingering flavours of apple and honey.* ¶ *D.*

★★★★ 1992 Ch. Coucheroy Rouge Graves, Bordeaux, Fr. £6.59. *Ripe raspberryish, typical Graves by Jacques Lurton.* ¶ *WFP, RM.*

★★★★ 1991 Gevrey Chambertin Vieilles Vignes Dom. Roy, Burgundy, Fr. £17.69. *Serious raspberry and cherry flavours. Good, intense Burgundy.* ¶ *RM.*

★★★★ 1989 Ch. de Lastours, Oak-aged, Corbieres, Fr. £6.79. *Rich, dark fruits, herbs and spices with smooth tannins.* ¶ *D, LB.*

★★★ 1991 Esporao Cabernet Sauvignon, Por. £4.69. *Stewed, brambly fruits, mossy with a firm tannic structure.* ¶ *G, BF.*

★★★★ 1991 Voss Zinfandel, Alexander Valley, California, US. £9.99. *Delicious jammy, leathery red made by Australians in California.* ¶ *RM, BF.*

★★★★★ 1991 Puligny Montrachet Dom. Louis Carillon, Burgundy, Fr. £16.99. *Nutty, buttery yet subtle. Built to last.* ¶ *WFC, CH.*

★★★★ 1977 Smith Woodhouse Vintage Port, Douro, Por. £20.91 *Youthful, spicy with deep fruit and really complex flavours. Well worth keeping.* ¶ *CC.*

★★★★★ Blandy's 10 Year Old Malmsey, Madeira Wine Company, Mad. £12.99. *Very complex, malty, Old English marmaladey, nutty wine. Very moreish.* ¶ *D, CC.*

54 Merchants

BRO   Brookshaws of Nantwich   ★★★

8-10 Hospital Street, Nantwich, Cheshire CW5 5RJ. Tel/Fax 01270 625302.
Independent Wine Merchant. **Opening hours:** Mon-Sat 0800-1700. **Delivery:** free
locally.

Mark Brookshaw's is a curious tale. As a delicatessen and specialist meat shop owner
for over 26 years, he quite reasonably liked to sell his customers jars of fruit in
brandy at Christmas. One day, his friendly local off licence (who had just introduced
a similar product), threatened to report him for selling alcohol without a licence.
Thus spurred, he went out and got one and now offers a tidy little range of Old and
New World wines, many of which will be familiar to customers of Adnams, a small
East Anglian firm not known for its specialist meats.

***** 1991 Meursault, Dom. Comtes de Lafon, Burgundy, Fr. £20.25. *Fabulous,
rich, complex nutty Meursault to drink now or keep for a decade.* ¶ **WMP.**
*** 1994 Les Terrasses de Guilhem Red, Aimé Guibert, Midi, Fr. £4.50. *Easy
going country wine from the maker of Mas de Daumas Gassac.* ¶ **PY, RM.**
***** 1989 Ch. D'Armailhac, Baron Philippe de Rothschild, Pauillac, Bordeaux Fr.
£18.75. *Classic blackcurranty, cedary claret from a ripe vintage.* ¶ **G, RMS.**
**** 1992 'M' Pinot Noir/Shiraz, Montara Estate, Aus. £5.75. *An unusual
blend; plummy and licoricey and very interesting.* ¶ **WFP.**
*** 1994 Campo Nuevo Tinto, Bodegas Agro Navarra, Sp. £3.19. *Very youthful
wine with a flavour of just-ripe plums.* ¶ **RM.**

BWI   Bute Wines   ★★★★

Mount Stuart, Rothesay, Isle of Bute, Argyll & Bute PA20 9LR. Tel 01700 502730 Fax
01700 505313 Also at 2 Cottesmore Gardens, London W8 5PR. Independent Wine
Merchant. Wine by the case only. **Opening hours:** Mon-Fri 0900-1700. **Delivery:**
free locally. **Services:** cellarage, *en primeur*, mail order, gift mailing, glass hire, ice.
No credit cards.

Antipodeans may be confused by the name. It does not, as they might surmise, refer
to a purveyor of extremely good vinous beverages, but to the ancestral isle of
Jennifer, Marchioness of Bute, one of Britain's most approachable aristocrats, and the
company she founded there. The core business is the supplying of Fine Wine mostly
from classic areas to private and trade customers up and down the land. Bordeaux is
particularly strongly represented, mostly in the very bankable vintages of 1988, 1989
and 1990, but the Rhône and Burgundy are pretty much blue chip too. Domaine de
l'Arlot and Domaine Dujac stand out, as do Jaboulet, Guigal and the more affordable
Weinert range from Argentina. Other attractions are the wine weekends on the
island with luminaries like Olivier Bernard from Domaine de Chevalier.

**** 1994 Palliser Estate Martinborough Sauvignon Blanc, N.Z. £10.81. *A really
classy Kiwi Sauvignon with ripe blackcurranty fruit.* ¶ **WMC.**
**** 1992 St Aubin Blanc, Louis Jadot, Burgundy, Fr. £12.95. *Lovely woody,
honeyed fruit flavours. Smooth and rich.* ¶ **D, FD.**
**** 1986 Dom. de Chevalier, Graves, Bordeaux, Fr. £23.63. *Classic, elegant
perfumed claret worth keeping a while longer.* ¶ **LB, CH.**
***** 1988 Spottswoode Cabernet Sauvignon, Napa Valley, California, US.
£33.10. *Pricy but good, mint and cassis Californian Cabernet.* ¶ **LB, CH.**
***** 1991 Clos de la Roche, Dom. Armand Rousseau, Burgundy, Fr. £30.06.
*Rich, concentrated wine with cassis fruit and damsons. Just what a Grand
Cru should be.* ¶ **CC, RM.**
***** 1989 Ch. Coutet, Sauternes, Fr. £16.89. *Great value sweet Bordeaux,
with flavours of dried apricot and marmalade.* ¶ **PF, PS.**
**** 1970 Warre's Vintage Port, Douro, Por. £36.23 *A lovely blend of dark
spices, soft sweet berry fruits and gentle oak.* ¶ **CS, CC.**

BUT   Butlers Wine Cellar   ★★★

247 Queens Park Road, Brighton, E. Sussex BN2 2XJ. Tel 01273 698724. Fax 01273 622761. Independent Wine Merchant. **Opening hours:** Tues, Wed 1000-1800, Thurs, Fri 1000-1900, Sat 0900-1900. **Delivery:** free locally. **Tastings:** regular in-store. **Services:** mail-order, glass hire.

And they complain that the British taste for eccentricity is dead. . just one look at The Butler's Journal produced by this bearded bohemian is proof to the contrary. 'Wine tasting as a contact Sport' on page 9 more or less sums it up. However, behind the beard and bravado is a very competent list with a wealth of old vintages – 1945 Sandeman Vintage Port, Krug 1976, Chateau Climens 1967, Chateau Lynch-Bages 1961 to name but a few – not to mention a compact and concise list of more up-to-date consumables. Try too Mr B's newly launched wine club whose newsletter promises 'articles, quizzes and offers'.

- **** 1992 Ch. Grand Puy Lacoste, Pauillac, Bordeaux, Fr. £9.75. *A soft and elegant wine showing its class even in an indifferent year.* ❚ **LB, CH.**
- **** 1989/90 d'Arenberg Old Vine Shiraz, McLaren Vale, Aus. £5.95. *Heaps of sweet fruit and peppery spices.* ❚ **D, RM.**
- *** 1992 Banfi Centine Rosso di Montalcino, Tuscany, It. £7.95. *A huge, gutsy wine. Chocolate, black cherries and dusky tannins.* ❚ **G, BF.**
- **** 1978 Gonzalo De Berceo, Gran Reserva Rioja, Sp. £14.50. *Lots of dark berry fruits and smoky oak.* ❚ **P, WMC.**
- **** 1994 Chablis, Servin, Burgundy, Fr. £8.95. *A cool, crisp wine – perfect for a summer's day.* ❚ **SM, S.**

ABY   Anthony Byrne Wines   ★★★★

Ramsey Business Park, Stocking Fen Road, Ramsey, Cambs PE17 1UR. Tel 01487 814555. Fax 01487 814962. Independent Wine Merchant. **Opening hours:** Mon-Fri 0900-1730. **Services:** cellarage.

Maintaining a far lower public profile than some of his competitors, Burgundy and Alsace lover Anthony Byrne enjoys a wine merchant's equivalent of superstar status among restaurateurs. He deserves recognition for the way in which he has helped to seduce restaurant lists throughout the country away from dull negociants to producers like Domaine de l'Arlot, Georges Clerget, Dubreuil Fontaine and Zind Humbrecht. The New World is more patchily covered, but the Rutherglen Muscats of Stanton and Killeen, Victorian Rieslings of Delatite and Paliser wines from New Zealand are, like the restaurants in which they are served, all worth a lengthy detour.

- ***** Champagne Drappier, Cuvée Speciale, Fr £11.43. *Rich, Slightly citrussy, classy fizz.* ❚ **AP, FD.**
- **** 1995 Santa Carolina Sauvignon Blanc, Lontue, Chi. £4.69. *Leafy Sauvignon with lovely ripe blackcurranty fruit.* ❚ **SM, CC.**
- **** 1993 Muscat d'Alsace, Dom. Zind Humbrecht, Alsace, Fr. £9.34. *Bags of spicy fruit, zesty and refreshing.* ❚ **O, CS.**
- ***** 1990 Gewürztraminer Clos Windsbuhl, Dom. Zind Humbrecht, Alsace, Fr. £15.99. *Fantastic, complex, spicy, tropical fruit. Alsace at its best.* ❚ **S, O.**
- ***** 1991 Côte Rôtie Brune et Blonde, E Guigal, Rhône, Fr. £20.99 *Ripe autumn fruit with lots of tasty new oak. Very classy red wine which will improve.* ❚ **G.**
- **** 1994 Brouilly, Les Celliers de Samsons, Beaujolais, Fr. £5.55. *Soft berry fruits, smooth and slightly smoky.* ❚ **EN, LB.**
- **** 1992 Nuits-Saint-Georges, Domaine de l'Arlot, Côte d'Or, Fr. £13.37. *Berries, oak and allspice. Lovely modern Burgundy at its best.* ❚ **RMS.**
- ***** 1992 Chambertin Grand Cru, Domaine Rossignol Trapet, Burgundy, Fr. £32.12. *Rich dark fruits, chocolate and dense spices. A huge wine, worth keeping.* ❚ **BF, CC.**

56 Merchants

DBY   Dennis Byrne   ★★★★

Victoria Buildings, 12 King Street, Clitheroe, Lancs BB7 2EP. Tel 01200 23152.
Independent Wine Merchant. **Opening hours:** Mon, Tues, Wed, Sat 0830-1800,
Thurs, Fri 0830-2000. **Delivery:** free locally. **Tastings:** in-store most weekends and
on request to groups. **Services:** en primeur, glass hire. No credit cards.

Two years ago this small family-run business in the beautiful Ribble Valley took
radical action to compete with the buying power of the large multiples. Costs were
slashed (hence the absence of glossy wine lists) and margins trimmed to the bone to
match and even beat prices on offer elsewhere. As a result of this brave approach,
sales have increased dramatically and many customers travel hundreds of miles to
shop with the Byrnes. Over a thousand wines are stocked with the fine Bordeaux and
Burgundy selection changing weekly as new bargains are snapped up. The New
World selection is impressive too, bristling with the likes of Henschke and Ridge.

★★★★★   E & E Sparkling Shiraz, S Australia, Aus. £12.99. *Extraordinary, spicy, oaky
red fizz with all sorts of summer pudding flavours.* ¶ **D, RM, CH.**

★★★★   1994 Neil Ellis, Elgin Vineyard Selection Sauvignon Blanc, SA. £5.99. *Lemon
and lime; quite a restrained wine from a newly developed region.* ¶ **AP, LS.**

★★★★★   1990 Piesporter Goldtropfchen Riesling Auslese, Reichsgraf Von Kesselstatt,
Mosel, Ger. £9.99. *Clean, refreshing ripe apple flavours.* ¶ **AP, PF.**

★★★★★   1990 Gewürztraminer Clos Windsbuhl, Domaine Zind Humbrecht, Alsace, Fr.
£15.99. *Peaches, lychees and apricots – gorgeously spicy!* ¶ **O, SP, CS.**

★★★★★   1992 Mount Edelstone Shiraz, Henschke, Eden Valley, Aus. £12.95.
Gorgeous concentrated wine with damsons and spice. Will last. ¶ **G, RMS.**

★★★★   1993 L A Cetto Petite Sirah, Baja California, Mex. £4.50. *Excitingly fresh
pepper and spice, full of primary red fruit flavours.* ¶ **SM, P.**

★★★★★   1993 Saintsbury Carneros Pinot Noir, California, US. £11.75. *This
raspberryish wine matches all but Burgundy's very best.* ¶ **WMP, D.**

★★★★★   Gonzalez Byass Mathusalem, Jerez, Sp. £18.99. *Liquid Christmas pudding! A
real mouthful of dried fruit and spice.* ¶ **D, PS.**

★★★★★   1976 Fonseca Guimaraens Vintage Port, Oporto, Por. £19.99. *Lovely rich,
classic port with stewed fruit, chocolate and spice. Still fresh.* ¶ **CH, CS.**

CWI   A Case of Wine   ★★★

Harford, Pumpsaint, Llanwrda, Dyfed SA. 19 8DT. Tel 01558 650671. Fax 01558
650671 Mobile 0378 929030. Independent Wine Merchant. Wine by the case only.
Opening hours: Mon-Fri 0800 till late, Sat 0900 till late, Sun 0900-1700.
Delivery: free locally. **Tastings:** regular in-store and tutored for private occasions
and colleges. **Services:** cellarage, glass hire, ice, gift wrapping.

Aldo Steccanella is a busy man; when he's not meeting local customers' orders, he's
out lecturing at local catering colleges, spreading the word about his true passion,
the wine of his native Italy. Given his enthusiasm, it seems almost churlish to
recommend picking up a few well-chosen bottles from Australia or South Africa – or
possibly a little something from a local Welsh vineyard.

★★★★   1994 Vernaccia di San Gimignano, Teruzzi e Puthod, Tuscany, It. £7.72.
Bone dry, yet richly flavoured lemony, almondy wine. ¶ **SF, WM.**

★★★★   1992 Millton Vineyard Chenin Blanc, Gisborne, NZ. £8.21. *Unusually serious
organic treatment for an unfashionable, yet classy grape.* ¶ **WMC, WFC.**

★★★★★   1993 Dolcetto d'Alba "Pian Romualdo", Giuseppe Mascarello, Piedmont, It.
£8.58. *A wild concoction of plums and cherries.* ¶ **P, FF, RM.**

★★★   1990 Señorio de Berbete Rioja Crianza, Bodegas Alavesas, Sp. £4.90. *A
generous wine full of sweet, rich fruit and oak.* ¶ **D, SP.**

★★★★   1992 Gewürztraminer Kirchheimer Geisskopf Beerenauslese, Emil Hammel,
Pfalz, Ger. £6.44. *Unusual German Gewurz – attractively lemony.* ¶ **CS, PF.**

CHF   Chippendale   ★★★★

15 Manor Square, Otley, West Yorks LS21 3AP. Tel/Fax 01943 850633.
Independent Wine Merchant. **Opening Hours:** Mon, Tues, Thurs, Fri 1000-1745,
Sat 0930-1700. **Delivery:** free locally. **Tastings:** regular in-store, "specials' for
discount members. **Services:** mail order, gift mailing, glass loan.

Michael Pollard is a wasted talent. Okay, so he's a really good wine merchant with a
nose for great value stuff across the board but, as we've previously mentioned, the
man's a natural writer with the kind of dry Yorkshire wit the wine – and the world –
needs. Fortunately, Mr P shares his talents pretty freely with his customers in the
form of a discursive monthly newsletter which is quite sufficient reason for joining
his mailing list and recently launched Discount Club. Join up now and we promise
you'll be hooked – if not on the prose style, then on wines like the Carignanissime de
Centeilles and Pierre Dumazet's brilliant Vin de Pays Viognier.

★★★★   1993 Martinborough Vineyard Sauvignon Blanc, NZ. £7.60. *Richer than many
        Kiwi Sauvignons: asparagus, gooseberry and lime.* ⅋ **O, SF.**
★★★   1994 Plaimont Jean des Vignes Demi-Sec, S W France, Fr. £3.25. *Delightful
        fresh off-dry white, full of lemon and orange flavours.* ⅋ **D, PY.**
★★★★   1992 Carignanissime de Centeilles, Minervois, Fr. £5.59. *An extremely
        dense brambly red wine, full of herby, earthy flavours.* ⅋ **BF, RMS.**
★★★★★   1993 Basedow Shiraz, S Australia, Aus. £6.99. *Spicy wine with some
        delicacy to it.* ⅋ **RM, BF, P, LB.**
★★★   Candidato Joven, Cosecheros y Criadores, Sp. £3.49. *Very fruity and youthful
        – this is a soft and gluggable wine ideal for parties.* ⅋ **PY, D.**

CWS   Co-op   ★★★

New Century House, P.O. Box 53, Manchester M60 4ES. Tel 0161 834 1212.
Supermarket Chain. 2011 branches. **Opening Hours:** normal trade hours.
Services: ice.

Following in the footsteps of a well known politician, cricket and Trollope lover, the
Co-op this year introduced its own customer charter to establish its role as a
'responsible retailer'. Meanwhile, wine buyer Arabella Woodrow has continued to
build up a range of wines to make many a so-called serious merchant envious – stuff
like the Leasingham Semillon from the Clare Valley, les Fiefs de Lagrange and
Domaine Rion Vosne Romanée. Whether you'll find these in your local store
depends almost as much on the tastes of the (more or less autonomous) manager as
on where you live. But even the most basic shops should offer some inexpensive but
increasingly worthwhile own-label wines from Spain and such New World novelties
as the Long Slim Chardonnay-Semillon from Chile. All we need now is a politicians'
charter and we'll be pretty well protected all round.

★★★★   1992 Co-op Sparkling Liebfraumilch, Rhine, Ger. £4.19. *A fresh and light
        grapey wine full of gentle bubbles.* ⅋ **D, PY.**
★★★★   Co-op Asti Spumante, Piedmont, It. £4.75. *Delicious peachy, muscat grapes
        – a very appealing example of a style that often disappoints.* ⅋ **D, PY, PF.**
★★★★   Champagne de Clairveaux Brut, Marne Et Champagne, Fr. £12.29. *Another
        winner from one of the best Champagne co-ops.* ⅋ **D, AP, LS.**
★★★   1994 Three Choirs New Release, Gloucester, Eng. £3.99. *Delightful
        hedgerow and elderflower with plenty of summer fruit.* ⅋ **AP, LS.**
★★★★   1995 Caliterra Sauvignon Blanc, Curico, Chi. £3.99. *Fresh Chilean Sauvignon
        – one of the first 1995 wines to hit the shelf.* ⅋ **WFC, D.**
★★★   Co-op Sauvignon Blanc, Cave de Rauzan, Bordeaux, Fr. £3.55. *Simple, clean
        and fresh; everything you expect from a modern Bordeaux white.* ⅋ **AP, PY.**
★★★★   1994 Chardonnay, Domaine Virginie, Midi, Fr. £3.49. *Softly oaky, easy-going
        wine with ripe slightly tropical fruit.* ⅋ **D, WM, FD.**

**** 1994 Kirkwood Chardonnay, Hugh Ryman/Penfolds, Komrat, Mol. £3.29. *Simple, melony, oaky wine. Party fare.* ¶ *D, PY.*

**** 1993 Augustus Chardonnay, Penedes, Sp. £9.49. *Rich, buttery pineapple and melon with a little honey on toast.* ¶ *WMC, SM.*

**** 1993 Bernkastler Badstube Riesling Kabinett, Reichsgraf von Kesselstadt, Mosel, Ger. £6.49. *Lovely green apples and lemon.* ¶ *D, AP, LS.*

**** 1994 Etchart Torrontes, Cafayate, Arg. £3.99. *Grapes and mangoes and limey freshness – from a grape rarely found outside Argentina* ¶ *AP, O, CS.*

**** 1992 Leasingham Domaine Cabernet Sauvignon/Malbec, S Australia, Aus. £6.49. *Rich tobbacoey cassis and serious ripe tannins.* ¶ *G, BF, RM.*

**** 1993 Chateau Reynella Cabernet Merlot, S Australia, Aus £6.75. *Balance and flavour knocks most petit chateaux into a cocked hat.* ¶ *WMP, RMS, D.*

**** 1991 Raimat Cabernet Sauvignon, Costers del Segre, Sp. £5.99. *Full ,sweet fruit complexity and the elegance of good barrel ageing.* ¶ *RM, SP, P.*

**** 1992 Thelema Cabernet Sauvignon, Stellenbosch, SA. £7.49. *Really good, rich cassis and mint with layerings of vanilla oak.* ¶ *LB, RMS, CS.*

*** 1993 Cranswick Estate Murrumbidgee Shiraz/Grenache, Aus. £3.49. *Light but gluggable red – rather like a fruity Cotes du Rhone.* ¶ *WMP, D.*

**** 1993 Baileys Shiraz, Victoria, Aus. £6.99. *Young and tannic, full of ripe loganberry fruit and developing smoky leather.* ¶ *G, RM, SP.*

*** Co-op Côtes Du Luberon, Celliers de Marrenon, Rhône, Fr. £3.49. *Simple, fresh peppery red fruit – strawberries and redcurrants.* ¶ *D, WMP.*

**** 1992 Crozes Hermitage, Louis Mousset, Rhône, Fr. £4.89. *Very easy-going Northern Rhône with lovely cherry fruit.* ¶ *Lb, SP, RM.*

*** 1994 Brown Brothers Tarrango, Victoria, Aus. £4.49. *Plummy, quite Beaujolais in style, with a touch of green pepper.* ¶ *WM, E, SM.*

**** 1993 Morgon Les Charmes, Gerard Brisson, Beaujolais, Fr. £6.79. *Packed with red berry fruit and a little smoky gamey character.* ¶ *LS, LB.*

*** 1990 Dealul Mare Classic Pinot Noir, Rom. £2.99. *Very easy going wine – like home-made raspberry jam.* ¶ *D, PY.*

**** 1993 Hamilton Russell Pinot Noir, Walker Bay, SA. £7.99. *Plummy, cherryish, lightly oaky wine from South Africa's top Pinot producer.* ¶ *RMS, CC.*

*** 1993 Oak Aged Tempranillo Rioja, Berberana, Sp. £4.39. *Soft, toffeeish wine with flavours of plum and strawberry.* ¶ *SM, WMP.*

COA   Brian Coad   ★★★

66 Cole Lane, Ivy Bridge, Devon PL21 0PN. Tel 01752 896 545. Fax 01732 691 160. Mobile: 0374 684 918. Answerphone outside office hours. **Delivery:** 1 case free within 40 mile radius of Ivy Bridge.

On second glance this apparently bald, description-free list reveals itself to contain such highly desirable wines as Burgundies from Carillon, Armand Rousseau and Méo-Camuzet as well as Bordeaux from Palmer, Beychevelle and Leoville LasCases, available in several vintages. In this company, the Loires, though good, appear a little less impressive, despite Mr Coad's evident pride in being the UK ambassador of the Confrerie des Fins Goussiers d'Anjou. Still, what's good for the Goussier's good for the decanter.

**** 1993 Chablis, Dom du Colombier, Guy Mothe, Burgundy, Fr. £8.65. *Serious young Chablis from a very reliable estate.* ¶ *S, WFC.*

***** 1991 Chassagne Montrachet, Dom. Louis Carillon, Burgundy, Fr. £14.70. *Maturing white Burgundy at its nutty best.* ¶ *WMC, E, SF.*

*** 1993 Maitre d'Estournel, St Estephe, Bordeaux, Fr. £5.95. *Youthful claret from Ch. Cos d'Estournel. Full of crunchy berry flavours.* ¶ *LB, RM.*

***** 1989 Vosne Romanee, Dom. Méo-Cazumet, Burgundy, Fr. £17.25. *Lovely oaky, complex red Burgundy with ripe mulberries and spice.* ¶ *WMP, RMS, BF.*

**** 1992 Coteaux de l'Aubance 'Les Trois Demoiselles', Dom. Richou, Loire, Fr. £14.00. *Crunchily fresh young wine from a top class producer.* ¶ *PF, CHO.*

CCL   Cockburns of Leith   ★★★

7 Devon Place, Edinburgh EH12 5HJ. Tel 0131 346 1113. Fax 0131 313 2607.
Independent Wine Merchant. **Opening Hours:** Mon-Fri 0900-1800, Sat 1000-1800,
Sun 1100-1700. **Tastings:** regular in-store, plus regular tutored. **Services:**
cellarage, mail order, glass loan, ice.

Cockburns hold the Scottish agencies for some very worthwhile wine producers,
including Warre's Port and Emilio Lustau's fine Sherries. If you are tempted by
these, and the likes of Caliterra from Chile, Rongopai from New Zealand and Rioja's
C.V.N.E., drop into Cockburn's Wine Emporium the next time you are in Edinburgh.
Prices, particularly on these agency wines, are competitive, and there are plenty of
other tasty little numbers including a good line in vintage Cognac and Armagnac.

**** 1993 Sancerre, Dom. du Petit Roy, Andre Dézat, Loire, Fr. £8.95. *Zingy and
       herbaceous peapod and hedgerow flowers.* ⅋ **S, LS, FD.**
*** 1993 Wyndham Estate Bin 222 Chardonnay, New South Wales, Aus. £5.99.
       Soft, buttery-ripe, obviously New World in style. ⅋ **WM, FF.**
**** 1990 Chablis 1er Cru Fourchaume, La Chablisienne, Burgundy, Fr. £10.50.
       Rich, biscuity yet lemony with a steely mineral edge. ⅋ **AP, LS, SF.**
*** 1993 Welmoed Pinotage, Stellenbosch, SA. £4.50. *Very agreeable crunchy
       berry and banana fruit - light and easy.* ⅋ **SM, D, PY.**
**** 1993 Wyndham Estate Bin 555 Shiraz, New South Wales, Aus. £5.99.
       Attractive cherryish, easy-going Aussie red. ⅋ **RM, RMS, CH.**
**** 1991 Craigmoor Shiraz, New South Wales, Aus. £6.99. *Quite European-style
       Aussie; ripe yet restrained, with good peppery berry flavours.* ⅋ **WMP, RM.**
***** Lustau Manzanilla Pasada de Sanlucar, Jerez, Sp. £11.75. *Wonderful dry
       nutty sherry with a savoury tang.* ⅋ **AP, SF.**

CNL   Connolly's   ★★★

Arch 13, 220 Livery Street, Birmingham B3 1EU. Tel 0121 236 9269. Fax 0121 233
2339. Independent Wine Merchant. **Opening Hours:** Mon-Fri 0900-1730, Sat 1000-
1400. **Delivery:** free locally. **Tastings:** regular in-store, plus monthly tutored
sessions. **Services:** mail order, gift mailing, glass hire, ice.

The Connolly household is nothing if not modest. Their new wine list came with the
reassuring news that they receive "small parcels of interesting wines from time to
time". However, unless you want something German with ambitions beyond
Liebfraumilch there is no need for concern. The French selection is particularly
colourful, with magnums of 1975 Mouton-Rothschild crowning a superb array of red
Bordeaux. If you are planning a celebration, you could opt for a jeroboam of Moët.
And you can even take advantage of the Connollys' offer to produce a personalised
wine series from any label you care to design yourself. How about that for service?

**** 1994 Houghton Wildflower Ridge Chenin Blanc, W Australia, Aus. £5.49.
       Apples, honey and citrus fruits. Very crisp and refreshing. ⅋ **D, WM.**
**** 1993 Three Choirs Estate Premium Dry, Gloucester, Eng. £3.99. *Fresh, crisp
       and very appley. Great value English wine.* ⅋ **AP, PY.**
***** 1991 Opus One, Mondavi/Rothschild, California, US. £43.50. *Beautifully
       made, with oak, cassis, eucalyptus and more than a hint of cedar.* ⅋ **LB, RMS.**
**** 1993 Bon Courage Shiraz, Robertson, SA. £5.59. *New Wave South African
       red with ripe fruit and spice.* ⅋ **LB, PY.**
**** 1991 Viñas de Gain Rioja, Cosecheros Alaveses, Sp. £5.49. *Good value,
       soft wine with a flavour of ripe plum and spice.* ⅋ **P. BF.**
**** 1989 Calem Late Bottled Vintage, Oporto, Por. £9.49. *Rich and plummy well-
       balanced flavours.* ⅋ **CC, CS.**
**** 1989 Ch. Poujeaux, Moulis, Bordeaux, Fr. £12.95. *Ripe claret with bags of
       soft cassis fruit. Classy.* ⅋ **LB.**

60 Merchants

COK   Corkscrew   ★★★★

Arch no 5, Viaduct Estate, Carlisle CA2 5BN. Tel/Fax 01228 43033. Independent Wine Merchant. **Opening Hours:** Mon-Sat 1000-1800. **Delivery:** free locally. **Tastings:** regular in-store, plus new wine club. **Services:** *en primeur*, gift mailing, glass hire.

This little gem of a merchant has been going from strength to strength over the last year. Its excellent range of wines from Bordeaux and Australia means it is truly a source of the best of both worlds, while the selection from Alsace, Spain, Italy and Chile is no less impressive.

★★★★★   1992 Mitchelton Print Label Shiraz, Victoria, Aus. £11.49. *Soft but concentrated berryish wine with good oak spice.* ❙ *BF, D.*

★★★★   1993 Morgan Pinot Noir, California, US. £11.99. *Burgundian-style Pinot with lovely raspberry fruit.* ❙ *CH.*

★★★★   1993 Talenti Rosso de Montalcino, Tuscany, It. £8.49. *Warm spicy fruit and hints of black cherry, tar and leather.* ❙ *P, RMS.*

★★★★   Seppelt Old Trafford, S Australia, Aus. £8.49. *Australian 'port'. Nutty, toffeed and rich. Really rather classy.* ❙ *CH.*

C&B   Corney & Barrow   ★★★★

12 Helmet Row, London EC1V 3QJ. Tel 0171 251 4051. Fax 0171 608 1373. Independent Wine Merchant. **Opening Hours:** Mon-Fri 0830-1800. Also at: 8 Academy Street, Ayr KA7 1HT. Tel 01292 267000. Fax: 01292 265903. **Opening Hours:** Mon-Sat 0930-1730. 194 Kensington Park Road, London W11 2ES. Tel 0171 221 5122 Fax 0171 221 9371. **Opening Hours:** Mon-Sat 1030-2000. 26 Rutland Square, Edinburgh EH1 2BW. Tel 0131 228 2233 Fax 0131 228 2243. Minimum one case. **Opening Hours:** Mon-Fri 0930-1730 (out of hours by special arrangement). **Delivery:** free locally. **Tastings:** regular in-store plus tutored tastings for customers on request. **Services:** cellarage, *en primeur*, mail order, gift mailing, glass hire.

"Tradition? Why, tradition is merely an experiment that has succeeded" – the words of Emile Peynaud, the Bordeaux guru, were quoted to us by Adam Brett-Smith as an illustration of his company's philosophy. Mr B-S took exception to the comment in last year's Guide that his firm's prices were higher than those of some of his competitors. Well, they are, but as we tried to say last year, very often the wines are like the fast cars so popular with Corney & Barrow's managing director: good or unusual enough to be beyond price. Wines like Tertre Roteboeuf, Trotanoy, Petrus and those of the Domaine de la Romanée Conti are all firmly in the Rolls Royce/Ferrari bracket: if you need to ask the price, you probably aren't a serious buyer. At the Lancia and Citroen level, however, there are good white Bordeaux, wines like Joseph Roty's rich Gevrey Chambertins, Simi's delicious Californian Chardonnay and the Palliser Estate Sauvignons from New Zealand and even a relatively inexpensive pair of wines from Switzerland. Like Ferrari drivers, Corney's customers enjoy the handling.

★★★★   Delamotte Brut, Champagne, Fr. £16.69. *Rich, lemon curdy, Chardonnay-based fizz.* ❙ *AP, PY.*

★★★★   1990 Tokaji Aszu 5 Puttonyos, The Royal Tokaji Wine Co, Hun. £15.86. *Modern Tokay with intense limey flavours. Sweet but not cloying.* ❙ *PS.*

★★★   Manzanilla de Sanlucar, Antonio Barbadillo, Jerez, Sp. £6.64. *Delicious yeasty, nutty, refreshing dry sherry.* ❙ *AP, PY.*

★★★★   1993 Pinot Grigio 'Grigio Luna', Cecilia Beretta, It. £5.76. *Attractive, gentle spicy white with a long lingering flavour.* ❙ *WFP, SF.*

★★★★   1992 Staton Hills Fumé Blanc, Washington State, US. £6.40. *Intensely flavoured wine with as much blackcurranty richness as a red. Characterful stuff from an underrated region.* ❙ *D.*

★★★★   1993 Dom. du Nozay, Sancerre, Loire, Fr. £8.99. *Classic, grassy, Loire style. Good with seafood.* ❙ *S.*

**** 1992 Ch. de Bachen, Tursan. South West, Fr. £9.45. *Brilliant mixture of New World oak and bone-dry European character. Like really good old fashioned White Rioja.* ¶ *G, RMS.*

***** 1992 Gewürztraminer Bollenberg, Theo Cattin, Alsace, Fr. £9.39. *Very unctuous wine with fabulous Turkish delight flavours. Quintessential Gewürztraminer.* ¶ *AP, WM.*

**** 1989 Ch. Michel de Montaigne, Bergerac, South West, Fr. £6.37 *Good, maturing, green peppery and plummy. Better than many a claret.* ¶ *BF, SM.*

***** 1992 Bourgogne Coulanges-la-Vineuse, Clos du Roi, Burgundy, Fr. £7.45. *Deep rosé in colour, but packed with creamy strawberry fruit. Great for picnics.* ¶ *CH, SM.*

**** 1990 Ch. Richotey, Fronsac, Bordeaux, Fr. £6.37. *Soft, toffeeish, plummy Merlot. A great alternative to St Emilion.* ¶ *LB .*

***** 1993 Ch de la Liquière, Cuvée des Amandiers, Faugéres, Midi, Fr. £5.80. *Rich, earthy country red with bags of gamey flavour.* ¶ *G.*

**** 1993 Late Harvest Vidal, Hillebrand, Ontario, Can. £6.11 (half). *Curious stuff with lots of acidity for late harvest wine. Very mango-like.* ¶ *PS.*

CEB   Croque-en-Bouche   ★★★★★

221 Wells Road, Malvern Wells, Worcester WR14 4HF. Tel 01684 565612.
Independent Wine Merchant. Wine by the case only. **Opening Hours:** any reasonable hour by appointment. **Delivery:** free locally. **Services:** mail order.

Croque-en-Bouche's list leaves us with the distinct impression that restaurateur Robin Jones has bought at least a case of every wine he has ever enjoyed, and now has so much stock to offer diners that he has been forced to start retailing wine in order to keep up with his buying habits. He demonstrates a magpie instinct for collecting the quirkiest and most exciting range of wines regardless of origin and with scant reference to reputation or price. Where else in England could you find every vintage of Guigal Côte Rôtie La Mouline from 1986 to 1976, Heitz Napa Cabernet 1973, Henschke Hill of Grace 1987, Savennières Coulée de Serrant 1969, or Chateau Chalon 1953 in 65cl bottles? We could go on: there are over 1,000 wines, each as mouthwateringly unusual as the last. Even more amazing are the restaurant prices, particularly in comparison to the all too frequent 300-500% mark-up of top London establishments. 'G' de Gilette 1958 would cost you £35.40 in the shop, and a mere £42.00 with your meal. At that kind of money, you could take your loved one by taxi from London to Malvern for an evening at the Croque-en-Bouche – Hugh Grant's favourite restaurant, apparently – drink Mr Jones dry, return by limo and still have change from the price of a dinner for two at one of London's ritziest joints!

**** Champagne Jacquesson Blanc de Blanc Brut, Fr. £19.40. *Classy, nutty, full flavoured Champagne from a little-known producer.* ¶ *AP, S.*

**** 1986 Lake's Folly Hunter Chardonnay, Aus. £17.60. *A cult wine in Australia.* ¶ *WFP, WM.*

**** 1991 Cloudy Bay Late-Harvest Riesling, NZ. £10.50. *Proof that the Sauvignon King can also make luscious sweet wines.* ¶ *AP, CC.*

***** 1976 Riesling Cuveé Frédéric Émile, Alsace, Fr. £34.00. *Great mature Riesling; with typical petrolly spice.* ¶ *O, LS.*

*** 1989 Ch. de Fonscolombe, Midi, Fr. £4.89. *Quite serious southern French wine with deep herby flavours.* ¶ *D.*

**** 1990 St Nicolas-de-Bourgueil, Jamet, Loire, Fr. £6.90. *Classic red Loire; blackcurrants and pleasantly earthy.* ¶ *D, SP.*

**** 1978 Negru de Purkar, Mol. £18. *Rich, porty wine from a grape variety little found outside Moldova.* ¶ *RMS.*

**** 1983 Ch. Labégorce-Zédé, Margaux, Bordeaux, Fr. £14.50. *Ready-to-drink cedary claret from an up-and-coming chateau.* ¶ *LB.*

62 Merchants

CUM   Cumbrian Cellar   ★★★★

1 St. Andrew's Square, Penrith, Cumbria CA11 7AN. Tel 01768 863664. Independent Wine Merchant. **Opening Hours:** Mon-Sat 0900-1730. **Delivery:** free locally. **Services:** mail order, gift mailing, glass hire.

All the weird and wonderful wine regions of the world are here with examples of vinous technology (or lack of it) from as far flung nations as Peru, Brazil, Morocco, Zimbabwe, China and even the odd (very odd) effort from the Crimea. But if you are tempted to consign the Cumbrian Cellar to the novelty department think again. France, Germany and Italy shore up the main part of the range, while Australia and New Zealand neatly sandwich the more outlandish wines between them.

- ***   1989 Tsingtao Chardonnay, China. £6.99. *A rare chance to taste Chinese Chardonnay. Drink soon.* ⏱ *LS.*
- ***   1989 Cousino Macul Cabernet Sauvignon Reserva, Antiguas, Chi. £7.10 *Traditional, quite earthy red – like old-fashioned claret.* ⏱ *RM.*
- ***   1987 Faustino V Rioja Reserva, Sp. £7.25. *Soft, quite jammy wine with sweet oak.* ⏱ *LB, D.*
- **** 1989 Jurançon Moelleux, Clos Girouilh, S.W. France, Fr. £5.50 (half). *Lovely honeyed wine with a hint of lime.* ⏱ *PS.*
- **** 1963 Cavendish Vintage Fortified Wine, SA. £7.50. *In South Africa they call this "port" – good old tawny style.* ⏱ *CH, D.*

D   Davisons   ★★★★

7 Aberdeen Road, Croydon, Surrey CR0 1EQ. Tel 0181 688 5939. Fax 0181 760 0390. Regional Chain. 76 branches. **Opening Hours:** Mon-Fri 1000-1400, 1700-2200, Sat 1000-1000, Sun 1200-1400, 1900-2100. **Delivery:** free locally. **Services:** gift mailing, glass loan, ice.

Despite the difficulties caused by exchange rates, semi-suicidal competition and cross-Channel shopping, Michael Davies is fundamentally both an optimist and a pragmatist. So, at a time when he has had neither reason, nor opportunity to buy in as much wine en primeur as he might have liked, Mr Davies has concentrated on investing in the freeholds of his shops and building a range of immediately drinkable New World wines. These should keep his customers going until the 1200 cases of 1982 claret and various vintage ports are deemed ready to be drunk. These shops are generally better staffed than most of their competitors and if they feel rather old fashioned and rustic, they are perhaps all the more welcoming for that.

- ***   Killawarra Brut, Southcorp, S Australia, Aus. £5.49. *Good, easy-going fizz.* ⏱ *LS, AP.*
- **** 1994 Caliterra Chardonnay, Curico, Chi. £3.99. *Well made lightly lemony modern wine.* ⏱ *D, LS.*
- **** 1994 Nuragus di Cagliari, Cantina Sociale di Dolianova, Sardinia, It. £3.99. *Pleasant, easy going, herby dry white. Perfect for a party.* ⏱ *PY.*
- ***   1994 Soave Classico Vigneto Colombara, Zenato, Veneto, It. £4.99. *Light but quite rich, almondy, brazil-nutty wine.* ⏱ *PY, LS.*
- ***** 1994 Nautilus Estate Marlborough Sauvignon Blanc, NZ. £7.99. *Spicy, gooseberryish wine with lots of ripe tropical fruit.* ⏱ *AP, LS.*
- **** 1994 Ironstone Semillon Chardonnay, W Australia, Aus. £5.99. *Stylish, peachy, lemony wine. Lighter bodied than many Australians.* ⏱ *WFC, PY.*
- ***   1993 Wyndham Estate Bin 222 Chardonnay, New South Wales, Aus. £6.45. *Soft, buttery-ripe, obviously New World in style.* ⏱ *WFC, S.*
- ***   1994 James Herrick Chardonnay, Midi, Fr. £4.99. *A Chablis-like Southern French wine from an Anglo-Australian-owned winery.* ⏱ *SF, WM.*
- ***   1994 Balaton Boglar Oaked Chardonnay, South Balaton, Hun. £3.29. *Good value, simple party wine.* ⏱ *P, WMP.*

**** 1994 Etchart Torrontes, Cafayate, Arg. £4.29. *Grapes and mangoes and limey freshness from a grape rarely found outside Argentina.* ⅋ **LS, PY.**

*** 1993 Parrots Hill Cabernet Sauvignon, S Australia, Aus. £5.59. *Ripe, blackcurrant jammy wine.* ⅋ **SP.**

*** 1991 KWV Cabernet Sauvignon, Cape, SA. £3.99. *Traditional South African red; earthy with more than a touch of leafy greenness.* ⅋ **SP, PY.**

**** 1991 Monteviña Cabernet Sauvignon, California, US. £6.79. *Classy blackcurranty wine with sweet oak and fresh mint.* ⅋ **BF, RMS.**

**** 1993 Wyndham Estate Bin 555 Shiraz, New South Wales, Aus. £6.45. *Attractive cherryish, easy-going Aussie red.* ⅋ **SP.**

**** 1991 Craigmoor Shiraz, New South Wales, Aus. £6.79. *Quite European-style Aussie; ripe yet restrained, with good peppery berry flavours.* ⅋ **BF, RM.**

*** 1990 Dealul Mare Classic Pinot Noir, Rom. £2.99. *Very easy going wine – like home made raspberry jam.* ⅋ **PY, FF.**

**** 1991 Montes Alpha, Curico, Chi. £8.49. *Classy, rich wine with good damson fruit and oak.* ⅋ **CC, BF.**

*** 1985 Rioja Coto de Imaz Gran Reserva, Sp. £7.99. *Modern, mulberryish. Mature with lots of soft oak.* ⅋ **P, RM.**

ROD   Rodney Densem   ★★★

Stapeley Bank, London Road, Nantwich, Cheshire CW5 7JW. Tel 01270 623665. Fax 01270 624062. Independent Wine Merchant. **Opening Hours:** Mon-Fri 0900-1800, Sat 0900-1730. **Delivery:** free locally. **Tastings:** regular in-store plus occasional tutored tastings by arrangement. **Services:** *en primeur*, mail order, gift mailing, glass hire.

Rodney Densem is not shy in his belief that the French are about to lead a major 'vinous revolution', a view that is amply reflected in an attractive range of good quality, good value wines from all around the country. Balance, however, is Rodney's middle name and the best of the Old World happily rubs shoulders with the best of the New. Chile, South Africa, Australia and New Zealand all get a look-in, but they face stiff competition from his small but well-priced range of Vin de Pays.

*** 1994 Neil Ellis Sauvignon Blanc, SA. £4.99. *Clean, fresh, mid-weight Sauvignon – crisp appley acidity and a lively zingy palate.* ⅋ **AP, PY.**

*** 1992 Petit Chablis, William Fevre, Burgundy, Fr. £6.98. *Serious Chablis with nothing 'Petit' about it at all.* ⅋ **WFC, S.**

*** 1992 Columbia Crest Merlot, Washington State, US. £8.45. *Rich, ripe plummy wine with loads of fruit.* ⅋ **LB, RMS.**

**** 1992 E&E Black Pepper Shiraz, S Australia, Aus. £11.45. *Intense, quintessentially Australian Shiraz. Rich, spicy and long.* ⅋ **SP.**

**** 1982 Dow's Quinta do Bomfim, Douro, Por. £14.25. *Vintage port style for little more than Late Bottled Vintage price.* ⅋ **CC, CH.**

DIR   Direct Wine Shipments   ★★★

5-7 Corporation Square, Belfast BT1 3AJ. Tel 01232 238700/243906. Fax 01232 240202. Independent Wine Merchant. **Opening Hours:** Mon, Tues, Wed, Fri 0900-1830, Thurs 0900-2000, Sat 0930-1700. **Delivery:** free on orders of 2 cases or more in Northern Ireland. **Tastings:** regular in-store, two six-week courses a year plus various illustrative tastings. **Services:** cellarage, *en primeur*, mail order, glass hire.

If you enjoy spending entire afternoons choosing a bottle (or ten) from an unfeasibly large selection of very fine wine, then Corporation Square, Belfast, is the place for you. The enthusiasm of the McAlindon brothers and their staff is catching and their events schedule competes with the Queen's, including lavish tastings (amongst them one for the Soroptimist Society. answers on a postcard), dinners, exam courses and – yes, you've guessed it – bridal evenings.

 ***   1994 Forrest Estate Marlborough Sauvignon Blanc, NZ. £8.25. *Lovely, herbaceous wine with typical Marlborough gooseberry fruit.* ¶ **WMC, D.** dxx

 ****   1992 Eden Ridge Shiraz, S Australia, Aus. £6.99. *Very approachable, perfumed wine with mulberry fruit.* ¶ **PY, RM.**

 ****   1990 Château de Domaine de l'Eglise, Pomerol, Fr. *Serious, figgy Merlot with enough tannin to make it a keeper.* £16.50. ¶ **RMS, LB.**

*****   1991 Bourgogne Rouge, Domaine Jean Gros, Fr. £6.99. *Great value; serve it as Vosne Romanée and few people will notice the difference.* ¶ **CC, BF.**

DD   Domaine Direct   ★★★★

29 Wilmington Square, London WC1X 0EG. Tel 0171 837 1142. Fax 0171 837 8605. Independent Wine Merchant. Wines by the case only, but may be mixed. **Opening Hours:** Mon-Fri 0830-1730. **Delivery:** free locally. **Tastings:** regular in-store. **Services:** cellarage, *en primeur.*

Curiously, as merchants like Oddbins discover Burgundy, long-established specialists in the region, Domaine Direct, have begun to explore other regions of France, Italy and the New World, adding three excellent and exclusive Californian producers – Spottswoode, Etude and Doug Nalle – to their showstopping Australian winery Leeuwin Estate. A policy of transferring wine straight from producer to consumer helps to keep prices down; with many wines on offer for less than £7.

 ***   1993 Pibaleau Touraine Azay-le-Rideau Blanc Sec, Loire, Fr. £5.58. *Dry, crisp and appley with a yeasty aroma.* ¶ **AP, LS.**

 ***   1993 Sauvignon de St. Bris, Jean-Hughes Goisot, Burgundy, Fr. £6.17. *Serious alternative to Sancerre from vineyards close to Chablis.* ¶ **WM, CH.**

 ****   1990 Leeuwin Estate 'Art Series' Chardonnay, Margaret River, Aus. £16.39. *Australia's top Chardonnay — like super-rich Puligny Montrachet.* ¶ **WFP, FF.**

 ****   1992 Nalle Zinfandel, Cal. £12.34. *Intense, spicy licoricy Zinfandel. California's 'own' grape at its best.* ¶ **SP, RM, CH.**

 ****   1992 Etude Pinot Noir, Cal. £14.69. *Full of summer fruits, young and crunchy with liquorice aroma.* ¶ **G, P.**

ECK   Eckington Wines   ★★★

2 Ravencar Road, Eckington, Sheffield S31 9GJ. Tel/Fax 01246 433213. Independent Wine Merchant. Wines by the case only. **Opening Hours:** Mon-Fri 0900-2100, Sat 0900-1800, Sun 0900-1500. **Delivery:** free locally. **Tastings:** regular in-store, plus tutored sessions on the first Tuesday of each month. **Services:** mail order. No credit cards.

This is the place to re-stock the cellar if it is looking a little vinously-challenged, especially if your preference is for exotic spicy reds such as the Norton Malbecs from Argentina, the Moroccan 1992 Rabbi Jacob Red and a very comprehensive selection of Chateau Musar from Lebanon. North America is well represented with the Saintsbury and Knudsen Erath Pinot Noirs and the stunning Opus One. For a mix'n'match solution ask about the Quarterly Wine Scheme, particularly the selection which includes the 1990 Oakville Estate Cuvée Sauvage Chardonnay.

 ****   1994 Wairau River Sauvignon Blanc, NZ. £7.55. *Top quality, gooseberryish New Zealand Sauvignon wih a subtler style than many.* ¶ **D, PY**

 ****   1982 Bodega Norton Malbec, Arg. £9.40. *An unusually good example of a spicy red wine grape which was once a major part of Bordeaux.* ¶ **LB, G.**

*****   1991 Rockford Basket Press Shiraz, S Australia, Aus. £8.99. *Concentrated wine from grapes grown on old vines and made using traditional equipment.* ¶ **G, CS.**

 ****   1986 L. A. Cetto Nebbiolo Reserva, Baja California, Mex. £7.65. *Made from an Italian grape grown in Mexico. Leathery, good value.* ¶ **G, RM**

EP   Eldridge Pope   ★★★

Weymouth Avenue, Dorchester, Dorset DT1 1QT. Tel 01305 251 251. Fax 01305 258 155. Regional Chain. 13 branches. **Opening Hours:** generally Mon-Fri 0900-1730, Sat 0900-1700, with local variations up to 2100. **Tastings:** regular in-store; also runs the Dorset Wine Society with lectures/tastings from October to May. **Services:** cellarage, *en primeur*, mail order, gift mailing, glass hire.

Eldridge Pope has been shipping wine since 1833 and is deeply traditional, with French wine still predominating. However the winds of change are blowing through Dorchester – witness "The Chairman's Exuberantly Fruitful New World Sauvignon", a wine to stand alongside "The Chairman's Classic, Flavoursome, Red Burgundy". The former is made for them by the excellent Redwood Valley Estate in New Zealand and is one of a greatly expanded range from Australia, New Zealand, Chile and California. Elsewhere, Château Cissac has been demoted – temporarily at least – from Chairman's Claret in favour of the more readily drinkable Château Beaumont nearby. Sorry, that should read "The Chairman's Traditional Mature Claret".

*** Cuvée de l'Ecusson, Bernard Massard, Lux. £7.05. *Creamy, off-dry, very attractive. A rare opportunity to drink Luxembourg fizz.* ¶ **AP, LS.**

*** 1994 Jurançon Sec Grain Sauvage, Cave de Jurançon, Fr. £4.99. *Dry, lemony, distinctively traditional South Western white.* ¶ **WM, WMC.**

**** 1994 Penfolds Organic Chardonnay Sauvignon Blanc, S Australia, Aus. £5.99. *Rich and plummy with flavours of apple and lime.* ¶ **D, O, PY.**

**** 1991 Volnay, Marquis d'Angerville, Burgundy, Fr. £14.35. *A fuller-bodied than usual Volnay, with ripe damsony fruit.* ¶ **D, O, PY.**

**** 1991 Lindemans Limestone Ridge Shiraz Cabernet, S Australia, Aus. £11.99. *Oak and liquorice. Concentrated and very Australian.* ¶ **CH, RM.**dxx

**** 1993 L.A.Cetto Petite Sirah, Baja California, Mex. £5.05. *Full of red fruit flavours with the addition of fresh pepper and spices.* ¶ **SP, P.**

**** 1992 Gundlach-Bundschu Zinfandel, Cal. £9.99. *Unpronounceable after a few glasses, but great, spicy Zinfandel all the same.* ¶ **G, BF.**

ELL   Ben Ellis   ★★★★

Brockham Wine Cellars, Wheelers Lane, Brockham, Surrey, RH3 3HJ. Tel 01737 842160. Fax 01737 843210. Independent Wine Merchant. **Opening Hours:** Mon-Fri 0900-1800, Sat 0930-1300. **Delivery:** free locally. **Services:** mail order, cellarage, glass loan.

'We never advertise' Mark Pardoe states proudly, relying on customers' loyalty to this three-man band. Looking at the range – good regional French wines, affordable and up-market Bordeaux and Burgundy (from producers like Rion and Girardin), and an unusually well chosen range from such New World producers as Warwick in South Africa, Ngatarawa in New Zealand and Plantagenet in Australia – it is easy to understand why they are loathe to stray.

***** Champagne Billecart-Salmon Brut, Fr. £17.97. *My favourite all round fizz. Subtle with just enough biscuity richness.* ¶ **PY, AP.**

*** 1993 Château Routas Luc Sorin, Côteaux Varois, Languedoc, Fr. £8.62. *Very well-made herby-fruity southern French wine.* ¶ **WMP, WFP.**

**** 1991 Jade Mountain Les Jumeaux, Napa, Cal, US. £11.99. *Very distinctive peppery, Rhône style Californian.* ¶ **LB, SP.**

**** 1993 Kanonkop Pinotage, Stellenbosch, SA. £8.76. *This is one of the best examples by the master of Pinotage.* ¶ **SP, SM.**

***** 1989 Nuits Saint Georges Grandes Vignes, Daniel Rion, Burgundy, Fr. £19.83 *Top class modern Burgundy. Berry flavours with sweet oak.* ¶ **RM,**

**** 1993 Au Bon Climat Pinot Noir, Santa Barbara, Cal. £11.99. *Stylish Southern Californian Pinot with cherries and a hint of horseradish.* ¶ **BF, RM.**

66 Merchants

EWC   Enotria Winecellars   ★★★★★

153-155 Wandsworth High Street, London SW18 4JB. Tel 0181 871 3979.
Independent Wine Merchant. **Opening Hours:** Mon-Fri 1130-2030, Sat 1000-2030.
Delivery: free locally. **Tastings:** regular in-store, plus tutored tastings and dinners.
Services: gift mailing, glass hire, ice.

Last year we reported the sale of Winecellars to Italian wholesalers Enotria. This year the deal was made more concrete by a change of name, which handily avoided any confusion with Greenalls' new Wine Cellar chain, but slightly removed the lustre from a favourite merchant. Still, what's in a name? What we care about is the wines and the range now offered by David Gleave and his team is better than ever. Italy is inevitably the focus of attention, with one of the most reliable and comprehensive tours of that infuriatingly complex country, and a team of producers like Isole e Olena, Roberto Voerzio and Puiatti. However the selection would be impressive if every single bottle of Italian wine were omitted, with wines as tasty as Thelema from South Africa, Shaw & Smith from Australia and Vino Noceto from California.

★★★   1994 Moscato d'Asti, Araldica, Piedmont, It. £3.75. *Fresh and extraordinarily grapey.* ¶ **PY, PF.**

★★★★★   1990 Brunello di Montalcino, Argiano, Tuscany, It. £16.25. *Intense, gamey, dark berryish wine with a long-lasting flavour.* ¶ **BF, CH.**

★★★   1994 Cortese Alasia, Araldica, Piedmont, It. £4.99. *Bone dry, herby wine. Refreshing.* ¶ **WMC, WFC.**

★★★★   1994 Soave Classico, Pieropan, Veneto, It. £6.95. *Rich, serious Soave from the master of the style. A creamy, texture and almondy flavours.* ¶ **WFC, FD.**

★★★★★   1993 Pinot Bianco, Jermann, Friuli, It. £10.69. *Rich, creamy dry wine with lovely perfumed spice.* ¶ **CH, FD.**

★★★★★   1994 Shaw & Smith Sauvignon Blanc, S Australia, Aus. £9.49. *Clean and soft with some complexity.* ¶ **D, PY.**

★★★★   1993 Salisbury Estate Show Reserve Chardonnay, Victoria, Aus. £8.49. *Rich, unashamedly Australian; a peachy, oaky mouthful.* ¶ **WM, CH.**

★★★★   1994 Bergerac Château Le Payral, Thierry Daulhiac, Bergerac, Fr. £5.29. *Fresh, lemony grassy refreshing wine.* ¶ **WMP.**

★★★★   1992 Langhi Shiraz, Mount Langhi Ghiran, Victoria, Aus. £9.95. *Soft and creamy , attractively flavoured with ripe blackberries.* ¶ **BF, PY.**

★★★★★   1991 Venegazzu della Casa, Gasparini, Veneto, It. £8.99. *Lovely Dundee Cake-in-a-glass. Rich, long, satisfying Italian red.* ¶ **P. WMP.**

★★★   1993 Montepulciano d'Abruzzo, Umani Ronchi, It. £4.29. *Earthy with tobacco overtones, stawberries and spices.* ¶ **PY, CH.**

★★★   1990 Villa de Vetrice Chianti Rufina Riserva, Tuscany, It. £5.49. *Fresh, herby young Chianti to drink with food.* ¶ **P, WFC.**

★★★★   1991 Barbera d'Asti 'Ceppi Storici', Piedmont, It. £5.49. *A mouthful of wild young summer pudding flavours.* ¶ **CH, CS.**

★★★   1993 Parrina Rosso, La Parrina, Tuscany, It. £5.99. *Great value tobacco and fresh herbs and plums.* ¶ **CH, RM.**

★★★★   1992 Ascheri Bric Milieu, Piedmont, It. £10.99. *Intense, gamey, tobaccoey red. Well worth keeing.* ¶ **BF, CH, G.**

★★★★★   1988 Allegrini Amarone, Veneto, It. £14.49. *Berries, raisins and dried apricots. A fascinating cocktail of flavours.* ¶ **WFP, RM.**

★★★★★   1991 Isole e Olena Cepparello, Tuscany, It. £17.95. *Brilliant Super Tuscan with herby blackcurranty fruit. Lingering and delicious.* ¶ **BF, CH.**

★★★★   1994 Capezzana Barco Reale, Tuscany, It. £6.49. *Intense, herby, berryish and delicious.* ¶ **WFP, RM.**

★★★★   1988 Quinta Do Crasto L B V, Oporto, Por. £11.99. *Lovely stewed-fruit port from a small estate.* ¶ **CC, CH.**

★★★★   1988 Tokaji Aszu 5 Puttonyos, Ch. Megyer, Hun. £12.99. *Intensely concentrated wine with honey, apricot and spice.* ¶ **CS, PS.**

EVI Evingtons ★★★

120 Evington Road, Leicester, LE2 1HH. Tel 0116 254 2702. Independent Wine Merchant. **Opening Hours:** Mon-Sat 0930-1800. **Delivery:** free locally. **Tastings:** local evening classes (standard and advanced) and courses for clubs, societies etc. **Services:** cellarage, *en primeur*, gift mailing, glass loan, ice.

Evingtons manage to offer a wide choice of wines, without either spreading themselves too thinly or getting bogged down in cumbersome lists. Instead they steer a middle course providing variety and interest from around the world in a fairly compact, tight range of wines. Look out for their Spanish and Italian sections, a good fund of new World fizz, and a nice little line in single quinta Ports.

- ★★★ 1993 Houghton Gold Reserve Verdelho, W Australia, Aus. £6.95. *Unusual lime marmalade flavours – a rich change from Chardonnay.* ¶ **WM, CH.**
- ★★★★ 1993 Conde de Valdemar Rioja Blanco, Martinez Bujanda, Sp. £8.15. *modern Spanish white with character.* ¶ **S, FO.**
- ★★★★ 1992 Tokay Pinot Gris Reserve Particulières, Kuehn, Alsace, Fr. £7.59. *Good combination of softness and acidity. Attractively spicy.* ¶ **AP, CS.**
- ★★★★ 1989 Château La Serre, Luc d'Arfeuille, Bordeaux, Fr. £17.95. *Serious maturing Bordeaux. Rich and complex.* ¶ **LB, G.**
- ★★★ 1992 Montes Cabernet Sauvignon, Chi. £4.65. *Good value blackcurranty wine.* ¶ **WM, RM.**

FAR Farr Vintners ★★★★

19 Sussex Street, Pimlico, London SW1V 4RR. Tel 0171 828 1960 Fax 0171 828 3500 Telex: 919940 Farr G. Independent Wine Merchant. Wines by the case only. **Office Hours:** Mon-Fri 1000-1800. **Services:** cellarage, *en primeur*, mail order, exports. Minimum order: £500.

When the owners of the Savoy decided to dispose of some 9,000 cases of its best wine it surprised no one that they called Farr Vintners. Here minimum orders are £500 and to get a discount you need to spend £2000. This policy doubtless helped raise Farr's turnover last year to over £15m, more than double that of their nearest competitor, though sales overseas will have played their part, as recognised by the receipt of this year's Queens' Award for Export Achievement. The firm defies anyone to find more competitive prices, and keeps theirs down by buying direct from producers, charging for delivery and playing the wine market as though they were buying and selling futures. However, stand by for price rises due to increasing demand, falling supply and the state of the pound. Get those Petrus orders in quickly.

FV Fernlea ★★★

7 Fernlea Road, Balham, London SW12 7RT. Tel 0181 673 0053. Independent Wine Merchant. **Opening Hours:** 1030-1800, Sat 1000-1800. **Delivery:** free locally. Despite offering a medley of fine wines from around the world, Fernlea vintners seem abnormally proud of one area in particular: Mexico, where they have found a quartet of worthwhile wines. Less adventurous drinkers should check out the excellent Clarets and Burgundies before plundering the Aussies and Californians.

- ★★★ 1993 Columbia Crest Sauvignon Blanc, California, US. £4.40. *Crisp, limey acidity, citrus fruits – bags of flavour.* ¶ **D, SM, S.**
- ★★★★ 1988 Ch. Lafon Rochet, Bordeaux, Fr. £11.22. *Maturing, serious claret. Cedary and complex.* ¶ **D, LB.**
- ★★★★★ 1990 Yarra Yerring No. 1 Cabernet, Victoria, Aus. £16.14. *Bailey Carrodus' awesome concoction of dense Cabernet fruit.* ¶ **CH, RMS, G.**
- ★★★★ 1992 L A Cetto Petit Sirah, Baja California, Mex. £4.15 *Delicious sweet fruits, smooth and long lasting.* ¶ **D, WM.**

FLM   Ferrers le Mesurier   ★★★

'Turnsloe', North Street, Titchmarsh, Kettering, Northants. NN14 3DH. Tel/Fax 01832 732660. Answerphone outside business hours. Independent Wine Merchant. Wines by the case only (may be mixed).

FLM make no secret of their dissatisfaction with the burdens placed upon the independent merchant by duty increases and cross-channel bootlegging. However, they are valiantly keeping their head above water with a well chosen, concise selection. The Stafford Ridge 1991 Rieslings and Chardonnays along with the Wirra Wirra Church Block superbly represent the New World while the Champagne Bruno Paillard Brut Premier Cuvée outclasses many a bigger name fizz.

★★★★	1994 Sancerre Andre Dezat et Fils, Loire, Fr. £7. *Crisp, lemon and lime Sauvignon. Complex and clean.* ⅋ **WFP, SF, CC.**
★★★	1994 Aotea Sauvignon Blanc, Gisborne, NZ. £5.25. *All the grassy, gooseberry flavours you only get from New Zealand.* ⅋ **WMC, D, E.**
★★★★★	1991 Lenswood Riesling, Stafford Ridge, South Australia, Aus. £6. *Petrolly, tropical fruits. Floral with a crisp acidity.* ⅋ **LS, SP.**
★★★	1992 Chinon Paul Buisse, Loire, Fr. £5. *Good, blackcurranty, summer-puddingy red.* ⅋ **RM, CC.**
★★★★	1993 Wirra Wirra Church Block, McLaren Vale, S Australia, Aus. £6.50. *Very well made, quite elegant berryish red with just enough oak.* ⅋ **LB, RM.**

FDL   Findlater Mackie & Todd   ★★★★

Deer Park Road, Merton Abbey London, SW19 3TU. Tel 0181 543 0966 Fax 0181 543 2415. Mail order only. Wine by the case only. **Opening Hours:** Mon-Fri 0900-1730. **Delivery:** Free on two cases or more, or £100 or more. **Services:** cellarage, en-primeur, mail order, gift mailing, glass hire, wedding service.

Still leading a relatively independent existence following its marriage to Waitrose, this mail-order specialist offers an excellent if largely traditional selection of wines at a wide range of prices. Bordeaux, with some surprisingly mature examples, is the mainstay, but the Rhône is well covered too. New World wines include the complex 1993 Mount Langhi Ghiran Riesling from Victoria and a host of mouthwatering Sauvignons from New Zealand, including 1993 Villa Maria and 1993 Brancott Estate.

★★★★	Champagne Duc de Marne Grand Cru Brut, Fr. £16.75. *Rich, biscuity, yeasty flavours with lots of ripe fruit.* ⅋ **D, WMC.**
★★★★	1992 Bacharacher Schloss Stahleck Riesling Kabinett, Mittelrhein, Ger. £6.99. *Floral, exotic fruits and crisp acidity.* ⅋ **O, CC.**
★★★★	1994 Thelema Mountain Sauvignon Blanc, Stellenbosch, SA. £7.55. *Delicious cool climate Sauvignon. Gooseberries and crisp acidity, very well made.* ⅋ **AP, S.**
★★★	1989/91 Rosé des Riceys, Alexandre Bonnet, Champagne, Fr. £13.75. *A deep coloured rosé, made in exceptional years. Mint and raspberries.* ⅋ **AP.**
★★★★	1989 Ch. Puygueraud, Côtes de Franc, Bordeaux, Fr. £7.85. *Rich and earthy claret, preferably to lay down for a couple of years.* ⅋ **LB, D.**
★★★	1993 Côtes-du-Rhône, Cave de Vignerons de Laudun, Fr. £3.99. *Plums and damsons, rich and warm.* ⅋ **WM, CH.**
★★★★	1991 Cosme Palaçio Tinto Rioja, Sp. £4.59. *Smooth, creamy oak with dark damson fruits.* ⅋ **WM, D.**
★★★★★	1991 Robert Mondavi Pinot Noir, Napa Valley, California, US. £8.99. *Dark, Smoky fruits and well balanced oak.* ⅋ **BF, RM.**
★★★★	1993 Ronco Sangiovese San Crispino, Romagna, It. £5.35. *Leathery and chocolatey. Plenty of dark berry fruit.* ⅋ **G, RM.**
★★★★	1987 Graham's Late Bottled Vintage, Oporto, Por. £9.89. *Lots of rich, sweet damson fruit. Lovely dark oak.* ⅋ **CC, CH, CS.**

LEF   Le Fleming   ★★★★

9 Longcroft Avenue, Harpenden, Herts AL5 2RB. Tel 01582 760125. Independent Wine Merchant. Wines by the case only. **Opening Hours:** 24-hour answerphone. **Delivery:** free locally. **Tastings:** regular in-store, plus tutored sessions for local clubs, schools, etc. **Services:** mail order, gift mailing, glass hire, ice. No credit cards.

Cherry Jenkins, the cheerful, well informed wine buyer, manager, salesperson and secretary of this one-woman operation has fought hard to head off the drift towards the Channel in search of more alcohol for less cash. Now offering tastings "at all times and at short notice", Cherry is also busily selling to restaurants. The ever growing Le Fleming list includes a well chosen range of French and New World wines, all reliable, never dull and sometimes a revelation.

- ★★★★   1992 Pinot Blanc, Domaine Zind Humbrecht, Alsace, Fr. £8.19. *Floral and spicy. Peaches and apricots.* ¶ **O, S.**
- ★★★   1991 Newtonian Cabernets, California, US. £7. *The Newton stable's second wine. Lovely damson and plum flavours.* ¶ **D, WM, G.**
- ★★★★   1991 Saint Joseph Rouge, Pierre Gaillard, Rhône, Fr. £9.20. *Herbs and spices with soft, ripe fruits.* ¶ **G, SP.**
- ★★★★★   1993 Rockford Dry Country Grenache, S Australia, Aus. £7.23. *Concentrated Grenache, packed with plum and strawberry fruit and spice.* ¶ **SP, O.**
- ★★★★   1993 Barco Reale, Villa di Capezanna, It. £5.80. *Young and intensely fruity. Chocolate and smoky wood.* ¶ **WFP.**

F&M   Fortnum & Mason   ★★★★

181 Piccadilly, London W1A 1ER. Tel 0171 734 8040. Fax 0171 437 3278. Department Store. **Opening Hours:** Mon-Sat 0930-1800. **Delivery:** free locally. **Tastings:** regular in-store. **Services:** cellarage, mail order, gift mailing.

Once the snooty source of overpriced, predictable wines, the store with the clock is now one of the best places in Britain to buy wine – thanks essentially to the efforts of down-to-earth wine buyer Annette Duce and her team. Today, the range is unrecognisable, with wacky Californians and Austrians from Bonny Doon and Willi Opitz respectively, affordable Faively Burgundies and such good value regional French wines as Ch. Routas from the Coteaux Varois at under a fiver.

- ★★★★   1985 Champagne Bollinger Grande Année Rosé, Fr. £37. *Doughy and yeasty with plenty of soft, ripe fruits and a biscuit crispness.* ¶ **AP, D.**
- ★★★★   1994 Fortnum and Mason Sancerre, Vacheron, Loire, Fr. £9.95. *Lovely gooseberry tang and gentle acidity.* ¶ **D, S, SM.**
- ★★★★   1988 Fortnum and Mason Margaux, Chateau Rausan Segla, Bordeaux, Fr £15.95. *Classy, quite approachable, blackberryish – good value.* ¶ **LB.**
- ★★★★   1993 Au Bon Climat Pinot Noir, California, US. £15.25. *Great Pinot Noir with a 'wild' berry flavour. Richly satisfying.* ¶ **SP, RMS.**
- ★★★★   Taylor's 20 Year Old Tawny, Oporto, Por. £28.75. *Lovely and nutty with orange peel flavours.* ¶ **CC, CH.**

FUL   Fullers   ★★★★

The Griffin Brewery, Chiswick Lane, London W4 2QB Tel 0181 996 2000. Fax 0181 995 0230. Regional Chain. 63 branches. **Opening Hours:** Mon-Sat 1000-2200, Sun 1200-1500, 1900-2200. **Delivery:** free locally. **Tastings:** regular in-store. **Services:** glass hire, ice, 4 minute wine chilling service.

The buying team at Oddbins must have mixed feelings when they see the growing success of this London brewery's wine shops. After all, Roger Higgs, the man who has built on an already very impressive range was, until last year, out there choosing wines for them. So, it is not surprising to see the arrival of handwritten blackboards and wines like the brilliant Fuente del Ritmo from Spain. One of the three remaining smaller chains in the south east of England, Fullers is a merchant to watch.

**** 1991 Seppelt Salinger, S Australia, Aus. £9.99. *Biscuity and yeasty with ripe fruit and crisp acidity.* ⁋ *D, AP.*

**** 1994 Vavasour Dashwood Sauvignon Blanc, Marlborough, NZ. £8.49. *Lovely ripe gooseberry fool in a glass.* ⁋ *D, EN, WMC.*

**** 1994 Grove Mill Sauvignon Blanc, Marlborough, NZ. £6.95 *Really ripe gooseberry and exotic passionfruit. Big, fat and balanced.* ⁋ *AP, E, WMC.*

**** 1994 Rosemount Estate Shiraz/Cabernet Sauvignon, S.E. Aus. £4.99. *Ripe blackberry fruits with peppery spices.* ⁋ *SP, BF.*

**** 1994 Saint Veran, Dom. des Deux Roches, Burgundy, Fr. £7. *A good rich white Burgundy with toffee and pineapple hints.* ⁋ *CH, WFC, BF.*

**** 1993 Catena Estate Chardonnay, Mendoza, Arg. £7.99. *Very attractive ripe juicy Chardonnay. Peachy.* ⁋ *WFP, SM.*

**** 1994 Caliterra Estate Casablanca Chardonnay, Chi. £4.99. *Good, oaky creamy wine full of peach and pineapple and restrained oak.* ⁋ *D, PY, SM.*

*** 1992 Ironstone Cabernet Sauvignon/Shiraz, W Australia, Aus. £5.99. *Luscious berry fruits, smoky and peppery.* ⁋ *SP, WM.*

**** 1992 Penfolds Bin 389 Cabernet Shiraz, S Australia, Aus. £8.99. *Blackcurrants, eucalyptus and pepper. Full and rich.* ⁋ *FF, BF.*

*** 1991 Oriachovitza Cabernet Sauvignon Reserve, Menada Stara Zagora, Bul. £3.19. *Soft, plummy, blackcurranty wine. Very easy-going.* ⁋ *PY, WMC, CH.*

**** 1993 Cono Sur Cabernet Sauvignon, Chimbarongo, Chi. £3.79. *Good, creamy, ripe cassis and plum with minty overtones.* ⁋ *BF, G, D.*

**** 1993 Stellenzicht Cabernet Sauvignon/Malbec, Stellenbosch, SA. £3.99. *Spicily herbaceous wine with some of the richness of blackcurrant jam.* ⁋ *LB*

**** 1993 Dieu Donne Cabernet Sauvignon, Franschhoek, SA. £4.99. *Blackberries, cassis and mint. Lovely glugging stuff.* ⁋ *BF.*

**** 1992 Fairview Cabernet Franc/Merlot Reserve, Paarl, SA. £5.6. *Pomerol blend from one of South Africa's most experimental winemakers.* ⁋ *RM, P.*

*** 1993 Chateau Reynella Shiraz, S. Australia, Aus. £6.99. *Fantastic berry, mint and eucalyptus combination with balanced oak.* ⁋ *G, G, D.*

**** 1990 Penfolds Grange, S Australia, Aus. £49 *Unmistakeably Australian. Packed with concentrated fruit, spice and oak. Leave for a decade.* ⁋ *D, RM.*

*** 1994 Fortant de France, Grenache Noir, Midi, Fr. £3.49. *A light peppery wine in the Côtes du Rhône style; rich and long.* ⁋ *O, WMP.*

*** 1994 Casa de la Vina Cencibel, Valdepeñas, Sp. £3.29. *Ultra-soft and gluggable jammy toffee wine.* ⁋ *LB.*

*** 1992 Gran Feudo Crianza, Bodegas Julian Chivite, Navarra, Sp. £3.99. *Soft and smooth, creamy fruit and gentle oak.* ⁋ *CH, D, RM.*

GAL   Gallery Wines   ★★★

The Gomshall Gallery, Gomshall, Surrey GU5 9LB. Tel 01483 203 795. Fax: 01483 203 282. Independent Wine Merchant. **Opening Hours:** Mon-Sat 1000-1800. **Delivery:** free locally.

As a traditionalist, Dirk Collingwood concentrates on France and the French. Don't bother looking for the fruits of flying winemaking, which is, in Mr C's view, the "scourge" of the wine trade, stripping each country's wines of their inherent character. Well maybe; all I'll say is that the Gallery list supports his case pretty well.

**** 1990 Graacher Himmelreich Riesling Auslese, F W Gymnasium, Mosel, Ger. £11.10. *Citrusy, floral fruits balancing an underlying sweetness.* ⁋ *PF, PS.*

*** 1988 Ch. Haut Bages Liberal, Pauillac, Bordeaux, Fr. £16.50. *Classy and maturing Bordeaux. Dark fruit, mossy and heavy tannins.* ⁋ *LB.*

*** 1994 Fleurie, Dom. Berrod Les Roches sur Vivier, Beaujolais, Fr. £4.70. *Youthful, light summer fruits. Good glugging.* ⁏ *D, O, LB.*

*** 1989 Santenay, Dom. Roger Belland, Burgundy, Fr. £9. *Delicious, plummy, wine with real Burgundian character.* ⁏ *RM.*

GON Gauntley's   ★★★★★

4 High Street, Exchange Arcade, Nottingham NG1 2ET. Tel 0115 941 7973. Fax 0115 950 9519. Independent Wine Merchant. **Opening Hours:** Mon-Sat 0830-1730. **Delivery:** free locally. **Tastings:** regular in-store plus frequent tutored tastings given by wine growers (especially from the Rhône). **Services:** cellarage, *en primeur*, mail order, gift mailing, glass hire.

Having conquered the Rhône, with a constantly changing but consistently dazzling selection of reds and whites, and the south and south west of France with great Bandol from Ch Pibarnon and Pic St Loup from Mas Brugière, Gauntleys has perhaps inevitably turned its attention to Burgundy. As you might expect, the list is already packed with stars such as Rene Engel, Lafarge and Pousse d'Or in Volnay and Georges Bryczek in Morey St Denis. The New World selection is growing, with wines from the brilliant Joseph Swan winery in California and Cullen, Dalwhinnie and John Irvin in Australia. To keep track of all this hectic activity, get on the Gauntleys mailing list; their updates are worth reading if only for the Dumas quotes.

***** 1989 Riesling Cuvée Frederic Emile, Trimbach, Alsace, Fr. £16.99. *Ripe, spicy Riesling with a fresh lime marmalade character.* ⁏ *AP, LS.*

**** 1990 Gewürztraminer Cuvée de Seigneurs de Ribeaupierre, Trimbach, Alsace, Fr. £15.99. *Classic Gewurz flavours of peaches and lychees.* ⁏ *AP, S.*

***** 1993 Domaine de l'Hortus, Jean Orliac, Midi, Fr. £5.90. *Excitingly spicy, concentrated wine. A real mouthful.* ⁏ *SP, PY.*

**** 1990 Château de Reignac Cuvée Prestige, Bordeaux, Fr. £7.50. *Ripe, berryish, cedary claret from a great vintage.* ⁏ *LB.*

***** 1991 Warwick Farm Trilogy, Stellenbosch, SA. £8.99. *Fine, concentrated blend of Cab Sauv/ Franc and Merlot. Chewy and flavoursome.* ⁏ *BF, RMS.*

**** 1991 St. Jean de Bebian, Coteaux du Languedoc, Fr. £12.50. *Classy Southern French wine with gamey richness.* ⁏ *D.*

MG Matthew Gloag   ★★★

Bordeaux House, 33 Kinnoull Street, Perth PH1 5EU. Tel 01738 621 101. Fax 01738 628 167. Independent Wine Merchant. **Opening Hours:** Mon-Fri 0900-1700. **Delivery:** free on orders of 1 case or more in Scotland and 2 cases or more in England. **Tastings:** for wine clubs. **Services:** gift mailing, glass hire.

While still maintaining an admirable list of Claret, Burgundy and Rhône, this Highland outpost has attempted to break their traditional mould by expanding the New World section. Thus the odd Shiraz from Australia squares up to a nice little Crozes-Hermitage and fruity Chardonnays from New Zealand take on the might of Meursault. There is a fair range of South African wines to boot, but as that wretched little girl called Dorothy used to put it, there's no place like home and, for many people, the hardest part will be bidding farewell to a phenomenal range of malts.

*** 1994 Brouilly Garanche, Eventail, Beaujolais, Fr. £6.49. *Fruity, seductive Beaujolais with a typical boiled sweet and banana character.* ⁏ *LB, SM.*

**** 1993 Bourgogne Pinot Noir, Domaine B. Bachelet, Burgundy, Fr. £7.99. *Great value Burgundy from a brilliant Gevrey Chambertin estate.* ⁏ *CC, BF.*

**** 1989 Allesverloren Estate Tinta Barocca, Swartland, SA. £7.47. *Made from a port grape that has great potential for leathery, pruney dry wines.* ⁏ *G, RMS.*

*** 1994 Marques de Aragon Garnacha Tinto Puro, Bodega Campo San Isidro, Calatayud, Sp. £3.69. *Young, peppery and full of dusty flavour.* ⁏ *SP, P.*

GH Goedhuis & Co ★★★★

6 Rudolf Place, Miles Street, London SW8 1RP. Tel 0171 793 7900. Fax 0171 793 7170. Independent Wine Merchant. Wine by the case only. **Opening Hours:** Mon-Fri 0900-1800. **Delivery:** free locally. **Services:** cellarage, *en primeur*, mail order, glass hire, ice.

Goedhuis (pronounced Goodhouse) & Co continue to flourish both among wine buffs in this country and in Japan where they have a number of loyal – or should that be royal – customers. The range of Burgundies is top class, with a number of small estates not seen elsewhere. There are equally select Rhône and Port sections – the Croft 1960 is a real pearl, for example – though even a well heeled Japanese customer might need to take out a small Rhône to buy it. Mr G's Bordeaux and Burgundy 'Bottle Bank' cellar plans are also worth looking into.

***** 1993 Puligny Montrachet, Dom. Louis Carillon, Burgundy, Fr. £19.50. *Perfect white Burgundy – biscuity-rich, with pineapple fruit and leafy freshness.* ▐ *WM.*

**** 1989 Ch. Beaumont, Bordeaux, Fr. £9.70. *Classy, gently oaky wine with cedary richness.* ▐ *LB.*

**** 1990 Notre Dame de Landiras, Bordeaux, Fr. £6.30. *Good, young, raspberry and cassis fruit from a Danish pioneer producer.* ▐ *D.*

**** 1993 Givry 1er Cru 'Clos de la Servoisine', Joblot, Burgundy, Fr. £10.77. *Jammy, slightly rustic. Full of flavour.* ▐ *BF, RMS.*

***** 1990 Ch. de Beaucastel, Châteauneuf du Pape, Rhône, Fr. £20.56. *The Château Latour of Chateauneuf. Rich, and full of berry and spice.* ▐ *LB.*

G&M Gordon and MacPhail ★★★

George House, Boroughbriggs Road, Elgin, Moray IV30 1JY. Tel 01343 545 110. Fax 01343 540 155. Shop: 58-60 South Street, Elgin, Moray, IV30 1JY. Independent Wine Merchant. **Opening Hours:** Mon-Fri 0900-1715, Sat 0900-1700. **Delivery:** free locally. **Services:** mail order, glass hire.

Gordon & MacPhail offer a very mixed bag of goodies and not so goodies, amongst the latter a rather terrifying range of Scottish wines, a Rhinequeen Liebfraumilch and what sounds to be an unusual grape-grain blend in Chateau 'Fourcas-Holsten'. In general, their spirit list is far more impressive than the range of wines, though there are some welcome inclusions. Cape Mentelle, Peter Lehmann and Mitchell are amongst those representing the great down under and there are some good fairly priced red Bordeaux such as Chateau Caronne-Ste Gemme.

**** 1992 Mitchell Cabernet Sauvignon, S Australia, Aus. £8.75. *Big, intense blackcurrant wine from the Clare Valley.* ▐ *RM, G.*

***** 1992 Cathedral Cellars Triptych, KWV, Cape, SA. £7.99. *Modern South African crunchy-berry fruit.* ▐ *BF, RMS.*

**** 1990 Delegat's Proprietors Reserve, Merlot, Hawkes Bay, N.Z. £10.45. *Lovely plummy fruit and oak. One of New Zealand's best reds – quite Bordeaux-like.* ▐ *G, LB.*

**** 1994 Ch. du Grand Moulas, Marc Ryckwaert, Rhône, Fr. £6.08. *Peppery and redcurranty. Very characterful wine.* ▐ *CH.*

GI   Grape Ideas   ★★★★

3-5 Hythe Bridge Street, Oxford, OX1 2EW Tel 01865 722 137. Independent Wine Merchant. **Opening Hours:** Mon-Fri 1000-1900, Sat 1000-1800. **Delivery:** free locally. **Tastings:** regular in-store, tutored sessions on request for wine clubs, societies, colleges, etc. **Services:** mail order, glass hire, ice.

There are many reasons why Oxford is a potentially attractive place to open a wine shop, but student grants are not among them. It is a fine balancing act to cater for colleges looking for a few cases of first growth with students wanting a few bottles of anything under three quid. Grape Ideas manages well and has recently acquired the UK Agency for Les Mille Vignerons, whose range includes Vin de Pays de Côteaux de Fontcaude, a good selection of reds and whites for £2.89 apiece. It has also taken on the full range of Selaks from New Zealand, whose Sauvignon-Semillon 1994 recently received the "Southern Hemisphere White Wine of the Year" award.

***	Grandin Brut, Loire, Fr. £5.95. *Clean, dry easy-going and slightly honeyed fizz.* ¶ **AP, PY.**	
****	1993 Château de Marsannay Cuvée Charles Le Temeraire Blanc, Burgundy, Fr. £10.75. *Well-balanced, lingering, fruity Burgundy.* ¶ **WFP, S.**	
****	1994 Selaks Marlborough Sauvignon Blanc-Semillon, NZ. £8.95. *Fine gooseberries and oak combination.* ¶ **WM, SP.**	
*****	1993 Plantagenet Mount Barker Shiraz, W Australia, Aus. £9.95. *Lean, peppery and smoky with red berry fruit.* ¶ **LB, SP.**	
****	1986 Reserva Especial, A A Ferreira, Douro, Por £9.99. *Traditional Portuguese-style, woody, nutty port.* ¶ **CC, CH.**	
***	1993 Chardonnay 'Oak Cask' Reserve, Trapiche, Arg. £3.99. *An oaky, buttery melony bargain.* ¶ **WM, SF.**	
***	1993 Côtes de Duras Sauvignon Vieilles Vignes, Berticot, SW France, Fr. £3.89. *A good value alternative to dry white Bordeaux.* ¶ **PY, WMC.**	
****	1993 Barraida Branco, Quinta de Pedralvites, Sogrape, Por. £5.99. *Creamy, lemony, modern Portuguese white.* ¶ **B.**	

GNW   Great Northern Wine Co

Unit 5 Granary Wharf, The Canal Basin, Leeds, W. Yorks. LS1 4BR Tel 0113 246 1200. Fax 0113 246 1209. Independent Wine Merchant. **Opening Hours:** Mon-Fri 0900-1800, Sat 0930-1700. **Delivery:** free locally. **Tastings:** regular in-store, monthly tutored sessions, annual wine fair in October. **Services:** cellarage, mail order, gift mailing, glass hire.

We "hard working, weather-worn Northerners rarely have much to smile about" Steve Day comments, which might give some potential customers reason to pause before indulging in a discussion with Mr D which, as he says, could last "anywhere between two minutes and two hours!" Fortunately, the quality of the Great Northern range with wines like the LA Cetto Mexican Chardonnay and Tour de Gendres Bergerac Rosé is good enough to raise the corners of any wine lover's mouth.

***	1994 Chateau Haut Rian Bordeaux Blanc, Bordeaux, Fr. £4.99. *Clean, dry, quite grassy.* ¶ **WM, S.**	
****	1994 Château Tours des Gendres Rosé, Bergerac, Fr. £4.99. *A deliciously fresh, blackcurranty and plummy pink wine, full of crunchy fruit.* ¶ **AP, LS.**	
****	1986 L A Cetto Nebbiolo Reserva, Baja California, Mex. £8.95. *A wonderful leathery concoction to worry many a producer of the kind of indifferent Barolo which features on the lists of so many Italian restaurants.* ¶ **SP.**	
****	1991 Viñas de Gain Rioja, Cosecheros Alaveses, Sp. £5.82. *Good value, soft wine with a flavour of ripe plum and spice.* ¶ **LB, P.**	
****	Don Zoilo Amontillado, Jerez, Sp. £8.99. *Delicious, rich sherry, full of nuts and caramel.* ¶ **AP, S.**	

GWW   Great Western Wine Co   ★★★

The Wine Warehouse, Wells Road, Bath, BA2 3AP. Tel 01225 448 428 Fax 01225
442 139. Independent Wine Merchant. **Opening Hours:** Mon-Fri 0900-1900, Sat
1000-1900. **Delivery:** Free locally. **Tastings:** regular in-store plus tutored events by
winemakers, beginners courses and tastings of Bordeaux Cru Classés. **Services:**
cellarage, en-primeur, mail-order, gift mailing, glass hire, ice.

Last year's prediction of a change of name to Network West Wines obviously failed
to materialize, although Great Western have moved to a grander station in life only
yards from their original home. Their selection should send any wine lover into
public transports of delight: plenty of good regional French wines at the lower end of
the price platform, and a comprehensive selection from Australia for under £6,
including Mitchelton and Rothbury Estate. From the US Beringer, Madrona and
Saintsbury are just the ticket, or, if you prefer something more traditional, why not
go for something along the line of Chapoutier's 1990 Côte Rôtie "Brune et Blonde".
Not exactly a super saver at £24.44, but well worth it. Clearly getting there!

★★★	1994 Dom. Saint Hilaire Sauvignon, Vin de Pays d'Oc, Fr. £4.49. *Light and crisp. Soft melony fruits. Made by Australians in France.* ‖ *D, CC.*
★★★	1993 Matua Valley Chardonnay, Judd Estate, NZ £9.34. *Lovely cool fruits and gentle, well-balanced oak.* ‖ *WM, FD.*
★★★	1987 Nuits Saint Georges 'Aux Murgers', Méo Camuzet, Burgundy, Fr. £25.85. *Mature and soft, smoky oak, raspberries and cherries.* ‖ *LB, E.*
★★★★	1992 Le Volte, Tenute dell'Ornellaia, Bolgheri, It. £7.75. *A – relatively – affordable taste of the rich complex style of the far dearer Ornellaia.* ‖ *CS,*
★★★	1994 Ch. Tour des Gendes Semillon/Sauvignon Blanc, Bergerac, Fr. £4.89. *Crisp and clean, pineapple and gooseberry.* ‖ *D, PY.*

PTR   Peter Green   ★★★

37 A/B Warrender Park Road, Edinburgh EH9 1HJ. Tel/Fax 0131 229 5925.
Independent Wine Merchant. **Opening Hours:** Mon-Fri 0930-1830, Sat 0930-1900.
Delivery: free locally. **Services:** mail order. No credit cards – Switch only.

While reserving judgement about Peter Green's stocking of KWV and Zonnebloem
which are not among the Cape's foremost ambassadors we would wholeheartedly
sanction almost every other wine on their list as being at the very least reliable and at
best truly excellent. The German selection is particularly impressive – get to grips
with a Lingenfelder Scheurebe Spatlese or one of the wines from Burklin-Wolf or
Furst von Metternich. Alsace and Bordeaux are well served and there are some fine
examples of mature (1986) Burgundy from folk like Rion and Trapet. Neither will the
excellent Italian or Australian range disappoint.

★★★★	1990 Pelorus, Cloudy Bay, N.Z. £11.25. *Crisp and refreshing bubbly, full of burnt toast and zesty, melony fruit flavours.* ‖ *AP, S.*
★★★	1994 Uitkyk Sauvignon Blanc, Stellenbosch, SA. £5.50 *Gooseberries and limes; grassy and slightly herby.* ‖ *WMC, D.*
★★★★	1989 Wachenheimer Gerümel Riesling Spätlese, Bürklin-Wolf, Rhine, Ger. £14.85. *Serious maturing Riesling with rich petrolly spice.* ‖ *CS, PF..*
★★★★	1992 Crozes Hermitage, Cave de Tain l'Hermitage, Rhône, Fr. £5.99. *Rich and smoky, with raspberryish sloes and tar.* ‖ *RM, CH.*
★★★★★	1990 Tignanello, Antinori, Tuscany, It. £22.20. *One of the original Super Tuscans. Rich, herby, blackcurranty and classy.* ‖ *LB.*
★★★★	Ramos Tinto Quinta da Urtiga Vintage Character Port, Douro, Por. £8.75. *Rich, Vintage-like port from a subsidiary of Roederer Champagne.* ‖ *CH, D.*

HAL   Hall Batson & Co   ★★★

168 Wroxham Road, Norwich NR7 8DE. Tel 01603 415115. Fax 01603 484096.
Independent Wine Merchant. **Opening Hours:** Mon-Fri 0900-1730, Sat 0930-1200.
Delivery: free locally. **Services:** mail order, free glass loan, free tastings, *en primeur* offers.

If attitude is anything to go by, Hall Batson and Co are destined for great things. At present, there are a few too many carelessly bought Woodbridge Californians and Wyndham Estate Australians on the list to put them on the front row of East Anglian merchants, but there are inventive forays into New Zealand and Eastern Europe and carefully listed good-value wines from classic European regions.

***** 1994 Hunters Sauvignon Blanc, Marlborough, NZ. £9.52. *Green pepper and gooseberry. A worthy rival to Cloudy Bay.* ¶ *D, WMC.*

*** 1993 River Route Cabernet Sauvignon/Merlot, Recas, Rom. £3. *Lovely stewed fruit, herbaceous and lightly tannic.* ¶ *PY, BF.*

**** 1991 Ch. La Nerthe, Rhône, Fr. £12.81. *Smoky fruits, white pepper and mint.* ¶ *G, RM.*

**** 1992 Bourgogne Pinot Noir Les Vignerons d'Igé, Mâcon, Burgundy, Fr. £6.11. *Berries and cherry flavours. Earthy spices.* ¶ *G, SM.*

HLV   Halves   ★★★

Wood Yard, off Corve Street, Ludlow, Shropshire, SY8 2PX. Tel 01584 877866. Fax 01584 877677. Independent Wine Merchant. Minimum order 24 half bottles. Office Hours: Mon-Fri 0900-1830, occasionally Sat mornings. **Delivery:** included in list price.

"Drinking halves as a matter of course is more a state of mind rather than of pocket." Tim Jackson, in a new berth following the sinking of The Wine Treasury where he used to display his wares, is the world's premier halvist. Of course halves are dearer – but cuter too, and as well as a comprehensive list, there are pre-selected cases, containing two, three or four halves each of various wines and sherries, although a true halvist festival would surely be easier to arrange with mixed dozens of 12 different wines.

*** 1991 Stoneleigh Chardonnay, Marlborough, NZ. £2.78 (half) *Honey and lemon curd, lots of citrussy fruit and crisp acidity.* ¶ *PY, WM.*

***** 1992 St Joseph, André Perret, Rhône, Fr. £5 (half). *Peppery, spicy and rich damson fruit.* ¶ *LB, CH.*

**** 1987 Lindemans Botrytis Semillon, S. Australia, Aus. £6.92 (half *sugar, oak and peaches. A bargain alternative to Sauternes.* ¶ *AP, PS.*

***** 1989 Vin de Constance, Klein Constantia, SA. £11.79. (50 cl). *Gorgeous, late harvest wine from one of the oldest vineyards in the New World.* ¶ *D*

**** 1986 Ch. Filhot, Sauternes, Fr. £10.19. (half) *Classic, maturing dried-apricotty wine.* ¶ *D, AP, CS, PS.*

HOK   Hammonds of Knutsford   ★★★

Warford Grange Farm, Pedley House Lane, Great Warford, Knutsford, Cheshire WA16 7SP. Tel 01565 872872. Fax 01565 872900. Independent Wine Merchant.
Opening Hours: Mon-Fri 0800-1800 or by appointment. **Delivery:** free locally.
Services: mail order, glass loan. No credit cards.

Skipping regretfully past the gargantuan number of fine whiskies, cognacs and spirits on offer here, one quickly realises that the wine section is unlikely to yield many undiscovered gems, but Guigal from the Rhône, Louis Latour from Burgundy, Schlumberger from Alsace and Mondavi from California dominate, disproving the old adage that familiarity breeds contempt. And there is a good selection of old Claret for the ultra-traditionalist.

***   Champagne Baron Edouard Massé, Fr. £12.50. *A lesser known label from the reliable and occasionally excellent house of Lanson.* ⁋ ***CC, AP.***

***   1991 Dom. Ott, Blanc des Blancs, Clos Mireille, Côtes de Provence, Fr. £14.95. *A rare, cult wine in France. Creamy and distinctive.* ⁋ ***FO, WMC.***

****   1985 Côte Rôtie Brune et Blonde, E. Guigal, Rhône, Fr. £22.95. *Rich baked fruits, herbs and white peppers in glorious abundance.* ⁋ ***G, RMS.***

*****   1993 Moulin-à-Vent Dom. Tour de Bief, Georges Duboeuf, Beaujolais, Fr. £7.05. *A delicate summer wine. Strawberries, cherries and cassis.* ⁋ ***AP, FF.***

****   1988 Marqués de Murrieta Rioja Tinto Reserva, Sp. £7.95. *Dark and woody, with plums and damsons.* ⁋ ***G, LB.***

HAR   Harrods   ★★★★

Knightsbridge, London, SW1X 7QX. Tel 0171 730 1234. Department Store. **Opening Hours:** Mon, Tues, Sat 1000-1800, Wed, Thurs, Fri 1000-1900. **Tastings:** regularly for members of the Gourmet Club and people on the mailing list. **Services:** gift-mailing, mail order, cellarage, *en primeur.*

"We have loads of funky kit here that you wouldn't believe." Andrew Montague, the Fred Flintstone lookalike who arrived at Harrods after a few years of attempting to promote Californian wines in Britain, is trying hard to continue the revolution begun last year by Nick Mason. We wonder quite what Harrods' customers make of such new wines as the brilliant Henschke Abbott's Prayer from Australia, Roederer Quartet fizz from California and Ata Rangi Pinot Noir from New Zealand. Still, if they prefer to stick to the old world, they can always try one of the starry range of red Rhônes which I reckon to be among the most funkily tasty wines in the universe.

*****   1983 Champagne Charles Heidsieck Blanc des Millenaires, Fr. £41. *Stunning, toasty and packed with crisp fruit.* ⁋ ***AP, D, S.***

*****   1994 Jackson Estate Sauvignon Blanc, Marlborough, NZ. £7.99. *Gorgeous ripe, gooseberryish wine from a vineyard opposite Cloudy Bay.* ⁋ ***WMC, D, S.***

****   1993 Chablis Dom. des Marrenniers, Bernard Legland, Burgundy, Fr. £8.49. *Good modern Chablis with pineappley fruit and complexity.* ⁋ ***FF.***

****   1993 Wakefield Clare Riesling, S. Australia, Aus. £4.99. *Floral, tropical fruits and a lovely, zesty acidity.* ⁋ ***CC, O, S.***

*****   1989 Meerlust Rubicon, Stellenbosch, SA. £10. *Fine concentrated claret style with rich raisiny fruit. Needs time.* ⁋ ***LB, G.***

****   1992 Marimar Torres Pinot Noir, Cal. £15.99. *Packed with raspberry and sweet oak. Creamily satisfying.* ⁋ ***WM, CH.***

*****   Quinta Da Ervamoira 10 Year Old Tawny, Ramos-Pinto, Douro, Por. £13.56. *Lovely plummy wine with a flavour of the darkest brown sugar.* ⁋ ***CC, CH.***

****   1986 Reserva Especial, A A Ferreira, Douro, Por. £9.99. *Traditional Portuguese-style, woody, nutty port.* ⁋ ***CC, CS.***

HN   Harvey Nichols   ★★★★

Knightsbridge, London, SW1. Tel 0171 235 5000. Department Store. **Opening Hours:** Mon-Fri 1000-2000, Sat 1000-1800. **Tastings:** regular in-store plus tutored sessions. **Services:** mail order, gift-mailing, gift-wrapping in store.

If there were an award for the chic-est place to buy wine in Britain, this has to be it. Within murmuring distance of the restaurant, cappuccino bar and the shelves of strawberry pasta and olive blossom honey, the wine shop on the fifth floor of "Harvey Nicks" ingeniously squeezes a surprising number of examples of the best of both worlds. The classics are secreted at the back of the shop, by the way, so are often overlooked. It says much for this shop that when *WINE Magazine* needed a representative set of top-class Cabernets from several countries and a handful of top-flight clarets for a tasting, they found them all here.

HAS   The Haslemere Cellar   ★★★

Rear of 2 Lower Street, Haslemere, Surrey, GU27 2NX. Tel 01428 645081. Fax 01428 645081. Independent Wine Merchant.**Opening Hours:** Tues-Sat 0930-1830, Sat 0900-1700.**Tastings:** regular tutored. **Delivery:** free locally and in Central London. **Services:** cellarage, glass loan.

Surrey drinkers are apparently turning back to claret, or at least that's the experience here, where they can choose such wines as Beychevelle 1983 and Margaux 1987. Others may prefer to delve into Alsace, the Rhône and Germany, including eight of Dr Loosen's best. There is also a good selection of Vins Doux Naturels, with both reds and whites from Banyuls.

- ★★★★ 1993 Soave Classico Superiore, Anselmi, Veneto, It. £6.95. *Proper Soave made from the superior Garganega rather than Trebbiano.* ‖ *WFC, FD.*
- ★★★★★ 1990 Wehlener Sonnenuhr Riesling Spatlese, Dr Loosen, Mosel, Ger. £9.75. *Wonderfully rich honeyed lemon with fine balance.* ‖ *AP, PF.*
- ★★★★★ 1966 Ch. Pavie, St Emilion Grand Cru, Bordeaux, Fr. £23.50. *Perfectly mature claret.* ‖ *LB, CH.*
- ★★★★★ 1991 Crozes-Hermitage "La Guiraude", Alain Graillot, Rhône, Fr. £11. *Wonderful white pepper, blackberry, leather and fine new oak.* ‖ *RMS, SP.*
- ★★★★★ 1961 Ch. Doisy-Daëne, Barsac, Bordeaux, Fr. £49. *Classic old Sauternes from an excellent year.* ‖ *CS, PF.*

HHC   Haynes Hanson and Clark   ★★★★

Sheep Street, Stow-on-the-Wold, Gloucs GL54 1AA. Tel 01451 870808. Also at 25 Eccleston Street, London, SW1W 9NP. Independent Wine Merchant. **Opening Hours:** Mon-Fri 0900-1800, Sat 0930-1700. **Delivery:** free locally. **Services:** *en primeur*, mail order, gift mailing, glass hire, ice.

Burgundy is principally the name and the game for HHC, who have settled into a new head office in the countryside. However, though their day-to-day work patterns may be a little more sedate, their list is still switched on to London pace with a dazzling array of top-quality Burgundy producers straight out of Anthony Hanson's updated and brilliant book on the region (Faber & Faber). California, Australia and South Africa are all ably represented and peddled keenly at their Eccleston Street shop, where employees still face the glare of city lights.

- ★★★★★ Champagne Louis Roederer Brut Premier, Fr, £22.25. *Rich, toasty and yeasty, with rich but not overstated, ripe fruit.* ‖ *D, AP, S.*
- ★★★★ 1993 Chauvigne Blanc d'Anjou, Dom. Richou, Loire, Fr. £6.15. *Bone dry Loire white from the Chenin grape. Elegant and lively.* ‖ *LS, WMC.*
- ★★★★ 1992 Louisvale Chardonnay, Devon Valley, Stellenbosch, SA. £8.99. *Great elegance and richness from the Cape's Chardonnay specialist.* ‖ *SF, WMC.*
- ★★★★★ 1992 Chassagne Montrachet, Gagnard Delagrange, Burgundy, Fr. £19.60. *Subtle white Burgundy built to last. Only a hint of oak.* ‖ *FD, S.*
- ★★★★ 1992 Domaine de Limbardie, VdP de Côteaux de Murviel, H Boukandoura, Fr. £4.90. *Crisp red fruit flavours, full of Southern sunshine.* ‖ *D, RM.*
- ★★★★★ 1990 Ch. Clos de l'Eglise, Pomerol, Bordeaux, Fr. £20.95. *Classic young Merlot-dominant Bordeaux. Subtle, complex and well worth keeping.* ‖ *LB.*
- ★★★★★ 1986 Hermitage La Chapelle, Jaboulet, Rhône, Fr. £17.95. *Monstrous deep purple wine, still needing time in the bottle – a genuine classic.* ‖ *G, RMS.*
- ★★★★ 1991 Plantagenet Mount Barker Shiraz, W. Australia, Aus. £9.55. *Lean, peppery and vegetal with delicious red berry fruit.* ‖ *SP, RM.*
- ★★★★★ 1992 Vosne Romanée, Dom Jean Grivot, Burgundy, Fr. £17.60. *Deep, rich, quite spicy Burgundy which needs time. Will be a classic.* ‖ *BF, CH.*
- ★★★★★ 1989 Volnay, Les Taillepieds, Burgundy, Fr. £24.10. *Good-value price. Brilliant, complex and subtle; delicately perfumed berry flavours.* ‖ *BF, CH.*

HW Hedley Wright & Co ★★★★

11 The Twyford Centre, London Road, Bishop's Stortford, Herts CM23 3YT. Tel 01279 506512. Fax 01279 657462. Independent Wine Merchant. **Opening Hours:** Mon-Wed 0900-1800, Thu-Fri 0900-1900, Sat 1000-1800. **Delivery:** free locally. **Tastings:** regular in-store, plus tutored events. **Services:** en primeur, glass hire, gift-mailing, ice.

Forget the Daniel le Brun Champagne-like fizz and gooseberryish Sauvignons from Jackson Estate in New Zealand, the Domaine de Cabasse Rhônes, the Montes Chileans and Churchill Graham ports. No, place an immediate order for a case of Pâté de Erizos, the tinned Chilean sea urchin pâté of which David Sandys Renton is inordinately proud. Okay, so when it was offered to the editor of the *Guide*, the pâté hit the spittoon faster than any wine, but Mr S-R earnestly believes in its aphrodisiac properties and, not having swallowed it, who can argue?

**** Taltarni Brut Taché, Victoria, Aus. £7.99. *Delicately pink wine with lovely, subtle, raspberryish, chocolatey flavours.* ¶ *AP, PY.*

***** 1994 Jackson Estate Sauvignon Blanc, Marlborough, NZ. £7.99. *Gorgeous ripe, gooseberryish wine from a vineyard opposite Cloudy Bay.* ¶ *D, SP.*

*** 1994 Montes Fumé Blanc, Curico, Chi. £4.85. *Gently zingy lemon character – and a mildly oaky flavour.* ¶ *O, WM, SF.*

**** 1994 Inglewood Show Reserve Verdelho, New South Wales, Aus. £9.49. *Very distinctive nutty, peachy and spicy wine with a hint of lime.* ¶ *D, O.*

**** 1991 William Wheeler Winery Zinfandel, California, US. £9.95. *Good, berryish, slightly eucalyptussy Zinfandel.* ¶ *P, G.*

**** 1990 Los Llanos Reserva, Valdepenas, Sp. £3.99. *Great modern Spanish red with ripe, berryish fruit.* ¶ *D, LB.*

**** Churchill's 10 Year Old Tawny, Douro, Por. £12.75. *Fresh, tangy port with flavours of ripe plum and orange-peel.* ¶ *CC, CH.*

HBR/BAR Heyman Barwell & Jones ★★★★

130 Ebury Street, London SW1W 9QQ. Tel 0171 730 0324. Fax 0171 730 0575. Independent Wine Merchant. **Opening Hours:** Mon-Fri 0900-1800. **Services:** mail order, en primeur, glass loan.

The greatest reason to celebrate the marriage of wholesalers Heyman Brothers and Barwell & Jones must surely be the dazzling selection of Burgundies, full of names like Mongeard-Mugneret and Armand Rousseau, a range of a dozen of Robert Weil's best wines from Germany, some excellent Montecillo Riojas from Spain and a set of ancient and modern Tokaji. There are also some tasty ports from the small firm of Burmester and seven single-domaine vintage Armagnacs, but the happy couple could be more adventurous in the New World. Beware prices that exclude VAT.

**** Champagne Ruinart Brut, Fr. £16.65. *Little known Grand Marque now finding increasing favour in the U.K.* ¶ *AP, LS.*

***** 1991 Chassagne Montrachet, Dom. Louis Carillon, Burgundy, Fr. £14.20. *Maturing white Burgundy at its nutty best.* ¶ *SF, D, WMC.*

***** 1990 Rheingau Riesling Spatlese, Weingut Robert Weil, Ger. £12.14. *Great, concentrated late harvest wine from a Japanese–owned estate.* ¶ *O, CC.*

**** 1990 Beaune 1er Cru "Les Chouacheux", Labouré Roi, Burgundy, Fr. £10.87. *Good value, raspberryish Pinot from a reliable negociant.* ¶ *RM, BF.*

***** 1989 Chambolle Musigny "La Combe d'Orvaux", Jean Grivot, Burgundy, Fr. £21.54. *Soft, perfumed damsony fruit. Fine Burgundy.* ¶ *RMS, BF.*

*** 1993 Bardolino Classico, Vigneto Tachetto, G. Rizzardi, It. £5.09. *Light, cherryish organic wine. Serve slightly chilled.* ¶ *D, WFP.*

**** 1983 Tokaji Szamorodni Sweet, Hegyalja Estate, Hun. £4.99 (50cl). *Nutty, with exciting lemon and lime marmalade flavours* ¶ *CC, PS.*

H&D   Hicks and Don   ★★★

The Brewery, Blandford St Mary, Dorset DT11 9LB. Tel 01258 456040. Fax 01258 450147. Independent Wine Merchant. **Opening Hours:** Mon-Fri 0900-1700 plus answerphone. **Delivery:** free for three cases or more. **Services:** cellarage, *en-primeur*, mail order, gift-mailing, glass hire.

The Hicks & Don wine list can tell you a good deal more than which wines they offer – look no further to find out just how useful sausage skins can be if you're caught short. The selection is good, with plenty of reliable if unexciting names in every country including several reasonably priced Chablis (Drouhin, Brocard etc). Much the same range is found in the 16 Woodhouse Wines shops which also belong to Hall & Woodhouse, the brewers who brought us Badger and Tanglefoot. Expect the wines to reach the standard of those ales over the next year, though, following the arrival of the talented Philip Clive from the very different world of Asda, it will be interesting to see how he fits in with Messrs Hick and Don, MWs both.

★★★	1992 Partridge Seyval Dry, Dorset, Eng. £5.85. *Enticing, dry, floral white from the hybrid Seyval grape. Perfect for a summer afternoon.* ¶ *AP, D.*	
★★★	1993 Chardonnay, Dom. Virginie, VdP D'Oc, Fr. £4.81. *Light, lemony Chardonnay, gently oaked and softly fruity.* ¶ *AP, LS.*	
★★★★	1994 Chatsfield Cabernet Franc, Mount Barker, W. Australia, Aus. £7.49. *Fragrant Cabernet Franc; cherries, chocolate and spice.* ¶ *WM, CH.*	
★★★★	1994 Gamay Noir, Fairview Estate, Paarl, SA. £4.75. *Delightfully fresh strawberry fruit with a hint of banana.* ¶ *E, LS.*	

HIG   High Breck Vintners   ★★★

Bentworth House, Bentworth, Nr. Alton, Hants, GU34 5RB. Tel 01420 562218. Fax 01420 563827. Independent Wine Merchant. **Opening Hours:** Mon-Fri 0930-1730, other times by arrangement. **Services:** glass loan.

At last, a wine merchant you can pop into after entertaining the kids at Alton Towers for the day. The list is not over-long, but there's enough here to keep you amused, with good red Loires, great value from the South-West and well-chosen Beaujolais. Eurosceptics should seek elsewhere however; there are no New World wines here. High Breck believe in France – sufficiently to import wines unavailable elsewhere.

★★★★	1990 Domaine de la Grave Blanc, Graves, Bordeaux, Fr. £9.60. *Aromatic and grassy Sauvignon, layered with well judged gentle oak.* ¶ *WM, WFC.*
★★★★	1992 Sancerre "Les Creux", Gitton, Loire, Fr. £9.79. *Fresh and nettley, showing the gun-flint flavours of the chalky "Calcaire" soil.* ¶ *S, FO.*
★★★	1990 Carta de Oro Rioja Crianza, Bodegas Berberana, Sp. £6.26. *Richly fruity and generously oaked – a good example of modern Rioja.* ¶ *LB.*
★★★★	1989 Saussignac La Croix Blanche, Ch. Richard, Bergerac, Fr. £6.99. *Good value, one of the more unusual alternatives to Sauternes.* ¶ *PS.*

JEH   J E Hogg   ★★★

61 Cumberland Street, EH3 6RA, Edinburgh. Tel 0131 556 4025. Independent Wine Merchant. **Opening Hours:** Mon-Fri 0900-1300 & 1430-1800, Sat & Wed 0900-1300. **Delivery:** free locally and in East Lothian. **Services:** glass hire.

Tastes are changing in Edinburgh, it seems. Chablis is on the up, as is the top end of the Burgundy spectrum and Mr H notes a major revival in interest in his Italian reds. With Allegrini's La Grola Valpolicella and Capezzana Barco Reale featuring among a plethora of goodies, this does not surprise us, but we are disappointed to learn that the fine German range is doing no better than "still hanging in there". Dr Prum, Dr Burklin Wolf and the Wegeler-Deinhard Estate all deserve better than this.

***** 1992 Babich Irongate Chardonnay, Hawkes Bay, NZ. £13. *Soft Chardonnay with tropical flavours and the freshness of lemon balm.* ¶ *D, FD, WM.*

**** 1990 Wegeler Deinhard Rhinegau Riesling Spätlese, Ger. £13. *Fresh fruits of peaches and lemons warmed by overtones of banana fritters.* ¶ *CC, O, PF, S.*

*** 1986 Viña Arana Rioja Reserva, La Rioja Alta, Sp. £8. *Soft and fruity, great for picnics.* ¶ *D, FF, PY.*

**** Don Zoilo Manzanilla, Jerez, Sp. £8. *Classic salty, tangy dry sherry. Serve very cold — and generously.* ¶ *D, PY, AP.*

HOL   Holland Park Wine Co   ****

12 Portland Road, London, W11 4LA. Tel 0171 221 9614. Fax 0171 221 9613.
Independent Wine Merchant. **Opening Hours:** Mon-Fri 1000-2030, Sat 0900-2030.
Delivery: free locally. **Tastings:** regular in-store plus a series of tutored tastings.
Services: cellarage, *en primeur*, mail order, gift-mailing, glass hire, ice.

James Handford MW has spent some money on recruitment with the addition of David Penny to the Holland Park workforce (he must be in for a pound). It has paid off with some sterling work in the Burgundy department with the 1992 Jean Pillot Chassagne-Montrachet and Gerard Thomas Meursault Blagny. To be frank we couldn't give tuppence if we never saw the 1992 Los Vascos white again so we are glad to note its disappearance from the list, though the red is commendable enough. There is an impressive array from Italy and the New World – especially the kiwis. Trip down to Holland Park and you'll be quids in.

*** 1994 Santa Helena Seleccion Directorio Oak Aged Chardonnay, Curico, Chi. £5.49. *Attractive, light, easy-going, quite French-style Chardonnay.* ¶ *CH, SM.*

***** 1992 Crichton Hall Chardonnay, Cal. £13.95 *Made by an Englishman. Buttery rich, very seductive wine.* ¶ *D, SF, LS, WFP.*

**** 1993 Rasteau Côtes du Rhône Villages, Cave de Rasteau, Rhône, Fr. £5.69. *Pepper and spice with ripe, jammy summer fruits.* ¶ *G, RMS, SP.*

**** 1993 Stoniers Pinot Noir, Mornington Peninsula, Aus. £7.99. *Classy, oaky, mulberryish wine with lovely vanilla oak.* ¶ *BF, WFP, D, CH.*

**** 1992 Ladoix Les Carrieres, Edmond Cornu, Burgundy, Fr. £13.50 *Raspberries and spearmint. Good value from a little -known village.* ¶ *WMP.*

HOP   Hopton Wines   ***

13 Teme Street, Tenbury Wells, Worcs, WR15 8BB. Tel/Fax 01584 810355.
Independent Wine Merchant. **Opening Hours:** Mon-Fri 1000-1300 & 1330-1900.
Sat 1000-1300 & 1415-1900. **Delivery:** free locally. **Services:** mail order, glass loan, *en primeur* offers, storage, hampers and giftware. No credit cards.

Mr Woodward's main objective this year is to keep trading in the face of the government's obstructive budgets. The list is centred around a core of château and domaine-bottled wine from privately owned properties in France, like Château de l'Hurbe in Fronsac, Château de Pic in Bordeaux and Domaine des Genaudières from the Loire, the majority of which are both unfamiliar and worth investigating.

*** 1990 St Veran, Dom. Gueugnon, Burgundy, Fr. £7.95. *Good value wine from an appellation neighbouring Pouilly Fuissé.* ¶ *E, S, SF, AP.*

*** 1992 Fairview Estate Chardonnay, Paarl, SA. £7.30. *Lemony, melony wine with some buttery richness.* ¶ *PY, LS, FF, FD.*

**** 1989 Ch. de Lamarque, Haut-Médoc, Bordeaux, Fr. £8.17. *Good, quite traditional claret with tarry cedary flavours.* ¶ *LB, RMS, CH.*

**** 1991 Fetzer Valley Oaks Cabernet Sauvignon, Cal. US. £7.97. *Clean, rich and full with typical dusty blackberry flavours.* ¶ *G, LB, RMS, WMP.*

**** 1981 Glorioso Gran Reserva Rioja, Bodegas Palacio, Sp. £9.04. *Lovely mature wine with gentle oakiness.* ¶ *AP, D.*

HOU   Hoults   ★★★

5 Cherry Tree Walk, The Calls, Leeds LS2 7EB. Tel 0113 2453393. Independent Wine Merchant. **Opening Hours:** Mon-Sat 1000-1830, Sun 1200-1500. **Delivery:** free locally. **Tastings:** regular in-store plus occasional tutored sessions for organisations. **Services:** mail order, gift mailing.

With outlets in Huddersfield and Leeds, this "pile it high and sell it cheap" outfit can now "out-Oddbins" its competitors to the tune of a £1 million turnover. £3.99 South Africans and Chileans are flying out of the door, holding hands with Penfolds 202 Riesling and Peter Lehman Grenache. At a more sedate pace, French wine under a tenner is proving a big hit. The buying efforts occasionally seem to be a bit hit or miss, but stick to the tried and tested and you'll find plenty of glorious bargains.

****   1993 Marc Brédif Vouvray, Loire, Fr. £10.99. *Dry, yet honeyed, appley wine. Ripe and good.* ¶ *AP, O.*

*****   1994 Rothbury Estate Marlborough Sauvignon Blanc, NZ. £6.99. *Immaculate – clean fresh gooseberries with a grapefruit edge.* ¶ *E, S, AP, D.*

***   1994 Lindemans Cawarra Semillon Chardonnay, S. Australia, Aus. £3.99. *A very easy mouthful: peaches and pineapples.* ¶ *D, AP, FF.*

*****   1990 Gewürztraminer Grand Cru Brand, Cave de Turckheim, Alsace, Fr. £14.99. *Rich, very lycheeish, satisfying wine. Lovely with fresh fruit.* ¶ *CS, O.*

****   1990 Château Ramage La Batisse, Bordeaux, Fr. £10.99. *A good value example of modern Bordeaux winemaking. Cedary and ripe.* ¶ *G, LB, RMS, CH.*

SHJ   S H Jones   ★★★★

27 High Street, Banbury, Oxon OX16 8EW. Tel 01295 251179. Fax 01295 272352. Independent Wine Merchant incorporating Philip Eyres and Associates. **Opening Hours:** Mon-Fri 0830-1800, Sat 0900-1800. Also at 9 Market Square, Bicester, Oxon OX6 7AA. Tel 01869 322448. **Opening Hours:** Mon-Sat 1000-2000. **Delivery:** free locally. **Tastings:** regular in-store, plus tutored sessions. **Services:** cellarage, *en primeur*, mail order, gift-mailing, glass hire, ice. N.B. Philip Eyres is now trading under S H Jones.

And here in the depths of deepest Oxfordshire, lurking under a façade of Cotswold stone we stumble across that most elusive of endangered species, "Independentus Wine Merchantus". Continually preyed upon by the much larger "Voracious Supermarketus" this much smaller animal has to adapt to survive by providing a more personal approach and competitively priced quality wines. Fortunately this one in Banbury, along with its mate in Bicester, seems in no danger if the wine list is anything to go by, and the association with Philip Eyres will help. Look out for an interesting selection of French Country Wines plus the Schlumberger Gewürztraminers and Rieslings, Pouilly Blanc Fumé, domaine Thibault and the organic Vouvray, le Haut Lieu from Huët.

****   1993 Chablis 1er Cru Montmains, Dom. des Menants, Jean-Marc Brocard, Burgundy, Fr. £10.50 *Buttery, typical Old World style.* ¶ *AP, WMC, WFP.*

****   1994 Brown Brothers Dry Muscat Blanc, Milawa, Victoria, Aus. £5.39. *Dry, grapey and limey wine. Very refreshing.* ¶ *AP, D.*

*****   1994 Chateau du Grand Moulas, Marc Ryckwaert, Rhône, Fr. £5.39. *Peppery, redcurranty and ripe.* ¶ *LB, SP, RMS.*

****   1992 Dom. du Vieux Telegraphe, H. Brunier, Rhône, Fr. £12.49. *Old - fashioned and full in style.* ¶ *CH, RM, G.*

****   1990 Los Llanos Reserva, Valdepeñas, Sp. £4.29. *Great modern Spanish red with ripe, berryish fruit.* ¶ *FF, D, IB.*

****   1993 Domaine Chanier Vouvray Moelleux, Loire, Fr. £5.59. *Rich, appley, sweetly honeyed wine, typical ultra-ripe Chenin Blanc.* ¶ *O, PF.*

JIC Just In Case ★★★★

1 The High street, Bishops Waltham, Hants SO32 IAB. Tel/Fax 01489 892969. Independent Wine Merchant. **Opening Hours:** Mon-Sat 0900-2100, Sun 1200-1400. **Delivery:** free locally. **Services:** mail order, glass loan, regular in-shop and tutored tastings, cellarage.

Commander Fred Woodfine founded Just in Case five years ago, after leaving the Royal Navy, and in 1993 David Moore was piped aboard, bringing with him an in- depth tactical assessment of the strengths and weakness of the Antipodean fleet. Last year in an exciting engagement Commander Woodfine captured the agency for Huntingdon Estate in Mudgee, regarded by Halliday and Evans of the Australian High Command as one of New South Wales' premier ships of the line. Manoeuvres in the Mediterranean have been progressing exceptionally well – "Roussanne", "Marsanne", "Chardonnay", and the powerful "Viognier" of the modern Domaine Virginie fleet are on their way to dry dock in Bishops Waltham, to join Jurancon's Domaine Cauhape, Château de Lastours from Corbières and Château Routas of the Côteau Varois.

★★★★	1992 St Aubin 1er Cru, Thomas, Burgundy, Fr. £10.85. *Honey and toffee oak. Smooth appley fruits and balancing acidity.* ⅊ **WFC, S.**	
★★★★	1991 Barbera d'Asti Ceppi Storici, Araldica, It. £4.99. *Leather and tobacco combined with chocolate and plummy fruit.* ⅊ **P, G.**	
★★★★★	1990 Cepparello, Isole e Olena, It. £17.85. *Heavy and intensely rich in style. Stewed dark fruit and cigar box flavours.* ⅊ **D, RM, WFP.**	
★★★★	1993 Thelema Reserve Chardonnay, SA. £9.55. *Thick, buttery oak and creamy fruit.* ⅊ **SM, CH.**	
★★★★	1992 Mount Langhi Ghiran Shiraz, Victoria, Aus. £8.35. *Perfect Aussie Shiraz — dark berry fruits, eucalyptus and peppery spice.* ⅊ **SP, RM, D.**	

J&B Justerini and Brooks ★★★★★

61 St. James's Street, London SW1A 1LZ. Tel 0171 493 8721. Fax 0171 499 4653. Independent Wine Merchant. **Opening Hours:** Mon-Fri 0900-1730 (open Sat during December). Also at 45 George Street, Edinburgh, EH2 2HT. **Delivery:** free for two cases or more on U.K. mainland. **Services:** cellarage, *en primeur*, mail order, gift-mailing, glass hire, ice.

J & B proudly declare that of their many former clients, Charles Dickens was a regular imbiber; asking for more here would seem particularly appropriate. Burgundy and Bordeaux remain remarkably exciting. J & B have restricted the supply of some of the more stunning Rhônes – Guigal's Côte Rotie, La Landonne/Mouline/Turque – which hopefully means they will be drunk by appreciative buyers rather than disappear to be gloated over by some bluebeard collector in his cavern. Germany deserves a special mention for an excellent range, the North American Chalk Hill Sauvignons and Chardonnays 1992 spice up the relatively sparse selection from California, and the unusual Dry River Sauvignon 1994 from New Zealand is a pleasure to see. J & B's prices aren't unreasonable and for the friendly service and experience of the staff they're definitely worth paying.

★★★★★	1988 Champagne Le Mesnil, Fr. £18.90. *A great example of Chardonnay-based Champagne, full of flavours of buttered toast. Classy.* ⅊ **CC, FD, AP, LS.**	
★★★	1992 Condrieu, E Guigal, Rhône, Fr. £22.90. *The Viognier at its best. Ultra-perfumed with lovely peachy favours.* ⅊ **FD, O, LS.**	
★★★★★	1992 Chassagne Montrachet 1er Cru, Jean Noel Gagnard, Burgundy, Fr. £25. *Incredibly concentrated, rich and complex.* ⅊ **E, WMC, WFP.**	
★★★★	1993 Mitchelton Reserve Marsanne, Victoria, Aus. £6.99. *Traditional in style and full of honeyed fruits - apricots and grapefruit.* ⅊ **AP, LS, FD.**	
★★★★	1993 Gewürztraminer Cuvée Théo, Domaine Weinbach, Alsace, Fr. £12.45. *An attractive spiciness combined with tropical fruits.* ⅊ **O, AP.**	

- **** 1992 Côtes du Rhône Cuvée des Capucines, Dom. du Vieux Chêne, Fr. £4.85. *A delicate wine with jammy soft fruit.* ¶ *CH, SP, WM.*
- ***** 1989 Côte Rôtie Brune et Blonde, E Guigal, Rhône, Fr. £18.90 *Forest fruits of sloes and loganberries mixed with spice.* ¶ *RMS, SP, G.*
- **** 1993 Fairview Shiraz Reserve, Paarl, SA. £7.85. *Refreshingly minty Shiraz, at once spicy and leafy.* ¶ *D, P, SP, BF.*
- **** 1990 Dom. Coste-Caumartin Pommard, Burgundy, Fr. £18. *Concentrated plums and dark stone fruits.* ¶ *BF, RMS, CC.*
- ***** 1992 Nuits St Georges 1er Cru Les St Georges, Domaine Robert Chevillon, Burgundy, Fr. £21. *Jam-packed full of raspberries. Delicious.* ¶ *CC, WFP, RMS.*
- ***** 1990 Brauneberger Juffer Sonnenuhr Auslese, Fritz Haag, Mosel, Ger. £17.90 *Great maturing Mosel Riesling with a "stony" flavour.* ¶ *PS.*
- ***** 1989 Vouvray Le Haut Lieu 1er Tri Moelleux Gaston Huet, Loire, Fr. £32. *Concentrated late harvest Chenin with lingering apple and honey.* ¶ *O, PF.*
- **** 1985 Delaforce Vintage Port, Douro, Por. £19.50. *Light and refreshing with good plummy fruit.* ¶ *CC, CH.*

KS Kwik Save ★★★

Warren Drive, Prestatyn, Clwyd, LL19 7HV. Tel 01745 887111. Fax 01745 882504. Supermarket Chain. **Opening Hours:** Mon-Sat 0830-1730 (late opening selected stores).

Angela Muir, the Kwik Saviour of Britain's wine drinkers, continues her crusade. Where other chains worry about the "glass ceiling" of £4.99, Ms Muir knows that, to her customers, every penny over £1.99 represents dangerous extravagance. Courageously, Ms Muir has on occasion de-listed such well known standards as Bordeaux Rouge and Côtes du Rhône when she could not find examples that came up to scratch. Even now we suspect that she would prefer customers to try her Portuguese discoveries rather than some of the lower priced efforts from France.

- **** Champagne Louis Raymond, Fr. £8.89. *One of the most impressive under-a-tenner Champagnes available on the high street.* ¶ *AP, S.*
- *** Pelican Bay Dry White, Aus. £2.95. *Juicily ripe tropical fruit flavours — a very simple easy Aussie.* ¶ *PY, D.*
- *** 1994 Marsanne, Domaine Fontenille, Virginie, VdP d'Oc, Fr. £3.29. *Clean and ripe with a good leafy character and hint of brazil nuts.* ¶ *SM, FD.*
- *** 1994 White Pacific Sauvignon, Curico, Chi. £2.59. *A light and grassy wine packed with fresh appley flavours.* ¶ *WMC, AP.*
- *** Landema Falls, Cinsault-Cabernet Sauvignon, SA. £2.69. *Light strawberry jam and lemon marmalade; pleasantly unusual.* ¶ *SP, WMC.*
- *** 1994 Angove's Chardonnay, S. Australia, Aus. £4.19 *Rich and spicy oak flavours with simple pineapple fruit.* ¶ *FD.*
- **** 1993 De Belfont, Cuvée Speciale Portan/Merlot, VdP de l'Aude, Fr. £2.79. *A light, berryish wine partly made from an unusual grape, the Portan. It has a country herb character and a chunky finish.* ¶ *PY.*
- *** 1994 Kwik Save Cabernet Sauvignon, Midi, Fr. £2.79. *Simple cassis and cherry fruit. Light and gluggable.* ¶ *PY, RM.*
- **** 1994 Cono Sur Cabernet, Chi. £3.69. *Rich cassis fruit and good vanilla oak, this is long and well-made.* ¶ *SP, WM.*
- *** 1994 Fortant de France, Grenache Noir, Midi, Fr. £3.39. *A light peppery wine in the Côtes du Rhône style; rich and long.* ¶ *RM, LB.*
- **** 1994 Pinot Noir, Domaine St. Martin, Virginie, VdP d'Oc, Fr. £3.99. *Lovely ripe raspberry and plum flavours and plenty of rich fruit.* ¶ *RMS.*
- *** 1994 Don Fadrique Cencibel, J Santos, La Mancha, Sp. £2.79. *"Fresh out of the vat", crisp acidity and tones of sloes and ripe dark berries.* ¶ *LB, P.*
- **** 1994 Alta Mesa, Estremadura, Por. £2.69. *Refreshingly crisp with a dark berry character and tones of tobacco and prunes.* ¶ *SP, PY.*

L&W Lay and Wheeler ★★★★★

6 Culver Street West, Colchester, Essex CO1 1JA. Tel 01206 764446. Fax 01206 560002. Independent Wine Merchant. **Opening Hours:** Mon-Sat 0830-1730. Also at Wine Market, Gosbecks Road, Colchester, Essex CO2 9JT. **Opening Hours:** Mon-Sat 0800-2000. In Scotland: Mackeanston House, Doune, Perthshire FKI6 6AX. Tel 01786 850414. Fax 01786 850414. **Delivery:** free on orders of two cases or more or on orders to the value of £150 or more. **Tastings:** regular in-store, plus tutored tastings and workshops. **Services:** cellarage, *en primeur*, mail order, gift- mailing, glass hire, ice.

Over the last few years Lay & Wheeler have sometimes been overshadowed by the vinous fireworks set off by their East Anglian neighbours Adnams. But these very different firms run a close race when it comes to seeking out and selling good wine. Lay & Wheeler's more sober approach – the BBC2 to Adnams' Channel 4 perhaps? – is reflected in the character of its staff and list. But behind the sobriety there is a great deal of excitement to be found, ranging from the opportunity customers were given to meet Mme de Lencquesaing and to taste nine vintages of her Pichon Longueville, to the mixed cases of New Zealand wines which offer a brilliant introduction to that country's styles. A remarkably safe place to choose a wine 'blind'.

- ★★★★★ 1988 J Jordan Winery Sparkling Wine, Cal. £16.25. *Lots of fresh fruit and toasty more vinous flavours.* ¶ **D, WFC.**
- ★★★★ 1994 Viña Santa Rita Sauvignon Blanc Reserva, Maule, Chi. £5.65. *Complex citrus and pineapple fruit flavours and well-balanced acidity.* ¶ **D, S.**
- ★★★ 1993 Buda Bridge Chardonnay, Gyongyos Estate, Hun. £3.95. *Richly honeyed with creamy fruit.* ¶ **PY, FD.**
- ★★★★★ 1992 Meursault Genevrières, Boisson-Vadot, Burgundy, Fr. £21.95. *Classy young Burgundy; fresh, with buttery nutty richness.* ¶ **WM, FD, S.**
- ★★★★ 1993 Zeltinger Schlossberg Riesling Kabinett, Selbach-Oster, Mosel, Ger. £8.50. *Refreshing tropical fruits, floral flavours and balanced acidityy.* ¶ **O, S.**
- ★★★★ 1992 Claridge Red Wellington, SA. £9.95. *Excellent Bordeaux blend, full of rich minerally berry fruit, made by the maverick Roger Jorgensen.* ¶ **LB.**
- ★★★★★ 1992 Henschke Mount Edelstone Shiraz, Eden Valley, Aus. £12.95. *Heaps of bright plum fruit, eucalyptus and white pepper.* ¶ **RM, FF.**
- ★★★★ 1991 Côtes Du Rhône Rouge, E Guigal, Rhône, Fr. £7.50. *Rich, damson fruit, herbs and spices.* ¶ **RM, CH.**
- ★★★★★ 1994 Julienas Domaine du Clos du Fief, Michel Tete, Beaujolais, Fr. £8.25. *Soft berry fruits, light and refreshing.* ¶ **O, D, FF.**
- ★★★★★ 1991 Domaine de l'Arlot Nuits St Georges Clos des Forêts, Burgundy, Fr. £26.95. *Smooth tannins balanced by opulent berry fruits.* ¶ **RM, E.**
- ★★★★ 1989 Lindemans Botrytis Semillon, S. Australia, Aus. £6.85 (half). *Barley sugar, oak and ripe peaches. Pure hedonism.* ¶ **CC, PF, PS.** ·

L&S Laymont and Shaw ★★★★

The Old Chapel, Millpool, Truro, Cornwall, TR1 1EX. Tel 01872 70545. Fax 01872 233051. Independent Wine Merchant. Mail order by the case only. **Opening Hours:** Mon-Fri 0900-1700. **Delivery:** free, mainland U.K., minimum one case. **Services:** cellarage, mail order, gift-mailing, glass hire.

In the introduction to their list, Laymont and Shaw quote Trollope who says, "There is no saying truer than that which declares that there is truth in wine." How true is the quote, then? No sleeping during the siesta for these hombres, dyed in the wool Hispanophiles that they are; this year they have thrown their sombreros into the ring with new wines from Montenovos and two new agencies – Castillo de Monjardin of Navarra and Valduero from Ribera del Duero. All this on top of one of the most comprehensive selections of Spanish wine and sherry outside Madrid.

* **** 1992 Castillo de Monjardin Chardonnay, Navarra, Sp. £6.99 *Full flavoured new wave Spanish white.* ⁙ *WM, FO.*
* **** 1989 Viña Ardanza Blanco, La Rioja Alta, Sp. £6.70. *Lovely old-fashioned Rioja. Soft, woody and ripe and very easy to drink.* ⁙ *WFC, FO.*
* *** 1994 Campo Nuevo Tinto, Bodegas Agro Navarra, Sp. £3.90. *Very youthful wine with a flavour of just-ripe plums.* ⁙ *P, FF.*
* **** 1990 Los Llanos Reserva, Valdepeñas, Sp. £4.39. *Great modern Spanish red with ripe, berryish fruit.* ⁙ *WFP.*
* ***** 1987 Rioja Reserva, Viña Ardanza, La Rioja Alta, Sp. £9.21. *Gentle, cherryish and strawberryish wine with lovely vanilla oak.* ⁙ *CH, BF.*
* **** 1987 Viña Val Duero Reserva, Bodegas Val Duero, Ribera del Duero, Sp. £9.58. *Smooth, matured oak balanced by light cherryish fruit.* ⁙ *G, RM.*

LAY   Laytons/André Simon   ★★★★

20 Midland Road, London NW1 2AD. Tel 0171 388 4567. Fax 0171 383 7419. Independent Wine Merchant. Also at 50-52 Elizabeth Street, Belgravia, London SW1W 9PB. Tel 0171 730 8108/9. Fax 0171 730 9284. 14 Davies Street, Mayfair London W1Y 1LJ. Tel 0171 499 9144. Fax 0171 495 2002. 21 Motcomb Street, Knightsbridge, London SW1X 8LB. Tel 0171 235 3723. Fax 0171 235 2062. **Opening Hours:** Mon-Fri 0900-1800, Sat 1000-1600. **Services:** cellarage, *en primeur*, mail order, gift-mailing, glass hire, ice.

What is there to say about a company whose chairman can recite the County Cricket Captains of the 1946 season to a man? Quite simply, the unique charm of Laytons and the associated André Simon shops lies in the irresistable wit and enthusiasm of their leader, gloriously plain to see in the selection and presentation of the wines. The acquisition of a spanking new claret cellar has added a strong range of mature Classed Growths to the already mighty Bordeaux collection, while second favourite, Italy has become the brunt of a tidal wave of extravagant price deals. The Rhône is looking consistently stronger, with some particularly attractive Châteauneuf-du-Papes while Laytons' strong suit remains its own-label Champagnes. What a pity that English cricket gives so few opportunities to open a bottle.

* **** Champagne Deutz Brut Cuvée Classic, Fr. £17.60. *Good, slightly chocolatey fizz; creamy and rich.* ⁙ *PY.*
* **** 1992 Condrieu, Delas Frères, Rhône, Fr. £22.05. *The Viognier at its best. Ultra-perfumed with lovely peachy favours.* ⁙ *O, FD, SM.*
* **** 1994 Gewürztraminer, Kientzheim, Dom. Blanck, Alsace, Fr. £9.77. *Floral, with apricots and peaches. Nicely spicy.* ⁙ *O, CS.*
* **** 1986 Ch. Fontaney, Margaux, Bordeaux, Fr. £9.40. *Smooth tannins, subtle berry fruits and herbaceous characteristics.* ⁙ *D, LB.*
* **** 1991 Vosne Romanée, Dom. Anne et François Gros, Burgundy, Fr. £20.60. *Rich, concentrated Burgundy with interesting new oak.* ⁙ *D, LB.*
* **** 1988 Barbera del Monferrato, Cassinis, Piedmont, It. £7.95. *Deliciously mature with dark fruits and smooth tannins. Ready to drink.* ⁙ *SP, G.*
* ***** 1983 Ch. Climens Premier Cru Classé, Barsac, Sauternes, Bordeaux, Fr. £40.61 *Lovely, mature, complex, honeyed wine. Still worth keeping.* ⁙ *D.*

LEA   Lea & Sandeman   ★★★★★

301 Fulham Road, London SW10 9QH. Tel 0171 376 4767. Fax 0171 351 0275. Independent Wine Merchant. **Opening Hours:** Mon-Fri 0900-2230, Sat 1000-2230. Also at 211 Kensington Church Street, London, W8 7LX. Tel 0171 221 1982. Fax 0171 221 1985. **Delivery:** free locally. **Tastings:** regular in-store plus special tastings for small groups of customers. **Services:** mail order, gift-mailing, glass hire/loan, ice.

If you are something of a sensualist, then visiting Lea & Sandeman may well make your day – and Charles Lea's. Always looking on the bright side of life (and Fulham

Road), he valiantly maintains that the Oddbins on the dark side serves to keep all beer swillers and gin soaks out of his nice shop, though you have to wonder what "type" his exhibitions of erotica attract...even the wine list now has its fair share of naked bodies to tempt you to sample voluptuous delights such as Chandon de Briailles, Domaine Georges Mugneret and Pommard Clos des Epeneaux, all of which will be appearing on the Burgundy list this year. Some 1994 virgin clarets will be available *en primeur* and the Rhône selection will be more magnificent than ever, although with the lira much weaker than the franc, Italy is looking even more seductive than usual. So that's Lea & Sandeman. How was it for you? P.S. regular customers report "less aloof service" at the Kensington shop.

**** Seppelt Pinot Rosé, S. Australia, Aus. £6.49. *A ripe, raspberryish toffeed rosé. Great value.* ¶ *AP, PY.*

**** 1993 Conde de Valdemar Rioja Blanco, Martinez Bujanda, Sp. £8.40. *Good modern Spanish white with character.* ¶ *LS, SM.*

**** 1989 Weinert Cabernet Sauvignon, Mendoza, Arg. £8.99. *Soft, Spanish-style Cabernet with attractive blackcurranty fruit.* ¶ *SP.*

*** 1991 Weinert Malbec, Mendoza, Arg. £7.52. *A typically spicy example of an underrated Bordeaux and Cahors black grape at home in Argentina.* ¶ *P, BF.*

***** 1990 Avignonesi Merlot, Tuscany, It. £18.62. *A top-class Italian answer to Pomerol. Plummy and herby, with sweet oak.* ¶ *LB.*

**** 1989 Pommard 1er Cru Clos des Epeneaux, Dom. Comte Armand, Burgundy, Fr. £23.95. *Ripe, mature, slightly gamey Burgundy. Will keep.* ¶ *BF, CH.*

**** 1992 Chianti Classico, Castello di Fonterutoli, Tuscany, It. £6.46. *Well-made, quite "serious" with herby, dried fruit flavours.* ¶ *P.*

**** 1990 Argiolas Turriga, Sardinia, It. £12.87. *Concentrated, complex, ripe-tasting wine, made to go with flavoursome Italian food.* ¶ *SP, P.*

***** 1990 Amarone Capitel Monte Olmi, Tedeschi, Veneto, It. £14.10. *Intense, wild berries, raisins and figs.* ¶ *G, RMS.*

**** Churchill's Finest Vintage Character, Douro, Por. £8.81. *A well-made, spicy, rich port.* ¶ *CH, CS.*

OWL   O W Loeb   ****

64 Southwark Bridge Road, London, SE1 0AS. Tel 0171 928 7750 . Fax 0171 928 1855. Independent Wine Merchant. **Opening Hours:** Mon-Fri 0900-1730 for telephone enquiries only. **Delivery:** free locally. **Services:** mail order, en primeur offers, storage. No credit cards.

There cannot be many more complete roll calls of the brightest and best from the Mosel than that offered by O W Loeb. Names like J J Prum, Friedrich Wilhelm Gymnasium, Willi Haag, Reichsgraf von Kesselstadt and C von Schubert usually only congregate in learned books on the region by Teutonophile wine scribes. To find them all, plus seven other M-S-R luminaries and a lexicon of similarly impressive estates from the Rhine, on the shelves of a single wine merchant is a rare and celebrated event. Loeb demonstates a similar mastery of Alsace, the Rhône and Burgundy, and has recently added a range of laudable French Country Wines to broaden appeal and extend the range of "less expensive wines".

**** 1991 Braunceberger Juffer Riesling Kabinett, Willi Haag, Mosel, Ger. £7.10. *Classy Mosel with pure, appley Riesling fruit.* ¶ *AP, S.*

***** 1993 Wehlener Sonnenuhr Riesling Auslese, J J Prum, Mosel, Ger. £16.65. *Fresh young wine, lusciously sweet but with the freshness of grapes.* ¶ *PF.*

**** 1990 Chinon Cuvée du Clos du Chêne Vert, Joguet, Loire, Fr. £10.70. *Maturing blackcurranty wine with a rich, lingering finish.* ¶ *WMP.*

**** 1991 Morey St Denis, Dom. Dujac, Burgundy, Fr. £17.35. *Concentrated, raspberryish wine with great complexity. Great, understated Burgundy.* ¶ *BF.*

**** 1990 Saint-Joseph Le Grand Pompée, Jaboulet, Rhône, Fr. £8.62. *Pure spice, with leathery richness.* ¶ *G, RM.*

LWE   London Wine Emporium   ★★★★

86 Goding Street, Vauxhall, London, SE11 5AW. Tel 0171 587 1302. Fax 0l71 587 0982. Independent Wine Merchant. **Opening Hours:** Mon-Fri 1000-1900, Sat 1000-1700. **Delivery:** free locally. **Tastings:** tutored on the third Monday of the month (except July, August and December). **Services:** mail order, glass hire.

1995 has been a busy year. David Rigg has been off making wine in the wild outdoors of Australia, whilst Colin Barnes has been beefing up the number of tastings held on the premises, fighting for a licence to sell by the bottle (finally granted), organising the first-ever Women in Wine festival and using the same name to launch a brief list of female winemakers (we want to know when short, left-handed, or balding vignerons will get similar treatment). Needless to say the company still has its list firmly footed in the New World, Australia in particular, but provides good drinking from winemakers of both sexes in the rest of the world, too.

- ★★★★ 1992 Lansdowne Chardonnay, Grove Mill Wine Co, Marlborough, NZ. £11.49. *Good Chardonnay with ripe tropical flavours.* ❙ **WFP, WM.**
- ★★★ 1994 Seppelt Moyston Semillon Chardonnay, S. Australia, Aus. £4.49. *Oaky, creamy wine with lovely peachy fruit.* ❙ **PY.**
- ★★★★★ 1992 Cullen Margaret River Cabernet Sauvignon/Merlot Reserve, W Australia, Aus. £11.79. *Bordeaux meets Australia in unusually restained style.* ❙ **G.**
- ★★★★ 1990 Chateau Grand Corbin, Alain Giraud, Bordeaux, Fr. £14.99. *Young, well-made claret with rich plummy fruit.* ❙ **LB.**
- ★★★ 1992 Welgemeend Estate Wine, Paarl, SA. £8.99. *Modern South African red with European style fruit.* ❙ **G, RMS.**
- ★★★★ 1988 Meerlust Merlot, Stellenbosch, SA. £9.99. *Soft plummy merlot with delightfully soft tannins and a gentle brackeny fruit.* ❙ **CH, BF.**
- ★★★★ Seppelt Old Trafford, S. Australia, Aus. £7.99. *Australian "port". Nutty, toffeed and rich. Really rather classy.* ❙ **CC, CH.**

LUV   Luvains Bottle Shop   ★★★

93 Bonnygate, Cupar, KY15 4LG. Tel/Fax 01334 654820. Independent Wine Merchant. **Opening Hours:** Mon-Sat 0900-1900, Sun 1200-1700. **Delivery:** free locally. **Tastings:** regular in-store plus tutored sessions. **Services:** glass loan, cellarage, ice.

"House of Lords (Not for Sale)" – unlike certain sections of the Lower House, we might add, before pointing out that the commodity in question is a deluxe whisky. As malt lovers, we have to admit to being gob-smacked by eight pages of whiskies, including no fewer than 14 separate bottlings of the Macallan and 18 of Springbank. The wine list is slightly less dazzling – until you get to the Bordeaux and, more particularly, the Italian selection where there are five vintages of Borgogno Barolo to be found, going back to 1961 and 1952. We also like anyone with the wit to subtitle Sardinia and Sicily respectively "Bandit Country" and "Real Bandit Country".

- ★★★ 1992 Chablis Premier Cru, Moreau, Burgundy, Fr. £10.79. *Lovely flinty, grassy flavours. Lemon, lime and pineapple fruit, slightly honeyed.* ❙ **S, FD.**
- ★★★★ 1994 Oyster Bay Sauvignon Blanc, NZ. £6.49. *Beautifully balanced gooseberry pineapple fruit. Delicately floral with a crisp acidity.* ❙ **S, D, WMC.**
- ★★★★ 1992 Savennieres Clos du Papillon, Loire, Fr. £8.99. *Classic dry Loire. - Honeyed, ripe melony fruits.* ❙ **D, S, WMC.**
- ★★★★ 1961 Barolo, G. Borgogno, Piedmont, It. £36.99. *Massive, dark and rich. Chocolate, cigar-box aromas and damson and plum fruit.* ❙ **G, RM, P.**
- ★★★★ 1991 Cape Mentelle Zinfandel, W. Australia, Aus. £9.69. *Gutsy, spicy fruit. Slightly earthy, well-balanced tannins.* ❙ **P, RM, G.**
- ★★★★ 1976 Fonseca Vintage Port £20.99. *Stunning and unusual flavours. Herbal spices, dried fruit and sweet fresh plums. Nutty wood.* ❙ **CC, CH, CS.**

MWW Majestic ★★★★

Odhams Trading Estate, St. Albans Road, Watford, Herts WD2 5RE. Tel 01923 816999 Fax 01923 819105. Wine Warehouse. Wine by the case only. **Opening Hours:** Mon-Sat 1000-2000, Sun 1000-1800. **Delivery:** free locally. **Tastings:** regular in-store, plus tutored sessions for local wine groups and clubs. **Services:** mail order, glass hire, ice.

As Britain's supermarkets contort themselves to sell wine at less than it costs to produce, ace wine dealer Tony Mason paradoxically continues to transform his growing chain of warehouses. Glossy leaflets, sober price lists with profiles of Bordeaux superstar Jean-Michel Cazes...it's all come a long way since the days when red-braced yuppies used to fill their GTis with Bulg Cab to drink with the Spag Bol. One characteristic remains consistent, though: it pays to pick and choose among the bargains. Sometimes Mr Mason seems to be more readily seduced by the marketing or the deal than the flavour in the bottle. Even so, this is now a very well-run organisation and, given the fact that it allows you to taste before you buy and runs frequent wine weekends, the risks of majesty are kept to a minimum.

★★★★	1992 Chateau Haut Mazières Blanc, Bordeaux, Fr. £4.99. *Easy, attractive New World style — lemon zest and creamy oak.* ¶ **WFC, PY.**
★★★	1994 Lindemans Cawarra Semillon Chardonnay, S Australia, Aus. £3.99. *A very easy mouthful: peaches and pineapples.* ¶ **WM, FF.**
★★★★	1993 Chablis Fourchaume, Boudin, Burgundy, Fr. £10.99. *Rich, full wine with leafy freshness.* ¶ **WM, S.**
★★★	1993 Moselland Classic Riesling, Mosel, Ger. £3.79. *Simple, light, fruity easy-going wine.* ¶ **AP.**
★★★★★	1990 Piesporter Goldtropfchen Riesling Auslese, Reichsgraf Von Kesselstatt, Mosel, Ger. £9.99. *Clean Mosel with lots of ripe apple flavour.* ¶ **PF, SM.**
★★★★	1992 Monopole Barrel Fermented Rioja, CVNE, Sp. £5.79. *Nutty, oaky with apricot and greengage fruit.* ¶ **SP, P.**
★★★★★	1992 Saumur Blanc Vieilles Vignes, Langlois Château, Loire, Fr. £9.99. *Honeyed with rich, appley flavours.* ¶ **O, PF.**
★★★★	1993 Lindemans Bin 45 Cabernet Sauvignon, S. Australia, Aus. £4.99. *Ripe, blackcurranty, great-value wine with quite obvious oak.* ¶ **BF, RMS.**
★★★★	1992 Jose Canepa Private Reserve Cabernet Sauvignon, Maipo, Chi. £5.49. *Lovely wine with intense blackcurranty fruit.* ¶ **BF, FF.**
★★★★	1992 Ridge Santa Cruz Mountains Cabernet Sauvignon, Cal. £15.49. *Intense but approachable wine with cassis and oak.* ¶ **BF, RM.**
★★★	1994 Cortenova Merlot, Grave del Friuli, Pasqua, It. £2.99. *Light, crisp, herbaceous red.* ¶ **LB, RMS.**
★★★★	1992 Monastère de Trignan, Coteaux du Languedoc, Fr. £4.29. *Terrific smoky raspberry and chocolate — a miniature Côte Rôtie!* ¶ **LB.**
★★★★	1990 Gigondas, Guigal, Rhône, Fr. £9.99. *Peppery, serious wine with brambly fruit.* ¶ **G, CH.**
★★★★★	1993 Robert Mondavi Pinot Noir, Cal. £9.99. *Top class New World Pinot with raspberries and gentle oak.* ¶ **P, RM.**
★★★★★	1992 Dom. Drouhin Oregon Pinot Noir, US. £16.95. *Real Burgundy style, with cherry and raspberry fruit and oak.* ¶ **SM.**
★★★★	1990 Salice Salentino Riserva, Cosimo Taurino, It. £4.99. *Dark, figgy and intense with honeyed stewed fruit and rich oak.* ¶ **P, CH.**
★★★★	1992 Rioja Tempranillo, Marqués de Griñon, Sp. £4.39. *Oak, spice and strawberries. Very flavoursome.* ¶ **LB, WMP.**
★★★	1988 Alentejo Tinto Velho, JM da Fonseca, Por. £4.69. *Intensely figgy and cedary.* ¶ **CC, CH.**
★★★★	1987 Lindemans Botrytis Semillon, S. Australia, Aus. £5.99. *Barley sugar, oak and ripe peaches. Pure hedonism.* ¶ **CS, PS.**
★★★★	Brown Brothers Reserve Liqueur Muscat, Milawa, Victoria, Aus. £7.99. *Raisins, dried fruit and molasses. Very indulgent stuff.* ¶ **PF, CHO.**

M&S   Marks and Spencer   ★★★★

47 Baker Street, London W1A 1DN. Tel 0171 935 4422 Fax 0171 487 2679.
Department Store, 283 branches. **Opening Hours:** vary from store to store. **Tastings:**
regular in-store. **Services:** mail order. No credit cards except M&S account card.

The winds of change we reported last year as blowing through the uninspiring M&S
cellars have been positively gale-like over the last 12 months. There are all sorts of
genuinely interesting wines on the shelves now, including some, like the Canyon Creek
range from Geyser Peak in California, Kaituna Hills from Montana in New Zealand
and Domaine Mandeville from France, which are unavailable elsewhere. Surprisingly
to those who know the profit margins on which M&S like to work – and the prices
charged in the past – the cost of buying a bottle here is now quite comparable to those
elsewhere. There is still work to be done, though; the buyers have not yet broken out of
the mould of focusing on large reliable suppliers. It is revealing to see how much
reliance is still placed on the KWVs and Girellis of this world – and how little time has
been spent on trying to find decent wine from 'Germany. M&S are however to be
congratulated for pioneering the use of plastic corks – and, incidentally, for the fact that,
in a recent survey, the British public have greater faith in the knickers-to-Niersteiner
chain than in the Church of England, politicians and, unsurprisingly, the press.

- ★★★★ St. Michael Prosecco, Zonin, Treviso Hills, It. £4.99. *Fresh and full of fruit, great-value fizz.* ¶ **D, AP.**
- ★★★ La Chablisienne Mousseux, Chablis, Fr. £8.99. *Buttery and rich, with a lovely crisp lemony acidity.* ¶ **FD, S, SF, WMP.**
- ★★★★ St Michael Chevalier de Melline, Union Champagne, Fr. £14.99. *Fresh, with some complex yeast characters.* ¶ **PY, FD, AP.**
- ★★★★ 1994 St Michael Mandeville Viognier, Midi, Fr. £4.99. *Great wine from a grape once restricted to high-priced wines from Northern Rhône.* ¶ **AP, D, WFC.**
- ★★★ 1994 St Michael Madeba Reserve Sauvignon, Robertson, SA. £4.99. *Less herbaceous than most New World Sauvignons. Topical fruit flavours.* ¶ **D, SF.**
- ★★★★ 1994 Montana Kaituna Hills Sauvignon Blanc, Marlborough, NZ. £4.99 *Gooseberries galore. Lovely, typical Kiwi Sauvignon .* ¶ **D, E, PY.**
- ★★★ 1994 St Michael Lontue Chilean Sauvignon Blanc, Hugh Ryman, San Pedro, Chi. £3.99. *Clean and fresh with subtle tropical fruit.* ¶ **AP, D, PY.**
- ★★★★★ 1994 St Michael Kaituna Hills Chardonnay, Montana, Gisborne, NZ. £4.99. *Wonderfully fresh flavours of melons, mangos and apricots.* ¶ **WM, SM, D, CH.**
- ★★★★ 1993 Rosemount Orange Vineyard Chardonnay, Aus. £8.99 *Impressive, quite lean, European-style Chardonnay from a new region.* ¶ **D, SM.**
- ★★★★ St Michael Chardonnay/Viognier, Les Vignerons Ardechois, Fr. £3.99 *A very unusual blend: fruit salady and fresh.* ¶ **CH, D, PY.**
- ★★★★ 1993 St Michael Rudesheimer Rosengarten, Franz Reh, Nahe, Ger. £3.99. *Lemon curd mixed with tropical fruits – quite a mixture!* ¶ **AP, LS.**
- ★★★ 1992 St Michael Deidesheimer Hofstuck Riesling, St Ursula, Pfalz, Ger. £4.99. *A fruity medley of caramel, pineapples and apples.* ¶ **PY, D, CC.**
- ★★★ 1994 St Michael Padthaway Riesling, Andrew Garrett, Aus. £4.99. *Ripe spicy fruit with beeswax and lemons.* ¶ **AP, SP, O.**
- ★★★★ 1991 St Michael Trapiche Red, Mendoza, Arg. £6.99. *Good value, juicy red from one of the biggest producers in Argentina.* ¶ **PY, RM, BF.**
- ★★★★ 1993 St Michael Maipo Cabernet Sauvignon Reserve, Carmen Vineyards, Chi. £4.99. *Ripe crunchy blackcurrants. A fruity mouthful.* ¶ **LB, RMS, WM.**
- ★★★★★ 1989 Chateau Gazin, Bordeaux, Fr. £14.99. *Classy, honeyed, plummy Merlot-based claret. Richly drinkable now but worth keeping.* ¶ **CH, RMS.**
- ★★★ 1982 Nuits St George, Louis Jadot, Burgundy, Fr. £12.99. *Very mature Burgundy with an attractively gamey character.* ¶ **BF, CH, CC.**
- ★★★★ St Michael Penascal, Hijos de Ant. Barcelo, Valladolid, Sp. £3.79 *Spicy yet soft with raspberries, prunes and strawberries.* ¶ **P, SP, CH.**
- ★★★★ 1993 Bleasdales Langhorne Creek Cabernet Sauvignon, S. Australia, Aus. £5.99. *Great value blackcurrant jammy wine.* ¶ **WMP, P, G.**

**** 1992 Les Fiefs de Lagrange, Bordeaux, Fr. £10.99. *The second label of Château Lagrange. Classy, cedary and rich.* ❚ *CH,G, IB.*

**** 1988 Ch. l'Hospitalet, Ch. Gazin, Bordeaux, Fr. £12.99. *Soft, mature wine with gently stewed plum fruit.* ❚ *RM, RMS.*

*** 1993 St Michael Shiraz, Rosemount, S. Australia, Aus. £5.99. *Hugely ripe, big, plummy and full of fruit with a peppery edge.* ❚ *LB, D, G.*

**** 1993 St Michael McLaren Vale Shiraz, Andrew Garrett, Aus. £5.50. *Ripe spicy, damsony wine. Immediately appealing.* ❚ *P, SP, BF.*

**** 1994 Fleurie, Cellier des Samsons, Beaujolais, Fr. £6.99. *Light but bursting with summer fruits; great for picnics.* ❚ *D, E, O, SM.*

MFW Martinez Fine Wines ★★★★

The Old Town Hall, 22 Union Street, Halifax HX1 1PR. Tel 01422 320022. Independent Wine Merchant. **Opening Hours:** Mon-Fri 1000-1800, Sat 0900-1800. Also at 36 The Grove, Ilkley, LS29 2EE. Tel 01943 603 241, and Corn Exchange Cellars, The Ginnel, Harrogate HG1 3HU. Tel 01423 501 783. **Opening Hours:** Mon-Fri 1000-1830. **Delivery:** free locally, nationwide at fixed charge. **Tastings:** three in-shop per year, plus tutored sessions. **Services:** mail order, fine wine offers, glass hire.

Martinez now has three shops, and a wine list to considerably brighten up cold northern nights. There is no bias towards countries Hispanic, as the name may suggest, though Spain and Chile are amply represented by wines such as the 1991 Bodegas Guelbenzu from Navarra, and Villard Merlot from the Cachapoal Region in Chile. There are excellent wines from Southern France – eg Château de Lastours "Fût de Chêne" – and the New World. The US is particularly impressive with wines like the Madrona Zinfandel, Saintsbury Pinot Noir and Newton Merlot.

**** 1990 Mountadam Sparkling Wine, Aus. £14.55. *From a (for Australia) high-altitude vineyard. Great, full-flavoured raspberry and pineapply wine.* ❚ *PY.*

**** 1992 Old Luxters Reserve, Chiltern Valley Winery, Oxon, Eng. £6.65. *With a name like an ale, this is a stylish, rich wine to match the Loire.* ❚ *SF, FO, LS.*

*** 1992 Ch. des Estanilles "Cuveé Tradition", Faugères, Fr. £6.25. *Rich, quite gamey, flavoursome wine from southern France.* ❚ *G, RM.*

**** 1989 Ch. Marbuzet, St Estephe, Bordeaux, Fr. £18.85. *Ripe, classic claret with green pepper, cassis and sweet oak.* ❚ *LB, RMS.*

*** 1991 Thelema Merlot, Stellenbosch, SA. £9.25. *Young wine from a great producer. Crunchy slightly unripe plums.* ❚ *BF, CH.*

***** 1990 Barolo "Bussia Soprana", Aldo Conterno, Piedmont, It. £24.95. *Top-class Barolo from a master producer: tobaccoey, plummy and intense.* ❚ *G.*

MYS Mayor Sworder ★★★★

381 Kennington Road London SE11 4PT. Tel 0171 735 0385. Fax 0171 735 0341. Independent Wine Merchant. **Opening Hours:** Mon-Fri 0830-1730. **Delivery:** free locally. **Tastings:** regular in-store. **Services:** cellarage, *en primeur*, mail order, gift-mailing, glass hire. No credit cards.

Having now fully assimilated Russell & McIver (its purchase of a couple of years ago), Mayor Sworder has donned stylish new clothes in the shape of an explanatory modern list, complete with pen-and-ink illustrations. However, long-standing customers will be reassured to see that, in the words of the song, "the fundamentals still apply". Characterful French regional wines, Burgundies and petit château Bordeaux all enjoy greater prominence than showstoppers from the New World and the wines have been chosen irrespective of hype and fashion, so there are white Santenays, Aligotés and a raft of individual whites from the Maconnais as well as an outstanding "basic" red Burgundy from Hubert de Montille. Prices are unusually fair.

***** 1989 Champagne de Venoge Brut, Fr. £25.99 *Intense, raspberryish, chocolatey fizz with a lovely lingering flavour.* ¶ **PY, D.**

**** 1994 Château Xanadu Semillon, W. Australia, Aus. £9.58. *Attractive, almost Sauvignon-like, herbaceous with hints of spice.* ¶ **WFC, FO.**

*** 1992 Zonnebloem Merlot, Stellenbosch Farmers' Winery, Cape, SA. £7.10. *Quite old fashioned, earthy wine.* ¶ **G, RM.**

**** 1990 Ch. Lanessan, Haut-Médoc, Bordeaux, Fr. £11.65. *Attractively traditional, unoaked wine with cedary flavour.* ¶ **LB, RMS.**

MTL   Mitchells Wine Merchant   ★★★★

354 Meadowhead, Sheffield, S. Yorks S8 7UJ .Tel 0114 274 5587. Fax 0114 274 8481. Independent Wine Merchant. **Opening Hours:** Mon-Thurs 0930-2000, Fri-Sat 0930-2030, Sun 1200-1400, 1900-2200. **Delivery:** free locally. **Tastings:** weekly in-store plus tastings and talks for groups and members of own wine club. **Services:** cellarage, mail order, gift-mailing, glass hire, ice.

Having run out of doors to stop and papers to weight, the word on the street is that the Mitchells are going to need to buy a new mantelpiece soon to cope with their ever-increasing array of awards. Not content with being mere Specialist Independent Off Licence Of The Year, they went on to win the overall prize of Off Licence Of The Year. The selections are strong from Italy, Spain and Bordeaux but it would be hard to overlook the New World as it occupies a third of the cellar. And, if you've a bit of time to kill while you're waiting for a claret to mature, you could always turn your hand to an exclusive jigsaw puzzle depicting the great man himself.

***** E & E Sparkling Shiraz, S Australia, Aus. £12.99. *Extraordinary spicy, oaky red fizz with all sorts of summer pudding flavours.* ¶ **O, D, CHO.**

**** 1994 Sauvignon, Philippe de Baudin, Hardy's, Midi, Fr. £4.49. *Rich, appley wine made at an Australian-owned domaine near Béziers.* ¶ **S, FO.**

***** 1993 Beringer Private Reserve Chardonnay, Cal. £14.49. *Stunning combination of hot buttered toast and honey.* ¶ **SM, CC, WMC.**

***** 1993 Moulin à Vent, Fut de Chêne, Georges Duboeuf, Beaujolais, Fr. £7.95 *Serious cherryish Beaujolais with sweet spicy oak.* ¶ **FF, WMP.**

***** 1989 Château Lascombes, Margaux, Bordeaux, Fr. £20. *Elegant young claret with violet perfume and ripe blackcurrant character.* ¶ **LB, CH.**

**** 1983 Warre's Vintage Port, Warre & C A S A, Douro, Por. £17.66. *Rich, finely balanced, delicate port.* ¶ **D, CH.**

MOR   Moreno   ★★★★

2 Norfolk Place, London W2 1QN. Tel 0171 706 3055. Fax 0171 724 3813. Independent Wine Merchant. **Opening Hours:** Mon-Sat 1000-2000. **Delivery:** free locally. **Tastings:** regular in-store, plus the Spanish Wine Club on the last Friday of every month. **Services:** mail order, gift-mailing, glass hire, ice.

Rivalling Laymont & Shaw for the mantle of Spanish Specialist Extraordinaire, Manuel Moreno's company is a haven for ranks of Riojas including all of the great names, with vintages running back to the early Sixties and beyond – even to 1942 in the case of Castillo Ygay – as well as the weird and the wonderful from the more esoteric regions and grape varieties of Spain. Most people wouldn't even dare to try to pronounce Txomin Etxaniz from Geritiaco Txakolina until they've drunk at least a bottle; less tongue-twisting but equally rare are wines from Almansa, Calatayud, Rias Baixas and Priorato. On more familiar ground, there is an excellent range of vintages from Torres Black Label, Jean Leon Cabernet and Vega Sicilia, and there is an increasingly impressive list from Portugal, not to mention the Wine of the Year, Ignacio Recabarran's Casablanca Vineyards Sauvignon Blanc.

*** 1992 Cava Parxet Extra Brut Gran Reserva, Bodegas Marqués de Alella, Sp. £7.99. *Rich, traditional Spanish fizz.* ∏ **PY.**

**** 1994 Marqués de Alella Allier, Sp. £15.99. *Serious oaky wine to compete with Burgundy.* ∏ **WFC, WM.**

**** 1994 Casablanca Sauvignon Blanc, White Label, Curico, Chi. £4.99. *Brilliant gooseberryish wine from a new region of Chile.* ∏ **S, WFC.**

*** Navajas Rosé, Bodegas Navajas, Rioja, Sp. £4.59. *Soft, creamy apricot, vanilla and strawberry flavours. Characterful.* ∏ **O, WMP.**

**** 1987 Masia Barril Classico Tinto, Masia Barril, Priorato, Sp. £12.99 *Very intense old-fashioned, spicy wine. Needs food.* ∏ **G, RMS, BF, CH.**

*** 1994 Marqués de Aragon Garnacha Tinto Puro, Bodega Campo San Isidro, Calatayud, Sp. £3.69. *"Serious"wine; young, peppery, delicious.* ∏ **LB.**

M&V   Morris and Verdin   ****

The Leathermarket, Weston Street, London SE1 3ER. Tel 0171 357 8866. Fax 0171 357 8877. Independent Wine Merchant. Wines by the case only. **Opening Hours:** Mon-Fri 0800-1800. **Delivery:** free locally. **Tastings:** occasional in-store, plus tutored. **Services:** cellarage, *en primeur*, mail order, glass hire. No credit cards.

Jasper Morris' leap across the pages of the London A-Z has considerably eased the congestion experienced previously at Churton Street. Now that his life is not in immediate danger of being ended prematurely by the effect of gravity on a case of Meursault Les Tessons, it is possible to say with some confidence that Jasper remains committed to providing quality wines bought directly from classic Burgundy domaines, châteaux and such eccentric New World wineries as Bonny Doon and Au Bon Climat. The wine list looks as strong as ever and it is worth noting that M&V have been appointed agents by Vega Sicilia (and their two new initiatives of Bodegas Alion and Bodegas Oremus). Keep a look-out for Vins du Pays, Rhône and Qupe's Chardonnay/Viognier blend from California.

*** 1993 Dom. San de Guilhem, Côtes de Gascogne, Fr. £4.70. *Good, leafy, quite appley wine. Great for everyday drinking.* ∏ **LS.**

*** 1994 Sylvaner, Vieilles Vignes, Dom Ostertag, Alsace, Fr. £6.90. *Rich, concentrated wine with peary perfumed fruit.* ∏ **FD.**

*** 1993 Château Routas Luc Sorin, Côteaux Varois, Languedoc, Fr. £8.20 *Very well made herby-fruity southern French wine.* ∏ **LS.**

*** Jade Mountain Mourvèdre, California, US. £12. *Spicy, intense with an interesting plum skin character.* ∏ **LB, RM.**

**** 1993 Qupé Syrah, Santa Barbara, California, US. £9.90. *Intense plummy and smoky-spicy wine. Very Rhône-like.* ∏ **O, BF.**

*** 1994 Clos de Gilroy, Bonny Doon, California, US. £7.30 *Pepper galore – with damson jam and a touch of vanilla.* ∏ **LB, RMS.**

**** 1993 St. Joseph, Clos Cuminaille, Pierre Gaillard, Rhône, Fr. £9.40. *The real thing. Lovely bramble, spicy Rhône Syrah.* ∏ **CH, RM.**

**** 1993 Au Bon Climat Pinot Noir, California, US. £12.50. *Great Pinot Noir with a wild berry flavour. Richly satisfying.* ∏ **RMS, BF, WM.**

**** 1993 Bourgogne Rouge Les Bons Batons, Patrice Rion, Burgundy, Fr. £8.50. *A classy Pinot Noir from one of the most go-ahead estates in the Côte de Nuits.* ∏ **CC, BF.**

***** 1992 Clos de la Roche Vielles Vignes, Dom. Ponsot, Burgundy, Fr. £46. *Yes, I know it's pricey, but it's a wonderfully complex wine with plenty of rich berry flavours.* ∏ **LB, BF.**

**** 1993 Douro Tinto, Quinta de la Rosa, Por. £4.90. *Australia meets Portugal: rich, concentrated berry fruits and spice.* ∏ **RM, G.**

***** 1990 Jurançon Noblesse, Dom. Cauhapé, Fr. £19.90. *Characterful, quite honeyed wine made from traditional grapes in the South-West.* ∏ **PS.**

**** 1988 Bonnezeaux La Chapelle, Ch. de Fesles, Loire, Fr. £19. *Luscious, super-ripe apricot and over-ripe pears and honey.* ∏ **CS, D, PS.**

MRN   Wm. Morrison Supermarkets   ★★★

Hilmore House, Thornton Road, Bradford BD8 9AX. Tel 01924 870000. Regional Supermarket Chain, 75 branches. **Opening Hours:** Mon-Fri 0830-2000, Sat 0830-1800, Sun 1000-1600. Hours vary. **Services:** glass hire.

It must be pleasant sometimes to be out of the direct firing line of the giant supermarkets whose discounting exocets are generally aimed at each other. Even so, Morrisons' customers are just as susceptible to the lure of £1.99 Liebfraumilch and £2.39 Australian whites as the rest of British humanity, so we applaud the efforts the chain is making to offer attractive, fairly priced wines. This is not as exciting a place in which to buy a bottle as, say, Booths, but the range is fundamentally sound.

NAD   Nadder Wine Co   ★★★

Hussars House, 2 Netherhampton Road, Harnham, Salisbury, Wilts SP2 8HE. Tel 01722 325418 Fax 01722 421617. Independent Wine Merchant. **Opening Hours:** Mon-Fri 0900-1800, Sat 0900-1300. **Delivery:** free within 50 miles of Central London and Salisbury for orders of £50 or over. **Services:** mail order, gift-mailing, glass hire, ice.

Jaffelin from Burgundy heads the charge of a host of new names to this list with California's Clos du Val, Australia's Taltarni and South Africa's Boschendal bringing up the rear. Amiable support is provided by regulars like Australia's Brown Brothers, Leon Beyer from Alsace, Foppiano from the US, and a host of good clarets from Bordeaux. Chris Gilbey, proprietor of said establishment, assures us rather worryingly that his prices are "buttock-numbingly" low – and that, even if you can't find a wine you like, Nadder can always offer you a massage. Or at least that's what he says.

- ★★★★ Brown Brothers Pinot/Chardonnay Brut, Milawa, Victoria, Aus. £9.95. *Very European style fizz with lovely bitter chocolate flavours. Classy.* ¶ *AP, LS.*
- ★★★ 1994 Dom. de Lacquy Blanc Vdp de Terroirs Landais, Midi, Fr. *Fresh, light, herby, enjoyable.* £4.15. ¶ *SF, D.*
- ★★★ 1991 Boschendal, Lanoy, Paarl, SA. £5.25. *A very soft, spicy blend of several red grapes; warm and alluring.* ¶ *BF, FF.*
- ★★★★ 1990 Château Villemaurine, Robert Giraud, Bordeaux, Fr. £17.95. *Good, soft, plummy claret.* ¶ *LB, RMS.*
- ★★★ 1993 Reif Estate Winery Vidal, Ontario, Can. £4.95. *Delightfully floral with a hint of honey and apple. Good summer drinking.* ¶ *AP, D.*

BWC   Le Nez Rouge   ★★★★

12 Brewery Road, London N7 9NH. Tel 0171 609 4711. Fax 0171 607 0018. Independent Wine Merchant. **Opening Hours:** Mon-Fri 0900-1730 (order office) shop by appointment. **Delivery:** free nationally. **Tastings:** a couple of large ones per year, plus various themed sessions. **Services:** mail order, *en primeur* offers.

"If you really just like fruit, why not drink pineapple juice with vodka? Nor do we believe that concentration is necessarily a virtue". Controversial words quoted from Joseph Berkmann's introduction to the Le Nez Rouge list. However much one could argue the toss on this one, we cannot deny that the wines are generally of a high calibre and, while there are lots of agreeable old world examples, quite a few of the others are dangerously concentrated and, wait for it...fruity! The core of the list is drawn from the agencies held by Berkmann Wine Cellars, the parent company, and includes the whole range from Georges Duboeuf as well as Coldstream Hills from Australia, an extensive range of reliable Burgundy and new South African finds Lievland and Buitenverwachting. Watch out, too, for the excellent mixed taster cases.

***** 1993 Beringer Private Reserve Chardonnay, Cal. £14.49. *Stunning combination of buttered toast and honey — massive complexity.* ⁋ **WMC.**

**** 1990 Vouvray Demi-Sec, Ch. Vaudenuits, Loire, Fr. £6.67. *Apples, green plums and honey — a gentle semi-sweet wine.* ⁋ **PF.**

**** 1994 Côtes Du Rhône Dom. des Moulins, Georges Duboeuf, Rhône, Fr. £4.62. *Good, down-the-line Côtes du Rhône; fresh and peppery.* ⁋ **SP, D.**

***** 1993 Moulin à Vent, Fut de Chêne, Georges Duboeuf, Beaujolais, Fr. £7.55. *Serious cherryish Beaujolais with sweet spicy oak.* ⁋ **SM, G**

**** 1993 Coldstream Hills Reserve Pinot Noir, Yarra Valley, Victoria, Aus. £12.49. *This could be Burgundy. Classic style with ripe fruit and oak.* ⁋ **BF.**

**** 1992 Morton Estate Hawkes Bay Cabernet/Merlot, NZ. £7.45. *Juicily ripe cassis fruit and a little herbaceous green pepper.* ⁋ **LB, SP.**

JN James Nicholson ★★★★★

27a Killyleagh Street, Crossgar, Co. Down, Northern Ireland. Tel 01396 830091. Independent Wine Merchant. **Opening Hours:** Mon-Sat 1000-1900. **Delivery:** free locally. **Tastings:** regular in-store, plus tutored sessions by visiting winemakers, seminars, dinners, etc. **Services:** en primeur, mail order, gift-mailing.

One of Britain's very best wine merchants, James Nicholson has the disadvantage of being separated from the mainland by a stretch of water. Much the same could, of course, be said for Sainsbury's branch in Calais, but the wine's better in Belfast and, as a customer of James Nicholson, you get the chance to meet thy (favourite wine) maker at tastings with the likes of Ian Hollick from Australia, Ernst Loosen of Germany and Francois Billecart-Salmon of Champagne. California is especially well covered, with wines like those of Laurel Glen, Kistler and Bonny Doon.

**** 1994 Casablanca Sauvignon Blanc, White Label, Curico, Chi. £4.79. *Brilliant gooseberryish wine from a new region of Chile.* ⁋ **D, LS.**

**** 1992 Dr Loosen Riesling, Mosel, Ger. £5.99. *A ripe and grapey wine full of refreshingly simple citrus and honey flavours.* ⁋ **AP, D.**

**** 1990 Château Lascombes, Margaux, Bordeaux, Fr. £13.95. *Classic Margaux which needs time to develop. Lovely blackberryish fruit.* ⁋ **LB, RMS.**

**** 1992 Laurel Glen Terra Rosa, Cal. £7.59. *Fabulous value — a really full, rich and fruity junior version of Patrick Campbell's Cabernet.* ⁋ **LB, D.**

**** 1992 Ridge Zinfandel Lytton Springs, Cal. £13.39. *Lovely spicy wine with hedgerow flavours. Great with game.* ⁋ **G, BF.**

***** 1993 Saintsbury Carneros Pinot Noir, Cal. £11.35. *This raspberryish wine matches all but Burgundy's very best.* ⁋ **BF, RMS, D.**

**** 1994 Heggies Botrytis Riesling, Eden Valley, Aus. £6.55 (half). *Concentrated, apricotty, limey wine. Honeyed, long and balanced.* ⁋ **CS, PF.**

N&P Nickolls and Perks ★★★★

37 High Street, Stourbridge, West Midlands DY8 ITA. Tel 01384 494518. Independent Wine Merchant. **Opening Hours:** Mon-Sat 0900-1800. **Delivery:** free nationally for five cases or more. **Tastings:** regular in-store and for company's own Stourbridge Wine Society. **Services:** cellarage, en primeur, gift-mailing, mail order, glass hire, ice.

Nickolls & Perks say that their list of fine wines is offered to selected clients at highly attractive trade prices (rather than vice versa). Should you be one of the "selected few" to be offered access to N &P's fine and rare stocks, you will not be disappointed with the Bordeaux and Champagnes. You might initially be a tad concerned about the financial benefit of being a chosen one, especially as prices listed are exclusive of VAT, but there is no gainsaying the quality of a range which includes wines like Henri Clerc's 1985 Batard Montrachet and Rene Engel's 1988 Vosne Romanée as well as a roll call of the great-and-good of Bordeaux. Bear in mind, though, that stocks of each wine are often as limited as the number of highly attractive clients.

NIC   Nicolas   ★★★

6 Fulham Road, London, SW3 6HG. Tel 0171 584 1450. Regional chain. Eight branches. **Opening Hours:** Mon-Fri 1100-2200, Sat 1000-2200, Sun 1200-1500, 1900-2200. **Delivery:** free locally. **Tastings:** regular in-store plus courses (ring 0171 586 1196 for details). **Services:** *en primeur*, mail order, gift-mailing, glass hire, gift wrapping, ice.

It has taken a while, but Nicolas is beginning to learn that being France's only major chain of wine shops does not give it an automatic right to success in Britain. While the shops are well managed by charming and informative – usually French – staff, the contents of the shelves could be described as *l'oeuf du curé – bon dans des parts*. Top-class Bordeaux and single-estate wines from other regions of France are worth spending time on, as are the sometimes surprisingly fairly priced Champagnes. Burgundies are less convincing, often revealing themselves to have been bought from the same *négociant* as some of the far cheaper offerings to be found in nearby supermarkets. Similarly, Nicolas' humbler wines, most particularly its Vins de Pays, are sometimes good, sometimes dull, revealing how little attention they receive in France. Depite these criticisms, it can be worth dropping into a Nicolas shop; the staff are keen and some of the special offers are very worthwhile – and the range could give you a few ideas on what to buy duty-free from one of their shops across the water. Incidentally, quite why Nicolas even attempts to sell non-French wines is a mystery; it does so with as much skill and enthusiasm as Margaret Thatcher might apply to singing the *Internationale*.

***   Champagne de Venoge Brut, Cordon Bleu, Fr. £11.90 *(half)*. *Excellent aroma of yeasty biscuits – will continue to improve in bottle.* ❦ **AP, SF.**
****   1992 Château d'Arcins, Haut Médoc, Bordeaux, Fr. £8.50. *Classy, quite traditional claret with green peppery appeal.* ❦ **LB, RM.**
*****   1964 Ch. Margaux, Bordeaux, Fr. £144.50. *A rare chance to taste one of the classic First Growths at a not entirely unreasonable price.* ❦ **BF, LB.**
***   1993 Beaujolais Villages Réserve Nicolas, Fr. £5.95. *Good, black chocolatey Gamay.* ❦ **E, SM, LS.**

NWR   Noble Rot   ★★★

18 Market Street, Bromsgrove, Worcs B61 8DA. Tel 01527 575606. Independent Wine Merchant. **Opening Hours:** Mon-Fri 1000-1900, Sat 0930-1830. **Delivery:** free locally. **Tastings:** regular in-store plus occasional tutored sessions and "wine fair-type" in May and November. **Services:** glass hire.

NRW have just been given permission to sell by the bottle as this goes to press, thereby offering their customers and themselves far greater freedom. Good value is indelibly stamped across the majority of the wines they stock, particularly the selection from Southern France. If you would prefer not to spend over £10 on a reliable bottle of wine, this is your kind of store.

****   1994 Villard Aconcagua Sauvignon Blanc, Casablanca Valley, Chi. £4.99. *Made by a Frenchman in Chile; grassy, like good Bordeaux Blanc.* ❦ **D, PY.**
****   1993 Chablis Domaine des Marrenniers, Bernard Legland, Burgundy, Fr. £8.99. *Good modern Chablis with lovely pineapply fruit.* ❦ **S, WFC.**
****   1994 La Serre Cabernet Sauvignon, Midi, Fr. £3.99. *Ripe crunchy blackcurrants. Good party wine.* ❦ **PY.**
****   1993 Bon Courage Shiraz, Robertson, SA. £5.59. *New Wave South African red with ripe fruit and spice.* ❦ **G, SP.**
****   1992 Nine Popes, Charles Melton, Barossa Valley, Aus. £9.99. *An awesome construction of peppery blackberry fruit and spice.* ❦ **G, RMS.**
***   1990 Carignano del Sulcis Riserva, "Rocca Rubia", Santadi, It. £8.99. *Enticing peppery explosion of pure Carignan fruit.* ❦ **P, SP.**

NI   Nobody Inn   ★★★★★

Doddiscombsleigh, Nr. Exeter, Devon EX6 7PS. Tel 01647 252394. Fax 01647 252978. Independent Wine Merchant. **Opening Hours:** Mon-Sun 1100-1430, 1900-2300, other times by arrangement. **Delivery:** free locally. **Tastings:** regular in-house, tutored once a month between October and March. **Services:** mail order, gift mailing, glass hire.

What is it about Britain's country hoteliers which turns them into such extraordinary vintners? Nick Borst Smith's cellar is an Aladdin's cave; his list an imbiber's encyclopedia to entice all but the faintest of heart to venture down the hazardously narrow country roads to make a personal visit. When you've worked your way through his wine list, turn your attention to the selection of malts – you'll have to agree that Nobody does it better.

★★★★ 1994 Casablanca Valley Sauvignon Blanc, Curico, Chi. £6.99. *Herbaceous and aromatic with plenty of clean, classy fruit.* ⅋ *D, SP.*

★★★★★ 1991 Erdener Prälat Riesling Kabinett, Dr. Loosen, Mosel, Ger. £10.61. *Genuinely classy Mosel Riesling; delicate and finely balanced. Drink now or keep awhile.* ⅋ *AP, D.*

★★★★ 1989 Weinert Cabernet Sauvignon, Mendoza, Arg. £9.82. *Soft, Spanish-style Cabernet with attractive blackcurranty fruit.* ⅋ *RMS, LB, CH.*

★★★★ 1989 Museo "1752" Juan Carrau, Cerro Chapeau, Uruguay. £6.12. *Rich, well-made, mulberryish wine from Uruguay.* ⅋ *BF, RMS.*

★★★★ 1988 Luigi Bosca Syrah, Mendoza, Arg. £8.31. *Proof that Argentina can make Syrah/Shiraz to compete with Australia and the Rhône.* ⅋ *SP.*

★★★★★ 1989 La Guirade, Crozes-Hermitage, Alain Graillot, Rhône, Fr. £21.77. *Utterly wonderful. A cocktail of immense blackberry fruit and pepper.* ⅋ *G.*

★★★★★ 1991 Ridge, Geyserville Vineyard, Sonoma Valley, Cal. £16.53. *Big beast of a blend.Mostly Zinfandel with a little Petit Syrah.* ⅋ *G, BF, RMS.*

★★★★ 1990 Dolcetto D'Alba, G. Mascarello & Figlio, It. £8.61. *Gorgeous crunchy cherry and wild smoky bacon.* ⅋ *RM, P.*

★★★★ 1989 Jasnières, Les Truffières, Jean-Baptiste Pinon, Loire, Fr. £15.20. *Classic Loire Chenin with flavours of honey and apples.* ⅋ *CS.*

★★★★ 1990 Jurancon Moelleux, Clos Uroulat, C. Hours, Fr. £15.05. *Rich creamy apricot and peach.* ⅋ *PF, PS.*

★★★★ Stanton & Killeen Rutherglen Muscadelle, Victoria, Aus. £5.86. *Hedonistic blend of nuts, tea leaves, raisins and caramel.* ⅋ *CHO.*

OD   Oddbins   ★★★★★

31-33 Weir Road, Wimbledon, London SW19 8UG. Tel 0181 944 4400. Fax 018l 944 4411. National Chain. 205 branches. **Opening Hours:** vary between Mon-Sat 1000-2100, Sun 1200-1500, 1900-2100. Fine Wine Shops: Farringdon Street and Notting Hill Gate in London; Cambridge, Oxford, Glasgow and Edinburgh. **Delivery:** free locally. **Tastings:** in all stores every Saturday, plus tutored and two wine fairs per year. **Services:** gift-mailing, en primeur, glass loan, ice.

"I just can't believe these people..." The observation was echoed by a score of winemakers and men and women from throughout the wine world who had come to London to pour wine at the annual Oddbins fair. "These people" were simply the most enthusiastically knowledgeable wine drinkers any of the well-travelled visitors had ever encountered. Oddbins remains an extraordinary training ground for anyone interested in wine – from the primary education of the inexpensive Aussies and French regional wines through the A-Level, great-value-for-£7.50 wines from just about everywhere, to the degree-level brilliant white Burgundies, rare clarets and rarer Australians and Californians on offer at the increasingly impressive Fine Wine shops. If you are going to buy from a chain, why go elsewhere? Will the show go on? The reason for raising the question lies in the disappearance to head office of John Ratcliffe, one of the architects of Oddbins' success. Is Mr R being groomed for higher things, or have Seagram, the Canadian distillers who own it, moved him out of the way to allow them to transform Oddbins into a more profitable – and duller – business offering greater shelf space to Seagram's own spirits and often unimpressive wine brands? I'd prefer to believe the first explanation, but a study of the way Seagram has run its other wine businesses would suggest that it might be naïve to do so. Gather ye rosés, reds and whites, while ye may...

**** 1992 Croser, Petaluma, S Australia, Aus. £10.49 *Classy Aussie fizz, with a very Champagne-like richness.* ¶ *AP, S, WMC.*

***** Champagne Bonnet, Carte Blanche, Fr. £13.49. *Rich in style, biscuity and toasty with luscious appley fruits.* ¶ *AP, D, S.*

***** Champagne Bonnet Rosé, Fr. £13.99. *Clean and refreshing with lots of summer fruits and a zesty tang.* ¶ *AP, EN, S.*

***** 1985 Champagne Moët et Chandon, Cuvée Dom Perignon, Fr. £58.49. *Classic, maturing fizz with loads of nutty richness.* ¶ *AP, EN, D.*

*** 1994 Puglian White, Cantele, It. £3.19. *Young and fresh with an invigorating citrussy touch. Great with pizza.* ¶ *P, PY.*

***** 1993 Condrieu Les Chaillets Vielles Vignes, Cuilleron, Rhône, Fr. £19.99. *Delicately floral with intense peachy, apricot flavours. Balancing acidity.* ¶ *O.*

*** 1992 Seaview Pinot Noir Chardonnay, S. Australia, Aus. £7.49. *Lovely and toasty, with lots of appley fruit. Great value fizz.* ¶ *D, AP, EN.*

**** 1994 Saint Veran, Dom. des Deux Roches, Burgundy, Fr. £7.69. *A good rich white Burgundy with toffee and pineapple hints.* ¶ *WMC, D.*

**** 1994 Penfolds Koonunga Hill Chardonnay, Penfolds, S. Australia, Aus. £4.99. *Rich, ripe, mango-ey and peachy wine with sweetly spicy oak.* ¶ *AP, CS, WFC.*

***** 1992 Chateau Tahbilk Chardonnay, Victoria, Aus. £6.49. *Rich and buttery oak with plenty of ripe pineappley fruit.* ¶ *WM, D.*

*** 1994 Aldridge Estate Semillon/Chardonnay, Cranswick Estate, New South Wales, Aus. £3.75. *Tangy gooseberry fruits with lovely toffee oak.* ¶ *D, PY.*

**** 1993 Stoniers Chardonnay, Mornington Peninsula, Aus. £7.99. *Classy, quite Burgundian Chardonnay. Buttery and peachy.* ¶ *SM, D, AP.*

**** 1993 Mâcon Vergisson, Dom. Roger Lasserat, Burgundy, Fr. £6.49. *Big and buttery , slightly vegetal, honeyed banana, caramel and nut.* ¶ *SM, D.*

**** 1993 St. Aubin 1er Cru Les Charmois, Dom. Bernard Morey, Burgundy, Fr. £12.99. *Concentrated floral apricot peach fruit, rustic and classy.* ¶ *D, S.*

***** 1992 Pouilly-Fuissé Tête de Cru, Dom. J A Ferret, Burgundy, Fr. £16.99. *A lovely mature, honeyed wine with crème caramel, butter and wax.* ¶ *AP, S.*

**** 1993 Glen Carlou Reserve Chardonnay, Paarl, SA. £9.99. *Rich and Burgundian with nutty tones of biscuits, bread and pineapple.* ¶ *CH, S.*

**** 1991 Newton Chardonnay, Napa Valley, California, US. £11.99. *Serious spicy oaky wine, with melony fruit and Burgundian biscuity richness.* ¶ *WFP.*

**** 1993 Burrweiler Altenforst Scheurebe Kabinett, Messmer, Pfalz, Ger. £5.99. *Delicately spiced, soft peachy fruit.* ¶ *O, EN.*

**** 1993 Mussbacher Esleshaut Rieslaner Spätlese, Müller-Catoir, Ger. £11.99. *Rich, long, honey and honeysuckle, spicy, exotic oriental style.* ¶ *O, PF, CC.*

**** 1994 Mount Hurtle Grenache Rosé, McLaren Vale, Aus. £4.99. *Lovely, slightly soft gingery fruit with brilliant clean flavours.* ¶ *AP, PY, D.*

**** 1994 Vredendal Cabaret, Olifants River, SA. £5.49. *Good, modern South African red with crunchy fruit.* ¶ *CH.*

**** 1993 Costières de Nîmes, Château Paul Blanc, Midi, Fr. £4.99. *Complex dark fruit, chocolate, smooth oak. Fantastic value.* ¶ *D, BF.*

***** 1993 Robertson's Well, Mildara, S. Australia, Aus. £7.49. *Rich, ripe, mouthfillling wine.* ¶ *RM.*

**** 1991 Stoniers Reserve Cabernet Sauvignon, Mornington Peninsula, Aus. £11.99. *Unusually — for Australia — subtle, blackberryish wine. Classy.* ¶ *SP.*

***** 1988 Orlando Jacaranda Ridge Cabernet Sauvignon, Orlando Wines, S. Aus. £17.49. *Sweet fruit, soft spices and new oak.* ¶ *RM, CH.*

**** 1993 Cono Sur Cabernet Sauvignon, Chimbarongo, Chi. £3.79. *Good, creamy, ripe cassis and plum with minty overtones.* ¶ **D, BF, LB.**

**** 1993 Stellenzicht Cabernet Sauvignon Block Series, Stellenbosch, SA. £4.99. *Fresh, leafy, blackcurranty. More French than New World.* ¶ **D, LB.**

**** 1991 Kanonkop Paul Sauer, Stellenbosch, SA. £10.99. *Intensely rich plum fruit, dark wood and spices.* ¶ **BF, G.**

**** 1993 Carmen Gold Reserve Cabernet Sauvignon, Chi. £9.99. *Ripe cassis fruit and lashings of oaky vanilla.* ¶ **RMS.**

**** 1991 Rouge Homme Cabernet Shiraz, Coonawarra, Aus. £4.99. *Intensely ripe, jammy and concentrated, full of cassis, spice and oak.* ¶ **SP, G.**

***** 1992 Penfolds Bin 28 Shiraz, S. Aus. £6.99. *Spice galore, with chocolate, blackcurrant and black cherry. Worth keeping.* ¶ **BF, G.**

**** 1992 Coldstream Hills Cabernet Merlot, Yarra Valley, Aus. £8.95. *Stewed plums, herbs and allspice.* ¶ **P, WMP.**

**** 1991 Lindemans Limestone Ridge Shiraz Cabernet, S Australia, Aus. £11.99. *Oak and liquorice are the keynotes here. Very Australian.* ¶ **P, SP.**

**** 1993 Stellenzicht Cabernet Shiraz, Stellenbosch, SA. £3.99. *A clean, ripe, berryish flavour full of cassis and spice.* ¶ **RM .**

**** 1993 Côtes du Rhône Genevrieres, Réméjeanne, Rhône, Fr. £6.99. *Stunning dark fruit, chocolate, mint and pepper.* ¶ **G, BF.**

*** 1993 Genus Shiraz, SA. £3.99. *Smoky and peppery and rather more like Pinotage than Shiraz.* ¶ **D, G.**

**** 1993 Madrona Zinfandel, California, US. £6.99 *Jammy, rich and spicy; a typical Zinfandel with ripe apple fruit.* ¶ **P, BF.**

**** 1990 Domaine Drouhin Oregon Pinot Noir, US. £16.99. *Real Burgundy style, with cherry and raspberry fruit and oak.* ¶ **BF.**

**** 1991 Marchesi de Frescobaldi Pomino Rosso, Tuscany, It. £7.99. *Cherries, blackcurrants and chocolatey spices.* ¶ **P, RM.**

*** 1994 Vega de Moriz, Valdepeñas, Sp. £3.29. *Ultra-soft and glugable jammy toffee wine.* ¶ **PY, BF.**

**** 1990 Rioja Faustino V, Bodegas Faustino Martinez, Sp. £6.99. *Creamy smooth, with gutsy fruit and rich woody tinges.* ¶ **RMS.**

**** 1993 Château Rieussec, Reserve Sauternes, Fr. £5.99 (half). *Thick and creamy. Orange peel, intensely aromatic fruit and honeyed oak.* ¶ **PF.**

PAL   Pallant Wines ★★★

7 High Street, Arundel, West Sussex BN18 9AD. Tel 01903 882288. Fax 01903 882801. Independent Wine Merchant. **Opening Hours:** Mon-Sat 0900-1800, Sun 1200-1400. **Delivery:** free locally. **Services:** mail order, catering available.

"Go Up-Market – Not Supermarket." Pallant's rallying cry echoes those of merchants up and down the land. However, Pallant's customers seem to have taken heed. Despite the additional burden of their location near the south coast and the inevitable erosion of sales of cheap wine and beer, the medium and upper price ranges are in good shape and sales of Champagne, Fine Claret and Burgundy are going particularly well. Pay particular attention to Rene Vanatelle's Château de Livey and Franz Haas' Moscato Rosa. There is also a fine delicatessen counter selling all manner of cheeses, breads, coffee beans, smoked fish etc. All highly pallantable.

*** 1989 Champagne Jules Mignon, Marne et Champagne, Fr. £18.75. *Biscuity nuttiness, honeyed fruits and crisp acidity.* ¶ **AP, EN, D.**

**** 1989 Graacher Himmelreich Kabinett, Friedrich Wilhelm Gymnasium, *Moselle*, Ger. £6.66. *Fresh, apple and lemon flavours; beautiful balance.* ¶ **LS.**

**** 1992 Simonsig Estate Pinotage, Stellenbosch, SA. £5.69. *Smoky spices and strawberry fruit.* ¶ **P, SM.**

*** 1991 Dolcetto d'Alba, Elio Altare, It. £7.88. *Plums and berries, tobacco and chocolate. Lovely leathery wine from the leader of the New Wave of winemaking in Piedmont.* ¶ **P, FF, SP.**

P   Parfrements   ★★★

68 Cecily Road, Cheylesmore, Coventry CV3 5LA. Tel 01203 503646. Independent Wine Merchant. Wines by the case only. **Opening Hours:** Mon-Fri 0900-1800, Sat 0900-1300, Sun 0900-1800. **Delivery:** free locally. **Tastings:** regular in-store, plus tutored sessions on request. **Services:** mail order, gift mailing, glass hire.

Worth being sent to Coventry for. Gerald Gregory's great range of Clarets and reasonably-priced Burgundy top this list with some excellent producers from the 'other world' such as Gundlach Bundschu from California, Dalwhinnie from Australia and Jackson Estate from New Zealand.

**** 1992 Jackson Estate Chardonnay, Marlborough, NZ. £7.41. *Cool climate fruit and a crisp acidity. Classy stuff.* ¶ **SM, D, EN.**

**** 1990 Cornas, Domaine Marcel Juge, Rhône, Fr. £11.52. *Serious, smoky, gamey wine. Built to last.* ¶ **G.**

***** 1987 Viña Ardanza, Rioja, Sp. £10. *Bags of succulent fruit balanced by lovely smooth tannins.* ¶ **SP, CS.**

***** 1991 Clancys, Peter Lehmann, Barossa Valley, Aus. £8.47. *Full, ripe berry fruits and black cherries. A touch of eucalyptus.* ¶ **WM, FF.**

PAV   The Pavilion Wine Co   ★★★★

3 Oak street, Heeley, Sheffield S8 9UB. Tel 0114 255 3301. Fax 0114 255 1010. Independent Wine Merchant. **Opening Hours:** Mon-Fri 0930-1800, Sat 0900-1700. **Delivery:** free locally. **Tastings:** regular in-store, plus wine-tasting circle. **Services:** cellarage, mail order, gift-mailing, glass hire, ice.

David Gilmour states proudly that 'there are no (or very few) great wines on our list: our strength lies in medium priced wines.' He is a little over modest in our view. Granted there is no Petrus or DRC, but wines like Domaine Manciat-Poncet in Charnay-les-Macon, Domaine Jayer-Gilles on the Hautes Cotes de Nuits and Domaine Antoine Gosset from Chinon are classics of their kind. There are also simple wines like Sauvignon d'Arjolle from Domaine Teisserenc which treads with panache the middle ground between the old fashioned local style and flying winemaker fruitiness. Australia is represented by four good estates: Goundrey, Pike's Polish Hill, Garry Farr and Cullens.

**** 1994 Soave Classico, Nino Pieropan, Veneto, It. £6.75. *Fresh, youthful fruit and cool acidity.* ¶ **FR, O, WFC.**

***** 1993 Viognier Dom. du Rieufrais, VdP Coteaux des Baronnies, Fr. £7.49. *Fantastic peaches and apricots. Delicate and floral.* ¶ **O, FD.**

**** 1992 Châteauneuf-du-Pape Dom. de Vieux Telegraphe, Rhône, Fr. £10.67. *Pepper and spice — with rich damson fruit.* ¶ **SP, RM.**

**** 1992 Santenay Clos de La Confrérie, Vincent Giradin, Burgundy, Fr. £11.95. *Oakily spicy wine – ripe with flavours of black cherries.* ¶ **WM, CH.**

THP   Thos Peatling   ★★★★★

Westgate House, Westgate Street, Bury St Edmunds, Suffolk IP33 1QS. Tel 01284 755948. Fax 01284 705795. Regional Chain. 27 branches. **Opening Hours:** vary from shop to shop. **Delivery:** free locally, nationally for two cases or more. **Tastings:** regular in-store, plus tutored sessions 4-6 times a year at the Bury St. Edmunds and Clerkenwell Road (London) branches; others as required. **Services:** cellarage, en primeur, glass loan. No credit cards.

Thos Peatling make it abundantly clear that claret is their first love, accounting for a sixth of their total wine sales (although Burgundy runs it a close race with nearly one bottle in every dozen). Whether there is a hard-core of clandestine fine claret drinkers in the sleepy Lovejoyesque towns of East Anglia remains to be discovered. However Peatling's are keen to provide for their New World fans, as sales of South African and South American wine rose last year by a half and a third respectively. The Australian and New Zealand wines didn't hang about either. All in all, what one of those Lovejoyesque dealers might call fine antiques and modern classics.

As we go to press, credible rumours are flying around the wine trade about a takeover of Peatlings by Thresher, as part of a deal between Greene King and Whitbread, Thresher's owners. I, for one hope that these stories come to nothing; Peatlings would be a sad loss for British wine drinkers.

**** 1986 Peatlings Bernkasteler Schlossberg Riesling Kabinett, Mosel, Ger. £8.99. *Light and fruity with a sweetish tinge.* ¶ *O, AP.*

*** 1993 Chardonnay Vino da Tavola Le Veritiere, It. £4.49. *Crisp, fresh fruit and New World style honeyed oak.* ¶ *WMC, D.*

***** 1990 Milmanda Chardonnay, Miguel Torres, Penedes, Sp. £16.99. *Buttery, toffee oak and peachy, lemony fruit.* ¶ *EN, FD, WMC.*

**** 1991 Brown Bros Semillon, Milawa, Victoria, Aus. £6.99. *Mandarins, lime and old English marmalade, plus sweet oak. Deliciously indulgent.* ¶ *D, WM.*

*** 1991 Vin de Pays Côteaux de La Cèze, Domaine Maby, S E France, Fr. £4.49. *Light and fruity. Some choclatey spice.* ¶ *WM, FF.*

**** 1985 Weinert Cabernet Sauvignon, Mendoza, Arg. £9.99. *Soft, Spanish-style Cabernet with attractive blackcurranty fruit.* ¶ *SP, WM.*

***** 1989 Château Lascombes, Margaux, Bordeaux, Fr. £13.99. *Elegant young claret with violet perfume and ripe blackcurrant character.* ¶ *LB, CH.*

**** 1991 Heathcote Shiraz, Hanging Rock, Victoria, Aus. £15.99. *Berry fruits, damsons and plums with a peppery, eucalyptus tinge.* ¶ *RM, SP.*

*** 1992 Fairview Shiraz, Paarl, SA. £5.49. *Refreshingly minty Shiraz – at once spicy and leafy.* ¶ *RMS, SP.*

***** 1992 Nuits St Georges Premier Cru, Domaine de l'Arlot, Burgundy, Fr. £11.99. *Top class Burgundy – perfumed, with summer pudding fruit.* ¶ *BF, D.*

**** 1992 Quady Winery Essensia Orange Muscat, California, US. £6.65. *Treacly orange peel flavours, rich and tangy.* ¶ *AP, PF, CH.*

**** Peatlings 20 Years Old Tawny, Por. £18.99. *Nutty and intensely woody. Gorgeous dark honeyed fruits.* ¶ *CC, CH.*

PST   Penistone Court   ★★★

Railway Station, Penistone, South Yorkshire S30 6HA. Tel 01226 766037. Fax 01226 767310. Independent Wine Merchant. **Opening Hours:** Mon-Fri 0900-1800, Sat 1000-1500. **Delivery:** free locally. **Tastings:** regular in-store. **Services:** mail order, glass hire.

Uneven in quality, the Penistone list impresses one moment and leaves us wondering the next. When Christopher Ward has put together such an impressive Spanish selection – CVNE, Contino, Imperial, Martinez Bujanda, Murietta, Berberana and Torres – why is the Australian range so run-of-the-mill, and the choice from South Africa practically devoid of any interest? Still, the above mentioned Spaniards, a well chosen Californian list and the entire Rhône selection (good, if all from Delas) and keen prices all tip the balance in favour of a visit to The Railway Station.

*** 1994 Bianco Di Custoza, Cavalchina, Veneto, It. £5.58 *Subtle, creamy and youthfully fresh.* ¶ *P, RM.*

***** 1990 Sonoma Cutrer Chardonnay Les Pierres, US. £14.28. *Ultra-classy, fine Meursault-lookalike. Worth keeping.* ¶ *D, SF, WM.*

***** 1991 Opus One, Mondavi/Rothschild, California, US. £42.28 *Beautifully made co-production between Mouton Rothschild and Mondavi, with oak, cassis, eucalyptus and more than a hint of cedar.* ¶ *LB.*

**** 1992 Banfi, Moscadello di Montalcino, Tuscany, It. £15. *Smooth and rich, with flavours of banana fritters, mandarins and some spice.* ¶ *CS, PS.*

P&G   Philglas & Swiggot   ★★★★

21 Northcote Road, London SW11 1NG. Tel 0171 924 4494. **Opening Hours:** Mon-Sat 1100-2100, Sun 1200-1500, 1900-2100. **Delivery:** free locally. **Tastings:** regular in-store, tutored sessions for groups and wine clubs on request. **Services:** glass loan, ice, gift mailing.

The fact that Karen Rogers' company runs an 'annual summer barbie and tasting' gives the game away. This is, if not actually an Antipodean colony, pretty close to being one. And why not, with wines like those of Balgownie, Campbells and Martinborough? Old World wines have to conform to the same criteria of flavour and value-for-money – which helps to explain the preponderance of offerings from the Rhone and Italy, though Burgundy is clearly a growing interest. Prices there might, however lead to a renaming of the company as Phil Smallglass and Sippit.

- ★★★   1993 Black Opal Chardonnay, Mildara, SE. Australia. £5.99. *Rich, very easy-going, peachy wine.* ¶ **SF,SM.**
- ★★★★   1992 Roo's Leap Shiraz Cabernet, Mildara, Aust. £5.99. *Big, spicy, berryish mouthful.* ¶ **FF, RM, D.**
- ★★★★   1993 Tunnel Hill Pinot Noir, Tarrawarra Vineyards, Aust. £7.99. *Berryish, plummy wine with gentle oak from the cool region of Yarra.* ¶ **BF, RM.**
- ★★★★   1990 Balgownie Estate Pinot Noir, Aust. £12.99. *Serious Pinot with good raspberryish fruit. Drink now.* ¶ **RMS, WMP, WFP.**

CPW   Christopher Piper   ★★★★

1 Silver Street, Ottery St. Mary, Devon EX11 1DB. Tel 01404 814139. Fax 01404 812100. Independent Wine Merchant. **Opening Hours:** Mon-Fri 0830-1300, 1400-1800, Sat 0900-1300, 1430-1700. **Delivery:** free locally. **Tastings:** regular in-store plus numerous tastings throughout the year (including three major ones and three wine-weekends). **Services:** bi-monthly news letter, cellarage, *en primeur*, mail order, gift mailing, glass hire.

Christopher Piper obviously bought the Tardis from the BBC after the last series of Doctor Who – how else can he can squeeze quite so many wines into the one shop and cellar? Still the inhabitants of Devon should thank heaven that he does, as they browse through his excellent range of Bordeaux and Burgundy, inspired choice of Beaujolais (Mr P's adopted homeland), and the tastiest examples from Italy and Germany. The New World is ably represented by the likes of Rongopai, Domaine Drouhin and Coldstream Hills. There is even a small selection of cooking wine.

- ★★★★★   1994 Hunters Sauvignon Blanc, Marlborough, NZ. £10.33. *Amazingly intense aromas of capsicum, tomato skin and gooseberry.* ¶ **D, O, PY.**
- ★★★★★   1991 Erdener Prälat Riesling Kabinett, Dr. Loosen, Mosel, Ger. £11.76 *A classy Mosel Riesling; delicately balanced with fine acidity.* ¶ **CC, O, SM.**
- ★★★★   1993 Albariño Lagar de Cervera, Rias Baixas, Galicia, Sp. £8.33. *Delightfully aromatic and beautifully balanced. One of Spain's best whites.* ¶ **P, O, D.**
- ★★★★   1994 Neethlingshof Gewürztraminer, Stellenbosch, SA. £5.12. *Spicy wine with a smell of parma violets. Lemony and deliciously perfumed.* ¶ **PY, O, SP.**
- ★★★★   1993 Saxenberg Estate Shiraz, Stellenbosch, SA. £7.70. *Inky black, dense and tannic Shiraz – chewy and intense.* ¶ **CH, P, RM.**
- ★★★★★   1992 Lytton Springs Zinfandel, Ridge Vineyards, Santa Cruz Mountains, US. £17.18 *Layers of wonderful complex wild bramble and spicy oak.* ¶ **LB, RMS.**
- ★★★★★   1993 Rockford Dry Country Grenache, S Australia, Aus. £8.37. *Serious low yield Grenache, packed with dense plum and strawberry fruit.* ¶ **LB, RM.**
- ★★★★   1993 Coldstream Hills Reserve Pinot Noir, Yarra Valley, Victoria, Aus£12.50. *This could be Burgundy. Classic style with ripe fruit and oak.* ¶ **CH, BF, WMP.**
- ★★★★   1985 Quarles Harris Vintage Port, Por. £16.40. *Richly mouthfilling young port from an underrated producer.* ¶ **CH, D.**

102 Merchants

TP   Terry Platt   ★★★★

Ferndale Road, Llandudno Junction, Gwynedd LL31 9NT. Tel (shop) 01492 872997 (office) 01492 592971. Fax 01492 592196. Independent Wine Merchant. **Opening Hours:** (shop) Mon-Sat 1000-2000, Sun 1200-1400; (office) Mon-Fri 0830-1730. **Delivery:** free locally. **Tastings:** regular in-store plus special tasting sessions and dinners. **Services:** mail order, gift mailing, glass hire.

The wine list at this venerable institution is on the verge of obesity. This year Jeremy Platt, son of Terry, has added yet more wines to the range stocked in their aptly named World of Wine shop. Intrepid explorers of global flavours can wander from Alsace (Schlumberger and Trimbach) and Champagne (Taittinger and Bollinger) to Monnow Valley in Wales, via Gray Monk from Canada, Blue Rock Estate from South Africa and Pujol from Uruguay. It's enough to make a wine lover drool.

★★★★	1992 Riesling QbA, Reichsgraf von Kesselstatt, Mosel, Ger. £6.89 *Youthful Mosel with lovely appley, steely fruit.* ¶ *O, SP, S.*	
★★★	1993 Gewürztraminer "Moulin Blanc", Dopff au Moulin, Alsace, Fr. £7.99. *Perfumed, classic Gewürz with fresh lychee fruit.* ¶ *O, SP, AP.*	
★★★	1993 Railroad Red Shiraz-Cabernet, Graham Beck, Robertson, SA. £5.39. *Spicy-berryish blend on a lighter scale than Australian versions.* ¶ *RM, D, BF.*	
★★★★★	1993 Qupé Syrah, Santa Barbara, California, US. £11.65. *Intense plummy and smoky-spicy wine. Very Rhône-like.* ¶ *CH, G, LB.*	
★★★★★	Quinta Da Ervamoira 10 Year Old Tawny, Ramos-Pinto, Douro, Por. £12.39. *Lovely plummy wine with a flavour of the darkest brown sugar.* ¶ *CC, CH.*	

PON   Le Pont de la Tour   ★★★★

The Butler's Wharf Building, 36D Shad Thames, Butler's Wharf, London SE1 2YE. Tel 0171 403 2403. Fax 0171 403 0267. Independent Wine Merchant. **Opening Hours:** Mon-Sat 1200-2030, Sun 1200-1500. **Delivery:** free locally. **Services:** mail order, gift-mailing, glass hire, ice.

Acting as both a retail outlet and the cellar for the restaurant, the layout of the shop strives to create a cellar atmosphere with both diners and shoppers welcome to browse at leisure. Should Michael Winner be forcibly ejected from the restaurant he could linger here over a finely chosen selection of bottles from virtually every wine producing region on earth. Though these are significantly cheaper than on the restaurant wine list, bargains here are few and far between.

★★★★★	1993 Pinot Bianco, Jermann, Friuli, It. £10.95. *Rich, creamy dry wine with lovely perfumed spice.* ¶ *FD, O.*
★★★★	1993 Soave Classico Superiore, Anselmi, Veneto, It. £6.95. *Proper Soave made from the superior Garganega rather than Trebbiano. Rich, with peary fruit.* ¶ *RM, P, WMP.*
★★★★★	1982 Château Gruaud Larose, Bordeaux, Fr. £59.50. *Classic, ripe, plummy and cedary. A great wine.* ¶ *LB, RMS, CH.*
★★★★	1990 Cornas Marcel Juge, Rhône, Fr. £14.95. ¶ *SP, LB. Serious, smoky, gamey wine. Built to last.* ¶ *G.*
★★★	1993 Bourgogne Rouge, Chopin Groffier, Burgundy, Fr. £9.95. *Young Burgundy with fresh mulberry fruit.* ¶ *P, FF, RM.*
★★★★★	1989 Charmes Chambertin, Domaine Dujac, Burgundy, Fr. £43. *Classy, berryish wine with subtle complex flavours and subtle oak.* ¶ *CH, RM, WFP, BF.*
★★★★★	1991 Venegazzu della Casa, Gasparini, Veneto, It. £9.95 *Lovely Dundee Cake-in-a-glass. Rich, long, satisfying Italian red.* ¶ *CH, P.*
★★★★	1991 Barbera d'Asti 'Ceppi Storici', Piedmont, It. £5.65 *A mouthful of summer pudding flavours.* ¶ *D, AP.*
★★★★	1983 La Rioja Alta Gran Reserva 904, Sp. £16.99. *Lovely, oaky traditional wine with soft strawberry fruit.* ¶ *P, WMP.*

POR — Portland Wine Co ★★★★

16, North Parade, Sale Moor, Greater Manchester M33 3JS. Tel 0161 962 8752. Fax 0161 905 1291. Independent Wine Merchant. **Opening Hours:** Mon-Sat 1000-2100, Sun 1200-1500 & 1900-2130. **Delivery:** free locally. **Tastings:** tutored events, regula tastings in Hale. **Services:** gift-mailing, glass loan, ice.

Geoff Dickinson is still clearly addicted to the Antipodes although there are signs that he is trying to wean himself off the habit by switching his attention to the potentially more dangerous (in cost terms) offerings from California. As for the Old World, Burgundy and Spain remain strong. For a friendly welcome and an extensive range of good Bordeaux visit the Hale branch, and, to taste your way through the range enquire about the great wine fair held annually in conjunction with Booth's of Stockport, at which you might meet the editor of this Guide. Computer-minded wine buffs may be interested to know that Portland have recently become UK distributor of 'Vindata', a computer wine database and cellar management system.

*** 1994 Red Cliffs Estate Chardonnay, Mildura, Victoria, Aus. £4.99. *Simple, tropically ripe wine with biscuity character.* ⁋ **D, FF, FO.**

**** 1992 Marimar Torres Chardonnay, California, US. £11.99. *Classy, creamy Chardonnay with melony fruit and gentle oak.* ⁋ **D, S, WFC, WMP, LS.**

**** 1993 Mitchelton 111 Shiraz/Grenache/Mourvedre, Victoria, Aus. £7.49. *Characterful, perfumed with pepper and blackberries.* ⁋ **SP, RM, WMP.**

***** 1992 Bonny Doon Muscat Canelli, Vin de Glaciere, Santa Cruz, US. £9.99 (half). *Sheer indulgence; honeyed, concentrated, grapey wine.* ⁋ **D, PF.**

**** Seppelt Old Trafford, S Australia, Aus. £7.99. *Australian 'port'. Nutty, toffee'd and rich. Really rather classy.* ⁋ **AP, D, CH, CC.**

QR — Quellyn Roberts ★★★

15 Watergate Street, Chester, Cheshire CH1 2LB. Tel 01244 310455. Fax 01244 346704. Independent Wine Merchant. **Opening Hours:** Mon-Sat 0845-1745. **Delivery:** free locally. **Services:** mail order, glass loan.

A neat little merchant tucked away under the wattle and daub archways of Chester, with a comprehensive range covering all the usual hot spots of the wine world. Particularly impressive are the South African reds. Despite the flood of SA wine in recent years, finding vintages of the more quality conscious 'boutique' wineries has not been easy, but Quellyn Roberts seem to have met the challenge admirably.

**** 1994 Delegats Chardonnay, Oyster Bay, NZ. £7.99. *Ripe tropical fruit bursting out of the glass, restrained only by firm oak.* ⁋ **SF, LS.**

***** 1985 Ch. Lynch-Bages, Pauillac, Bordeaux, Fr. £35.25. *A truly excellent claret, drinking superbly at the moment.* ⁋ **LB, RM.**

*** 1993 Côtes du Rhône Villages, Cellier des Dauphins, Rhone, Fr. £5.15. *Simple, crunchy and spicy strawberry fruit.* ⁋ **SP, WMP, D.**

***** Quinta Da Ervamoira 10 Year Old Tawny, Ramos-Pinto, Douro, Por. £13.75. *Lovely plummy wine with a flavour of moscavado sugar.* ⁋ **CH, CC.**

R — R S Wines ★★★★

32, Vicarage Road, Southville, Bristol BS3 1PD. Tel:01179 631780. Fax 01179 533797. Independent Wine Merchant. **Opening Hours:** Mon-Fri 0900-1900. **Delivery:** free locally. **Tastings:** regular in-store. **Services:** cellarage, *en primeur*, glass hire. No credit cards.

Raj Soni's wine list has a bespoke feel to it, as opposed to the familiar trotting out of standard definitions from the "wine merchant description phrasebook," – the publicity-blurb-descriptions accusation from last year's Guide has obviously been heeded. The emphasis is on unusual yet good-value wines such as Châteaux Le

Livey and Clos Labarde. Burgundy includes the buttery Givry Blanc 1er Cru, Domaine Thevenot Le Brun Noble Pinot Beurot and Maison Pierre Bourée Gevrey Chambertin. Australia fields the 1992 Cape Mentelle Zinfandel and Bethany Estate's 1989 Shiraz. But enough of all that wine; to be really honest, the bottle on my shopping list has nothing to do with grapes – it's the Ardberg 1975 Islay, Cask Strength.

***** 1993 Thelema Mountain Reserve Chardonnay, Stellenbosch, SA. £9.30. *Really stunning, generously oaked Chardonnay.* ¶ *WMC, SF.*

**** 1994 Bethany Estate Late Harvest Riesling, S Australia, Aus. £5.95. *Luscious, baked apple flavours – with brown sugar and cloves!* ¶ *PF.*

**** 1991 Weinert Malbec, Mendoza, Arg. £7.99. *A typically spicy example of an underrated Bordeaux and Cahors grape at home in Argentina.* ¶ *RM.*

***** 1992 Cape Mentelle Zinfandel, Margaret River, W Australia, Aus. £8.95. *A rare and highly successful outing for this Californian grape.* ¶ *G, RMS.*

**** 1993 L A Cetto Petite Sirah, Baja California, Mex. £4.75. *Excitingly fresh pepper-and-spice nose, full of primary red fruit flavours.* ¶ *SP, P, PY.*

*** Fino de Sanlucar, Antonio Barbadillo, Jerez, Sp. £4.75. *Fresh, dry and rather savoury — excellent with calamares.* ¶ *LS, S.*

RAE   Raeburn Fine Wines   ★★★★★

21-23 Comely Bank Road, Edinburgh EH4 1DS. Tel 0131 332 5166. Fax 0131 332 5166. Independent Wine Merchant. **Opening Hours:** Mon-Sat 0930-1800, Sun 1230-1700. **Delivery:** free locally. **Tastings:** tutored tastings at The Vaults in Leith. Details on application. **Services:** cellarage, *en primeur*, mail order, glass hire.

In May, when the wine press was rushing about like the white rabbit between tastings, Zubair Mohamed travelled down to London to open a few wines from the little-known Joseph Swan winery in California. It says much for Mr Mohamed that the turn-out for that low key event was 100 times more impressive than for the swanky launch Robert Mondavi held a few months earlier. Raeburn is quite simply one of the most highly regarded merchants on either side of the border – and a great source for stylish wine, irrespective of its nationality and prestige.

**** Vouvray Mousseux, Société Huët, Loire, Fr. £10.50. *Softly foaming appley-honeyed, very classy stuff.* ¶ *AP, D, PY.*

**** 1989 Viognier, La Jota Vineyards, Napa Valley, California, US. £19.80. *Perfumed, very classy wine from a rising star among grapes.* ¶ *SP, D.*

***** 1989 Meursault, Francois Jobard, Burgundy, Fr. £21.95. *Lovely, nutty, slightly pineapply wine. Very classy.* ¶ *WM, WFC.*

***** 1991 Minervois Ch. de Violet 'Cuvée Clovis', Midi, Fr. £5.75. *H.H. Munro's favourite wine, a rich and haunting medley of wild herbs.* ¶ *RM, G.*

***** 1989 Vieux Ch. Certan, Pomerol, Thienpont, Bordeaux, Fr. £37. *Ultra-fine Pomerol; richly fruity plum and spice.* ¶ *LB, BF.*

**** 1987 Brokenwood Estate Cabernet Sauvignon, Hunter Valley, Aus. £9.95. *Hunter Cabernet is rare. This is rich, ripe and long.* ¶ *RMS, RM.*

**** 1992 Warwick Estate Cabernet Franc, Stellenbosch, SA. £7.99. *Delightfully concentrated chocolate and bramble fruit.* ¶ *RM, P.*

**** 1991 Cornas, Noel Versat, Rhône, Fr. £14.95. *Deep purple, with hedonistically intense smoky tannic fruit.* ¶ *G, RMS.*

***** 1988 Joseph Swan Zinfandel, Sonoma County, California, US. £9.99. *Dense brambly fruit, beginning to soften into opulent richness.* ¶ *G, RM.*

*** 1992 Carignane, Rochioli Vineyards, Russian River Valley, California, US. £8.99. *Big, intense, spicy wine with damsons and cherries.* ¶ *BF, LB.*

**** 1991 Pommard, Jean-Marc Boillot, Burgundy, Fr. £14.99. *Serious Burgundy. Still a little tough, but with lovely fruit.* ¶ *BF, CH, CS.*

*** 1988 Bourgogne Passetoutgrain, Henri Jayer, Burgundy, Fr. £7.95. *A mixture of Pinot Noir and Gamay from a top producer – this is a mature and smooth wine.* ¶ *SM, E, D.*

RAM — Ramsbottom Victuallers ★★★

16-18 Market Place, Ramsbottom, Bury, Lancs. BL0 9HT. Tel 01706 825070. Independent Wine Merchant. **Opening Hours:** Wed-Sat 1000-1730, 1930-2200, Sun 1230-1500. **Delivery:** free locally. **Tastings:** wine of the week every Saturday, plus tutored tastings with supper in the adjoining restaurant (next series: Sept '95-Easter '96).

Chris Johnson emerges unscathed from the chaos and disruption associated with a major re-build of a delicatessen and wine cellar, with an extensive and appetising selection of wines. Even though Italy and Spain are no longer as strong, there is plenty of mileage left in the the New World, Rhone, Alsace, Bordeaux and Burgundy. A treasure in a part of the world often fonder of beer than Beaune.

*** Champagne Cattier Brut, Chigny-les-Roses 1er Cru, Fr. £17.95. *Really lovely small grower's Champagne full of soft summer fruit.* ‖ *AP, D.*
***** 1992 Basedow Shiraz, S Australia, Aus. £6.65. *Spicy wine with some delicacy to it.* ‖ *G, RM.*
**** 1982 Morey St. Denis Grand Cru, Dom. Ponsot, Burgundy, Fr. £45. *Mature, plummy wine with soft complex mulberryish flavours.* ‖ *BF, CS.*
**** 1989 Coteaux du Layon Chenin Blanc, Clos de St. Catherine, Baumard, Fr. £21. *Intense, honeyed, appley wine.* ‖ *CS, PF.*

RD — Reid Wines ★★★★

The Mill, Marsh Lane, Hallatrow, Nr. Bristol BS19 3DN. Tel 01761 452645. Fax 01761 453642. Independent Wine Merchant. **Opening Hours:** Mon-Fri 1000-1800, Sat by arrangement. **Delivery:** free locally and in central London. **Tastings:** occasional in-store plus 'vertical/horizontal, regional and comparative' tastings at The Mill or in a local restaurant. **Services:** cellarage, mail order, gift mailing, glass hire.

The three Muscat-eers Boobbyer, Baker and Wood continue to dazzle and enthral on their mission to rescue wine lovers from disappointment. Brushing their curled Aloxe from their eyes they proceed without a fearful Beaune in their bodies. Recent Fleuries of action have resulted in a consolidation of their reputation as an excellent source of old and rare Bordeaux, Burgundy, Rhône and Loire wines. Their derring-do has not been limited to Europe and a Soave leap across the hemisphere has directed well-deserved attention to many of the New World wines. With such a cast, plus a script from Bill Baker, who could give the world's greatest wine writers a run for their money, wine aficionados can sleep soundly in their beds at Nuits.

**** 1993 Pinot Bianco, Jermann, Friuli, It. £10.99. *Rich, creamy dry wine with lovely perfumed spice.* ‖ *WM, LS.*
***** 1985 Ch. de Fieuzal Blanc, Bordeaux, Fr. £13.50 (half). *Absolutely stunning white Graves; rich and creamy with lingering oak.* ‖ *WMC, WFC.*
**** 1994 Bonny Doon Ca' del Solo Malvasia Bianca, California, US. £7.60. *A really distinctively grapey blend of Californian and Italian flavours.* ‖ *SP, AP.*
***** 1984 Niebaum Coppola Rubicon, California, US. £16.95. *Francis Ford Coppola's wonderful Cabernet-based red made from a top vintage.* ‖ *G, RMS.*
***** 1961 Ch. Mouton Rothschild, Pauillac, Bordeaux, Fr. £395.00. *A really great wine from a great vintage. Share with your best friend.* ‖ *BF, LB, CH.*
*** 1993 Sancerre Rouge Les Cailliers, Domaine Vacheron, Loire, Fr. £9.50. *Beautifully elegant, fragrant red made from Pinot Noir.* ‖ *SM, E.*
***** 1959 Ch. D'Yquem, Sauternes, Bordeaux, Fr. £350.00. *Almost bound to be let down by any food – try it with the best Foie Gras you can find.* ‖ *AP, D.*
**** 1988 Vin Santo Selvapiana, Tuscany, It. £11.75. *Ideally drunk with sweet almond biscuits, this is liquid amber heaven.* ‖ *D, PS.*

RES   La Reserve ★★★★

56 Walton Street, London SW3 1RB. Tel 0171 589 2020. Fax 0l71 581 0250. Independent Wine Merchant. **Opening Hours:** Mon-Sat 0930-2100. **Delivery:** free locally. **Tastings:** regular in-store and tutored. **Services:** *en primeur*, cellarage, cellar construction advice, valuation, mail order, gift-mailing, glass hire, ice.

The Mark Reynier group, which includes La Reserve, Le Sac à Vin and Le Picoleur, was put on this earth to serve the oenological tastes of the great and good. The wealth of mature claret, ports, Burgundies and Italian reds offered over the last year has changed little, except perhaps in age. Some of the younger vintages, particularly from Spain, California and Australia, provide excellent drinking and though hardly cheap, represent attractive value. I would also recommend exploring the Walton Street cellar – a discrete hideaway in which the bottles sold in the shop can be drunk at shop prices. Ideal for those Chelsea Cinq-à-Sept rendezvous.

★★★★ 1992 Chablis, Dom. Jean Collet, Burgundy, Fr. £9.50. *Delicate and steely, with citrusy fruit and a touch of honey.* ‖ *FD, S, SM.*

★★★★ 1985 Ch. Pavie, St. Emilion, Bordeaux, Fr. £37. *Open, mature fruit with a smoky earthiness. Lovely mature claret.* ‖ *LB.*

★★★★ 1988 Grgich Hills Zinfandel, California, US. £13.50. *Full and plummy, spicy and herbaceous.* ‖ *G, BF, CH.*

★★★★★ 1993 Stoniers Reserve Pinot Noir, Mornington Peninsula, Aus. £11.99. *Soft, smoky fruits and classy use of oak.* ‖ *G, WM, CH.*

★★★★ 1986 Ch. Rabaud Promis, Sauternes, Bordeaux, Fr. £19.50. *Rich and creamy, with honeyed oak and exotic fruit flavours.* ‖ *PF, PS, CS, AP.*

HR   Howard Ripley ★★★★★

35 Eversley Crescent, London N21 1EL. Tel/Fax 0181 360 8904. Independent Wine Merchant. Wines by the case only (whole/mixed). **Opening Hours:** Mon-Fri 0900-2200, Sat 0900-1630, Sun 0900-1130. **Delivery:** free locally. **Services:** *en primeur*, mail order, glass hire. No credit cards.

In the latest edition of the Burgundy Bible Howard Ripley has again come up trumps with an exquisite selection to force Burgundy lovers to get down on their knees in praise of the twin gods Pinot Noir and Chardonnay. Interesting developments from last year include the decision to list affordable wines from the Côte Chalonnaise as well as offerings from the domaine vineyards of Faiveley, one of Burgundy's most highly respected merchants. Other familiar names from the Old Testament include the Domaine Leflaive and Guy Amiot, while the arrival of Bruno Clavelier in Vosne-Romanee indicates that the Good Book is still being written. We are not worthy.

★★★★ 1980 Meursault 1er Cru Perrières, Robert Ampeau, Burgundy, Fr. £24. *Creamy, nuttily mature, quite old fashioned wine.* ‖ *S, WMC*

★★★★★ 1993 Bâtard-Montrachet, Dom Ramonet, Burgundy, Fr. £52. *Pricy but glorious; lean but biscuity and complex. Give it time.* ‖ *WMC, WFC.*

★★★★★ 1993 Gevrey Chambertin Cuvée Vielles Vignes, D. Bachelet. Burgundy, Fr. £15.50. *Lovely cherry-and-plum wine with a touch of oak.* ‖ *BF, RM*

★★★★ 1993 Gevrey-Chambertin Cuvée Vieilles Vignes, Alain Burguet, Burgundy, Fr. £20. *Classic, intense Burgundy with raspberry fruit.* ‖ *G, CH.*

★★★★ 1990 Corton Marechaudes Dom Chandon de Briailles, Burgundy, Fr. £24. *Great, quite tough wine which needs time to open out.* ‖ *RMS.*

★★★★★ 1993 Grands Echézeaux, Engel, Burgundy, Fr. £34. *Spice galore. Great, complex wine built to last.* ‖ *G, RMS, CS.*

★★★★ 1993 Chambolle-Musigny, Alain Hudelot-Noellat, Burgundy, Fr. £13. *Very youthful, packed with raspberry and mulberry fruit and oak.* ‖ *BF, WM.*

★★★★★ 1990 Volnay Clos du Château des Ducs, Michel Lafarge, Burgundy, Fr. £33. *Volnay at its plummy-violetty best.* ‖ *BF, RMS.*

RBS   Roberson   ★★★★★

348 Kensington High Street, London W14 8NS. Tel 0171 371 2121. Fax 017l 371 4010. Independent Wine Merchant. **Opening Hours:** Mon-Sat 1000-2000, Sun 1200-1500. **Delivery:** free locally. **Tastings:** regular in-store, plus tutored sessions with producers or suppliers. **Services:** *en primeur*, mail order, glass hire, ice.

There is always a perverse pleasure in watching Kensingtonian pin-striped gentlemen and ladies-who-lunch buy their clarets from a shop that looks spookily like a cross between a scene from Mad Max and a Gaudi design musem. Why brave such confusion? The answer is in the row upon row of fine wines occupying the bent metal and curled steel racks that line the shop's walls. Among them are vintages of Bordeaux from 1924, Burgundies from 1945 and even vintage ports from 1927, not to mention the younger fare listed below. Roberson's is as much a museum as a merchant, though the exhibits can be legally removed – by those who have the wherewithall.

★★★★★ 1985 Champagne Moët et Chandon, Cuvée Dom Perignon, France £58. *Classic, maturing fizz with loads of nutty richness.* ‖ **AP.**

★★★★★ 1994 Pewsey Vale Eden Valley Riesling, S Australia, Aus. £7.50. *Ripe, appley, limey Riesling from a coolish high altitude vineyard.* ‖ **AP, LS.**

★★★★ 1992 Dr Loosen Riesling, Mosel, Ger. £6.50. *A ripe and grapey wine full of refreshingly simple citrus and honey flavours.* ‖ **CC.**

★★★★ 1990 Gattinara, Giuseppe Bianchi, Piedmont, It. £7.95. *Intense, berryish, tobaccooey alternative to Barolo.* ‖ **RM, G.**

★★★★ 1989 Weinert Cabernet Sauvignon, Mendoza, Arg. £10.95. *Soft, Spanish-style Cabernet with attractive blackcurrant fruit.* ‖ **BF, RM.**

????? 1928 Corton Clos du Roy, Grand Cru, Vergne, Burgundy, Fr. £90. *No, I have no idea what this tastes like; please write and let me know.* ‖ **D.**

★★★★★ 1982 Ch. Labégorce Zédé, Bordeaux, Fr. £19.95. *Lovely mature claret with the gentle blackberry fruit of Margaux.* ‖ **D.**

★★★★ 1991 Marqués de Griñon, Dominio de Valdepusa, Cabernet Sauvignon, Sp. £10.95. *Deep, rich concentrated fruits with oak.* ‖ **SP, P.**

★★★★ 1993 Au Bon Climat Pinot Noir, California, US. £14.95. *Great Pinot Noir with a 'wild' berry flavour. Richly satisfying.* ‖ **LB.**

★★★★ 1990 Hogue Cellars Merlot, Columbia, US. £10.95. *Good, plummy wine with tasty oak – from an underrated region.* ‖ **LB, RM.**

RW   The Rogers Wine Company   ★★★

20 Lower Street, Sproughton, Ipswich, Suffolk IP8 3AA Tel/Fax 01473 748464. Independent Wine Merchant. **Opening Hours:** visits by appointment only. **Delivery:** free locally. **Services:** mail-order, glass loan, *en primeur* offers. No credit cards.

It takes a brave man to launch a wine company in the recession years, especially one dealing mainly at the upper end of the market, but the risk obviously didn't deter Michael Rogers back in 1992. Four years on he is still going, due in part to a list that places the emphasis on quality rather than quantity. Not strictly for explorers of the brave New World but there is the odd surprise.

★★★ 1994 Ch. le Raz, Sauvignon Sec, Bergerac, Fr. £4.65. *Clean, quite grassy, Bordeaux Blanc-style wine. Refreshing.* ‖ **WMC, PY.**

★★★★ Muscat de Rivesaltes, Dom. de Força Real, Fr. £5.65. *A subtler alternative to Muscat de Beaumes de Venise. Lovely curranty stuff.* ‖ **PS, CHO.**

★★★★★ 1989 Ch. Rieussec 1er Grand Cru, Sauternes, Fr. £45.95. *Sheer class; complex flavours of dried apricot, oak and sweet plums.* ‖ **PS.**

★★★★ 1992 Laforêt Rouge Pinot Noir, J. Drouhin, Burgundy, Fr. £7.30. *Good value, anything but 'basic', red Burgundy. Certainly a wine to match many a Beaune.* ‖ **LB.**

RTW   Rose Tree Wine Co   ★★★★

15 Suffolk Parade, Cheltenham, Glos. GL50 2AE. Tel 01242 583732. Fax 01242 222159. Independent Wine Merchant. **Opening Hours:** Mon-Fri 0830-1900, Sat 0900-1800. **Delivery:** free locally. **Tastings:** regular in-store plus sessions for local wine clubs. **Services:** en primeur, mail order, gift mailing.

If this merchant's list were a house, an estate agent might describe it as bijoux and compact, with lovely little areas of Claret and Burgundy, elegant Rhônes, a collection of Italian treasures, and a delightful view of the upper end of the Australian, Portuguese and Spanish markets, plus access to some lovely sherry.

★★★★★ 1989 Weinert Carrascal, Mendoza, Arg. £7.47. *Well-made young wine with good berry fruit.* ¶ **SP, RMS.**

★★★★ 1993 Los Cameros Pinot Noir, Cameros Creek, California, US. £8.86. *Lovely fruits – strawberries and cherries dominate.* ¶ **G, RM.**

★★★★ 1988 Amarone Classico della Valpolicella Speri, Casa Girelli, Veneto, It. £9.40. *Rich, concentrated wine – at once pruney and raisiny, yet dry.* ¶ **SP, P.**

★★★ 1991 Carta de Oro Rioja Tinto, Bodegas Berberana, Sp. £5.48. *Soft, ripe, inviting Spanish red.* ¶ **SP, CH.**

★★★★ Brown Brothers Reserve Muscat, Milawa, Victoria, Aus. £10.99. *Raisins, dried fruit and molasses. Very indulgent stuff.* ¶ **PS, S.**

SAF   Safeway   ★★★★

Safeway House, 6 Millington Road, Hayes, Middlesex UB3 4AY. Tel 0181 848 8744 Fax 0181 5731865. Supermarket Chain. 362 branches. **Opening Hours:** Mon-Sat 0800-2000 (2100 on Friday), Sun 1000-1600. **Services:** glass hire, ice.

While most of the wine trade forgot the short-lived attempt to launch a National Wine Week, Liz Robertson and her team at Safeway kept its own version of it alive, twice a year – in May and late September – selling wines otherwise unavailable. Just as obstinately, Ms Robertson and her team have remained true to the cause of organic wine, sponsoring the annual Organic Wine Challenge which the editor of the Guide has had the sometimes uncomfortable honour of chairing. These, though, are sidelines to the daily business of selling wine and this is something the chain is now doing very well, thanks partly to the removal of wine racks from most stores which has allowed a broader proportion of the range to be offered in each shop. Given the constraints of price points under which all the supermarkets now struggle, the average level of quality is high and Safeway is to be congratulated for continuing its policy of selling 'young vatted' red wines from several countries.

★★★ Safeway Australian Brut, Southcorp, S Australia, Aus. £4.99. *Lively, refreshing wine with lots of fruit salady freshness.* ¶ **AP, PY.**

★★★ Safeway Cava Brut, Freixenet, Penedes, Sp. £4.99. *Soft, quite fresh, traditional Spanish fizz for people who find the Aussie version too flavoursome and fruity.* ¶ **PY.**

★★★★ Cuvée Napa, Mumm, California, US. £8.79. *Ripe, quite serious Californian fizz with lovely appley, berryish flavours.* ¶ **LS, CC.**

★★★ 1994 Bianco di Verona, Ilasi Co-op, It. £2.79. *Light, green and clean – a well-made basic wine.* ¶ **P, WFP.**

★★★★ Safeway Vin Blanc, Domaines Virginie, VdP de l'Herault, Fr. £3.65. *A simple creamy wine, clean and rich with good length.* ¶ **PY.**

★★★★ 1994 Philippe de Baudin Sauvignon, VdP d'Oc, Fr. £4.49. *Clean and ripe with really intense cassis leaf and gooseberry fruit.* ¶ **WMC, S.**

★★★ 1994 Chapel Hill Barrique-Fermented Chardonnay, Kym Milne, Balaton, Hun. £4.99. *Lean classic chardonnay characters and lots of oak.* ¶ **WM, LS.**

★★★ 1994 Safeway Australian Chardonnay, SE Australia, Aus. £3.99. *A light unoaked chardonnay with agreeable 'jelly cube' fruit.* ¶ **WFP, SF.**

**** 1994 Boschendal Chardonnay, Paarl, SA. £6.55. *Creamy, rich and nutty with serious oak and crisp ripe fruit.* ¶ **WM, WFC.**

*** 1994 Chardonnay (Oak Aged), Hugh Ryman, VdP d'Oc, Fr. £3.99. *Clean and creamy, a typical commercial style of Chardonnay.* ¶ **WM, S.**

**** 1992 Safeway Pouilly Fuissé, Luc Javelot, Burgundy, Fr. £8.99. *Rich and long with ripe, nutty fruit and creamy, commercial oak.* ¶ **S.**

**** 1993 Mercurey 'Les Mauvarennes', Dom. Faiveley, Burgundy, Fr. £9.99. *Well-oaked with a great length of rich nutty fruit, butter and toast. Good value Southern Burgundy.* ¶ **CH, WFC.**

*** 1993 Meursault 'Les Grands Charrons', Dom. Michel Bouzereau, Burgundy, Fr. £12.99. *A good, rather lean style.* ¶ **WMC, S.**

**** 1994 The Millton Vineyard Barrel-fermented Chardonnay, Gisborne, NZ. £7.99. *A very rich and spicy wine with tropical fruit.* ¶ **LS.**

**** 1988 Puligny Montrachet, Aymeric Alexis, Burgundy, Fr. £12.99. *A mature and quite old fashioned wine, nutty, concentrated, rustic and long.* ¶ **SF, AP.**

*** 1994 Czech Pinot Blanc, Nick Butler & Mark Nairn, Moravia, Cze. £3.49. *Soft, fresh and light. Pleasant party wine.* ¶ **PY.**

*** 1994 Jacques Lurton Rosé d'Anjou, Loire, Fr. £3.39. *Jammy, crisp and rather dry for an Anjou rosé, this is interesting stuff.* ¶ **AP, LS.**

**** 1994 Laperouse, Penfolds/Val d'Orbieu, Midi, Fr. £4.49. *A rich, ripe and creamy wine with hints of lemon curd. Characterful.* ¶ **WM, FF.**

*** 1993 Dom. Roche Vue, Minervois, Fr. £3.89. *A gutsy, earthy wine with tough tannins and traditional rustic character.* ¶ **G.**

*** 1992 Domaine Marbrières, Faugères, Fr. £4.39. *A herby wine, dry and pleasant with rich earthy fruit.* ¶ **P.**

**** 1993 La Cuvée Mythique, VdP d'Oc, Fr. £5.99. *A characterful wine, packed with good plummy spicy fruit.* ¶ **LB.**

**** 1993 Wolf Blass Yellow Label Cabernet Sauvignon, S Australia, Aus. £6.99. *Big, quite obvious Aussie white with tropical fruit and oak.* ¶ **BF, RMS.**

*** 1994 Safeway Merlot, VdP des Coteaux de l'Ardeche, Fr. £3.19. *Serious Merlot, full of toffee, spice and firm tannins. Will soften well.* ¶ **RM.**

*** 1994 Kirkwood Cabernet/Merlot, Hugh Ryman, Mol. £3.49. *Lots of ripe berry fruit and lingering oak flavours.* ¶ **LB.**

**** 1993 Penfolds Rawson's Retreat Bin 35, Ruby Cabernet/Shiraz, Aus. £4.45. *A good ripe and rich wine with length and well-judged oak.* ¶ **SP, P.**

*** 1993 Gorchivka Vineyard Cabernet Sauvignon, Rousse, Bul. £3.35. *A ripe and jammy Cabernet, well-made and creamy with some wood.* ¶ **G, LB.**

***** 1993 Penfolds Organic Cabernet/Merlot, Clare Valley, S Australia, Aus. £6.99. *Ripe cassis and green pepper, well made and long.* ¶ **RMS.**

*** 1991 Vina Albali Cabernet Sauvignon, Valdepenas, Sp. £6.99. *Good sweet oak, a good Spanish style, rich with honey & plum.* ¶ **SP, CH.**

*** 1994 Safeway Côtes du Luberon, Hugh Ryman, Rhône, Fr. £3.19. *Clean and simple with rich flavours typical of the style.* ¶ **P, RM.**

**** 1994 Fortant de France Syrah Rosé, Midi, Fr. £3.99. *Spicy berry fruit, pepper and redcurrant. This is good stuff.* ¶ **AP, LS.**

**** 1993 Ch. La Tour de Beraud, Costières de Nimes, Midi, Fr. £3.55. *A rich and peppery, spicy Syrah, very much in the Rhône style.* ¶ **SP. P.**

*** 1993 Ch. Montner, Côtes du Roussillon Villages, Midi, Fr. £3.59. *Good, rather tough Syrah fruit with some licorice and good length.* ¶ **RMS, RM.**

**** 1994 Galet Vineyards Syrah, Midi, Fr. £3.99. *A big, rich, jammy and smoky wine full of sweet fruit and great length.* ¶ **SP.**

*** 1993 Châteauneuf du Pape 'La Source Aux Nymphes', Rhône, Fr. £7.99. *A classically jammy Châteauneuf full of creamy strawberry fruit.* ¶ **P.**

*** 1993 Wildflower Ridge Shiraz, W Australia, Aus. £5.69. *Rich, spicy and sweetly ripe with crisp acid and good length.* ¶ **G, RMS.**

*** 1992 Safeway Casa di Giovanni, Calatrasi, VdT di Sicilia, It. £3.55. *A good characterful wine, with tones of rich tobacco, nuts and herbs.* ¶ **P.**

**** Safeway 10 Years Old Tawny Port, Oporto, Por. £9.99. *Clear, pale brick-red, with intense fruits. Sweetly balanced.* ¶ **CH, D.**

JS   Sainsbury's   ★★★★

Stamford House, Stamford Street, London SE1 9LL. Tel 0171 921 6000. Fax 0171 921 6988. Supermarket Chain. 365 branches in the UK, plus one in the Mammouth superstore in Calais. **Opening Hours:** Mon-Fri 0800-2000, Sat 0800-1800, Sun 1000-1600. **Services:** mail order via Sainsbury's magazine Tel 0800 716129, ice in some stores.

Around two years ago, the British wine trade resounded to the calls of what was privately known as the 'BBC' campaign after its stated aim to 'Bring Back Cheesman'. Well, coincidentally or not, within days of the revelation that Tesco had finally drawn level with the long-standing champion, the man who created Sainsbury's reputation as a seller of serious wines over a decade ago, was back at his old desk at the head of the department. It is too early, as we go to press, to discern how Mr C's return will change life within a supermarket whose chairman has never made a secret of his own interest in wine. Hopefully, though, it will halt a widely complained-of trend towards bullying wine producers into making wine to hit British price points. Unfortunately, with the best will in the world, maintaining wine standards while the pound falls, the chancellor squeezes and customers refuse to pay a little extra, is little easier than flowing water uphill. Which helps to explain how Sainsbury's came to sell the highly disapointing Tarrawingee wines from Australia whose only raison-d'etre was their cheapness. On the other hand, the policy of using Hugh Ryman, Geoff Merill and Peter Bright as flying winemakers has paid off handsomely; Sainsbury's Merrill-made Italian range leaves most competitors' standing. Their Wine Direct mail-order service is back too – after a rocky start – with rather more impressive wines than those offered by Tesco's similar service. It is still too early, however, to say which of the chains is doing the best job on the internet. Perhaps readers would like to let us know their experiences.

★★★   Sainsbury's Champagne Demi-Sec, Fr. £12.45. *Good malty character with some sweet cherry fruit.* ¶ **CC, D, PF.**

★★★★   Sainsbury's Champagne Extra Dry, Fr. £12.95. *Softly malty with chocolate tones on top of sweetly ripe Pinot fruit.* ¶ **AP, LS.**

★★★★   Sainsbury's Blanc de Noirs Champagne, Fr. £11.99. *Very good sweetly honeyed chocolate flavours.* ¶ **LS, PF, PY.**

★★★★   Champagne Mercier Demi-Sec, Fr. £15.99. *A great example of soft, honeyed fizz. Drink with light, creamy puddings.* ¶ **PF, CC**

★★★★   1994 Danie de Wet Grey Label Chardonnay, Robertson, SA. £5.45. *Buttery and chocolatey - like aged Champagne, with some minty oak.* ¶ **SF, WMP.**

★★★   Sainsbury's Trebbiano Garganega, VdT del Veneto, It. £2.99. *Ripe, greengage and honey flavours. Better value than much Soave.* ¶ **AP, D, LS.**

★★★   1994 Bianco di Custoza, Geoff Merrill, Veneto, It. £3.45. *Nutty and greengagey with lively acid and lots of fruit.* ¶ **AP, PY.**

★★★   1993 Ch. Les Bouhets, Bordeaux Blanc, Fr. £4.15. *Strongly grassy, crisp, catty nose with earth and gooseberry tones.* ¶ **LS, WM**

★★★   1993 Sainsbury's Sancerre, Dom. Henry Pellé, Loire, Fr. £6.95. *Attractively herby with nice ripe gooseberry fruit and good soft acid.* ¶ **S, FO.**

★★★★   1994 Grove Mill Sauvignon Blanc, Marlborough, NZ. £6.95. *Really ripe gooseberry and exotic passionfruit. Big, fat and balanced.* ¶ **SP, O.**

★★★★   1994 Villa Maria Sauvignon Blanc, Marlborough, NZ. £5.95. *Ripe, tropical and full of gooseberry fruit - well balanced and rich.* ¶ **SP, LS.**

★★★★   1994 Sainsbury Chardonnay, Cernavoda, Rom. £3.49. *Quite aromatic with a fat finish and nice length.* ¶ **WM, WMC.**

★★★   Geoff Merrill Sainsbury's Chardonnay delle Tre Venezie, Veneto, It. £3.75. *Nice, lemony nose; spritzy, uncomplicated flavours.* ¶ **AP, LS.**

★★★   1994 Chardonnay Atesino, Barrique Aged, Geoff Merrill, VdT, It. £4.99. *Toasty and leesy pineapple. Better than most S. French Chards.* ¶ **WM, D.**

★★★   Sainsbury's White Burgundy, Fr. £4.99. *Biscuit tones with a slight Bergamot character and hints of candied peel.* ¶ **FD, D.**

*** 1993 Mâcon Chardonnay, Dom. Les Ecuyers, Burgundy, Fr. £6.95. *Ripe tropical fruit, full of pineapple, honey and mango flavours.* ¶ **S, SF.**

*** 1994 Denman Estate Hunter Valley Chardonnay, New South Wales, Aus. £4.99. *Ripe and toasty with pineapple fruit and crisp acidity.* ¶ **WM.**

*** 1994 Rosemount Estate Chardonnay Semillon, SE Australia, Aus. £5.49. *Toasty tang of Semillon behind the creamy Chardonnay.* ¶ **SM, WMC.**

**** 1990 Geoff Merrill Chardonnay, S Australia, Aus. £7.95. *Impressively toasty with a limey tang. Tasting good but drink up.* ¶ **WFC, WFP.**

**** 1994 Matua Chardonnay, Eastern Bays, NZ. £6.99. *Ripe and pineappley with hints of mint, butter and toast.* ¶ **SP, SF.**

*** 1994 Boschendal Chardonnay, Paarl, SA, £6.45. *Creamy, rich and nutty with serious oak and crisp ripe fruit.* ¶ **SM, WMC.**

*** 1994 Santa Rita Estate Reserve Chardonnay, Maipo, Chi. £5.25. *Big, ripe, toasty, rich pineapple. Creamy, oaky and better than many Aussies.* ¶ **FD.**

*** 1983 Erdener Treppchen Riesling Spätlese, Moselland, Ger. £4.99. *Limey, honeyed, lean and appley with a great acid/sweetness balance.* ¶ **AP, D.**

**** Sainsbury's Alsace Pinot Blanc, Fr. £4.25. *Honeyed, ripe and attractive with good lemon flavours.* ¶ **SP.**

**** 1994 Mount Hurtle Grenache Rosé, McLaren Vale, Aus. £4.99. *Lovely, slightly soft gingery fruit with brilliant clean flavours.* ¶ **SM, WMP.**

*** 1994 Dom. de la Tuilerie Merlot Rosé, H. Ryman, Fr. £3.99. *Herby and crisp, with an extra dimension of soft, honeyed fruit.* ¶ **AP, PY.**

*** Kourtaki Vin de Pays de Crète Red, Gre. £2.99. *Dark peppery Grenache-style wine with raisiny fruit and soft tannins.* ¶ **RM.**

*** 1989 Bulgarian Reserve Cabernet Sauvignon, Lovico Suhindol Region, Bul. £3.39. *Very coconutty American oak and rich blackcurrant fruit.* ¶ **LB, CH.**

*** Sainsbury's Mendoza Cabernet Sauvignon/Malbec, Arg. £3.49. *Pleasant tarry and fragrant with smoky, ripe, mulberry fruit.* ¶ **LB, RM.**

**** 1993 Santa Carolina Merlot Gran Reserva, San Fernando, Chi. £5.25. *Serious Merlot: rich with ripe blackcurrants and raisins and coconut oak.* ¶ **RM, D.**

*** 1991 Santa Carolina Cabernet Sauvignon Reserva, Maipo, Chi. £5.25. *Intense Ribena, treacle and a wealth of sweet ripe fruit flavours, with a touch of tar.* ¶ **LB.**

*** 1992 Ch. La Vieille Cure, Fronsac, Bordeaux, Fr. £7.95. *Very herbaceous – showing effects of the vintage, but with nice new oak.* ¶ **LB, BF.**

**** 1990 Ch. Fournas Bernadotte, Haut Médoc, Bordeaux, Fr. £7.45. *Ripe and blackcurranty with soft tannins –drinking really well.* ¶ **RM, RMS.**

**** 1990 Ch. Cantemerle, Haut Médoc, Bordeaux, Fr. £14.95. *Blackcurrant and malt with treacley intensity. Soft and drinking beautifully.* ¶ **BF, RM.**

**** 1988 Ch. Grand-Puy-Lacoste, Pauillac, Grand Cru Classé, Fr. £16.95. *Hard blackcurranty core, austere and fairly tannic. Lovely in 3 yrs time.* ¶ **G, LB.**

**** 1992 St. Hallett Cab Sauv/Franc/Merlot, Barossa Valley, S Australia, Aus. £6.95. *Rich, big, Bordeaux blend. Ripe and oaky.* ¶ **RM, LB.**

*** 1993 Cabernet Sauvignon Atensino, Barrique Aged, Geoff Merrill, It. £4.99. *Crunchy blackcurrants and smooth oak.* ¶ **LB, D**

*** 1993 Chais Baumière Syrah, VdP d'Oc, Fr. £4.45. *Ripe raspberry fruit and leather character with firm tannins.* ¶ **SP, RM.**

*** Sainsbury's Crozes Hermitage, Rhône, Fr. £4.79. *Dark flavours of chocolate, malt and creosote.* ¶ **G, SP.**

*** 1994 Fleurie, La Madone, Albert Dorival, Beaujolais, Fr. £6.95. *Rich soft and meaty – just what a good Cru Beaujolais ought to be.* ¶ **SM, WMP.**

**** South Bay Vineyards California Pinot Noir, US. £4.99. *Warm bramble and spicy vanilla bouquet.* ¶ **WFP, CH.**

*** Sainsbury's Teroldego Rotaliano, Geoff Merrill, It. £3.99. *Ripe strawberry and plum, with some serious meaty flavours.* ¶ **E, LS.**

**** Sainsburys Old Oloroso, Gonzalez Fernandez, Jerez, Sp. £3.35. *Lovely nutty tones with a suggestion of oranges.* ¶ **CH.**

**** Sainsburys Vintage Character Port, Taylor's, Oporto, Por. £6.49. *Chocolate, nuts and raisins; a lovely smooth, mature port.* ¶ **CH.**

SAN   Sandiway   ★★★★

Chester Road, Sandiway, Cheshire CW8 2NH. Tel 01606 882101. Fax 01606 888407. Independent Wine Merchant. **Opening Hours:** Mon-Fri 0900-1300, 1400-2200, Sat 0900-2200, Sun 1200-1400, 1900-2200. **Tastings:** regular in store, 'seasons' of tutored tastings with visiting speakers, plus sessions for local companies and groups. **Services:** gift mailing, glass loan.

Graham Wharmby runs a rather eccentric little outfit in rural Cheshire. After Christmas he decided that they had a little too much stock, so he organised a sale. The discount increased the more you bought; starting at 1% for one bottle, 2% for two.... all the way up to 20% for 20 bottles. In two days he had solved his stock problem and presented himself with another one... so watch out for some new wines on the shelf this summer. Sandiway do not have a list so you will have to mosey up to the shop to have a look around. While you are there, you might consider joining the Sandiway S.S. (Sediment Society – for the dregs of the wine world) and risk being invited to one of Mr Wharmby's dangerously exciting evening tastings under the guidance of a winemaking guru (Last up was John Williams – not the guitar legend but the owner-winemaker at Frog's Leap in California – "a hoot" apparently).

- ★★★   Vouvray Brut, Moncontcour, Loire, Fr. £8.60. *Gently foaming appley wine with tinges of honey and lemon.* ¶ **AP.**
- ★★★★ 1994 Pfeiffer Carlyle Estate Riesling, Victoria, Aus. £5.75. *Light fruity aromas of apple and citrus with a refreshing grapefruit tang.* ¶ **AP, LS.**
- ★★★   1992 Ca'Dei Filari Chardonnay, Friuli, It. £4.95. *Lovely and simple; a light lemony Chardonnay.* ¶ **AP, WM.**
- ★★★★ 1990 Ch. Sénéjac, Médoc, Bordeaux, Fr. £9.95. *Deliciously ripe and stylish, but with the legs to last at least another five years.* ¶ **LB, CH.**
- ★★★★ 1988 Ch. Musar, Bekaa Valley, Leb. £7.99. *A potential great – remniscent of the famous 1972 and 1977 vintages.* ¶ **G, SP, RMS.**
- ★★★★ Quinta de La Rosa Finest Reserve, Oporto, Por. £9. *Plummy, intense, cherryish port with more than a touch of spice.* ¶ **CH, CS.**

SEB   Sebastopol Wines   ★★★

Sebastopol Barn, London Road, Blewbury, Oxon. OX11 9HB. Tel 01235 850471. Fax 01235 850776. Independent Wine Merchant. **Opening Hours:** Tues-Sat 1030-1730. **Delivery:** free locally. **Services:** mail order, glass loan, *en primeur* offers, accessories.

'We look forward to seeing you in the barn'. Barbara Affleck's invitation is a tempting one – considering what she has to offer. Stuff like Château Beaucastel – of which there are no fewer than nine vintages – Domaine Leroy Burgundies, Grange galore and Selvapiana Tuscans. By now you will have probably got the picture and will be already happily barn-dancing your way to Blewbury.

- ★★★★★ 1983 Savennières, Dom. de la Bizolière, Soulez, Loire, Fr. £6.29. *First class organic wine. Rich, dry honeyed Chenin.* ¶ **CS, PF.**
- ★★★★★ 1992 Puligny-Montrachet Les Garennes, Olivier Leflaive, Burgundy, Fr. £18.98. *Lovely, leafy, oaky wine. Classy white Burgundy.* ¶ **WMC.**
- ★★★★ 1989 Riesling Bergheim 'Engelgarten', Marcel Deiss, Alsace, Fr. £8.59. *Serious appley Riesling with a little petrolly maturity.* ¶ **S, FO.**
- ★★★★★ 1991 Henschke Cabernet/Merlot, Abbott's Prayer, Lenswood, Aus. £13.95. *Finely crafted and full of flavour. A real Aussie classic.* ¶ **G, LB.**
- ★★★★★ 1985 Ch. Haut-Bages-Liberal, Pauillac, Bordeaux, Fr. £14.59. *Richly fruity ripe claret, full of velvety-smooth tannins.* ¶ **BF, CH.**
- ★★★★ 1991 Côtes du Ventoux 'La Vieille Ferme', Jean Perrin, Rhône, Fr. £4.29. *Delicious crunchy red fruit and smoky, gamey, spice.* ¶ **SP, RM.**
- ★★★★★ 1989 Ch. de Beaucastel, Châteauneuf-du-Pape, Rhône, Fr. £29.95. *Massively complex beast – a brooding monster.* ¶ **G, SP, RMS.**

SK — Seckford ★★★★

2 Betts Avenue, Martlesham Heath, Ipswich, Suffolk IP5 7RH. Tel 01473 626681 Fax 01473 626004. Independent Wine Merchant. **Opening Hours:** Tues–Sat 1000-1800. **Delivery:** free locally. **Tastings:** regular in-store and tutored, plus organised events. **Services:** en primeur, glass loan, gift-mailing.

The cosy atmosphere of Seckford is amply reflected in the small but perfectly formed range of wines on offer by the case. Organised in neat little sections it is particularly good on affordable Claret (with the exception of the odd case of Latour) but is equally well-turned out as far as its Australian wines are concerned. Wine is sold exclusively by the case but if you don't like your purchase you won't have to give it to the elderly aunt for Christmas. Seckford will exchange it for something tastier.

- ★★★★ 1990 Angelo's Old Vine White, Russian River, California, US. £9.50. *Richly aromatic white blend with great concentration of flavour.* ¶ **WM, SP.**
- ★★★★★ 1989 Dr Loosen Riesling Spatlese, Mosel, Ger. £8.95. *Wonderful Riesling combining the ripeness of the vintage with Mosel elegance.* ¶ **AP, D.**
- ★★★★ 1989 Ch. Pitray, Côtes de Castillon, Bordeaux, Fr. £7.25. *Plummy ripeness and genuine elegance. Classy.* ¶ **RM, BF.**
- ★★★★★ 1992 Bourgogne Passetoutgrain, Henri Jayer, Burgundy, Fr. £7.95. *Light and fruity blend of Pinot Noir with Gamay.* ¶ **SM, WMC.**
- ★★★★★ 1988 Barolo, Aldo Vajra, Piedmont, It. £14.39. *Still mighty tannic, but softening into sumptuous wild fruit and gamey flavours.* ¶ **G, RMS.**

SEL — Selfridges ★★★★

400 Oxford Street, London W1A 1AB. Tel 0171-629 1234 Fax 0171-495 8321. Department Store. **Opening Hours:** Mon-Sat 0930-1900 (Thurs until 2000). **Delivery:** free nationally for orders over £100 or on any value order for 12 Bottles or more to Selfridges Gold Account Customers. **Tastings:** daily in-store between 1300-1800. 4 tutored tastings per annum through Gold Account Privilege. **Services:** mail order, gift mailing, free glass hire, export, wine fair.

William Longstaff, Wine and Spirits Buyer, "enthusiasm boiling over", aims to make Selfridges the most exciting retailer in the wine trade. While we welcome the pepping-up of the list and the introduction of tutored tastings and vineyard visits, there is still a long way to go before Mr L and his team come anywhere near rivalling the ambience of an Oddbins store, or of offering anything like the consistently thrilling and maverick Adnams store. Still, the range is one of the most comprehensive around and if you are after Vintage Grand Cuvée Champagne in gift boxes at not wholly unreasonable prices, or what must be the broadest selection of Israeli wines outside Tel Aviv, then jump on a No. 88 bus forthwith.

- ★★★★ Pongracz Brut, Bergkelder, Coastal Region, SA. £9.99. *Classy, very rich, Champagne-like fizz in a similarly classy bottle.* ¶ **AP, LS, D.**
- ★★★★★ 1992 Crichton Hall Chardonnay, California, US. £11.99. *Made by an Englishman. Buttery rich, very seductive wine.* ¶ **WMC, WM.**
- ★★★★ 1993 Jermann 'Where The Dreams Have No End', VdT, Friuli, It. £35. *Italian superstar's top white; not cheap but creamily fascinating.* ¶ **D, O.**
- ★★★★★ 1989 Meerlust Rubicon, Stellenbosch, SA. £10.29. *Fine concentrated claret style with rich raisiny fruit and soft silky tannins.* ¶ **BF, RMS.**
- ★★★★ 1990 Ernst & Julio Gallo Northern Sonoma Estate Cabernet Sauvignon, California, US. £32. *Big, very blackcurranty wine with subtle oak; at once classy and fruitily Californian.* ¶ **LB, RMS.**
- ★★★★ 1991 Saintsbury Reserve Carneros Pinot Noir, California, US. £22.99. *Very rich, with up-front spice and rich plum and damson fruit. Fantastic.* ¶ **BF, CS.**
- ★★★★ 1991 Sauternes Baron Philippe, Bordeaux, Fr. £12.99. *Creamy, rich and honeyed with good fresh fruit.* ¶ **D, PS.**

SHW   Shaws of Beaumaris   ★★★★

17 Castle Street, Beaumaris, Anglesey, Gwynedd LL58 8AP. Tel 01248 810328. Fax 01248 810328. Independent Wine Merchant. **Opening Hours:** Mon-Sat 1000-1730, Wed 1000-1300. **Delivery:** free locally. **Services:** glass loan.

P.G. Shaw is a self-confessed fanatic when it comes to Italian wines. Look for the 1991 Barbera d'Asti, Ceppi Storici, the 1988 Valpolicella La Grola, Allegrini, the Vino Nobile di Montepulciano and the Roero Arneis, Malvira. Bordeaux and Burgundy are perfectly acceptable and there is a comprehensive range of good Beaujolais. The wines are chosen to represent value and when they do creep over the £20 mark they are worth their inclusion. Representatives from Australia and California are strong and it is interesting to see the Welsh Cariad wines on the list.

★★★★   David Wynn Brut, Aus. £7.99. *Good value, easy going, quite fruity fizz from Adam Wynn.* ¶ *AP, LS.*

★★★★   1993 Sancerre, Andre Dézat, Loire, Fr. £9.35. *Proper Sancerre, with clean fruit, steeliness and creamy length. Subtle and good.* ¶ *CC, S.*

★★★★   1989 Edna Valley Chardonnay, California, US. £8.99. *Masterful buttery Chardonnay from south of San Francisco. Deliciously Californian.* ¶ *WFP, SF.*

★★★★   1993 Albariño Lagar de Cervera, Rias Baixas, Galicia, Sp. £7.99. *Delightfully aromatic and beautifully balanced. One of Spain's best white wines.* ¶ *P, S.*

★★★★   1993 Clos de Centeilles, Caragnanissime de Centeilles, Minervois, Fr. £5.85. *Proof that the Carignan can produce rich ripe, spicy reds.* ¶ *LB, RMS.*

★★★★   1988 Valpolicella 'La Grola', Allegrini, Veneto, It. £8.85. *Serious Valpolicella with highly concentrated cherry and plum-skin fruit.* ¶ *P, SP.*

ES   Edward Sheldon   ★★★

New Street, Shipston-on-Stour, Warwickshire CV36 4EN. Tel 01608 661409. Fax 01608 663166. Independent Wine Merchant. **Opening Hours:** Mon-Fri 0900-1900, Sat 0900-1700. **Delivery:** free locally. **Tastings:** regular in-store. **Services:** *en primeur*, mail order, gift mailing, glass hire.

A very traditional merchant with a touching faith in the way the world ought to be run. "If the Mayor of Ste Croix du Mont doesn't know how to make good wine,who does?" asks the list. Well, we know of all sorts of French mayors and big-wigs within the Appellation Contrôlée authorities who make rotten wine. Fortunately, in the case of Ste Croix du Mont, Edward Sheldon are absolutely on the button - the mayor's Ch. de Berbec is better than many a Sauternes. Rhônes from Beaucastel are impressive too, as are the Coopers Creek New Zealand wines. Enthusiasts for old fashioned Burgundy will like the reds here, too, but lovers of exciting wines from California should look elsewhere. Maybe Napa should appoint a better winemaker as mayor.

★★★★   Champagne Joseph Perrier, Cuvée Royale Rosé, Fr. £19.78. *Lovely, soft, maturing pink fizz with raspberry fruit.* ¶ *AP.*

★★★★   1994 Ch. Thieuley Blanc, Cuvée Francis Courselle, Bordeaux, Fr. £6.58. *Rich, honeyed, peachy wine with a touch of gooseberry.* ¶ *LB, G.*

★★★★★ 1989 Dr. Loosen Riesling Graacher Himmelreich, Mosel, Fr. £7.85. *The Mosel and the Riesling at their most refreshing, limey appley best.* ¶ *AP, S.*

★★★★★ 1992 E & E Black Pepper Shiraz, Barossa Valley Winery, Aus. £12.78. *Explosive plum and damson fruit from 70-year-old vines.* ¶ *RM, SP.*

★★★★   1992 Fairview Cabernet Franc/Merlot Reserve, Paarl, SA. £7.49. *Serious blend from one of South Africa's most experimental winemakers.* ¶ *G, RMS.*

★★★★★ 1985 Graham's Vintage Port, Grahams, Douro, Portugal £20.99. *Superbly rich and concentrated port.* ¶ *CC, CS.*

★★★★   1989 Ch. Gruaud Larose, St. Julien, Bordeaux, Fr. £27.12. *Ripe, cedary wine from a ripe vintage. Needs at least five years.* ¶ *LB, CH.*

SAS   Sherston Wine Company   ★★★

97 Victoria Street, St Albans AL1 3TJ. Tel 01727 858841. Independent Wine Merchant. **Opening Hours:** Tues-Fri 1130-1900, Sat 0930-1800. **Delivery:** free locally. **Tastings:** regularly. **Services:** glass hire.

Perfect proof that size really doesn't matter. The relatively tiny list packs an amazing number of virile wines from all over the world within its pages; not least a marvellous range from almost all of Italy's principal wine regions, including Sicily and Sardinia. Spain is also given a rather hefty weighting with some prize wines from producers such as Castello Ygay and CVNE, and there are some great wines from Portugal that contribute to making this the Iberian wine lovers' guide to heaven.

***   1994 Bianco Di Custoza, Cavalchina, Veneto, It. £5.89. *Subtle, creamy and youthfully fresh.* ¶ *WFP, LS.*
***   1994 Verdicchio di Castelli di Jesi, Santa Barbara, Marche, It. £6.99. *Fresh young wine, with a herby-limey tang.* ¶ *SP.*
****   1991 Hermitage Rouge, E Guigal, Rhône, Fr. £21.99. *Serious, quite 'wild' tasting young Hermitage which will soften with time.* ¶ *RM, RMS.*

SV   Smedley Vintners   ★★★★

Rectory Cottage, Lilley, Luton, Beds. LU2 8LU. Tel 01462 768214. Fax 01462 768332. Independent Wine Merchant. Wine by the case only. **Opening Hours:** Mon-Fri 0900-1830, Sat, Sun 0900-1800. **Delivery:** free locally. **Services:** cellarage, *en primeur*, mail order, gift mailing, glass hire, ice. No credit cards.

"The days of the small merchant may be numbered... but we continue to survive, grow and to make a profit." Upbeat words from Mr Smedley who is the very embodiment of the "small wine merchant" and, as I declared in the guide last year, one of my favourites. Still strong on Italy, with wines from Antinori and Prunotto, he also has the Montes range from Chile, William Wheeler from California and a new selection from Domaine Saint Pierre in the Rhône. Mr. S would love to carry a wider range but at the moment "the economics do not make sense".

****   Champagne Laurent Perrier Brut, Fr. £16.25. *Delicate, peachy fruits. Soft and yeasty – complex and delicious.* ¶ *D, AP, S.*
****   1993 St. Veran, Rodet, Burgundy, Fr. £5.88. *Good value Burgundy. Buttery oak balanced by fresh fruits and crisp acidity.* ¶ *D, WM, FD.*
*****   1994 Jackson Estate Sauvignon Blanc, Marlborough, NZ. £8.23. *Gorgeous ripe, gooseberryish wine from a vineyard opposite Cloudy Bay.* ¶ *O, WMC.*
****   1994 Jackson Estate Chardonnay, Marlborough, NZ. £8.11. *Lovely tropical fruit. Richly mouthfilling.* ¶ *WM, LS.*
*****   1992 Mitchelton Reserve Marsanne, Victoria, Aus. £7.40. *One of the white grapes of the Rhône; peachy, floral, rich and fascinating.* ¶ *SF.*
***   1992 Wheeler Winery Merlot, California, US. £9.52. *Good, quite approachable plummy cherryish Merlot.* ¶ *G, RMS.*
****   1991 Weinert Malbec, Mendoza, Arg. £8.20. *A typically spicy example of an underrated Bordeaux and Cahors black grape — at home in Argentina.* ¶ *SP.*
****   1991 Rocca Rubia Carignano del Sulcis, Santadi, Sardinia, It. £9.33. *Rich, intense warm-climate wine with berry fruit and pepper.* ¶ *P, SP.*
****   1991 Tignanello, Antinori, Tuscany, It. £21.15. *The classic Super Tuscan, wth ripe, slightly earthy plummy fruit. Complex and tasty.* ¶ *RM P.*
****   1990 Prunotto Barolo Cru Bussia, Piedmont, It. £12.34. *Serious Barolo, built to last, with intense leathery berryish flavours.* ¶ *SP, P.*
****   1990 Tokaji Aszu 5 Puttonyos, The Royal Tokaji Wine Co, Hun. £14.08. *Good, modern Tokay with intense limey flavours. Sweet but not cloying.* ¶ *PF, PS.*
****   Churchill's 10 Year Old Tawny, Douro, Por. £12.22. *Fresh, tangy port with flavours of ripe plum and orange-peel. Delicious served cool.* ¶ *CC, CS.*

SMF   Somerfield   ★★★

Somerfield House, Hawkfield Business Park, Whitchurch Lane, Bristol BS14 OTJ. Tel 0117 935 9359. Fax 0117 978 0629. Supermarket Chain. 617 branches. **Opening Hours:** Mon-Sat 0830-1800 (some stores open until 2000 during the week), Sat 0830-1800, Sun 1000-1600. **Tastings:** regular in-store.

As the people behind nuclear power stations have discovered, it is not enough simply to devise a new name; you have to go out selling it to the public. Which helps to explain why, having transformed most of their Gateway stores into smart new Somerfields, the powers-that-be indulged in the most agressive bout of wine discounting Britain has ever seen. For the first time, bottles were openly being sold below cost in an effort both to attract new customers and to persuade existing shoppers to find a little space in their baskets for wine. Angela Mount is a good buyer, as is evident from many of the wines in her range; the supposed bargains however, often did credit neither to Somerfield nor the region from which they came.

****   Prince William Champagne, Fr. £11.79. *Clean, dry and refreshing fizz.* ❙ *AP, LS.*

***   Touraine Rosé Brut, Cave de Viticulteurs de Vouvray, Loire, Fr. £5.99. *Crisp and light with apple and raspberry flavours.* ❙ *SF.*

****   1988 Champagne Lanson Vintage, Fr. £23.99. *Very classy maturing Champagne which would be worth keeping for another few years.* ❙ *AP, S.*

****   Martini Brut Special Cuvée, Martini & Rossi, Pessione, It. £5.99. *Clean, citrussy, dry fizz.* ❙ *WFP, PY.*

***   1993 Somerfield Muscadet de Sèvre Et Maine, Jean Beauquin, Loire, Fr. £2.99. *Well-balanced, slightly sweet and appley Muscadet.* ❙ *LS, FO.*

****   1994 Dom. Bordeneuve VdP des Côtes de Gascogne Blanc, Yves Grassa, Fr. £3.49. *Clean peary wine from the master of this style.* ❙ *S, PY, AP.*

****   1994 Domaine La Tuiliere Chardonnay, VdP d'Oc, Hugh Ryman, Fr. £3.99. *Fresh, modern, nicely understated melony pineappley wine.* ❙ *WM, S.*

****   1994 José Canepa y Cia Sauvignon Blanc, Maipo, Chi. £3.69. *Fresh, leafy, slightly tropical flavour. Bordeaux meets New Zealand.* ❙ *S, PY.*

****   1994 Le Piat d'Or Chardonnay, Piat Pere et Fils, Midi, Fr. £3.99. *Rich and creamy fruit flavours. A Piat d'Or worth drinking!* ❙ *PY.*

****   1994 Somerfield Chardonnay, VdP de l"Herault, Delta Domaines, Fr. £3.89. *A refreshing citrussy Chardonnay.* ❙ *WFP, WM.*

****   1994 Viña Santa Rita Reserva Chardonnay, Maipo, Chi. £5.05. *Soft, ripe, quite easy going wine.* ❙ *WM, S.*

***   Somerfield Liebfraumilch, Rheinberg Kellerei, Rheinhessen, Ger. £2.45. *Light, grapey and simple.* ❙ *SP, PY.*

***   1992 Somerfield Rheinhessen Spätlese, Rheinberg Kellerei, Ger. £3.49. *Fresh fruit aroma with peaches and honey flavours.* ❙ *CC, S.*

****   1994 Gewürztraminer, Caves de Turkheim, Alsace, Fr. £4.99. *Good, perfumed rich and classic.* ❙ *AP, LS.*

****   1994 Laperouse, Penfolds/Val d'Orbieu, Midi, Fr. £4.49. *A rich, ripe and creamy wine with hints of lemon curd. Characterful.* ❙ *SP.*

***   Somerfield Corbières, Val D'Orbieu, Midi, Fr. £2.99. *Good value, fresh, quite rustic wine. A perfect party red.* ❙ *PY, LS.*

***   1992 Domaine d'Abrens, Maison Jeanjean, Minervois, Fr. £3.35. *Earthy, slightly leathery wine; ideal for drinking with cold meat.* ❙ *LB, CH.*

***   Somerfield Claret, Louis Eschenauer, Bordeaux, Fr. £3.29. *An unusually ripe-tasting basic claret; green peppery with some blackcurrant.* ❙ *LB.*

***   1994 Val d'Orbieu Syrah Rosé, Midi, Fr. £3.05. *Good, peppery, berryish refreshing and dry.* ❙ *WM, AP.*

****   1993 Jacob's Creek Shiraz/Cabernet, Orlando Wines, S E Australia, Aus. £4.29. *Simple, ripe jammy mouthful.* ❙ *G, SP.*

***   1990 Châteauneuf-du-Pape Domaine de la Solitude, Rhône, Fr. £8.99. *Clean, fruity and fresh.* ❙ *LB, RM.*

* * * 1995 Cape Selection Pinotage, Vinimark, Stellenbosch, SA. *Strawberries and bananas; South Africa's answer to 'Nouveau'.* £3.49. ¶ *P, RMS.*
* * * 1991 Caves de Buxy, Burgundy, Fr. £4.99. *Concentrated succulent berry fruits.* ¶ *HC.*
* * * * 1990 Chianti Classico Montecchio, Tuscany, It. £4.05. *Tasty wine with good, herby flavours.* ¶ *LS, P.*
* * * * 1990 Taurino Salice Salentino Riserva, Puglia, It. £5.05. *Hefty, tobaccoey wine with heaps of flavour.* ¶ *HC, G.*
* * * * 1991 Alianca Bairrada Reserva, Caves Alianca, Por. £3.49. *Rich, tobaccoey wine with a touch of spice. Could be worth keeping.* ¶ *SP, G.*
* * * * 1993 El Dragon Tempranillo, Berberana, Sp. £4.19. *Fruity nose with spice and cooked aromas; will last well.* ¶ *LB.*
* * * * 1987 Viña Albali Valdepeñas Gran Reserva, Bodegas Felix Solis, Valdepeñas, Spain £4.99. *Soft, maturing, quite rich and earthy.* ¶ *LB, HC.*
* * * * Castillo de Liria Moscatel, Gandia, Valencia, Sp. £3.19. *Lovely fresh grapey, honeyed wine. Sweet but not in the least bit cloying.* ¶ *PS.*
* * * * 1989 Château Bastor-Lamontage, Sauternes, Fr. £7.69. *Great-value sweet Bordeaux, with flavours of dried apricot and marmalade.* ¶ *PF, PS.*
* * * * Somerfield Amontillado Sherry, Perez Megia, Jerez, Sp. £4.19. *Lovely, rich caramel, nuts and toffee combination.* ¶ *S, AP.*
* * * * Somerfield Cream Sherry, Perez Megia, Jerez, Sp. £4.19. *Balanced sweet and nutty sherry.* ¶ *AP.*
* * * * Tawny Royal Oporto, Royal Oporto Wine Company, Oporto, Por. £5.39. *Well-balanced fruity, toffee'd Port.* ¶ *CC.*

SOM Sommelier Wine Co ★★★★

The Grapevine, 23 St. George's Esplanade, St Peter Port, Guernsey, Channel Islands GY1 2BG. Tel 01481 721677. Fax 01481 716818. Independent Wine Merchant. **Opening Hours:** Mon-Thurs 1000-1730. Fri 1000-1800. Sat 0930-1730. **Delivery:** free locally. **Tastings:** regular tastings for clubs plus an evening class. **Services:** *en primeur*, mail order, gift mailing.

"We always hope that you have as much enjoyment drinking the wines as we did finding them." So says Richard Allisette and goes on to claim that every wine he stocks has been tasted at least once, usually two or three times. However much fun the selection process, it obviously pays off when you look at the list. Every single wine would be welcomed into the *Guide*'s cellar, particularly Conterno's Piedmontese offerings, Ridge Zinfandel or Pieropan's Recioto di Soave. Bear in mind, though, before you get too overexcited, that Sommelier is located on Guernsey and their prices are subject only to Channel Islands duty and no VAT.

* * Vouvray Brut, Didier Champalou, Loire, Fr. £5.99. *Crisp and fresh fruity style. A touch of honey and bananas.* ¶ *D, AP.*
* * * * 1994 Neudorf Moutere Semillon, Nelson, NZ. £9.50. *More like ripe Sauvignon than Semillon, with gooseberries and barely ripe peaches.* ¶ *D, S.*
* * * * 1993 Chablis Vieilles Vignes, Gilbert Picq, Burgundy, Fr. £9.95. *Green, grassy and steely with lovely fresh fruit.* ¶ *S, AP, WFC.*
* * * * 1994 Bethany Estate Late Harvest Riesling, S Australia, Aus. £5.20 (half). *Luscious, baked apples – complete with brown sugar and cloves! Great winemaking from the Germanic region of Barossa.* ¶ *PF.*
* * * * 1990 Capitel San Rocco Rosso, Tedeschi, Veneto, It. £5.80. *Leathery with dark cherry fruits, tobacco and chocolate.* ¶ *P, WM.*
* * * 1994 David Wynn Shiraz, S Australia, Aus. £5.30. *Medium-bodied, ripe berryish, peppery wine to drink with lamb.* ¶ *SP, G.*
* * * * 1991 Saintsbury Reserve Carneros Pinot Noir, California, US. £17.95. *Smoky herbs and pepper. Luscious, full fruits.* ¶ *WM, CH, D.*
* * * * Quinta de La Rosa Finest Reserve, Oporto, Por. £8.40. *Plummy, intense, cherryish port with more than a touch of spice.* ¶ *CH, CS.*

SPR · Spar · ★★★

32-40 Headstone Drive, Harrow, Middlesex HA3 5QT. Tel 0181 863 5511. Fax 0181 863 0603. Supermarket Chain. 2350 branches. **Opening Hours:** vary between: Mon-Sun 0800-2200/2300. **Delivery:** at discretion of individual stores. **Tastings:** occasional in-store, available on request. **Services:** glass hire, ice (selected stores). Credit cards at discretion of individual stores.

With 1.3m customers passing through its 2350 shops, Spar is, like the Co-op, potentially one of the strongest forces in British wine retailing. Also like the Co-op, it remains handicapped by the autonomy of shop managers and the tendency of customers to restrict their purchasing to rather less hedonistic fare than wine. But, as we've mentioned in previous editions of the *Guide*, Philippa Carr is not easily dissuaded from her crusade to get good, interesting wines onto those shelves. And just look at the list below to see what you might find if you are lucky enough to wander into a Spar shop whose manager has become a member of the Carr lobby.

- ★★★ Spar Viognier, Val d'Orbieu, Midi, Fr. £4.99. *Floral and richly perfumed with apricots, peaches and banana.* ¶ *D, O, CH.*
- ★★★★ 1994 Orlando Chardonnay, S. E. Australia, Aus. £5.25. *Buttery and honeyed with rich fruit.* ¶ *WMC, D.*
- ★★★★ 1994 Neethlingshof Gewürztraminer, Stellenbosch, S.A. £4.39. *Spicy wine with a smell of parma violets. Lemony and deliciously perfumed.* ¶ *O, SP, CH.*
- ★★★ Spar Rosé de Syrah, Val d'Orbieu, Midi, Fr. £3.35. *Crisp and fresh with full red fruits — strawberries and cream.* ¶ *D, PY.*
- ★★★★ 1993 Lindemans Bin 45 Cabernet Sauvignon, S. Australia, Aus. £4.99. *Ripe, blackcurranty, great value wine with quite obvious oak.* ¶ *WM, BF, CH.*
- ★★★ 1993 Corbans Wines Cooks Cabernet Sauvignon, Hawkes Bay, NZ. £4.99. *Luscious blackberry fruit, spearmint and spice.* ¶ *WMC.*
- ★★★ 1990 Ribera del Duero Senorio de Nava Crianza, Sp. £5.99. *Rich damson fruit, caramelly oak and smooth tannins.* ¶ *P, SP.*
- ★★★ Spar Old Cellar L.B.V. Port, Symington Group, Por. £7.19. *Sweet plum fruit, dark tobaccoey tannins and herbs.* ¶ *CC, CH.*

SUM · Summerlee · ★★★

Summerlee Road, Finedon, Northampton NN9 5LL. Tel/Fax 01933 682221. Independent Wine Merchant. **Opening Hours:** Mon-Fri 0915-1230. **Delivery:** free locally (plus London, Oxford and Cambridge) for two cases or more. **Services:** cellarage, *en primeur*, mail order, gift mailing, glass hire. No credit cards.

A new location and new partners sees Summerlee march into 1996 in even better shape. Freddy Price is still the buyer, a fact reflected in the excellent European selection, most especially the impressive list of fine German wines. Paul Anheuser, Schloss Saarstein, Balthasar Ress and Max Ferd Richter are not names that will be recognised in many households, but now that we've got VE day out of the way, perhaps the Great British punter will begin to recognise the merits of fine Mosel wines and there'll be a bit less Blue Nun over the white cliffs of Dover.

- ★★★ 1990 Ch. d'Arlay, Fleur du Savignin, Côtes de Jura, Fr. £7.13. *Nutty, rich wine from an unusual grape variety.* ¶ *LS.*
- ★★★★ 1991 Chassagne Montrachet Vieilles Vignes, B. Morey, Burgundy, Fr. £12.40. *Toffee and buttery oak; rich ripe fruits and crisp acidity.* ¶ *D, WM.*
- ★★★★★ 1989 Graacher Himmelreich Riesling Spätlese, Max Ferd Richter, Mosel, Ger. £9.45. *Floral, peachy fruits with a honeyed sweetness.* ¶ *SP, O.*
- ★★★★ 1992 Serriger Schloss Saarsteiner Riesling Kabinett, Mosel, Ger. £8.07. *Apricots and melons, tropical fruits and a lemon zest.* ¶ *O, WMC.*
- ★★★★ 1985 Ch. Léoville Barton, St Julien, Bordeaux, Fr. £22.09. *Beautifully matured, earthy claret. Classic cigar-box flavours and smooth tannins.* ¶ *LB.*

T&W T&W ★★★

51 King Street, Thetford, Norfolk IP24 2AU. Tel 01842 765646. Independent Wine Merchant. **Opening Hours:** Mon-Fri 0930-1730, Sat 0930-1300. **Delivery:** free locally. **Tastings:** regular in-store. **Services:** cellarage, *en primeur*, mail order, gift mailing, glass hire.

The "other" East Anglian merchant, T&W is commendable for its eccentric support for similarly eccentric producers like Willi Opitz and Umathum in Austria, Roberto Bava in Italy and Kent Rasmussen in California, all of whom make wines quite unlike those of their neighbours. More conservative customers should have no fear though; the range of classics is unusually sound, with some particularly attractive old vintages.

★★★★ 1991 Dom. de la Bongran Cuvée Tradition, Selection E. J. Thevenet, Burgundy, Fr. £12.95. *Buttery, toffee oak and crisp appley fruit.* ¶ **D, SM.**

★★★★★ 1989 Kent Ramussen Pinot Noir, Carneros, California, US. £13.95. *Soft, summer fruits and smooth, smoky tannins.* ¶ **WM, D, CH.**

★★★★★ 1992 Weisser Schilfmandl Muskat, Vin Paille, Opitz, A. £34.95. *Extraordinary wine made from grapes dried on straw mats. An experience.* ¶ **D.**

★★★★★ 1992 Umathum St Laurent, A. £16.55. *Serve this blind and your guests will swear that it's a top class mulberryish Pinot Noir.* ¶ **WM, D, CH.**

★★★★★ 1988 Barbera d'Asti, Bava, Piedmont, It. £5.80. *Dark plum and damson fruit, tobacco and chocolate. Lovely smooth wine.* ¶ **P, RM, SP.**

TAN Tanners ★★★★

26 Wyle Cop, Shrewsbury, Shropshire SY1 1XD. Tel 01743 232007. Fax 01743 344401. Independent Wine Merchant. **Opening Hours:** Mon-Sat 0900-1800. **Delivery:** free locally. **Tastings:** regular in-store, plus tutored sessions with the likes of Gerard Jaboulet, Ernst Loosen. **Services:** *en primeur*, mail order, gift mailing, glass hire, ice.

Four retail outlets either side of the Welsh border represent the public face of this enthusiastic and go-ahead company which was founded in 1872. The headquarters and main shop are at Wyle Cop in Shrewsbury in an extremely attractive Dickensian cellar which has been in continuous use as a wine merchants since 1842. Not content with the image of an agreeable provincial wine merchant, Tanners have developed a business that now sees two-thirds of their trade coming from the restaurant and hotel sector, and a wine list that reaches 12,000 homes up and down the country. They are also extremely active in organising or participating in events, dinners, fairs and tastings around the region, and are one of the relatively few merchants who make buying '*en primeur*' an exciting, reassuring and cost-effective exercise.

★★★★ Champagne Joseph Perrier, Cuvée Royale Rosé, Fr. £22. *Lovely, soft, maturing pink fizz with raspberry fruit.* ¶ **D, AP.**

★★★★ Pongracz Brut, Bergkelder, Coastal Region, SA. £8.99. *Classy, very rich, Champagne-like fizz in a very classy bottle.* ¶ **D, AP, S.**

★★★★★ 1992 Babich Irongate Chardonnay, Hawkes Bay, NZ. £12.99. *Soft, ripe Chardonnay with tropical flavours and the freshness of lemon balm.* ¶ **WMC.**

★★★★★ 1989 Dr. Loosen Riesling Graacher Himmelreich, Mosel, Ger. £7.49. *The Mosel and the Riesling at their most refreshing, limey appley best.* ¶ **O, CC.**

★★★★ 1992 Domaine St Eulalie Minervois, Midi, Fr. £3.70. *Good value, flavoursome country red.* ¶ **WFP, G.**

★★★★ 1991 Craigmoor Shiraz, New South Wales, Aus. £6.99. *Quite European-style Aussie; ripe yet restrained, with good peppery berry flavours.* ¶ **SP, RM.**

★★★★ 1991 Rioja Conde de Salceda Fourth Crianza, Vina Salceda, Sp. £4.30. *A rich cocktail of mulberry and oak flavours. Deliciously Spanish.* ¶ **P, G.**

★★★★ Jose Maria Da Fonseca Succs, Moscatel Do Setubal 20 Yr Old, Por. £11.95. *Mature nutty oak balanced by fresh orange peel and berry fruits.* ¶ **C, CH, PS.**

120 Merchants

CT   Charles Taylor   ★★★★

Cornwall Road, Waterloo, London SE1 8TW. Tel 0171 928 8151 Fax 0171 928 3415. Independent Wine Merchant. **Opening Hours:** Mon-Fri 0900-1700. **Delivery:** free locally. **Services:** *en primeur*, mail order.

Charles Taylor, Master of Wine, continues to expand his eponymous company by the simple expedient of concentrating his efforts in one area and sticking to it – and of trusting his own taste for fairly conservative wine flavours. With the exception of the Redbank Winery and Evans and Tate from Australia, all of Mr Taylor's selection is chosen from France, chiefly Burgundy, but with forays into Alsace, the Loire, Champagne and the Rhône. The properties and domaines whose wines he sells are chiefly little-known traditionalists of mostly unimpeachable quality, including the likes of Ancien Domaine Auffray, Gerard Thomas and Lucien Boillot. There is plenty here for the enthusiast who is prepared to buy by the case.

★★★★   Champagne Fernand Bonnet Carte d'Or, Blanc de Blancs Brut, Fr. £13.20. *Lovely, lemony, creamy fizz with real class.* ⑪ *CC, FD, S.*

★★★★   1992 Ch. Thieuley Blanc, Cuvee Francis Courselle, Bordeaux, Fr. £7.30. *Crisp, appley and fresh with gentle acidity.* ⑪ *WFC, WM.*

★★★   1993 Chablis, Dom. Alain Geoffroy, Burgundy, Fr. £7.75. *Lovely flinty, melony Chablis, honeyed and crisp. Perfect for a picnic.* ⑪ *SM, S, WFC.*

★★★★   1992 Puligny Montrachet, Dom. Louis Carillon, Burgundy, Fr. £16.10. *Biscuity rich, with pineapple fruit and leafy freshness.* ⑪ *WMC, AP, LS.*

★★★★   1993 Gnangara Shiraz, Evans & Tate, W Australia, Aus. £6.35. *Young, quite old fashioned Shiraz; decidedy Rhône-like.* ⑪ *RMS, CH, SP.*

★★★★   1992 St. Aubin 1er Cru 'La Chateniére', Dom. Gérard Thomas, Burgundy, Fr. £10.70 *Classy raspberryish rustic Pinot.* ⑪ *RM, CH, CC, WFP.*

★★★★   1989 Coteaux du Layon Rochefort, Moelleux, Dom. de la Motte, Loire, Fr. £9.30. *Lovely mature, honeyed wine. Classic sweet Loire.* ⑪ *O, PF.*

★★★★★   1990 Chambertin, Dom. Rossignol-Trapet, Burgundy, Fr. £33.78. *Great wine. Complex, cherryish Burgundy with a hint of gameyness.* ⑪ *WM, P.*

TO   Tesco   ★★★★

Wines & Spirits Department, Tesco Stores Ltd, P.O. Box 18, Delamare Road, Cheshunt, Waltham Cross, Herts EN8 9SL. Tel 01992 632222. Supermarket Chain. 520 branches in the UK. **Opening Hours:** vary.

Celebrating the moment when it drew level with or overtook Sainsbury (statistics vary), this year, Tesco was also able to congratulate itself on the success of its first wine and beer shop in Calais, the launch of its internet service and the coup of securing the exclusivity of Malcolm Gluck's own-blend 'Superplonk' wines from Spain. More important, perhaps, was the expansion of the smart 'Metro' shops in such unexpected spots as Canary Wharf (home, incidentally of the *Daily* and *Sunday Telegraph*) and the introduction of a loyalty card. Initially mocked by competitors as a credit card version of the old Green Shield stamps, the card soon proved to be one of the cleverest retailing ideas of the 1990s. Used properly, it will enable Tesco to know precisely the kind of wine each of its cardholders has been buying regularly and occasionally, enabling the chain to learn about the changing patterns of the way we eat and drink. We would predict that, by the time the next *Guide* hits the streets, at least one of Tesco's competitors will have followed in its wake. As for Tesco's current range of wines, there are well chosen efforts across the board – especially at the higher end of the price scale (where they sell more wine than one might expect) – but, as elsewhere, too many of the cheaper wines taste as though they were bought on price. Pioneering flying winemaker wines from Brazil and Canada and cleverly resealable cartons win more points for originality than for pure quality and value.

**** Champagne Mercier Demi-Sec, Fr. £15.99. *A great example of soft, honeyed fizz. Drink with light, creamy puddings.* ¶ **CC, PF.**

**** Champagne Herbert Beaufort, Fr. £14.99 *Toasty and rich, balanced by fresh citrus fruit and crisp acidity.* **D, AP.**

*** Tesco Prosecco VdT del Veneto, It. £3.49. *Clean, peppery, quite herby wine with a slightly peary flavour.* ¶ **AP, LS.**

*** Tesco South African Sparkling wine, Madeba, Robertson, SA. £6.99. *Some creaminess and oak – more like white wine with bubbles than fizz.* ¶ **FD, FO.**

*** Tesco Canadian White Wine, J Worontschak, Can. £3.99. *Clean, fruit-salady dry wine with a fat, peachy texture.* ¶ **LS, AP, PY.**

*** 1993 Ch. de Passavant Anjou Blanc, Loire, Fr. £3.99. *Honey and lemon! Good, traditional Loire white. Rich, yet dry.* ¶ **AP, D, LS.**

*** 1995 Gôiya Kgeisje, Sauvignon-Chardonnay, Western Cape, SA. £3.79. *A fresh, peary wine with a lovely creamy finish.* ¶ **WM, PY, FF.**

**** 1994 Caliterra Sauvignon Blanc, Curico, Chi. £3.99. *Clean, gooseberry-cream wine; aromatic, refreshing and long.* ¶ **SM, AP, WFP.**

**** 1993 Petit Chablis, Louis Josse, Burgundy, Fr. £6.49. *Good, real Chablis character with slatey dryness and buttery richness.* ¶ **E, WM, SF.**

*** 1994 Leopard Creek Chardonnay, Paarl, SA. £3.99. *Pleasant, creamy wine with good Macon Blanc style. Slightly off-dry.* ¶ **D, PY, WFC.**

*** Tesco Robertson Chardonnay Colombard, SA. £3.99. *Pleasant, light appley wine with a touch of Chardonnay creaminess.* ¶ **PY, SF.**

**** 1994 Caliterra Estate Casablanca Chardonnay, Chi. £4.99. *Good, oaky creamy wine full of peach and pineapple and restrained oak.* ¶ **FF, LS, SM.**

*** 1994 Tesco Clare Valley Riesling, Mitchells, S Australia, Aus. £4.99. *Good, lime jelly Riesling, typically Australian. An easy-going mouthful.* ¶ **O, S, AP.**

*** 1994 De Wetshof Estate Rhine Riesling, Robertson, SA. £4.99. *Dry, limey, and earthy, with a hint of icing sugar and a touch of greenness.* ¶ **LS, PY.**

*** 1992 Trittenheimer Apotheke Riesling Kabinett, F W Gymnasium, Mosel, Ger. £5.59 *Lovely honeyed, appley Riesling with crisp lemony acidity .* ¶ **CC, O.**

*** 1994 Dom Chancel Côtes du Luberon Rosé, Midi, Fr. £3.99. *Good, juicy rosé with red fruit flavours of blackberries and plums.* ¶ **FD, SP, LS.**

*** Moroccan Red Wine, Zenatta, Mor. £2.99. *Rich, tobaccoey, and quite Portuguese in style; plum skins and currants.* ¶ **RM, WMP.**

*** Tesco Canadian Red, Niagara Peninsula, Can. £3.99. *Quite rich, spicy, crunchy-berryish, very jammy, very commercial.* ¶ **IB, RM, D.**

*** 1993 Chartron la Fleur, Ch Moulin des Arnauds, Bordeaux, Fr. £3.99. *Soft, easy Merlot, full of gentle plummy fruit; good-value stuff.* ¶ **LB, RMS, WMP.**

*** 1993 Tesco Buzet, SW France, Fr. £3.99. *Soft, juicy minty blackcurrant Cabernet Franc plus soft, toffeeish Merlot.* ¶ **BF, RM,PY.**

*** 1989 Ch. Labégorce, Margaux, Bordeaux, Fr. £14.99. *Good, ripe and cedary young wine with lovely blackberryish fruit. Cedary, good.* ¶ **G, RMS, LB.**

*** 1993 Leopard Creek Cabernet/Merlot, SA. £3.99. *A rich, ripe, juicy blackcurrany wine. Australian-style South African.* ¶ **D, PY, RM.**

*** 1993 Caliterra Cabernet Merlot, Curico, Chi. £5.99. *Intense, slightly minty cassis. Attractive and very blackcurranty.* ¶ **LB, D, RMS.**

*** 1993 Errazuriz Don Maximiano Cabernet Reserva, Chi. £6.99. *Rich black cherry and cassis with good oak. Quite long and complex.* ¶ **WM, SP.**

**** 1992 Crozes Hermitage, Cave de Tain l'Hermitage, Rhône, Fr. £5.99. *Rich and smoky, raspberryish sloes and tar.* ¶ **CH, G, LB, WMP.**

*** 1994 Ch de Beaulieu, Coteaux d'Aix en Provence, Midi, Fr. £3.99. *Good peppery Grenache and juicy damsony fruit.* ¶ **LB, G, WMP.**

*** Tesco McLaren Vale Grenache, S Australia, Aus. £3.99. *Bags of deep, licoricey fruit, pepper and great length.* ¶ **D, RM.**

**** 1991 Penfolds Kalimna Bin 28 Shiraz, Aus. £6.99. *Lovely, sweet licoricey wine with oak and very concentrated dark spicy fruit.* ¶ **D, G, RMS, LB.**

***** 1992 Maglieri McLaren Vale Shiraz, Aus. £6.99. *Good, supercharged Rhône style. Lovely intense cigary spice and fruit.* ¶ **CH, RM, SP.**

**** 1993 Yalumba Bush Vine Grenache, Barossa Valley, Aus. £6.99. *Softly peppery and oakily spicy. Lovely long wine with dark berry fruit.* ¶ *D, SP, G.*

**** 1992 Rosemount Balmoral Syrah, McLaren Vale, Aus. £16.49. *Huge spicy, peppery Syrah with good oak. Very Rhône-like.* ¶ *G, LB, RM.*

*** 1994 Brown Brothers Tarrango, Victoria, Aus. £4.49. *Plummy, quite Burgundian, with a tough of green pepper.* ¶ *WMP, RM.*

*** 1993 Echo Hills Baden Pinot Noir, Ger. £3.49. *Dark rosé, creamy, off-dry, commercial German Piat d'Or.* ¶ *WFP, PY.*

*** Tesco California Pinot Noir, US. £4.29. *Good, rich squashy raspberry fruit. Serious wine at a lighthearted price.* ¶ *D, PY, WMP.*

**** 1991 Villa Pigna Cabernasco VdT, Marches, It. £5.99. *Rich and deep with blackcurrants and blackberries and a mouthful of oak.* ¶ *RM, P.*

*** 1988 Viña Mara Rioja Reserva, Sp. £5.49. *A soft, oaky commercial style, rather traditional and not over fruity.* ¶ *WFP, WMP, P.*

*** 1991 Tesco Dão Tinto, Por. £2.99. *Light, tobaccoey wine, attractive and perfumed.* ¶ *P, PY, WMP.*

*** 1993 Beaumes de Venise, Rhône, Fr. £4.99. *An unusual red Beaumes-de-Venise, this is a rich wine, good and peppery.* ¶ *CH, RM, SP.*

**** Tesco Finest Pale Amontillado, Sanchez Romate, Jerez, Sp. £4.99. *Nutty, crisp and lively with an intense dry finish.* ¶ *SF, SM, AP.*

***** Yalumba Museum Show Reserve Rutherglen Muscat, Victoria, Aus. £6.89 *Ginger, Dundee-cake aromas and lovely sweet spices.* ¶ *CHO, CS, D, PF.*

TH   Threshers   ★★★★

Sefton House, 42 Church Road, Welwyn Garden City, Herts AL8 6RJ. Tel 01707 328244. National Chain. 594 branches. **Opening Hours:** Mon-Sat 0900-2200, Sun 12-1500, 1900-2200. **Delivery:** free locally, nationally at cost. **Tastings:** occasional in-store plus sessions for local organisations. **Services:** glass loan, ice.

Congratulations to Thresher for one of the more innovative moves of the year: bringing in its own Sauvignon Blanc Nouveau from Chile, less than three months after the harvest and just in time for people to enjoy it on a hot summer's day – and for doing so at an attractive £3.95 a bottle. This is precisely the sort of thing chains like Thresher should be doing, as is the ongoing effort to promote the marriage of "Wine with Food". Slightly less congratulation-worthy is Thresher's loudly touted "no quibble" guarantee which invites customers to return for replacement any bottle they do not like. It is a laudable idea, but one which actually offers nothing one might not find at a long list of independent merchants throughout the country. These are however, very easy places in which to find good wine, and staff training is having an effect (though we wondered about the employee who innocently wondered what kind of wood had been used to mature a wine whose label bore the legend "unoaked").

**** Seppelt Imperial Rosé, S Australia, Aus. £4.99. *Lively, refreshing, fruit-filled fizz.* ¶ *LS, PY.*

**** 1992 Croser, Petaluma, S Australia, Aus. £10.49. *Classy Aussie fizz, with a very Champagne-like richness.* ¶ *WFP.*

**** Champagne Le Mesnil, Blanc de Blancs Fr. £13.95. *A great example of Chardonnay-based Champagne, full of flavours of buttered toast.* ¶ *AP, S.*

**** 1986 Champagne Moët & Chandon Brut, Champagne, France. £24.45. *Strawberries and cream. A fresh, crisp Champagne.* ¶ *CC, WM.*

**** Moscato Spumante Frassino, Santero, Piedmont, It. £3.79. *Lovely fresh, grapey fizz. Drink well chilled as an aperitif.* ¶ *AP.*

**** 1994 Kings Canyon Sauvignon Blanc, H Ryman/Arciero, California, US. £3.99. *Zippy gooseberry fruit flavours. Rich character.* ¶ *WMC, O.*

*** 1994 Penfolds Semillon Chardonnay, S Australia, Aus. £4.99. *Delicious and succulent well-balanced blend.* ¶ *WM, PY.*

*** 1989 Preslav Khan Krum Reserve Chardonnay, Bul. £3.59. *The belatedly improved Bulgarian Chardonnay we've all been waiting for.* ¶ *FF.*

*** 1994 Soleil d'Or Chardonnay, Vin de Pays d'Oc, H Ryman, Fr. £3.99. *Fresh, easy-going, melony wine. Good for parties.* ¶ *PY, WM.*

*** 1994 Penfolds Bin 202 Riesling, Aus. £3.99. *Very fresh – fruit salad and lime marmalade flavours.* ¶ *PY, S.*

*** Butlers Blend Pinot Gris Riesling, Kiskoros Winery/Nick Butler, Hun. £2.99. *Dry, ripe and fresh.* ¶ *SP, O.*

*** 1992 Wynns Coonawarra Estate Riesling, S Australia, Aus. £5.99. *Rich, refeshing ripely grapey Riesling.* ¶ *CC.*

*** 1992 Riesling Gueberschwihr, Domaine Zind Humbrecht, Alsace, Fr. £7.29. *A fine elegant Alsatian Riesling.* ¶ *AP.*

*** 1994 Villa Maria Private Bin Riesling, Marlborough, NZ. £5.99. *Interesting apple and lemon flavours.* ¶ *LS, S.*

*** 1993 Sharpham Barrel-Fermented, Devon, Eng. £8.99. *Oaky, lemony and dry English wine.* ¶ *CC.*

*** Retsina Kourtaki Of Attica, D. Kourtakis, Gre. £3.59. *A typical piney, lemony, example, fresh and good.* ¶ *S.*

**** 1994 Etchart Torrontes, Cafayate, Arg. £4.99. *Grapes and mangoes and limey freshness – from a grape rarely found outside Argentina.* ¶ *LS, PY.*

*** 1993 Rkatsiteli Hincesti, H Ryman/Penfolds, Mol. £2.99. *Easy going, off-dry wine made from an indigenous Moldovan grape variety.* ¶ *PY.*

**** 1992 Domaine St Eulalie Minervois, Midi, Fr. £4.19. *Good value, flavoursome country red.* ¶ *G, RM.*

**** 1994 Prosperity Red, Firestone Vineyards, California, US. £4.99. *A fruity, jammy mouthful.* ¶ *RMS, FF.*

*** 1992 Tollana Black Label Cabernet Sauvignon, S Australia, Aus. £4.99. *Jammy, simply blackcurrant and damson flavours.* ¶ *LB, RM.*

*** 1991 Caliterra Reserva Cabernet Sauvignon, Curico, Chi. £5.99. *Ripe blackcurrant and oak. Quite stylish.* ¶ *SP, P.*

***** 1993 Warwick Farm Trilogy, Stellenbosch, SA. £8.99. *Fine, concentrated blend of Cab Sauv/Franc and Merlot. Chewy and flavoursome. Riper than many South African reds.* ¶ *G, RMS.*

*** 1993 Côtes du Ventoux La Mission, Rhône, Fr. £2.99. *Good, peppery, inexpensive alternative to Côtes du Rhône.* ¶ *FF, PY, SP, RM.*

***** 1992 Penfolds Bin 28 Shiraz, S Australia, Aus. £6.59. *Spice galore, with chocolate, blackcurrant and black cherry. Worth keeping.* ¶ *SP, G.*

*** 1991 Penfolds Magill Estate Shiraz, S Australia, Aus. £12.99. *Plums, oak and spice combination.* ¶ *BF, RM.*

*** Nitra Winery St Laurent, Carl Reh, Nitra Region, Slovakia. £3.29. *Raspberryish, Beaujolais-like party red.* ¶ *PY, FF.*

***** 1990 Nuits-Saint-Georges, Clos de l'Arlot, Côte d'Or, Fr. £27.99. *Berries, oak and allspice. Lovely modern Burgundy at its best.* ¶ *BF, RMS.*

*** 1993 Montepulciano d'Abruzzo, Umani Ronchi, It. £3.79. *Earthy tobacco and strawberries; a good spicy, old fashioned rustic wine.* ¶ *SP, P.*

*** 1994 Santara Dry Red, Conca de Barbera, Concavins/Hugh Ryman, Sp. £2.99. *Oaky, jammy black cherryish wine.* ¶ *BF, PY.*

*** Alandra Herdade, Esporao Vinho Branca, Por. £3.49. *Concentrated citrussy flavours with smoky aromas.* ¶ *CH.*

*** J P Tinto, Vino de Mesa, J P Vinhos, Pinhal Novo, Por. £2.99. *Good value, herby, plummy red.* ¶ *FF, PY, D.*

*** 1993 Valdemar Vino Tinto, Martinez Bujanda, Rioja, Sp. £3.99. *Soft delicate raspberry flavours.* ¶ *SP, PY.*

*** 1990 Raimat Tempranillo, Costers del Segre, Sp. £6.19. *Good fruits and interesting oak.* ¶ *D.*

*** Don Zoilo Oloroso, Jerez, Sp. £7.99. *Nutty, burnt sugar aroma and a rich, ripe taste.* ¶ *S, AP.*

*** Bright Brothers Port, Douro, Por. £4.99. *Rich, sweet damson fruit and nutty oak.* ¶ *CH, CC.*

*** Dow's 10 Year Old Tawny, Douro, Por. £7.49. *A full and rewarding, richly flavoured Port.* ¶ *CC, CS.*

124 Merchants

HOT   House of Townend   ★★★★

Red Duster House, 101 York Street, Wincolmlee, Hull, N. Humberside HU2 0QX. Tel 01482 26891. Fax 01482 587042. Independent Wine Merchant. **Opening Hours:** Mon-Sat 1000-2200, Sun 1200-1400. **Delivery:** free locally. **Tastings:** regular in-store, tutored sessions for groups plus monthly tastings for own wine club. **Services:** cellarage, *en primeur*, mail order, gift mailing, glass hire, ice.

Upon the first reading of the Rt Hon John E Townend MP's list (printed on white rather than green paper), anyone with Ayes to see and a Noes to smell will appreciate the excellent rare wines unassumingly rubbing shoulders with their more available peers. Oh yes. Take for example the 1947 Chateau Lafite-Rothschild, 1er Cru Pauillac, the 1963 Quinta do Noval Vintage Port (in no risk of losing its deposit) and the slightly more affordable white 1991 Nuits St Georges, Clos de L'Arlot. However, on the opposition benches there lurks the 1992 Californian Sutter Home Sauvignon Blanc. There is a good, traditional selection of Bordeaux but the Burgundies get the votes for consistent quality. Whether the Westminster Gin at £8.22 will remain in the cabinet for longer than seven days is anyone's guess but as the late Harold Wilson said "a week is a long time in politics". Or as the Rt Hon Mr Townend might prefer, "Re-order, Re-order".

★★★★	Merchant Vintners' Baron de Beaupré Champagne, Ellner, Fr. £13.75. *Soft, creamy bubbles and easy, soft flavours. Gulpable!* ¶ *AP, D.*
★★★★	1994 Pipers Brook Ninth Island Chardonnay, Tasmania, Aus. £7.99. *Unoaked, Chablis-like, appley-pineappley Chardonnay. Deliciously un-Australian.* ¶ *S, FD.*
★★★★	1993 Bourgogne Aligoté, Domaine des Manants, Jean-Marc Brocard, Burgundy, Fr. £5.50. *A good example of a dry, yet creamy, white wine.* ¶ *FD.*
★★★★	1989 Côtes Du Rhône Cuvée Privée, Cellier des Dauphins, Rhône, Fr. £6.35. *Spicy complex wine with pepper galore and lots of berry fruit.* ¶ *SP, RM.*
★★★★	5 Year Old Dry Madeira, d'Oliveira, Mad. £9.59. *Baked fruits, cashews and walnuts with fresh orange and apricot fruit .* ¶ *CH, D.*

TRO   Trout Wines   ★★★

Nether Wallop, Stockbridge, Hampshire SO20 8EW. Tel/Fax 01264 781472. Independent Wine Merchant. **Opening Hours:** Mon 0930-1300, Tues-Fri 0930-1300, 1700-2000, Sat 0930-1300, 1400-2000. **Delivery:** free locally. **Services:** glass hire.

Nearly two years old and growing fast, this trout is becoming a big fish in its small Hampshire pond. Its feeding habits are diversifying and it is now often seen to rise to tempting homemade cakes and jams – as well as the more usual fare of fine wines from around the world. Drouhin Burgundies and Crozes Hermitage Blanc from Delas are liable to provoke a feeding frenzy, and Trout has been known to leap out of the water completely at the merest sniff of Masi's Campo Fiorin Valpolicella. Pack your landing net and head off to Nether Wallop.

★★★★	Champagne Le Brun de Neuville Brut, Cuvée Selection, Fr. £15.50. *Classy biscuit tones and fresh lemony acidity.* ¶ *AP, D, LS.*
★★★	1990 Crozes Hermitage Blanc Delas, Rhône, Fr. £4.50. *Nutty, distinctive and very rare.* ¶ *LS, WM.*
★★★	1993 Greciano Pellegrino, Sicily, It. £4.99. *A most unusual Sicilian white with a lovely, lightly fruity style.* ¶ *D.*
★★★	1990 Minervois, Dom. La Tour Boisée, Cuvée Marie Claude, Fr. £6.95. *Minervois in a claret style made from Syrah and Carignan.* ¶ *RM, SP.*
★★★	1988 Oak Knoll Pinot Noir, California, US. £10.95. *One of the most successful Oregon Pinots – very Burgundian in style.* ¶ *BF.*
★★★★	Quinta de La Rosa Finest Reserve, Oporto, Por. £9. *Plummy, intense, cherryish port with more than a touch of spice.* ¶ *CH, CC.*

TUR   Turville Valley Wines   ★★★★

The Firs, Potter Row, Great Missenden, Bucks. HP16 9LT. Tel 01494 868818.
Independent Wine Merchant. **Opening Hours:** Mon-Fri 0900-1730. **Delivery:** free
locally. **Services:** cellarage, *en primeur*, mail-order.

Whatever your experience in wine, you know that when a merchant's list starts off
with a vintage from the last century it is likely to be "serious". An even graver tone is
lent to the proceedings when you realise the merchant also has a whole section
devoted to "Big bottles" which does not refer to two-litre jugs of Lambrusco. Such is
the case with Turville Valley Wines whose list is a vinous version of Debretts.
Vintages of Yquem, for instance, date back as far as 1861, the Domaine de la
Romanee Conti listings begin at 1945 and Chateau Margaux kicks off with 1929; their
Port section has to be seen to be believed and they certainly have one of the most
comprehensive collections of Madeira on this planet. The New World gets a little
sniff with older vintages of Grange Hermitage from Australia, but strictly speaking
this is a haven and heaven for traditionalists. All credit though to Michael Raffety and
Christopher Davis, who rarely let the prices exceed the digits of the vintage.

UBC   Ubiquitous Chip   ★★★★

8 Ashton Lane, Glasgow G12 8SJ. Tel 0141 334 5007. Fax 0141 337 1302.
Independent Wine Merchant. **Opening Hours:** Mon-Fri 1200-2200, Sat 1100-2200.
Services: cellarage, mail order, glass loan.

One of our little tricks when deciding which merchants are worthy of a
paragraph of weak puns in the *Guide* is to apply the "South African Test", since
the health of this section is often indicative of the energy and vision of a
company's wine buying over the last couple of years. The Chip comes up
trumps in this test with a short punchy selection, reflecting but not overplaying
the range of new flavours from Mandelaland. Mulderbosch Sauvignon is here
(better than Cloudy Bay?) as is the excellent 1991 Warwick Trilogy, Neil Ellis
Cabernet and Hamilton Russell Pinot Noir. Rest assured, the rest of the world is
equally well represented, and there's a fine selection of bottled beer and an
outstanding (possibly unrivalled?) range of rare malt whiskies.

* ★★★★ 1994 Mulderbosch Sauvignon Blanc, Stellenbosch, SA. £7.80. *Twice voted the world's best Sauvignon; most of it is exported to America.* ¶ **AP, O.**
* ★★★ 1989 Bandol Rosé, Mas de la Rouvière, Bunan, Fr. £7.85. *Powerful and richly flavoured rosé at its best with food.* ¶ **SM, WMP.**
* ★★★ 1992 Fitou Terre Rouge Domaine Terre Ardente, Midi, Fr. £4.95. *Rich oak and lots of spicy fruit.* ¶ **BF, WMP.**
* ★★★ 1993 Figaro, Aimé Guibert, VdP de l'Hérault, Fr. £3.60. *Simple warm fruity Southern red with good spicy flavours.* ¶ **D, PY.**
* ★★★★ 1993 Château Lamarche "Lute", Bordeaux Superieur, Fr. £6.75. *Better than average "petit château" claret; plums and green pepper.* ¶ **LB.**
* ★★★★ 1992 L A Cetto Cabernet Sauvignon, Baja California, Mex. £4.50. *Excitingly fresh pepper and spice nose, full of real fruit flavours.* ¶ **SP, BF.**
* ★★★★★ 1978 Ch. Haut Brion 1er Grand Cru Classé, Bordeaux, Fr. £126. *An absolute stunner; knocks spots off every other wine from the vintage.* ¶ **LB.**
* ★★★★ 1988 Elderton "Command" Shiraz, S Australia, Aus. £12. *Front-of-mouth fruit flavours; ripe, rich and delicious. Fruity wine with excellent balance. Easy drinking.* ¶ **G, BF.**
* ★★★★ 1993 L A.Cetto Petite Sirah, Baja California, Mex. £4.50 *Excitingly fresh pepper and spice nose, full of primary red fruit flavours.* ¶ **SP, BF.**
* ★★★★ 1986 Gnangara Shiraz, Evans & Tate, Swan Valley, Aus. £8.25. *Leathery, smoky Shiraz; wonderfully rustic and evocative.* ¶ **G, BF.**
* ★★★★ 1992 Redwood Valley Estate Late Harvest Rhine Riesling, Nelson, NZ. £6.40 (half). *Lusciously intense, creamy lemon meringue.flavours.* ¶ **PS, CC.**

U   Unwins   ★★★

Birchwood House, Victoria Road, Dartford, Kent DA1 5AJ. Tel 01322 272711 Fax 01322 294469. National Chain. 300 branches. **Opening Hours:** vary between: Mon-Fri 0900-2200, Sat 0900-2200, Sun 1200-1500, 1900-2200. **Delivery:** free locally. **Tastings:** regular in store, occasional tutored tastings. **Services:** mail order, gift mailing, glass hire, ice.

Last year, we wondered whether Unwins might be smartening itself for a prospective suitor: someone like Greenall's Wine Cellar chain, for example. Well, no wedding bells have been heard yet though, up in Warrington, there's certainly an engagement ring waiting to go on somebody's finger. Meanwhile, at Unwins all sorts of things are going on. There are one-off parcels of "Undiscovered" wines, listings of bottles from Western Australia, Argentina and even British Columbia, regional ales of the month and exclusive 25-year-old malt whiskies. Even more surprisingly, Unwins also takes pride in becoming "much more competitive on price", introducing wines at £1.99 and £2.09. These are still not the most exciting shops on the high street, but they're a lot more enticing than they've been in our drinking memory.

****	Champagne Duchatel Blanc de Blancs Brut, A Thienot, Fr. £14.99. *Bready, yeasty, complex nose with light lemon fruit character on palate.* ¶ *AP, LS.*
****	Asti Spumante, Sperone, It. £4.99. *Soft grapey, floral nose; rich gentle palate, sweet but pleasantly balanced.* ¶ *PF, AP, CHO.*
***	1994 Soave Classico, Rocca Sveva, Veneto, It. £3.99. *Light lemony and dry, a very good, easy white.* ¶ *LS.*
****	1993 Matua Valley Sauvignon Blanc, Hawkes Bay, NZ. £7.69. *Nice light fruity nose; pleasant aging gooseberry. Good fruit palate with length and upfront flavours. A clean wine with a soft finish.* ¶ *O, S.*
****	Cuvée One Pinot Noir Chardonnay, Yalumba, S Australia, Aus. £8.29. *Nice fresh, zingy nose with good fruit, crisp and attractive on palate. Clean finish with citrus and grapefruit character.* ¶ *D, CHO.*
****	1993 Etchart Torrontes, Cafayate, Arg. £4.49. *Grapes and mangoes and limey freshness — from a grape rarely found outside Argentina.* ¶ *SP, O.*
***	Minervois Domaine de l'Estagnol, Les Chais Beaucairois, Midi, Fr. £3.49. *Herby smoky wine with simple, enjoyable red fruit.* ¶ *SP, WMP.*
****	1993 Penfolds Koonunga Hill Shiraz Cabernet Sauvignon, S Australia, Aus. £5.99. *Lovely rich jammy red fruit and soft vanilla oak.* ¶ *D, PY.*
***	1994 Jose Canepa Cabernet Sauvignon, Maipo, Chi. £4.49. *Tobaccoey, herby rich blackcurrant fruit.* ¶ *LB.*
****	1992 Crozes Hermitage, Louis Mousset, Rhône, Fr. £5.49. *Very easy-going Northern Rhône with lovely cherry fruit.* ¶ *BF, RM.*
****	1994 Fleurie Domaine des Carrières, Ets Loron Et Fils, Beaujolais, Fr. £6.99. *Restrained, youthful nose. Fresh, lively cherries and good acidity.* ¶ *D, SM.*
****	1993 Pinot Noir, Bichot, Burgundy, Fr. £5.49. *Attractive raspberry and mint aromas. Hints of licorice and spice. Full, juicy fruit. Easy drinking.* ¶ *BF.*
****	1994 Chianti Villa Selva, Tuscany, It. £3.99. *Excellent fresh black cherry and stalky vegetal fruit.* ¶ *P, RM.*
***	1994 Giordano Barbera del Piemonte, It. £3.99. *Easy-going wild berryish red.* ¶ *P, PY.*
****	1988 Giordano Barolo, Giordano, Piedmont, It. £8.49. *Nicely mature, earthy and evocative explosion of wild spicy fruit.* ¶ *G, RM.*
***	1994 Pedras Do Monte, Palmela Cooperative, Terras do Sado, Por. £3.79. *Good, young, plummy, appley new wave Portuguese red.* ¶ *FF, SP.*
****	1992 Quinta do Manjapao, Torres Vedras, Por. £4.49. *Clean, interestingly tobaccoey and plummy red.* ¶ *WMP, RM.*
****	1985 Castillo Fuentemayor Gran Reserva, Age, Age, Rioja, Spain. £6.79. *Clean fruity nose with some spice; good balance, nice fruit and grip.* ¶ *LB.*
****	1989 Vouvray Moelleux, Cave des Viticulteurs du Vouvray, Loire, Fr. £9.99. *Classic Chenin Blanc nose; honey, apples and a minerally backbone.* ¶ *PF.*

***** 1992 Eiswein Neusiedlersee, Weinkellerei Burgenland, Aus. £7.89 (half). *Extraordinarily concentrated, tropical fruit and a touch of ginger.* ¶ **CS, PS.**

**** Taylor's 10 Year Old Tawny, Oporto, Por. £14.99 *Tangily refreshing port; chocolatey, with lots of plummy orangey fruit.* ¶ **CH. CC.**

V&C Valvona and Crolla ★★★★★

19 Elm Row, Edinburgh EH7 4AA. Tel 0131 556 6066. Fax 0131 556 1668. Independent Wine Merchant. **Opening Hours:** Mon, Tues, Wed, Sat 0830-1800, Thurs, Fri 0830-1930. **Delivery:** free locally. **Tastings:** regular in-store, informal weekly tastings, plus yearly programme of tutored sessions. **Services:** mail order, gift mailing, glass hire, corporate tastings.

The Auld Alliance between Scots and French gets far too much press; what about the Newer Alliance between Scotland and Italy – as demonstrated by great restaurants, ice cream and, thanks to the Contini brothers, a brilliant delicatessen and wine shop? Okay so there are as few non-Italian wines here as you'd find in an oenoteca in Venice or Rome – but the wines are far better chosen than they would almost ever be in Italy where big names and tradition would weigh more heavily in the balance than quality and value for money. When you come to think of it, what could be more perfect than a blend of Scots, er, carefulness, with Italian flair?

**** 1994 Nuragus di Cagliari, Cantina Sociale di Dolianova, Sardinia, It. £3.99. *Pleasant, easy going, herby dry white. Perfect for a party.* ¶ **D, PY.**

*** 1991 Uccellanda Bianco, Bellavista, Lombardy, It. £23.99. *Rich creamy fruit and toffee flavours.* ¶ **WFC, D.**

**** 1991 Venegazzu della Casa, Gasparini, Veneto, Italy. £8.99. *Lovely Dundee Cake-in-a-glass. Rich, long, satisfying Italian red.* ¶ **D, P.**

**** 1990 Aglianico Del Vulture Riserva, d'Angelo, Basilicata, It. £10.99. *Intense, leathery, herby wine from a warm part of Southern It.* ¶ **WM, P.**

**** 1991 Marchesi de Frescobaldi Pomino Rosso, Tuscany, It. £8.99. *Lovely new-wave Italian red with ripe berry fruit.* ¶ **FF, PY, P, RM.**

**** 1990 Antinori Tenute Marchese Chianti Classico, Tuscany, It. £10.99. *Lovely jammy fruit; chocolate and cigar-box flavours.* ¶ **P, D, WM.**

**** 1990 Prunotto Barolo Cru Bussia, Piedmont, It. £20.50. *Serious Barolo, built to last, with intense leathery berryish flavours.* ¶ **SP, G.**

**** 1988 Masi Agri cola Mazzano Amarone Della Valpolicella, Veneto, It. £19.95. *Ultra-serious, concentrated, mature wine; bitter cherryish and gamey.* ¶ **D, CH.**

**** 1988 Banfi Poggio all Oro Brunello di Montalcino Riserva, Banfi, Tuscany, It. £23.99. *Good, leathery, plum-skinny and mouthfilling.* ¶ **P, BF.**

HVW Helen Verdcourt ★★★★

Spring Cottage, Kimbers Lane, Maidenhead, Berks. SL6 2QP. Tel 01628 25577. Independent Wine Merchant. Wine by the case only. **Opening Hours:** anytime – with the help of the answerphone. **Delivery:** free locally. **Tastings:** sessions monthly for three local wine clubs. **Services:** cellarage, *en primeur*, mail order, gift mailing, glass hire. No credit cards.

Pocket Wine Guide? You want to get yourself a pocket wine merchant, mate! Berkshire residents take note; Helen Verdcourt packs a lifetime of erudition into a compact twelve pages of closely typed text. No glossy photos or elaborate tasting notes here, but wine after wine of the highest calibre. Ms Verdcourt has shied away from many of her old French favourites this year as the last four vintages have caused most fine red wines to be a little light and out of balance, but numbered among the exceptions are the 1991 Cote Roties. Look instead to Italy for Vietti Castiglione Fallettoís fine Piedmontese reds, California's Ridge and Newton or new South African superstar Saxenberg.

*** 1988 Auxey Duresses, Jaffelin, Burgundy, Fr. £8.65. *Gorgeous honeyed peaches and melons, with soft and creamy wood.* ¶ *D, WMC.*

*** 1995 Oyster Bay Sauvignon Blanc, NZ. £6.55. *A really classy Kiwi Sauvignon with ripe blackcurranty fruit.* ¶ *D, S.*

**** 1993 St Hallett Cabernet Sauvignon, S Australia, Aus. £6.99. *Delicious, easy going summer pudding flavours with freshly ground pepper.* ¶ *P, WM.*

**** 1988 Ch. Ramage la Batisse, Bordeaux, Fr. £10.60. *Delicious, dark fruit and earthy, leathery wood. Will keep.* ¶ *LB, CH.*

**** 1988 Hermitage Rouge, E Guigal, Rhône, Fr. £13.60. *Serious, quite 'wild' tasting Hermitage which will soften further with time.* ¶ *RM, SP.*

VW   Victoria Wine   ★★★★

Dukes Court, Duke Street, Woking, Surrey GU21 5XL. Tel 01483 715066. Fax 01483 755234. National Chain. 1531 branches. **Opening Hours:** vàry between: Mon-Sat 1000-2200, Sun 1200-1500, 1900-2200. **Services:** gift delivery 'Post Haste' (a bit like Interflora with bottles), glass loan, ice, gift vouchers, full exchange guarantee.

As over two dozen shops throughout the country have been transformed into smart new Victoria Wine Cellars, Allied Domecq's chain has taken on a decidedly perky allure. Years after watching their arch rival Thresher, develop its Wine Rack chain, Victoria Wine can now field a range of recognisable shops in which anyone with a serious interest in wine can feel at home. Shops with Victoria Wine signs are more confusing, as they may prove to be "destination wine shops" which sell decent, if smaller ranges of wines and "neighbourhood drinks shops" in which the focus is far more heavily on beer and tobacco. Throughout the better shops, the range has improved too, with wines like the own-label Deakin Estate range from Australia and the La Serre wines from southern France and well-chosen Bordeaux (promoted after a tough tasting, by the author of this *Guide*). Hard-bitten observers within the wine trade question the multinational owner's commitment to Victoria Wine; I suspect that much will depend on them making rather more money over the next year or so than they are thought to be bringing in at present – and wish them well.

**** Champagne Lanson Black Label, Fr. £17.49. *Delicately dry and toasty with soft pineapple fruits.* ¶ *D, AP, S.*

***** 1989 Victoria Wine Vintage Champagne, Marne et Champagne, Fr. £18.99. *Great value doughy, yeasty fizz. Lots of rich fruit.* ¶ *D, AP.*

**** 1994 Mondoro Asti, Barbero, Piedmont, It. £6.49. *Appley, grapey fruit. Full bodied and crisply dry.* ¶ *PY, D.*

*** Lindauer Rosé, Montana, Marlborough, NZ. £6.99. *Strawberry, raspberry fruit and a fresh zesty acidity.* ¶ *AP, D, PY.*

**** 1994 Lenotti Bianco di Custoza, Veneto, It. £3.99. *Creamy, slightly peary, fresh wine. Good value.* ¶ *WM, PY.*

*** 1994 Big Franks White, Midi, France £4.25. *Full, grapey fruit and tropical aromas. Tangy lemon and lime freshness.* ¶ *WM, PY, D.*

**** 1994 Stoneleigh Sauvignon Blanc, Marlborough, NZ. £5.99. *A brilliant asparagus and gooseberry aroma; classic Kiwi Sauvignon.* ¶ *WMC, S, D.*

**** 1994 Gabriel Meffre Galet Vineyards Chardonnay, Rhône, Fr. £3.99. *Toffee aromas and young, tropical fruit.* ¶ *PY, WM.*

**** 1994 Deakin Estate Colombard Chardonnay, Victoria, Aus. £3.99. *Good value, easy-going party wine with a lime marmalade flavour.* ¶ *PY, D.*

**** 1994 Penfolds Koonunga Hill Chardonnay, Penfolds, S Australia, Aus. £4.99. *Rich, ripe, mango-ey and peachy wine with sweetly spicy oak.* ¶ *SM, WM, D,*

**** 1994 Basedow Chardonnay, S Australia, Aus. £6.99. *Buttery and rich, with lovely tropical ripeness.* ¶ *SM, CH.*

**** 1993 Montana Wines Church Road Chardonnay, Hawkes Bay, NZ. £7.99. *Perfectly balanced toffee richness and fresh appley fruit.* ¶ *SF, SM, WM.*

*** 1992 Ernest & Julio Gallo Northern Sonoma Estate Chardonnay, California, US. £19.99. *Full mango peach fruit and buttery, creamy wood.* ¶ *D, EN, WMC.*

**** 1994 Fortant de France Chardonnay, Skalli, Midi, Fr. £3.99. *Soft but creamy, with buttery oak and plenty of apricot and pineapple fruit – from the Languedoc Roussillon pioneers of this kind of varietal wine.* ¶ **D, EN, WM.**

**** 1993 Wolf Blass Silver Label Riesling, S. Australia, Aus. £5.29. *Tropical, floral aromas with a balancing acidity.* ¶ **O, CC.**

**** 1988 Kiedricher Sandgrub Riesling Kabinett, Schloss Groenesteyn, Rheingau, Ger. £6.49. *Pineapple and apricot fruit. Floral and zesty.* ¶ **CH, O.**

*** 1994 Big Frank's Red, Midi, Fr. £4.25. *Full, ripe berry fruit and weighty, but balanced tannins.* ¶ **D, RM..**

**** 1993 La Cuvée Mythique, VdP d'Oc, Fr. £6.49. *A characterful wine, packed with good plummy spicy fruit.* ¶ **G, P.**

*** 1994 La Fortuna Malbec, Viña La Fortuna, Lontue, Chi. £4.99. *Smooth and mellow plum fruits and caramelly oak.* ¶ **P, LB.**

**** 1993 Merlot Chais Cuxac, Val d'Orbieu, Midi, Fr. £4.99. *Soft, easy-going and plummy.* ¶ **G, RMS.**

**** 1991 Wynns Coonawarra Estate Cabernet Sauvignon, S. Australia, Aus. £7.99. *Classic Coonawarra, with rich cassis flavours and minty eucalyptus.* ¶ **WM, WMC, D.**

**** 1994 Victoria Wine Claret, Calvet, Bordeaux, Fr. £3.79. *Earthy, herbaceous and plummy. Tannins need time.* ¶ **PY, LB.**

**** 1992 Ch. d'Arcins, Cru Bourgeois, Bordeaux, Fr. £6.99. *Leather and tobacco with rich berry fruits.* ¶ **RM, D.**

**** 1993 Stellenzicht Cabernet Sauvignon/Malbec, Stellenbosch, SA. £3.99. *Spicily herbaceous wine with some of the richness of blackcurrant jam.* ¶ **BF.**

***** 1993 Basedow Shiraz, S Australia, Aus. £6.79. *Spicy wine with some delicacy to it.* ¶ **SP, G.**

**** 1990 Côte Rôtie Brune et Blonde, E. Guigal, Rhône, Fr. £18.99. *Ripe autumn fruit with lots of new oak. Classy red wine which will improve.* ¶ **G, LB.**

**** 1993 Bougogne Rouge 'Charles de France', Jean Claude Boisset, Fr. £5.99. *Soft, young summer fruits with slightly smoky wood.* ¶ **G, SM.**

*** 1993 Montepulciano d'Abruzzo, Umani Ronchi, It. £3.99. *Earthy tobacco and strawberries; a good spicy, old fashioned rustic wine.* ¶ **P, G.**

*** 1990 Villa de Vetrice Chianti Rufina Riserva, Tuscany, It. £5.49. *Fresh, herby young Chianti which needs food.* ¶ **P, WM, CH.**

**** Palo Cortado, Sanchez Romato, Jerez, Sp. £3.99 (half). *Dry, yet honeyed; fascinating nutty sherry.* ¶ **AP, S.**

*** Pellegrino Marsala Garibaldi Dolce, Sicily, It. £5.99. *Nuts, treacle and sultanas. Rich and spicy fruit.* ¶ **CHO, CC, PS.**

*** Cockburn's Special Reserve, Oporto, Por. £7.99. *Sweet, ripe damson fruit and spicy, herbal aromas.* ¶ **CC. CH, CS.**

***** 1990 Dow's Crusted Port, Douro, Por. £10.99. *A great alternative to vintage port. Plummy with a hint of ginger.* ¶ **CC, CH, CS.**

***** Yalumba Museum Show Reserve Rutherglen Muscat, Victoria, Aus. £6.99. *Australian Liqueur Muscat at its gingery, Dundee Cakey, spicy best.* ¶ **D, CH.**

LV   La Vigneronne   ★★★★

105 Old Brompton Road, London SW7 3LE. Tel 0171 589 6113. Independent Wine Merchant. **Opening Hours:** Mon-Fri 1000-2100, Sat 1000-1900. **Delivery:** free locally. **Tastings:** regular in-store plus an average of two evening tutored sessions given by Liz Berry MW. **Services:** cellarage, en primeur, mail order, gift mailing.

A London landmark for countless British wine lovers and overseas visitors who rely on its shelves to provide interesting examples of Old and New World alike. Despite worried rumours that the shop was for sale, nothing has changed; the range of wines, the tutored tastings and, dare I say, service which was described by one customer as *'de haut en bas'*. This is a shame, as anyone who determindly charts such an uncommercial course through strange and exciting waters deserves the support of every wine lover in the land.

VLG Village Wines ★★★

6 Mill Row, High Street, Bexley, Kent DA5 1LA. Tel 01322 558772. Fax 01322 558772. Independent Wine Merchant. **Opening Hours:** Mon-Fri 1000-1800, Sat 1000-1700. **Delivery:** free locally. **Services:** mail order, glass loan, *en primeur* offers, gift pack, bar service.

One of the more entertaining wine lists we encountered this year – who else boldly enquires of their customers, "Are you short of vintage port?"– and sends out invitations decorated by a drawing of "Beau Jollie" to join the Worshipful Mayor and Mayoress of Bexley at a tasting? Those untempted by the prospect of rubbing shoulders with civic dignitaries should, however, read the list and take particular note of one of Britain's best ranges of serious German single estate wines. Elsewhere, the range is pretty mixed with too many KWVs and Sutter Homes to win real approval.

★★★	1986 Mehring Blattenberg Kabinett Riesling/Scheurebe, Alfons Sebastiani, Mosel, Ger. £5.49. *Tropical mango fruit and crisp acidity.* ⁋ *O, AP.*
★★★★	1992 Tim Adams Semillon, Clare Valley, S Australia, Aus. £9.98. *Rich and honeyed with zesty citrus fruit to balance.* ⁋ *D, WM, SM.*
★★★★	1975 Negru de Purkar, Mol. £8.98. *Stunningly dense exotic red from Moldavia. Tastes like 30 year old Cru Classe claret.* ⁋ *RM, LB, D.*
★★★	1988 Ch. Giscours, Margaux, Bordeaux, Fr. £19.95. *Earthy, jammy fruit and smoky tannins. Will keep.* ⁋ *D, LB.*
★★★	1992 Rosso Cornero, Umani Ronchi, Marches, It. £4.29. *Good value, tobaccoey, pruney and flavoursome.* ⁋ *SP, P.*

VLN Villeneuve Wines ★★★★

1 Venlaw Court, Peebles EH45 8AE Tel 01721 722500. Fax 01721 729922. Independent Wine Merchant. **Opening Hours:** Mon-Thurs 0900-2000, Fri-Sat 0900-2100. **Delivery:** free nationally. **Services:** mail order, glass loan, cellarage.

"Anyone who buys a bottle of wine at £1.39 should be rounded up and shot!" So says Kenneth Vanna, proprietor of Villeneuve Wines, campaigner against ridiculous rates of duty and obviously a supporter of the moderate view on life and all things green and pleasant. Still it's an attitude that has helped produce an exciting list of wines and propel him towards thoughts of a second retail shop over the coming year. A particularly good range of Californian wines and some nice Aussie heavyweights.

★★★	1992 Jurancon Sec, Clos Guirouilh, S W France, Fr. £5.99. *Refreshingly crisp and youthful with lemony, mango fruits.* ⁋ *FD, D, PY.*
★★★★	1995 Caliterra Sauvignon Blanc, Curico, Chi. £2.99. *Gooseberries and grapefruit, with a grassy acidity.* ⁋ *D, S, WMC.*
★★★★	1990 Marimar Torres Chardonnay, Sonoma County, California, US. £13.99. *Rich, buttery oak and fresh tropical fruit.* ⁋ *D, FF, WM.*
★★★★	1994 Rose of Virginia, Charles Melton, Aus. £6.62. *A dark, rich rosé – perfect for those winter evenings.* ⁋ *AP, D.*
★★★★	Johnstone Reserve Claret, Nathaniel Johnstone, Bordeaux, Fr. £4.39. *Jammy fruits and earthy, herby spice.* ⁋ *LB.*
★★★★	1990 Grande Escolha, Quinta do Cotto, Por. £11.99. *Big and beefy, with dark cherry fruits.* ⁋ *RM, G.*
★★★★	1992 Saintsbury Pinot Noir, Carneros, California, U.S. £12.99. *Smoky spices with lovely fresh strawberry, blackcurrant fruits and smooth tannins.* ⁋ *WM, CH.*
★★★★	1991 Fetzer Zinfandel, California, U.S. £5.52. *Dark and plummy; weighty oak and lovely spice.* ⁋ *SP, RM.*
★★★★★	1981 Ch. Yquem, Sauternes, Bordeaux, Fr. £140. *A once-in-a-lifetime experience.* ⁋ *PS.*

VDV   Vin du Van ★★★★

Colthups, The Street, Appledore, Kent TN26 2BX. Tel 01233 758 727. **Opening Hours:** Mon-Sun 0900-1800. Independent Wine Merchant. Minimum order 4 bottles (no minimum in Appledore). **Delivery:** free locally. **Services:** mail order, gift mailing. No credit cards.

Ian Brown informs us that approximately 60% of his customers are doctors or surgeons, largely as a result of a successful mail order campaign in a learned surgical magazine. A scan of the list would reveal that Mr Brown has taken the scalpel to the Spanish section in its entirety (a bitter pill for Hispanophiles to swallow), leaving the theatre of operations free for his first true love – the wines of the Antipodes. Mr B had obviously been at the laughing gas before writing his list – his wine descriptions had us in stitches. Ryecroft Flame Tree Cabernet Shiraz might lead to Campbell's Rutherglen Bobbie Burns Shiraz 1991/2, in which case we would prescribe a dose of the efficacious Yarra Yering No 2 Shiraz. Give V-du-V a check-up, or better still, order a sample case.

★★★★	1985 Seppelt Show Sparkling Shiraz, S Australia, Aus. £11.75. *Ultra concentrated wine with all sorts of ripe hedgerow fruits.* ⑪ **AP.**	
★★★	1992 Ngatarawa Sauvignon Blanc, NZ. £6.95. *Sancerre style – grassy and crisp, with asparagus and gooseberry fruit.* ⑪ **D, AP, S.**	
★★★★	1992 Cloudy Bay Late Harvest Riesling, NZ. £7.95 (half). *Orange peel and peachy fruit with a wonderfully delicate sweetness.* ⑪ **PF.**	
★★★	1990 Willespie Verdelho, Aus. £7.85. *Soft tropical fruits and a limey, grapey richness. Cool and subtle.* ⑪ **WM, D.**	
★★★★★	1993 Hardy's Coonawarra Cabernet Sauvignon, S Australia, Aus. £5.95. *Classic Aussie Cabernet: blackcurrants, cassis, eucalyptus and spice.* ⑪ **D.**	
★★★★	Yalumba Cuvée Prestige Sparkling Cabernet, Aus. £8.75. *Yes, fizzy blackcurrants is this. Great on a summer's day.* ⑪ **D.**	
★★★★	1992 'M' Pinot Noir/Shiraz, Montara Estate, Aus. £4.99. *An unusual blend; plummy, licoricey and very interesting.* ⑪ **SP, P.**	

VER   Vinceremos ★★★★

65 Raglan Road, Leeds LS13 3JT. Tel 0113 2431691. Fax 0113 2431693. Independent Wine Merchant. Wine by the case only. **Opening Hours:** Mon-Fri 0900-1730, Sat: occasionally open – call first. **Delivery:** free locally. **Services:** mail order, glass hire (locally).

If there was a Guardian Good Wine Guide for "right-on" wine merchants, then Vinceremos would be top of the list. Last year they won more medals for organic wines at the International Wine Challenge and the Organic Wine Challenge than any other merchant and they are justifiably proud of their Millton Vineyard range, and the wines from Domaine Richeaume, as well as the excellent Eden Ridge Australians. To celebrate their tenth anniversary this year they are planning a series of special offers and have grown sufficiently to move to bigger premises.

★★★★	1994 Pinot Gris/Riesling, Bocsa, Kiskoros, Hun. £2.95. *A cool crisp wine with tropical fruit and gooseberries.* ⑪ **PY, FD.**
★★★★	1994 Chenin Blanc Barrel Fermented, Millton Vineyard, Gisborne, N.Z. £5.99. *Lovely soft, peachy and grassy.* ⑪ **WMC, SM.**
★★★★	1992 Dom. Richeaume Syrah, Henning Hoesch, Provence, Fr. £7.99. *Smoky and rich fruits with a sprinkling of white pepper.* ⑪ **P, RM, G.**
★★★★	Rabbi Jacob, Sincomar, Rabat, Mor. £3.49. *Soft, quite earthy, attractive, old-fashioned red.* ⑪ **BF, RM.**
★★★★	1993 Vacqueyras Domaine le Clos de Caveau, Gerard Bungener, Rhône, Fr. £5.99. *Hefty red with masses of damson fruit and peppery spices.* ⑪ **RM.**
★★★★	1993 Valréas Domaine de La Grande Bellane, Jean Couston, Rhône, Fr. £6.35. *Blackcurrants, chocolate and tobacco galore.* ⑪ **G, RM, SP.**

VT   The Vine Trail   ★★★★

5 Surrey Road, Bishopston, Bristol BS7 9DJ. Tel/Fax 0117 9423946. Independent Wine Merchant. **Opening Hours:** by arrangement. **Delivery:** free locally. **Tasting:** in-store, private tutored tastings available, with or without food. **Services:** cellarage, mail order. No credit cards.

The Vine Trail import a relatively small range of hand crafted wines directly from remote family-owned French vineyards. They also have a rather unusual approach to the layout of their wine list, arranging it as a tour through each wine region in turn. When you set off through the Dordogne, you will be recommended Domaine de Perreau's Montravel Blanc and when striding on to Burgundy, the wines of Daniel Barraud represent Mâcon, and Jean Philippe Fichet is one of the recommended growers from the Côte de Beaune. Explorers of French wine should lace up their hiking boots forthwith and set off to Bristol.

★★★	1993 Montravel Blanc Sec, Domaine de Perreau, Bergerac, Fr. £4.25. *Buttery Semillon and crisp gooseberry Sauvignon combined.* ¶ **SM, CH.**	
★★★★	1992 Condrieu, André Perret, Rhône, Fr. £15.75. *Exquisitely delicate, tropical and floral. Will develop further.* ¶ **D, O.**	
★★★★	1992 Meursault, Jean Philippe-Fichet, Burgundy, Fr. £13.75. *Roast hazelnuts and ripe pineapple; intense, rich and persistent.* ¶ **WFC, S.**	
★★★★	1989 Ch. Monbousquet, St Emilion, Bordeaux, Fr. £12.15. *John Arlot's favourite claret – tobacco leaf aromas from the Cabernet Franc.* ¶ **LB.**	
★★★★	1990 Jurançon 'Clos Thou', R Lapouble-Laplace, SW France, Fr. £12.55. *Honeyed apricot with a refreshing acidity – 100% Petit Manseng.* ¶ **AP, D.**	

VR   Vintage Roots   ★★★

Sheeplands Farm, Wargrave Road, Wargrave, Berks RG10 8DT. Tel 01734 401222. Fax 01734 404814. Independent Wine Merchant. **Opening Hours:** Mon-Fri 0900-1800, plus answerphone. **Delivery:** free locally. **Services:** mail order, gift mailing, glass hire.

"Organic – the way wine should be." A worthy statement with which we would heartily concur opens the Vintage Roots list, and indeed every wine listed has been produced in a way that could be described to a greater or lesser degree, as organic. The problem all too frequently associated with "green" wine is that the lack of recourse to some form of chemical intervention leaves the vines open to disease and the wine to bacterial infection. When this can be avoided, either by good fortune or alternative methods, the resulting wine can be very good indeed and may retain much more individual and expressive flavour. Lance Pigott and Neil Palmer have put together a creditable range of mostly French and some Italian, Spanish and New World wines, including the excellent Penfold's organic range, and Milton Vineyard from New Zealand. You could also try out their enticing beer, cider, cognac and.... chocolate.

★★★★	1988 Champagne Fleury, Fleury, Fr. £18.95. *Crisp, toasty fizz with appley, grapey fruit.* ¶ **AP, D, S.**	
★★★★	1989 Lessini Durello, Fongaro, Veneto, It. £9.25 *Toasty and honeyed with crisp, fresh peachy fruit.* ¶ **D, WFC.**	
★★★	1993 Macabeu Col. Leccio, Albert I Noya, Penedes, Sp. £7.75. *Creamy oak and zesty citrus fruit.* ¶ **SM, D.**	
★★★	1992 Meursault, Jean Javillier, Burgundy, Fr. £12.99. *Toffee'd and honeyed oak with delicate lime and mango fruit.* ¶ **WM, S, D.**	
★★★★	1991 Chateau Pech-Latt Vieilles Vignes, Corbieres, SW France, Fr. £5.95. *Rich, gamey wine, packed with flavour.* ¶ **LB, G.**	
★★★★	1993 Chateau La Canorgue, J.P. Margan, Provence, Fr. £6.50. *Lovely dark fruit, smoky spices and an earthy richness.* ¶ **LB, D.**	

W Waitrose ★★★

Doncastle Road, Southern Industrial Area, Bracknell, Berkshire RG12 8YA. Tel 01344 424680. South-of-England-based Supermarket Chain. 111 branches. **Opening Hours:** vary from store to store.

Still by far the most traditional supermarket in Britain – the one which resisted illegal Sunday opening – Waitrose probably remains the most reliable. Despite an unaccustomed zest for marketing (previously thought infra dig) and a regular influx of wines not seen elsewhere, this is not the place to look for gratuitous novelties or batches of 'new wave' wines from long-established countries. Indeed, the style of some of the Bordeaux on offer here is closer to that of an old-fashioned City merchant than you might find chez Adnam or Oddbin. Which, for lovers of well chosen examples of more conservative wines will come as welcome news.

**** Champagne Devaux Cuvée Rosé, Fr. £13.95. *Lovely, fresh strawberry fruit and delicate creamy bubbles – attractively elegant.* ¶ *AP, D, PF.*

**** 1989 Waitrose Vintage Champagne, F. Bonnet, Fr. £14.75. *Delightfully balanced lemon and apple fruit with a hint of bready yeast.* ¶ *AP, LS.*

**** 1994 Montenuevo Sauvignon Blanc, Maipo, Chi. £3.49. *Fresh, leafy, slightly tropical flavour. Bordeaux meets New Zealand.* ¶ *WM, LS, PY.*

**** 1994 Vdp d'Oc Chardonnay Boisé, Maurel Vedeau, Midi, Fr. £4.49. *Restrained, lemon and pineapple; ripe but not blowsy.* ¶ *WM, WFC.*

**** 1994 Pipers Brook Ninth Island Chardonnay, Tasmania, Aus. £7.99. *Unoaked, appley Chardonnay. Deliciously un-Australian.* ¶ *S, FD.*

**** 1993 Chablis 1er Cru Beauroy, La Chablisienne, Fr. £9.95. *A wine of impressive depth – good rich, yet elegant fruit.* ¶ *LS, WMC.*

**** 1993 Waitrose Gewürztraminer, Cave de Beblenheim, Alsace, Fr. £5.75. *Elegantly spicy and grapefruity.* ¶ *SP, O.*

**** 1994 Tokay Pinot Gris Clos de Hoen, Cave Vinicole de Beblenheim, Alsace, Fr. £4.99. *Lightly fruity and floral with honey and lemon.* ¶ *SP, O.*

**** 1993 Stellenzicht Cabernet Sauvignon Block Series, Stellenbosch, SA. £3.99. *Well-made tasty Cabernet packed with berry fruit.* ¶ *LB, D.*

**** 1993 Cono Sur Cabernet Sauvignon, Chimbarongo, Chi. £3.69. *Good, creamy, ripe cassis and plums with minty overtones.* ¶ *FF, PY.*

**** 1995 Avontuur Pinotage, Stellenbosch, SA. £4.79. *Latest vintage of this commendably smoky, chewy wine.* ¶ *SP, RM.*

*** 1994 Waitrose Côtes-du-Rhône, Cave de Laudun, Rhône, France. £3.25. *Lovely commercial style full of soft red fruit.* ¶ *D, PY, FF.*

*** Don Hugo, Bodegas Vitorianas, Sp. £2.99. *A simple but juicy red, full of tasty fruit and agreeable wood.* ¶ *PY.*

**** Castillo de Liria Moscatel, Gandia, Valencia, Sp. £3.35. *Lovely fresh grapey, honeyed wine. Sweet but not in the least bit cloying.* ¶ *PF.*

*** Waitrose Solera Jerezana Dry Oloroso, Lustau, Jerez, Sp. £4.95. *Wonderfully nutty and richly flavoured, raisiny sherry.* ¶ *AP.*

*** Waitrose Fine Tawny, Smith Woodhouse, Douro, Por. £5.75. *Good plum and prune fruit with a persistent flavour.* ¶ *CH.*

***** Blandy's 10 Year Old Malmsey, Madeira Wine Co., Mad. £14.45. *Deep, dark, complex and malty – Seville oranges and moscovado sugar.* ¶ *D. CH.*

WAW Waterloo Wine Co ★★★★

6 Vine Yard, Borough, London SE1 1QL. Tel 0171 403 7967. Fax 0171 357 6976. Independent Wine Merchant. **Opening Hours:** Mon-Fri 1000-1830, Sat 1000-1700. **Delivery:** free locally. **Tastings:** regular in-store and tutored sessions on request. **Services:** glass hire, ice.

Letting bygones be bygones, the Waterloo Wine Co wish it to be known that they do now stock a Napoleon brandy. The rest of their range, however, has remained more or less in the status quo, offering a comprehensive selection of good quality and value wines especially from southern France and the (unusually comprehensively covered) Loire. Plans are afoot, however, to refine the list over the coming year and concentrate more on specific regions. No doubt one on which they will continue to focus will be Waipara West in New Zealand where the company has its own vineyard.

**** Champagne Le Brun de Neuville Cuvée Selection, Fr. £12.75. *An excellent, big-flavoured and classy Champagne with yeast and biscuit.* ¶ *AP, LS, D.*

**** 1992 Domaine la Tour Boisée Rouge, Minervois, Fr. £4.25. *A classy blend of Syrah and Carignan.* ¶ *RM, SP*

**** 1990 Ch. Héléne Cuvée Ulysses, Marie Héléne Gau, Corbières, Fr. £5.70. *Quite serious, gamey, toffee'd wine.* ¶ *BF.*

**** 1993 Stoniers Pinot Noir, Mornington Peninsula, Aus. £7.99. *Classy, oaky, mulberryish wine with lovely vanilla oak.* ¶ *WMC, WMP.*

***** 1993 Mark Rattray Pinot Noir, Waipara, NZ. £11.49. *Lovely intense wild, plummy, oaky wine from an up-and-coming New Zealand producer.* ¶ *SM.*

**** 1990 Aurelio Settimo Barolo, Piedmont, It. £10.25. *Concentrated cherryish, smoky wine.* ¶ *G, LB.*

WAC   Waters Wine Merchants   ★★★

Collins Road, Heathcote, Warwick, Warwickshire CV34 6TF. Tel 01926 888889. Fax 01926 887416. Independent Wine Merchant. Wine by the case only. **Opening Hours:** Mon-Fri 0900-1700, Sat 0900-0030. **Delivery:** free locally. **Services:** glass loan, ice.

Waters, (née Waters of Coventry) is now firmly settled into its new home in Warwick where it offers a great range of clarets and surprisingly reasonably-priced Burgundy. The ubiquitous and generally uninspiring Mondavi Woodbridge and Sutter Home wines are thankfully supplemented by more interesting Californian fare from Ridge and Dry Creek. Similarly, we'd recommend sidestepping the Zonnebloem South Africans and heading straight for the Boschendals. This patchiness and tendency to take a producer's complete range is apparent elsewhere, but there are enough good wines here for us to say that these are Waters worth taking.

***** 1989 Champagne de Venoge Brut, Fr. £24.39. *Intense, raspberryish, chocolatey fizz with a lovely lingering flavour.* ¶ *D, AP.*

*** 1991 Pouilly Fumé, de Ladoucette, Loire, Fr. £10.27. *Deeply concentrated gooseberry fruit; wonderfully smoky.* ¶ *S, FO.*

**** 1992 Coudoulet de Beaucastel Blanc, Côtes de Rhône, Fr. £10.73. *Ripe, peachy and spectacularly balanced Rhône white.* ¶ *LS, WMC.*

*** 1992 Concha Y Toro Merlot, Rapel, Chi. £3.99. *Plummy, easy-going red. Good party fare.* ¶ *D, PY, LB.*

*** Ridge Paso Robles Zinfandel, Montebello, California, US. £8.38. *Ridge's entry-level Zin — full of brambley promise.* ¶ *SP.*

WES   Wessex Wines   ★★★★

88, St Michael's Trading Estate, Bridport, Dorset DT6 3RR. Tel 01308 427177. Fax 01308 424343. Independent Wine Merchant. Wine by the case only. **Opening Hours:** Mon-Sat 0900-1230, Sun and afternoons "on call". **Tastings:** regular in-warehouse, plans for tutored tastings. **Services:** gift mailing, glass hire, ice.

Mike Farmer assures us that the absence of the all too appropriate Thomas Hardy from his list is for commercial rather than literary reasons, and far from the madding regularity with which the same producers turn up elsewhere, his list continues to promote more obscure wines. His regional and southern French examples are particularly appealing, including the brilliant Château de Lastours "Cuvée Simone Descamps". The new "Wine Warehouse" is bigger and better, and the "taste before you buy" policy should encourage anyone looking for bargains to try here first.

*** 1993 Bellefontaine Terret, VdP des Côtes de Gascogne, Fr. £3.35. *Fresh, herby dry wine. Good "Old World" flavour.* ⟍ **AP, LS.**

*** 1994 Bourgogne Blanc, Boutinot, Fr. £5.19. *Fresh, young, quite pineappley Chardonnay.* ⟍ **WM, SF.**

*** 1991 Minervois, Dom. Les Combelles, J.P. Henriques, Fr. £4.39. *Unusually "serious" Minervois with rich berry fruit.* ⟍ **G, BF.**

***** 1989 Corbières, Ch. de Lastours, Cuvée Simone Descamps, Fr. £4.95. *Even more serious Corbières, from a home for the mentally handicapped.* ⟍ **RM, SP.**

*** 1989 Ch. Tourteran, Haut-Médoc, Bordeaux, Fr. £7.11. *Nicely made, ripe blackcurranty wine; beginning to mature.* ⟍ **LB.**

*** 1992 Chénas, Dom. de Chassignol, Jacques Depagneux, Beaujolais, Fr. £5.79. *Rich, cherryish Beaujolais from a lesser-known village.* ⟍ **SM, LS.**

WHI   The White Horse Inn   ★★★★

Chilgrove, Nr Chichester, West Sussex. Tel 01243 535219. Fax 01243 535301. Independent Wine Merchant. **Open for collections:** Tues-Sat 1100-2230, Sun mornings by arrangement. **Services:** Ice, glasses.

There are some truly great wines on the White Horse Inn wine list. Among the gems are a fantastic selection of Humbrecht and Schlumberger vendanges tardives, several Huët and Poniatowski Vouvrays, Cloudy Bay and Kumeu River from New Zealand and, from California, Quivira Zinfandel, Matanzas Creek Merlot. And – for the more financially adventurous – Stags Leap Cask 23 Cabernet Sauvignon. If you are going to eat at the inn, there is no extra charge on the wine, so why not splash out and wash down your steak with a drop of 1947 Chateau Lafite?

***** 1990 Bâtard Montrachet, Jean Noel Gagnard, Burgundy, Fr. £55. *Great, biscuity wine; white Burgundy at its best. Worth keeping.* ⟍ **WFC.**

***** 1991 Kumeu River Chardonnay, Auckland, NZ. £13.45. *Wonderfully opulent and very convincingly Burgundian Chardonnay.* ⟍ **WM, CH.**

***** 1989 Savennières, Clos du Papillon, Yves & Pierre Soulez, Loire, Fr. £14.95. *Lovely Chenin Blanc with appley freshness and nuts.* ⟍ **PF.**

**** 1990 Maximiner Grunhauser Herrenberg Spatlese, von Schubert, Mosel, Ger. £15.50. *Stylish, 'slatey' Riesling with grapey perfumed appeal.* ⟍ **AP, S.**

***** 1990 Barolo 'Bussia Soprana', Aldo Conterno, Piedmont, It. £24.50. *Top class Barolo from a master producer: tobaccoey, plummy and intense.* ⟍ **CH.**

WOC   Whitesides of Clitheroe   ★★★

Shawbridge Street, Clitheroe, Lancs. BB7 1NA. Tel 01200 22281. Fax 01200 27129. Independent Wine Merchant. **Opening Hours:** Mon-Sat 0900-2130. **Delivery:** free locally. **Tastings:** regular in-store. **Services:** gift mailing, glass hire.

Despite a printed list which barely strays beyond the pedestrian (though it's good to see Willespie, Grove Mill and Jackson Estate sticking their heads up among such stock favourites as Brown Brothers, Lindemans, Penfolds, etc.), the shop on Shawbridge Street is a veritable Aladdin's cave with labyrinthine shelving featuring rows and rows of wine to have Jilly Goolden looking for a new Thesaurus.

**** 1994 Grove Mill Sauvignon Blanc, Marlborough, NZ. £7.69. *Really ripe gooseberry and exotic passionfruit. Big, fat and balanced.* ⟍ **HC.**

***** 1990 St. Veran Cuvée Prestige, Dom. Roger Lasserat, Burgundy, Fr. £9.50. *Maturing, quite creamy Southern Burgundy. Serious.* ⟍ **SF, S.**

**** 1988 Graacher Himmelreich Auslese, F.W. Gymnasium, Ger. £11.50. *Elegant, honeyed wine with floral perfume and petrolly spice.* ⟍ **AP, PS.**

*** 1994 Brouilly Garanche, Eventail, Beaujolais, Fr. £6.69. *Fruity, seductive Beaujolais with a typical boiled sweet and banana character.* ⟍ **AP, LS.**

**** 1988 Pommard Clos des Epeneaux, Comte Armand, Burgundy, Fr. £21.50. *Fine, mature red Burgundy, with gameyness and raspberry fruit.* ∥ *LB, RMS.*

***** Yalumba Museum Show Reserve Rutherglen Muscat, Victoria, Aus. £7.25. *Australian Liqueur Muscat at its gingery, Dundee Cakey, spicy best.* ∥ *PS.*

**** 1979 Graham's Malvedos Vintage Port, Por. £17.45. *A (relatively) affordable taste of the perfumed Graham's style of port.* ∥ *CC, CS.*

WIK   Wickham & Co   ★★★★

New Road, Bideford, Devon, EX39 2AQ. Tel 1237 473292. Fax 01237 472471. Independent Wine Merchant. **Opening Hours:** Mon-Fri 0900-1700, Sat 0900-1300. **Delivery:** free locally. **Services:** mail order, glass loan.

Wickham first began shipping port and Madeira as early as 1817. These days they have somewhat by-passed the port in favour of a jack-of-all trades approach to their range. The great and good of Bordeaux, Burgundy and the Rhône are forced to compete for customers' attention with upstarts from the colonies and, in this case, as elsewhere, it is probably the Australians who come out on top, followed closely by a range of excellent wines from the oldest of the New World nations, South Africa.

**** 1993 Chablis, Dom. des Manants, Jean Marc Brocard, Burgundy, Fr. £6.50. *Serious Chablis; lean and made for shellfish.* ∥ *S.*

**** 1993 Etchart Torrontes, Cafayate, Arg. £4.28. *Unusual but satisfying aromatic wine from a grape unique to Argentina.* ∥ *D, PY.*

**** 1992 Pinot Gris, Schlumberger, Alsace, Fr. £7.75. *Lovely; intensely spicy with typical Alsace perfume.* ∥ *AP, S.*

**** 1991 Crozes Hermitage 'Les Meysonnieres' Rouge, Chapoutier, Rhône, Fr. £7.64. *Blackberryish wine; concentrated with attractive oak.* ∥ *CH, RMS.*

*** 1993 Mitchells Peppertree Shiraz, Clare Valley, S Australia, Aus. £6.75. *An Australian classic, with lovely spicy brambley fruit.* ∥ *SP, BF.*

**** 1992 Saxenburg Estate Pinotage, Stellenbosch, SA. £5.46. *Full of brambles and plums.* ∥ *SP, RM.*

WBU   The Wine Bureau   ★★★★

5 Raglan Street, Harrogate, HG1 1LE. Tel 01423 527772. Fax 01423 563077. Independent Wine Merchant selling by the case. **Opening Hours:** mainly Mon-Sat 0900-1700 – but "flexible". **Delivery:** free locally. **Tastings:** in store. **Services:** mail order, glass loan, ice, cellaring.

The retail arm of oddly named wholesalers 'The Tannin Level', and situated in a genteel corner house in similarly genteel Harrogate, the Wine Bureaucrats are clearly mining a rich – in all senses of the word – seam of Yorkshire wine enthusiasm. There are exciting up-market wines here you'd scour the rest of the country to find; wines like Dulong's innovative Rebelle, Jermann's extraordinary perfumed, buttery "Where the Dreams Have no End" white and the Goldwater Estate wines from Waiheke Island off the shore of Auckland in New Zealand. The list is small but informative and entertaining; be sure to ask about the X-rated tasting notes for the E&E Shiraz...

**** 1993 Sauvignon de St Bris, Burgundy, Fr. £6.05. *Wonderfully fresh, clean Sancerre-style wine.* ∥ *D, AP.*

***** Rebelle Cuvée No. 3, Fr. £9.95. *An Australian-style blend of Syrah and Cabernet – made in a decidedly Bordeaux-style way.* ∥ *D, PY, AP.*

**** 1992 Enate Tinto Crianza, Somontano, Sp. £5.75. *A red combining the best of its two components, Cabernet and Tempranillo.* ∥ *P, WM.*

***** 1991 E & E Black Pepper Shiraz, S. Australia, Aus. *A huge and intensely concentrated combination of pepper, rich fruit and eucalyptus.* ∥ *D, BF, LB.*

**** 1994 Babich Hawkes Bay Sauvignon Blanc £6.35, Hawkes bay, NZ. *Fresh and crisp with typical Kiwi gooseberry and melon fruit.* ∥ *RM, CC.*

TWB   The Wine Business   ★★★

Unit 2, Chelsea Wharf, 15 Lots Road, London, SW10 0QF. Tel 0171 351 6856 Fax 0171 351 0030. Independent Wine Merchant. **Opening Hours:** Mon-Fri 0900-2000, Sat 1100-1500. **Delivery:** free locally. **Tastings:** in-store. **Services:** mail order, glass loan, ice.

This single branch, independent wine warehouse operation close to the picturesque power station and Chelsea Harbour (annual hang-out of the UK wine trade during the International Wine Challenge), used to be known as London Wine Ltd. It does a better job than most at offering a short, punchy range from most of the major corners of the globe. There are no real surprises here; the buzzword is reliability, so prepare yourself for a Louis Latour lineup representing Burgundy, Georges Duboeuf taking care of Beaujolais, and the Australian range being limited to Jacobs Creek and Lindemans.

* ***   1994 Torres Gran Viña Sol, Penedes, Sp. £5.25. *Fresh melon and a little soft peachy banana fruit. Refreshing.* ▮ *D, LS.*
* ***   1994 Dom. de Papolle, VdP des Côtes de Gascogne, Fr. £3.67. *Crisp and refreshing appley wine with zing.* ▮ *D, PY, AP*
* ***   1993 Chateau Angelin, R M D I, Midi, Fr. £4.20. *Good well-made stuff; lightly fruity and well balanced.* ▮ *D.*
* ****   1994 Fleurie, Georges Duboeuf, Beaujolais, Fr. £8.10. *Lovely fresh raspberry fruit with a suggestion of spice and chocolate.* ▮ *SM, E, WMP.*
* ***   1993 Marimar Torres Pinot Noir, California, US. £15.99. *Packed with raspberry and sweet oak. Creamily satisfying.* ▮ *RM, CC.*

WC   Wine Cellar   ★★★

P.O. Box 476, Loushers Lane, Warrington, Cheshire WA4 6RR. Tel 01925 444555. Fax 01925 415474. Regional Chain. 30 branches. **Opening Hours:** Mon-Sat 1000-2200, Sun 1200-1400, 1900-2200. **Delivery:** free locally. **Tastings:** regular in-store. **Services:** glass hire, consumer wine fairs.

Wouldn't it be nice if Warrington had something to be known for apart from being the home of heavily marketed Wodka and the headquarters for the Cellar 5 chain of beer 'n fag shops? Well, as predicted in last year's *Guide*, Greenalls, the firm behind the spirit and the shops has now bravely entered the world of real wine, with its new mini chain of – so far – mostly northern-based Wine Cellar shops. Looking like a cross between Next boutiques and spruced-up Wine Racks, topped with Oddbins-style graphics and wine list, these shops are a welcome addition to the high street – as is an impressive list of wines put together from scratch by Kevin Wilson (the buyer who took William Low out of the dark age). Only one cloud hovers on the horizon, in the shape of rumours from 'reliable City sources' that the new-born chain is to be taken over by Thresher. I, for one, would prefer to believe Greenalls' denials. We shall see.

* ***   Seaview Brut, Penfolds, Aus. £5.75. *A lovely, rich mouthful of good yeasty flavours and fine Pinot fruit. One of the best value fizzes around.* ▮ *AP, PY.*
* ***   1993 Viura Hermanos Lurton, Rueda, Sp. £4.49. *Clean ripe and tangy, this is very well made in a good commercial style.* ▮ *SP, RM.*
* ****   1990 Meursault, Dom. Matrot, Burgundy, Fr. £17.49. *The real thing; nutty, yeasty and long with rich tones of burnt butter.* ▮ *CH, SF.*
* ****   1992 Dr Loosen Riesling, Mosel, Ger. £5.99. *A ripe and grapey wine full of refreshingly simple citrus and honey flavours.* ▮ *O, CC.*
* ***   1991 Cabernet Sauvignon, Quinta de Pancas, Por. £5.99. *Good rich flavours of cassis & oak; well made and well balanced.* ▮ *LB, G.*
* ***   1993 Gigondas, Cave de Vacqueyras, Rhône, Fr. £6.99. *Good peppery wine, long rich and spicy, very typical.* ▮ *G, LB.*
* ***   1994 Valdepenas Sin Crianza, Casa de la Vina, Sp. £3.49. *Good, ripe and well made; this is a soft, plummy and gently spicy wine.* ▮ *SP, P.*

TWH   The Wine House   ★★★★

10 Stafford Road, Wallington, Surrey SM6 9AD. Tel 0181 669 6661. Fax 0181 401 0039. Independent Wine Merchant. **Opening Hours:** Tues-Sat 1000-1800, Sun 1200-1400. **Delivery:** free locally. **Tastings:** regular in-store, plus wine-tasting circle. **Services:** Glass hire, ice.

The Rodkers have no illusions about the attraction of big, "safe" names and the propensity of customers to buy by price. Section A of their list exemplifies wine available for under a fiver, including David Wynn's Red or Les Terrasses de Guilhem from Mas de Daumas Gassac. Spain is well represented in Section B by Cosme Palaçio, and Guelbenzu Enate, and Portugal by Luis Pato and others of his calibre. Masi's Campo Fiorin and Maculan's Brentino Breganze Rosso set the pace for Italy and from France the likes of Gaillard's 1989 St Joseph, Ermitage de Chasse-Spleen 1988 and Faiveley's Bourgogne Pinot Noir make up a French multiple choice extravaganza. The pricier red Bordeaux (Section C) are a little too orientated towards 1984 and 1987, but are nevertheless worth a second glance for beauties such as Château Vray Croix de Gay 1985 and Château Beychevelle 1989.

***   Denbies Estate Wine, Surrey, Eng. £4.35. *Good value, clean, grapey, grapefruity English wine.* ¶ **WM.**

***   1993 Galestro, Antinori, Tuscany, It. £4.99. *Cool, crisp white with fresh, clean fruit.* ¶ **D, PY, WMC.**

***   1993 Nobilo White Cloud, NZ. £3.50. *Zippy youthful fruit with a lovely lemony tang.* ¶ **PY, SM.**

****   1985 Bairrada, Luis Pato, Por. £5.90. *Beautifully balanced, rich red, with dark cherry fruits and smooth oak.* ¶ **RM, G.**

****   1992 Fleur de Carneros Pinot Noir, California, US. £8.75. *Smoky oak and summer pudding fruits.* ¶ **SM, WMC.**

WR   Wine Rack   ★★★★

Sefton House, 42 Church Road, Welwyn Garden City, Herts AL8 6RJ. Tel 01707 328244. National Chain. 118 branches. **Opening Hours:** Mon-Sat 0900-2200, Sun 1200-1500, 1900-2200. **Delivery:** free locally, nationally at cost. **Tastings:** occasional in-store plus sessions for local organisations. **Services:** glass loan, ice.

A star performer and a refreshing addition to the high street when Whitbread gave birth to it as a brother to Thresher a few years ago, Wine Rack has more recently seemed a little less exciting. Indeed, this year, unkind critics have occasionally gone so far as to nickname it "Beer Rack" on account of the wide range of ales which sometimes appear to have supplanted the wines. But look beyond the cans and you will find a long list of *International Wine Challenge* award-winners and a range which includes particularly impressive selections of wines from Alsace, Bordeaux, Chile and New Zealand, as well as the full Thresher range. Even so, compared to Bottoms Up – whose range is very similar – there is a significant risk of the stocks of the bottle you want in any given shop being very limited. The store's management's efforts to educate its staff are supplemented via its "Book of Knowledge" which should enable even the least sparky of assistants to answer your trickier questions.

****   1988 Champagne Lanson Vintage, Fr. £23.99. *Very classy maturing Champagne which would be worth keeping for another few years.* ¶ **AP, D.**

****   Cuvée Napa Brut, Mumm, California, US. £8.99. *Lots of fresh fruit and doughy, yeasty aromas. Great value fizz.* ¶ **AP, D.**

****   1994 Villard Aconcagua Sauvignon Blanc, Casablanca Valley, Chi. £4.99. *Made by a Frenchman in Chile; grassy and like Bordeaux Blanc.* ¶ **SF, LS.**

****   1993 Sauvignon Salices, J. & F. Lurton, Midi, Fr. £3.99. *Deliciously crisp and fruity Sauvignon, floral and fresh.* ¶ **LS, AP.**

**** 1993 Red Cliffs Estate Chardonnay, Mildura, Victoria, Aus. £4.99. *Simple, tropically ripe wine with some biscuity almost Burgundian character.* ∥ *FD.*

**** 1993 Martinborough Vineyard Chardonnay, NZ. £10.99. *Loads of fantastic tropical fruit tempered by serious vanilla oak.* ∥ *WMC.*

***** 1990 Gewürztraminer Grand Cru Brand, Cave de Turckheim, Alsace, Fr. £11.59. *Rich, very lycheeish, satisfying wine. Lovely with fresh fruit.* ∥ *O.*

**** 1988 Ch. d'Angludet, Margaux, Bordeaux, Fr. £14.99. *Lovely jammy fruit and earthy oak. Will keep.* ∥ *LB, G.*

**** 1991 Ch. Bouscassé, Alain Brumont, S W France, Fr. £6.69. *Classic Madiran with fruity yet slightly tough flavour. Tastily traditional.* ∥ *RM, SP.*

**** 1991 Rosso Conero San Lorenzo, Umani Rònchi, It. £5.59. *Complex black cherry, damson fruit. Chocolate and cigar-box aromas with smooth tannins.* ∥ *P, RM.*

***** 1989 Gran Sangre de Toro, Miguel Torres, Penedes, Sp. £5.49. *Seductive wine with vanilla oak, spice and ripe squashy strawberries.* ∥ *LB.*

**** 1992 Chapel Hill Shiraz, McLaren Vale, Aus. £7.99. *Ultra-ripe, soft smoky Shiraz you could enjoyably spread on toast.* ∥ *RMS, CHO.*

**** 1992 Morgan Pinot Noir, California, US. £12.99. *Burgundian-style Pinot with lovely raspberry fruit.* ∥ *SM, BF.*

***** 1989 Vouvray Sec Le Haut Lieu, Gaston Huët, Loire, Fr. £7.49. *Concentrated chenin with lingering flavours of apple and honey.* ∥ *CC.*

**** Don Zoilo Manzanilla, Jerez, Sp. £7.99. *Classic salty, tangy dry sherry. Serve very cold – and generously.* ∥ *AP.*

***** Gonzalez Byass Mathusalem, Jerez, Sp. £18.99. *Liquid Christmas pudding! A real mouthful of dried fruit and spice.* ∥ *D.*

**** 1977 Smith Woodhouse Vintage Port, Douro, Por. £20.91. *Youthful, spicy with deep fruit and really complex flavours. Well worth keeping.* ∥ *CH, CS.*

WSC The Wine Schoppen ****

See Barrels and Bottles.

WSO The Wine Society *****

Gunnels Wood Road, Stevenage, Herts, SG1 2BG. Enquiries: Tel 01438 741177 Fax 01438 741392. Orders: Tel 01438 740222 Fax: 01438 761167. Wine Club – £20 Life Membership. **Opening Hours:** Mon-Fri 0900-1730, Sat 0900-1600. **Delivery:** free nationally for 1 case or more. **Tastings:** regular in-store and tutored, plus organised events and customers' club. **Services:** *en primeur*, cellarage, mail order, glass hire.

If you fancy buying leek and almond relish from Normandy, wood roasted piquillo peppers or rocket sauce made from rucoletta, extra virgin olive oil, almonds, capers and anchovies, you've come to the right place. The point about specialities like these is that they really seem to have been introduced because they suit the tastes of the members. This embodiment of democracy is just as evident in one of the best ranges of Ancient and Modern wines anywhere – a standard of service which is, according to members, second to none and, of course, the opportunity to save duty by collecting your purchases from the Society's increasingly successful outlet in Hesdin, near Calais.

**** 1994 Casablanca Valley Chardonnay, Curico, Chile. £6.95. *Lovely modern, fresh pineappley, melony wine with gentle oak.* ∥ *WFC, LS.*

*** 1988 Riesling Cuvée Frederic Emile, Trimbach, Alsace, Fr. £15. *Delicious apple and honey flavours. A classic Alsace Riesling.* ∥ *AP.*

**** 1991 Basedow Shiraz, S Australia, Aus. £5.60. *Spicy wine with some delicacy to it.* ∥ *G, SP.*

*** 1991 Alentejo, Carvalho Ribeiro Ferriera, Por. £4.45. *Meaty, characterful stuff from a – hitherto – little-known region of Portugal.* ∥ *P, PY.*

**** 1991 Viñas de Gain Rioja, Cosecheros Alaveses, Sp. £5.50. *Good value, soft wine with a flavour of ripe plum and spice.* ∥ *RMS, P.*

***   1994 Chardonnay Alasia, Araldica, Piedmont, It. £4.95. *Simple, fruity Chardonnay.* ⁙ *LS, WMP.*

***   1993 Dom. du Moulin Rigaud Minervois, Midi, Fr. £4.25. *Rich, toffee, plum and berry fruits. Characterful.* ⁙ *RM.*

****   1934 Niepoort Colheita Port, Douro, Por. £120. *The Society offers cheaper ports, but this extraordinary old Tawny is a treasure.* ⁙ *LB, RMS.*

WMK   Winemark   ★★★

3 Duncrue Place, Belfast, Northern Ireland BT3 9BU. Tel 01232 746274. Fax 01232 748022. Independent Wine Merchant. **Opening Hours:** Mon-Sat 0930-2100 **Delivery:** free locally. **Tastings:** regular in-store, plus tutored tastings for wine club and groups. **Services:** mail order, gift mailing, glass hire.

The largest off-licence chain in Northern Ireland with 73 stores, Winemark is tapping a rich vein of success. A generally strong selection tends to rely in the main on wines from big producers like Hardy's, Gallo and Turkheim. Where the choice is extended significantly beyond the ordinary, such as the top end of the German list, you will, though, find some real gems. Everything depends on you the customer: if Winemark can sell wines like Muller Catoir, Mas de Daumas and Clos du Val, then the buyers might be tempted to "Oddbinsize" the more modest segments of the list.

****   1993 Pouilly Fumé Les Loges, Guy Saget, Loire, Fr. £7.79. *Crisp and fresh, slightly spicy grapey, peachy fruit.* ⁙ *D, S, SM.*

***   1994 Solana Torrontes & Treixadura, Alanis B&B & Mitchelton Wines, Sp. £4.29. *Easy-going, appley dry white wine from two unusual grapes.* ⁙ *S, D.*

***   1991 Oriachovitza Cabernet Sauvignon Reserve, Menada Stara Zagora, Bul. £3.19. *Soft, plummy, blackcurranty wine. Very easy-going.* ⁙ *SP, G.*

***   1993 Château Malijay Les Genevrières, D V S M, Rhône, Fr. £5.49. *Wonderful peppery spices, spearmint and rich fruit.* ⁙ *RMS.*

***   1985 Campo Viejo Rioja Gran Reserva, Rioja, Sp. £7.99. *Smooth, matured tannins and lovely earthy fruit.* ⁙ *RMS, SP.*

WIN   The Winery/Les Amis du Vin   ★★★★

Clifton Road, Maida Vale, London W9 1SS. Tel 0171 286 6475. Fax 0171 495 4473 Independent Wine Merchant/Wine Club. **Opening Hours:** Mon-Fri 10.30-20.30, Sat 10.00-1800 **Delivery:** free locally. **Tastings:** regular in-store. **Services:** mail order, gift-mailing, glass hire, ice.

This pharmacy-turned-wine shop around the corner from Lords offers ordinary mortals the chance to buy by the bottle wine otherwise sold wholesale by the Forte's subsidiaries Griersons and Geoffrey Roberts. It also remains one of the few places in Britain to find big-name and hard-to-find mature Californian wines, many of which are good value for money – though they tend to cost over £10 a bottle. There are good Australians from Petaluma and Yalumba, New Zealanders from Delegats and some impressive Italians too, but France is a major focus, especially Champagne, Burgundy, the Rhône and South.

*****   1994 Nautilus Estate Marlborough Sauvignon Blanc, NZ. £6.95. *Spicy, gooseberryish wine with lots of ripe tropical fruit.* ⁙ *WMC, PY.*

*****   1991 Petaluma Chardonnay, S Australia, Aus. £9.95. *Beautifully balanced appley fruit and creamy oak. Ready to drink.* ⁙ *WM, WMC.*

*****   1990 Cuvaison Merlot, California, US. £15.95. *All you could wish for in a Merlot. Intensely plummy with smooth, spicy oak.* ⁙ *LB, WM.*

****   1992 Côtes Du Rhône, A Ogier & Fils, Rhône, Fr. £5.50. *Classy, clean raspberry flavours.* ⁙ *G, RMS.*

*****   1991 Don Jacobo Rioja Crianza, Bodegas Corral, Sp. £5.50. *Good ripe fruit with soft oak.* ⁙ *SP, P.*

WWI Woodhouse Wines

See Hicks & Don.

WRW Wright Wine Co ★★★★

The Old Smithy, Raikes Road, Skipton, N. Yorks BD23 1NP. Tel 01756 700886. Fax 01756 798580. Independent Wine Merchant. **Opening Hours:** Mon-Sat 0900-1800. **Delivery:** free locally. **Tastings:** occasional in-store. **Services:** gift mailing, glass hire, ice. No credit cards.

A creditable and well thought out range of wines and spirits, put together with the minimum of fuss and fanfare. The list is not designed to chuckle over, nor to wow you with stunning photographs – all you will find here are wine names and prices – but getting to know the Wright Wine Co's range may well pay dividends, particularly if you are a cocktail barman looking for rare ingredients. Wine lovers may be more interested in a great range of Burgundy, plenty of good classed growth eighties claret and a solid selection of Aussies and Californians.

★★★★ 1988 Champagne Pol Roger Extra Dry, Pol Roger, Champagne, Fr. £26.50. *Richly toasty with delicious fresh pineapple fruit.* ¶ *AP, D, S.*

★★★ 1990 Hautes Côtes de Nuits Blanc, Pinot Beurot, Thevenot le Brun, Burgundy, Fr. £11.50. *Creamy, with citrusy, honeyed aromas.* ¶ *WM, SM.*

★★★★★ 1991 Warwick Farm Trilogy, Stellenbosch, SA. £8.95. *Fine, concentrated blend of Cab Sauv/Franc and Merlot. Chewy and flavoursome.* ¶ *LB.*

★★★★ 1989 Cornas, J. Vidal-Fleury, Rhône, Fr. £10.30. *Serious, smoky wine with ripe berry fruit. Spicy and ready to drink.* ¶ *G.*

★★★★ 1994 Brouilly Château Thibault, Loron et Fils, Beaujolais, Fr. £7.70. *Soft, ripe raspberry and strawberry fruit. Smooth tannins.* ¶ *D, FF, WM.*

YAP Yapp Bros ★★★★★

The Old Brewery, Mere, Wiltshire BA12 6DY. Tel 01747 860423. Fax 01747 860929. Independent Wine Merchant. **Opening Hours:** Mon-Fri 0900-1700, Sat 0900-1300. **Delivery:** free on orders of 2 cases or more. **Services:** gift mailing, glass hire.

Notable wine writers have penned less worthy and informative volumes than the beautifully illustrated Yapp wine list. All credit goes to Robin and Judith Yapp who, for over a quarter of a century, have provided their customers with the best the Rhône and the Loire have to offer. It may be specialist to the point of absurdity, but they offer more choice from just two regions than many merchants manage to give from across the world.

★★★ 1992 Gros Plant, La Maisdonnière, Bernard Baffreau, Loire, Fr..£5.25. *Bone dry traditional Loire white. Screams for shellfish.* ¶ *S.*

★★★★ 1992 Hermitage Blanc, Grippat, Rhône Fr. £17.25. *Rich, floral, spicy wine. Drink now or leave for a decade.* ¶ *RM, SP.*

★★★ 1992 Azay le Rideau Rosé, Gaston Pavy, Loire, Fr. £6.25. *Fresh, but quite 'serious' pink to drink with food.* ¶ *FD, LS.*

★★★★★ 1991 Domaine de Trévallon Eloi Dürrbach, Provence, Fr. £21.25. *Fascinating, complex wine; spicy and lingering.* ¶ *RMS, SP.*

★★★ 1994 Ch. de Crémat Rouge, Charles Bagnis, Provence, Fr. £16.95. *Pricy but fascinating, made near Nice from grapes grown almost nowhere else.* ¶ *LB.*

★★★★★ 1993 Hermitage, Chave, Rhône, Fr. £22.50. *Serious, mature wine built to last. Gamey and concentrated and just beginning to soften.* ¶ *RM, G.*

★★★★★ 1993 Cornas, Clape, Rhône, Fr. £13.25. *Classic, smoky, leathery Syrah to keep or drink with strong game right now.* ¶ *G, RM.*

★★★★ 1994 Crozes Hermitage, Alain Graillot, Rhône, Fr. £8.75. *A wine to compete with pricier Hermitage. Rich, modern and intensely brambley.* ¶ *RM, SP.*

**** 1993 Côte Rôtie, Jasmin, Rhône, Fr. £16.95. *Concentrated, leathery wine with deep berry flavours.* ¶ *SP, RM.*

*** 1992 Coteaux d'Ancenis Pierre Guidon, Loire, Fr. £5.65. *A rare chance to taste the Gamay away from its home in Beaujolais. Cherryish.* ¶ *WM,D.*

**** 1989 Jasnières, Les Truffières, Jean-Baptiste Pinon, Loire, Fr. £15.25. *Classic Loire Chenin with flavours of honey and apples.* ¶ *D, S.*

**** 1993 Bonnezeaux Domaine de la Sansonnière Cuvée Mathilde, Loire, Fr. £26.75. *Honey and apricots. Lovely young Late Harvest wine.* ¶ *WM, SM, S.*

YOR   York Wines   ★★★★

Wellington House, Sheriff Hutton, York YO6 IQY. Tel 01347 878716. Fax 01347 878546. Independent Wine Merchant. **Opening Hours:** Tues 1000-1700 Wed-Sat 1000-2000. **Delivery:** free on orders of 1 case or more. **Services:** mail order, glass loan.

Second division football teams are often far more exciting than the big boys. The players might not be household names but they still score goals and their transfer fees are affordable. The York team looks strong this year; the French trio of Corbières, Cahors and Bergerac are reliable in midfield, and one or two of the Eastern Europeans are exciting, if occasionally a little volatile. Up-front, the experience of the strikers Ch de Ferrand and Champagne "Charlie" Gremillet guarantees results, and the young 16 year old Quinta do Bomfim from Portuguese team Dow's is solid in goal.

*** 1993 Chardonnay 'Le Veritiere', GIV, It. £5.15. *A very appealing Chardonnay, 15% barrel fermented and full of fresh, zingy fruit.* ¶ *FD, SM.*

*** 1990 Taltarni Shiraz, Victoria, Aus. £7.45. *Black cherry and plum fruit, lovely sweet oak and minty aromas.* ¶ *RM, SP.*

**** 1990 Cumaro VdT, Umani Ronchi, Marches, It. £10.65. *Rich modern wine with deep brambley fruit.* ¶ *LB, G.*

**** 1987 CVNE Rioja Reserva, Sp. £7.85. *Tobacco and chocolate, creamy oak and rich berry fruits.* ¶ *P, SM.*

NY   Noel Young   ★★★★

56, High Street, Trumpington, Cambridge CB2 2LS. Tel 01223 844744. Fax 01223 844736. Independent Wine Merchant. **Opening Hours:** Mon-Sat 1000-2100, Sun 1200-1400. **Delivery:** free locally. **Tastings:** regular in-store, plus "winemaker evenings". **Services:** en primeur, mail order, gift mailing.

How many merchants offer you the chance to compare the flavour of two southern French whites made from the Terret, to sample the Scrabble lover's favourite Cuvée Bixintxo from Irouléguy, or carry out a comparative tasting of nine different (first class) New Zealand Sauvignon blancs, late harvest wines from Austria, serious Burgundies and more affordable French regional wines? All the more region for any budding wine student to go up to Cambridge. As for Noel Young, I'd readily award a double first.

**** 1993 Alois Kracher Traminer, Neusiedlersee, A. £9.59. *Floral, tropical fruit and soft spicy aromas.* ¶ *O, AP.*

**** 1994 Bonny Doon Ca' del Solo Malvasia Bianca, California, US. £7.99. *Perfumed, dry yet grapey, blend of Californian and Italian flavours.* ¶ *D, S.*

**** 1992 Chateau Bouscassé, Alain Brumont, S W France, Fr. £6.99. *Interesting classic Madiran with fruity yet slightly tough flavour. Tastily traditional.* ¶ *G.*

***** 1992 E&E Black Pepper Shiraz, S Australia, Aus. £13.29. *Intense, quintessentially Australian Shiraz. Rich, spicy and long.* ¶ *G, CH.*

**** 1993 Au Bon Climat Pinot Noir, California, US. £13.49. *Great Pinot Noir with a 'wild' berry flavour. Richly satisfying.* ¶ *SM, G.*

***** 1987 Alois Kracher Scheurebe, Alois Kracher, Neusiedler See, A. £20. *Perfumey fruit, rich and full bodied. Slightly spicy.* ¶ *O, SP, CH.*

A-Z

HOW TO READ THE ENTRIES

Tim Adams[1] (Clare Valley, Australia) Highly successful producer of rich,
peachy SEMILLON[2] and deep-flavoured SHIRAZ 88 90 91 92.[3]*****[4] Semillon
1993 £9[5] (AUC)[6] Shiraz 1990 £10-11 (MG, SEL).

1 Names of producers appear in red (grape varieties are framed in red; wine
terms appear in SMALL CAPITALS).
2 Words that have their own entry elsewhere in the A-Z appear in SMALL BOLD
CAPITALS.
3 Only those vintages that are good have been listed.
4 Where specific wines are mentioned they are rated from * to *****
according to value for money.
5 Prices are rounded up to the nearest 50p and represent those quoted as we
go to print in July 1995. Prices from producers and merchants other than
the ones we mention may vary. Prices marked with an * refer to the
average cost at auction.
6 Stockists. See pages 30/31 for an explanation of merchants codes. If the
merchant is not featured in the Guide, the telephone number will appear.
(Note: even if not specifically stated, many of the wines mentioned may
also be available from supermarkets and high street wine merchants).

Abboccato (Italy) SEMI-DRY. *** Tesco Orvieto Classico, Barbi £3.50 (TO).
Abfüller/Abfüllung (Germany) BOTTLER/BOTTLED BY.
Abocado (Spain) SEMI-DRY.
Abbruzzi (Italy) Region on the east coast. Often dull TREBBIANO whites. Finer
MONTEPULCIANO reds. *** 1994 Tollo Montepulciano d'Abruzzo £2.50 (A).
AC (France) See APPELLATION CONTROLEE.
Acacia (CARNEROS, California) One of California's historically sometimes
uneven producers; now decidely improved. CHARDONNAY and PINOT NOIR.
**** 1993 Chardonnay £12 (BI) *** 1989 Pinot Noir £11 (MWW, WR).
Acetic acid THIS VOLATILE ACID (CH_3COOH) FEATURES IN TINY PROPORTIONS IN
ALL WINES. CARELESS WINEMAKING CAN RESULT IN WINE BEING TURNED INTO
ACETIC ACID - A SUBSTANCE BETTER KNOWN AS VINEGAR.
Acidity ESSENTIAL NATURAL BALANCING COMPONENT (USUALLY TARTARIC) THAT GIVES
FRESHNESS. IN HOTTER COUNTRIES (AND SOMETIMES COOLER ONES) IT MAY BE ADDED.
Aconcagua Valley (CHILE) Central valley region noted for its blackcurranty
CABERNET SAUVIGNON. *** 1991 Don Maximiano Cabernet Sauvignon Reserva,
Errazuriz Estate £7 (OD).
Tim Adams (Clare Valley, Australia) Highly successful producer of rich,
peachy Semillon and deep-flavoured Shiraz. 88 90 91 92. ***** Semillon
1993 £9 (AUC) ***** 1993 Aberfeldy £12 (AUC).
Adega (Portugal) WINERY – EQUIVALENT TO SPANISH BODEGA.
Adelaide Hills (Australia) Cool, high-altitude vineyard region, long known
for top-class lean RIESLING and SEMILLON but now more famous for
varieties such as SAUVIGNON BLANC, CHARDONNAY and PINOT NOIR and for
sparkling wine such as CROSER. 82 88 90 91 92. ***** Petaluma Chardonnay
1992 £10.50 (OD) **** 1993 Semillon, Henschke £9 (BOO, DBY).
Graf Adelmann (Wurttemberg, Germany) One of the best producers in the
region, making good *** red wines from such grapes as the TROLLINGER,
Lemberger and Urban. Look for Brüssele'r Spitze wines.

Aglianico Thick-skinned grape grown by the Ancient Greeks but now more or less restricted to Southern Italy, where it produces dark, hefty TAURASI and AGLIANICO DEL VULTURE.

Aglianico del Vulture (BASILICATA, Italy) Tannic, licoricey-chocolatey blockbusters made on the hills of an extinct volcano. Give them a decade – and a plateful of tasty food. 85 86 87 88 90. **** 1990 Aglianico Del Vulture, d'Angelo £7 (RBS) *** 1990 Aglianico del Vulture, Le Vigne Basse £6 (WSO).

Agricola vitivinicola (Italy) WINE ESTATE.

Aguja (Leon, Spain) So-called 'needle' wines, ultra-rare outside Spain, which owe their slight SPRITZ to the addition of ripe grapes to the fermented wine.

Ahr (Germany) Northernmost ANBAUGEBIET, producing light red wines little seen in the UK. *** 1990 Walporzheimer Klosterberg, QbA £5.50 (WSC).

Airén (Spain) The most widely planted variety in the world – and one of the very dullest. With modern winemaking methods it can produce commercial stuff, which explains why flying winemakers are so often to be found in Spanish plains.

Coteaux d'Aix-en-Provence (France) A recent AC region made famous by the decision of the ex-owner of CH. LA LAGUNE to compete with Bordeaux at his Ch Vignelaure, a property which, until its recent purchase, has failed to live up to its early potential. Elsewhere, look for light, floral whites, and fruity reds and dry rosés using BORDEAUX and RHONE varieties. 89 90 91 92 93. *** 1992 Château Romanin £9 (LNR).

Ajaccio (CORSICA, France) This would-be independent island has far too many appellations – there's politics for you – but the tangily intense reds and the oaked whites made by Comte Peraldi are better than mere holiday fare. Look out too for wines from Gie Les Rameaux.

Albana di Romagna (Italy) Improving but traditionally dull white wine which, for political reasons, was made Italy's first white DOCG, thus making a mockery of the whole Italian system of denominations. *** 1994 'ICROPPI' £5 (EWC).

Albariño (Spain) The Spanish name for the Portuguese Alvarinho. And the name of the peachy-spicily wine made from it in Galicia. Arguably Spain's best, most interesting, white. *** 1993 Lagar De Cervera, Rias Baixas, Lagar De Fornelos £9 (L&W).

Aleatico (Italy) Red grape producing sweet, Muscat-style, often fortified wines. Gives name to DOCs A. di Puglia and A. di Gradoli. **** 1988 Aleatico di Sovana Avignonese £14 (half) (V&C).

Alella (Spain) DO district of Catalonia, producing better whites (from grapes including the XAREL-LO) than reds. **** 1993 Marques de Alella Clásico, Parxet £6 (ADN, MOR, WSO, MG).

Alenquer (OESTE, Portugal) Coolish region producing good reds from the PERIQUITA, Muscaty whites from the FERNÃO PIRES and increasingly successful efforts with more familiar varietals from France. **** 1991 Quinta de Pancas Cabernet, Producao de Vinhos de Quinta £6 (TH, WR, BU) *** 1994 Casa de Pancas Chardonnay, Producao de Vinhos de Quinta £6 (SMF).

Alentejo (Portugal) Up-and-coming province north of the Algarve in which good red BORBA is made, Australian-born David Baverstock produces his juicy red ESPERAO, JM da Fonseca makes Morgado de Reguengo and Peter BRIGHT, another Aussie, has long produced Tinta da Anfora, former Red Wine of the Year. **** 1994 Esporão, Finagra £3 (TH,WR, BU) **** 1992 Borba, Co-op de Borba £3 (TO) **** 1988 Tinto Velho, JM da Fonseca £4 (MWW).

Alexander Valley (SONOMA, California) Appellation in which SIMI, JORDAN, Murphy Goode and GEYSER PEAK are based. Good for approachable reds and classy (especially in the case of ***** SIMI) CHARDONNAYS.

Algarve (Portugal) Denominated for political reasons. If there were no beaches and tourists to hand, the wines here would be well-nigh unsaleable.

Algeria Hearty, old-fashioned mostly red wines produced by state-run cooperatives.

Caves Aliança (Portugal) Reliable producer of modern BAIRRADA, DOURO and better-than-average DAO. **** 1991 Alianca Bairrada Reserva, £4 (DBY) (SMF, BTH).

Alicante (VALENCIA, Spain) Hot region producing generally dull stuff apart from the sweetly honeyed Moscatels that appreciate the heat. *** Tesco Moscatel De Valencia, Gandia £3.50 (TO).

Alicante-Bouschet Unusual dark-skinned and dark-fleshed grapes traditionally popular as a (usually illegal) means of dyeing pallid reds made from nobler fare. In Australia, Rockford use it to make tiny quantities of good rosé that is sadly only available at the winery. Reds *** 1992 Topolos £10 (Bl).

Aligoté (BURGUNDY France) The region's lesser white grape, making dry, sometimes sharp, white wine traditionally mixed with cassis to make KIR. When lovingly handled and given a touch of oak it can make a fair imitation of basic Bourgogne Blanc, but loving hands rarely have time for Aligoté. Also grown in Eastern Europe, where they think a lot of it 91 92 93 94. **** 1993 Domaine Daniel Rion £8 (M&V) **** 1993 Jean-Marc Brocard, Domaine des Manants £5.50 (ADN).

Allegrini (VENETO, Italy) Go-ahead top-class producer of single-vineyard VALPOLICELLA and SOAVE. **** 1988 Amarone Classico della Valpolicella £11 (EWC) *** 1991 La Grola Valpolicella, Allegrini £7.50 (EWC) **** 1991 Recioto Classico £13) (L&W).

Allier (France) SPICY OAK MUCH FAVOURED BY MAKERS OF WHITE WINE.

Almacenista (Jerez, Spain) FINE, OLD, UNBLENDED SHERRY FROM A SINGLE SOLERA – THE SHERRY EQUIVALENT OF A SINGLE MALT WHISKY. LUSTAU ARE SPECIALISTS. **** Oloroso Anada 1918 Solera (Pilar Aranda y Latorre), Emilio Lustau £12 (L&W).

Almansa (Spain) Warm region noted for softish reds which can be almost black, thanks to the red juice of the grapes used here.

Aloxe-Corton (BURGUNDY, France) COTE DE BEAUNE commune producing slow-maturing, majestic but at times toughly uninspiring reds (including the GRAND CRU CORTON) and potentially sublime but equally slow-developing whites (including Corton Charlemagne). Invariably pricy; variably great. 78 85 88 89 90 92 (red) 88 89 90 92 93 (white). **** Corton-Pougets Grand Cru, Domaine des Heritiers, Louis Jadot 1989 £30 (TH) **** 1990 Aloxe Corton Tollot-Beaut £22 (ADN) ***** 1992 Corton Charlemagne, Bonneau de Martray £40 (L&W).

Alsace (France) Northerly region enjoying a warm micro-climate that enables producers to make riper-tasting wines than their counterparts across the Rhine, despite often huge yields per acre and the most generous CHAPTALISATION allowances in France. The wines are named after the grapes – PINOT NOIR, GEWURZTRAMINER, RIESLING, TOKAY/PINOT GRIS, PINOT BLANC (known as Pinot d'Alsace) and (rarely) MUSCAT. In the right hands, the 50 or so GRAND CRU vineyards should yield better wines though their name on a label offers no guarantee of quality. Late harvest, off-dry wines are labelled VENDANGE TARDIVE and SELECTION DES GRAINS NOBLES. References to Reserve and Selection Personnelle often mean nothing. 83 85 86 88 89 90 92. See individual grape varieties for recommendations.

Altare, Elio (PIEDMONT, Italy) The genial Svengali-like leader of the BAROLO revolution. Followers like CLERICO and ROBERTO VOERZIO now run him a very close race. **** 1990 Nebbiolo £8 (V&C).

Altesino (TUSCANY, Italy) First class producers of Brunello di Montalcino and oaky Vino da Tavola Cabernet ('Palazzo') and Sangiovese ('Altesi'). **** 1990 Palazzo Altesi Rosso, £15 (DBY).

Alto-Adige (Italy) Aka Italian Tyrol and Sudtirol. DOC for a range of mainly white wines, often from Germanic grape varieties. Also light and fruity reds made from the LAGREIN and Vernatsch. Not living up to its promise of the early 1980s when it was considered to be one of the most exciting regions in Europe, though a few producers are showing what could – and should – be done. 90 91 92 93 94. **** 1991 Cabernet Riserva Schlosshof, Viticoltori Alto Adige £6 (WIN).

Alvarinho (Portugal) White grape aka ALBARINO; at its fresh, lemony best in VINHO VERDE blends and in the DO Alvarinho de Monção. *** Vinho Verde, Quinta da Aveleda £6 (AV).

Amabile (Italy) SEMI-SWEET.

Amador County (California) Region noted for intensely-flavoured, old-fashioned ZINFANDEL. Depressingly, the obsessional mania to promote the NAPA region has helped to ensure that few examples of these often far more interesting wines reach UK shores. In the US, look out for Amador Foothills Winery's old-vine ZINFANDELS. *** 1989 Sutter Home Reserve Zinfandel £7.50 (MTL, DBY).

Amaro (Italy) BITTER.

Amarone (VENETO, Italy) ALSO 'BITTER', USED PARTICULARLY TO DESCRIBE RECIOTO. BEST KNOWN AS AMARONE DELLA VALPOLICELLA. *** 1990 Recioto Amarone Delle Valpolicella, Brigaldara £12 (GNW) ***** Amarone, Capitel Monte Olmi, Tedeschi £16 (ADN).

Amberley Estate (W. AUSTRALIA) Young estate with good SEMILLON and CABERNET-MERLOT blend. **** 1994 Semillon-Sauvignon Blanc £9 (DBY) (ADN).

Amézola de la Mora (RIOJA, Spain) Eight-year-old estate promising classy red RIOJA in which, unusually, GRENACHE plays no part.

Amity (OREGON, USA) High quality producer of PINOT NOIR.

Amiral de Beychevelle See CHATEAU BEYCHEVELLE.

Amontillado (JEREZ, Spain) Literally 'like Montilla'. In Britain, pretty basic medium-sweet sherry; in Spain, fascinating dry, nutty wine. **** Don Zoïlo £8 (DBY, TH) ***** Amontillado Del Duque, Gonzalez Byass £19 (MTL, DBY).

Amoroso (JEREZ, Spain) SWEET SHERRY STYLE DEVISED FOR THE BRITISH.

Robert Ampeau (BURGUNDY, France) MEURSAULT specialist who also produces fine traditional reds, including first class POMMARD. *** 1980 Meursault 1er Cru Perrieres £24 (HR).

Ampurdan-Costa Brava (CATALONIA, Spain) A great place for a holiday. Ignore the wines – but if you do trip over a dull white, remember that this is one of the main sources of juice for the sparkling winemakers of the PENEDES. So now you know why those CAVAS taste the way they do.

Amtliche Prufüngsnummer (Germany) OFFICIAL IDENTIFICATION NUMBER SUPPOSEDLY RELATING TO QUALITY. (IN FACT, TO GET ONE, WINES HAVE TO HAVE SCORED 1.5 OUT OF 5 IN A BLIND TASTING). APPEARS ON ALL QBA/QMP WINES.

Anbaugebiet (Germany) TERM FOR 11 LARGE WINE REGIONS (EG RHEINGAU). QBA AND QMP WINES MUST INCLUDE THE NAME OF THEIR ANBAUGEBIET ON THEIR LABELS, A STIPULATION THAT DOESN'T HELP SIMPLIFY GERMAN WINE LABELLING.

Coteaux d'Ancenis (LOIRE, France) Light reds and deep pinks from the CABERNET FRANC and GAMAY, and MUSCADET-style whites. 89 90 92. *** 1992 Coteaux d'Ancenis Pierre Guidon £6 (YAP).

Andalucia (Spain) The hot southern part of the country in which the wines of JEREZ, MONTILLA and MALAGA are made. Non-fortified wines are far less impressive.

Anderson Valley (CALIFORNIA) Small cool area within MENDOCINO, good for white and sparkling wines. Do not confuse with the less impressive Anderson Valley in New Mexico. *** 1992 Gewürztraminer, Husch £8 (J&B).

Ch. l'Angélus (BORDEAUX, France) Flying high since the late 1980s, this is a ST EMILION to watch; classy, plummy and skilfully oaked. The second label Carillon d'Angelus is also well worth seeking out. 82 83 84 86 88 89 90 91. **** 1992 £28 (NIC).

The Angelus See WIRRA WIRRA.

Anghelu Ruju (SARDINIA, Italy) Intensely nutty-raisiny, port-'n-lemony wine made by Sella & Mosca from old CANNONAU grapes. *** 1981 £12 (V&C).

Ch. d'Angludet (BORDEAUX, France) CRU BOURGEOIS made by Peter Sichel (the merchant responsible for CH. PALMER). Classy cassis-flavoured, if slightly earthy MARGAUX-like wine that can be drunk young but is worth waiting for. **** 1979 £14.50 (RD).

Angoves (SOUTH AUSTRALIA) MURRAY RIVER producer with improving, good-value CHARDONNAY and CABERNET. *** 1995 Nanya Creek Red £4 (N&P).

Paul Anheuser (NAHE, Germany) One of the most stalwart supporters of the TROCKEN movement, and a strong proponent of the RIESLING, this excellent estate is also unusually successful with its RULANDER and PINOT NOIR.

Anjou (LOIRE, France) The source of many dry and DEMI-SEC whites, mostly made from the CHENIN BLANC grape with up to 20% CHARDONNAY or SAUVIGNON. The rosé is almost always awful but there are good, light, cla5ety, CABERNET reds. For the best, look out for Anjou-Villages in which the GAMAY is not permitted. 85 86 90 92 93 94. *** 1992 Chateau Passavant Anjou Blanc £4 (TO).

Annata (Italy) VINTAGE.

Año (Spain) YEAR, PRECEDED BY A FIGURE – eg 5 – WHICH INDICATES THE WINE'S AGE AT THE TIME OF BOTTLING. BANNED BY THE EC SINCE 1986.

Anselmi (VENETO, Italy) Source of SOAVE Classico good enough to disprove the generally dismal rule, as well as serious sweet examples. *** 1993 Soave Classico Superiore £6 (UBC).

Antinori (TUSCANY, Italy) A pioneer merchant-producer who has improved the quality of CHIANTI with its widely available examples such as Villa Antinori and Pèppoli while spearheading the SUPER-TUSCAN revolution with superb wines like TIGNANELLO and SOLAIA. **** 1991 Antinori Tignanello £20.50 (L&W).

AOC (France) See APPELLATION CONTROLEE.

AP (Germany) See AMTLICHE PRUFUNGSNUMMER.

Appellation Contrôlée (AC/AOC) (France) INCREASINGLY QUESTIONED DESIGNATION FOR 'TOP QUALITY' WINE: GUARANTEES ORIGIN, GRAPE VARIETIES AND METHOD OF PRODUCTION – BUT NOT QUALITY.

Aprémont (Eastern France) Floral, slightly PETILLANT white from skiing region. 93 94. *** 1992 Les Rocailles £6.50 (THP).

Apulia (Italy) See PUGLIA.

Aquileia (FRIULI-VENZIA-GIULIA, Italy) DOC for easy-going, single-variety reds, rosés and whites made from a wide range of grapes. The REFOSCO can be plummily refreshing.

Ararimu (AUCKLAND, NEW ZEALAND) See MATUA VALLEY.

Arbin (SAVOIE, France) Red wine made from Mondeuse grapes. This is one that tastes best in its more usual context (after skiing rather than after work).

Arbois (Eastern France) AC region. Light reds from Trousseau and PINOT NOIR, dry whites from the JURA, most notably VIN JAUNE and fizz.

Viña Ardanza (RIOJA, Spain) Fairly full-bodied red made with a high proportion (40 per cent) of GRENACHE; good oaky white, too. **** 1987 Reserva, La Rioja Alta £9 (ADN).

Coteaux de l'Ardèche (RHONE, France) Light country reds and whites, mainly from the SYRAH and CHARDONNAY grapes by certain Burgundians 88 89 90 91 92. *** 1994 Les Terrasses Blanc £4 (YAP).

Argentina Now beginning to compete in quality as well as quantity with its Andean neighbour, Argentina, the world's fourth biggest wine producing nation makes CABERNET and MERLOT reds which often have a touch more backbone than the Chileans – as well as some unusually successful spicy MALBEC. CHARDONNAYS are improving too, thanks to the efforts of firms like Trapiche and Catena where Californian-born Paul Hobbs is having a similarly beneficial influence to the one he has shown at VALDIVIEZO in Chile. Look out too for grapey whites made from the Muscat-like Torrontes. 84 85 86 88 90 91 93. **** 1988 Luigi Bosca Syrah, Leoncio Arizu £8 (NI, JAR) **** 1992 Catena Estate Cabernet Sauvignon £8 (BI, FUL) **** 1991 Weinert Malbec £8 (SV, GI) *** 1994 Bodega Norton Sangiovese £5 (BOO, MTL) **** 1994 Etchart Torrontes £4 (CWS, TH, WR,U).

Argyll Oregon fizz from Brian Croser (of PETALUMA). One of the classiest offerings from the New World. **** Argyll Brut £12 (LAV).

Ch. d'Arlay (JURA, France) Reliable producer of nutty VIN JAUNE and light, earthy-raspberryish PINOT NOIR. **** 1966 Vin Jaune £24 (RD).

Domaine de l'Arlot (BURGUNDY, France) Brilliant, recently constituted NUITS ST GEORGES estate which belongs to the same French insurance company as Chateaux LYNCH BAGES and PICHON LONGUEVILLE. Lovely, purely defined modern reds and a rare example of white Nuits St Georges to make a Meursault-maker weep into his barrels. ***** 1991 Nuits St Georges 1er Cru, Clos l'Arlot £23 (L&W).

Arneis (PIEMONTE, Italy) Spicy indigenous white variety, used to make good, unoaked wines. **** 1993 Cru San Michele, Deltetto £8 (EWC).

Ch. l'Arrosée (BORDEAUX France) Small, well-sited ST EMILION property with fruitily intense wines. **** 1989 £22.50 (J&B).

Arrowfield (HUNTER VALLEY, Australia) Producer of ripe, full-flavoured CHARDONNAY. *** Arrowfield Show Reserve Chardonnay 1993 £8 (W).

Arrowood (SONOMA, California) Producer of excellent CHARDONNAY and good CABERNET made by the former winemaker of CHATEAU ST JEAN.

Arroyo (RIBERA DEL DUERO, Spain) A name to watch for well-made, intensely flavoursome reds.

Arruda (OESTE, Portugal) Fresh, inexpensive BEAUJOLAIS-style reds which help to win friends for Portugal. *** Sainsbury's Arruda £3 (JS).

Ascheri (PIEDMONT, Italy) New-wave producer ; impressive single-vineyard, tobacco n'berry wines. *** 1992 Bric Milieu £9 (EWC) *** 1991 Barolo £8 (OD).

Asciutto (Italy) DRY.

Asenovgrad (BULGARIA) Demarcated northern wine region. Reds from CABERNET SAUVIGNON, MERLOT and MAVRUD. 85 87 88 89 90 91. *** 1991 Asenovgrad Mavrud £3 (WIW).

Ashton Hills (Adelaide Hills, Australia) Small up-and-coming winery whose winemaker, Stephen George, is producing subtle, increasingly creditable CHARDONNAY. *** 1990 Ashton Hills Chardonnay £8 (AUC).

Assemblage (France) THE ART OF BLENDING WINE FROM DIFFERENT GRAPE VARIETIES IN A CUVEE. ASSOCIATED WITH BORDEAUX AND CHAMPAGNE.

Assmanhausen (RHEINGAU, Germany) If you like sweet PINOT NOIR, this is the place. For me even the light dry versions are rarely worth a detour.

Asti (PIEDMONT, Italy) Town famous for sparkling SPUMANTE, lighter MOSCATO D'ASTI and red BARBERA D'ASTI. *** Fontanafredda NV £6 (widely available).

Astringent MOUTH-PUCKERING. MOSTLY ASSOCIATED WITH YOUNG RED WINE. SEE TANNIN.

Aszu (HUNGARY) THE SWEET 'SYRUP' MADE FROM DRIED AND (ABOUT 10-15 PER CENT) 'NOBLY ROTTEN' GRAPES (SEE BOTRYTIS) USED TO SWEETEN TOKAY.

Ata Rangi (MARTINBOROUGH, NEW ZEALAND) Inspiring small estate with high quality PINOT NOIR and NEW ZEALAND's only successful SHIRAZ. **** 1991 Pinot Noir £17 (J&B).

Coteaux de l'Aubance (LOIRE, France) Light wines (often semi-sweet) grown on the banks of a LOIRE tributary. 83 85 88 89 90 92 93 *** Domaine de Bablut Moelleux, C Daviau £15.50 (ADN).

Au Bon Climat (SANTA BARBARA, County California, US) Top quality producer of characterfully flavoursome, if sometimes slightly horseradishy, PINOT NOIR and classy CHARDONNAY. A great example of what Santa BARBARA can do – and yet another blow to NAPA hype. ***** 1993 Pinot Noir 'La Bauge' £17 (M&V) **** 1993 Chardonnay £15 (BWS).

Domaine des Aubuisiers (LOIRE, France) Superb VOUVRAY domaine producing impeccable wines, ranging from richly dry to lusciously sweet. ***** 1993 Vouvray Demi-sec £7 (OD).

Auckland (NEW ZEALAND) All-embracing designation which once comprised over 25 per cent of the country's vineyards. Often wrongly derided by Marlborophiles who have failed to notice how good the wines of KUMEU RIVER can be, as well as the ones produced by Goldwater Estate on Waiheke Island. **** 1993 Goldwater Chardonnay £9 (MWW).

Aude (South-West France) Prolific département traditionally producing much ordinary wine. Now CORBIERES and FITOU are improving as are the VINS DE PAYS, thanks to plantings of new grapes (such as the VIOGNIER) and the efforts of go-ahead firms like Skalli (FORTANT DE FRANCE). 88 89 90 91 92 93. ** L'Estagnon Vin de Pays de l'Aude £3.50 (TH).

Ausbruch (Austria) TERM FOR RICH BOTRYTIS WINES WHICH ARE SWEETER THAN BEERENAUSLESEN BUT LESS SWEET THAN TROCKENBEERENAUSLESEN.

Auslese (Germany) MOSTLY SWEET WINE FROM SELECTED RIPE GRAPES USUALLY AFFECTED BY BOTRYTIS. THIRD RUNG ON THE QmP LADDER. THE BEST EXAMPLES COME FROM NEUSIEDLERSEE AND RUST.

Ch. Ausone (BORDEAUX, France) Pretender to the crown of top ST EMILION, this estate which owes its name to the Roman occupation can produce some of the tastiest, most complex claret. ***** 1989 £68 (ADN).

Austria Home of all sorts of whites, ranging from dry SAUVIGNON BLANCS, greengagey GRUNER-VELTLINERS and ripe RIESLINGS to luscious late-harvest wines. Reds are less successful, but the lightly fruity PINOT-NOIR-like ST LAURENTS are worth seeking out. 83 85 87 88 89 90 91 93 94. See WILLI OPITZ.

Auxerrois Named after the main town in northern BURGUNDY, this is the Alsatians' term for a fairly dull local variety that may be related to the SYLVANER, MELON DE BOURGOGNE or CHARDONNAY. In Luxembourg it is the name for the PINOT GRIS. Grown, with little success, in Luxembourg, and with rather more in Britain. *** Wooton Auxerrois 1992 £5.50 (WSO).

Auxey-Duresses (BURGUNDY, France) Best known for its buttery whites but produces greater quantities of raspberryish if rather rustic reds. A slow developer. 83 85 87 88 89 90 92 93. *** 1993 Louis Jadot £11 (TH).

Quinta da Aveleda (Penafiel, Portugal) Estate producing serious dry VINHO VERDE. *** Aveleda Vinho Verde £5 (L&W).

Avelsbach (MOSEL-SAAR-RUWER, Germany) RUWER village producing delicate, light-bodied wines. 83 85 86 87 88 89 90 92.

Avignonesi (TUSCANY, Italy) Classy producer of VINO NOBILE DI MONTALCINO, SUPER-TUSCANS such as Grifi, a pure MERLOT, serious CHARDONNAY and SAUVIGNON whites and an unusually good VIN SANTO. *** 1990 Avignonesi Merlot, Avignonesi £18 (LEA, RD, V&C).

Avize (CHAMPAGNE, France) Village known for fine white grapes.

Ay (CHAMPAGNE, France) Ancient regional capital growing mainly black grapes. 79 82 83 85 88 89. **** Bollinger NV £22 (widely available).

Ayala (CHAMPAGNE, France) Underrated producer which takes its name from the village of Ay. **** Château d'Ay Brut NV £15 (LAV, WIN).

Ayl (MOSEL-SAAR-RUWER, Germany) Distinguished SAAR village producing steely wines. 85 86 87 88 89 90 92 93. *** 1991 Ayler Kupp, Riesling Kabinett Bischöfliche Priesterseminar £8 (ADN).

Azienda (Italy) ESTATE.

Babich (Henderson, NEW ZEALAND) The rich 'Irongate' CHARDONNAY is the prize wine here, but the SAUVIGNON BLANC is good, too, and the reds improve with every vintage. **** 1992 Babich Irongate Cabernet Sauvignon/Merlot £13 (DBY, SEL).

Bacchus White grape, a MÜLLER-THURGAU x RIESLING cross, making light, flowery wine. Grown in Germany and also England. See DENBIES.

Domaine Denis Bachelet (BURGUNDY, France) Classy small GEVREY CHAMBERTIN estate making cherryish wines that are as good young as with five or six years of age. **** 1993 Cuvée Vielles Vignes £15.50 (HR).

Backsberg (PAARL, South Africa) A CHARDONNAY pioneer, making a richly Burgundian version and slightly less exciting reds. *** 1992 Backsberg Merlot £5 (DBY, TO).

Bad Durkheim (RHEINPFALZ, Germany) Chief RHEINPFALZ town, producing some of the region's finest whites, plus some reds 83 85 88 89 90 91 92.

Bad Kreuznach (NAHE, Germany) Chief and finest wine town of the region, giving its name to the entire lower NAHE. 83 85 88 89 90 91 92. *** 1989 Kreuznacher Bruckes Riesling Auslese, Schloss Plettenberg, £9 (TH, WR, BU).

Badacsony (HUNGARY) Wine region renowned for full-flavoured whites.

Baden (Germany) Warm (well, relatively) southern region in which it is possible to use ripe grapes to make dry (TROCKEN) wines, usually from grapes other than the Riesling. Some good PINOT NOIRS are being produced, too, by Karl-Heinz Johner, former winemaker at LAMBERHURST, but there is little to set the world alight.

Baden Winzerkeller (**ZBW**) (Germany) Huge co-op whose reliability has done much to set Baden apart from the rest of Germany. If you must have dry German whites, this is the place. *** Co-op Baden Dry White £3.50 (CWS).

Baga (Portugal) High-quality, spicily fruity red grape varieties – used in Bairrada. *** 1990 Sogrape Reserva Bairrada Red £5 (GI).

Bailey's (North-East VICTORIA, Australia) Traditional producer of good Liqueur Muscat and hefty, old-fashioned SHIRAZ. Current wines are a little lighter and less impressive. *** 1992 Shiraz £5.50 (OD).

Bairrada (Portugal) DO wine region south of Oporto, traditionally producing dull whites and tough reds, often from the BAGA. Revolutionaries like SOGRAPE, LUIS PATO and ALIANCA are proving what can be done. Look for spicy, blackberryish reds and creamy whites. 85 88 89 90 92. See BAGA.

Balance HARMONY OF FRUITINESS, ACIDITY, ALCOHOL AND TANNIN. BALANCE CAN DEVELOP WITH AGE BUT SHOULD BE EVIDENT IN YOUTH, EVEN WHEN, THROUGH ACIDITY OR TANNIN FOR EXAMPLE, WINES MAY APPEAR DIFFICULT TO TASTE.

Balaton (HUNGARY) Wine region producing fair-quality reds and whites. *** Co-op Hungarian Country Red £3 (CWS).

Anton Balbach (Erben Rheinhessen, Germany) Potentially one of the best producers in the region – especially for its late-harvest wines. **** Niersteiner Klostergarten Riesling Kabinett 1990 £7.50 (ADN).

Balbás (RIBERA DEL DUERO, Spain) Small producer of juicy TEMPRANILLO reds and rosé.

Ch. Balestard-la-Tonnelle (Bordeaux, France) Good, quite traditional ST EMILION, built to last.

Balgownie (VICTORIA, Australia) One of Victoria's most reliable producers of lovely intense blackcurranty CABERNET in GEELONG. CHARDONNAYS are big and old-fashioned and PINOT NOIRS are improving. *** 1992 Balgownie 1er Cuvée Shiraz Cabernet £5 (OD).

Balthasar Ress (HATTENHEIM, Germany) Classy producer blending delicacy with concentration. **** 1990 Johannisberger Erntebringer Riesling Kabinett £7 (SUM).

Ban de Vendange (France) OFFICIALLY SANCTIONED HARVEST DATE.

Bandol (Provence, France) AOC red and rosé. MOURVEDRE reds are
particularly good and spicy. Worth keeping. Whites, though improving, are
uninspiring 83 85 86 89 90 92 93.

Bannockburn (GEELONG, Australia) Gary Farr uses his experience making
wines at DOMAINE DUJAC in BURGUNDY to produce concentrated, toughish
**** PINOT NOIR at home. The CHARDONNAY is good, too, if slightly big for
its boots. 85 86 88 90. **** 1992 Chardonnay £10 (ADN, LEA) **** 1990 Pinot
Noir £13 (ADN).

Banyuls (Provence, France) France's answer to tawny port. Fortified,
GRENACHE-based VIN DOUX NATUREL, ranging from off-dry to lusciously
sweet. The RANCIO style is rather more like MADEIRA. 82 85 86 88 89 90 91
92. *** 1978 Banyuls Vieilles Vignes, Vendage Tardive, Domaine du Mas Blanc
£20 (WSO).

Barbadillo (JEREZ, Spain) Great producer of FINO and MANZANILLA. **** Palo
Cortado £13 (MG).

Barbaresco (PIEDMONT Italy) DOCG red from the NEBBIOLO grape, with
spicy fruit plus depth and complexity. Traditionally approachable earlier
(three to five years) than neighbouring BAROLO but, in the hands of men
like ANGELO GAJA and in the best vineyards, potentially of almost as
high a quality – and even higher prices! 82 83 84 85 86 87 88 89 90 92.
*** 1990 Marina Macarino Barbaresco Campo Quadro, £10 (WAW).

Barbera (PIEDMONT, Italy) Grape making fruity, spicy, characterful wine
(eg B. d'Alba & B. d'Asti), usually with a flavour reminiscent of cheese-
cake with raisins. Now in California, Mexico and (at BROWN BROS)
Australia 86 87 88 89 90 92. **** 1993 Barbera d'Alba "Vignota", Conterno
Fantino £8 (ADN).

Barca Velha (DOURO, Portugal) Portugal's most famous red, made from port
varieties by FEIRREIRA. It's tough stuff, but plummy enough to be worth
keeping – and paying for. **** 1982 Barca Velha "Ferreirinha" £33 (CEB).

Bardolino (VENETO, Italy) Light and unusually approachable for a traditional
DOC Italian red. Commercial versions are often dull as ditchwater but at
best are Italy's answer to Beaujolais – refreshing with a hint of bitter cherries.
Best drunk young unless from an exceptional producer. See MASI. 88 89 90
91 92. *** 1993 Bardolino Classico Tacchetto, Guerrieri-Rizzardi £5 (BAR).

Guy de Barjac (RHONE, France) A master of the SYRAH grape, producing
some of the best, smokiest examples around. ***** 1991 Cornas £16 (L&W).

De Bartoli (SICILY, Italy) If you want to drink MARSALA rather than use it in
cooking, this is the name to remember. The raisiny Bukkuram, made from
PASSITO Muscat grapes is an alternative delight.

Barolo (PIEDMONT, Italy) Noblest of DOCG reds, made from NEBBIOLO. Old-
fashioned versions are undrinkably dry and tannic when young but, from a
good producer (like BORGOGNO) and year, can last and develop
extraordinary complexity. Look out also for examples from MASCARELLO,
ALDO CONTERNO, CLERICO, ROBERTO VOERZIO, ELIO ALTARE and
FONTANAFREDDA. Modern versions are ready earlier, but still last. 83 85 86
87 88 89 90 92. *** 1985 Barolo Pio Cesare £9 (RBS).

Baron de Ley (RIOJA, Spain) Small RIOJA estate whose wines, partly aged in
French oak, take several years to 'come round'. Less dazzling than it would
like to be. *** 1987 Baron De Ley Rioja Crianza £7 (TH, BU, WR).

Barossa Valley (Australia) Big, warm region north-east of Adelaide which is
famous for traditional SHIRAZ, 'ports' and RIESLINGS which age to oily
richness. CHARDONNAY and CABERNET have moved in more recently and the
former makes subtler, classier wines in the increasingly popular higher
altitude vineyards of the ADELAIDE HILLS overlooking the Valley.
See KRONDORF, ROCKFORD, MELTON, PENFOLDS, PETER LEHMANN. 80 84 86 87
90 91 92.

Barrique FRENCH BARREL, PARTICULARLY IN BORDEAUX, HOLDING 225 LITRES. TERM USED IN ITALY TO DENOTE BARREL AGEING.

Jim Barry (CLARE VALLEY, Australia) Producer of the dazzling, spicy, mulberryish Armagh SHIRAZ, the stratospheric price of which was once justified with admirable frankness by the words 'We've got a ****ing lifestyle to support you know'.

Barsac (BORDEAUX, France) AC neighbour of SAUTERNES, with similar, though not quite so rich, SAUVIGNON/SEMILLON dessert wines. 75 76 83 86 88 89 90 91. *** 1991 Château Climens £21.50 (TH, WR, BU).

Barton & Guestier (BORDEAUX, France) Increasingly commercial BORDEAUX shipper. Now Seagram-owned. *** 1990 '1725' Bordeaux Rouge £5 (OD).

Basedows (SOUTH AUSTRALIA) Producer of big, concentrated SHIRAZ and CABERNET and ultra-rich SEMILLON and CHARDONNAYS. Unashamedly Australian. **** 1993/4 Semillon £6 (VW, BI) **** 1994 Chardonnay £7 (VW, BI) **** 1993 Shiraz £7 (BI).

Basilicata (Italy) Southern wine region chiefly known for AGLIANICO DEL VULTURE and some improving VINI DA TAVOLA 85 86 87 88 90 91 92. *** 1990 Aglianico Del Vulture Riserva, d'Angelo £9 (RBS, V&C).

Von Bassermann-Jordan (RHEINPFALZ, Germany) Traditional producer often using the fruit of its brilliant vineyards to produce TROCKEN RIESLINGS with more ripeness than is often to be found in this style. **** Forster Jesuitgarten Riesling Spätlese 1988 £8 (VW) **** Forster Kirchenstück Riesling Spätlese 1993 £14 (BI).

Bastardo (Portugal) Red grape used widely in port and previously in Madeira, where there are a few wonderful bottles left. Shakespeare refers to a wine called 'Brown Bastard'.

Ch. Bastor-Lamontagne (SAUTERNES, France) Remarkably reliable, classy and surprisingly inexpensive alternative to the big name properties among which it is situated. **** 1989 £8 (half) (BWI, SMF).

Ch. Batailley (BORDEAUX, France) Approachable, quite modern PAUILLAC with more class than its price might lead one to expect. *** 1982 £25 (DIR).

Bâtard-Montrachet (BURGUNDY, France) Biscuity-rich white GRAND CRU shared between CHASSAGNE and PULIGNY MONTRACHET. Often very fine; always very expensive. 78 79 81 82 83 85 86 87 88 89 90 92. ***** 1993 Domaine Ramonet £52 (HR).

Coteaux des Baux-en-Provence (Provence, France) Inexpensive fruity reds, whites and rosé of improving quality, plus the cult DOMAINE DE TREVALLON, which shows what can be done round here. 85 86 88 89 90 91 92. ***** 1991 Domaine de Trévallon Eloi Dürrbach £21 (YAP).

Bava (PIEDMONT, Italy) Innovative producer making good MOSCATO, BARBERA and, reviving indigenous grapes such as the rarely grown raspberryish Ruche and the Erbaluce. **** 1992 Ruche di Castagnole Monferrato, Cantine Bava "Casa Brina" £10 (ADN).

Ch. de Beaucastel (RHONE, France) The top estate in CHATEAUNEUF-DU-PAPE, using organic methods to produce richly gamey-spicy reds and rare but fine creamy-spicy whites. **** 1991 Château de Beaucastel Rouge £13.50 (M&V, L&W).

Beaujolais (BURGUNDY, France) Light, fruity red from the GAMAY, good chilled and for early drinking; BEAUJOLAIS-VILLAGES is better, and the 10 Crus better still. With age, these can taste like (fairly ordinary) BURGUNDY, though I can't see why this is a prized quality when it means sacrificing the boiled sweet and banana flavour of them when they are young. See BEAUJOLAIS-VILLAGES, MORGON, CHENAS, BROUILLY, COTE DE BROUILLY, JULIENAS, MOULIN A VENT, FLEURIE, REGNIE, ST AMOUR, CHIROUBLES. 88 89 91. *** 1993 Beaujolais Georges Duboeuf £5 (widely available).

Beaujolais Blanc (BURGUNDY, France) From the CHARDONNAY, rarely seen under this name. Commonly sold as ST VERAN. 87 88 90 91 92 93.

Beaujolais-Villages (BURGUNDY, France) From the north of the region, fuller-flavoured and more alcoholic than plain BEAUJOLAIS, though not necessarily from one of the named Cru villages. Good plain BEAUJOLAIS from a quality-conscious producer can outclass many a 'Villages'. 85 88 89 91. *** 1993 Georges Duboeuf £5 (M&S, TO).

Beaulieu Vineyard (NAPA Valley, California) Historic winery, famous from the turn of the century and now owned by UK giant Grand Metropolitan. The Georges de Latour Private Reserve Cabernet can be impressive and keeps well, and recent vintages of Beautour were improved possibly by the efforts of the late, great Andre Tchelistcheff. Other wines are memorably and unworthily ordinary. Pronounced 'Bow-Ly-ew' or, more confidently, 'Bee-Vee' in the US. *** 1991 Beaulieu Vineyards Rutherford Cabernet Sauvignon, £9 (JEH).

Beaumes de Venise (Rhône, France) COTES DU RHONE village producing spicy dry reds and better-known sweet, grapey fortified VIN DOUX NATUREL from the MUSCAT. (white) 88 89 90 91 (red) 86 88 89 90 91 *** 1993 Muscat de Beaumes de Venise, Caves des Vignerons £8 (OD).

Beaune (BURGUNDY, France) Large, reliable commune for soft, raspberry-and-rose-petal PINOT NOIR with plenty of PREMIERS but strangely no GRANDS CRUS. The walled city is the site of the famous Hospices charity auction. Also (very rare) whites made with great success by JOSEPH DROUHIN. 78 80 82 83 85 87 88 89 90 92.

JB Becker (RHEINGAU, Germany) One of Germany's only successful producers of ripe, classy PINOT NOIR (here known as SPATBURGUNDER). *** 1991 Riesling Spätlese Dienheimer Kreuz, Bruder Dr Becker £8 (WMK).

Beerenauslese (Germany) LUSCIOUS SWEET WINES FROM SELECTED RIPE GRAPES (BEEREN), HOPEFULLY AFFECTED BY BOTRYTIS. **** 1991 Heinrich & Kracher Beerenauslese £13 (L&W).

Bekaa Valley (LEBANON) War-torn region in which Serge Hochar grows the grapes for his CH. MUSAR wines. *** 1987 Ch. Musar £8 (widely available).

Ch. Belair (BORDEAUX, France) CH. AUSONE's stablemate. Lighter in style and not always up to the mark, but still a classy, long-lived ST EMILION. **** 1985 £22 (ADN).

Bellet (Provence, France) Tiny AC behind Nice producing fairly good red, white and rosé from local grapes including the Rolle, the Braquet and the Folle Noir. (Excessively) pricy and rarely seen in the UK. *** 1994 Ch. de Crémat, Charles Bagnis £17 (YAP).

Bendigo (VICTORIA, Australia) Great warm region for big-boned, long-lasting reds with intense berry fruit. See BALGOWNIE, JASPER HILL and PASSING CLOUDS. **** 1993 Water Wheel Bendigo Shiraz £7 (AUC).

Bentonite TYPE OF CLAY USED AS A CLARIFYING AGENT TO REMOVE IMPURITIES BEFORE BOTTLING. POPULAR AS A NON-ANIMAL-DERIVED FINING MATERIAL.

Berberana (RIOJA, Spain) Increasingly dynamic producer of a range of juicier, fruitier young-drinking styles as well as the improving Carta de Plata and Carta de Oro Riojas. *** 1993 Rioja Berberana Oak Aged Tempranillo £4 (SAF).

Bereich (Germany) VINEYARD AREA, SUBDIVISION OF AN ANBAUGEBIET. ON ITS OWN INDICATES SIMPLE QbA WINE, eg NIERSTEINER. FINER WINES ARE FOLLOWED BY THE NAME OF A GROSSLAGE SUBSECTION; EVEN BETTER ONES BY THE NAMES OF INDIVIDUAL VINEYARDS.

Bergerac (BORDEAUX, France) Lighter, often good-value alternative to everyday CLARET or dry white BORDEAUX, revolutionised in the 1980s by CH. DE LA JAUBERTIE, former stationery magnate Henry Ryman's property and the place where his son, the ubiquitous Hugh, the flying winemaker, first cut his vinous teeth. Fine, sweet MONBAZILLAC is produced here, too 89 90 91 92. **** 1993 Clos l'Envège Côtes de Bergerac, Yves Pages £5 (AV).

Bergkelder (Cape, South Africa) Huge winery that still matures and bottles wines for such top-class Cape estates as MEERLUST, which, like its counterparts in BORDEAUX and California really ought to bottle their own.

Even so, the Bergkelder's own Stellenryck wines are worth watching out for, the cheaper Fleur du Cap range is likeable enough and Pongrasz fizz is first class. **** 1992 Fleur Du Cap Merlot, Bergkelder £7 (DBY, N&P, EP, HHC).

Beringer Vineyards (NAPA Valley, California) Big Swiss-owned producer notable for two CABERNETS (**** Knights Valley and ***** Private Reserve) and increasingly impressive Burgundy-like Chardonnay.
***** 1993 Beringer Private Reserve Chardonnay, £14.50 (MTL, BWC, OD).

Bernkastel (MOSEL-SAAR-RUWER, Germany) Town and vineyard area on the MITTELMOSEL making some of the finest RIESLING (including the famous Bernkasteler Doktor) and a lake of poor-quality wine 83 85 86 88 89 90 91 92 93. *** 1994 Rudolf Müller, Asda Bereich Bernkastel £2.50 (A).

Berri Renmano (RIVERLAND, Australia) Big producer now associated with THOMAS HARDY. Reliable, inexpensive reds and whites – though the recently released 'unwooded' CHARDONNAY tastes as though it strayed into an oak barrel. **** 1992 Renmano Chardonnay Bin Reserve 124, £7 (NY, U).

Best's Great Western (VICTORIA, Australia) Under-appreciated winery in GREAT WESTERN making delicious concentrated SHIRAZ from old vines, attractive CABERNET and rich CHARDONNAY. *** 1994 Best's Great Western Chardonnay £10 (DBY).

Bethany (BAROSSA, South Australia) Impressive small producer of knockout SHIRAZ. ***** 1991 Shiraz £9 (OD).

Ch. Beychevelle (BORDEAUX, France) An over-performing Second Growth which belongs to an insurance company. Very typical ST JULIEN with lots of cigar-box character. The second label, Amiral de Beychevelle can be a worthwhile buy. 88 89 90 94. **** 1989 Ch. Beychevelle £28 (J&B).

Léon Beyer (ALSACE, France) Serious producer of lean, long-lived wines.
*** 1992 Gewürztraminer £8.50 (WSO).

Bianco di Custoza (VENETO, Italy) Widely exported DOC, a reliable, crisp, light white from a blend of grapes. A better value alternative to most basic SOAVE. 93 94. *** 1993 Sainsbury Bianco di Custoza, Geoff Merrill GIV £3.50 (JS).

Maison Albert Bichot (BEAUNE, France) Big NEGOCIANT with excellent CHABLIS and VOSNE ROMANEE, plus a range of perfectly adequate wines sold under a plethora of other labels. *** Pinot Noir £5.50 (U).

Biddenden (Kent, England) Maker of the usual range of Germanic grape wines but supreme master in this country of the peachy Ortega.

Billecart-Salmon (CHAMPAGNE, France) Possibly the region's best all-rounder for quality and value. The one Champagne house whose subtle but decidedly ageable non-vintage, vintage and rosé I buy without hesitation. Superlative. **** Brut £18 (OD).

Bingen (RHEINHESSEN, Germany) Village giving its name to a RHEINHESSEN BEREICH that includes a number of well-known GROSSLAGEN. 76 83 85 88 89 90 91 92. *** 1993 Binger St Rochuskapelle Kabinett £3.50 (WSC).

Binissalem (Mallorca, Spain) The holiday island is proud of its demarcated region, though why, it's hard to say. Jose Ferrer's and Jaime Mesquida's wines are the best of the bunch.

Biondi-Santi (TUSCANY, Italy) Big-name property; supreme underperformer.
*** Brunello di Montalcino 1985 £38 (V&C) *** 1971 £125 (V&C).

Biscuity FLAVOUR OF BISCUITS (eg DIGESTIVE OR RICH TEA) OFTEN ASSOCIATED WITH THE **CHARDONNAY** GRAPE, PARTICULARLY IN **CHAMPAGNE** AND TOP-CLASS MATURE **BURGUNDY**, OR WITH THE YEAST THAT FERMENTED THE WINE.

Black Muscat Grown chiefly as a table grape, also produces very mediocre wine – except that made at the QUADY winery in California.
**** Elysium, Quady Winery 1988 £6 (HLV, ES, U, MWW).

Blagny (BURGUNDY, France) Tiny source of good unsubtle red (sold as Blagny) and potentially top-class white (sold as MEURSAULT, PULIGNY MONTRACHET, Blagny, Hameau or Piece sous le Bois). *** 1981 Blagny Piece sous le Bois, Rouge, Leflaive £9 (ABY).

Blain-Gagnard (BURGUNDY, France) Excellent producer of creamy, modern CHASSAGNE MONTRACHET. ***** 1993 Chassagne-Montrachet 1er cru, Morgeot £10 (DD) ***** 1988 Bâtard-Montrachet £39 (DD).

Blanc de Blancs WHITE WINE, USUALLY SPARKLING, MADE SOLELY FROM WHITE GRAPES. IN CHAMPAGNE, DENOTES 100 PER CENT CHARDONNAY.
***** Champagne Taittinger Comtes de Champagne 1986 £60 (SEL) **** Le Mesnil Blanc De Blancs Brut N V £14 (TH, WR, BU, J&B).

Blanc de Noirs WHITE (OR PINK) WINE MADE FROM BLACK GRAPES. *** 1990 Champagne de Venoge, Blanc de Noirs £23 (WAC, MYS) *** Waitrose Blanc de Noirs Champagne, Alexandre Bonnet £12 (W).

Blandy's (MADEIRA, Portugal) Brand owned by the Madeira Wine Company and named after the sailor who began the production of fortified wine here. Brilliant old wines. **** Blandys 5 Year Old Malmsey Madeira £12 (OD, BOO).

Blanquette de Limoux (MIDI, France) MÉTHODE CHAMPENOISE sparkler, which, when good, is appley and clean. Best when made with a generous dose of CHARDONNAY, as the local MAUZAC tends to give it an earthy flavour with age. The local Aimery cooperative is one of the most modern in France and quality is improving. **** Blanquette Méthode Ancestrale, Producteurs de Blanquette, £5 (A).

Wolf Blass (BAROSSA VALLEY, Australia) German immigrant who prides himself on making immediately attractive 'sexy' (his term) reds and whites by blending wines from different regions of South Australia and allowing them plentiful contact with new oak. Varying label colours indicate expense and expertise, with black signifying the peak of the range. **** 1991 President's Selection Cabernet Sauvignon £10 (MTL, DBY, EP, P&G).

Blauburgunder (Austria) The Austrian term for PINOT NOIR, making light, often sharp reds.

Blauer Portugieser (Germany) Red grape used in Germany and Austria to make light, pale wine.

Côtes de/Premières Côtes de Blaye (BORDEAUX, France) A ferry-ride across the river from St Julien, this is clay-soil territory with patches of limestone which should make respectively for good Merlot and white (sold as Blaye or BORDEAUX Blanc) wines. Sadly, so far, poor winemaking has prevented many estates from living up to this potential. Progess is being made though. 85 86 88 89 90 93. *** 1993 Ch Bertinerie £6 (OD).

Schloss Böckelheim Southern region of the Nahe producing varied fare. Wines from the Kupfergrube vineyard and the State Wine Domaine are worth buying. *** 1990 Schloss Böckelheimer Kupfergrube Riesling Auslese £14 (OWL).

Bodega (Spain) WINERY OR WINE CELLAR; PRODUCER.

Body USUALLY USED AS 'FULL-BODIED', MEANING A WINE WITH MOUTH-FILLING FLAVOURS AND PROBABLY A FAIRLY HIGH ALCOHOL CONTENT.

Jean-Claude Boisset (BURGUNDY, France) Fast-growing NEGOCIANT which has recently bought the impressive JAFFELIN negociant, plus the previously dull BOUCHARD AINE. Its own wines and those of the latter firm are improving and they are usefully exploring new regions further south. The appointment of local superstar Bernard Repolt as chief winemaker is beginning to be repaid with better Burgundies. *** 1992 Mercurey Blanc Tastevine £8 (W).

Bolla (VENETO, Italy) Producer of plentiful, adequate VALPOLICELLA and SOAVE and smaller quantities of impressive single vineyard wines like its Jago and Creso. **** 1986 Amarone Classico £12 (V&C).

Bollinger (CHAMPAGNE, France) Great, family-owned firm at AY, whose wines need age. The luscious and rare Vieilles Vignes is made from pre-PHYLLOXERA vines, while the nutty RD was the first late-disgorged Champagne to hit the market. Best buy: the vintage. **** 1988 £34 (BU, MTL, DBY, BU).

Bommes (BORDEAUX, France) SAUTERNES Commune and village containing several PREMIERS CRUS. 75 76 79 80 81 83 86 88 89 90. **** 1990 Château Rabaud Promis, Premier Cru £23 (BI).

Ch. le Bon-Pasteur (BORDEAUX, France) The impressive private estate of Michel Rolland, who acts as consultant for half his neighbours in Bordeaux as well as producers in almost every other winegrowing region in the universe. 82 83 85 88 89 90 91 93. **** 1989 £30 (F&M).

Domaine Bonneau du Martray (BURGUNDY, France) Largest grower of Corton-Charlemagne and a reliable producer thereof. Also produces a classy red GRAND CRU CORTON. **** 1992 Corton-Charlemagne £37 (OD).

Bonnezeaux (LOIRE, France) Delicious sweet whites produced from the CHENIN BLANC which last forever. 71 76 83 85 88 89 90 92. 1993 Domaine de la Sansonniére Cuvée Mathilde £27 (YAP).

Bonny Doon Vineyard (SANTA CRUZ MOUNTAINS, California) Randall Grahm, the original 'Rhône Ranger' has an affection for Italian varieties which is increasingly evident in a range of characterful red, dry and late harvest whites. ***** 1992 The Catalyst £6 (OD) *** 1992 Cinsault £15.50 (ADN) **** 1992 Ca Del Solo Malvasia Bianca £7.50 (M&V, SAN, POR, HN, NY).

Borba (ALENTEJO, Portugal) See ALENTEJO.

Bordeaux (France) Largest quality wine region in France, producing reds, rosés and deep pink CLAIRETS from CABERNET SAUVIGNON, CABERNET FRANC, PETIT VERDOT, and MERLOT, and dry and sweet whites from (principally) blends of SEMILLON and SAUVIGNON. Bordeaux Supérieur denotes slightly riper grapes. Dry whites from regions like the MÉDOC and SAUTERNES where they are not part of the mainstream activity are sold as Bordeaux Blanc, so even the efforts by Chateaux Yquem, Margaux, and Lynch Bages are sold under the same label as the most basic supermarket blended white. Bordeaux Superieur is merely red wine made from (slightly) riper grapes. 82 83 85 86 88 89 90 93 94. See GRAVES, MEDOC, POMEROL, ST.EMILION, etc.

Borgogno (PIEDMONT, Italy) Resolutely old-fashioned BAROLO producer whose wines develop a sweet, tobaccoey richness with age. In their youth though, they're often not a lot of fun. ***** 1987 Barolo Riserva £9 (RBS).

De Bortoli (RIVERINA, Australia) Fast-developing firm (following its move into the YARRA VALLEY) which startled the world by making a Botrycised peachy, honeyed SEMILLON which beat CH. YQUEM in a tasting – and by making it in the unfashionable RIVERINA. **** 1991 Windy Peak Cabernet Merlot £5.75 (SAF) *** St Michael Australian Brut Sparkling Wine £5 (M&S).

Boschendal (Cape South Africa) Modern winery producing some of the Cape's best fizz and fast-improving whites. *** NV Brut Sparkling £10 (SUM) *** 1993 Grand Cuvee Sauvignon Blanc £6 (TO).

Botrytis BOTRYTIS CINEREA, A FUNGAL INFECTION THAT ATTACKS AND SHRIVELS GRAPES, EVAPORATING THEIR WATER AND CONCENTRATING THEIR SWEETNESS. VITAL TO SAUTERNES AND THE FINER GERMAN AND AUSTRIAN SWEET WINES. SEE SAUTERNES,TROCKENBEERENAUSLESE.

Bottle-fermented COMMONLY FOUND ON THE LABELS OF US SPARKLING WINES TO INDICATE THE METHODE CHAMPENOISE; GAINING WIDER CURRENCY. BEWARE, THOUGH – IT CAN INDICATE INFERIOR 'TRANSFER METHOD' WINES.

Bouchard Aîné (BURGUNDY, France) For a long-time, an unimpressive merchant, recently taken over by BOISSET and now under the winemaking control of the excellent Bernard Repolt of JAFFELIN. Watch this space.

Bouchard Père et Fils (BURGUNDY, France) Traditional merchant with some great vineyards. Wines – apart from the Beaune de l'Enfant Jesus and LA ROMANEE are generally less impressive. *** 1983 Clos Vougeot £15 (RD).

Bouquet OVERALL SMELL, OFTEN MADE UP OF SEVERAL SEPARATE AROMAS.

Côtes de Bourg (BORDEAUX, France) Clay-soil region just across the water from the MEDOC and an increasingly reliable source of good value, if somewhat fast-maturing MERLOT-dominated plummy reds. Whites are much less impressive. 85 86 88 89 90 92. *** 1991 Ch. Rousset £6 (ADN).

Bourgueil (Loire, France) Red AC in the Touraine area, producing crisp, grassy-blackcurranty 100 per cent Cabernet Franc wines; can age well in good years. 83 85 86 88 89 90 92. *** 1992 Les Barroirs Couly-Dutheil £6 (U).

Bouvet-Ladubay (LOIRE, France) Producer of good LOIRE fizz and better SAUMUR CHAMPIGNY reds. *** Saumur Brut, Bouvet Ladubay £9 (SEL).

Bouvier (Austria) Characterless variety used to produce tasty but mostly simple late-harvest wines.

Bouzeron (BURGUNDY, France) Village in the COTE CHALONNAISE, principally known for ALIGOTE which is supposedly at its best here. 88 89 90 92. *** 1994 Aligoté de Bouzeron, A. de Villaine £8.50 (ADN).

Bouzy Rouge (CHAMPAGNE, France) Sideline of a black grape village: an often thin-bodied, rare and overpriced red wine which, despite what they say, rarely ages. 88 89 90 92. *** 1988 Andre Clouet £15 (T&W).

Bowen Estate (COONAWARRA, Australia) Producer proving that COONAWARRA can be as good for SHIRAZ as CABERNET. **** 1992 Shiraz £9 (AUC).

Domaines Boyar (Bulgaria) Privatised producers especially in the SUHINDOL region – selling increasingly impressive 'Reserve' reds under the LOVICO label. Other wines are less reliably recommendable *** 1990 Bulgarian Reserve Merlot £3.50 (JS).

Brachetto d'Acqui (PIEDMONT, Italy) Eccentric Muscatty red grape. Often frizzante. *** 1993 Araldica £5 (V&C).

Ch. Branaire-Ducru (BORDEAUX, France) A very Revival in the 1980s for this fourth-growth ST JULIEN Estate. 82 83 85 86 88 89 90. **** 1982 £32 (J&B).

Brand's Laira (COONAWARRA, Australia) Underperforming, traditional producer. **** Cabernet Sauvignon 1993 £95 (WAV).

Ch. Brane-Cantenac (BORDEAUX, France) Perennial under achieving MARGAUX, though the second label, the discouragingly named Château Notton can be a worthwhile buy. 85 86 88 89 90 91. *** 1978 £38 (NIC).

Braquet (MIDI, France) Grape variety used in Bellet. *** Ch. de Crémat 1994 Charles Bagnis £17 (YAP).

Brauneberg (MOSEL-SAAR-RUWER, Germany) Village best known in the UK for the Juffer vineyard. ***** 1993 Brauneberger Juffer-Sonnenuhr Riesling Kabinett, Fritz Haag £10 (L&W).

Brazil Country in which large quantities of fairly light-bodied wines are produced in a region close to Puerto Allegre, where it tends to rain at harvest time. Progress is being made, however, following the efforts of Australian flying winemaker John Worontschak who produced unexceptional own-label wine there for Tesco. The Palomas vineyard on the Uruguayan border has a state-of-the-art winery and a good climate. The wines have yet to reflect those advantages however.

Breaky Bottom (Sussex, England) One of Britain's best, making SEYVAL to rival dry wines from the LOIRE.

Georg Breuer (Rheingau, Germany) Innovative producer with classy RIESLINGS and high quality RULANDER. **** 1989 Rüdesheimer Berg Rottland Trockenbeerenauslese £79 (half) (OD).

Bricco Manzoni (PIEDMONT, Italy) Non-DOC oaky red blend of NEBBIOLO and BARBERA grapes grown on vines which could produce BAROLO. Drinkable young. 83 85 86 87 88 89 90 92. **** 1988 Valentino Migliorini £13 (V&C).

Bridgehampton (LONG ISLAND, New York State, US) Producer of first class MERLOT and CHARDONNAY to worry a Californian.

Bridgewater Mill (ADELAIDE HILLS, South Australia) More modest sister winery to PETALUMA. Also a wonderful restaurant in which to stop for lunch. **** 1993 Bridgewater Mill Chardonnay £6 (OD, TH).

Bright Australian-born Peter Bright of the J Pires winery makes top-class Portuguese wines, including Tinta da Anfora and QUINTA DA BACALHOA, plus a growing range in countries such as Spain and Chile made under the Bright Brothers label. **** Sainsbury's do Campo Tinto, Peter Bright £3 (JS).

Jean-Marc Brocard (BURGUNDY, France) Classy CHABLIS producer with well-defined individual vineyard wines. **** 1993 Chablis Premier Cru 'Montmains', Domaine des Manants £11 (ADN) *** 1993 Chablis £7 (OD).

Brokenwood (HUNTER VALLEY, Australia) Starry source of great SEMILLON, SHIRAZ and even (unusually for the HUNTER VALLEY) CABERNET. ***** 1991 Shiraz £8 (NY).

Brouilly (BURGUNDY, France) Largest of the ten BEAUJOLAIS Crus producing pure, fruity GAMAY 85 88 89 91. **** 1994 Brouilly, Les Celliers de Samsons, £5.50 (ABY).

Ch. Broustet (BORDEAUX, France) Rich, quite old-fashioned, well-oaked BARSAC 2ème Cru. *** 1989 £20 (OWL).

Brown Brothers (North-east VICTORIA, Australia) Family-owned and Victoria-focused winery with a penchant for exploring new wine regions and grapes. Wines are rarely better than four star, though the SHIRAZ can hit five, and the liqueur Muscat has, coincidentally, been doing that since the purchase of the old All Saints winery in RUTHERGLEN. The ORANGE MUSCAT and FLORA remain a delicious mouthful of liquid marmalade and the Tarrango, though slightly less light-hearted than when it was first produced, is still a great alternative to Beaujolais. *** 1994 Tarrango £5 (W, VW) *** King Valley Chardonnay 1992 £7.50 (OD).

Bruder, Dr Becker (RHEINHESSEN, Germany) Known in Germany for TROCKEN RIESLINGS, but a good source of late-harvest wines and well-made SCHEUREBE **** 1993 Scheurebe Dienheimer Tafelstein Kabinett £5 (SAF).

Brunello di Montalcino (TUSCANY, Italy) Prestigious DOCG red from a SANGIOVESE clone. Needs at least five years to develop complex and intense fruit and flavour. 83 85 87 88 89 90 91. ***** 1990 Brunello di Montalcino Castello Banfi £15 (MWW) *** 1986 Brunello di Montalcino Riserva, Poggio all'Oro, Banfi £24 (V&C).

Brut DRY, PARTICULARLY OF CHAMPAGNE AND SPARKLING WINES. BRUT NATURE/SAUVAGE/ZERO ARE EVEN DRIER, WHILE 'EXTRA-SEC' IS PERVERSELY APPLIED TO (SLIGHTLY) SWEETER FIZZ.

Bual (MADEIRA) Grape producing a soft, nutty wine – wonderful with cheese. **** Blandy's 5 Year Old Bual, Madeira Wine Company, £12 (BOO).

Buçaco Palace Hotel (Portugal) Red and white wines made from grapes grown in BAIRRADA and DAO which last forever but cannot be bought outside the Disneyesque Hotel itself.

Bucelas (Portugal) DO area near Lisbon, best known for its intensely coloured, aromatic, bone-dry whites which rarely reach Britain.

Buena Vista (CARNEROS, California) One of the biggest estates in CARNEROS, this is an improving producer of Californian CHARDONNAY, PINOT NOIR and CABERNET. Look out for Reserve wines.

Bugey (East France) SAVOIE district producing a variety of wines, including white Roussette de Bugey from the grape of that name. *** Vin de Bugey, Crussy Blanc de Blanc (Sparkling) £7.50 (WSO).

Von Buhl (RHEINPFALZ, Germany) One of the area's best estates, due partly to vineyards like the Forster Jesuitengarten. See FORST. ***** 1985 Forster Jesuitengarten Riesling Spatlese £10 (OWL).

Buitenverwachting (Constantia, South Africa) Enjoying a revival since the early 1980s, this show-piece organic winery of CONSTANTIA, with its organic approach is making particularly tasty whites.

Bulgaria Developing quickly since the advent of privatisation and flying winemakers. Even so, the good-value, but less than brilliant, country wines, CABERNET SAUVIGNON and MERLOT with which it has made its reputation, have yet to be bettered. MAVRUD is the traditional red variety. 81 83 84 85 86 87. *** 1987 Sliven Bulgarian Cabernet Sauvignon, Vini Sliven £3.50 (VW).

Bull's Blood (EGER, HUNGARY) The red wine, aka Eger Bikaver, which, gave defenders the strength to fight off Turkish invaders is mostly anaemic stuff now but privatisation promises better things. *** St Ursula £3 (SMF).

Burdon (JEREZ, Spain) The brand used by Luis Caballero for his top-class range of sherries.

Grant Burge (BAROSSA, South Australia) Dynamic producer and owner of BASEDOWS. **** 1992 Shiraz £6 (AUC).

Burgenland (AUSTRIA) Wine region bordering Hungary, climatically ideal for fine, sweet Auslesen and Beerenauslesen. *** 1992 Eiswein Neusielersee Weinkellerei Burgenland £7 (OD, U).

Alain Burguet (BURGUNDY, France) One-man domaine which proves how good plain GEVREY CHAMBERTIN can be without the help of new oak. Look for his Vieilles Vignes. **** 1993 Gevrey Chambertin Vieilles Vignes £20 (HR).

Burgundy (France) Home to PINOT NOIR and CHARDONNAY; wines ranging from banal to sublime, but never cheap. (red) 78 83 85 88 89 90 91 92 (white) 85 86 88 89 90 92 93.

Bürklin-Wolf (RHEINPFALZ, Germany) Impressive estate with great organic RIESLING vineyards. **** 1989 Forster Pechstein Riesling Auslese £24 (THP).

Buttery RICH FAT SMELL OFTEN FOUND IN GOOD CHARDONNAY (OFTEN AS A RESULT OF MALOLACTIC FERMENTATION) OR IN WINE THAT HAS BEEN LEFT ON ITS LEES.

Buxy (Cave des Vignerons de) (BURGUNDY, France) Cooperative with fair value oaked Bourgogne Rouge and Montagny Premier Cru. Current vintages are sadly rather less dazzling than in the past. *** 1993 Montagny 1er Cru, Cave de Buxy £6.50 (TO) *** 1991 Somerfield Red Burgundy, £5 (SMF).

Buzbag (Turkey) Rich, dry, red wine. Rarely well made and often oxidised.

Côtes de Buzet (BORDEAUX, France) AC region adjoining BORDEAUX, producing light clarety reds, and duller whites from SAUVIGNON. 88 89 90 92. *** 1992 Domaine de la Croix, Vignerons de Buzet £3.50 (TO).

Ca' dei Frati (LOMBARDY, Italy) One of Italy's finest white wine producers, both of LUGANA and CHARDONNAY-based fizz. **** 1994 Dal Cero £8 (V&C).

Ca' del Bosco (LOMBARDY, Italy) Classic, if pricy BARRIQUE-aged CABERNET/MERLOT blends, fine CHARDONNAY and good PINOT BIANCO/PINOT NOIR/ CHARDONNAY METHODE CHAMPENOISE FRANCIACORTA from perfectionist producer Maurizio Zanella. **** 1990 Franciacorta £10 (V&C). ***** 1987 Pinero £38 (V&C) **** 1989 Chardonnay £23 (V&C).

Ca' del Pazzo (TUSCANY, Italy) Ultra-classy oaky SUPER-TUSCAN with loads of ripe fruit and oak. **** 1990 Caparzo £15 (V&C).

Cabardès (MIDI, France) Up-and-coming region north of Carcassonne using traditional Southern and BORDEAUX varieties to produce good, if rustic reds. *** 1992 Cabardès Domaine de Caunettes Hautes £4.50 (DIR, U).

Cabernet d'Anjou/de Saumur (LOIRE, France) Light, fresh, grassy, blackcurranty rosés, typical of their grape, the CABERNET FRANC. 85 86 87 88 89 90 92. *** Tesco Cabernet de Saumur, Caves de Vignerons de Saumur £4 (TO).

Cabernet Franc Kid brother of CABERNET SAUVIGNON; blackcurranty, but more leafy. Best in the LOIRE, Italy, and partnering CABERNET SAUVIGNON and particularly MERLOT in ST. EMILION. See CHINON and TRENTINO.

Cabernet Sauvignon The great red grape of BORDEAUX, where it is blended with MERLOT and other varieties. The most successful red varietal, grown in every reasonably warm winemaking country. See BORDEAUX, COONAWARRA, CHILE, NAPA. etc.

Cadillac (BORDEAUX, France) Sweet but rarely luscious (non-BOTRYTIS) old-fashioned SEMILLON AND SAUVIGNON whites for drinking young and well-chilled. *** 1990 Château du Juge £7 (AV).

Cafayate (ARGENTINA) See ETCHART.

Cahors (South-west France) 'Rustic' BORDEAUX-like reds produced mainly from the local TANNAT and the COT (MALBEC). Some examples are frankly Beaujolais-like while others are tannic, and quite full-bodied, though far lighter than they were in the days when people spoke of 'the black wines of Cahors'. 83 85 88 89 90 91. *** 1992 Cahors, Clos La Coutale £6.50 (NIC).

Cairanne (RHONE, France) Named COTES DU RHONE village for good, peppery reds. 82 83 85 88 89 90 91. *** 1994 Côtes du Rhône Villages, Domaine de la Presidente, Max Aubert £6 (SV, MWW).

Calabria (Italy) The 'toe' of the boot, making CIRO from the local Gaglioppo reds and GRECO whites. CABERNET and CHARDONNAY are promising too, especially those made by LIBRANDI. *** 1990 Librandi Cirò £4.50 (SMF).

Calem (DOURO, Portugal) Quality-conscious Portuguese-owned producer with a British winemaker. The speciality COLHEITA tawnies are among the best of their kind. **** 1987 Calem Colheita £14 (THP, JEH).

Calera (SANTA BENITO, California, US) Maker of some of California's best PINOT NOIR from individual vineyards such as Jensen, Mills, Reed and Selleck. The CHARDONNAY and VIOGNIER are pretty special, too. **** 1993 Central Coast Chardonnay £11 (MWW).

Caliterra (CURICO, CHILE) Go-ahead winery, making particular progress with its whites, thanks to the efforts of winemaking superstar Ignacio Recabarren. **** 1991 Cabernet Sauvignon Reserva, Vina Caliterra £6 (TH, BU, ECK) *** 1994 Casablanca Chardonnay £4.50 (DBY, CWS).

Ch. Calon-Segur (BORDEAUX, France) Traditional ST ESTEPHE that doesn't always live up to its 3rd Growth status and can be dauntingly tough. Lasts well though. 82 83 85 86 88 89 90. *** 1986 £18 (ABY).

Camille-Giroud (BURGUNDY, France) Little-known, laudably old-fashioned merchant with no great love of new oak and small stocks of great mature wine which prove that good BURGUNDY doesn't need it.

Campania (Italy) Region surrounding Naples, best known for TAURASI, LACRYMA CHRISTI and GRECO DI TUFO. 85 86 87 88 90 91 92.

Campillo (RIOJA, Spain) A rare example of RIOJA made purely from TEMPRANILLO, showing what this grape can do. The white is less impressive. *** 1982 Rioja Gran Reserva £10 (TO).

Campo Viejo (RIOJA, Spain) A go-ahead, often underrated bodega whose RESERVA and GRAN RESERVA are full of rich fruit. Albor, the unoaked red (pure TEMPRANILLO) and white (VIURA) are first-class examples of modern Spanish winemaking, while the Reserva 1988 is a good example of why it is often worth not spending the extra on a GRAN RESERVA. **** 1994 Albor Rioja £4 (BOO, DBY) *** 1985 Rioja Gran Reserva £7.50 (MTL, DBY, SMF).

Canada Surprising friends and foes alike, British Columbia and, more specifically, Ontario are producing good CHARDONNAY, RIESLING, improving PINOT NOIRs and more regularly, intense Ice Wines, usually from the Vidal grape. *** 1993 Stonechurch Vineyards Vidal £5 (TP).

Cannonau di Sardegna (SARDINIA, Italy) Heady, robust, dry-to-sweet, DOC red made from the Cannonau, a clone of the GRENACHE. 82 83 84 85 86 88 89 90 91 92. **** 1989 Sella & Mosca £6 (V&C).

Ch. Canon (BORDEAUX, France) First rate property whose subtle wines are wonderful examples of the ST EMILION at their best. Worth seeking out in difficult vintages. 82 83 85 86 88 89 90 91. **** 1966 la Gaffelière £17 (RD).

Canon Fronsac (BORDEAUX, France) Small AC bordering on POMEROL for attractive reds from increasingly good value if rustic Petits Châteaux. 82 85 86 88 89 90 92 93. *** 1992 Château Moulin Pey Labrie £8 (BKW).

Ch. Cantemerle (BORDEAUX, France) A (5ème) CRU CLASSE situated outside the main villages of the MEDOC. Classy, perfumed wine with bags of blackcurrant fruit. 83 85 86 87 88 89 90. **** 1989 £20 (BBR).

Cantenac (BORDEAUX, France) Commune within the appellation of MARGAUX whose Châteaux include PALMER. 82 83 85 86 88 89 90.

Canterbury (NEW ZEALAND) Despite early success with PINOT NOIR by St Helena, this cool area of the South Island is best suited to highly aromatic RIESLING and CHABLIS-like CHARDONNAY. Look for wines from GIESEN Amberly Estate, Larcomb, St Helena and Waipara Springs.

Cantina (Sociale) (Italy) WINERY COOPERATIVE.

Cape Mentelle (MARGARET RIVER, Australia) Brilliant Western Australian sister to CLOUDY BAY, with impressive SEMILLON-SAUVIGNON, SHIRAZ, CABERNET and, remarkably, a wild, berryish ZINFANDEL to shame many a Californian. **** 1994 Semillon Sauvignon £8 (TO) **** Shiraz 1992 £9 (J&B).

Capel Vale (MARGARET RIVER, Australia) Just outside the borders of MARGARET RIVER (demonstrating the dubious value of New World appellations); good source of RIESLINGS, GEWURZTRAMINERS and improving reds such as the Baudin blend. **** 1992 Chardonnay, £11 (M&S).

Villa di Capezzana (TUSCANY, Italy) Conte Ugo Contini Bonacossi not only deserves credit for getting Carmignano its DOCG, he also helped to promote the notion of CABERNET and SANGIOVESE as compatible bedfellows, thus helping to open the door for all those priceless – and pricy – SUPER-TUSCANS. *** 1988 Carmignano Riserva, Tenuta di Capezzana £10 (EWC).

Capsule THE SHEATH COVERING THE CORK ON A WINE BOTTLE WHICH, SINCE THE BANNING OF LEAD, IS USUALLY MADE OF PLASTIC OR A TYPE OF TIN.

Caramany (PYRENEES, France) New AC for an old section of the COTES DU ROUSSILLON-VILLAGES. VIGNERONS CATALANS produce a good example.

Carbonic Maceration SEE MACERATION CARBONIQUE.

Ch. Carbonnieux (BORDEAUX, France) Until recently, the whites here aged well but lacked fresh appeal in their youth. Since 1991, however, they are beginning to compete with CH. FIEUZAL and LA LOUVIERE and the raspberryish reds are becoming some of the most reliable in the region 85 86 88 89 90 91. *** 1992 (red) £13 (WR, BU).

Carcavelos (Portugal) Sweet, usually disappointing fortified wines from a DO region close to Lisbon. Rare in Britain.

Carema (PIEDMONT, Italy) Wonderful, perfumed NEBBIOLO produced in limited quantities. ***** 1988 Nera Eticchetta Ferrando £13 (V&C).

Carignan Prolific red grape making usually dull, coarse wine for blending, but classier fare in CORBIERES and FITOU. In Spain it is known as Cariñena and Mazuelo, while Italians call it Carignano. **** 1994 Minervois, Carignanissime de Centeilles, Domergue £6 (ADN).

Louis Carillon & Fils (BURGUNDY, France) Superlative modern PULIGNY estate producing impeccable wines. ***** 1993 Puligny-Montrachet 1er Cru, Champs Canet £27 (L&W).

Cariñena (Spain) Important DO of Aragon for rustic reds, high in alcohol and confusingly made, not from the Cariñena (or CARIGNAN) grape but mostly from the Garnacha Tinta. Also some whites. 88 89 90 91 92. *** 1988 Cariñena, San Valero £4 (SAF).

Carmenet Vineyard (SONOMA, California) Excellent and unusual winery tucked away in the hills and producing long-lived, very BORDEAUX-like but (unusually for California) very approachable reds, and (even more unusually for California) good SEMILLON-SAUVIGNON whites and Cabernet Franc. **** 1991 Cabernet Franc, £15 (DBY).

Carmignano (TUSCANY, Italy) Exciting alternative to CHIANTI, in the same style but with the addition of CABERNET grapes. 82 83 85 86 87 88 89 90 91. See VILLA DI CAPEZZANA.

Carneros (California) Small, cool, high-quality region shared between the NAPA and SONOMA Valleys, and producing top-class CHARDONNAY and PINOT NOIR. 85 86 87 88 89 90 91. ***** 1993 Saintsbury Carneros Pinot Noir, £12 (DBY, ADN).

Carneros Creek (California) Producer of ambitious but toughly disappointing PINOT NOIR under this name and the far better (and cheaper) berryish Fleur de Carneros. *** 1993 Fleur de Carneros Pinot Noir £8 (RTW).

Carr Taylor (Sussex, England) One of England's more businesslike estates with a worthwhile fizz. *** 1990 Medium Dry Superior £5 (SAS).

Ch. Carras (MACEDONIA, Greece) Until recently the only internationally visible Hellenic effort at modern winemaking. Disappointing when compared with HATZIMICHALIS. *** Château Carras Red 1990 £8.50 (SEL).

Casa (Italy, Spain, Portugal) FIRM OR COMPANY.

Casa vinicola (Italy) FIRM BUYING AND VINIFYING GRAPES.

Casablanca (CHILE) New region in ACONCAGUA; a magnet for quality conscious winemakers and producing especially impressive SAUVIGNONS, CHARDONNAYS and GEWURZTRAMINERS, especially from producers like CALITERRA, Santa Carolina, Santa Emiliana, Villard and Casablanca. Watch out for reds too, from these wineries plus SANTA RITA and CONCHA Y TORO.

Viña Casablanca (Chile) Go-ahead winery in the region of the same name, showcasing the talents of winemaker Ignacio Recabarren. **** 1994 Sauvignon £5 (TH).

Caslot-Galbrun (LOIRE, France) Top-class producer of serious, long-lived red Loires. **** 1992 Bourgueil La Hurolaie £5 (WSO).

Castellare (TUSCANY, Italy) Innovative small CHIANTI CLASSICO estate whose SANGIOVESE/MALVASIA NERA I Sodi di San Niccoló VINO DA TAVOLA is worth seeking out. **** 1991 I Sodi di San Niccoló £17 (LAV, WIN).

Castell'in Villa (TUSCANY, Italy) Producer of powerful CHIANTI CLASSICO RISERVA and a VINO DA TAVOLA called Santa Croche.

Furstlich Castell'sches Domanenamt (FRANKEN, Germany) Prestigious producer of typically full-bodied FRANKEN dry whites. *** 1988 Casteller Kirchberg, Müller-Thurgau £10 (F&M).

Castellblanch (CATALONIA, Spain) Producer of better-than-most CAVA, provided you catch it very young. *** Cava £5.50 (TH, WR, BU).

Casteller (TRENTINO, Italy) Pale red, creamy-fruity wines for early drinking.

Castelli Romani (LATIUM, Italy) Frascati-like whites produced close to Rome. Reds are dull.

Castello dei Rampolla (TUSCANY, Italy) Good CHIANTI producer whose wines need time to soften.

Castello della Sala (UMBRIA, Italy) Antinori's rather over-priced but sound CHARDONNAY and good SAUVIGNON and Procanico blend. *** 1993 Borro della Sala £8 (V&C).

Castello di Volpaia (TUSCANY, Italy) High-quality CHIANTI estate with SUPER-TUSCAN Coltassala. **** 1990 Coltassala £14 (ADN).

Castellogiocondo (TUSCANY, Italy) High-quality Brunello estate. *** 1992 Rosso Di Montalcino, Campo ai Sassi £5 (W) **** 1988 £13 (LAV).

Vignerons Catalans (ROUSSILLON, France) Dynamic cooperative with decent, inexpensive wines. *** 1994 Safeway Côtes Du Roussillon Villages, £3 (SAF).

Catalonia (Spain) The semi-autonomous region in which is found the PENEDES, PRIORATO and the little-known CONCA DE BARBERA, TERRA ALTA and COSTERS DEL SEGRE.

Cat's pee DESCRIBES THE TANGY SMELL OFTEN FOUND IN TYPICAL – AND FREQUENTLY DELICIOUS – MULLER-THURGAU AND SAUVIGNON.

Domaine Cauhapé (South West France) Extraordinary JURANCON producer of excellent VENDANGE TARDIVE and dry wines from the MANSENG grape. **** 1992 Vendanges "10 novembre" £13 (M&V).

Cava (Spain) FIZZ PRODUCED BY THE METHODE CHAMPENOISE BUT HANDICAPPED BY INNATELY DULL LOCAL GRAPES AND AGEING WHICH DEPRIVES IT OF FRESHNESS. AVOID VINTAGE VERSIONS AND LOOK INSTEAD FOR ANA DE CODORNIU AND RAIMAT CAVA – BOTH MADE FROM CHARDONNAY – OR WELL-MADE EXCEPTIONS TO THE EARTHY RULE AS JUVE I CAMPS AND CONDE DE CARALT AND THE FOLLOWING EXAMPLES: *** 1990 Torre Del Gall, Gran Reserva Brut, Cava Chandon £8 (VW) *** Segura Viudas Cava Brut Reserva £6 (OD).

Cave (France) CELLAR.

Cave Co-operative (FRANCE) COOPERATIVE WINERY.

Caymus Vineyards (NAPA Valley, California, US) Traditional producer of concentrated, Italianate reds (including a forceful ZINFANDEL) and a characterful CABERNET FRANC. Liberty School is the second label.

Domaine Cazes (ROUSSILLON, France) Maker of great MUSCAT DE RIVESALTES, rich marmaladey stuff which makes most BEAUMES DE VENISE taste very dull. ******* 1992 Muscat de Rivesaltes, Domaine Cazes £10.50 (HN, PON, LV).

Cellier des Samsons (BURGUNDY, France) Source of better-than-average BEAUJOLAIS. ******* 1994 Fleurie, Cellier Des Samsons £7 (TH, WR, BU).

> **Cencibel** The name for TEMPRANILLO in VALDEPENAS.

Central Valley (California, US) Huge, irrigated region controlled by winemaking giants who annually make nearly three quarters of the state's wines without, so far, producing anything to compete with the fruit of very similar regions Down Under. HUGH RYMAN's Kings Canyon SAUVIGNON shows what Aussie-style winemaking can achieve, but QUADY's fortified and sweet wines are still the best wines here. ******** Starboard (Batch 88) Quady Winery £9 (half) (MWW) ******** 1994 Kings Canyon Sauvignon £5 (TH).

Central Valley (CHILE) The region in which most of CHILE's wines are made. It includes MAIPO, RAPEL, MAULE and CURICO, but not the newly fashionable cool-climate region of CASABLANCA which is in ACONCAGUA, further north.

Cépage (France) GRAPE VARIETY.

Cepparello (TUSCANY, Italy) Brilliant, pure SANGIOVESE VINO DA TAVOLA made by Paolo de Marchi of ISOLE E OLENA.

Ceretto (PIEDMONT, Italy) Big producer of mid-quality BAROLOS and more impressive single-vineyard offerings. ******* 1990 Barolo Zonchera £16 (V&C) ******* 1988 Bricco Rocche Prapo £24 (V&C).

Cérons (BORDEAUX, France) Bordering on SAUTERNES with similar, less fine, but cheaper wines. 82 85 86 88 89 90. ******* 1989 Château de Cérons £17 (NIC).

Ch. Certan de May (BORDEAUX, France) Top-class POMEROL estate with subtly plummy wine. ********* 1989 £47 (C&B).

LA Cetto (Baja California, Mexico) With wines like LA CETTO's tasty CABERNET and spicy-soft PETITE SIRAH, it's hardly surprising that Baja California features on lists rather more often than many big names from that slightly more northerly region across the US frontier. ******** 1992 Cabernet Sauvignon £5 (DBY, EP) ********* 1993 Petite Sirah, £5 (CWS, DBY, EP).

Chablais (VAUD, Switzerland) A good place to find PINOT NOIR rosé and young CHASSELAS (sold as Dorin).

Chablis (BURGUNDY, France) Often overpriced and overrated white, but fine examples offer a steely European finesse that New World CHARDONNAYS rarely capture. GRANDS CRUS should show extra complexity. 78 79 81 85 86 87 88 89 90 92 93. ******** 1992 Vieilles Vignes, La Chablisienne £8 (TH) ******** 1988 1er Cru Vaillon, Etienne & Daniel Defaix £16 (L&W).

La Chablisienne (BURGUNDY, France) Cooperative selling everything from PETIT CHABLIS to GRANDS CRUS under a host of labels. Rivals the best estates in the appellation. See CHABLIS.

Chai (France) CELLAR/WINERY.

Chalone (MONTEREY, California) Under the same ownership as ACACIA, EDNA VALLEY and CARMENET, this 25-year old winery is one of the big names for PINOT NOIR and CHARDONNAY and even PINOT BLANC. After a rocky period when wines displayed some dodgy wood flavours – and the arrival of heavy investment from the Château Lafite Rothschilds, it's right back on form with long-life, very Burgundian wines. ******* Chardonnay 1993 £20 (LAV).

Chalonnais/Côte Chalonnaise (BURGUNDY, France) Source of lesser-known, less complex Burgundies – GIVRY, MONTAGNY, RULLY and MERCUREY. Potentially (rather than always actually) good-value. 85 86 87 88 89 90 92 93. ******** 1993 Rully Blanc 1er Cru Les Clous, Olivier Leflaive £10 (L&W).

Chambers Rosewood (RUTHERGLEN, Australia) Competes with Morris for the crown of best Liqueur MUSCAT maker. The Rosewood is worth seeking out. **** Chambers-Rosewood Rutherglen Liqueur Muscat £6 (half) (ADN).

Chambertin (BURGUNDY, France) Ultra-cherryish and damsony GRAND CRU whose name was adopted by the village of GEVREY. Already famous in the 14th century, later it was Napoleon's favourite – though he drank it with water. Chambertin Clos-de-Bèze, Charmes-Chambertin, Griottes-Chambertin, Latricières-Chamberin, Mazis-Chambertin and Ruchottes Chambertin are all neighbouring GRANDS CRUS. **** 1993 Gevrey-Chambertin Cuvée Vieilles Vignes, Alain Burguet £20 (HR).

Chambolle Musigny (BURGUNDY, France) COTE DE NUITS village whose wines are sometimes more like perfumed examples from the COTE DE BEAUNE. Criticism of quality in recent years drove producers to tighten up the appellation tastings in 1993. Watch this space. 78 83 85 88 89 90 92. ***** 1993 1er Cru Les Amoureuses, Domaine Roumier £35 (HR)

Champagne (France) Source of the finest and greatest (and most jealously guarded) sparkling wines, from the PINOT NOIR, PINOT MEUNIER and CHARDONNAY grapes. See individual listings.

Champigny (LOIRE, France) See SAUMUR.

Domaine Chandon de Briailles (Burgundy, France) Good SAVIGNY-LES-BEAUNE estate whose owner is related to the original Chandon of the Champagne house. **** 1990 Corton Marechaudes Grand Cru £24 (HR).

Chanson (BURGUNDY, France) Long-established but undistinguished merchant. *** 1989 Beaune Bastion Premier Cru, £14 (ES).

Chapel Hill (MCLAREN VALE, South Australia) Pam Dunsford's impressively rich – some say too rich – reds and whites have recently been joined by a similarly noteworthy but leaner unoaked CHARDONNAY. **** 1992 Cabernet Sauvignon £9 (AUC) **** 1994 Unwooded Chardonnay £8 (AUC).

Chapel Hill (Balatonboglar, HUNGARY) Label used for adequate rather than inspiring wines made in Hungary by flying winemaker Kym Milne. *** Sainsbury's Hungarian Country White Wine £3 (JS).

Chapoutier (RHONE, France) Family-owned merchant rescued from its faded laurels by a new generation of Chapoutiers who are using more or less organic methods. *** 1994 Belleruche, £8 (DBY).

Chaptalisation THE LEGAL (IN SOME REGIONS) ADDITION OF SUGAR DURING FERMENTATION TO BOOST A WINE'S ALCOHOL CONTENT.

Charbono Obscure grape variety grown in CALIFORNIA but thought to come from France. Makes interesting, very spicy, full-bodied reds at Inglenook and DUXOUP WINEWORKS. **** 1992 Duxoup £11 (BI).

Chardonnay The great white grape of BURGUNDY, CHAMPAGNE and now the New World. As capable of fresh simple charm in BULGARIA as of buttery, hazelnutty richness in MEURSAULT. See under producer headings.

Charmat THE INVENTOR OF THE CUVE CLOSE METHOD OF PRODUCING CHEAP SPARKLING WINES. SEE CUVE CLOSE.

Charta (RHEINGAU, GERMANY) RHEINGAU SYNDICATE USING AN ARCH AS A SYMBOL TO INDICATE DRY (TROCKEN) STYLES OFTEN APPARENTLY ACIDIC ENOUGH TO REMOVE ENAMEL FROM TEETH. SPATLESE AND PREFERABLY AUSLESE VERSIONS ARE MADE FROM RIPER GRAPES. KABINETTS ARE FOR KEEN LEMON-SUCKERS.

Chartron & Trébuchet (BURGUNDY, France) Good, recently founded, small merchant specialising in white Burgundies. *** 1993 Chardonnay £7 (LAY).

Chassagne-Montrachet (BURGUNDY, France) COTE DE BEAUNE Commune making grassy, biscuity, fresh yet rich whites and mid-weight, wild fruit reds. Pricy but less so than neighbouring PULIGNY and just as recommendable. 86 88 89 90 92 93. *** 1991 Chassagne Montrachet Blanc Louis Latour £14 (MWW).

Ch. Chasse-Spleen (BORDEAUX, France) CRU BOURGEOIS CHATEAU whose wines can, in good years, rival those of many a CRU CLASSE. 82 83 85 86 89 90 91 92. **** 1985 £18 (ADN) **** 1990 £18 (BI).

Chasselas Widely grown, prolific white grape making light, often dull wine principally in Switzerland, eastern France and Germany. Good examples are rare. *** 1992 Pouilly, Cepage Chasselas, Guyot £7 (YAP).

Domaine du Chasseloir (LOIRE, France) Makers of good domaine Muscadets
*** 1993 £6 (WSO).

Château (usually BORDEAUX) LITERALLY 'CASTLE'; VINEYARD OR WINE ESTATE.

Château-Chalon (JURA, France) Speciality JURA AC for a VIN JAUNE which should keep almost indefinitely. *** 1986 Bourdy £29 (NIC).

Château-Grillet (RHONE, France) Tiny appellation consisting of a single estate and producer of once great, now disappointing VIOGNIER white. Wines from neighbouring Condrieu are better value. *** 1991 £27 (YAP).

Châteauneuf-du-Pape (RHONE, France) Traditionally the best reds (rich and spicy) and whites (rich and floral) of the SOUTHERN RHONE. Thirteen varieties can be used for the red, though purists still favour GRENACHE. (reds) 78 81 83 85 86 88 89 90 91. Recommended: CH. DE BEAUCASTEL, CHAPOUTIER Barbe Rac, FONT DE MICHELLE, GUIGAL, RAYAS.

Gerard Chave (RHONE, France) The best estate in HERMITAGE? Certainly but the wines demand patience. NB: labels read JL Chave; the eldest son in alternate generations is thus named, so it is thought unnecessary to print anything else in between times. 82 83 85 88 89 90. ***** 1985 Hermitage £36.50 (ADN) ***** 1982 £33 (YAP, DIR).

Chavignol (LOIRE, France) Village within the commune of SANCERRE.
**** 1990 "La Grande Côte" F Cotat £15 (ADN).

Chénas (BURGUNDY, France) Good but least well-known of the original BEAUJOLAIS Crus. 88 89 90 91. *** 1994, George Duboeuf £6 (BWC, DBY).

Chêne (France) OAK, AS IN FUTS DE CHENE (OAK BARRELS).

Chenin Blanc Honeyed white grape of the LOIRE, whose wines vary from bone-dry to very sweet and long-lived. Grown successfully in SOUTH AFRICA, NEW ZEALAND and AUSTRALIA, and in California at DRY CREEK. See VOUVRAY, QUARTS DE CHAUMES, BONNEZEAUX, SAUMUR.
**** 1994 Houghton Wildflower Ridge Chenin Blanc, £5.50 (MTL, DBY).

Ch. Cheval Blanc (BORDEAUX, France) Supreme ST EMILION property, unusual in using more CABERNET FRANC than MERLOT. Great, complex stuff. 81 82 85 86 89 90 93 ***** 1993 £37 (L&W).

Domaine de Chevalier (BORDEAUX, France) Great PESSAC-LEOGNAN estate which proves itself in difficult years. The rich, SAUVIGNON-influenced white is superlative oaked BORDEAUX while the restrained, raspberryish red is superlative classy CLARET. 85 86 87 88 89 90 93 ***** 1989 (red) £29 (ADN).

Cheverny (LOIRE, France) Light, floral whites from SAUVIGNON and CHENIN BLANC and now, under the new 'Cour Cheverny' appellation, wines made from the limey local Romarantin grape. 76 83 85 86 88 89. *** 1993 Sauvignon de Cheverny, Cazin £7 (L&W).

Chianti (Classico, Putto, Rufina) (TUSCANY, Italy) SANGIOVESE-dominant DOCG. Generally better than pre-1984, when it was customary to add wine from further south and mandatory to put dull white grapes into the vat with the black ones. The cockerel or cherub, respectively the insignia of the Classico and Putto growers are supposed to indicate a finer wine than the basic Chianti sold in straw-covered *fiasco* bottles, and the producers in the Rufina area claim that their region makes better stuff, too. Trusting good producers is a far safer bet. Look for ANTINORI, ISOLE E OLENA, Castello di Ama, CASTELL'IN VILLA, CASTELLARE, RUFFINO, CASTELLO DEI RAMPOLLA, CASTELLO DI VOLPAIA, FRESCOBALDI, SELVAPIANA. 83 85 86 87 88 89 90 91 93.

Chiaretto di Bardolino (LOMBARDY, Italy) Sadly rare in the UK: refreshing, berryish light reds and rosés from around Lake Garda. *** 1993 Chiaretto Classico Bardolino, Rosato £4.50 (HBR).

Chile Rising source of juicy blackcurranty CABERNET and (potentially even better) MERLOT, SEMILLON, CHARDONNAY and SAUVIGNON. See SANTA RITA, CASABLANCA, CONCHA Y TORO, ERRAZURIZ, CALITERRA, MONTES and COUSINO MACUL.

Chinon (LOIRE, France) CABERNET FRANC-based reds, rosés and whites that are light and grassy when young. Reds from a hot summer can age for up to 10 years 86 88 89 90 92. See OLGA RAFFAULT and COULY-DUTHEIL.

Chiroubles (BURGUNDY, France) One of the BEAUJOLAIS Crus; drinks best when young and full of almost nouveau-style fruit. 91 92 93. *** 1994 Chiroubles Music £6 (ABY).

Julian Chivite (NAVARRA, Spain) Innovative producer whose reds and rosés easily outclass many of those from big name Rioja bodegas. **** 1989 Reserva Tinto £4.50 (TH, WR, BU).

Chorey-lès-Beaune (BURGUNDY, France) Modest raspberry and damson reds once sold as Côte de Beaune Villages and now appreciated in their own right. Look for TOLLOT BEAUT and the Ch. de Chorey. 85 86 88 89 90 92.

Churchill Graham (DOURO, Portugal) Small **** dynamic young producer founded by Johnny Graham whose family once owned a rather bigger port house. *** Churchill's Finest Vintage Character Port £9 (SV, DBY, LEA).

Chusclan (RHONE, France) Named village of Côtes du Rhône with maybe the best rosé of the area. *** Co-op Côtes du Rhône, Co-op Chusclan £3 (CWS).

Cinsaut/Cinsault Prolific, hot climate, fruity red grape with high acidity, often blended with GRENACHE. One of the 13 permitted varieties of CHATEAUNEUF-DU-PAPE, and also in the blend of CHATEAU MUSAR in the Lebanon. **** 1992 Bonny Doon Vineyard Cinsault £15.50 (ADN) .

Cirò (CALABRIA, Italy) Hefty southern red made from the Gaglioppo, dull white and rosé. **** 1990 Librandi Ciro Riserva Ducca San Felice, £9 (EWC).

Ch. Cissac (BORDEAUX, France) Traditional CRU BOURGEOIS, close to ST ESTEPHE, making tough wines that last. Non tannin-freaks should stick to ripe vintages. Very popular among the pinstriped customers of El Vinos. 82 83 85 86 88 89 90. *** 1989 £11 (J&B, OD).

Ch. Citran (BORDEAUX, France) Improving CRU BOURGEOIS thanks to major investment by the Japanese.

Bruno Clair (BURGUNDY, France) MARSANNAY estate with good FIXIN, GEVREY-CHAMBERTIN, MOREY-ST-DENIS and SAVIGNY. *** Marsannay Rosé 1991 £8.50 (RD). **** 1991 Chambertin, Clos de Bèze, Grand Cru £33 (J&B).

Clairet The derivation of 'claret' – very light red wine, almost rosé. *** 1993 Château Bonnet Bordeaux Clairet £5 (TH).

Clairette Dull, white, workhorse grape of southern France used for CLAIRETTE DE DIE.

Clairette de Die (RHONE, France) Pleasant, if rather dull, sparkling wine. The Cuvée Tradition made with MUSCAT is invariably far better; grapey and fresh – like a top-class French Asti Spumante. *** Georges Aubert Clairette de Die Tradition Methode Dioise Ancestrale £7 (U).

Auguste Clape (RHONE, France) One of the masters of CORNAS. Great, intense, long-lived wines. ***** 1993 Cornas £13 (YAP).

la Clape (LANGUEDOC ROUSSILLON, France) Little known cru within the Coteaux de Languedoc with tasty Carignan-based reds and soft, creamy whites.

Clare Valley (Australia) Well-established, slatey soil region enjoying a renaissance with high-quality RIESLINGS that age well and deep-flavoured SHIRAZ, CABERNET and MALBEC (look for PETALUMA, PENFOLDS, MITCHELLS,

Leasingham, TIM ADAMS, TIM KNAPPSTEIN, Pikes, LINDEMANS). 80 84 86 88 89 90 91 92. **** 1994 Tim Knappstein Clare Valley Riesling £5 (OD) ****1993 Penfolds Clare Estate Chardonnay £6 (OD).

Claret ENGLISH TERM FOR RED **BORDEAUX**. SEE UNDER SEPARATE BORDEAUX CHATEAU HEADINGS.

Clarete (Spain) TERM FOR LIGHT RED WINE – FROWNED ON BY THE EC.

Ch. Clarke (BORDEAUX, France) A good rather than great CRU BOURGEOIS estate recently founded by a Rothschild connected with neither Lafite nor Mouton. *** 1988 £10 (PST).

Classico (Italy) MAY ONLY BE USED ON A CENTRAL, HISTORIC AREA OF A **DOC**, EG CHIANTI CLASSICO, VALPOLICELLA CLASSICO.

Raoul Clerget (BURGUNDY, France) Old-fashioned BURGUNDY NEGOCIANT.

Clerico, Domenico (PIEDMONT, Italy) Superb new wave BAROLO and DOLCETTO producer, with Arte, a terrific NEBBIOLO/BARBERA blend.

Climat (BURGUNDY, France) AN INDIVIDUAL VINEYARD.

Ch. Climens (BORDEAUX, France) Gorgeous, quite delicate BARSAC which easily outlasts many heftier SAUTERNES. 83 86 88 89 90 91. ***** 1989, £42 (J&B) ***** 1983 £31 (Bl).

Clone SPECIFIC STRAIN OF A GIVEN GRAPE VARIETY. FOR EXAMPLE, MORE THAN 300 CLONES OF PINOT NOIR HAVE BEEN IDENTIFIED.

Clos (France) LITERALLY, A WALLED VINEYARD – AND OFTEN A FINER WINE.

Clos de la Roche (BURGUNDY, France) One of the most reliable GRANDS CRUS in the COTE D'OR. ***** 1989 Domaine Armand Rousseau £28 (ADN).

Clos de Tart (BURGUNDY, France) GRAND CRU vineyard in MOREY ST DENIS exclusively made by Mommessin. Others might do more with it, but it does age well. **** 1988 Domaine Mommessin £63 (F&M, RD).

Clos de Vougeot (BURGUNDY, France) GRAND CRU vineyard divided among more than 70 owners, some of whom are decidedly uncommitted to quality. But who cares when the world is full of people ready to buy the label? Sensible wine drinkers will seek out names like DOM RION, JOSEPH DROUHIN, JEAN GROS, LEROY, MEO CAMUZET, FAIVELEY, Arnoux and Confuron. **** 1987 Drouhin £17 (RD).

Clos des Papes (RHONE, France) Top class CHATEAUNEUF DU PAPE estate. *** Châteauneuf du Pape Rouge £14 (Bl).

Clos du Bois (SONOMA, California) Top flight producer whose 'Calcaire' CHARDONNAY (named, like Chalk Hill, after the chalky soil of BURGUNDY of which there is none in California) and Marlstone CABERNET-MERLOT are particularly fine. ***** 1993 Chardonnay, Calcaire Vineyard £16 (WIN, LAY).

Clos du Roi (BURGUNDY, France) BEAUNE PREMIER CRU that is also part of CORTON GRAND CRU. **** 1993 Beaune 1er Cru Clos Du Roi, Chateau Philippe-Le-Hardi £12 (ABY).

Clos du Val (NAPA Valley, California) Bernard Portet, brother of Dominique, who runs TALTARNI in Australia, makes good STAGS LEAP reds – including CABERNET and MERLOT – that develop well with time. *** 1991 Pinot Noir £11 (DBY, RD). **** 1991 Zinfandel Stags Leap District £10 (DBY, RD).

Clos Floridène (BORDEAUX, France) Classy oaked white GRAVES made by superstar Denis Dubourdieu. The second label – 'Le Second de Clos Floridène'– is worth buying, too. **** 1993 £12 (OD).

Clos René (BORDEAUX, France) POMEROL estate making intensely concentrated, spicy wines. **** 1988 £15.50 (J&B).

Clos St-Georges (BORDEAUX, France) SAUTERNES-like wine produced just outside that appellation. 86 88 90. *** 1990 £7 (JS).

Cloudy Bay (MARLBOROUGH, NEW ZEALAND) Under the same (now largely French) ownership as CAPE MENTELLE, this is the ten-year-old cult winery that proved how classily the Sauvignon can perform in MARLBOROUGH. The CHARDONNAY is equally impressive as are the rare late-harvest wines and the leanish reds are improving. The PELORUS fizz is (for some, too much of) a buttery mouthful. ***** SAUVIGNON BLANC is widely but briefly available to those on merchant's waiting lists. *** 1990 Pelorus £13 (VW).

J F Coche-Dury (BURGUNDY, France) A superstar MEURSAULT producer whose basic reds and whites outclass his neighbours' supposedly classier fare. **** Bourgogne Rouge 1992 £13 (L&W).

Cockburn-Smithes (DOURO, Portugal) Well known for the unexceptional Special Reserve but producer of great vintage and up-market tawny port. **** 1985 Vintage Port £25 (THP).

Codorniu (CATALONIA, Spain) Humungous fizz maker whose Ana de CODORNIU is a reasonable CHARDONNAY-based CAVA. The dull prestige cuvée is popular in Spain. Unsurprisingly the Californian effort tastes… well, Cava-ish, despite using Champagne varieties (widely available).

Colares (Portugal) DO region near Lisbon for heavy, tannic red wines. The vines are grown in deep sand. Rare in the UK. *** 1983 Chitas £11 (SEL).

Colchagua Valley (CHILE) CENTRAL VALLEY region in which LOS VASCOS and UNDURRAGA are located.

Coldstream Hills (YARRA VALLEY, Australia) Lawyer turned winemaker and wine writer James Halliday makes stunning PINOT, great (Reserve) CHARDONNAY and increasingly impressive CABERNET-MERLOTS. Proof that critics can make as well as break. **** 1992 Cabernet Merlot £9 (W) *** 1990 Cabernet Sauvignon £10 (M&S). ***** 1993 Pinot Noir £8.50 (OD).

Colheita (Portugal) HARVEST OR VINTAGE – PARTICULARLY USED TO DESCRIBE TAWNY PORT OF A SPECIFIC YEAR.

Marc Colin (BURGUNDY, France) Large family estate with vineyards in ST-AUBIN, SANTENAY CHASSAGNE and a small chunk of LE MONTRACHET. A class act. **** 1993 Chassagne-Montrachet Blanc £15 (OD).

Collards (AUCKLAND, NEW ZEALAND) Small producer of lovely pineappley CHARDONNAY and appley CHENIN BLANC.

Colle/colli (Italy) HILL/HILLS.

Colli Berici (VENETO, Italy) DOC for red and white – promising CABERNETS.

Colli Orientali del Friuli (FRIULI-VENEZIA GIULIA, Italy) Lively single-variety whites and reds from near the Yugoslav border. Subtle, honeyed and very pricy Picolit, too. 85 88 89 90 91 92. **** La Viarte Pinot Grigio 1993/4 £9 (BI).

Collio (FRIULI-VENEZIA GIULIA, Italy) High altitude region with a basketful of white varieties, plus those of BORDEAUX and red BURGUNDY. Refreshing and often unshowy. Recommended producers: JERMANN, Puiatti.

Collioure (LANGUEDOC-ROUSSILLON, France) Intense RHONE-style red, often marked by the MOURVEDRE in the blend. *** Clos de Paulilles 1990 £7 (OD).

Colombard White grape grown in south-west France principally for distillation into Armagnac and more recently for good, light modern whites by YVES GRASSA and PLAIMONT. Also planted in AUSTRALIA (PRIMO ESTATE) and the US, where it is known as FRENCH COLOMBARD and used by E&J GALLO to make their only reasonably priced recommendable wine. *** 1993 E&J Gallo French Colombard £4 (widely available) **** 1994 Primo Estate £6 (AUC).

Columbia Crest (WASHINGTON STATE, US) Affordable producer of MERLOT and second label of CH. STE MICHELLE. *** 1989 Chardonnay £8 (RBS).

Columbia Winery (Washington, US) Producer of good, CHABLIS-style CHARDONNAY and GRAVES-like SEMILLON; subtle single-vineyard CABERNET, especially good MERLOT, SYRAH and Burgundian PINOT NOIR. *** 1988 Merlot £8 (HBJ) *** 1992 Pinot Noir Woodburne Cuvée £10 (HBJ).

Commandaria (CYPRUS) Traditional dessert wine with rich raisiny fruit *** St John, Keo £5 (U).

Commune (France) SMALL DEMARCATED PLOT OF LAND NAMED AFTER ITS PRINCIPAL TOWN OR VILLAGE. EQUIVALENT TO AN ENGLISH PARISH.

Conca de Barberà (CATALONIA, Spain) Cool region where large amounts of bulk wine are made. Torres's is impressive but pricy Milmanda is also produced here, as is Hugh Ryman's rather cheaper Santara. *** 1992 Milmanda Chardonnay £22.50 (SEL) *** 1994 Santara Chardonnay £4 (VW, JS).

Concha y Toro (MAIPO, CHILE) Fast improving, thanks to the efforts of winemaker Gaetana Carron and investment in CASABLANCA. Greatest successes so far have been the CABERNETS. Best wines are sold under Don Melchior, Marques de Casa Concha and Casillero del Diablo labels.
*** 1990 Marqués de Casa Concha Cabernet Sauvignon £7 (TAN).

Conde de Caralt (CATALONIA, Spain) One of the best names in CAVA. Catch it young. *** Somerfield Cava £5 (SMF) *** Tanners Cava Brut £6.50 (TAN).

Conde de Valdemar (RIOJA, Spain) See MARTINEZ BUJANDA.

Condrieu (RHONE, France) Potentially fabulous pricy pure VIOGNIER. A cross between dry white wine and perfume. Far better than the ludicrously hyped and high-priced CHATEAU GRILLET next door. Vernay is the top producer. 86 87 88 89 90 91 92 93. **** 1993 Geoges Vernay £18 (OD).

Consejo Regulador (Spain) SPAIN'S ADMINISTRATIVE BODY FOR THE ENFORCEMENT OF THE DO LAWS.

Consorzio (Italy) PRODUCERS' SYNDICATE, OFTEN USING THEIR OWN SEAL OF QUALITY.

Constantia (SOUTH AFRICA) The first wine region in the first New World country. Until recently, the big name here was the government-run and undistinguished ** Groot Constantia. Now KLEIN CONSTANTIA produces wines which go much further to explain this region's enduring reputation.

Aldo Conterno (PIEDMONT, Italy) A truly top class BAROLO estate from individual vineyards as well as top class BARBERA. Nobody does it better.
**** 1992 Nebbiolo delle Langhe "Il Favot" £13 (EWC).

Contino (RIOJA, Spain) CVNE-owned RIOJA ALAVESA estate whose wines have more fruit and structure than most. Some recent bottlings have been disappointing. *** 1988 Reserva £11 (L&W).

Coonawarra (SOUTH AUSTRALIA) Extraordinary cool(ish) red-soil region in the middle of nowhere. Produces great blackcurranty-minty CABERNET and underrated SHIRAZ as well as big CHARDONNAYS and full-bodied RIESLING. Still Australia's only internationally acknowledged top-class mini-region. (red) 82 84 85 86 87 88 90 91 92. See PETALUMA, PENFOLDS, WYNNS, ROUGE HOMME, PARKER ESTATE, LINDEMANS, KATNOOK.

Coopers Creek (AUCKLAND, NEW ZEALAND) Good, individualistic whites including Coopers Dry, a CHENIN-SEMILLON blend, CHARDONNAY, SAUVIGNON and RIESLING. **** 1994 Chardonnay £6 (MWW).

Copertino (Italy) Richly fascinating, intensely berryish wine made from the NEGROAMARO. **** 1991 Sainsbury's Copertino Riserva £4 (JS).

Corbans (Henderson, NEW ZEALAND) Big winery (encompassing Cooks). Good rich MERLOT reds. **** 1992 Private Bin Merlot £10 (VW).

Corbières (MIDI, France) Fast-improving though short-lived red wines, moving from rustic to RHONE in style. Whites and rosés have further to go. 85 86 88 89 90 91 92. **** Château Combe Loubière, 1993 £4 (ES).

Corked UNPLEASANT MUSTY SMELL AND FLAVOUR, CAUSED BY FUNGUS ATTACKING CORK. ALMOST ALWAYS GETS WORSE ON CONTACT WITH OXYGEN.

Cornas (RHONE, France) Dark red from the SYRAH grape, hugely tannic when young but worth keeping. 76 78 79 82 83 85 88 89 90 91. Look for: CLAPE, Tain Cooperative, JUGE, DE BARJAC, Colombo. ***** Clape 1988 £18 (CEB).

Corsica (France) Mediterranean island making robust reds, whites and rosés under a raft of appellations (doled out to assuage rebellious islanders). Vins de Pays (de l'Ile de Beauté) are often more interesting.

Cortese (Italy) Grape used in PIEMONTE and to make GAVI.

Corton (BURGUNDY, France) GRAND CRU hill potentially making great, intense, long-lived reds and – as Corton Charlemagne – whites. The supposedly uniformly great vineyards run a suspiciously long way round the hill. Reds can be very difficult to taste young; many never develop. **** 1986 Corton Grand Cru, Domaine Tollot-Beaut £24 (J&B).

Corvo (SICILY, Italy) Ubiquitous producer of pleasant reds and whites.
    *** Duca di Salaparuta 1992 £6 (V&C).

Ch. Cos d'Estournel (BORDEAUX, France) In ST ESTEPHE, but making wines
    with PAUILLAC richness and fruit, this is top class BORDEAUX. Spice is the
    hallmark. 82 83 85 86 88 89 90 ***** 1986 £26 (BBR).

Cosecha (Spain) HARVEST OR VINTAGE.

Cossart Gordon (MADEIRA, Portugal) High quality brand used by the
    Madeira Wine Co. **** 5 Year Old Sercial Madeira £12 (J&B).

Costers del Segre (CATALONIA, Spain) Denomination more or less created
    for RAIMAT.

Costières de Nimes (MIDI, France) Up-and-coming region which can make
    reds to match the northern Rhône. *** 1993 Ch Paul Blanc Rouge £5 (OD).

Costières du Gard (South-west France) Fruity reds, rarer whites and rosés.
    Surprisingly hard to find in the UK.

Cot The red grape of CAHORS and the Loire. aka MALBEC.

Côte de Beaune (Villages) Geographical distinction for the southern half of
    the COTE D'OR. With the suffix 'Villages', indicates red wines from one or
    more of the villages in the Côte de Beaune. Confusingly, wine labelled
    simply 'Côte de Beaune' comes from a small area around BEAUNE itself and
    often tastes like wines of that appellation. These wines (red and white) are
    rare. 79 80 82 83 85 87 88 89 90 92.

Côte de Brouilly (BURGUNDY, France) One of the BEAUJOLAIS Crus; distinct
    from BROUILLY and often finer. Floral and ripely fruity; will keep for a few
    years. 88 89 90 91 92 93. **** 1994 Brouilly Chateau des Tours, £8 (CPW).

Côte de Nuits (BURGUNDY, France) Northern, and principally 'red' end of the
    COTE D'OR. The suffix 'Villages' indicates wine from one or more of the
    communes in the area. 78 80 82 83 84 85 86 87 88 89 90 92.

Côte des Blancs (CHAMPAGNE, France) Principal CHARDONNAY-growing
    area. 78 83 85 86 88 90. *** Champagne Le Mesnil Blanc de Blancs £14 (TH).

Côte d'Or (BURGUNDY, France) Geographical designation for the central,
    finest slopes running down the region, encompassing the COTE DE NUITS
    and COTE DE BEAUNE. See under various BURGUNDY entries.

Côte Rôtie (RHONE, France) Powerful, smoky yet refined SYRAH (possibly
    with a touch of white VIOGNIER) reds from the northern RHONE, divided
    into two principal hillsides, the 'Brune' and 'Blonde'. They need at least six
    (better 10) years. Best producers: GUIGAL GERIN, ROSTAING, Champet,
    JAMET, JASMIN, Burgaud, Dervieux-Thaize. 78 79 82 83 85 88 89 90 91.

Côte(s), Coteaux (France) HILLSIDES – PREFIXED TO, eg BEAUNE, SHOULD
    INDICATE FINER WINE.

Coteaux Champenois (CHAMPAGNE, France) Appellation for the madly over-
    priced still wine of the area. Mostly thin, light and acidic; justification for
    putting bubbles into this region's wines. LAURENT PERRIER's is better than
    most, but it's still only worth buying in the ripest vintages. 88 89 90 92.

Côtes du Rhône (Villages) (France) Large APPELLATION for medium and
    full-bodied spicy reds produced mostly in the southern part of the RHONE
    Valley. The best supposedly come from a set of better villages (and are sold
    as CdR Villages) though some single domaine 'simple' COTES DU RHONES
    outclass many Villages wines. GRENACHE is the key red wine grape but the
    SYRAH is gaining ground. Whites which can include new wave VIOGNIERS
    are improving. 88 89 90 91 92. *** 1990 Côtes du Rhône Villages Vidal-Fleury
    £7 (MWW). *** 1994 Chateau La Diffre, Seguret £5 (VW).

Cotesti (ROMANIA) Easterly vineyards growing some French varieties.

Cotnari (ROMANIA) Traditional white dessert wine.

El Coto (RIOJA, Spain) Small estate producing good, medium-bodied El Coto
    and Coto Imaz reds. *** 1985 Rioja Coto de Imaz Gran Reserva £8 (D).

Coulure VINE DISORDER CAUSED BY ADVERSE CLIMATIC CONDITIONS WHICH CAUSES
    REDUCED YIELDS (AND POSSIBLY HIGHER QUALITY) AS GRAPES SHRIVEL AND FALL.

Couly-Dutheil (LOIRE, France) High-quality CHINON estate with vines literally just behind the château in which Henry II imprisoned Eleanor of Aquitaine, his scheming wife. **** 1992 Chinon Rosé £6 (MWW).

Pierre Coursodon (RHONE, France) One of the best producers in ST JOSEPH. ***** 1991 Saint Joseph L'Olivaie £10 (BU).

Cousino Macul (MAIPO, CHILE) The only producer in CHILE to master traditional methods. Reds are more successful than whites. *** 1990 Antiguas Reserva Cabernet Sauvignon £6 (ADN, CWN) *** 1991 Merlot £5 (TO).

Ch. Coutet (BORDEAUX, France) Delicate neighbour to CH. CLIMENS, often making comparable wines: Cuvée Madame is top flight. 82 83 85 86 88 89 90. **** 1988 £20 (BBR).

Cowra (NEW SOUTH WALES, Australia) Up-and-coming region, making a name for itself with CHARDONNAY. Will one day eclipse its better known but less viticulturally ideal neighbour, the HUNTER VALLEY. **** 1993 Rothbury Estate Cowra Vineyards Chardonnay £6 (JS).

Cranswick Estate (South-east Australia) Successful RIVERLAND producer making reliable inexpensive wines widely available under the Barramundi label. *** 1993 Sauvignon £4 (MWW).

Cream sherry POPULAR STYLE (THOUGH NOT IN SPAIN) PRODUCED BY SWEETENING AN OLOROSO. THE NAME IS ATTRIBUTED TO A VISITOR TO HARVEYS WHO PREFERRED ONE OF THE COMPANY'S SHERRIES TO THE THEN POPULAR 'BRISTOL MILK'. 'IF THAT'S THE MILK', SHE JOKED, 'THIS MUST BE THE CREAM'.

Crémant (France) IN CHAMPAGNE, LIGHTLY SPARKLING. ELSEWHERE, eg CREMANT DE BOURGOGNE, DE LOIRE AND D'ALSACE, **METHODE CHAMPENOISE** FIZZ.
**** Mayerling Brut Crémant d'Alsace, Cave de Turckheim £8 (BOO, DBY, U)
*** Dom de Martinolles Crémant de Limoux, Vignobles Vergnes £8 (VER).

Criado y Embotellado (por) (Spain) GROWN AND BOTTLED (BY).

Crianza (Spain) LITERALLY 'KEEPING' – 'CON CRIANZA' MEANS AGED IN WOOD – OFTEN PREFERABLE TO THE RESERVAS AND GRAN RESERVAS WHICH ARE HIGHLY PRIZED BY SPANIARDS BUT TO BRITONS CAN TASTE DULL AND DRIED-OUT.

Crisp FRESH, WITH GOOD ACIDITY.

Croft (Spain/Portugal) Port and sherry producer making highly commercial but rarely memorable wines in either style. *** Sainsbury's Late Bottled Vintage Port, Croft 1987 £7 (JS) *** Croft Vintage Port 1982 £18.50 (VW).

Croser Made by Brian Croser of PETALUMA in the PICCADILLY VALLEY, this is one of the New World's most CHAMPAGNE-like fizzes. Becoming less lean as the proportion of PINOT NOIR increases. **** 1992 £11 (VW, OD).

Crouchen (France) Obscure grape capable of producing agreeable whites. Known as Clare Riesling in AUSTRALIA and Paarl Riesling in SOUTH AFRICA. *** 1992 White Clare, Wakefield Wines £5 (U, RAE, W, DBY).

Crozes-Hermitage (RHONE, France) Up-and-coming appellation on the hills behind supposedly greater HERMITAGE. Smoky, blackberryish reds are pure SYRAH. Whites (made from MARSANNE and ROUSSANNE) are creamy but less impressive. And they rarely keep. Recommended: CHAPOUTIER (including White), DELAS, GRAILLOT, Pochon, Tain cooperative, TARDY & ANGE.

Cru Bourgeois (BORDEAUX) WINES BENEATH THE CRUS CLASSES, SATISFYING CERTAIN REQUIREMENTS, WHICH CAN BE GOOD VALUE FOR MONEY AND, IN CERTAIN CASES, BETTER THAN SUPPOSEDLY CLASSIER CLASSED GROWTHS. *** 1993 Ch. Tour Haut Caussan, Haut Medoc £9 (ADN).

Cru Classé (BORDEAUX) THE BEST WINES OF THE MEDOC ARE CRUS CLASSES, SPLIT INTO FIVE CATEGORIES FROM FIRST (TOP) TO FIFTH GROWTH (OR CRU) IN 1855. THE GRAVES, ST EMILION AND SAUTERNES HAVE THEIR OWN CLASSIFICATIONS.

Cru Grand Bourgeois/Exceptionnel (France) AN ESTATE-BOTTLED HAUT-MEDOC CRU BOURGEOIS, WHICH IS SUPPOSEDLY AGED IN OAK BARRELS. TERM IS THE SAME AS CRU BOURGEOIS SUPERIEUR, THOUGH EXCEPTIONNEL WINES MUST COME FROM THE AREA ENCOMPASSING THE CRUS CLASSES. FUTURE VINTAGES WILL NOT BEAR THIS DESIGNATION AS IT HAS FALLEN FOUL OF THE EC.

Hans Crusius (NAHE, Germany) One of the most famous estates in Germany run by Hans and his son Dr Peter Crusius. Famous for a clarity and depth of flavour, strongly marked by the soil and preserved by careful, traditional winemaking. Big old oak casks are the norm with many of the wines. Better TROCKEN wines than most, thanks to the use of riper grapes. 85 86 88 89 90 92 93. **** 1993 Traiser Rotenfels Riesling Spätlese £10 (L&W).

Crusted port AFFORDABLE ALTERNATIVE TO VINTAGE PORT, A BLEND OF DIFFERENT YEARS BOTTLED YOUNG AND ALLOWED TO THROW A DEPOSIT. **** 1987 Grahams Crusted Port £11 (TO) *** 1989 Booths Crusted Port £10 (BTH).

Cullens (Margaret River, Australia) Brilliant estate run by mother and daughter team of Di and Vanya Cullen. Source of stunning SAUVIGNON-SEMILLLON blends, claret-like reds and Burgundian CHARDONNAY. ***** 1994 Sauvignon Blanc £11 (ADN) **** 1992 Cabernet Sauvignon/ Merlot Reserve £11 (DBY, ADN, LWE, DIR).

Curico (CHILE) Wine region in which TORRES, SAN PEDRO and CALITERRA have vineyards. Rapidly being eclipsed by CASABLANCA.

Cuvaison (NAPA Valley, California, US) Swiss-owned winery with high-quality CARNEROS CHARDONNAY, increasingly approachable MERLOT and now, good PINOT NOIR. Calistoga Vineyards is a second label. *** 1991 Chardonnay £13 (MWW).

Cuve close THE THIRD-BEST WAY OF MAKING SPARKLING WINE, WHERE THE WINE UNDERGOES SECONDARY FERMENTATION IN A TANK AND IS THEN BOTTLED. ALSO CALLED THE CHARMAT OR TANK METHOD.

Cuvée/(de Prestige) MOST FREQUENTLY A BLEND PUT TOGETHER IN A PROCESS CALLED ASSEMBLAGE. PRESTIGE CUVEES ARE (PARTICULARLY IN CHAMPAGNE) SUPPOSED TO BE THE CREAM OF A PRODUCER'S PRODUCTION.

CVNE (RIOJA, Spain) COMPANIA VINICOLA DEL NORTE DE ESPANA IN FULL, 'COO-NAY' IN SHORT: A LARGE OPERATION BY THE OWNERS OF CONTINO, PRODUCING THE EXCELLENT VINA REAL IN CRIANZA, RESERVA; IMPERIAL OR GRAN RESERVA IN THE BEST YEARS, AND A LIGHT CVNE TINTO. UNTIL RECENTLY, CONSISTENT, HIGH-QUALITY WINES, THOUGH SOME RECENT RELEASES HAVE BEEN SLIGHTLY LESS DAZZLING. **** 1987 CVNE Viña Real Rioja Reserva £9 (WSO).

Didier Dagueneau (LOIRE, France) The iconoclastic producer of some of the best, steeliest POUILLY FUME. Prices are high worth paying. **** 1993 Pouilly Fumé Pur Sang, £17 (ABY).

Dão (Portugal) Once Portugal's best known wine region – despite the dullness of its wines. Today, thanks to a few pioneering producers like SOGRAPE, both reds and whites are improving. Even so, BAIRRADA is intrinsically more interesting. 88 89 90 92. *** 1991 Co-op Dão, Sogrape £3 (CWS).

Kurt Darting (RHEINPFALZ, Germany) One of Germany's band of new wave producers who care more about ripe flavour than making excessive quantities of tooth-scouringly dry wine. Men like Darting deserve every true German wine lover's support. ***** 1992 Forster Schnepfenflug Huxelrebe Trockenbeerenauslese £12 (OD) **** 1992 Durckheimer Hochberg Riesling Spätlese £7 (OD).

Réné Dauvissat (BURGUNDY, France) One of the best estates in CHABLIS. Watch out for other Dauvissats – the name is one of the many used by the LA CHABLISIENNE Cooperative. **** 1993 Chablis 1er Cru Lechet £13 (TAN).

Dealul Mare (ROMANIA) Carpathian region once known for whites, now producing surprisingly good reds from 'noble' varieties such as the Pinot Noir. *** 1990 Classic Pinot Noir £3 (CWS, MRN, D).

Etienne & Daniel Defaix (BURGUNDY, France) Classy, traditional CHABLIS producer, making long-lived wines with a steely bite. **** 1990 Chablis, £12 (L&W) *** 1988 Chablis Premier Cru 'Les Lys' £17 (L&W).

Dégorgée (dégorgement) THE REMOVAL OF THE DEPOSIT OF INERT YEASTS FROM CHAMPAGNE AFTER MATURATION. SEE RD.

Deidesheim (RHEINPFALZ, Germany) Distinguished wine town noted for flavoursome RIESLINGS. *** 1992 St Michael Deidesheimer Hofstuck Riesling, St Ursula £5 (M&S).

Delas Frères (RHONE, France) Often underrated NEGOCIANT whose red individual vineyard wines can rival those of GUIGAL and the reconstructed CHAPOUTIER. ***** 1991 Hermitage Cuvée Marquise de la Tourette £17 (LAY) **** 1989 Côte Rôtie, Seigneur de Maugiron £17 (LAY).

Delatite (Central VICTORIA, Australia) Producer of lean-structured, long-lived wines. *** 1992 "Dead Man's Hill" Gewürztraminer £7 (AUC) **** 1992 Devil's River Cabernet/Merlot £7 (AUC, TO).

Delegats (AUCKLAND, NEW ZEALAND) Family firm which has hit its stride recently with impressively ripe reds, especially plummy MERLOTS. The second label is 'Oyster Bay'. **** 1993 Oyster Bay Chardonnay £8 (MWW) **** 1991 Proprietor's Reserve Cabernet Sauvignon £9 (MWW).

Demi-sec (France) MEDIUM-DRY.

Denbies (Surrey, England) Dynamic co-production between a UK landowner and a South African winery owner (of La Bri). Part tourist attraction, part winery it has so far produced good dry wines and far better sweet ones. **** 1991 Noble Harvest £16 (SEL).

Deutches Weinsiegel (Germany) SEALS OF VARIOUS COLOURS AWARDED FOR MERIT TO GERMAN WINES, USUALLY PRESENT AS NECK LABELS. TO BE TREATED WITH CIRCUMSPECTION.

Deutscher Tafelwein (Germany) TABLE WINE, GUARANTEED GERMAN AS OPPOSED TO GERMANIC-STYLE EC TAFELWEIN.

Deutz (CHAMPAGNE, France; Spain, New Zealand, California) One of the first of the Champenois to try to make better than adequate wine overseas. The New Zealand Deutz Marlborough Cuvée, made with MONTANA, is back on form and the Californian Maison Deutz is a rich winner too, but keep an eye out for the classily subtle Cuvée William Deutz Champagne. *** Deutz Marlborough Cuvée Brut, Montana Wines Ltd £10 (OD).

Diabetiker Wein (Germany) INDICATES A VERY DRY WINE WITH MOST OF THE SUGAR FERMENTED OUT (AS IN A DIAT LAGER), THUS SUITABLE FOR DIABETICS.

Disznókó (TOKAY, Hungary) Newly consituted estate run by Jean Michel Cazes of CH LYNCH BAGES. Top class modern sweet Tokay is being made, but the dry, lemony wines made from the Furmint are arguably even more interesting. *** Disznókó Tokaji Furmint £5 (TH, BU).

Diamond Creek (NAPA Valley, California) Big Name producer with good vineyards (Gravelly Meadow, Red Rock Terrace and Volcanic Hill) but tough wine which demands patience.

DLG (Deutsche Landwirtschaft Gesellschaft) BODY AWARDING MEDALS FOR EXCELLENCE TO GERMAN WINES – FAR TOO GENEROUSLY.

DO Denominaci/on/ão de Origen (Spain, Portugal) DEMARCATED QUALITY AREA, GUARANTEEING ORIGIN, GRAPE VARIETIES AND PRODUCTION STANDARDS.

DOC Denominacion de Origen Califacada (Spain) LUDICROUSLY, AND CONFUSINGLY, SPAIN'S NEWLY LAUNCHED HIGHER QUALITY EQUIVALENT TO ITALY'S DOCG SHARES THE SAME INITIALS AS ITALY'S LOWER QUALITY DOC WINES. SO FAR, RESTRICTED TO RIOJA – GOOD, BAD AND INDIFFERENT – AND OF NO RELEVANCE TO ANYONE SEEKING REASSURANCE WHEN BUYING SPANISH WINE.

DOC(G) Denominazione di Origine Controllata (é Garantita) (Italy) QUALITY CONTROL DESIGNATION BASED ON GRAPE VARIETY AND/OR ORIGIN. 'GARANTITA' IS SUPPOSED TO IMPLY A HIGHER QUALITY LEVEL IN MUCH THE SAME WAY THAT ITALIAN POLITICIANS AND BUSINESSMEN ARE NOT SUPPOSED TO EXCHANGE BRIBES.

Ch. Doisy-Daëne (BORDEAUX, France) Fine BARSAC property whose wines can be more restrained than those of some of its neighbours. 82 85 86 88 89 90. **** 1989 £21.50 (BBR, ADN).

Ch. Doisy-Dubroca (BORDEAUX, France) Underrated **** SAUTERNES estate producing ultra-rich wines at often attractively low prices. Sadly hard to find in the UK. 82 85 86 88 89 90.

Ch. Doisy-Védrines (BORDEAUX, France) Reliable BARSAC property which made a stunningly concentrated 1989 (and a less impressive 1990). 82 85 85 88 89. *** 1989 £26 (BBR).

Dolcetto (d'Alba, di Ovada) (PIEDMONT, Italy) Red grape making anything from soft, everyday wine to more robust, long-lasting DOCs. In all but the best hands, worth catching young. 83 85 86 88 89 90 92.
∗∗∗ 1994 Dolcetto d'Asti Alasia, Araldica £5 (EWC) ∗∗∗ 1993 Dolcetto d'Alba, Aurelio Settimo £5 (WAW).

Dôle (Switzerland) Appellation of VALAIS producing attractive, rather than stunning reds from the PINOT NOIR and/or GAMAY. Best bought by people who have plenty of Swiss currency and who like very light wines to knock back after a day on the piste. ∗∗∗ Dôle du Valais, Provins Valais £10 (C&B).

Dom Pérignon (CHAMPAGNE, France) Top-end of MOET ET CHANDON's Champagne, named after the Abbey cellarmaster who is erroneously said to have invented the CHAMPAGNE method. Impeccable. (Moët will disgorge older vintages to order for customers' birthdays and anniversaries. Write and ask). ∗∗∗∗∗ £60 (OD etc).

Domaine (France) WINE ESTATE, CAN ENCOMPASS A NUMBER OF VINEYARDS.

Domaine Carneros (NAPA Valley, California) TAITTINGER's US fizz – produced in a perfect and thus ludicrously incongruous replica of the Champagne house's HQ in France. The wine, however, is one of the best New World efforts by the Champenois. ∗∗∗∗ Brut £14 (RBS).

Domaine Chandon (NAPA Valley, California) MOET & CHANDON's long established but until recently under-performing Californian winery has a first class winemaker who has finally been allowed to compete with her counterpart at DOMAINE CHANDON in Australia. Not yet available in Britain.

Domaine Chandon (YARRA VALLEY, Australia) Sold as Green Point in the UK, this is the winery whose winemaker Tony Jordan proved to its owners, MOET & CHANDON (though they hate to admit it) that Aussie grapes grown in a variety of cool climates can make wine that's every bit as good as all but the best CHAMPAGNE. Improving with every vintage – and now joined by a creditable, CHABLIS-like still Colonades CHARDONNAY. ∗∗∗∗ 1991 Green Point, £10.50 (W, MWW, JS, VW, BWS).

Domaine Drouhin (OREGON, US) BURGUNDY producer's highly expensive investment in the US that's finally producing world-beating reds, thanks to Veronique Drouhin's skill and personal commitment and some of OREGON's best vineyards. The 1990 beat a top class array of Burgundies – including several of Drouhin père's company's wines – to take the International Wine Challenge Trophy in 1994. ∗∗∗∗∗ 1990 Pinot Noir £17 (OD).

Domecq (JEREZ/RIOJA Spain) The biggest sherry house and producer of the once ultra-reliable, recently variable La Ina FINO, the rare but wonderful 51-1A AMONTILLADO and an attractively gentle red RIOJA.

Dominus (NAPA Valley, US) Christian MOUEIX's modestly named competitor to OPUS ONE has always been a heftily tannic CABERNET. Since 1989 that TANNIN has been matched by fruit, making for wine in which it is easier to believe. Even so, wines like the 1987 need to be left to themselves for several years. Unless you need a 1987 red you know will still be alive and kicking for a 21st birthday in 2008, buy one of M. MOUEIX's far more approachable BORDEAUX. 89 90 91 92. ∗∗∗ 1988 £30 (L&W).

Dopff 'Au Moulin' (ALSACE, France) Underrated NEGOCIANT whose GRAND CRU wines are among the most concentrated around. ∗∗∗∗ 1993 Gewürztraminer "Moulin Blanc" £8 (TP).

Dopff & Irion (Alsace, France) Not to be confused with its more recommendable namesake. ∗∗∗ 1993 Riesling £6 (EP).

Dosage THE ADDITION OF SWEETENING SYRUP TO NATURALLY DRY CHAMPAGNE.

Douro (Portugal) The great port region and river, producing much demarcated and increasingly good table wines thanks partly to the efforts of SOGRAPE and Australians David Baverstock (at QUINTA DE LA ROSA) and PETER BRIGHT. SEE BARCA VELHA 85 88 89. ∗∗∗∗ 1993 Quinta de la Rosa £5 (M&V) ∗∗∗ Bright Brothers Douro Red £5 (TH).

Doux (France) SWEET.

Dow (DOURO, Portugal) One of the big two (with TAYLORS) and under the same family ownership as WARRES, SMITH WOODHOUSE and GRAHAMS. Great vintage port and similarly impressive tawny. The Quinta do Bomfim wines offer a chance to taste the Dow's style affordably. 63 66 70 77 80 83 85 91. **** Dow's Vintage Port 1980 £19 (HLV, DBY) *** Dow's Late Bottled Vintage 1989 £8 (BOO, MTL, W, SMF).

Jean-Paul Droin (BURGUNDY, France) Good, small CHABLIS producer with approachable, 'modern' wines. *** 1991 Chablis Fourchaume £16 (F&M).

Dromana Estate (MORNINGTON PENINSULA, Australia) Ace viticulturalist, Gary Crittenden has pioneered this region, with leanish CHARDONNAY and raspberryish PINOT, both of which might benefit from less of the viticultural expertise Mr C unashamedly uses to achieve high yields per vine.

Joseph Drouhin (BURGUNDY, France) One of the very best NEGOCIANTS in BURGUNDY with a range of first class reds and whites including a rare white BEAUNE from its own Clos des Mouches, top class CLOS DE VOUGEOT and unusually (for a NEGOCIANT) CHABLIS. The Marquis de Laguiche MONTRACHET is sublime. **** 1990 Savigny les Beaune £12 (OD) **** 1993 Montagny Blanc £9 (WES).

Pierre-Jacques Druet (LOIRE, France) Reliable BOURGUEIL producer making characterful individual cuvées. **** 1993 Les Cent Boisselées £8 (ADN).

Dry Creek (SONOMA, California) A rare example of a Californian AVA region whose wines have an identifiable quality and style. Look out for Sauvignon Blanc and Zinfandel – from wineries like Dry Creek, DUXOUP, Quivira, Nalle and Rafanelli.

Dry River (MARTINBOROUGH, NEW ZEALAND) Small estate with a particularly impressive PINOT GRIS.

Georges Duboeuf (BURGUNDY, France) The 'king of BEAUJOLAIS' who introduced the world to the boiled sweet flavour of young GAMAY at a time when most commercial versions tasted like CHATEAUNEUF DU PAPE. A wide range of good examples from individual growers, vineyards and villages. Reliable Nouveau, good straightforward MACONNAIS white single domaine Rhônes and now the biggest plantation of VIOGNIER in the world. **** 1994 Côtes Du Rhône Domaine des Moulins £5 (BWC) **** 1994 Fleurie £7-8 (MTL, BWC, TO).

Duc de Magenta (BURGUNDY, France) Classy estate now managed by JADOT.

Duckhorn (NAPA Valley, California) Vaunted producer who thankfully seems to be moving away from the intentionally impenetrable style of his highly priced MERLOT. This may dismay collectors and wine snobs who presumably derive similar pleasure from cold showers and being beaten with birch twigs; as a wine *drinker*, I'll open a bottle to celebrate. *** 1992 Merlot £18 (L&W) *** 1990 Cabernet Sauvignon £17 (L&W).

Ch. Ducru-Beaucaillou (BORDEAUX, France) SUPER SECOND ST JULIEN with a less-obvious style than peers such as LEOVILLE-LAS-CASES and PICHON LALANDE. Second wine is Croix-Beaucaillou. 85 86 88 89 90 91 92 **** 1990 £28 (BBR).

Domaine Dujac (BURGUNDY, France) Cult BURGUNDY producer with fine, long-lived, if sometimes rather pallid wines from MOREY ST DENIS including CLOS DE LA ROCHE. Now helped by Gary Farr of BANNOCKBURN in Australia busily investing time and effort into vineyards in Southern France. **** 1989 Morey St Denis £19 (ADN) **** 1993 Chambolle-Musigny £17 (HR).

Dumazet (RHONE, France) Top flight Northern RHONE producer making fewer than 200 cases of perfumed Condrieu per year from his one acre plot of steeply sloping vineyards. Buy this instead of CHATEAU GRILLET. **** 1993 Condrieu £14 (BI).

Dumb AS IN DUMB NOSE, MEANING WITHOUT SMELL.

Dunn Vineyards (NAPA Valley, California) Tough, forbidding CABERNETS from HOWELL MOUNTAIN for the very, very patient collectors who've run out of DUCKHORN MERLOT and DOMINUS.

Côtes de Duras (BORDEAUX, France) Inexpensive whites from the
SAUVIGNON, often better value than basic BORDEAUX Blanc. 88 89 90 92
*** 1993 Oak Aged Landerrouat £4 (SAF).

Durbach (BADEN, Germany) Top vineyard area of this ANBAUGEBIET.

Durif See PETITE SIRAH. *** 1991 Morris Durif £10 (ADN, WTR).

Jean Durup (BURGUNDY, France) Modern estate whose owner believes in
extending vineyards of CHABLIS into what many claim to be less
distinguished soil, and not using new oak. The best wines are sold under
the Ch de Maligny label. **** 1991 Chablis Château de Maligny £8 (WR).

Duxoup Wine Works (SONOMA, California) Inspired winery-in-a-shed,
producing very good PINOT NOIR, CHARBONO and fine SYRAH from bought-
in grapes. Not a name to drop among US collectors; they prefer tougher
fare from more château-like edifices. **** 1992 Charbono £11 (BI)
**** 1992 Carneros Pinot Noir, Hudson Vineyard £13 (BI).

Echézeaux (BURGUNDY, France) GRAND CRU vineyard between CLOS DE
VOUGEOT and VOSNE ROMANEE and more or less an extension of the latter
commune. The village of Flagey Echezeaux on the wrong – relatively
vineless – side of the *Route Nationale* apparently takes its name from the
'flagellation' used by the peasants to gather corn in the 6th century. The
famous producers of what ought to be wonderfully spicy, rich wines are
the DOMAINE DE LA ROMANEE-CONTI and HENRI JAYER. GRANDS-ECHEZEAUX
should be finer. 76 78 80 83 85 86 88 89 90 92. **** 1993 Grands Echézeaux
Grand Cru, Engel £34 (HR).

Edelfäule (Germany) BOTRYTIS CINEREA, OR 'NOBLE ROT'.

Edelzwicker (ALSACE, France) Generic name for a blend of grape varieties.
The idea of blends is coming back – but not the name (see HUGEL).

Eden Ridge (SOUTH AUSTRALIA) Organic wines made by MOUNTADAM
**** 1992 Shiraz £7.50 (BOO, DBY, JAR).

Eger Bikaver (Eger, Hungary) See BULLS BLOOD.

Einzellage (Germany) SINGLE VINEYARD; MOST PRECISE AND OFTEN THE LAST PART
OF A WINE NAME, FINER BY DEFINITION THAN A GROSSLAGE.

Eiswein (Germany) The ultimate, ultra-concentrated late-harvest wine, made
from grapes naturally frozen on the vine. Rare and hard to make (and
consequently very pricy) in Germany but more affordable in Austria and,
increasingly, Canada. Intensely delicious but often with worryingly high
levels of acidity. ***** 1992 Neusiedlersee, Weinkellerei Burgenland £7.50
(OD, U) ***** 1991 Kiedricher Wasseros Riesling, Robert Weil £50 (HBJ).

Eitelsbach (MOSEL-SAAR-RUWER, Germany) One of the top two Ruwer wine
towns, site of the famed Karthäuserhofberg vineyard. **** 1989
Eitelsbacher Marienholz Riesling, Bischofliches Konvikt £85 (J&B).

Elaborado y Anejado Por (Spain) 'MADE AND AGED FOR'

Elba (Italy) Island off the Tuscan coast making full dry reds and whites.

Elbling Inferior Germanic white grape.

Elgin (South Africa) Coolish – Burgundy-like – apple-growing country which
is rapidly attracting the interest of top producers. Will probably eventually
overshadow all but the best parts of Stellenbosch and Paarl.

Eléver/éléveur TO MATURE OR 'NURTURE' WINE, ESPECIALLY IN THE CELLARS OF
THE BURGUNDY NEGOCIANTS, WHO ACT AS ELEVEURS.

Neil Ellis (Stellenbosch, South Africa) One of the Cape's best new wave
winemakers and a pioneer of the new region of ELGIN. *** 1992 St Michael
Merlot/Cabernet Sauvignon, Jan Coetzee/Neil Ellis £5 (M&S).

Eltville (Rheingau, Germany) Town housing the RHEINGAU state cellars and
the German Wine Academy, producing good RIESLING with backbone 83 85
88 89 90 91 92 93. **** 1990 Sonnenberg Riesling Spätlese Hirt Gebhardt
£8.50 (FDL).

Emerald Riesling (California) Bottom of the range white cross grape (RIESLING x MUSCADELLE), at best fresh, fruity but undistinguished. Popular in the Central Valley in California.

Emilia-Romagna (Italy) Region around Bologna best known for LAMBRUSCO; also the source of ALBANA, SANGIOVESE DI ROMAGNA and PAGADEBIT.

En primeur NEW WINE, USUALLY BORDEAUX. SPECIALIST MERCHANTS BUY AND OFFER WINE 'EN PRIMEUR' BEFORE IT HAS BEEN RELEASED; CUSTOMERS RELY ON THEIR MERCHANTS JUDGEMENT TO MAKE A GOOD BUY – OR WAIT UNTIL ODDBINS, CHRISTIES OR SOTHEBYS SELL PRECISELY THE SAME WINE FOR THE SAME PRICE A YEAR OR SO AFTER EVERYBODY ELSE HAS TIED UP THEIR CASH BUYING IT EN PRIMEUR. IN THE US AND AUSTRALIA, WHERE PRODUCERS LIKE MONDAVI AND PETALUMA ARE SELLING THEIR WINE IN THIS WAY, THE PROCESS IS KNOWN AS BUYING 'FUTURES'.

English wine Produced from grapes grown in England (or Wales), as opposed to BRITISH WINE, which is made from imported concentrate. Quality has improved in recent years, as winemakers have developed their own personality, changing from semi-sweet, mock-Germanic to mock-dry Loire and now, increasingly to aromatic-but-dry and late harvest. Best wines are being made by BREAKY BOTTOM, THAMES VALLEY VINEYARDS, Bruisyard, THREE CHOIRS, CARR TAYLOR, Chiltern Valley and DENBIES.

Enoteca (Italy) LITERALLY, WINE LIBRARY OR, NOWADAYS, WINE SHOP.

Entre-Deux-Mers (BORDEAUX, France) Once a region of appalling medium dry wine from vineyards between the cities of BORDEAUX and Libourne. Now a slowly up-and-coming source of basic BORDEAUX Blanc and principally dry SAUVIGNON. Reds are sold as BORDEAUX Rouge. Both reds and whites suffer from the difficulty grapes can have in ripening here in cool years. 88 89 90 92. *** 1993 Chateau Bonnet, A Lurton £6 (TH, WR).

Epernay (CHAMPAGNE, France) Home of CHAMPAGNE houses such as MERCIER, MOET & CHANDON, PERRIER JOUET and POL ROGER.

Erbach (Rheingau, Germany) Town noted for fine, full RIESLING, particularly from the Marcobrunn vineyard. 85 86 88 89 90 91 92 93 *** 1989 Erbacher Marcobrunn Riesling Kabinett-Staatsweinguter Eltville £9 (AV).

Erbaluce di Caluso (PIEDMONT, Italy) Dry, quite herby, wine made from the Erbulace grape (see BAVA).

Erden (MOSEL-SAAR-RUWER, Germany) Northerly village producing full, crisp, dry RIESLING. In the BERNKASTEL BEREICH, includes the famous Treppchen vineyard. 83 85 86 88 89 90 91 92. **** 1989 Erdener Treppchen, Riesling Kabinett, Dr Loosen £10 (ADN).

Errazuriz (ACONCAGUA Valley, CHILE) One of CHILE's big name producers and owner of CALITERRA. Wines should improve from the 1995 vintage, following the arrival of a winemaker from New Zealand. *** 1991 Don Maximiano Cabernet Sauvignon £7 (DBY) *** 1994 White Cabernet £2.95 (KS).

Erzeugerabfüllung (Germany) BOTTLED BY THE GROWER/ESTATE.

Esk Valley (HAWKES BAY, NEW ZEALAND) Under the same ownership as VIDAL and VILLA MARIA. Successful with BORDEAUX-style reds and juicy rosé. **** 1992 Esk Valley Reserve Merlot/Malbec/Cabernet Franc £14.

Esperão (ALENTEJO, Portugal) Revolutionary wines made by Australian winemaker, David Baverstock. SEE ALENTEJO.

Espum/oso/ante (Spain/Portugal) SPARKLING.

Esters CHEMICAL COMPONENTS IN WINE RESPONSIBLE FOR A VARIETY OF ODOURS.

Estufa THE VATS IN WHICH MADEIRA IS HEATED, SPEEDING MATURITY AND IMPARTING ITS FAMILIAR 'COOKED' FLAVOUR.

Eszencia (HUNGARY) ESSENCE OF TOKAY, LOW-ALCOHOL (3%) MADE FROM INDIVIDUALLY PICKED, RAISINY AND (PARTLY) NOBLY ROTTEN GRAPES. ONCE PRIZED FOR ITS EFFECTS ON THE MALE LIBIDO. NOW VIRTUALLY UNOBTAINABLE, EVEN BY THOSE WHO CAN SEE THE POINT IN DOING ANYTHING WITH THE OUTRAGEOUSLY EXPENSIVE SYRUP APART FROM POURING IT OVER ICE CREAM. THE EASIER-TO-FIND ASZU ESZENCIA, THE SWEETEST LEVEL OF TOKAY IS A MORE SENSIBLE BUY.

Arnaldo Etchart (ARGENTINA) Dynamic producer, benefiting from advice by Michel Rolland of POMEROL fame and investment by its new owners Pernod Ricard. The key wine here though is the grapey white TORRONTES.

Etna (Italy) From the Sicilian volcanic slopes, hot-climate, soft, fruity DOC reds, whites and rosés. Can be flabby.

Ch. l' Evangile (BORDEAUX, France) A classy POMEROL which can, in great vintages like 1988, 1989 and 1990, sometimes rival its neighbour PETRUS, but in a more tannic style. Back on form after patchy years in the 1980s. 82 83 85 86 88 89 90 *** 1982 £70 (TVW).

Evans Family (HUNTER VALLEY, Australia) Len Evans of ROTHBURY VINEYARDS' own estate. Good rich CHARDONNAY and SEMILLON as characterful and generous as their maker.

Evans & Tate (WESTERN AUSTRALIA) Much improved producer following its move from the hot SWAN VALLEY into the cooler MARGARET RIVER. **** 1994 Inglewood Two Vineyards Wooded Chardonnay £7 (SV).

Eventail de Vignerons Producteurs (BURGUNDY, France) Reliable source of BEAUJOLAIS. *** 1994 Domaine des Esservies, Eventail £5.50 (FWF) *** 1994 Côte de Brouilly Bonnege, Eventail £6.50 (R).

Eyrie Vineyards (WILLAMETTE VALLEY, OREGON, USA) Pioneering PINOT NOIR producer whose success in a blind tasting of Burgundies helped to attract JOSEPH DROUHIN to invest his francs on a vineyard here.

Fairview Estate (PAARL, SOUTH AFRICA) Go-ahead estate where Charles Back makes a range of good value wines more open-mindedly than some of his neighbours. **** 1993 Shiraz Reserve, Charles Back £7 (ADN, J&B, ADN, THP);**** 1992 Cabernet Franc/Merlot Reserve, Charles Back £5.50 (ES, FUL).

Joseph Faiveley (BURGUNDY, France) Modern negociant with particular strength in his backyard vineyards in the COTE DE NUITS and NUITS ST GEORGES in particular. *** 1991 Fortnum And Mason Red Burgundy £8. **** 1987 Nuits St Georges Clos de la Maréchale £18. (MWW).

Ch. de Fargues (SAUTERNES, France) Elegant wines made by the winemaker at CH. D'YQUEM – and a good alternative.

Fat HAS A SILKY TEXTURE WHICH FILLS THE MOUTH. MORE FLESHY THAN MEATY

Fattoria (Italy) ESTATE, PARTICULARLY IN TUSCANY.

Faugères (MIDI, France) Good, full-bodied reds and some (less interesting) whites and rosés. With neighbouring ST CHINIAN, a major cut above the surrounding Coteaux du Languedoc. 88 89 90 91 92 *** 1993 Domaine de Lascaux £5 (OD) *** 1993 Faugères 'Reserve', Les Mille Vignerons, £4 (GI).

Faustino Martinez (RIOJA, Spain) Dependable RIOJA producer with excellent (GRAN) RESERVAS, fair whites and a decent CAVA. 81 82 85 87. **** 1990 Rioja Faustino V, £6.50 (DBY, BU, OD) **** 1987 Martinez Bujanda Rioja Garnacha, Martinez Bujanda £10 (TH WR BU).

Favorita (PIEDMONT, Italy) Traditional variety from PIEDMONT transformed by modern oenological practice. Crisp delicate floral whites.

Felsina Berardenga (TUSCANY, Italy) High quality CHIANTI estate, known for its *** 1990 Chianti Classico Riserva, Felsina Geradenca £11.50 (L&W) **** 1992 Felsina Beradenga Chianti Classico, £8.50 (DBY).

Fendant (Switzerland) See CHASSELAS.

Fermentazione naturale (Italy) 'NATURALLY SPARKLING' BUT, IN FACT, INDICATES THE CUVE CLOSE METHOD.

Fernão Pires (ALENTEJO, Portugal) MUSCAT-like white grape, used to greatest effect by Peter Bright of JP Vinhos – See ALENTEJO.

Ferreira (DOURO, Portugal) Traditional Portuguese port producer, equally famous for its excellent tawnies as for its BARCA VELHA, Portugal's best traditional unfortified red. **** Ferreira Duque de Braganca 20 Year Old Tawny, Ferreira £25 (DBY).

Sylvain Fessy (BEAUJOLAIS, France) Reliable small producer with wide range of crus. **** 1994 Brouilly Domaine des Samsons £8 (LAV, WIN) *** 1994 St Amour £9.50 (LAV, WIN).

Fetzer (MENDOCINO, California) The best of the bigger Californian wineries, one of the few which really tries to make good wine at (relatively) lower prices and a laudable pioneering producer of organic wines. Recently taken over but still run by the family. ***** 1993 Vineyards Reserve Chardonnay £13 (OD) **** 1992 Stony Brook Cabernet Sauvignon £5 (SAF) **** 1993 Vineyards Santa Barbara County Pinot Noir £7 (W, BKW).

William Fèvre (BURGUNDY, France) Quality CHABLIS producer who has been a reactionary in his resistance to expanding the region and a revolutionary in his use of new oak. **** Chablis 1992 £10.50 (F&M).

Ch. de Fieuzal (BORDEAUX, France) PESSAC LEOGNAN property regularly making great whites and lovely raspberryish reds. Abeille de Fieuzal is the (excellent) second label. 82 85 86 88 89 90 92. **** 1992 Chateau de Fieuzal, £11 (SAF).

Ch. Figeac (BORDEAUX, France) Forever in the shadow of its neighbour, CHEVAL BLANC, but still one of the most characterful and best-made St Emilions. 82 83 85 88 89 90. **** 89 £27.50 (THP).

Finger Lakes (NEW YORK STATE, US) Cold region whose producers struggle (sometimes effectively) to produce good Vinifera, including late harvest RIESLING. Hybrids such as SEYVAL BLANC are more reliable, though late-harvest RIESLINGS can be good.

Fining THE CLARIFYING OF YOUNG WINE BEFORE BOTTLING TO REMOVE IMPURITIES, USING A NUMBER OF AGENTS INCLUDING ISINGLASS AND BENTONITE.

Finish WHAT YOU CAN STILL TASTE AFTER SWALLOWING.

Fino (Spain) Dry, delicate SHERRY, the finest to aficionados. Drink chilled and within two weeks of opening. See LUSTAU, BARBADILLO, HIDALGO and GONZALEZ BYASS. *** Co-op Pale Dry Fino Luis Caballero £4 (CWS).

Firestone (SANTA YNEZ, California) Good producer – particularly of good value MERLOT and SAUVIGNON and late harvest RIESLING – in Southern California. *** Prosperity White £5 (TH, WR, BU); **** Prosperity Red £5 (DBY, TH, WR, BU).

Fitou (MIDI, France) Long considered to be an up-market CORBIERES and still a quite reliable southern AC, making reds largely from the CARIGNAN grape. Formerly dark and stubborn, the wines have become more refined, with a woody warmth, though they never quite shake off their rustic air. 89 90 91 92 93. *** 1992 Fitou Domaine de La Colombe, Producteurs Du Mont Tauch £4 (TO) *** 1993 Safeway Fitou, Les Chais Beaucairois £3.50.

Fixin (BURGUNDY, France) Northerly village of the COTE DE NUITS, producing lean, tough, uncommercial reds which can mature well. 85 87 88 89 90 92. **** 1993 Louis Jadot £11 (VWC).

Flabby LACKING BALANCING ACIDITY.

Fleurie (BURGUNDY, France) One of the 10 BEAUJOLAIS Crus, ideally fresh and fragrant, as its name suggests. Best vineyards within it include La Madonne and Pointe du Jour. 92 93 94 **** 1994 F Verpoix £7 (A) **** 1994 Georges Duboeuf £7 (TO).

Flor YEAST WHICH GROWS NATURALLY ON THE SURFACE OF SOME MATURING SHERRIES, MAKING THEM POTENTIAL FINOS.

Flora Grape, a cross between SEMILLON and GEWURZTRAMINER best known in BROWN BROTHERS ORANGE MUSCAT and Flora. *** Late Harvest Orange Muscat & Flora, Brown Brothers 1993 £5.50 (OD, MWW, TH, U, FUL).

Flora Springs (NAPA Valley, California) Good, unusual SAUVIGNON BLANC (Soliloquy) and MERLOT, CABERNET SAUVIGNON & CABERNET FRANC blend (Trilogy). **** 1984 Trilogy £16 (T&W).

Emile Florentin (RHONE, France) Ultra-traditional, ultra-tannic St. Joseph, *** 1988 Clos de L'Arbalestrier £14 (ADN).

Flying Winemakers YOUNG (USUALLY) ANTIPODEANS WHO ARE ANNUALLY AND INCREASINGLY DESPATCHED TO WINERIES (ESPECIALLY COOPERATIVES) WORLDWIDE TO MAKE BETTER AND MORE RELIABLE WINE THAN THE HOME TEAM. OFTEN, MERELY KEEPING TANKS AND PIPES CLEAN IS A MAJOR PART OF THE JOB – AS IS THE AVOIDANCE OF LEAVING TRUCKLOADS OF GRAPES TO COOK IN THE SUN WHILE WINERY WORKERS ENJOY THEIR FOUR-HOUR LUNCH. NAMES TO LOOK FOR ON LABELS INCLUDE JACQUES LURTON (WHOSE LABEL IS HERMANOS LURTON), HUGH RYMAN (RECOGNISABLE BY THE INITIALS HDR), KYM MILNE, GEOFF MERRILL, PETER BRIGHT (BRIGHT BROTHERS), JOHN WORONTSCHAK AND NICK BUTLER.

Folle Noir (MIDI, France) Traditional grape used to make BELLET.

Fonseca (DOURO, Portugal) Now a subsidiary of TAYLORS but still independently making great port; in blind tastings the 1976 regularly beats supposedly classier houses' supposedly finer vintages. See also GUIMARAENS. ***** 1976 Fonseca Guimaraens £20 (DBY, OD) **** Bin 27, Vintage Character £8.50 (MTL, L&W, W, F&M).

JM Fonseca Internacional (Est, Portugal) Big, highly commercial offshoot of the even bigger and more commercial Grand Metropolitan. Principal wines are Lancers, the MATEUS-lookalike semi-fizzy, semi-sweet pinks, and whites sold in mock-crocks and fairly basic commercial fizz produced by a process known as the RUSSIAN CONTINUOUS.

J M da Fonseca Successores (Est, Portugal) Unrelated to the port house of the same name and no longer connected to JM da Fonseca Internacional. A family-run firm which, with Alianca and SOGRAPE, is one of Portugal's big three dynamic wine companies. Top red wines include Pasmados, PERIQUITA (made from the grape of the same name) Quinta da Camarate, Terras Altas Dao and the CABERNET-influenced 'TE' Garrafeiras. Dry whites are less impressive, but the sweet old Moscatel de Setubal are luscious classics. **** 1988 Garrafeira 'Te', Jose Maria da Fonseca Succs, £7 (DBY).

Font de Michelle (RHONE, France) Reliable producer of a lightish-bodied red CHATEAUNEUF-DU-PAPE and tiny quantities of a brilliant, almost unobtainable, white. **** 1992 Cuvée Etienne £16 (WR).

Fontana Candida (LAZIO, Italy) Good producer, especially for FRASCATI. The top wine is Colle Gaio which is good enough to prove the disappointing nature of most other wines from this area. **** 1992 Villa Fontana, £4 (W).

Fontanafredda (PIEDMONT, Italy) Big producer with impressive Asti Spumante and very approachable (especially single-vineyard) *** Barolo. *** Asti Spumante £8.50 (F&M, HAR, LV, DBY, V&C).

Forst (RHEINPFALZ, Germany) Wine town producing great, concentrated RIESLING. Famous for the Jesuitengarten vineyard 75 76 79 83 85 86 88 89 90 92 93 **** 1988 Forster Jesuitgarten Riesling Spätlese, Basserman-Jordan £8.50 (VW).

Fortant de France (MIDI, France) Good quality, revolutionary brand owned by SKALLI and specialising in varietal wines from LANGUEDOC ROUSSILLON. Will improve still further when its own winemakers take over every aspect of production. **** 1994 Chardonnay £4 (VW,) 1994 Syrah £4 (BOO).

Les Forts de Latour (PAUILLAC, France) Second label of CHATEAU LATOUR, bottle-aged for 3 years prior to release. Not, as is often suggested, made exclusively from the juice of young vines and wine which might otherwise have ended up in bottles labelled CH LATOUR – there are vineyards whose grapes are grown specially for Les Forts – but still often better than other classed growth chateaux.

Ch. Fourcas-Hosten (BORDEAUX, France) CRU BOURGEOIS estate in LISTRAC producing firm old-fashioned wine with plenty of 'grip' for tannin fans.

Franciacorta (LOMBARDY, Italy) DOC for good, light, French-influenced reds but better noted for sparklers made to sell at the same price as CHAMPAGNE. 85 86 88 89 90 92. *** 1991 Franciacorta Rosso Fantecolo, Il Mosnel £7.50 (V&C) *** Bellavista Franciacorta Cuvée Brut, £13 (V&C).

Franciscan Vineyards (NAPA Valley, California) Reliable NAPA winery whose Chilean owner, Agustin Huneeus, has not only pioneered wines using their own yeast with his great, Burgundy-like 'Cuvée Sauvage' CHARDONNAY but has also punctured the pretentious balloons of some of his neighbours – including those who tried to create a 'RUTHERFORD BENCH' appellation. ***** 1991 Chardonnay Cuvée Sauvage £10 (OD).

Ch. de Francs (Bordeaux, France) Well-run estate which makes great value crunchy, blackcurranty wine and, with Ch Puygeraud, helps to prove the worth of the little-known region of the Côtes de Francs. **** 1992 £7 (TH, WR, BU).

Franken (Germany) ANBAUGEBIET making characterful, sometimes earthy, dry whites, traditionally presented in the squat flagon-shaped 'bocksbeutel' on which the Mateus bottle was modelled. One of the key varieties is the SYLVANER which helps explain the earthiness of many of the wines. The weather here does make it easier to make dry wine than in many other regions, however. 83 85 86 87 88 89 90 91 92 93. *** 1989 Iphofer Burgweg Silvaner, Ernest Gebhardt Sommerhausen Am Main £6 (WSC).

Frascati (Italy) Clichéd dry or semi-dry white from LATIUM, with few exceptions (those made by GEOFF MERRILL and Fontana Candida). At best soft and clean and with a fascinating 'sour cream' flavour. More usually dull. Drink within 12 months of vintage. *** 1994 Frascati Superiore, Pichini £4 (CWS) *** 1994 Villa Simone £6 (BI).

Freixenet (CATALONIA, Spain) Giant in the CAVA field and strong supporters of the campaign to preserve the role of traditional Catalonian grapes in fizz. Its big-selling Cordon Negro is just about as good a justification for adding CHARDONNAY to the blend as anyone who likes refreshing wine could ever require. *** Cordon Negro £6 (widely available).

Frescobaldi (TUSCANY, Italy) Family estate with classy wines including CASTELGIOCONDO, the CABERNET SAUVIGNON Mormoreto and the rich white Chardonnay Pomino Il Benefizio. **** 1991 Pomino Rosso £9 (V&C, VW, OD). *** 1991 Castello Di Nipozzano £6.50 (DBY, U, BH).

Friuli-Venezia Giulia (Italy) Northerly region containing a number of DOCs which focus on single-variety wines like MERLOT, CABERNET (mostly FRANC) PINOT BIANCO, PINOT GRIGIO and TOCAI. 85 88 89 90 91 92 93 94. *** Collio Sauvignon, Enofriulia, £7 (DWS).

Frizzante (Italy) SEMI-SPARKLING especially LAMBRUSCO.

Frog's Leap (NAPA Valley, California) Winery whose owners combine winemaking skill with the kind of humour that is too rarely encountered in the NAPA Valley (their slogan is 'Time's fun when you're having flies'). Tasty ZINFANDEL and unusually good SAUVIGNON. **** 1991 Frog's Leap Cabernet Sauvignon, £14 (BOO, DBY).

Fronsac/Canon Fronsac (BORDEAUX, France) POMEROL neighbours, regularly producing rich, intense, affordable wines. They are rarely subtle, but, with good winemaking from men like Christian Moueix of Ch Petrus (a great believer in these regions) they can be some of the best buys in Bordeaux. Canon Fronsac is supposedly the better of the pair. 85 86 88 89 90. **** 1990 Ch Roulet, Canon Fronsac £7.50 (L&W).

Côtes du Frontonnais (South-West France) Up-and-coming inexpensive red (and some ROSE); full and fruitily characterful. 85 86 88 89 90 93. *** 1993 Côtes du Frontonnais, Michel de L'Enclos £4 (U).

Ch. Fuissé (BURGUNDY, France) Jean-Jacques Bincent is probably the best producer in this commune, making wines comparable to some of the best of the COTE D'OR. The Vielles Vignes has the distinction of lasting as long as a good Chassagne-Montrachet but the other cuvées run it a very close race. **** 1993 Les Combettes £15 (MTL, BWC, OD).

Fumé Blanc Name adapted from POUILLY FUMÉ by ROBERT MONDAVI to describe his oaked SAUVIGNON. Now widely used for this style. *** 1992 Beringer Fumé Blanc £6 (MTL, BWC, OD, SE).

Fürmint Lemony white grape, used in Hungary for TOKAY and, given modern winemaking, good dry wines. See Royal Tokay Wine Co and DISZNOKO.

Fûts de Chêne (élévé en) (France) OAK BARRELS (MATURED IN).

Jean-Noel Gagnard (BURGUNDY, France) Thanks to the French inheritance laws which dish out estates equally between all heirs, and to the Burgundian winemakers' habit of marrying the sons and daughters of neighbouring vignerons, this is a domaine with vineyards spread far and wide across CHASSAGNE-MONTRACHET. Best of all is the BATARD-MONTRACHET, of which he has nearly an acre, but all are impeccably made – as is his red SANTENAY. **** 1992 Chassagne Montrachet 1er Cru, Jean Noel Gagnard £25 (BWI).

Jacques Gagnard-Delagrange (BURGUNDY, France) A top class producer in Chassagne-Montrachet with vines in both the BATARD MONTRACHET and MONTRACHET. A domaine to follow for those who like their wines delicately oaked. **** 1992 Chassagne-Montrachet £23 (OD). ***** 1992 Bâtard-Montrachet Grand Cru £50 (OD).

Gaillac (South-west, France) Light, fresh, good-value reds and whites, produced using GAMAY and SAUVIGNON grapes. Reds can rival BEAUJOLAIS. 88 89 90 91. *** 1993 Gaillac Rouge, Dom. Guillejon £5.50 (NIC).

Gaja (PIEDMONT, Italy) The man who proved that the previously modest region of Barbaresco could make wines which were saleable at prices higher than those asked for first-growth clarets, let alone the supposedly classier neighbouring region of BAROLO. Individual vineyard reds are of great quality and the CHARDONNAY is the best in Italy. Whether they're worth these prices, though, is another question. ***** 1988 Barbaresco Sorì San Lorenzo £69 (V&C) ***** 1988 Chardonnay, Gaia & Rey £34 (V&C).

Galestro (TUSCANY, Italy) There is no such thing as Chianti Bianco – the light, grapey stuff that is made in the Chianti region is sold as Galestro. *** 1990 Villa Antinori Chianti Classico, Antinori £7 (DBY, MWW).

E & J Gallo (CENTRAL VALLEY, California) The world's biggest wine producer; annual production is around 60 per cent of the total Californian harvest and more than the whole of Australia or CHAMPAGNE. At the top end, there is now some pretty good but ludicrously pricy CABERNET and CHARDONNAY from Gallo's own huge 'Northern Sonoma Estate', a piece of land which was physically re-contoured by their bulldozers. With the exception of the French COLOMBARD, the rest of the range, though much improved and widely stocked, is basically unrecommendable. **** 1992 Ernest & Julio Gallo Northern Sonoma Estate Chardonnay £20 (SEL).

Gamey SMELL OR TASTE REMINISCENT OF HUNG GAME. PARTICULARLY ASSOCIATED WITH OLD PINOT NOIRS AND SYRAHS. POSSIBLY AT LEAST PARTLY ATTRIBUTABLE TO THE COMBINATION OF THOSE GRAPES' NATURAL CHARACTERISTICS WITH OVERLY GENEROUS DOSES OF SULPHUR DIOXIDE BY WINEMAKERS. MODERN EXAMPLES OF BOTH STYLES SEEM TO BE DISTINCTLY LESS GAMEY THAN IN THE PAST.

Gancia (PIEDMONT, Italy) Reliable producer of Asti Spumante and good, dry Pinot di Pinot PINOT BLANC fizz. *** Gancia Pinot Di Pinot £7.50 (BLN).

Vin de pays du Gard (MIDI, France) Huge VIN DE TABLE producing area with one fair VDQS, COSTIERES DU GARD. 89 90 91 92.

Garrafeira (Portugal) INDICATES A PRODUCER'S 'RESERVE' WINE, SELECTED AND GIVEN EXTRA TIME IN CASK (MINIMUM 2 YEARS) AND BOTTLE (MINIMUM 1 YEAR). ***** 1988 Garrafeira TE, Jose Maria da Fonseca £7 (DBY).

Vin de Pays des Côtes de Gascogne (South-West, France) The region of the Three Musketeers – and a town called Condom – was once only known for ARMAGNAC. Today, thanks largely to the efforts of YVES GRASSA, the PLAIMONT cooperative and HUGH RYMAN, it produces good-value, fresh, floral whites and good light reds, but is having a tough time competing with the warmer vineyards of LANGUEDOC ROUSSILLON.*** Co-op Vin De Pays des Côtes de Gascogne, Grassa £3 (CWS).

Rolly Gassmann (ALSACE, France) Fine producer of subtle, long-lasting wines which are sometimes slightly marred by an excess of SULPHUR DIOXIDE. **** 1990 Auxerrois Moenchreben £9 (THP).

Gattinara (PIEDMONT, Italy) Red DOC from the NEBBIOLO – varying in quality but reliably full-flavoured and dry. 85 88 89 90 92 93. *** 1989 Cantina Sociale di Gattinara £6.50 (SEL).

Gavi (TUSCANY, Italy) Generally unexceptional dry white from the CORTESE grape. Compared by Italians to white Burgundy with which it and the creamily pleasant Gavi di Gavi share a propensity for high prices. 88 90 91 92 93. **** 1993 Gavi di Gavi, La Minaia, Bergaglio £10 (F&M).

Ch. Gazin (BORDEAUX, France) POMEROL property that has become far more polished since the mid 80s. 82 85 86 88 89 90 91. **** 1989 £15 (M&S).

Geelong (VICTORIA, Australia) Cool region pioneered by Idyll Vineyards (makers of old-fashioned reds) and rapidly attracting notice with BANNOCKBURN'S and Scotchman Hill's PINOT NOIRS. 88 89 90 91 92 93.

Geisenheim (RHEINGAU, Germany) Town and the home of the German Wine Institute wine school, once one of the best in the world but long overtaken by more go-ahead seats of learning in France, California and Australia. 83 85 88 89 90 91 92 93. **** Schlossgarten Riesling Spatlese, 1990 £11 (WSO).

Generoso (Spain) FORTIFIED OR DESSERT WINE.

Gentilini (Cephalonia, Greece) Nick Cosmetatos's modern white wines, made using classic Greek grapes and French varieties should be an example to all his countrymen who are still happily making and drinking stuff which tastes as fresh as an old election manifesto.

Gevrey Chambertin (BURGUNDY, France) Best-known big red CÔTE DE NUITS commune; very variable, but still capable of superb, plummy cherryish wine. The top GRAND CRU is LE CHAMBERTIN but, in the right hands, PREMIERS CRUS like Les Cazetiers can beat this and the other GRANDS CRUS. Best producers include VALLET FRERES, ALAIN BURGUET, DENIS BACHELET, Roty, ROSSIGNOL-TRAPET, ARMAND ROUSSEAU, DUJAC, Philippe Leclerc Dugat, Esmonin, and LEROY, Magnien and Maume. 78 80 82 83 85 88 89 90 92. **** 1989 Gevrey Chambertin Vallet Frères £19.50 (BOO, DBY) *** 1992 Gevrey Chambertin, Domaine Rossignol Trapet £13 (ABY).

> **Gewürztraminer** White (well, slightly pink) grape, making dry-to-sweet, full, oily-textured, spicy wine, best in Alsace, but also grown in Australasia, Italy, the US and Eastern Europe. Easily recogniseable by its perfumed parma violets-and-lychees character.

Geyser Peak (ALEXANDER VALLEY, California) Australian winemaker Darryl Groom revolutionised Californian thinking in this once Australian-owned winery with his SEMILLON-CHARDONNAY blend ('You mean Chardonnay's *not* the only white grape in the world?'), and decent reds which show an Aussie attitude towards ripe TANNIN. A name to watch. *** Canyon Road Chardonnay £6 (M&S).

Ghiaie della Furba (TUSCANY, Italy) Great Cabernet-based SUPER TUSCAN from VILLA DI CAPEZZANA. *** 1989 £15 (V&C).

Giaconda (North East VICTORIA, Australia) Small producer hidden away in the hills, making impressive PINOT NOIR and CHARDONNAY.

Bruno Giacosa (PIEDMONT, Italy) One of Italy's best winemakers in the region, with a large range, including BAROLOS (Vigna Rionda in best years) and BARBARESCOS (Santo Stefano, again in best years). Recent success with whites, including a SPUMANTE. *** 1989 Barolo £20 (V&C).

Giesen (CANTERBURY, NEW ZEALAND) Small estate, with particularly appley RIESLING from CANTERBURY and SAUVIGNON from MARLBOROUGH.

Gigondas (RHONE, France) CÔTES DU RHÔNE commune, producing good-value, reliable, full-bodied, spicy/peppery, blackcurranty reds which show the GRENACHE at its best. A good competitor for nearby CHATEAUNEUF. 79 82 83 85 86 88 89 90 91. *** 1991 Domaine Cayron, Michel Faraud £10 (ADN).

Ch. Gilette (BORDEAUX, France) Eccentric, unclassified but classed-growth quality SAUTERNES kept in tank (rather than cask) for 20 or 30 years. Rare and expensive. ***** 1970 Ch. Gilette, Crème de Tête (C&B, when available).

Gippsland (VICTORIA, Australia) Up-and-coming coastal region where wineries like Bass Philip and Nicholson River are producing fascinating and quite European-style wines. Watch out for good Pinot Noirs.

Giropalette MACHINES WHICH, IN MÉTHODE CHAMPENOISE, AUTOMATICALLY PERFORM THE TASK OF REMUAGE. USED BY ALL BUT A VERY FEW PRODUCERS, DESPITE THE EFFORTS OF THE BIG HOUSES TO CONCEAL THE FACT FROM THE TOURISTS WHO TROOP THROUGH THEIR CELLARS.

Gisborne (NEW ZEALAND) North Island vine-growing area since 1920s. Cool, wettish climate, mainly used for (good) CHARDONNAY. An ideal partner for Marlborough in blends – or it would be if New Zealand's winemakers didn't generally take an apartheid-minded view of cross-regional blending. 89 90 91 93 94. Recommended: COOPERS CREEK, Matawhero (variable), MILLTON (organic), *** 1994 Millton Vineyard Chardonnay £8 (SAF).

Ch. Giscours (BORDEAUX, France) MARGAUX property which, despite the lovely blackcurranty wines it produced in the late 1970s and early 1980s remains on the threshold of competition with the best. Purchase in 1995 by a Dutchman may revive its fortunes. *** 1988 £33 in magnums (VW).

Givry (BURGUNDY, France) CÔTE CHALONNAISE commune, making typical and affordable, if rather jammily rustic, reds and creamy whites. French wine snobs recall that this was one of King Henri IV's favourite wines, forgetting the fact that a) he had many such favourites and b) his mistress happened to live here. Look for wines from Steinmaier, Joblot, Thénard and Mouton. 83 85 87 88 89 90 92 93. **** 1993 Givry 1er Cru Clos de la Servoisine, Joblot £12 (GH).

Glen Ellen (SONOMA VALLEY, California) Recently-purchased dynamic family firm producing large amounts of good commercial CHARDONNAY under its 'Proprietor's Reserve' label for Californiaphiles who like tropical fruit juice – and who dislike GALLO's dull offerings. Reds are approachable and good value. The Benziger range is better. **** 1993 Glen Ellen Proprietor's Reserve Chardonnay £4.50 (CWS, W, TO).

Ch. Gloria (ST JULIEN, BORDEAUX, France) One of the first of the super CRUS BOURGEOIS, looking less stunning nowadays. 82 83 85 86 88 89 90 91. *** 1989 £17 (BBR).

Golan Heights (Israel) Until recently almost the only non-sacramental wines in Israel were made by Carmel, who produced one of the least palatable SAUVIGNONS I have ever encountered. Today, Carmel wines are greatly improved, thanks to competition from this enterprise at which Californian expertise is used to produce good KOSHER CABERNET and MUSCAT. Quite how it will fare following the land restitution implicit in a peace treaty, no one knows. **** 1990 Yarden Cabernet Sauvignon £12.50 (SEL).

Goldwater Estate (AUCKLAND, NEW ZEALAND) BORDEAUX-like red wine specialist on Waiheke Island whose wines are expensive but every bit as good as many similarly-priced French offerings. **** 1990 Goldwater Cabernet Merlot, Goldwater £17 (MTL).

Gonzalez Byass (JEREZ, Spain) Producer of the world's best-selling **Fino** (*** Tio Pepe), this winery also makes some of the finest, most complex, traditional sherries available to mankind. ***** Matusalem Oloroso Muy Viejo, Gonzalez Byass £19 (MTL, DBY) ***** Amontillado Del Duque, Gonzalez Byass £19 (MTL, DBY).

Goulburn Valley (VICTORIA, Australia) Small, long-established region reigned over by the respectively ancient and modern CHÂTEAU TAHBILK and MITCHELTON both of whom make great MARSANNE. **** 1993 Mitchelton Goulburn Valley Reserve Marsanne £7 (W, MTL, OD).

Goundrey (WESTERN AUSTRALIA) Young winery in the up-and-coming region of MOUNT BARKER, making fruity but not overstated CHARDONNAY and CABERNET. *** 1994 Goundrey Wines Langton Chardonnay, £5 (BOO).

Graach (MOSEL-SAAR-RUWER, Germany) MITTELMOSEL village producing fine wines. Best known for Himmelreich vineyard. DEINHARD, JJ PRUM, FRIEDRICH-WILHELM-GYMNASIUM and VON KESSELSTADT are names to look out for. 83 85 86 88 89 90 91 92 93. **** 1992 Graacher Himmelreich Riesling Kabinett, Reichsgraf von Kesselstatt £6 (A).

Graham (DOURO, Portugal) Sweetly delicate wines, sometimes outclassing the same stable's supposedly finer but heftier DOWS. Malvedos is the SINGLE QUINTA. **** 1979 Graham's Malvedos £16 (MTL, MWW, TAN) *** Graham's 10 Year Old Tawny Port £15 (SEL).

Alain Graillot (RHONE, France) Producer who should be applauded for shaking up the sleepy, largely undistinguished appellation of CROZES HERMITAGE using grapes from rented vineyards. All the reds are excellent, and La Guiraude is the wine from the top vineyard. **** 1994 Crozes Hermitage £9 (YAP).

Gran Reserva (Spain) A QUALITY WINE AGED FOR A DESIGNATED NUMBER OF YEARS IN WOOD AND, IN THEORY, ONLY PRODUCED IN THE BEST VINTAGES. **** 1986 Ochoa Navarra Gran Reserva, Ochoa, £9.50 (MTL).

Grand Cru (France) THE FINEST VINEYARDS. OFFICIAL DESIGNATION IN BORDEAUX, BURGUNDY AND ALSACE. VAGUE IN BORDEAUX AND SOMEWHAT UNRELIABLE IN ALSACE. IN BURGUNDY: A SINGLE VINEYARD WITH ITS OWN AC, eg MONTRACHET.

Ch. du Grand Moulas (RHONE, France) Classy, unusually complex, COTES DU RHONE property. *** 1993, Marc Rykwaert, £5.50 (L&W, ADN).

Grand Vin (BORDEAUX, France) THE FIRST (QUALITY) WINE OF AN ESTATE – AS OPPOSED TO ITS SECOND LABEL.

Ch. Grand-Puy-Ducasse (BORDEAUX, France) Excellent wines from fifth-growth PAUILLAC property. 82 83 85 86 88 89 90. **** 1985 £16 (THP).

Ch. Grand-Puy-Lacoste (BORDEAUX, France) Top class Fifth Growth owned by the Borie family of DUCRU-BEAUCAILLOU and right up there among the super seconds. One of the best value wines in the region. 82 83 85 86 88 89 90. *** 1989 £17 (THP).

Grande Rue (BURGUNDY, France) Recently promoted GRAND CRU in VOSNE-ROMANEE, across the track from ROMANEE-CONTI (hence the promotion). However the Domaine Lamarche to whom this MONOPOLE belongs is a long-term under-performer. *** 1983 £42 (T&W).

Grandes Marques SUPPOSEDLY SIGNIFICANT SYNDICATE OF THE MAJOR CHAMPAGNE MERCHANTS CAST IN ASPIC AND INCLUDING FIRMS WHICH EXIST IN NO MORE THAN NAME. ITS FIRST ATTEMPT AT A QUALITY CHARTER INADVERTENTLY REVEALED HOW CONSERVATIVE AND – IN REAL TERMS – QUALITY UNCONSCIOUS IT IS.

Grands-Echézeaux (BURGUNDY, France) One of the best GRAND CRUS in BURGUNDY, see ECHEZEAUX.

Yves Grassa (South-west, France) Pioneering producer of VDP de Côtes de Gascogne. **** 1994 Domaine Bordeneuve Vin de Pays des Côtes de Gascogne Blanc £3.50 (SMF).

Alfred Gratien (CHAMPAGNE, France) Good CHAMPAGNE house, using traditional methods. Also owner of less impressive LOIRE fizz-maker, Gratien et Meyer, based in Saumur. *** 1985 £21 (WSO).

Grave del Friuli (FRIULI-VENEZIA GIULIA, Italy) DOC for young-drinking reds and whites. CABERNET and MERLOT are increasingly successful. 85 86 87 88 90 91 92 93. *** 1992 Merlot, Ladino £4 (ADN).

Graves (BORDEAUX, France) Large, southern region producing vast quantities of white, from good to indifferent. Reds have a better reputation for quality, particularly since most of the best whites come from the northern part of the Graves and are sold as PESSAC LEOGNAN. (red) 78 79 81 82 83 85 86 88 89 90 (white) 85 86 88 89 90 92, 93. **** 1993 Graves Rouge Baron Philippe de Rothschild, £6.50 (MTL) *** Tesco White Graves, Yvon Mau £4 (TO).

Great Western (VICTORIA, Australia) Region noted for SEPPELT's fizzes including the astonishing 'Sparkling Burgundy' SHIRAZES for BEST'S and for the wines of MOUNT LANGI GHIRAN. *** Seppelt Great Western Brut £5 (BOO, DBY, WR, BU).

Greco di Tufo (Italy) From CAMPANIA, best-known white from the ancient GRECO grape; dry, characterful southern wine. **** Antonio Mastroberardino Nova Serra 1993 £13.50 (V&C).

Green Point (Yarra, Australia) See DOMAINE CHANDON.

> **Grenache** Red grape of the RHONE (aka Garnacha in Spain) making spicy, peppery, full-bodied wine provided yields are kept low. Also increasingly used to make rosés across Southern France and California. *** 1994 Fortant de France £4 (MWW, FUL).

Marchesi de Gresy Good producer of single vineyard BARBARESCO. *** Camp Gros Martinenga £13 (LAV).

Grgich Hills (NAPA VALLEY, California) Pioneering producer of CABERNET SAUVIGNON, CHARDONNAY AND FUME BLANC. The name is a concatenation of the two founders – Mike Grgich (who made the French-beating 1972 Ch. Montelena Chardonnay) and Austin Hills, rather than a topographical feature. **** 1988 Cabernet Sauvignon £15 (EP) *** 1989 Zinfandel £12 (EP).

> **Grignolino** (PIEDMONT, Italy) Red grape and its modest, but refreshing, cherryish wine, eg the DOC Grignolino d'Asti. Drink young. 90 91 92 93. *** 1993 Aldo Conterno £9 (V&C).

Jean-Louis Grippat (RHONE, France) An unusually great white RHONE producer in HERMITAGE and ST JOSEPH. His reds in both APPELLATIONS are less stunning, but still worth buying in their subtler-than-most way. Look out too for his ultra-rare Cuvée des Hospices St Joseph Rouge. **** 1992 Hermitage Blanc £17 (YAP).

Jean Grivot (BURGUNDY, France) Top class VOSNE ROMANEE estate whose winemaker Etienne has recently escaped from the spell of Lebanese guru OENOLOGIST Guy Accad which made for wines which appeared to need longer to develop. **** 1990 Nuits-Saint Georges, Les Lavières, £26 (L&W).

Schloss Groenesteyn (RHEINGAU, Germany) Now underperforming, this RHEINGAU estate was once highly-rated. *** 1988 Kiedricher Sandgrub Kabinett Riesling £6.50 (VW).

Jean Gros (BURGUNDY, France) Great VOSNE ROMANEE producer, with unusually reliable CLOS VOUGEOTS. **** 1989 Vosne Romanée £21 (WR, BU).

> **Gros Lot/Grolleau** Workhorse grape of the LOIRE, particularly ANJOU, used for white, rosé and base wines for sparkling SAUMUR. *** 1992 Azay le Rideau Rosé, Gaston Pavy £6 (YAP).

> **Gros Plant (du Pays Nantais)** (LOIRE, France) Light, sharp white VDQS wine from the western Loire. In all but the best hands, serves to make even a poor MUSCADET look good. 89 90 92 93. *** 1992 La Maisdonnière, Bernard Baffreau £5 (YAP).

Grosslage (Germany) WINE DISTRICT, THE THIRD SUBDIVISION AFTER ANBAUGEBIET (EG RHEINGAU) AND BEREICH (EG NIERSTEIN). FOR EXAMPLE, MICHELSBERG IS A GROSSLAGE OF THE BEREICH PIESPORT.

Ch. Gruaud-Larose (BORDEAUX, France) One of the stars of the Cordier stable. Rich but potentially slightly unsubtle. Buy in good years. 82 83 85 86 88 89 90. *** 1985 £35 (SEL).

> **Grüner Veltliner** Spicy white grape of Austria and Eastern Europe, producing light, fresh, aromatic wine – and for WILLI OPITZ an extraordinary late harvest version. 87 88 89 90. **** 1993 Grüner Veltliner Trockenbeerenauslese, Willi Opitz £25.50 (T&W).

Guerrieri-Rizzardi (VENETO, Italy) Solid organic producer, with good AMARONE and single vineyard SOAVE Classico. *** 1992 Bardolino Classico Superiore £6 (F&M) *** 1992 Soave Classico Costeggiola £7 (SEL).

Guigal (RHONE, France) Still the yardstick for RHONE Reds, despite increased competition from CHAPOUTIER. His extraordinarily pricy single vineyard La Mouline, La Landonne and La Turque wines are still ahead of the young turks. The basic Côtes du Rhône is also well worth looking out for. 81 82 83 85 88 89 90. *** 1982 Hermitage Rouge, E Guigal, £22.50 (CEB) **** Côte Rôtie, Côtes Brune Et Blonde 1982 £21.50 (CEB).

Guimaraens (DOURO, Portugal) Associated with FONSECA; under-rated porthouse producing good wines. ***** 1976 Fonseca Guimaraens, £20 (DBY, OD) **** Bin 27, Fonseca Guimaraens, £8.50 (MTL, L&W, W, F&M).

Ch. Guiraud (BORDEAUX, France) SAUTERNES classed-growth, recently restored to original quality and now back in the pack who trail in the wake of Yquem. 82 83 85 86 88 89 90. *** 1988 £28.50 (J&B).

Gundlach-Bundschu (SONOMA VALLEY, California) A good source of well-made, juicy MERLOT and spicy ZINFANDEL. *** Zinfandel 1992/3 £8 (EP) Rhinefarm Vineyards Merlot 1992 £11 (EP).

Louis Guntrum (RHEINHESSEN, Germany) Family-run estate with a penchant for SYLVANER.

Gutedel (Germany) GERMAN NAME FOR THE CHASSELAS GRAPE.

Gyöngyös Estate (HUNGARY) The ground-breaking winery in which HUGH RYMAN first produced drinkable Eastern European SAUVIGNON and CHARDONNAY. *** 1994 Chardonnay £3.50 (CWS, MWW, JS).

Fritz Haag (MOSEL-SAAR-RUWER, Germany) Top class, small estate with classic RIESLINGS. ***** 1990 Brauneberger Juffer-Sonnenuhr Riesling Auslese £19 (L&W).

Halbtrocken (Germany) OFF-DRY. RISING STYLE INTENDED TO ACCOMPANY FOOD. USUALLY A SAFER BUY THAN TROCKEN IN REGIONS LIKE THE MOSEL, RHEINGAU AND RHEINHESSEN, BUT STILL OFTEN AGGRESSIVELY ACIDIC STUFF. LOOK FOR QbA OR AUSLESE VERSIONS. *** 1993 Riesling Halbtrocken, W Haag £8. (L&W).

Hallgarten (RHEINGAU, Germany) Important town near Hattenheim producing robust wines including the – in Germany – well regarded produce from SCHLOSS VOLLRADS. **** 1986 Hallgartener Schonhell Qba, Matuschka Greiffenclau £5.50 (EP).

Hamilton Russell Vineyards (WALKER BAY, South Africa) Pioneer of impressive PINOT NOIR and CHARDONNAY at a winery in Hermanus at the southernmost tip of the Cape. *** 1993 Hermanus Pinot Noir, £8 (CWS) **** 1994 Chardonnay, £7.50 (AV).

Hardy (SOUTH AUSTRALIA) Or more properly BRL Hardy, as the merged Berri-Renmano/Hardys is now known, is the second biggest wine producer in Australia, encompassing HOUGHTON and MOONDAH BROOK in WESTERN AUSTRALIA, Leasingham in the CLARE, the improved but still underperforming Redman in COONAWARRA, HARDY's itself and Chateau Reynella. HARDY's range is reliable throughout, including the commercial Nottage Hill and multi-regional blends, though the wines to look for are the top-of-the-range Eileen and Thomas Hardy. The Chateau Reynella wines made from MCLAREN VALE fruit and – in the case of the reds – using basket presses are good, quite lean examples of the region. *** 1994 Chateau Reynella Chardonnay, £7 (DBY) **** 1992 Eileen Hardy Shiraz, £10 (DBY, ADN) **** 1994 Moondah Brook Verdelho £5 (MTL, DBY).

Haro (RIOJA, Spain) Town at the heart of the RIOJA region.

Harveys (JEREZ, Spain) Maker of the ubiquitous *** Bristol Cream £6.50 (widely available).

Hattenheim (RHEINGAU, Germany) One of the greatest JOHANNISBERG villages, producing some of the best German RIESLINGS. 76 79 83 85 88 89 90. *** Nussbrunnen, Riesling Kabinett, Von Simmern 1992 £8.50 (ADN).

Hatzimichalis (Atalanti, Greece) The face of future Greek winemaking? Hopefully. This small estate produces top-notch CABERNET SAUVIGNON, MERLOT and fresh, dry Atalanti white. *** 1994 Chardonnay, £8 (GWC).

Haut Poitou (LOIRE, France) Often boring yet (quite) good value SAUVIGNON and CHARDONNAY whites and even less exciting reds. 89 90 92 93. *** 1994 Sauvignon Blanc de Haut Poitou, Caves de Haut Poitou £4 (SMF).

Ch. Haut-Bages-Averous (BORDEAUX, France) Second label of Ch LYNCH BAGES. Good value blackcurranty PAUILLAC. **** 1989 £18 (WR, BU, MWW).

Ch. Haut-Bages-Liberal (BORDEAUX, France) Top class small PAUILLAC property in the same stable as CHASSE-SPLEEN. 82 83 85 86 88 89 90.
**** 1988 £14 (TAN).

Ch. Haut-Bailly (BORDEAUX, France) Little known PESSAC-LEOGNAN property consistently making reliable, long-lived quite traditional wines, including an unusually good 1994. **** 1989 £16 (ADN, THP).

Ch. Haut-Batailley (BORDEAUX, France) Subtly-styled fifth-growth PAUILLAC from the same stable as DUCRU BEAUCAILLOU and GRAND PUY LACOSTE. 85 86 88 89 90. *** 1989 £14 (M&V).

Ch. Haut-Brion (BORDEAUX, France) Pepys' favourite and still the only non-MEDOC First Growth. Situated in the GRAVES on the outskirts of BORDEAUX (with a great view of the gasworks). Wines can be tough and hard to judge young but, at their best they develop a rich, fruity perfumed character which sets them apart from their peers. 1989 was especially good, as – compatitively – were 1993 and 1994. The white is rare and often sublime. 78 82 85 86 88 89 90 93 94. ***** 1988 £52 (J&B).

Ch. Haut-Marbuzet (BORDEAUX, France) A CRU BOURGEOIS which thinks it's a CRU CLASSE. Well-made, immediately imposing wine with bags of oak. Decidedly new-wave ST ESTEPHE. 82 83 85 86 88 89 90 92. **** 1992 Chateau Haut Marbuzet, Duboscq £13 (DBY, BKW).

Haut-Médoc (BORDEAUX, France) Large APPELLATION which includes nearly all of the well-known Crus Classés. Basic HAUT-MEDOC should be better than plain MEDOC. 78 81 82 83 85 86 88 89 90 91. *** 1983 Ch Cissac, Louis Vialard £11 (CWS).

Hautes Côtes de Beaune (BURGUNDY, France) Sound, soft, strawberry PINOT NOIR hailing from a group of villages situated in the hills above the big-name communes. Worth buying in good vintages; in poorer ones the grapes have problems ripening. Much of the wine seen outside the region is made by one of Burgundy's improving cooperatives. 85 86 87 88 89 90 92. *** 1991 Hautes Côtes de Beaune Rouge, Labouré Roi £5 (SMF) *** 1992 Hautes Côtes de Beaune Blanc, J.C Rateau £9 (VR).

Hautes Côtes de Nuits (BURGUNDY, France) Slightly tougher than HAUTES COTES DE BEAUNE, particularly when young. White wines are very rare. 85 86 87 88 89 90 92. *** 1993 Hautes Côtes de Nuits Blanc, E. Giboult £9 (VR).

Hawkes Bay (NEW ZEALAND) Major North Island vineyard area which is finally beginning to live up to the promise of producing top-class reds. Whites can be fine too, though rarely achieving the bite of MARLBOROUGH. Top producers include TE MATA, DELEGATS, MORTON ESTATE, ESK VALLEY, VIDAL, NGATARAWA, and BABICH. 87 89 90 91. **** 1994 Delegats Hawkes Bay Cabernet Sauvignon/Merlot, £12 (DBY) **** 1994 Morton Estate Hawkes Bay Pinot Noir £7.50 (BWC) ***** 1992 Babich Irongate Chardonnay, £13 (DBY, JEH, TAN).

Heemskerk (TASMANIA, Australia) Until recently associated with ROEDERER in the making of Jansz, this is a producer of (good) Aussie fizz and also the source of some good, sturdy reds. *** 1991 Heemskerk Jansz Brut £12.50 (ADN, TO).

Charles Heidsieck (CHAMPAGNE, France) A rare example of a CHAMPAGNE house which managed to match a rise in price with a corresponding rise in quality. Today the non-vintage is amongst the best value around, though strangely harder to find than one might expect. The Blanc de Blancs is first class too. **** NV £20 (TO).

Heitz Cellars (NAPA Valley, California) One of the great names of California and the source of stunning reds in the 1970s. Current releases of the flagship Martha's Vineyard Cabernet taste unacceptably musty, however, as do the traditionally almost-as-good Bella Oaks. In the US, such criticisms are treated as lèse-majesté (Robert Parker is circumspect in his comments), so collectors queue up every year to buy these wines as they are allowed on to the market. The late Geoffrey Roberts, Heitz's last importer into the UK, had no doubts that there was a problem. Current vintages are almost unfindable here.

Henschke (ADELAIDE HILLS, Australia) One of the world's best. From the long-established Hill of Grace with its 130-year-old vines and (slightly less intense) Mount Edelstone SHIRAZes to the new Abbott's Prayer MERLOT-CABERNET from Lenswood, the Henschke and Tilly's Vineyard white blend, there's not a duff wine in the cellar, and the reds last forever. Compare and contrast with HEITZ. **** 1992 Abbotts Prayer Merlot/Cabernet Sauvignon, £13 (BOO, DBY) ***** 1992 Mount Edelstone Shiraz, £13 (BOO, DBY).

Vin de pays de l' Hérault (MIDI, France) Largest vine-growing *département*, producing some 20 per cent of France's wine, nearly all VIN DE PAYS or VDQS, of which COTEAUX DU LANGUEDOC is the best known. Also the home of the extraordinary MAS DE DAUMAS GASSAC, where no expense is spared to produce wines which far surpass 'country wines' to compete with the best from supposedly far greater regions. The potential in this area is enormous. Watch this space. 82 83 85 86 88 89 90 91 93.

Hermitage (RHONE, France) Top-class, long-lived northern Rhône wines; superb, complex (SYRAH) reds and sumptuous, nutty (MARSANNE and ROUSSANE) whites. Also, the old Australian name for SYRAH and, confusingly, the South African term for CINSAULT. Best producers: CHAPOUTIER (since 1990), JABOULET AINE, CHAVE, DELAS (individual vineyard wines), SORREL, GRIPPAT, GUIGAL, VIDAL-FLEURY. 76 78 79 82 83 85 88 89 90 91. *** 1991 Hermitage Rouge, E Guigal, £22 (WR, BU, L&W, SAS).

The Hess Collection (NAPA VALLEY, California) High class CABERNET producer, high in the Mount Veeder hills. The lower-priced MONTEREY wines are worth buying too.

Hessische Bergstrasse (Germany) Smallest ANBAUGEBIET, rarely seen in the UK, but capable of fine EISWEINS and dry SYLVANERS which can surpass those of nearby Franken.

Hidalgo (MANZANILLA/JEREZ, Spain) Specialist producer of impeccable dry 'La Gitana' sherry and a great many own-label offerings. **** Sainsbury's Manzanilla Pasada, Bodegas Del Ducado £3.50 (JS).

Hochfeinste (Germany) 'VERY FINEST'.

Hochgewächs QbA (Germany) RECENT OFFICIAL DESIGNATION FOR RIESLINGS WHICH ARE AS RIPE AS A QmP BUT CAN STILL ONLY CALL THEMSELVES QbA. THIS FROM A NATION SUPPOSEDLY DEDICATED TO SIMPLIFYING WHAT ARE ACKNOWLEDGED TO BE THE MOST COMPLICATED LABELS IN THE WORLD.

Hochheim (RHEINGAU, Germany) Village whose fine RIESLINGS gave the English the word 'HOCK'. *** 1993 Hochheimer Domdechaney Riesling Spatlese Staatsweinguter Eltville, £11 (TAN).

Hock ENGLISH NAME FOR RHINE WINES, DERIVED FROM HOCHHEIM IN THE RHEINGAU. *** 1994 Safeway Hock £2.50 (SAF).

Hogue Cellars (Washington State, US) Dynamic YAKIMA VALLEY producer of good CHARDONNAY, RIESLING, MERLOT and CABERNET.

Hollick (COONAWARRA, Australia) A good, traditional producer; the Ravenswood is particularly worth seeking out. **** 1991 Cabernet Sauvignon £8.50 (BOO).

Hospices de Beaune (BURGUNDY, France) Charity hospital, whose wines (often CUVEES or blends of different vineyards), are sold at an annual charity auction, the prices supposedly – though less and less often – setting the tone for the COTE D'OR year. Observers have had to be pretty charitable too in recent years when discussing the wines, few of which have been anywhere near up to scratch. 1994 brought a new, very expensive, high-tech winery, however, and the welcome return of winemaker Andre Porcheret. The effect on the wines was instant. Even so, be aware that although price lists often merely indicate 'Hospices de Beaune' as a producer, all of the wines bought at the auction are matured and bottled by local merchants, some of whom are more scrupulous than others.

Houghton (SWAN VALLEY, Australia) Long-established subsidiary of HARDYS. Best known for its CHENIN-based rich white blend, sold Down Under as 'White Burgundy'. The wines to watch though are the ones from the MOONDAH BROOK vineyard. *** 1994 Gold Reserve Verdelho, £7.50 (DBY, POR, EVI, AV) *** 1992 Gold Reserve Cabernet Sauvignon, £7.50 (MTL, DBY).

Von Hovel (SAAR, Germany) 200-year-old estate with fine RIESLINGS from great vineyards. These repay the patience they demand.

Howell Mountains (NAPA, California) Hillside region to the north of NAPA, capable of fine whites and reds from La Jota. See DUNN.

Alain Hudelot-Noëllat (BURGUNDY, France) A great winemaker whose generosity with oak is matched, especially in his GRAND CRU RICHEBOURG and ROMANEE ST VIVANT by intense fruit flavours. **** 1993 Chambolle-Musigny £13 (HR).

Huelva (Spain) DO of the Extremadura region, producing rather heavy whites and fortified wines.

Gaston Huët (LOIRE, France) Long-time mayor of VOUVRAY and one of the very few producers who has consistently produced top quality individual vineyard examples of SEC, DEMI-SEC and MOELLEUX wines. His non-vintage fizz, though only made occasionally, is top class too. ***** 1989 Vouvray Le Haut Lieu 1er Tri Moelleux £32 (WR, BU).

Hugel et Fils (ALSACE, France) Reliable NEGOCIANT whose wines rarely reach great heights. Look out for the Jubilee wines and – hard-to-find – late harvest offerings. Gentil is a recommendable revival of the tradition of blending different grape varieties. **** 1993 Gentil £5 (JS).

Hungary Country previously known for its famous TOKAY, infamous BULL'S BLOOD, and OLASZ RIZLING. Now a popular destination for FLYING WINEMAKERS like HUGH RYMAN and KYM MILNE – a country to watch. **** 1994 Egri Csillagok Cabernet Sauvignon, £3 (U) **** 1988 Tokaji Aszu 5 Puttonyos, Chateau Megyer £14.50 (DBY).

Hunter Valley (Australia) The best-known wine region in Australia is ironically one of the least suitable parts in which to make wine. When the vines are not dying of heat and thirst they are drowning beneath the torrential rains which like to fall at precisely the same time as the harvest. Even so, the SHIRAZes and SEMILLONs – traditionally sold as 'Hermitage', 'Claret', 'Burgundy', 'Chablis' and 'Hunter Valley Riesling' – can develop remarkably. Best producers: LAKE'S FOLLY, BROKENWOOD, ROTHBURY ESTATE, ROSEMOUNT, TYRRELLS, MCWILLLIAMS, LINDEMANS, Reynolds, EVANS FAMILY, Petersons. (red) 83 86 87 88 90 91 92 (white) 83 86 87 88 90 91 92 93. *** 1994 Rothbury Estate Chardonnay, £6 (DBY, CWS, FUL).

Hunter's (MARLBOROUGH, NEW ZEALAND) One of MARLBOROUGH's most consistent producers of ripe fruity SAUVIGNON BLANCS. **** 1993 Sauvignon Blanc £9.50 (WR, BU).

Huxelrebe Minor white grape, often grown in England but proving what it can do when harvested late in Germany. ***** 1992 Forster Schnepfenflug Trockenbeerenauslese, Kurt Darting £13 (half) (OD).

Hybrid CROSS-BRED GRAPE VITIS VINIFERA (EUROPEAN) x VITIS LABRUSCA (NORTH AMERICAN) – AN EXAMPLE IS SEYVAL.

Hydrogen sulphide NATURALLY OCCURRING GAS GIVEN OFF BY ESPECIALLY YOUNG RED WINE, RESULTING IN SMELL OF ROTTEN EGGS. OFTEN CAUSED BY INSUFFICIENT RACKING. IF YOU SUSPECT A WINE OF HAVING THIS SMELL, YOU MAY BE ABLE TO REMOVE IT BY ADDING A PENNY (OR ANY OTHER COPPER COIN).

Vin de Pays de l' Ile de Beauté (CORSICA, France) Picturesque name for improving wines thanks to outsiders such as LAROCHE. Often better than this island's APPELLATION wines. *** 1993 Pinot Noir 'L', Laroche £4 (EP).

Imbottigliato nel'origine (Italy) ESTATE-BOTTLED.

Imperiale (BORDEAUX, France) LARGE BOTTLE CONTAINING ALMOST SIX AND A HALF LITRES OF WINE (EIGHT AND A HALF BOTTLES). CHERISHED BY COLLECTORS PARTLY THROUGH RARITY, PARTLY THROUGH THE GREATER LONGEVITY THAT LARGE BOTTLES ARE SUPPOSED TO GIVE THEIR CONTENTS. MIND YOU, IT HELPS IF YOU CAN EMPLOY ARNOLD SCHWARZENEGGER TO DO THE POURING RATHER THAN TAKING IT IN TURNS WITH A LONG STRAW.

Inferno (Italy) Lombardy DOC, chiefly red from NEBBIOLO, which needs to be aged for at least five years. *** 1990 Nino Negri £6.50 (V&C).

Inglenook Vineyards (NAPA, California) Once-great winery which like BEAULIEU, hardly benefitted in quality terms from being owned by a division of UK giant Grand Metropolitan. The great Gothic building and vineyards belong appropriately to Francis Ford Coppola while the brand has been sold on to a US firm with little evident love of fine wine.

Inniskillin (ONTARIO, Canada) Long-established winery with good Ice Wines (made from the Vidal grape), a highly successful Chardonnay and a rare example of a good MARECHAL FOCH. ***1993 Maréchal Foch £6 (AV).

Institut National des Appellations d'Origine (INAO) FRENCH ADMINISTRATIVE BODY WHICH DESIGNATES AND POLICES QUALITY. QUIETLY REACTING TO CRITICS OUTSIDE (AND TO A LESSER EXTENT WITHIN) FRANCE WHO WANT TO KNOW WHY APPELLATION CONTROLEE WINES ARE SO OFTEN INFERIOR TO THE NEW WAVE OF VINS DE TABLE OVER WHICH THIS BODY HAS NO AUTHORITY.

Irancy (BURGUNDY, France) Little-known, light reds and ROSÉS near CHABLIS from a blend of grapes including the PINOT NOIR and the little-known César. Curiously, Irancy has AC status whereas SAUVIGNON DE ST BRIS, a nearby source of superior whites, is merely a VDQS region.

Iron Horse Vineyards (SONOMA, California) One of the best sparkling wine producers in the NEW WORLD, thanks to cool climate vineyards. Reds and still whites are increasingly impressive too. *** 1989 Chardonnay £14 (NI).

Irouléguy (South-west, France) Earthy, spicy reds and ROSÉS, duller whites. *** 1990 Domaine Mignaberry Rouge £7 (ABY).

Isinglass FINING AGENT DERIVED FROM THE STURGEON.

Isole e Olena (TUSCANY, Italy) Brilliant, small CHIANTI estate with a pure SANGIOVESE SUPER-TUSCAN, CEPPARELLO and Italy's first (technically illegal) SYRAH. 83 86 88 89 90 91. **** 1991 Cepparello, £18 (DBY, EWC, ABY).

Israel Once the source of appalling stuff, but the new-style Varietal wines are improving. See GOLAN HEIGHTS.

Ch. d' Issan (BORDEAUX, France) Recently revived MARGAUX third growth with recogniseable blackcurrant CABERNET SAUVIGNON intensity. 82 83 85 86 89 90. *** 1989, £18 (J&B).

Italian Riesling/Riesling Italico Not the great RHINE RIESLING, but another name for the unrelated WELSCHRIESLING, LUTOMER AND LASKI RIZLING, going under many names, and widely grown in Northern and Eastern Europe. At its best in AUSTRIA.

Paul Jaboulet Aîné (RHONE, France) NEGOCIANT-owner of the illustrious HERMITAGE LA CHAPELLE and producer of good COTES DU RHONE and CHATEAUNEUF DU PAPE. Reliable but now overshadowed by GUIGAL and the reconstructed CHAPOUTIER. Even so, on its day, the La Chapelle can blow almost everything else out of the water. **** 1985 Hermitage La Chapelle £27 (CEB) ***** Hermitage La Chapelle 1970 £75 (CEB).

Jackson Estate (MARLBOROUGH, NEW ZEALAND) Next-door neighbour to CLOUDY BAY and producer of SAUVIGNON which is giving that superstar estate a run for its money. **** 1994 Marlborough Sauvignon Blanc £8 (BOO) **** 1994 Marlborough Chardonnay £9 (DBY).

Louis Jadot (BURGUNDY, France) Good, sometimes great, BEAUNE NEGOCIANT with especially good vineyards in Beaune itself and in Chassagne and Puligny Montrachet. Whites are the most impressive. **** 1993 Marsannay Blanc, £9 (WR, BU) **** 1989 Corton £25 (TH, WR, BU).

Jaffelin (BURGUNDY, France) Small NEGOCIANT recently bought from DROUHIN by BOISSET. Particularly good at supposedly 'lesser' appellations. **** 1992 Monthelie £8.50 (OD) *** 1992 Saint Romain £8 (OD).

Joseph Jamet (RHONE, France) Top-class COTE ROTIE estate. **** 1992 Côte Rotie, £17.50 (DBY).

Vin de Pays du Jardin de la France (LOIRE, France) Marketing device to describe some 50 million bottles of VINS DE PAYS from the LOIRE. *** 1994 Chardonnay, Donatien Bauhaud £3.50 (SAF).

Robert Jasmin (RHONE, France) Traditionalist COTE ROTIE estate, eschewing new oak. **** 1993 Côte Rôtie £17 (YAP).

Jasnières (LOIRE, France) Rare, bone-dry and – even rarer – MOELLEUX sweet CHENIN BLANC wines from TOURAINE. Buy carefully; poorly made wines offer an expensive chance to taste the CHENIN at its worst. 88 89 90 92. **** 1989 Les Truffières, Jean-Baptiste Pinon £9 (YAP).

Jasper Hill (Bendigo, Australia) Winery in Heathcote with a deserved cult following for both reds and whites. ***** 1992 Georgia's Paddock Shiraz, £15 (ADN).

Ch de la Jaubertie (South-west, France) Pioneering BERGERAC property established by Henry Ryman and now under his son, HUGH RYMAN's winemaking control. Reliable alternative to SANCERRE. Reds are less successful. **** 1991 Blanc £5 (VW).

Henri Jayer (BURGUNDY, France) Cult winemaker whose top COTE DE NUITS reds rival those of the DOMAINE DE LA ROMANEE CONTI. Now retired but still represented on labels referring to Georges et Henri, and as an influence on the wines of MEO CAMUZET. ***** 1989 Echezeaux £43 (J&B).

Robert Jayer-Gilles (BURGUNDY, France) Henri Jayer's cousin, whose top wines – including a Nuits St Georges les Damodes and an Echezeaux – bear comparison with those of his more famous relative. (His whites – particularly the aligoté are good, too). *** 1992 Hautes-Cotes de Beaune £13 (OD).

Jekel Vineyards (ARROYO SECO, California) Founded and still run by Bill Jekel, a famous critic of TERROIR, but now under the same ownership as FETZER. CABERNETS and CHARDONNAYS are better nowadays than the very commercial RIESLING and are worth following if you accept their slightly herbaceous style. *** 1992 Sanctuary Estate Cabernet Sauvignon £12 (W) **** 1993 Gravelstone Vineyard Chardonnay £10.50 (ADN, W).

Jerez (de la Frontera) (Spain) Centre of the Sherry trade, gives its name to entire DO sherry-producing area. See GONZALEZ BYASS, LUSTAU, HIDALGO, BARBADILLO.

Jermann (FRIULI-VENEZIA GIULIA, Italy) Brilliant, innovative winemaker with a knack of getting outrageous flavours – and prices – out of every white grape variety he touches. Look out for his Vintage Tunina, a blend of Tocai, Picolit and Malvasia, and the 'Where the Dreams have no End' white blend plus Capo Martino, a single-vineyard blend of PINOTS. **** 1992 Where The Dreams Have No End £29.50 (PON, SEL, EWC).

Jeroboam LARGE BOTTLE – IN CHAMPAGNE CONTAINING THREE LITRES (FOUR BOTTLES); IN BORDEAUX, IT CAN BE FOUR AND A HALF LITRES (SIX BOTTLES). DO CHECK BEFORE WRITING YOUR CHEQUE.

Jesuitengarten (RHEINGAU, Germany) One of Germany's top vineyards – well-handled by BASSERMANN-JORDAN. **** 1988, Forster Jesuitgarten Riesling Spätlese Bassermann-Jordan £8.50 (VW).

Jeunes Vignes DENOTES VINES TOO YOUNG FOR THEIR CROP TO BE SOLD AS AN APPELLATION CONTROLEE WINE, EG THE CHABLIS SOLD UNDER THIS LABEL BY THE CHABLISIENNE COOPERATIVE.

Jobard (BURGUNDY, France) Great small white wine estate. **** 1991 Meursault 'Genevrières' £24.50 (ADN).

Charles Joguet (LOIRE, France) One of the top-class names for red LOIRE, making wines that can last. ✱✱✱ 1990 Chinon, Clos du Chêne Vert £11 (OWL).

Johannisberg (RHEINGAU, Germany) Village making superb Riesling, which has lent its name to a BEREICH covering all the RHEINGAU. 75 76 79 83 85 88 89 90 91 92 93. ✱✱✱ 1993 Erntebringer Riesling Kabinett QmP R Muller £5 (TAN).

Johannisberg Riesling CALIFORNIAN NAME FOR RHINE RIESLING.

Karl-Heinz Johner (BADEN, Germany) The former winemaker at LAMBERHURST, now making good oaky Pinot Noir in southern Germany.

Jordan (SONOMA, California) SONOMA winery surrounded by the kind of hype more usually associated with NAPA. Table wines – from the ALEXANDER VALLEY – rarely warrant a long letter home from an open-minded wine lover, but they're decent enough and the 'J' fizz, though inevitably pricy, is of CHAMPAGNE quality. ✱✱✱✱ 1988 'J', Jordan Winery £16 (L&W).

Toni Jost (MITTELRHEIN, Germany) A new-wave producer with (well-sited) vines in Bacharach and a penchant for experimenting (successfully) with new oak barrels. ✱✱✱ 1993 Bacharacher Schloss Stahleck Riesling £7 (W).

Jug wine AMERICAN TERM FOR QUAFFABLE VIN ORDINAIRE, ESPECIALLY FROM THE CENTRAL VALLEY IN CALIFORNIA.

Marcel Juge (RHONE, France) Producer of one of the subtlest, classiest examples of CORNAS. ✱✱✱ 1990 Cornas £9 (EP).

Juliénas (BURGUNDY, France) One of the 10 BEAUJOLAIS CRUS, producing classic, vigorous wine which often benefits from a few years in bottle. 88 89 90 91. ✱✱✱✱ 1994 Julienas Domaine Du Clos Du Fief, Michel Tete £8 (L&W)

Juliusspital Weingut (FRANKEN, Germany) Top-class estate whose profits go to care for the poor and sick. A good source of RIESLING and SYLVANER. ✱✱✱ 1985 Iphoefer Julius-Echter Sylvaner Spätlese £10 (OWL).

Jumilla (Spain) Improving DO region, traditionally known for heavy, high-alcohol wines but increasingly making lighter ones. ✱✱✱✱ 1994 Sainsbury's Jumilla, Agapito £3.50 (JS).

Cotes de Jura (Eastern France) Region containing ARBOIS and SAVOIE, home of the SAVAGNIN grape and best known for specialities such as VIN GRIS, VIN JAUNE and VIN DE PAILLE.

Jurançon (South-west, France) Rich, dry apricotty white and excellent long-living sweet wines made from the GROS and PETIT MANSENG which are grown almost nowhere else. 86 87 88 89 90 91. ✱✱✱✱ 1991 Dom Cauhapé Vendange Tardive £9.50 (half) (WSO) ✱✱✱ 1993 Dom. Cauhapé Sec £8 (M&V).

Juvé y Camps (CATALONIA, Spain) The exception which proves the rule – by making and maturing decent CAVA from traditional grapes. ✱✱✱ 1990 Reserva de la Familia £8 (L&S).

Kabinett FIRST STEP IN GERMAN QUALITY LADDER, FOR WINES WHICH FULFIL A CERTAIN NATURAL SWEETNESS. ✱✱✱ 1989 Steinberger Riesling, Staatsweinguter Eltville £9.50 (THP).

Kaiserstuhl (BADEN, Germany) Finest BADEN BEREICH with top villages producing rich, spicy RIESLING and SYLVANER from volcanic slopes. ✱✱✱ 1991/2 Boetzinger Silvaner (Organic) Weingut Zimmerlin £4 (WSC).

Kallstadt (RHEINPFALZ, Germany) Village containing the best-known and finest vineyard of Annaberg, making luscious, full RIESLING.

Kalterersee (Italy) Germanic name for the Lago di Caldaro in the SUDTIROL/ALTO ADIGE.

Kanonkop (STELLENBOSCH, South Africa) Traditional estate with a modern approach reponsible for one of the very few Pinotages which shows real class. The light red blend, 'Kadette', is good, and BORDEAUX-style 'Paul Sauer' is one of the Cape's very best. ✱✱✱✱ 1991 Kanonkop Paul Sauer £11 (OD).

Katnook Estate (COONAWARRA, Australia) Small estate belonging to large (non-vinous) corporation which allows it the freedom to make the commercial Deakin Estate wines as well as such innovative stuff as a late harvest COONAWARRA CHARDONNAY (VW) as well as top-class COONAWARRA Merlot and Cabernet. ✱✱✱✱ 1992 Cabernet Sauvignon £10 (BI).

Kellerei/kellerabfüllung (Germany) CELLAR/PRODUCER/ESTATE-BOTTLED.

Kendall-Jackson (Clear Lake, California) High profile producer which has made a fortune by cleverly making supposedly classy CHARDONNAY and SAUVIGNON which are actually decidedly off-dry. *** 1992 Chardonnay Vintners Reserve £8 (MWW) *** 1991 Cabernet Sauvignon Vintners Reserve £8 (MWW).

Kenwood Vineyards (SONOMA VALLEY, California) A classy SONOMA winery with good single vineyard CHARDONNAYS, impressive, if tough, CABERNETS (including wine made from the author Jack London's vineyard) and brilliant ZINFANDEL. Sadly, unlike the Kendall Jacksons, these are hard to find in the UK. (Imported by Gillie Richards 01273 692 573).

> **Kerner** White grape, a RIESLING-cross, grown in Germany and now England.

Von Kesselstatt (MOSEL-SAAR-RUWER, Germany) Fine, though large, improving collection of four Riesling estates spread between the Mosel, Saar and Ruwer. **** 1992 Graacher Himmelreich Riesling Kabinett £6 (A).

Kiedrich (RHEINGAU, Germany) Top village high in the hills whose vineyards can produce great, intense RIESLINGS. 83 85 88 89 90 91 92 93. **** 1988 Schloss Groenesteyn, Kiedricher Sandgrub Riesling Kabinett £6.50 (VW).

Kientzheim (ALSACE, France) Village noted for its RIESLING. *** 1992 Riesling Kaefferkopf, Caves Vinicole de Kientzheim Kaysersberg £8 (ABY).

Kiona (WASHINGTON STATE, US) Small producer in the middle of nowhere with a penchant for intensely flavoured late harvest wines. *** Chardonnay 1990 £7 (OD) **** Late-Harvest Gewürztraminer 1993 £6 (OD).

Kir A BLEND OF WHITE WINE WITH A DASH OF CASSIS SYRUP INVENTED BY CANON KIR, THE THEN MAYOR OF DIJON, AS A MEANS OF DISGUISING THE OFTEN OTHERWISE UNPALATABLY ACIDIC LOCAL **ALIGOTE**. WITH SPARKLING WINE (PROPERLY **CHAMPAGNE**), A KIR ROYALE.

Kistler (SONOMA, California) Probably California's top CHARDONNAY producer, with a range of individual vineyard wines and improving PINOTS. BURGUNDY quality at BURGUNDY prices. **** 1992 Chardonnay 'Dutton Ranch' £21.50 (ADN).

Klein Constantia (CONSTANTIA, South Africa) Small go-ahead estate on the site of the great 17th-century CONSTANTIA vineyard. Wines, especially the SAUVIGNON, are not quite living up to the hype the estate has received, nor the prestige of the Constantia estate. Even so, they're light years ahead of Groot Constantia, the old-fashioned state-owned domain next-door. **** 1993 Estate Chardonnay £7 (DBY, W, SEL).

Klusserath (MOSEL-SAAR-RUWER, Germany) Small village best known in UK for Sonnenuhr and Konigsberg vineyards. 76 79 83 85 88 89 90 91 92.

Tim Knappstein (CLARE VALLEY, Australia) Long-time master of CLARE RIESLING whose name lost a little lustre during a period of ownership by MILDARA-BLASS. Now, rather more happily in the PETALUMA stable. Apart from CLARE wines, look out for the brilliant SAUVIGNON and promising PINOT NOIRS from LENSWOOD. **** 1993 Tim Knappstein Lenswood Chardonnay, Tim Knappstein £10 (OD).

Knudsen-Erath (OREGON, US) One of the better pioneers of this region but still far from earth-shattering.

Kracher (Neusiedlersee, Austria) Source of great (very) late-harvest wines including a very unusual effort with CHARDONNAY. ***** 1993 Chardonnay & Welschriesling Nouvelle Vague £25 (NY).

Krems (Austria) Town and WACHAU vineyard area producing Austria's most stylish Rieslings from terraced vineyards. *** 1990 Kremser Wachtberg Traminer, Weingut Undhof £7 (HAR).

Kreuznach (NAHE, Germany) Northern BEREICH, with fine vineyards around the town of BAD KREUZNACH. *** 1989 Bruckes Riesling Auslese, Schloss Plettenberg £9 (TH, WR, BU).

Domaine Kreydenweiss (ALSACE, France) Top-class organic producer with
particularly good PINOT GRIS and RIESLING. ******* 1992 Gewürztraminer Kritt
Selection Des Grains Nobles (half) £29 (LV) ******* 1992 Kritt Klevner £10 (LV).

Krondorf (BAROSSA VALLEY, Australia) Well-regarded winery specialising in
unashamedly traditional, big, Barossa styles. ******** 1992 Krondorf Show
Reserve Cabernet Sauvignon £9 (TO, VW, OD).

Krug (CHAMPAGNE, France) At its best, the CHATEAU LATOUR of CHAMPAGNE.
Great vintage wine, extraordinary ROSE and pure CHARDONNAY from the
Clos de Mesnil vineyard. Theoretically the best non-vintage on the market,
thanks to the inclusion of greater proportions of aged reserve wine.
**** NV £60 (OD etc).

Kuentz-Bas (ALSACE, France) Reliable producer, especially of PINOT GRIS and
GEWURZTRAMINER. ******** 1991 Tokay Pinot Gris Cuvee Tradition £9 (J&B).

Kumeu River (AUCKLAND, NEW ZEALAND) Innovative young winemaker (one
of the few Antipodeans to have worked a harvest at Ch. Petrus), Michael
Brajkovich is successful with a wide range of wines, including a very
unusual dry BOTRYTIS SAUVIGNON which easily outclasses many a dry wine
from SAUTERNES. ******** 1993 Chardonnay £15 (BEN) ******** 1992 Sauvignon
Blanc £10.50 (BEN) ******** 1990/1 Merlot Cabernet £13 (BEN).

Franz Künstler (RHEINGAU, Germany) A new superstar producer who is
showing the big name estates of the Rheingau what they ought to be doing
with their RIESLING. ******** 1993 Hochheimer Hofmeister Riesling Kabinett £8 (OD)

KWV (South Africa) Huge cooperative formed by the South African
government at a time when surplus wine seemed set to flood the industry
and maintained by the National Party when it needed to keep the members
of the big wine cooperatives, well, cooperative. Fast losing control over the
industry and belatedly improving the quality of its wines including a
respectable CHENIN BLANC and red Roodeberg blend as well as the
worthwhile Cathedral Cellars range. ******* 1994 Roodeberg Blanc, £4 (DBY).

Labouré-Roi (BURGUNDY, France) Highly successful and very commercial
NEGOCIANT, responsible for some quite impressive wines. Quality is
rarely less than respectable – which explains why so many retailers sell
these wines under their own names (a NUITS ST GEORGES address at the
foot of the label and an unfamiliar name such as Cottin Frères or Vaucher
is often the tell-tale sign). 85 88 89 90 91 92. ******* 1990 Nuits St Georges
£10 (SMF).

Labrusca (ITALY) VITIS LABRUSCA, THE NORTH AMERICAN SPECIES OF VINE, MAKING
WINE WHICH IS OFTEN REFERRED TO AS 'FOXY'. ALL VINIFERA VINE STOCKS ARE
GRAFTED ON TO PHYLLOXERA-RESISTANT LABRUSCA ROOTS, THOUGH THE VINE
ITSELF IS BANNED IN EUROPE AND ITS WINES, THANKFULLY, ARE ALMOST
UNFINDABLE.

Lacryma Christi (Campania, Italy) Literally, 'tears of Christ', the melancholy
name for some amiable, light, rather rustic reds and whites. Those from
Vesuvio are DOC. 86 87 88 89 90 92. ******* 1992 Antonio Mastroberardino
£12.50 (V&C).

Michel Lafarge (BURGUNDY, France) One of the very best producers in
Volnay – and indeed BURGUNDY. Fine, long-lived modern wine.
***** 1990 Volnay 1er Cru Clos du Chateau des Ducs £33 (HR).

Ch. Lafaurie-Peyraguey (BORDEAUX, France) Much-improved SAUTERNES
estate that has produced creamy, long-lived wines in the 80s and in 1990.
82 85 86 88 89 90. ******** 1987 £14 (THP).

Ch. Lafite-Rothschild (BORDEAUX, France) Often almost impossible to taste
young, this PAUILLAC FIRST GROWTH is still one of the monuments of the
wine world – especially since the early 80s. Earlier vintages such as 1970,
though, were disappointing and the 1962 – though faded now – was a
far more enjoyable wine than the more vaunted 1961, which still sells for
a fortune. Save your money and buy the brilliant 1990 instead. Possibly
a better 1994 than MOUTON too. 81 82 85 86 88 89 90. ******** 1992
£31.50 (L&W).

Ch. Lafleur (BORDEAUX, France) Christian MOUEIX's pet POMEROL. A tiny property with very old vines making traditional ultra-concentrated wine which, since 1981, has often been on a level with the wine Moueix makes down the road at PETRUS. 83 85 89 90. ***** 1983 £110 (FAR).

Ch. La Fleur-Petrus (BORDEAUX, France) For those who find PETRUS a touch too hefty, not to mention a touch unaffordable, this next-door neighbour offers gorgeously accessible POMEROL flavour (in PETRUS terms) a bargain price. 82 83 85 86 87 88 89 90 92. **** 1992 £22 (C&B).

Dom. des Comtes Lafon (BURGUNDY, France) The best domaine in MEURSAULT, with great vineyards in VOLNAY and a small slice of MONTRACHET. Wines last forever. ***** 1992 Volnay Santenots £24.50 (M&V) **** 1990 Meursault Clos de la Barre £36 (HAS).

Ch. Lafon-Rochet (BORDEAUX, France) A long-lived traditional ST ESTEPHE fourth growth which tends to be good, if a little tough, in all but the ripest vintages – surprising for a close neighbour of the more come-hitherish Cos d'Estournel. 82 83 85 86 88 89 90. *** 1988 £11 (FV).

Alois Lageder (Alto-Adige, Italy) New-wave producer of high quality, if pricy, examples of the kind of wine the Alto Adige ought to be producing. *** 1994 Chardonnay 'Buchholz' £9 (PON).

Lago di Caldaro (TRENTINO-ALTO ADIGE, Italy) Also known as the Kalterersee, using the local Schiava grape to make cool, light reds with slightly unripe, though pleasant fruit.

Ch. Lagrange (BORDEAUX, France) A once under-performing second growth St Julien which now shows what an injection of Japanese cash and local know-how (from Michel Delon of LEOVILLE-LASCASES) can do. Look out for Les Fiefs de Lagrange, the impressive second label. 82 85 86 88 89 90. *** 1992 Les Fiefs de Lagrange £11 (MTL, M&S).

Ch. La Lagune (BORDEAUX, France) A third growth MEDOC without a famous village! La Lagune is a bit of an oddity, almost as close to the north of BORDEAUX as HAUT BRION is to the south. Lovely, accessible wines which last well and are worth buying even in poorer years. 82 83 85 86 88 89 90. ***** 1986 £20.50 (L&W).

Lake County (California) Vineyard district salvaged by improved irrigation techniques and now capable of some fine wines as well as Kendall Jackson's highly commercial efforts. 86 87 88 89 90 92. *** 1992 Cabernet Sauvignon Kah-Nock-Tie, Konocti Winery £5 (BI).

Lake's Folly (HUNTER VALLEY, Australia) Meet Max Lake, surgeon-turned-winemaker-cum writer/researcher who has wonderful theories about the sexual effects of sniffing various kinds of wine. Pioneer of CHARDONNAY and still a rare success with CABERNET SAUVIGNON. Wines are now made by Max's son, Stephen. **** 1991 Lakes Folly, Chardonnay £13.50 (L&W).

Lalande de Pomerol (BORDEAUX, France) Bordering on POMEROL with similar, but less fine wines. Still generally better than similarly priced ST EMILIONS. Some good-value PETITS-CHATEAUX. 85 86 88 89 90 93. *** 1990 Chateau des Annereaux, Milhade et Fils £10 (DBY).

Lamberhurst (Kent, England) One of the first English vineyards and still one of the more reliable, though rarely the most innovative. *** 1994 Monarch, £3.50 (TH, WR).

Lambrusco (EMILIA-ROMAGNA, Italy) Famous/infamous low-strength (7.5 per cent) sweet, fizzy UK and North American version of the fizzy dry red wine favoured in Italy. The real thing – fascinating with its dry, unripe cherry flavour – is easily spotted thanks to its cork (the sweet stuff comes with a screw-cap). *** Lambrusco Secco Grasparossa, Chiarli £4 (V&C).

Landwein (Germany) A RELATIVELY RECENT QUALITY DESIGNATION – THE EQUIVALENT OF A FRENCH VIN DE PAYS FROM ONE OF 11 NAMED REGIONS (ANBAUGEBIET). OFTEN DRY.

Ch. Lanessan (BORDEAUX, France) Old-fashioned CRU BOURGEOIS made by people who hate the flavour of new oak. A surprisingly long-lived argument for doing things the way they used to be done. *** 1987 £7 (EP).

Langhe (PIEDMONT, Italy) A range of hills; when preceded by 'Nebbiolo delle', indicates declassified BAROLO and BARBARESCO.

Ch. Langoa-Barton (BORDEAUX, France) LEOVILLE BARTON's (slightly) less complex kid brother. Often one of the best bargain classed growths in BORDEAUX. Well made in poor years. 82 85 88 89 90 91 92 94. ******** 1989 £21 (L&W).

Coteaux du Languedoc (MIDI, France) A big appellation which has become a popular source of fast-improving everyday reds from RHONE and southern grapes. 88 89 90 91 92. ******* Spar Coteaux du Languedoc, Val d'Orbieu £3.50 (SMF).

Languedoc-Roussillon (MIDI, France) One of the world's largest wine regions and, until recently, a major source of the wine lake. But a combination of government-sponsored up-rooting and keen activity by FLYING WINEMAKERS and (a few) dynamic producers has turned this into the world's most worrying competitor for the NEW WORLD. The region includes appellations like CORBIERES and MINERVOIS, but the stuff you're most likely to encounter is VIN DE PAYS D'OC.

Lanson (CHAMPAGNE, France) Producer of average-to-okay non-vintage 'Black Label' and sublime vintage fizz. ******* 1988 £24 (OD etc).

Laroche (BURGUNDY, France) Good CHABLIS NEGOCIANT with some enviable vineyards of its own including PREMIERS and GRANDS CRUS. Reliable southern French CHARDONNAY VIN DE PAYS D'OC and innovative wines from CORSICA. ******* 1993 Chablis Montmains £11 (FV).

Ch Lascombes (BORDEAUX, France) Much improved, subtle, second growth Margaux which often exemplifies the perfumed character of this appellation. ******** 1989 £14 (THP).

Laski Riesling/Rizling (Former Yugoslavia) Yugoslav name for poor-quality white grape, unrelated to the RHINE RIESLING, aka WELSCH, OLASZ and Italico. ******* Lutomer Laski Rizling £3 (A).

Ch. de Lastours (LANGUEDOC, France) Combined winery and home for the mentally handicapped, and proof that CORBIERES can produce wine to rival BORDEAUX. Look out for the Cuvée Simone Descamps. ******** 1990 Fûts de Chêne £6.50 (BOO, DBY, POR).

Late Harvest MADE FROM (RIPER) GRAPES PICKED AFTER THE MAIN VINTAGE. ******** 1993 Madrona Late Harvest Riesling £5 (ADN, BKW).

Late-bottled vintage (port) (LBV) (DOURO, Portugal) OFFICIALLY, PORT WHICH HAS BEEN BOTTLED FOR FOUR OR SIX YEARS AFTER A SPECIFIC (USUALLY NON-DECLARED) VINTAGE. THE MOST WIDELY AVAILABLE, COMMERCIAL 'MODERN' STYLE, PIONEERED BY TAYLORS IS TREATED PRETTY MUCH LIKE RUBY AND VINTAGE CHARACTER AND FILTERED BEFORE BOTTLING SO IT NEEDS NO DECANTING. HOWEVER IT BEARS VERY LITTLE RESEMBLANCE TO REAL VINTAGE OR EVEN CRUSTED PORT. FORTUNATELY WARRES AND SMITH WOODHOUSE MAKE 'TRADITIONAL' – UNFILTERED – LBV WHICH CAN BE A GREAT ALTERNATIVE TO VINTAGE. ******* 1989 Graham's £10 (BOO, TH, OD) ******** 1989 Smith Woodhouse £8 (OD).

Latium/Lazio (Italy) The vineyard area surrounding Rome. Avoid most of its FRASCATI, although there are some exciting BORDEAUX-style reds. 88 89 90 92 93. ******* Rosso, Casale del Giglio 1992 £3 (SMF).

Louis Latour (BURGUNDY, France) Underperforming NEGOCIANT who still pasteurises his – consequently muddy-tasting – reds, treating them in a way no quality-conscious New World producer would dream of. Whites, however, including CORTON CHARLEMAGNE, can be sublime. ******** Puligny Montrachet 1976 £28.50 (RD).

Ch. Latour (BORDEAUX, France) First Growth PAUILLAC which can be very tricky to judge when young but which develops majestically. Recently bought (by a Frenchman) from its British owners, Allied Domecq. LES FORTS DE LATOUR is the – often worthwhile – SECOND LABEL. 82 85 86 88 89 90. ******** 1986 £54 (BI).

Ch. Latour-à-Pomerol (BORDEAUX, France) A great value, tiny (3,500-case) POMEROL under the same ownership as CH PETRUS and the same MOUEIX winemaking. It is a little less concentrated than its big brother but around a quarter of the price. 82 83 85 86 87 88 89 90. **** 1989 £30 (C&B).

Laudun (RHONE, France) Named village of COTES DU RHONE, with some atypical fresh, light wines and attractive rosés. *** 1993 Waitrose Côtes-du-Rhone, Cave de Laudun £3.50 (W).

Laurel Glen (SONOMA Mountain, California) Small, hillside-estate wines made by Patrick Campbell. A winery to watch for its ripe-flavoured, BORDEAUX-like reds that are well respected by true Californian wine lovers though, inevitably, not by the wretched collectors. Terra Rosa is the accessible SECOND LABEL. **** 1992 Terra Rosa £8 (JN, WC).

Laurent-Perrier CHAMPAGNE, France) One of the more reliable larger houses with particularly recommendable ROSE. *** N.V. £18 (widely available).

Ch. Laville-Haut-Brion (BORDEAUX, France) Exquisite white Graves that will last for 20 years or more. 82 83 85 86 88 89 90. **** 1989 £75 (BWI).

Coteaux du Layon (LOIRE, France) Whites from the CHENIN BLANC grape which are slow to develop and long lived. Lots of lean dry wine but the sweet BONNEZEAUX and QUARTS DE CHAUME are superior. **** 1970 'Faye', Ravouin-Cesbron £15 (ADN).

Lazio See LATIUM.

Lean LACKING BODY.

Lebanon Chiefly represented in the UK by the remarkable CHATEAU MUSAR, made in BORDEAUX style but from CABERNET SAUVIGNON, CINSAULT and SYRAH. 80 81 82 86 87 89 90. **** 1988 Ch Musar £9 (ADN).

Lees or lie(s) THE SEDIMENT OF DEAD YEASTS LET FALL AS A WHITE WINE DEVELOPS. SEE SUR LIE. *** 1994 Conilland Muscadet Du Sevre Et Maine "Sur Lie" Domaine du Petit Chateau £5.50 (HW).

Leeuwin Estate (MARGARET RIVER, Australia) Showcase winery (and concert venue) and producer of one of Australia's priciest and longest-lived CHARDONNAYS. Other wines are less dazzling. ***** 1990 Leeuwin Estate Art Series Chardonnay £16 (DD).

Domaine Leflaive (BURGUNDY, France) The late Vincent Leflaive was the uncriticable superstar of white Burgundy – despite the fact that wines ranged from dilutely disappointing to richly sublime. The next generation is using organic methods – to live up to the domaine's potential? **** 1991 Puligny Montrachet 'Clavoillon' £25.50 (ADN).

Olivier Leflaive (BURGUNDY, France) The NEGOCIANT business launched by Vincent LEFLAIVE's nephew. High class white wines with greater reliability than those of the domaine. *** 1993 Meursault £11 (ADN).

Peter Lehmann (BAROSSA VALLEY, Australia) Locally respected as the grand (not so) old man of the BAROSSA VALLEY, Peter Lehmann and his son Doug make the kind of intensely concentrated SHIRAZS, CABERNETS, SEMILLONS and CHARDONNAYS which amply make up in character what they lack in subtlety. ***** 1992 Clancy's Barossa Valley Red, £7 (BOO, DBY) **** 1990 Cabernet Malbec £15 (DBY).

Length HOW LONG THE TASTE LINGERS IN THE MOUTH.

Lenswood (Australia) Newly developed high-altitude region near Adelaide, proving its potential with SAUVIGNON, CHARDONNAY, PINOT NOIR and even (in the case of HENSCHKE's Abbott's Prayer), MERLOT and CABERNET SAUVIGNON. Pioneers include STAFFORD RIDGE and KNAPPSTEIN who also makes good PINOT NOIR. **** 1993 Tim Knappstein Chardonnay £10 (OD).

Léognan (BORDEAUX, France) Leading village of GRAVES with its own AC, PESSAC-LEOGNAN. *** 1992 Clos Grivet, Pessac-Léognan £8 (ADN).

Leon (Spain) North-western region producing acceptable dry, fruity reds and whites. *** 1986/9 Palacio de Léon £3.50 (VW).

Jean Leon (CATALONIA, Spain) American pioneer of CHARDONNAY and CABERNET and still – thanks to Hispanic conservatism – one of the few to succeed with these varieties. *** 1979 Cabernet Sauvignon £12.50 (POR).

Ch. Léoville-Barton (BORDEAUX, France) One of the classiest bargains in BORDEAUX. A fairly priced, reliably stylish ST JULIEN second growth whose wines are among the best in the MEDOC, especially in 1994. LANGOA BARTON is the sister property. 82 83 86 88 89 90. **** 1989 £24 (BWI).

Ch. Léoville-Las-Cases (BORDEAUX, France) Impeccably made ST JULIEN Super-Second which often matches its neighbour CH LATOUR. The second label, Clos du Marquis, is worth buying too, as is the CRU BOURGEOIS, Ch Potensac. 83 84 85 86 88 89 90. **** 1983 £31.50 (ADN).

Ch. Leoville-Poyferré (BORDEAUX, France) Improving toughly traditional ST JULIEN property steadily approaching the class of its neighbour LEOVILLE LAS-CASES. The second label, Moulin Riche, is a more approachable wine and is a worthwhile buy. 82 83 85 86 87 88 89 90 . **** 1990 £17 (BUT).

Dom Leroy (BURGUNDY, France) Organic domaine in VOSNE-ROMANEE recently founded by the former co-owner of the DOMAINE DE LA ROMANEE-CONTI making red wines which compete with those of that illustrious estate. ***** Nuits St. Georges, Lavières £29 (HR) ***** 1991 Vosne-Romanée 1er Cru, Les Beaux Monts £46 (HR).

Lie(s) SEE LEES/SUR LIE.

Liebfraumilch (Germany) Seditious exploitation of the QbA system. Good examples are pleasant, but most are alcoholic sugar water bought on price alone. Responsible for the ruination of the German wine market in the UK.

Limestone Ridge see LINDEMANS.

Limousin (FRANCE) OAK FOREST THAT PROVIDES BARRELS THAT ARE HIGH IN WOOD TANNIN. BETTER, THEREFORE, FOR RED WINE THAN FOR WHITE.

Limoux (MIDI, France) New APPELLATION for CHARDONNAYS which were previously sold as VIN DE PAYS d'Oc. See BLANQUETTE.

Lindauer (MARLBOROUGH, New Zealand) See MONTANA. *** Montana Lindauer Brut £7 (MTL, TO, VW).

Lindemans (Australia) Once PENFOLDS' greatest rival, now its subsidiary (aren't they all?) Noted for long-lived HUNTER VALLEY SEMILLON and SHIRAZ, COONAWARRA reds and good-value multi-region blends such as the internationally successful Bin 65 CHARDONNAY and Bin 45 CABERNET.
**** 1991 St George Cabernet Sauvignon £12 (BOO, DBY, WR, BU))
***** 1987 Botrytis Semillon £6 (BOO, DBY, MWW, L&W).

Karl Lingenfelder (RHEINPFALZ, Germany) Great new wave RHEINPFALZ producer of a special RIESLING, SCHEUREBE and an unusually successful PINOT NOIR. **** 1993 Scheurebe Kabinett Trocken £10 (ADN).

Jean Lionnet (RHONE, France) Classy CORNAS producer whose Rochepertuis is a worthwhile buy. **** 1992 Cornas, Domaine de Rochepertuis £17 (HBJ).

Liqueur de Tirage (CHAMPAGNE, France) THE YEAST AND SUGAR ADDED TO BASE WINE TO INDUCE SECONDARY FERMENTATION (AND HENCE THE BUBBLES) IN BOTTLE.

Liqueur d'Expedition (CHAMPAGNE, France) SWEETENING SYRUP FOR DOSAGE.

Liquoreux (France) RICH AND SWEET.

Liquoroso (Italy) RICH AND SWEET.

Lirac (RHONE, France) Peppery, TAVEL-like rosés, and increasingly impressive deep, berry-fruit reds. 80 81 85 89 90 91. *** 1992 Lirac Rouge, Ch D'Aqueria £7 (MWW).

Listel (LANGUEDOC, France) Big producer based on partially organic vineyards grown on sandy beaches close to Sète. Best wines are the rosé ('Grain de Gris') and low alcohol sparkling MUSCAT (Petillant de Raisin). *** 1994 Gris de Gris £4 (WMK).

Listrac (BORDEAUX, France) Small commune in the HAUT-MEDOC, near MOULIS, though quite different in style. Clay makes this good MERLOT country, though this isn't always reflected in the vineyards. Too many wines are toughly unripe. See CHATEAUX CLARKE, FOURCAS-HOSTEN & FOURCAS-DUPRE. 82 83 85 86 88 89 90. *** 1989 Ch. Fourcas-Loubaney, Listrac £10 (J&B).

Livermore (Valley) (California) Warm climate vineyard area with fertile soil producing full, rounded whites, including increasingly fine CHARDONNAY. *** 1990 Wente Brothers Estate Reserve Chardonnay, £11 (BBR).

Coteaux du Loir (LOIRE, France) Clean vigorous whites from a LOIRE tributary; JASNIERES is little seen but worth looking out for. 85 89 90 92 94.

Loire (France) An extraordinary variety of wines come from this area – dry whites such as MUSCADET and the classier SAVENNIERES, SANCERRE and POUILLY FUME; grassy, summery reds; buckets of ROSE – some good, most dreadful; glorious sweet whites and very acceptable sparkling wines.

Lombardy (Italy) The region (and vineyards) around Milan, known mostly for sparkling wine but also for increasingly interesting reds, and the whites of LUGANA.*** 1993 Franciacorta Bellavista £8.50 (V&C).

Long Island (NEW YORK, USA) A unique micro-climate where fields once full of potatoes are now yielding classy MERLOT and CHARDONNAY.

Dr Loosen (MOSEL-SAAR-RUWER, Germany) New Wave RIESLING producer. Probably the best and most reliable in the Mosel. **** 1992 Riesling Qba, £6 (DBY, ADN) **** 1989 Riesling Graacher Himmelreich £7.50 (TAN).

Lopez de Heredia (RIOJA, Spain) Ultra-traditional winery producing old fashioned Viña Tondonia white and GRAN RESERVA reds. *** Viña Tondonia Reserva Tinto 1985 £10 (MOR).

Los Llanos (VALDEPENAS, Spain) Commendable modern exception to the tradition of dull Valdepeñas. **** 1990 Reserva £4 (MTL, HW).

Los Vascos (COLCHAGUA VALLEY, CHILE) Estate belonging to Eric DE ROTHSCHILD of CH. LAFITE, which ought to be a flagship for CHILE. The CABERNET is good if uninspiring; the white disappointing, to say the least. *** 1992 Cabernet Sauvignon £6 (L&W).

Loupiac (BORDEAUX, France) Bordering on SAUTERNES, with similar but less fine wines. 83 85 86 87 88 89 90. **** 1990 Domaine du Noble, Loupiac £9 (H&D).

Ch. La Louvière (BORDEAUX, France) Andre LURTON's best known GRAVES property. Reliable, rich, modern whites and reds. 82 85 86 88 89 90. **** 1988 Rouge £15 (OD).

Lubéron (Côtes du) (RHONE, France) Reds, like light COTES DU RHONE, pink and sparkling wines; the whites CHARDONNAY-influenced. A new APPELLATION and still good value. 90 91 92 93. *** 1994 Côtes du Luberon Red, Cellier de Marrenon £4 (ABY, TH, WR, BU).

Ludon (BORDEAUX, France) HAUT-MEDOC VILLAGE and Commune. 81 83 85 86 88 89 90. ***** 1989 Ch La Lagune £20 (C&B).

Lugana (LOMBARDY, Italy) Grown on the shores of Lake Garda, smooth, pungent white wine, a match for food. LOMBARDY's best wine 90 91 92. **** 1994 Lugana Cru Villa Flora, Zenato £5 (W, D, C&B).

Lugny (BURGUNDY, France) See MACON.

Pierre Luneau (LOIRE, France) A rare beast: a top class Muscadet producer. Wines are sadly hard to find outside France.

Lungarotti (Umbria, Italy) Innovative producer who more or less created the TORGIANO denomination. **** 1985 San Giorgio, Rosso Dell'Umbria £18 (V&C).

Lurton (Jacques) Son of the owner of CH. LA LOUVIERE and Ch. Bonnet in ENTRE DEUX MERS who, having made a success there (especially with his whites), now makes wine all over the world. Look out for Hermanos Lurton wines from Spain. **** 1993 Hermanos Lurton Rueda Sauvignon Blanc £4 (OD).

Lussac-St-Emilion (BORDEAUX, France) A potentially worthwhile satellite of ST EMILION. 82 83 85 86 88 89 90. *** Lussac-St-Emilion ACP Sichel £6 (TAN).

Emilio Lustau (JEREZ, Spain) Great sherry producer, particularly noted for individual ALMECANISTA wines. **** Fortnum and Mason Manzanilla £7 (F&M) *** Lustau Sherry Cream, £3 (MTL, ES) *** Waitrose Oloroso £5 (W).

Lutomer (Slovenia) Wine-producing area still known mostly for its (very basic) LUTOMER RIESLING, but now doing better things with CHARDONNAY.

Luxembourg Source of pleasant, fresh, white wines from ALSACE-like grape varieties. **** Cuvée de l'Ecusson, Bernard Massard £7 (EP).

Ch. Lynch-Bages (BORDEAUX, France) Reliably over-performing Fourth Growth PAUILLAC which belongs to Jean-Michel Cazes, the man responsible for the success of CH. PICHON BARON. The (very rare) white is worth seeking out too. 82 83 85 86 88 89 90. **** 1988 £25 (BI).

Coteaux du Lyonnais (RHONE, France) Just to the south of BEAUJOLAIS, making some very acceptable good value wines from the same grapes. Best producers: Descottes, DUBOEUF, Fayolle. 91 92, 93 94.

Macedonia (Greece) Considered – by Greeks – to be the quality region of the north. *** 1993 Xinomavro Naoussa £4 (SAF).

Macération carbonique TECHNIQUE IN WHICH UNCRUSHED GRAPES FERMENT UNDER PRESSURE OF A BLANKET OF CARBON DIOXIDE GAS TO PRODUCE FRESH, FRUITY WINE. USED IN BEAUJOLAIS, SOUTH OF FRANCE AND BECOMING INCREASINGLY POPULAR IN THE NEW WORLD. *** 1993 Garnacha Veganueva Vinicola Navarra £4 (OD).

Mâcon/Mâconnais (BURGUNDY, France) Avoid unidentified 'rouge' or 'blanc' on wine lists. MACONS with the suffix VILLAGES, SUPERIEUR or PRISSE, VIRE, LUGNY or CLESSE should be better and can afford some pleasant, good-value CHARDONNAY. 91 92 93. *** 1994 Mâcon Superieur Rouge Les Epillets, Cave de Lugny £5 (W) *** 1994, Mâcon Villages Blanc George Duboeuf £6 (LNR).

Maculan (VENETO, Italy) A superstar producer of blackcurranty CABERNET BREGANZE, an oaked PINOT BIANCO-PINOT GRIGIO-CHARDONNAY blend called Prato di Canzio and the lusciously sweet TORCOLATO. *** 1994 Breganze di Breganze £8 (MTL).

Madeira (Portugal) Atlantic island producing fortified wines – usually identified by style: BUAL, SERCIAL, VERDELHO or MALMSEY. Most is ordinary stuff for use by mainland European cooks and, more rarely finer fare for drinking by wine drinkers who appreciate the unique marmeladey character of good Madeira. Also home to the Madeira Wine Company, owners of the Rutherford & Miles, BLANDY, Leacock and COSSART GORDON labels. This well-run quasi-monopolistic company now belongs to the Symingtons who, with DOWS, GRAHAMS, WARRES etc, have long had a similar role in the DOURO. Other producers to look out for include Henriques & Henriques and Barros e Souza. **** Blandy's 5 Year Old Bual £12 (BOO) **** Cossart Gordon 10 Year Old Malmsey £14 (BBR, C&B).

Maderisation DELIBERATE PROCEDURE IN MADEIRA, PRODUCED BY THE WARMING OF WINE IN ESTUFAS. OTHERWISE UNDESIRED EFFECT, COMMONLY PRODUCED BY HIGH TEMPERATURES DURING STORAGE, RESULTING IN A DULL, FLAT FLAVOUR TINGED WITH A SHERRY TASTE AND COLOUR.

Madiran (South-west, France) Robust country reds made from the TANNAT grape, tannic when young, but worth ageing. 82 85 86 88 89 90. **** 1989 Ch de Crouseilles £8 (U). *** 1985 Domaine de Pierron, Plaimont £6 (DBY).

Ch. Magdelaine (BORDEAUX, France) ST EMILION Estate owned by JP MOUEIX and neighbour to CH. AUSONE, producing reliable, rich wines. 82 85 86 89 90. **** 1988 £22 (TAN).

Magnum LARGE BOTTLE CONTAINING THE EQUIVALENT OF TWO BOTTLES OF WINE (ONE AND A HALF LITRES IN CAPACITY).

Maipo (CHILE) One of four viticultural regions identified by the Chilean Ministry of Agriculture. Contains many good producers, including Canepa, COUSINO MACUL, Peteroa, SANTA CAROLINA, SANTA RITA, UNDURRAGA, VINA CARMEN.

Maitre de chai (France) CELLAR MASTER.

Malaga (Spain) Andalusian DO producing raisiny dessert wines of varying degrees of sweetness, immensely popular in the 19th century. **** 1885 Solera, Scholtz Hermanos £4.50 (half) (SEL, W).

Ch. Malartic-Lagravière (BORDEAUX, France) PESSAC-LEOGNAN estate, bought a few years ago by LAURENT PERRIER, improving new-wave whites; reds need time. (red) 70 75 82 83 85 86 88 89 90 (white) 82 83 85 86 87 88 89 90 91 92. **** 1982 Red £88 (mag) (BWI).

Malbec Red grape, now rare in BORDEAUX but widespread in ARGENTINA and CAHORS, where it is known as the COT or AUXERROIS. *** 1991 Luigi Bosca Malbec Leonico Arizu £7 (NI) *** 1992 Trapiche Malbec Reserve £5 (DBY) **** 1993 Leasingham Domaine Cabernet Malbec £6.50 (HBR, OD).

Malolactic Fermentation SECONDARY FERMENTATION IN WHICH APPLEY MALIC ACID IS CONVERTED INTO THE 'SOFTER', CREAMIER LACTIC ACID. COMMON IN BURGUNDY; VARYINGLY USED IN THE NEW WORLD WHERE NATURAL ACID LEVELS ARE OFTEN LOW. RECOGNISABLE IN EXCESS AS A BUTTERMILKY FLAVOUR.

Ch de la Maltroye (BURGUNDY, France) Classy modern CHASSAGNE-based estate with fingers in 14 AC pies around BURGUNDY, all of whose wines are made by JL PARENT. **** 1992 Santenay La Comme 1er Cru £13 (OD).

Malvasia Muscatty white grape vinified dry in Italy (as a component in FRASCATI for example), but far more successfully as good, sweet traditional MADEIRA, where it is known as MALMSEY. It is not the same grape as MALVOISIE (see below). **** 1992 Ca Del Solo Malvasia Bianca, Bonny Doon £8 (NY, M&V, DBY, RD).

Malvoisie (LOIRE, France) Local name for the PINOT GRIS 89 90 92. *** Malvoisie 1993 Pierre Guindon £6 (YAP).

La Mancha (Spain) Big region producing mostly dull and old-fashioned but in recent times increasingly clean modern wine. **** 1993 Fuente del Ritmo Barrel Aged Tempranillo Bodegas Centro Españolas £4 (W, TH, BU, WR) *** 1994 La Mancha Tempranillo, Santiago Martinez £11.50 (A, TO, SAF, W).

Manzanilla Dry, tangy SHERRY – a FINO-style wine widely (though possibly mistakenly) thought to take on a salty tang from the coastal BODEGAS of Sanlucar de Barrameda. **** Don Zoilo Manzanilla £8 (DBY, TH, WR, BU, JEH) *** Tesco Superior Manzanilla Sanchez Romate £3 (half) (TO).

Maranges (BURGUNDY, France) New hillside appellation promising potentially affordable if rustic COTE D'OR wines. **** 1991 Maranges La Fussière £13.50 (NIC). .

Marc RESIDUE OF PIPS, STALKS AND SKINS AFTER GRAPES ARE PRESSED – OFTEN DISTILLED INTO A FIERY UNWOODED BRANDY OF THE SAME NAME, eg MARC DE BOURGOGNE.

Marches (Italy) Central region on the Adriatic coast best known for ROSSO CONERO and good, dry, fruity VERDICCHIO whites. (red) 85 86 87 88 89 90 92 93 (white) 89 90 91 92.

Marcillac (South-West, France) Full-flavoured country reds principally from the Fer grape – may also contain CABERNET and GAMAY.

Margaret River (Australia) Cool(ish) vineyard area on the coast of WESTERN AUSTRALIA, gaining notice for CABERNET SAUVIGNON and CHARDONNAY. Also Australia's only ZINFANDEL from CAPE MENTELLE (best known wineries are MOSS WOOD, CAPE MENTELLE, LEEUWIN, CULLEN, PIERRO, VASSE FELIX and Château Xanadu). 86 87 89 90 93.

Margaux (BORDEAUX, France) Large commune with a concentration of CRUS CLASSES including CHATEAU MARGAUX. Sadly, wines which should be deliciously blackberryish are variable, partly thanks to the diverse nature of the soil and partly through producers' readiness to sacrifice quality for the sake of yields. Curiously, though, if you want a good 1983, this vintage succeeded better here than elsewhere in the MEDOC. 78 79 81 82 83 85 86 88 89 91. **** Ch Palmer 1991 £30 (NIC).

Ch. Margaux (BORDEAUX, France) Peerless First Growth back on form since the dull 1970s and producing intense wines with cedary perfume and velvet softness when mature. The second wine, Pavillion Rouge (red and matching white) is worth buying too. 66 78 79 80 81 82 83 85 86 88 89 90. **** 1992 £30 (OD) **** 1991 £49 (BI).

Marlborough (NEW ZEALAND) Important wine area with cool climate in the South Island making excellent SAUVIGNON, CHARDONNAY and improving MERLOT and PINOT NOIR. Notable for CLOUDY BAY, contender for the best SAUVIGNON in the world; other good names include HUNTER'S, VAVASOUR, JACKSON ESTATE, Cellier le Brun and MONTANA. 90 91 92 93.

Côtes du Marmandais (South-west, France) Uses the BORDEAUX red grapes plus GAMAY, SYRAH and others to make pleasant, inexpensive, if rather rustic wines. *** 1991 Cocumont Co-operative £3 (SMF).

Marne et Champagne (CHAMPAGNE, France) Huge unglamorous producer which, for some reason, is usually omitted from books on CHAMPAGNE, which prefer to focus on companies with more active public relations departments. Owns Besserat de Bellefon, LANSON and ALFRED ROTHSCHILD labels and seems to be able to provide really good own-label wines (eg Victoria Wine 1989 Champagne) for buyers prepared to pay the price. ***** 1989 Victoria Wine Vintage Champagne £19 (VW) **** André Simon Champagne Brut NV £10 (MTL).

Marqués de Cáceres (RIOJA, Spain) Modern French-influenced BODEGA making fresher-tasting wines than many of its neighbours. A good, if anonymous, new-style white has been joined by a promising oak-fermented version and a pleasant ROSE (Rosado). **** 1990 Crianza Tinto £6 (L&W).

Marqués de Griñon (LA MANCHA, Spain) Dynamic exception to the dull LA MANCHA rule, making wines which often outclass RIOJA. The high quality juicy CABERNET-MERLOT and fresh white RUEDA have now been joined by Durius, a blend from RIBERA DEL DUERO. **** Rioja Tempranillo 1992 £5 (MWW, RBS).

Marqués de Monistrol (CATALONIA, Spain) Single-estate CAVA. Better than most. *** Brut Rosé £8 (VW).

Marqués de Murrieta (RIOJA, Spain) Until recently the best old-style oaky white (sold as Castillo Ygay), though recent efforts have been disappointing. The red, at its best, is one of the most long-lived elegant of Riojas – look out for old Castillo Ygays from the 1960s. *** 1990 Tinto Reserva £8 (DBY, L&W, J&B, TAN).

Marqués de Riscal (RIOJA, Spain) Famous, but for a long time flawed, property that seems to be getting its act together at last. The whites are already better and the 1994 Rueda SAUVIGNON is right on target to be one of the best made whites in Spain. *** Rioja Reserva 1989 £7 (VW).

Marsala (SICILY) Dark, rich, fortified wine from SICILY essential in a number of recipes, such as zabaglione. DE BARTOLI make stuff worth drinking. *** Pellegrino Garibaldi Dolce £6 (W, TH, OD, TO).

Marsannay (BURGUNDY, France) Pale red and ROSE from the PINOT NOIR plus elegant affordable CHARDONNAY. 85 87 88 89 90 92. *** 1991 Chateau de Marsannay Cuvée Charles Le Témeraire Rouge Noemie Vernaux £12 (GI).

Marsanne The grape usually responsible (in blends with ROUSSANNE) for most of the northern RHONE white wines. Also successful in the GOULBURN VALLEY in Victoria for CHATEAU TAHBILK and MITCHELTON and in California for BONNY DOON. 85 86 88 89 90 91 92. *** 1994 Domaine Virginie £5 (ADN, M&V) **** 1993 Mitchelton Reserve £7 (W, OD, MTL, SV) ***** 1994 Chateau Tahbilk £6 (OD).

Martinborough (NEW ZEALAND) Up-and-coming North Island region for PINOT NOIR and CHARDONNAY. Recommended: ATA RANGI, Dry River, MARTINBOROUGH VINEYARD, PALLISER ESTATE.

Martinborough Vineyard (NEW ZEALAND) Producer of the best Kiwi PINOT NOIR and one of the best CHARDONNAYS. Wines can be extraordinarily Burgundian in style. **** Pinot Noir 1993 £11 (OD, L&W, DBY) *** 1992 Chardonnay £11 (OD, L&W).

Martinez Bujanda (RIOJA, Spain) New-wave producer of fruit-driven wines sold as Conde de Valdemar. Probably the most consistently recommendable producer in Rioja. **** 1989 Cabernet Sauvignon £12 (MTL, TH, WR, BU) **** 1993 Conde de Valdemar Rioja Blanco £7 (MTL, DBY, EVI).

Martini (PIEDMONT, Italy) Good Asti Spumante from the producer of the vermouth house which invented 'lifestyle' advertising – still we're all guilty of something. *** Asti Spumante £5 (CWS).

Louis Martini (NAPA, California, US) Grand old name with superlative long-lived CABERNET from the MONTE ROSSO vineyard. Hard to find in Britain.

Marzemino (Italy) Spicy red grape *** 1993 Trentino Marzemino £5 (BOO).

Mas de Daumas Gassac (LANGUEDOC-ROUSSILLON, France) Ground-breaking Vin de Pays with an eccentric, complex red blend of half a dozen varieties (including PINOT NOIR and CABERNET) and white made from a blend that includes VIOGNIER. ***** 1994 Blanc £16 (ADN, OD) **** 1991 Rouge £11 (ADN, OD).

Bartolo Mascarello (PIEDMONT, Italy) Great ultra-traditional BAROLO specialist whose rose-petally wine proves that the old ways can compete with the new.

Giuseppe Mascarello (PIEDMONT, Italy) Top class BAROLO estate (unconnected with that of Bartolo), producing characterful wine from individual vineyards. Great DOLCETTO **** 1990 Dolcetto d'Alba £9 (NI).

Masi (ITALY) VALPOLICELLA producer with reliable, affordable reds and whites and single-vineyard wines which serve as justification for the existence of Valpolicella as a denominated region. **** 1991 Campo Fiorin £8 (L&W).

Massandra (CRIMEA, CIS) Producer of good but not great CABERNET and source of great, historic, dessert wines which were sold at a memorable Sothebys auction. **** 1938 White Muscat £70 (THP).

Master of Wine (**MW**) ONE OF A SMALL NUMBER OF PEOPLE (AROUND 200) WHO HAVE PASSED A GRUELLING SET OF TRADE EXAMS.

Matanzas Creek (SONOMA, California, US) Top-class complex CHARDONNAY, good SAUVIGNON and high-quality accessible MERLOT. Good SAUVIGNON, too. **** 1990 Sauvignon, Sonoma County £12 (HHC).

Mataro See MOURVEDRE **** 1992 Ridge Vineyards £13 (ADN) *** Tesco Australian Mataro, Kingston Estate £4 (TO, BOO).

Mateus (Portugal) Highly commercial pink and white off-dry, FRIZZANTE wine made by SOGRAPE, sold in bottles traditional in FRANKEN, Germany, and with a label depicting a palace with which the wine has no connection. A 50-year-old marketing masterpiece (widely available).

Thierry Matrot (BURGUNDY, France) Top-class white producer with great white and recommendable red BLAGNY. **** 1991 Meursault £15 (C&B).

Matua Valley (AUCKLAND, NEW ZEALAND) Reliable maker of great (MARLBOROUGH) SAUVIGNON, (Judd Estate) CHARDONNAY and MERLOT. Also producer of the even better ARARIMU red and white. **** 1994 Sauvignon Blanc £6 (U) **** 1992 Smith Dartmoor Cabernet Sauvignon £8 (W).

Ch. Maucaillou (MEDOC, France) CRU BOURGEOIS producing approachable wines to beat some CRUS CLASSÉS. **** 1989 £12 (JS).

Mauzac (France) Characterful, wild, floral, white grape used in southern France for Vins de Pays and GAILLAC. *** 1993 Domaine Lamoure Vin de Pays de l'Aude £4 (MWW).

Mavrodaphne Greek red grape and the wine made from it. Dark and strong, it needs ageing to be truly worth drinking. *** 1993 Kourtakis Mavrodaphne of Patras £4 (W, BTH).

Mavrud (BULGARIA) Traditional red grape and the characterful, if rustic, wine made from it. *** 1990 Zlatovrach Reserve Mavrud Asenovgrad £3 (JS).

Maximin Grünhaus (MOSEL-SAAR-RUWER, Germany) 1,000-year-old estate with intense RIESLINGS. **** 1992 Abtsburg Riesling Trocken £10 (L&W).

Mayacamas (NAPA, California) Long-established winery on MOUNT VEEDER with tannic but good CABERNET and long-lived, rich CHARDONNAY. ✯✯✯✯ 1985 Cabernet Sauvignon £23 (LAV).

McLaren Vale (SOUTH AUSTRALIA) Region close to Adelaide renowned for European-style wines, but possibly too varied in topography, soil and climate to create its own identity. ✯✯✯✯ 1993 Hardy's Chateau Reynella Cabernet Merlot £7 (CWS, OD, ECK, DBY) ✯✯✯✯ 1991 Mount Hurtle Shiraz, Geoff Merrill £6 (OD) ✯✯✯✯ Chapel Hill Unwooded Chardonnay 1994 £8 (AUC).

McWilliams (NEW SOUTH WALES, Australia) HUNTER VALLEY-based evidently non-republican firm with great, traditional ('Elisabeth') SEMILLON and ('Philip') SHIRAZ which need time. Fortified wines can be good, too. ✯✯✯✯ 1989 Elizabeth Semillon £7 (DBY, ADN, TO, JS).

Médoc (BORDEAUX, France) Area encompassing the region of BORDEAUX south of the GIRONDE and north of the town of BORDEAUX in which the CRU CLASSES are made as well as far more ordinary fare. As a generic term, should be better than basic BORDEAUX and less good than HAUT-MEDOC. Personal experience sadly tends to suggest that this hierarchy is as reliable as a modern royal mariage. 82 83 85 86 88 89 90.

Meerlust (STELLENBOSCH, South Africa) One of the Cape's very best estates. Classy MERLOTS and a BORDEAUX-blend called 'Rubicon' both of which will hopefully one day benefit from being bottled on the estate rather than by the BERGKELDER. ✯✯✯✯ 1989 Merlot £10 (BOO, DBY, PTR) ✯✯✯✯ 1989 Rubicon £10 (HAR, SEL, DBY, BOO).

Gabriel Meffre (RHONE, France) Sound commercial RHONE and, now, southern French producer. ✯✯✯✯ 1994 Galet Vineyards Chardonnay £4 (VW, W).

Charles Melton (BAROSSA VALLEY, Australia) Small-scale producer of lovely still and sparkling SHIRAZ and world-class rosé called 'Rosé of Virginia', as well as Nine Popes, a wine based on, and mistakenly named after, Châteauneuf du Pape. ✯✯✯✯✯ 1995, Rosé of Virginia £7 (ADN).

Mendocino (California, US) Northern, coastal wine county successfully exploiting cool microclimates to make 'European-style' wines, thanks, especially to the efforts of FETZER and SCHARFENBERGER. 86 87 88 90 91 92.

Mendoza (ARGENTINA) Capital of principal wine region. Source of good rich reds from firms including Trapiche, Catena, St Felicien, Finca Flichman and San Telmo. ✯✯✯✯ 1992 Trapiche Cabernet Sauvignon £4.50 (DBY).

Ménétou-Salon (LOIRE, France) Bordering on SANCERRE making similar if earthier, less pricy SAUVIGNON as well as some decent PINOT NOIR. (red) 87 88 89 90 92. ✯✯✯✯ 1994 Clos des Blanchais Domaine Henry Pellé, £8 (DBY, ADN).

Méo-Camuzet (BURGUNDY, France) Brilliant COTE DE NUITS estate with top-class vineyards and intense, oaky wines, which were for a long time, until his retirement, made by the great HENRI JAYER. ✯✯✯✯✯ 1991 Vosne Romanée 1er Cru Les Chaumes £27 (GH).

Mercaptans SEE HYDROGEN SULPHIDE.

Mercier (CHAMPAGNE, France) Subsidiary/sister company of MOET & CHANDON and producer of improving but pretty ordinary fizz.

Mercurey (BURGUNDY, France) Good-value if rustic wine from the COTE CHALONNAISE. Reds are tough but can be POMMARD-like and worth waiting for, while the nutty, buttery whites can be similar to MEURSAULT. 85 87 88 89 90 92. ✯✯✯✯ Mercurey Les Puillets 1993, Chateau Philippe-Le-Hardi £8 (ABY).

Merlot Red grape making soft, honeyed, even toffee-ish wine with plummy fruit, especially when planted in clay soil. Used to balance the tannic CABERNET SAUVIGNON throughout the MEDOC, where it is actually the most widely planted grape, as it is in POMEROL and ST EMILION, where clay also prevails. Also increasingly successful in California (especially for NEWTON), WASHINGTON STATE, VENETO, HUNGARY and Australia. ✯✯✯✯✯ 1992 Corbans Private Bin Merlot £8 (VW) ✯✯✯ 1990 Ch des Annereaux Lalande de Pomerol, Milhade et Fils £10 (ES).

Geoff Merrill (McLaren Vale, Australia) The ebulliant mustachioed winemaker who has nicknamed himself 'The Wizard of Oz'. Impressive if restrained (arguably too much so) Semillon-Chardonnay and Cabernet in McLaren Vale and, in 1993, a range of Italian wines for Sainsbury. Botham and Gower's favourite (vinous) tipple. **** 1992 Mount Hurtle Shiraz £6 (OD) **** Sainsbury's Chardonnay delle Tre Venezie £4 (JS).

Méthode Champenoise NOW RESTRICTED BY LAW TO WINES FROM CHAMPAGNE BUT IN EFFECT A METHOD USED FOR ALL QUALITY SPARKLING WINES; LABOUR-INTENSIVE, BECAUSE BUBBLES ARE PRODUCED BY SECONDARY FERMENTATION IN BOTTLE, RATHER THAN IN A VAT OR BY THE INTRODUCTION OF GAS. THUS BOTTLES MUST BE INDIVIDUALLY 'DEGORGED' TOPPED UP AND THEN RECORKED.

Methuselah SAME SIZE BOTTLE AS AN IMPERIALE, (SIX LITRES). USUALLY APPLIED TO CHAMPAGNE.

Meursault (Burgundy, France) Superb white Burgundy; the Chardonnay ideally showing off its nutty, buttery richness in full-bodied dry wine. Like Nuits St Georges and Beaune it has no Grands Crus but great Premiers Crus such as Charmes, Perrières and Génévrières. There is a little red wine here too, some of which is sold as Volnay. 81 82 85 86 88 89 90 92. *** 1992 Jean Javillier Meursault £13.

Ch de Meursault (Burgundy, France) See Patriarche.

Ch Meyney (Bordeaux, France) Improving St Estephe property, richer in flavour than some of its neighbours. 82 85 86 88 89 90. *** 1988 £12 (THP).

Domaine Michel Niellon (Burgundy, France) An estate which ranks consistently among the top five white Burgundy producers. Elegant and amazingly concentrated wines. **** 1990 Chassagne Montrachet £24 (OD).

Domaine Michelot-Buisson (Burgundy, France) One of the great old Meursault properties. A pioneer of estate bottling – and of the use of new oak. Wines are rarely subtle, but then they never lack typical Meursault flavour either. **** 1993 Meursault £13 (OD).

Mildara Blass (South Australia) A highly dynamic company with good Coonawarra wines and the very commercial Jamieson's Run. Sometimes labels seem to resemble those of competitors' wines. Subsidiaries include Wolf Blass, Yellowglen (uninspiring fizz) and Balgownie.

Millton Estate (New Zealand) James Millton is an obsessive, not to say masochist. He loves the hard-to-make Chenin Blanc and uses it to make first class organic wine near Auckland. Sadly, in Britain, we'd rather buy his Chardonnay. **** 1994 Barrel Fermented Chardonnay £8 (SAF).

Minervois (South-west, France) Firm, fruity and improving suppertime reds – Corbiere's (slightly) classier cousin. 88 89 90 91. **** 1994 Carignanissime de Centeilles, Boyer-Domergue £6 (ADN, OD) *** 1992 Domaine St Eulalie Minervois, £4 (TH, WR, BU, TAN).

Mis en Bouteille au Château/Domaine (France) BOTTLED AT THE ESTATE.

Ch la Mission-Haut-Brion (Bordeaux, France) Tough but rich reds which can rival its supposedly classier neighbour Haut Brion. 82 85 86 88 89 90. **** 1988 £46 (J&B).

Mitchell (Clare Valley, Australia) Good producer of Riesling and of the Peppertree Shiraz, one of the Clare Valley's best reds **** 1992 Cabernet Sauvignon £7 (L&W, SHJ, G&M, ADN) **** 1992 Watervale Riesling £6 (ADN, L&W, G&M).

Mitchelton (Goulburn Valley, Victoria, Australia) Modern producer of Marsanne and Semillon which has recently been bought by Petaluma. Late harvest Rieslings are also good, as is a Beaujolais-style red, known as Cab Mac. The Preece range – so named after the former winemaker – is also worth seeking out. **** 1993 Preece Chardonnay £6 (MTL, MWW) **** 1992 Preece Cabernet Sauvignon £6 (MWW).

Mittelhaardt (Rheinpfalz, Germany) Central and best Bereich of the Rheinpfalz 86 87 88 89 90 91 92.

Mittelmosel (Mosel-Saar-Ruwer, Germany) Middle and best section of the Mosel, including the Bernkastel Bereich. 85 86 87 88 89 90 91 92.

Mittelrhein (Germany) Small, northern section of the RHINE. Good RIESLINGS that are sadly rarely seen in the UK. 83 85 86 88 89 90 91 92 93.
  **** 1993 Bacharacher Schloss Stahleck Riesling Kabinett Toni Jost £6 (OD).

Moelleux (France) SWEET. ********* 1989 Vouvray Le Haut Lieu 1er Tri Moelleux Gaston Huët £32 (WR, BU) ******* 1993 Domaine Chanier, Vouvray £5 (SHJ, ADN).

Moët & Chandon (CHAMPAGNE, France) The biggest producer in Champagne. DOM PERIGNON, the top wine and Vintage Moët are reliably good and new CUVEES of Non-Vintage show a welcome reaction to recent criticism of inconsistency. See TORRE DE GALL, DOMAINE CHANDON, GREEN POINT. ******** NV £19 (OD etc).

Moillard (BURGUNDY, France) Middle-of-the-road NEGOCIANT whose best, really quite decent wines are sold under the 'Domaine Thomas Moillard' label. ******** 1991 Beaune-Grèves £15 (BBR).

Moldova Young republic next to ROMANIA whose vinous potential is being exploited by HUGH RYMAN. ******* 1992 H Ryman Rochu de Hincesti £3 (L&W).

Monbazillac (South-west, France) BERGERAC AC which is using the grapes of sweet BORDEAUX to make improving, inexpensive alternatives to SAUTERNES 83 85 86 88 89 90 91. ******* 1993 Domaine Du Haut Rauly £4 (CWS).

Robert Mondavi (NAPA, California, US) Pioneering producer of great Reserve CABERNET and PINOT NOIR and back-on-form CHARDONNAY, and inventor of oaky Blanc Fumé SAUVIGNON. The Woodbridge wines – apart from the Zinfandel – are less interesting and in Britain crazily overpriced. ********* 1993 Reserve Pinot Noir £22 (MWW) ********* 1990 Reserve Cabernet £30 (MWW).

Mongeard-Mugneret (BURGUNDY, France) A source of invariably excellent and sometimes stunningly exotic red BURGUNDY. ******* 1993 Bourgogne Passetoutgrains £5 (MWW).

Monica (di Cagliari/Sardegna) (Italy) Red grape and wine of SARDINIA producing drily tasty and fortified spicy wine. ******* Tesco Monica di Sardegna £3.50 (TO).

Monopole (France) LITERALLY, EXCLUSIVE – IN BURGUNDY DENOTES SINGLE OWNERSHIP OF AN ENTIRE VINEYARD.

Montagne St Emilion (BORDEAUX, France) A 'satellite' of ST EMILION. Often good-value reds which can outclass supposedly finer fare from St Emilion itself. Drink young. 85 86 88 89 90 92. ******* 1993 Comte de Perjan £5 (OD).

Montagny (BURGUNDY, France) Tiny hillside COTE CHALONNAISE commune producing good, lean CHARDONNAY that can be a match for many POUILLY FUISSES. PREMIER CRUS are not from better vineyards; they're just made from riper grapes. 83 85 87 88 89 90 92 93. ******* 1993 Montagny 1er Cru Montcuchot, Cave de Buxy £6 (SAF, MWW).

Montalcino (TUSCANY, Italy) Village near Sienna known for BRUNELLO DI MONTALCINO, Chianti's big brother whose reputation was largely created by the BIONDI SANTI estate whose wines no longer deserve the prices they command. Altesino, FRESCOBALDI and Banfi offer better value, as does the lighter ROSSO DI MONTALCINO. ******** 1990 Poggio Antico Brunello di Montalcino 1990 £20 (C&B).

Montana (MARLBOROUGH, NEW ZEALAND) Huge firm with tremendous SAUVIGNONS and GEWURZTRAMINERS (sadly unavailable in the UK), improving CHARDONNAYS and good-value LINDAUER fizz. Reds are getting there, too, but still tend to be on the lean and green side. Look out for the recently launched, smartly packaged, quite high priced, single-estate wines such as the Brancott Sauvignon. ******** Lindauer Brut £7 (OD, TO, MTL, VW) ******** 1993 Brancott Estate Marlborough Sauvignon Blanc £11 (OD, BKW, EP).

Monte Real Made by Bodegas Riojanos, generally decent, richly flavoured and tannic RIOJA. ******* 1988, Reserva Tinto Bodegas Riojanas £7 (ABY).

Montecillo (RIOJA, Spain) Classy wines including the oddly named – to Anglophones at least – Viña Monty. The Cumbrero Blanco white is good, too. ******** Gran Reserva 1986 £7 (OD).

Montée de Tonnerre (BURGUNDY, France) Excellent CHABLIS PREMIER CRU ***1990 Chablis 1er Cru Montée de Tonnerre, Regnard £13 (PRG).

Montefalco Sagrantino (UMBRIA, Italy) Intense cherryish red made from the local Sagrantino grape. ****1990 Sagrantino del Montefalco Brogal Vini £6 (BI).

Château Montelena (NAPA, California) Its two long-lived CHARDONNAYS (from NAPA and, rather better ALEXANDER VALLEY) make this one of the more impressive producers in the state. The vanilla-and-blackcurranty CABERNET is too impenetrable, however. ****1978 Chardonnay £25 (LV).

Montepulciano (Italy) Confusingly, both a red grape used to make red wines in central and South-east Italy, (Montepulciano d'ABRUZZI etc) and the name of a town in TUSCANY (see VINO NOBILE DI MONTEPULCIANO).

Monterey (California, US) Underrated region south of San Francisco, producing potentially good if sometimes rather grassy wines. ****1993 Monterey Vineyard Classic £5 (OD).

Montes (Curico, CHILE) Go-ahead winery with improving reds (including the flagship Alpha) and improved SAUVIGNON. Nogales is another label. ***1995 Villa Montes Sauvignon Blanc £4 (HW, SV, DBY) *** 1994 Montes Alpha Chardonnay £8 (HW).

Monteviña (California, US) Good ZINFANDEL from AMADOR COUNTY, reliable CABERNET and a FUME BLANC to make ROBERT MONDAVI weep. ****1992 Fumé Blanc £5 (WMK).

Monthélie (BURGUNDY, France) Often overlooked COTE DE BEAUNE village producing potentially stylish reds and whites. 83 85 87 88 89 90. ****1990 'Les Duresses', Monthelie Douhairet £14 (M&V).

Montilla-Moriles (Spain) DO region producing SHERRY-type wines in SOLERA systems, often so high in alcohol that fortification is unnecessary. Good examples easily match poor sherry but sadly the ones on sale in Britain have been chosen to compete with cheap 'British' 'sherry'. *** Safeway Dry Montilla, Alvear £3 (SAF) *** Somerfield Montilla Pale Cream, Perez Banquero £3.

Hubert de Montille (BURGUNDY, France) A lawyer-cum-winemaker whose VOLNAYS and POMMARDS are unusually fine and long-lived. ****1992 Bourgogne Rouge £12 (MYS).

Montlouis (LOIRE, France) Neighbour of VOUVRAY making similar, lighter-bodied, dry, sweet and sparkling wines. 85 88 89 90. ****1989 Vendages Tardives, J&M Berger £15 (YAP) ****1985 Mousseux J&M Berger £8 (YAP).

Le Montrachet (BURGUNDY, France) With its neighbours (BATARD-M, CRIOTS-BATARD-M, BIENVENUE- BATARD-M AND CHEVALIER-M) shares vineyards between PULIGNY and CHASSAGNE which can make the greatest and the priciest dry white in the world. Big, biscuity, potentially brilliant. ****1991 Domaine Comtes de Lafon £127 (ADN).

Cotes de Montravel (South-west, France) Source of dry and sweet whites and reds which are comparable to neighbouring BERGERAC.

Ch Montrose (BORDEAUX, France) Back-on-form ST ESTEPHE renowned for its intensity and longevity. More typical of the appellation than COS D'ESTOURNEL but often less approachable in its youth. Especially good in 1994. 82 83 85 86 88 89 90. ****1989 £28 (J&B).

Ch Montus (MADIRAN, France) Ambitious producer with carefully oaked examples of the TANNAT grape and PACHERENC DE VIC BILH. Bouscassé is a cheaper, more approachable label. ****1991 'Fûts de Chêne' £9.50 (BU).

Moondah Brook (SWAN VALLEY, WESTERN AUSTRALIA) An untypically (for the baking Swan) cool vineyard belonging to HOUGHTONS (and thus HARDYS). The star wines are the wonderful, tangy VERDELHO and richly oaky CHENIN BLANC which are brilliant. The CHARDONNAY and reds are less impressive. ****1994 Chenin Blanc £5 (DBY) ****1994 Verdelho £5 (DBY, MTL).

Mór (HUNGARY) Hungarian town making clean, aromatic white wines from a blend including the TRAMINER. ***1993 Safeway Hungarian Country Wine, A'gos £3 (SAF).

Morellino di Scansano (TUSCANY, France) Amazing cherry 'n' raspberry, young-drinking red made from a clone of SANGIOVESE. **** 1987 Riserva Le Pupitre £7 (OD).

Pierre Morey (BURGUNDY, France) Top-class MEURSAULT producer known for the power and concentration of his wines. **** Meursault 1er Cru Les Perrières 1993 £25 (HR).

Morey St Denis (BURGUNDY, France) COTES DE NUITS village which produces deeply fruity, richly smooth reds, especially the GRAND CRU 'Clos de la Roche. **** 1993 Domaine Dujac £17 (HR).

Morgon (BURGUNDY, France) One of the 10 BEAUJOLAIS CRUS. Worth maturing, as it can take on a delightful chocolate/cherry character. 88 89 90 93. **** 1993 Morgon Les Charmes, Gerard Brisson £7 (CWS) **** 1993 Domaine des Moulins £8 (NIC).

> **Morio Muskat** White grape grown in Germany and Eastern Europe and making simple, grapey wine. *** Somerfield Morio Muskat, St Ursula Wenkellerei £3 (SMF).

Mornington Peninsula (Australia) Some of Australia's newest and most southerly vineyards, close to Melbourne and under threat from housing developers. Good for PINOT NOIR, minty CABERNET and juicy CHARDONNAY though the innovative (but as yet unavailable in the UK) T'Galant is leading the way with other varieties. See STONIERS and DROMANA. 87 88 90 91 92.

Morris of Rutherglen (VICTORIA, Australia) Extraordinarily successful producer of Liqueur MUSCAT and TOKAY (seek out the Show Reserve) and intense DURIF, both still and, along with SHIRAZ, weirdly sparkling. **** Liqueur Muscat £9 (DBY) *** 1991 Morris Durif £10 (ADN).

Morton Estate (Waikato, NEW ZEALAND) Top-class producer of SAUVIGNON, CHARDONNAY and LOIRE/BORDEAUX-style reds. *** 1992 Chardonnay White Label £7 (BWC, DBY, CPW).

Moscatel de Setubal see SETUBAL.

Mosel-Saar-Ruwer (MSR) (Germany) Major region surrounding the three rivers that make up its name, capable of superbly elegant RIESLINGS which differ noticeably in each of the three regions. 76 78 82 83 85 88 89 90 91 92. **** 1993 Fritz Haag Riesling Halbtrocken £8 (L&W) **** 1991 Bernkasteler Badstübe Riesling Kabinett, Selbach-Oster £8.50 (L&W).

Mosel/Moselle (Germany) River and loose term for MOSEL-SAAR-RUWER wines, equivalent to the 'HOCK' of the RHINE. Not to be confused with the usually uninspiring Vins de Moselle produced on the French side of the river. Arguably, the best wine region in Germany today.

Moselblumchen (Germany) MOSEL-SAAR-RUWER equivalent to the RHINE's LIEBFRAUMILCH.

Lenz Moser (Austria) Big producer with a broad range, including particularly crisp dry whites and luscious sweet dessert wines. *** 1992 Pinot Blanc £4 (SAF).

Moss Wood (MARGARET RIVER, WESTERN AUSTRALIA) Pioneer producer of PINOT NOIR and CABERNET; only the CABERNET has lived up to early promise. The **** SEMILLON, though, is reliably good. **** 1991 Cabernet Sauvignon £12 (F&M) **** 1993 Chardonnay Margaret River £12 (F&M).

JP Moueix (BORDEAUX, France) Top-class NEGOCIANT/PRODUCER, Christian MOUEIX specialises in POMEROL and ST EMILION and is responsible for PETRUS, LA FLEUR-PÉTRUS, Bel Air, Richotey and DOMINUS in California. **** Château Bel Air 1993 £40 (C&B).

Moulin-à-Vent (BURGUNDY, France) One of the 10 BEAUJOLAIS CRUS – big and rich at its best and which, like MORGON, benefits from ageing a few years. 89 90 91 92. **** 1993 Fût de Chêne Georges Duboeuf £8 (MTL, LNR).

Moulis (BORDEAUX, France) Red wine village of the HAUT-MEDOC; like LISTRAC, with good-value CRUS BOURGEOIS. 85 86 88 89 90. See CHATEAU CHASSE-SPLEEN.

Mount Barker (WESTERN AUSTRALIA, Australia) Cooler climate southern region with great RIESLING, VERDELHO, IMPRESSIVE CHARDONNAY and restrained SHIRAZ. **** 1992 Goundrey Mount Barker Cabernet Sauvignon/Merlot £6.50 (BOO, SV, WSO, BBR).

Mount Langhi Ghiran (GREAT WESTERN, Australia) A maker of excellent cool-climate RIESLING, peppery SHIRAZ and very good CABERNET, though both the latter can be a touch lean. **** 1991 Shiraz £8 (EWC, DBY, OD).

Mount Mary (YARRA, Australia) Dr Middleton makes PINOT NOIR and CHARDONNAY that are unpredictably BURGUNDY-like in the best and worst sense of the term. The clarety Quintet blend is more reliable. *** 1991 Quintet £25 (AUC).

Mountadam (EDEN VALLEY, SOUTH AUSTRALIA) Son of DAVID WYNN (the 'saviour' of COONAWARRA), Adam makes classy Burgundian CHARDONNAY and PINOT NOIR (both still and sparkling) and an impressive blend called 'The Red'. Also worth seeking out are the EDEN RIDGE organic wines and the fruity DAVID WYNN range especially the unoaked CHARDONNAY. **** 1993 Chardonnay £12 (BOO, DBY, WR, BU) **** 1990 Mountadam Sparkling £17 (ADN) **** 'The Red' 1991 £16 (JAR).

Mount Veeder (NAPA, California, US) Convincing hillside appellation where MOUNT VEEDER Winery, Ch. Potelle, HESS COLLECTION and MAYACAMAS all produce impressive reds.

Mourvèdre Floral-spicy RHONE grape usually found in blends. Increasingly popular in France and California where, as in Australia, it is called MATARO. See PENFOLDS and RIDGE. **** 1992 Penfolds Shiraz-Mourvèdre 'Bin 2' Penfolds £5 (BOO, DBY, OD).

Mousse THE BUBBLES IN CHAMPAGNE AND SPARKLING WINES.

Mousseux (France) SPARKLING. VIN MOUSSEUX TENDS TO BE CHEAP AND UNREMARKABLE. *** GF Cavalier Brut, Caves De Wissembourg £4 (SAF, OD).

Mouton Cadet (BORDEAUX, France) A brilliant commercial invention by Philippe de Rothschild who used it to profit handsomely from the name of his first growth with which it has no discernable connecton. The white, though better than in the past, has even less of a *raison d'être*.

Ch. Mouton Rothschild (BORDEAUX, France) Brilliant First Growth PAUILLAC with gloriously complex flavours of roast coffee and blackcurrant. Since the early 1980s, equal to the best in the MEDOC, though some prefer the less obvious, less oaky style of Lafite. 70 75 81 82 85 88 89 90. **** 1981 £52 (BI).

Mudgee (NEW SOUTH WALES, Australia) Australia's first APPELLATION region, though heaven knows why. This high-altitude, isolated area is making far better wines than the robust, often clumsy stuff it used to, but it's still not a name to look out for. 82 84 88 89 90 91 92. **** 1994 Montrose Chardonnay £6.50 (THP) **** 1989 Montrose Wines Cabernet Sauvignon £6.50 (THP).

Muga (RIOJA, Spain) Producer of good old fashioned Riojas, of which Prado Enea is the best. *** 1985 Rioja Prado Enea £14.50 (DBY).

Müller-Catoir (RHEINPFALZ, Germany) Great, new-wave producer using new-wave grapes as well as RIESLING. Wines of all styles are impeccable and packed with flavour. Just what Germany needs to remind the world of what it can do. ***** 1993 Haardter Herrenletten Riesling Spätlese £10 (OD) **** 1992 Haardter Mandelring Scheurebe Spätlese £9 (OD).

Egon Müller-Scharzhof (MOSEL-SAAR-RUWER, Germany) Top-class Saar producer. **** 1993 Scharzhofberger Riesling Spätlese £14 (L&W).

Müller-Thurgau Workhorse white grape, a RIESLING x SYLVANER cross – also known as RIVANER – making much unremarkable wine in Germany, but yielding some gems for producers like MULLER CATOIR. Very successful in England. **** 1992 Langenlonsheimer Müller-Thurgau Kabinett, Willi Schweinhardt £5 (OD).

Champagne Mumm/Mumm Napa (CHAMPAGNE, France/NAPA, California)
Maker of slightly improved Cordon Rouge CHAMPAGNE and far better
CUVEE NAPA out west. The ROSE is better than the white and the WINERY
LAKE is best. **** Cuvée Napa £9 (OD) **** Cuvee Napa Rosé £9 (OD).

Muré (ALSACE, France) Producer of full-bodied wines, especially from the Clos
St Landelin vineyard. **** 1993 Gewürztraminer Côtes de Rouffach £7 (LNR).

Murfatlar (ROMANIA) Major vineyard and research area having increasing
success with CHARDONNAY. *** 1994 Barrel Fermented Chardonnay £3.49 (DBY).

Murphy-Goode (ALEXANDER VALLEY, California) CHARDONNAYS. Classy
producer of quite Burgundian style whites which sell at – for California –
affordable prices. **** 1991 Chardonnay £9 (ADN).

Murray River Valley (Australia) The area ranging between VICTORIA and
NEW SOUTH WALES which produces much of the Antipodes' cheapest wine
– a great deal of which is to be found in UK retailers' own-label bottles.

Murrumbidgee (NEW SOUTH WALES, Australia) Area formerly known for
bulk dessert wines, now improving irrigation and vinification techniques to
make good table wines and some stunning BOTRYTIS-affected sweet wines
for DE BORTOLI, Kingston Estate and LINDEMANS.

Château Musar (Ghazir, Lebanon) Serge Hochar makes a different red every
year, varying the blend of CABERNET, CINSAULT and SYRAH. The style veers
wildly between BORDEAUX, the RHONE and Italy, but there's never a risk of
becoming bored. Good vintages easily keep for a decade. The CHARDONNAY-
based whites are less than dazzling, though. *** 1988 £9 (ADN).

Muscadelle Spicy ingredient in white BORDEAUX, aka TOKAY in Australia
*** 1994 Van Loveren Blanc de Noir Muscadelle £3.50 (TO).

Muscadet (LOIRE, France) Area at the mouth of the LOIRE making dry, appley
white from the MELON DE BOURGOGNE. Clean, yeasty, slightly sparkling and
decidedly refreshing when good, which, sadly, is rare. New legislation and
a new 'Côtes de Grandlieu' appellation may help to improve matters. We'll
see. SUR LIE should be better. May be barrel-fermented. See SEVRE-ET-
MAINE.

Muscat à Petits Grains Aka FRONTIGNAN, the best variety of MUSCAT
and the grape responsible for MUSCAT DE BEAUMES DE VENISE, Muscat de
Rivesaltes, Asti Spumante, Muscat of SAMOS, RUTHERGLEN Muscats and dry
ALSACE Muscats. *** Cuvée Antoine, Muscat de Beaumes de Venise £8 (VW).

Muscat of Alexandria Grape responsible for MOSCATEL DE SETUBAL,
MOSCATEL DE VALENCIA and sweet SOUTH AUSTRALIANS. Also known as
Lexia. **** Setubal 20 year old, Jose Maria da Fonseca Succs £19 (TAN).

Muscat Ottonel MUSCAT variety grown in Middle and Eastern Europe.
*** 1981 Muskat Ottonel Alois Kracher £22 (NY).

Musigny (BURGUNDY, France) Potentially wonderful but more often
disappointing GRAND CRU from which CHAMBOLLE MUSIGNY takes its
name. **** 1993 Ch de Chambolle-Musigny £48 (HR).

Domaine Mussy (BURGUNDY, France) Top-class, tiny POMMARD estate with
very concentrated wines from that village, Beaune and Volnay. **** 1988
Beaune 1er Cru Montremenots £14 (HR).

Must UNFERMENTED GRAPE JUICE .

MW SEE MASTER OF WINE .

Nackenheim (RHEINHESSEN, Germany) Village in the NIERSTEIN BEREICH,
producing good wines but better known for its debased GROSSLAGE, Gutes
Domtal.

Nahe (Germany) ANBAUGEBIET producing wines which can combine delicate flavour with full body. 87 88 89 90 91 92. **** 1992 Kreuznacher Kronenberg Riesling Kabinett £4 (WSO).

Naoussa (Greece) Region producing dry red wines, often from the XYNOMAVRO grape. *** E. Tsantalissa, Naoussa, £5 (GWC).

Napa (California) Named after the American-Indian word for 'plenty', this is a region with plentiful wines ranging from ordinary to sublime. Too many are hyped; none is cheap. In the future, APPELLATIONS within NAPA, such as CARNEROS, STAGS LEAP AND MT VEEDER, and other nearby regions (like SONOMA) will take greater prominence when it is realised that parts of the county will never make spectacular wine. (red) 85 86 87 88 90 91 92 94 (white) 85 86 87 88 90 91 92 93.

Navajas (RIOJA, Spain) Small producer making reds and oaky whites worth keeping. *** 1991 Navajas Rioja Crianza Tinto £5 (DBY, WAW, MG, MOR).

Navarra (Spain) Northern DO, traditionally for ROSÉS and heavy reds but now producing better value, exciting wines, easily rivalling and often surpassing those from neighbouring RIOJA, where prices are often higher. Look out too for innovative CABERNETS and CABERNET blends. 85 86 87 88 89 90 91. *** 1992 Gran Feudo Crianza Bodegas Julian Chivite, £4 (BOO, DBY, FUL).

Nebbiolo Great red grape of Italy, producing wines which are slow to mature but become richly complex and fruity, epitomised by BAROLO and BARBARESCO aka SPANNA. Resembles the Pinot Noir in making wines whose flavour varies enormously depending on the soil in which it is grown. **** 1986 Nebbiolo, LA Cetto £9 (DBY).

Nederburg (PAARL, SOUTH AFRICA) Huge producer with plentiful commercial wines including an improving CHARDONNAY. Edelrood is a fair red blend; but the Edelkeur late harvest wines are the gems of the cellar. Sadly, the best wines are hard to find as they are only sold at the annual Nederburg Auction, one of the major events of the South African social calendar. *** 1994 Nederburg Special Late Harvest £5 (half) (DBY) **** 1988 Nederburg Private Bin 161 £11 (SEL).

Négociant (-Eléveur) (France) A MERCHANT WHO BUYS (MATURES) AND BOTTLES WINE.

Négociant-manipulant (NM) (CHAMPAGNE, France) BUYER AND BLENDER OF WINES FOR CHAMPAGNE, IDENTIFIABLE BY NM NUMBER MANDATORY ON LABEL.

Negroamaro (Italy) A Puglian grape that produces warm, gamey reds. Found in SALICE SALENTINO and COPERTINO. *** Salice Salentino Riserva 1990 Candido £6 (BU, OD).

Nelson (South Island, NEW ZEALAND) Small region, a glorious bus-ride to the north-west of MARLBOROUGH, in which NEUDORF and REDWOOD VALLEY make increasingly impressive wines.

Nemea (Peleponnese, Greece) Improving cool(ish) climate region for reds made from the Agiorgitiko grape. *** 1992 Boutari Nemea £3.50 (DBY).

Neuchâtel (Switzerland) Lakeside region. Together with Les Trois Lacs a source of good red and rosé, PINOT NOIR and CHASSELAS and CHARDONNAY whites. Good producers include Château d'Auvernier and Porret.

Neudorf (NELSON, NEW ZEALAND) Pioneering small-scale producer of beautifully made CHARDONNAY, SEMILLON, RIESLING and PINOT NOIR. **** 1994 Moutere Semillon, £10 (ADN, SEL, SOM).

Neusiedlersee (Austria) BURGENLAND region on the Hungarian border, source of great late harvest wines and increasingly good whites and reds. See WILLI OPITZ . **** 1992 Eiswein Neusiedlersee Weinkellerei Burgenland £7 (OD, U).

Nevers (France) SUBTLEST OAK – FROM A FOREST IN BURGUNDY.

New South Wales (Australia) Major wine-producing state which is home to the famous HUNTER VALLEY, along with the COWRA, MUDGEE, ORANGE and MURRUMBIDGEE regions.

New York State (US) See FINGER LAKES and LONG ISLAND.

New Zealand Superstar nation with proven SAUVIGNON BLANC and CHARDONNAY and increasingly successful reds.

Newton Vineyards (NAPA, California) High altitude vineyards with top-class CHARDONNAY, MERLOT and CABERNET which are now being made with help from MICHEL ROLLAND (look for the unfiltered examples). **** 1993 Newtonian Chardonnay £8 (DBY, TH, WR, BU).

Ngatarawa (HAWKES BAY, New Zealand) A small superstar winery with impressive reds and even better CHARDONNAYS and LATE HARVEST whites. (The 'g' is silent by the way and the emphasis is on the second 'a').

Nicholson River (GIPPSLAND, Australia) The temperamental GIPPSLAND climate ensures that this estate has a frustratingly small production, however its efforts have been repaid over and over by stunning CHARDONNAYS.

Niebaum Coppola (NAPA, California) You've read the book and seen the movie. Now taste the wine. The *Dracula* and *Godfather* director's own estate which now includes the appropriately Gothic Inglenook winery also has some of the oldest vines in the state and makes intensely concentrated CABERNETS to suit those of a patient disposition. **** 1990 Cabernet Franc £8 (RD) **** 1982 Rubicon £16 (RD).

Niederhausen Schlossböckelheim (NAHE, Germany) State-owned estate producing highly concentrated RIESLING from great vineyards. **** 1993 Niederhauser Hermannsberg Riesling Spätlese £10 (L&W).

Niepoort (DOURO, Portugal) Small, independent, port house making subtle vintage and particularly impressive COLHEITA tawnies. A name to watch. **** 1987 LBV Port £11 (BI) **** 1978 Colheita £20 (BI).

Nierstein (RHEINHESSEN, Germany) Village and (with PIESPORT) BEREICH best known in the UK. Some very fine wines, obscured by the notoriety of the reliably dull GÜTES DOMTAL. 83 85 88 89 90 91 92 93. **** 1993 Niersteiner Pettenthal Riesling Auslese W.G. Metternich £7 (A).

Nikolaihof (Niederösterreich, Austria) Producer of some of the best GRUNER VELTLINERS and RIESLINGS in Austria.

Nitra (SLOVAKIA) Promising hilly region, especially for PINOTS BLANC, GRIS and NOIR. *** St Laurent, Nitra Winery/Carl Reh £3 (HCK, TH, WR, BU).

Nobilo (Huapai, NEW ZEALAND) Family-owned firm making good OAKY CHARDONNAY from GISBOURNE (to be found on British Airways) and a pleasant commercial off-dry White Cloud blend. *** 1993 White Cloud £5 (AV, CWS, MWW) **** 1991 Dixon Vineyard Chardonnay £9 (AV).

Noble rot POPULAR TERM FOR BOTRYTIS CINEREA.

North-East Victoria (Australia) The region to find the liqueur-MUSCAT producers of RUTHERGLEN and GLENROWAN, including MORRIS, CHAMBERS and BAILEYS as well as BROWN BROTHERS and their pioneering cooler climate vineyards.

Nose SMELL.

Nouveau NEW WINE, MOST POPULARLY USED OF BEAUJOLAIS.

Nuits St Georges (BURGUNDY, France) Commune producing the most CLARET-like of red Burgundies, properly tough and lean when young but glorious in age. Whites are good but ultra-rare. 82 83 85 88 89 90 92. *** 1982 Nuits St Georges Louis Jadot £13 (M&S) **** 1991 Domaine de l'Arlot Clos des Forêts £25 (ABY, L&W).

Nuragus di Cagliari (SARDINIA, Italy) Good value, tangy distinctively floral wine from the Nuragus grape. **** 1994 Dolianova £4 (L&W, W, D, V&C).

NV NON-VINTAGE, MEANING A BLEND OF WINES FROM DIFFERENT YEARS.

Oaky FLAVOUR IMPARTED BY OAK CASKS WHICH WILL VARY DEPENDING ON THE SOURCE OF THE OAK (AMERICAN IS MORE OBVIOUSLY SWEET THAN FRENCH). WOODY IS USUALLY LESS COMPLIMENTARY.

Ochoa (NAVARRA, Spain) New-wave producer of fruitily fresh CABERNET, TEMPRANILLO and VIURA. **** 1986 Navarra Gran Reserva £9 (DWS, MTL) **** 1991 Tempranillo £6 (MWW).

Ockfen (MOSEL-SAAR-RUWER, Germany) Village producing some of the best, steeliest, wines of the SAAR-RUWER BEREICH, especially Rieslings from the Bockstein vineyard. *** 1992 Ockfener Scharzberg Riesling, Rheinart £4 (RTW).

Oechsle (Germany) SWEETNESS SCALE USED TO INDICATE THE SUGAR LEVELS IN GRAPES OR WINE.

Oenology/ist THE STUDY OF THE SCIENCE OF WINE AND THOSE WHO ADVISE WINEMAKERS.

Oeste (Portugal) Western region in which a growing number of fresh, light, commercial wines are being made, of which the most successful has undoubtedly been ARRUDA. *** Arruda, NV £3 (JS).

Oesterich (RHEINGAU, Germany) Source of good RIESLING. **** 1988 Hochheim, Deinhard Heritage Collection £7 (CNL).

Oidium INSIDIOUS FUNGAL INFECTION OF GRAPES, CAUSING THEM TO TURN GREY AND SHRIVEL.

Olarra (RIOJA, Spain) Unexceptional producer whose whites are pleasantly adequate. *** 1990 Sainsbury's Rioja Crianza Bodegas Olarra £4 (JS).

Olasz Rizling (HUNGARY) Term for the inferior WELSCHRIESLING.

Oloroso (JEREZ, Spain) STYLE OF FULL-BODIED SHERRY, DRY OR SEMI-SWEET **** Waitrose Solera Jerezana Dry Oloroso, Lustau £5 (W) ***** Matusalem Old Oloroso, Gonzalez Byass £19 (MTL, DBY).

Oltrepò Pavese (Italy) LOMBARDY DOC made from grapes including the characterfully spicy-fruity red Gutturnio and the local white Ortrugo. Fugazza is the most famous producer.

Omar Khayyam (Maharashtra, India) CHAMPAGNE-METHOD wine that has more than novelty value – but drink it young. The producer's cheeky name – 'Champagne India' – is a source of considerable annoyance to the Champenois but they, in the shape of Piper Heidsieck, were happy enough to sell the Indians their expertise. Besides, Moët and Mumm still shamelessly sell their South American wines as 'Champaña' and 'Champanha', so they're playing off a pretty weak wicket. *** Omar Khayyam £7 (DBY, NY).

Ontario (Canada) The best wine region in Canada. Look out for bottles with VQA stickers which guarantee quality and provenance. **** 1992 Klose Vineyard Chardonnay, Inniskillin Wines £10 (AV).

Willi Opitz (Austria) Odd-ball petfood manufacturer-turned-producer of a magical mystery tour of LATE HARVEST and straw-dried wines, including an extraordinary BOTRYTIS red wittily labeled 'Opitz One'. ***** 1993 Weisser Schilfmandl Muscat Das Original £40 (T&W) ***** 1993 Opitz One (red) £30 (T&W).

Oppenheim (RHEINHESSEN, Germany) Village in NIERSTEIN BEREICH best known, though often unfairly, for unexciting wines from the Krottenbrunnen. Elsewhere produces soft wines with concentrated flavour. 76 83 85 86 88 89 90 91 92. **** 1992 Weingut Kuhling-Gillot Oppenheimer Sacktrager Riesling £14 (WSC).

Opus One (NAPA, California, US) CLARET-like co-production between MOUTON ROTHSCHILD and ROBERT MONDAVI. Classy and very claret-like wine; decidedly more successful so far than DOMINUS – but it will have to be. The latter wine is still produced in rented space in another producer's winery, while the recently completed OPUS ONE winery, excavated into land to the side of the main road through NAPA, has been described as the world's most expensive hole in the ground. Mind you they never suspected they'd hit water down there. **** 1991 £41 (CNL, DBY, HAR, PRG, BEN).

Orange (NEW SOUTH WALES, Australia) (Very) recently developed coolish region which, with Cowra, is likely to eclipse the Hunter Valley as a major quality wine region of this state. For a taste of things to come, try the classy and quite European style Orange Chardonnay made by Philip Shaw of Rosemount from vineyards of which he is the proud co-owner. **** 1994 £8 (JS, M&S).

> **Orange Muscat** Yet another highly eccentric member of the MUSCAT family, this is the one which is best known for dessert wines in California and VICTORIA, including the delicious BROWN BROTHERS Late Harvest Orange Muscat & Flora. *** 1993 Late Harvest Orange Muscat & Flora, Brown Brothers £6 (OD, U, MWW, TH, FUL) **** 1994 Essencia, Quady Winery £6 (THP, HLV, ES).

Oregon (US) Fashionable cool-climate wine-producing state best known for endearingly bearded, be-sandled winemakers, at least a few of whom have been known to grow marijuana as keenly as their speciality, PINOT NOIR. Of the latter, with the exception of the DOMAINE DROUHIN, few examples surpass a good producer's basic BOURGOGNE Rouge, despite the high price. The CHARDONNAYS are even less successful, thanks to the planting of a late-ripening CLONE as recommended by experts from California. A conspiracy theorist might suspect inter-state sabotage. 83 85 86 87 88 90 91 92. **** 1992 Domaine Drouhin Oregon Pinot Noir £17 (OD, MWW).

Oriachovitza (BULGARIA) Major source of (fairly) reliable CABERNET SAUVIGNON and MERLOT. 87 88 89 90 91. *** 1991 Reserve Oriachovitza Cabernet Sauvignon Reserve Menada Stara Zagora £3 (A, FUL, WMK, THP).

Orlando (SOUTH AUSTRALIA) Huge, French-owned (Pernod-Ricard) producer of the world-beating and surprisingly reliable Jacob's Creek wines. The RF range is good, but the Gramps, Flaxmans, Lawsons and Jacaranda Ridge wines are undoubtedly the ones to look for. ***** 1988 Jacaranda Ridge Cabernet Sauvignon £18 (OD).

Orléanais (LOIRE France) A vineyard area around Orléans in the Central Vineyards region of the LOIRE, specialising in unusual white blends of CHARDONNAY and PINOT GRIS, and reds of PINOT NOIR and CABERNET FRANC. **** Vin d'Orléanais Blanc, Covifruit 1993 £5 (YAP) *** 1993 Rouge £5 (YAP).

Ornellaia (TUSCANY, Italy) BORDEAUX-blend SUPER TUSCAN from the brother of Pierro ANTINORI. Serious wine worth maturing for another few years. ***** 1992 £26 (EWC).

Orvieto (Italy) White Umbrian DOC responsible for a quantity of dull wine. Orvieto Classico is better. Look out for SECCO if you like your white wine dry; AMABILE if you have a sweet tooth. 89 90 91 92. *** 1994, Orvieto Classico Scambia £5 (Bl).

Osbourne (JEREZ, Spain) Producer of a good range of sherries including a brilliant Pedro Ximenez. **** Fino Quinta £6 (HBR) **** Amontillado Solera £17 (HBR).

Domaine Ostertag (ALSACE, France) Poet and philosopher Andre Ostertag presides over this superb Alsace Domaine. **** 1992 Gewürztraminer Fronholz £11 (M&V).

Overgaauw (STELLENBOSCH, South Africa) MERLOT pioneer who also makes Overtinto 'port', one of the best fortified wines in the Cape. *** 1994 Sylvaner £4 and **** 1989 Merlot £5 (FTH).

Oxidation THE EFFECT (USUALLY DETRIMENTAL, OCCASIONALLY – AS IN SHERRY – INTENTIONAL) OF OXYGEN ON WINE.

Oyster Bay (MARLBOROUGH, New Zealand) See DELEGATS.

Paarl (South Africa) Warm region in which BACKSBERG and BOSCHENDAL make a wide range of appealing wines. Hotter and drier than neighbouring STELLENBOSCH. *** 1994 Paarl Heights Colombard, Boland Wynkelder £3 (BOO, DBY, POR).

Pacherenc-du-Vic-Bilh (South-West, France) Dry or fairly sweet white wine made from the PETIT and GROS MANSENG. A speciality of MADIRAN growers. Very rarely seen, worth trying. **** 1988 Pacherenc-du-Vic-Bilh Collection Plaimont £5 (EP).

Padthaway (SOUTH AUSTRALIA) Vineyard area just north of COONAWARRA specialising in CHARDONNAY and SAUVIGNON, though reds work well here too. 86 87 88 90 91 92. **** 1993 St Hilary Chardonnay, Orlando Wines £8 (DBY) **** 1992 Lindemans Padthaway Chardonnay £8 (TH, WR, ABY, DBY).

Pagadebit di Romagna (EMILIA-ROMAGNA, Italy) Dry, sweet and fizzy whites from the plummy Pagadebit grape. **** 1993 Celli £5 (WSC).

Pais Very basic Chilean red grape and its wine. Rarely exported.

Bodegas Palacio (RIOJA, Spain) Underrated bodega with stylish fruit-driven reds and distinctively oaky whites. *** 1993 Rioja Cosme Palacio £5 (OD).

Palate THE TASTE OF A WINE.

Palatinate (Germany) Obsolete term for the RHEINPFALZ.

Palazzo Altesi (TUSCANY, Italy) Oaky Super Tuscan made from pure Sangiovese by ALTESINO. **** 1990 Altesino Palazzo Altesi Rosso £15 (DBY).

Pale Cream (Spain) HEAVILY SWEETENED PALE SHERRY WHICH ALLOWS BRISTOL CREAM FANS TO LOOK AS THOUGH THEY'RE SIPPING TIO PEPE. *** Tesco Finest Solera Pale Cream Sherry, Sanchez Romate £5 (TO).

Palette (PROVENCE, France) AC rosé and light white, well liked by holidaymakers in Nice, St Tropez and Cannes who are so used to paying a fiver for a coffee that they don't notice paying more for a pink wine than a serious claret. *** 1992 Ch Simone £16 (YAP).

Palliser Estate (MARTINBOROUGH, NEW ZEALAND) Source of classy SAUVIGNON BLANC and CHARDONNAY from the up-and-coming region of MARTINBOROUGH. **** 1994 Sauvignon Blanc £9 (DBY, TH, ABY) **** 1993 Chardonnay, Martinborough £11 (ABY, DBY).

Ch Palmer (BORDEAUX, France) Wonderfully perfumed Third Growth MARGAUX which stands alongside the best of the MEDOC and often outclasses its more highly ranked neighbours. The 1983s are a good buy – more than can be said for most MEDOCS of that vintage. 82 83 85 86 88 89 90. ***** 1989 £35 (BI).

Palo Cortado (Spain) A rare SHERRY wine pitched between an AMONTILLADO and an OLOROSO. **** Tesco Superior Palo Cortado, Sanchez Romate £4 (TO).

Palomino (Spain/SOUTH AFRICA) White grape responsible for virtually all fine Sherries – and almost invariably dull white wine, when unfortified.

Parellada (Spain) Dullish grape used for CAVA. At its best in TORRES' Viña Sol, but more thanks to winemaking than any innate quality.

Dom Parent (BURGUNDY, France) POMMARD-based grower/NEGOCIANT with claims to be the oldest in the world to have remained in the hands of the same family – and certainly the only one to include Thomas Jefferson among its former clients. Wines are quite old-fashioned too, but attractively so in their fruit-packed way. *** 1986 Pommard Premier Cru Les Epenots £12 (F&M).

Pasado/Pasada (Spain) TERM APPLIED TO OLD OR FINE FINO AND AMONTILLADO SHERRIES. WORTH SEEKING OUT.**** Sainsburys Manzanilla Pasada, Vinicola Hidalgo £3 (half) (JS).

C J Pask (HAWKES BAY, NEW ZEALAND) CABERNET pioneer with good CHARDONNAY and SAUVIGNON. **** 1993 Cabernet/Merlot £8 (L&W, SHJ) *** 1993 Chardonnay £8 (L&W, SHJ).

Paso Robles (San Luis Obispo, California) Warmish, long-established region, good for ZINFANDEL, RHONE and Italian varieties. Plus increasingly successful CHARDONNAYS and PINOTS. Watch this space. *** 1993 Wild Horse Chardonnay £9 (OD). *** 1990 Wild Horse Pinot Noir £8 (OD).

Pasqua (VENETO, Italy) Producer whose wines are fairly priced and among the most reliable and fairly priced in the region. *** 1994 Chardonnay del Veneto £3.50 (MWW).

Passetoutgrains (BURGUNDY, France) Wine supposedly made of two-thirds GAMAY, one-third PINOT NOIR – though few producers respect these proportions. Once the Burgundians' daily red – until they decided to sell it and drink cheaper wine from other regions. 86 87 88 90 92. **** 1992 Bourgogne Passetoutgrains £6.50 (M&V).

Passing Clouds (BENDIGO, Australia) 'We get clouds here, but it never rains...' Despite what some may find a fairly hideous label, this is one of Australia's most serious red blends. A wine worth keeping. **** 1990 Shiraz/Cabernet £10 (ADN).

Passito (Italy) SWEET RAISINY WINE, USUALLY MADE FROM SUN-DRIED GRAPES. NOW BEING USED IN AUSTRALIA BY PRIMO ESTATE. **** 1993 Passito Di Pantelleria, Carlo Pellegrino & C. Spa £10 (W, BH, WSO).

Frederico Paternina (RIOJA, Spain) Ernest Hemingway's favourite bodega – which is just about the only reason to buy its wine nowadays. (Just think how much ongoing publicity it would be enjoying if his daughter had been conceived after a bottle of Rioja rather than Margaux.)

Luis Pato (BAIRRADA, Portugal) One of Portugal's rare superstar winemakers, proving, among other things, that the BAGA grape can make first class spicy, berryish reds. **** 1991 Quinta do Riberinho Tinto £5 (ADN) *** 1991 João Pato £6.50 (BU).

Patriarche Huge merchant whose name is not a watchword for great BURGUNDY. The Château de Meursault domaine however, produces good MEURSAULT, Bourgogne Blanc, VOLNAY and Beaune. **** 1992 Volnay Clos Des Chênes, Domaine du Château de Meursault £15 (HAR, BOO).

Pauillac (BORDEAUX, France) One of the four famous 'communes' of the MEDOC, Pauillac is the home of Châteaux LATOUR , LAFITE and MOUTON-ROTHSCHILD as well as the two PICHONS and LYNCH BAGES. The epitome of full-flavoured, blackcurrant BORDEAUX; very classy (and expensive) wine. 78 79 81 82 83 85 86 88 89 90.

Pauly-Bergweiler (MOSEL-SAAR-RUWER, Germany) Ultra-modern winery with good, modern RIESLING.

Ch Pavie (BORDEAUX, France) Classy, impeccably made, plummily rich but complex ST. EMILION wines. The neighbouring Pavie Decesse is similar but a shade less impressive. A good 1994. 82 83 85 86 88 89 90 91. ***** 1985 £35 (NIC).

Pécharmant (South-west, France) In the BERGERAC area, producing light, BORDEAUX-like reds. Worth trying. 85 86 88 89 90 91. **** 1992 Ch Tiregand £6 (JS).

Pedro Ximenez (PX) White grape, dried in the sun for sweet, curranty wine and used in the production of the sweeter sherry styles favoured by Britain's diminishing band of sherry drinkers. Also produces a very unusual wine at DE BORTOLI in Australia ***** Cream of Cream Sherry, Argueso Valdespino £9 (SAF).

Pelorus (New Zealand) Showy New Zealand fizz. See CLOUDY BAY.

Pelure d'Oignon (France)'ONION SKIN'; ORANGEY-BROWN TINT OF SOME ROSE.

Penedés (Spain) Largest DOC of Catalonia with varying altitudes, climates and styles. Table wines are improving disappointingly slowly, however, despite the early example of TORRES. More importantly, this is the centre of the CAVA industry. **** 1989 Torres Gran Sangre de Toro £7(WR, TWB, U, BU) *** Somerfield Cava, Conde de Caralt £5 (SMF).

Penfolds (South Australia) The world's biggest premium wine company with a high quality range at every price level. Previously a red wine specialist but rapidly proving equally skilful with whites. (Also owns WYNNS, Seaview, ROUGE HOMME, LINDEMANNS, Tullochs, Leo Buring SEPPELT, Uncle Tom Cobbley and all). ***** 1988 Grange Bin 95 £46.50 (ADN, MWW) ***** Bin 707 Cabernet Sauvignon 1991 £15 (TO, U) **** 1992 Coonawarra Cabernet Sauvignon £9 (BOO, DBY, VW, SMF, OD). **** 1992 Chardonnay £7 (TH, MWW, OD, FUL, WR).

Penley Estate (SOUTH AUSTRALIA) High Quality COONAWARRA estate with rich Chardonnay and very blackcurranty Cabernet ***** 1991 Penley Estate Cabernet Sauvignon £9 (AUC).

le Pergole Torte (TUSCANY, Italy) Long-established pure SANGIOVESE, oaky SUPER TUSCAN. **** 1988 Montevertine £25 (V&C).

Periquita (Portugal) Spicy, tobaccoey grape – and the wine J M DA FONSECA makes from it. **** 1991 £4 (TO, OD, WR, W, MWW).

Perlé/Perlant (France) LIGHTLY SPARKLING.

Perlwein (Germany) SPARKLING WINE.

Pernand-Vergelesses (BURGUNDY, France) Commune producing rather jammy reds but fine whites, including some of the best buys on the COTE D'OR. 82 83 85 88 89 90 92. **** 1992 Blanc, Olivier Leflaive £9 (ADN) **** 1988 1er Cru Rouge Ile des Vergelesses, Dom. Chandon des Briailles £12 (HR).

André Perret (RHONE, France) Producer of notable CONDRIEU and decent ST JOSEPH. **** 1994 Condrieu Coteaux de Chery £19 (ADN).

Perrier-Jouët (CHAMPAGNE France) Currently underperforming Champagne house which coincidentally belongs, like that of other underperformer MUMM, to Canadian distillers Seagram. Sidestep the non-vintage for the genuinely worthwhile – and brilliantly packaged – Belle Epoque prestige fizz. **** 1988 Perrier Jouet £20 (OD).

Pesquera (RIBERA DEL DUERO, Spain) US guru Robert Parker dubbed this the CH PETRUS of Spain. Well, maybe. Others might just say that it's a top class TEMPRANILLO often equal to VEGA SICILIA and the best of RIOJA. **** 1990 Tinto, Alejandro Fernandez £11 (C&B). **** 1992 Pesquera, Fernandez £10 (OD)

Pessac-Léognan (BORDEAUX, France) GRAVES Commune containing most of the finest chateaux. 82 83 85 86 88 89 90. Try CHATEAU FIEUZAL, DOMAINE DE CHEVALIER, LA LOUVIERE or **** 1992 Ch. Haut Lagrange £8 (OD).

Petaluma (ADELAIDE HILLS, SOUTH AUSTRALIA) High-tech creation of BRIAN CROSER, Australia's top winemaker. Top class CHARDONNAYS from Piccadilly, high in the ADELAIDE HILLS, CLARE RIESLINGS (particularly good when LATE HARVEST) and CABERNETS made in COONAWARRA – and, in the case of the 'Sharefarmers' on the wrong side of the Coonawarra fence. **** 1992 Coonawarra Red £11 (OD, TH) **** 1993 Petaluma Chardonnay £11 (OD, TH).

Pétillant LIGHTLY SPARKLING.

Petit Chablis (BURGUNDY, France) (Theoretically) less fine than plain CHABLIS. 85 86 87 88 89 90 91. *** 1993 Petit Chablis, Domaine Jean Goulley £7 (WR, BU).

Petit château (BORDEAUX, France) LOOSE TERM FOR MINOR PROPERTY, SUPPOSEDLY BENEATH CRU BOURGEOIS.

Petit Verdot (France) Spicy, tannic, hard-to-ripen variety used in minute proportions in red BORDEAUX and (rarely) California.

Ch. Petit Village (BORDEAUX, France) Classy, intense blackcurranty-plummy POMEROL. Worth keeping. 82 85 86 87 89 90. **** 1989 £35 (J&B).

Petite Sirah Red grape, aka DURIF in the MIDI and grown in California. Nothing to do with the SYRAH but can produce very good, spicy red (neat or in blends by good producers like RIDGE and FETZER). See also MORRIS in Australia. **** 1991 L.A.Cetto Petite Sirah £5 (CEL, TAN, CWS, EP, THP).

Petrolly A NOT UNPLEASANT OVERTONE OFTEN FOUND IN MATURE RIESLING.

Ch Pétrus (BORDEAUX, France) Priciest (but best?) of all clarets. Ultra-concentrated voluptuous JP MOUEIX POMEROL hits the target especially well in the USA and Belgium. 82 83 85 88 89 90. **** 1988 £100 (C&B).

Pfaffenheim (ALSACE, France) Fast improving ALSACE Co-op which is already hitting the big time. **** 1992 Riesling, Hornstein £5 (ADN) **** 1992 Gewürztraminer, Hornstein £6 (ADN).

Pfalz (Germany) See RHEINPFALZ.

Pfeffingen (RHEINPFALZ, Germany) Good source of impeccably made RIESLING and SCHEUREBE.

Joseph Phelps (NAPA, California) Innovative winery – one of the first to introduce RHONE varieties (SYRAH and VIOGNIER) and a rare producer of late harvest RIESLING. The Insignia and Eisele CABERNETS are good, if tough. **** 1990 Le Mistral £14 (L&W) **** 1993 Viognier £12 (L&W).

Philipponnat (CHAMPAGNE, France) Small producer famous for Clos des Goisses but notable for Vintage and rosé. ***** 1988 Grand Blanc £27 (WAV) **** Le Reflet Brut £23 (WAV).

Phylloxera Vastatrix DASTARDLY LOUSE THAT WIPED OUT EUROPE'S VINES IN THE 19TH CENTURY. FOILED BY THE PRACTICE OF GRAFTING VINIFERA VINES ONTO RESISTANT AMERICAN ROOTSTOCK. ISOLATED POCKETS OF PRE-PHYLLOXERA AND/OR UNGRAFTED VINES STILL EXIST IN FRANCE (IN A VINEYARD BELONGING TO BOLLINGER AND ON THE SOUTH COAST – THE LOUSE HATES SANDY SOIL), PORTUGAL (IN QUINTA DA NOVAL'S 'NACIONAL' VINEYARD) AUSTRALIA AND CHILE. ELSEWHERE, A NEW BREED – 'PHYLLOXERA B' – IS SO DEVASTATING AREAS OF CALIFORNIA THAT NAPA VALLEY GROWERS WHO (MOSTLY) PLANTED ON INSUFFICIENTLY RESISTENT ROOTSTOCK WILL HAVE TO REPLANT UP TO 90% OF THEIR VINES. WHICH, THOUGH TRAGIC FOR A GREAT MANY QUALITY-CONSCIOUS PRODUCERS OUGHT TO TEACH THE OVER-CONFIDENT SCIENTISTS AT THE UNIVERSITY OF CALIFORNIA A LESSON IN HUMILITY. MAYBE NEXT TIME THEY WON'T DISREGARD WARNINGS FROM THE FRENCH.

Piave (VENETO, Italy) DOC in VENETO region, including reds made from a BORDEAUX-like mix of grapes. 88 89 90 91 92 93.

Ch Pichon Longueville (BORDEAUX, France) An under-performing Second Growth PAUILLAC until 1988. Aka Pichon Baron. Following purchase by the giant AXA insurance company (which now owns CH SUDUIRAUT, CLOS DE L'ARLOT, CANTENAC BROWN, PETIT VILLAGE and QUINTA DA NOVAL) and the arrival of Jean-Michel Cazes and winemaker Daniel Lioze, has moved it right into the front line, alongside and sometimes ahead of CH PICHON-LALANDE, once the other half of the estate. Wines are intense and complex. LYNCH BAGES tastes great – and remains great value – until you see what the same winemaker achieves here with better-sited vines. Les Tourelles, the second label, is often a good value alternative. 85 86 88 89 90. **** 1992 £11 (MTL, WR).

Ch Pichon-Lalande (BORDEAUX, France) Famed 'Super Second' still often referred to as Pichon Longueville (Comtesse de) Lalande. A tremendous success story, thanks to the unswerving efforts of its owner, Mme de Lenquesaing, top class winemaking and the immediate appeal of its unusually high MERLOT content. Classy, long-lived wine, back on form after the departure of the winemaker M Godin. **** 1990 £30.50 (BI).

Piedmont/Piemonte (Italy) Increasingly ancient-and-modern north-western region producing old-fashioned, tough, tannic BAROLO and BARBARESCO and increasing amounts of brilliant new-style, fruit-packed wines. Also the source of OLTREPO PAVESE, ASTI SPUMANTE and DOLCETTO D'ALBA. **** 1994 Chardonnay del Piemonte Vino da Tavola, Giordano £4 (M&S) **** Asti Spumante, Sperone £5 (U) *** 1989 Barolo, Terre del Barolo £7 (DBY, CWS).

Pieropan (Italy) SOAVE's top producer who more or less invented single vineyard wines here. *** 1994 Soave Classico, Pieropan £7 (EWC) **** 1990 Recioto di Soave, Le Colombare (half) £11 (L&W).

Pierro (MARGARET RIVER, Australia) Small estate with superlative, MEURSAULT-like CHARDONNAY. One of the classiest in the Antipodes, and a name to watch.

Piesport (MOSEL-SAAR-RUWER, Germany) With its GROSSLAGE Michelsberg, a region infamous for dull German wine bought by people who think themselves above LIEBFRAUMILCH. Try a single vineyards – Guntersley or Goldtroppchen – for something more memorable. 85 86 87 88 89 90 91 92. **** 1990 Piesporter Goldtropfchen Riesling Auslese, Reichsgraf von Kesselstatt £10 (MWW) ****1993 Piesporter Goldtropfchen Kabinett £5 (L&W).

Pikes (SOUTH AUSTRALIA) Top class estate in CLARE with especially good RIESLING and SHIRAZ. and unusually successful SAUVIGNON. A name to follow. **** 1992 Pikes Sauvignon Blanc £7 (JAR).

Pineau de la Loire (Loire, France) Local name for the CHENIN BLANC grape.*** 1993 Pineau de la Loire, Oisly et Thésée £5 (WSO).

Pinot Blanc Never quite as classy or complex as PINOT GRIS or CHARDONNAY, but fresh, creamy and adaptable: a bit like CHARDONNAY without all that fruit flavour. Widely grown, at its best in ALSACE (PINOT D'ALSACE), the ALTO ADIGE, elsewhere in Italy (as Pinot Bianco), and in Germany and Austria (as Weissburgunder). In California, a synonym for MELON DE BOURGOGNE and quite widely planted in Eastern Europe. **** 1992 Pinot Blanc, Zind Humbrecht £7 (LV, TH, ABY) **** 1992 Pinot Bianco 'Haberlehof', Alois Lageder £9 (EWC).

Pinot Chardonnay Misleading name for CHARDONNAY. Still used by TYRRELLS in Australia. Do not confuse with Pinot-Chardonnay, which is a description of a sparkling blend of PINOT NOIR and CHARDONNAY.

Pinot Gris White grape of uncertain origins, making full, rather heady, spicy wine. Best in ALSACE (also known as TOKAY D'ALSACE), Italy (as PINOT GRIGIO) and Germany (as Rülander or Grauburgunder). **** 1993 Sainsburys Pinot Grigio, Atesino, GIV £3.50 (JS) **** 1992 Tokay Pinot Gris Reserve Particuliere, Kuehn £7 (LV, EVI).

Pinot Meunier Dark pink-skinned grape that plays an unsung but major role in CHAMPAGNE, where it is the most widely planted variety. Grown in England as the Wrotham Pinot or Dusty Miller. BESTS in VICTORIA produce a Varietal wine from it, as, inevitably, does the wondrous Mr Grahm at BONNY DOON **** 1993 Bonny Doon £6 (OD).

Pinot Noir Black grape responsible for all of the world's greatest red BURGUNDY and in part for sparkling white CHAMPAGNE. Also grown in the New World with varying success. This depends largely on finding sites in which the climate is neither too warm (heat gives stewed plum flavours) or too cold; and winemakers with the patient dedication which might otherwise have destined them for a career in the church or psychiatric nursing. Buying PINOT NOIR is like Russian Roulette, but once you've got a taste for that complex, raspberryish flavour, you'll go on pulling that expensive trigger. See OREGON, CARNEROS, YARRA, SANTA BARBARA, BURGUNDY ***** 1992 Sanford Pinot Noir £14 (BEN, BH) ***** 1989 Gevrey Chambertin Vallet Frères £19.50 (BOO, DBY).

Pinotage Spicy PINOT NOIR x CINSAULT cross used in SOUTH AFRICA and (now very rarely) NEW ZEALAND. Good old examples are brilliant but rare; most taste muddy and rubbery. **** 1991 Simonsig Pinotage £6 (W) **** 1993 Kanonkop Pinotage £7 (TO).

Piper Heidsieck (CHAMPAGNE, France) Greatly improved Champagne, though the ultra-dry Brut Sauvage is an acquired taste and the US Piper Sonoma decidedly undistinguished. **** 1985 Champagne Piper Heidsieck, Heidsieck Cuvée Sauvage £20 (MTL).

Pipers Brook Vineyards (TASMANIA, Australia) Dr Andrew Pirie is a top class pioneering producer of CHARDONNAY, PINOT NOIR AND PINOT GRIS and a great publicist for an island mainland Aussies like to leave off maps. Ninth Island, the second label, includes an excellent unoaked CHABLIS-like CHARDONNAY. **** 1994 Chardonnay £8 (DBY, W, HOT).

Fernão Pires (Portugal) Muscatty grape, used to great effect by PETER BRIGHT of the JOAO PIRES winery.

Joao Pires (Portugal) Winemaker PETER BRIGHT shows that it is possible to make distinctive local styles using clean modern technology. Sadly, too few Portuguese producers have followed the example set by such internationally successful wines as Bright's Tinta da Anfora.

Plantagenet (MOUNT BARKER, Australia) Good producer of CHARDONNAY, RIESLING, CABERNET and lean SHIRAZ in this new region in the south-west corner of Australia. **** 1993 Omrah Vineyard Chardonnay £8 (GI, W, FDL).

Plovdiv (BULGARIA) Region for – so far – unexceptional MAVRUD, CABERNET and MERLOT. *** 1989 Cabernet Sauvignon £3 (TH, BU, WR).

Podravski (SLOVENIA) Source of dreaded LJUTOMER RIZLING and far better MUSCAT and PINOT GRIS.

Pol Roger (CHAMPAGNE, France) One of the most reliable producers, with subtle Non-Vintage, spectacular Cuvée Winston Churchill and an unusually good Demi-Sec. **** 'White Foil' Non-Vintage £20 (TO, OD, WR, MTL, BU) **** 1988 Extra Dry £27.5 (HLV, ABY, WRW)

Pomerol (BORDEAUX, France) With ST EMILION, the BORDEAUX for lovers of the MERLOT grape, which predominates in its rich, soft, plummy wines. CHATEAU PETRUS is the big name but wines like PETIT VILLAGE and CLOS RENE abound. None are cheap because production here is often limited to a few thousand cases a year (in the MEDOC, 20-40,000 is a common figure even among the big names). However, quality is far more consistent than in ST EMILION and the flavours far richer, spicier and plummier than all but the best of that larger, more disparate commune. See PETRUS and MOUEIX.

Pomino (TUSCANY, Italy) A small DOC within the CHIANTI RUFINA region and virtually a monopoly for FRESCOBALDI who make a buttery unwooded white PINOT BIANCO-CHARDONNAY, the oaky-rich Il Benefizio and a tasty SANGIOVESE-CABERNET red. **** 1991 Il Benefizio £11 (ADN).

Pommard (BURGUNDY, France) Variable quality commune, theoretically with a higher proportion of old vines, making slow-to-mature, then solid and complex reds. There is a rumoured tradition of using grapes from the less well-sited vineyards on the other side of the *route nationale*. 85 88 89 90 92. **** 1er Cru Rugiens de Courcel 1993 £19 (HR) **** 1993 1er Cru Les Jarollières, Jean Marc Boillot £19.50 (GH).

Pommery (CHAMPAGNE, France) Returned-to-form big-name with rich, full flavoured style. The top label, Louise Pommery white and rosé are both tremendous. ***** Louise Pommery Prestige Cuvée £39 (BI) **** Brut 1989 Vintage £20 (BI) **** Brut Royal £18 (BI).

Ponsot (BURGUNDY, France) Top class estate particularly for CLOS DE LA ROCHE and (rare) white MOREY ST DENIS. ***** 1991 Latricières-Chambertin £50 (L&W).

Ch Pontet-Canet (BORDEAUX, France) Rich, concentrated Fifth Growth Pauillac. 82 83 85 86 88 89 90. **** 1985 £14 (OD).

Ponzi (OREGON, USA) For some, the ideal combination: a producer of good PINOT NOIR and even better beer. Sadly, only the former can be bought in the UK.

Port (Portugal) FORTIFIED, USUALLY RED WINE MADE IN THE UPPER DOURO VALLEY. COMES IN SEVERAL STYLES; SEE **TAWNY**, **RUBY**, **LBV**, **VINTAGE**, **CRUSTED** AND **WHITE**. ***** 1990 Dow's Crusted Port, Dows £11 (BOO, ADN, W, VW) ***** 1985 Graham's Vintage Port, Grahams £21 (DBY, ES).

Pouilly Fuissé (BURGUNDY, France) White beloved by the Americans, and so sold at vastly inflated prices. POUILLY VINZELLES, POUILLY LOCHE and other MACONNAIS wines are more affordable and often just as good, though top class POUILLY FUISSE from producers like CHATEAU FUISSE Dom Noblet, or Domaine Ferret can compete with the best of the COTE D'OR. 85 86 87 88 89 90 92 93. *** 1992 Winemark, Paul Boutinot £7 (WMK) *** 1992 Pouilly Fuissé, Dom. Corsin £11 (ADN).

Pouilly Fumé (LOIRE, France) Potentially ultra-elegant SAUVIGNON BLANC with classic gooseberry fruit and 'smoky' overtones derived from flint ('Silex') sub-soil. Like SANCERRE, rarely repays cellaring. Ladoucette is the big name here, though his widely-available example of the appellation is unremarkable. If you want to see what he and the appellation can do, splash out instead on his Baron de 'L' – or buy one of our recommendations. 88 89 90 92 93. ***** 1993 'Pur Sang' Didier Dagueneau £17 (ABY) **** 1993 Domaine Jean Claude Chatelain £6 (CT).

Ch Poujeaux (BORDEAUX, France) Up-and-coming plummy-blackcurranty wine from MOULIS. 82 85 86 88 89 90. *** 1988 £10.50 (FDL).

Pourriture noble (France) SEE BOTRYTIS CINEREA or NOBLE ROT.

Prädikat (Germany) AS IN QUALITATSWEIN MIT PRADIKAT (QMP), THE HIGHER QUALITY LEVEL FOR GERMAN WINES INDICATING A GREATER DEGREE OF RIPENESS.

Precipitation THE CREATION OF A HARMLESS DEPOSIT, USUALLY OF **TARTRATE** CRYSTALS, IN WHITE WINE WHICH THE GERMANS ROMANTICALLY CALL DIAMONDS.

Premier Cru PRINCIPALLY A BURGUNDY RANKING, INDICATES WINES THAT ARE BETTER THAN PLAIN VILLAGE LEVEL AND SECOND ONLY TO A **GRAND CRU**. IN COMMUNES LIKE MEURSAULT, BEAUNE AND NUITS ST GEORGES WHICH HAVE NO GRAND CRU, THE TOP PREMIERS CRU (LIKE BEAUNE GREVES AND THEURONS, VOLNAY SANTENOTS, MEURSAULT PERRIERES, GENEVRIERES AND CHARMES AND NUITS ST GEORGES LES ST GEORGES) CAN BE GOOD ENOUGH TO LEAVE YOU WONDERING ABOUT THE SYSTEM.

Premières Côtes de Bordeaux (France) Up-and-coming riverside APPELLATION for reds and (often less interestingly) sweet whites. **** 1990 Chateau De Berbec, M Camille Brun £6 (ES, WR, OD, TH) *** Somerfield Premieres Côtes de Bordeaux, Yvon Mau £4 (SMF).

Ch Prieuré-Lichine (BORDEAUX, France) Improving Fourth Growth MARGAUX with good blackcurranty fruit. The consultant here is the great Michel Rolland, but cynics still wonder about an estate which can afford a new helicopter landing pad but which has yet to line some of its concrete tanks. 82 85 86 88 89 90 91. **** 1989 £20 (THP).

Primeur (France) NEW WINE, eg BEAUJOLAIS PRIMEUR or, as in 'en primeur' wine which is sold while still in barrel.

Primitivo di Mandura (PUGLIA, Italy) Spicy, plummy red made from the Primitivo, supposedly another name for the ZINFANDEL *** 1993 Primitivo del Salento Le Trulle, Centele/Kym Milne £4 (TO, TH, VW, SAF, OD).

Primo Estate (SOUTH AUSTRALIA) Second generation Italian immigrant Joe Grilli has created an extraordinarily imaginative venture among the fruit farms of the Adelaide Plains. His passion-fruity yet dry COLOMBARD may be the best example of this unloved grape in the world, his (tiny production) sparkling SHIRAZ, made with large doses of reserve wine produced by longer-established wineries is top class, as are the BORDEAUX-blends he makes as if he were in the VENETO, using grapes partially dried in the sun. We need more Joe Grillis, men and women who cause headaches for the big company bean-counters and official legislators who'd prefer a neat and tidily predictable world. *** 1994 Colombard £6 (AUC) **** 1992 Shiraz £7 (AUC).

Priorato (CATALONIA, Spain) Heftily alcoholic reds and (rare) whites from CARINENA and GARNACHA grapes grown in a very warm region. New wave producers are bringing a touch of class. *** 1993 Scala Dei Novell Tinto £5 (MOR).

Producteurs Plaimont (South-West, France) Extremely reliable cooperative from the Côtes de St Mont region in Armagnac producing an excellent and affordable range of BORDEAUX-lookalike reds and whites with some use of local grapes. 1993 Côtes de Saint Mont, Les Haut de Bergelle rouge £5 (L&W).

Propriétaire (Récoltant) (France) VINEYARD OWNER-MANAGER.

Prosecco di Conegliano (VENETO, Italy) Soft, sometimes slightly earthy dry and sweet sparkling wines made from the PROSECCO grape and often served from bottles containing the yeast which has made them fizz. Less boisterous than ASTI SPUMANTE and often less fizzy. An interesting taste of the past. **** Carpene Malvoti £14 (EWC).

Côtes de Provence Improving, good value fruity rosés and whites and ripe spicy reds. For some reason, a region with as much appeal to organic winemakers (like our two recommendations) as to fans of Mr Mayle's rural tales. 85 86 87 88 89 90 91. **** 1991 Terres Blanches Aurelia, Noel Michelin £7 (ABY) **** 1992 Domaine Richeaume Syrah, Henning Hoesch, £8 (VER).

Provence (France) Southern region producing a quantity of honest, country wine with a number of minor ACs. Rosé de Provence should be dry and fruity with a hint of peppery spice. **** 1990 Ch Pibarnon, Bandol £10.50 (ABY) **** 1990 Mas de Gourgonnier Reserve du Mas £7 (UBC).

J J Prüm (MOSEL-SAAR-RUWER, Germany) Top RIESLING producer with fine Wehlener vineyards. **** 1989 Wehlener Sonnenuhr Riesling Kabinett £10 (JN).

S A Prüm (MOSEL-SAAR-RUWER, Germany) Separate MOSEL estate with very respectable wines though none of the class of JJ's best.

Prunotto (Piedmont, Italy) Improving BAROLO producer recently bought by ANTINORI. **** 1989 Barolo £20 (V&C) **** 1993 Barbera d'Alba, Fiulot £6 (L&W).

Puglia (Italy) Hot region which is beginning to make some pretty cool wines thanks partly to the efforts of Flying Winemakers like Kym Milne. **** 1994 Chardonnay del Salento, Centele/Kym Milne £4 (TO, VW, OD) **** 1989 Salice Salentino, Candido £5 (EWC).

Puisseguin St Emilion (BORDEAUX, France) Satellite of ST EMILION making similar, MERLOT-dominant wines which, if drunk young, are often far better value. 85 86 88 89 90. **** 1992 Ch. Durand Laplagne £6 (ADN).

Puligny-Montrachet Aristocratic white COTE D'OR Commune that shares the MONTRACHET vineyard with CHASSAGNE. At its best, wonderfully complex buttery CHARDONNAY with a touch more elegance than Meursault. 78 79 81 83 85 86 88 89 90 92 93. ***** 1992 1er Cru Les Truffieres £24 (HR) **** 1993 1er Cru Les Folatières, Gérard Chavy et Fils £17 (OD) **** 1991 Maroslavac-Leger £15 (M&S).

Putto (Italy) As in CHIANTI Putto: wine from a consortium of growers who use the cherub (putto) as their symbol. Taken very seriously in Italy but rather less so by open-minded lovers of Italian wine elsewhere, who prefer to go by producers rather than consortia.

Puttonyos (HUNGARY) THE MEASURE OF SWEETNESS (FROM 1 TO 6) OF TOKAY. **** 1983 Tokaji Aszu 5 Puttonyos, Tokaji Hegyalja £11.50 (J&B) **** 1957 Tokaji Aszu 6 Putts £52.50 (ADN).

PX See PEDRO XIMENEZ

Pyrenees (VICTORIA, Australia) One of the classiest regions in VICTORIA, thanks to the efforts of TALTARNI and DALWHINNIE. **** 1992 Taltarni Merlot £9 (DBY).

Pyrénées Orientales (LANGUEDOC-ROUSSILLON, France) Big region including ROUSSILLON and RIVESALTES. Source of increasingly interesting VINS DE PAYS. **** 1993 Côtes de Roussillon, Domaine Gauby £5 (WR).

Pyrus see LINDEMANS.

QbA (Germany) Qualitätswein bestimmter ANBAUGEBIET: basic quality German wine meeting certain standards from one of the 11 ANBAUGEBIET, eg RHEINHESSEN.

QmP (Germany) QUALITÄTSWEIN MIT PRADIKAT: QbA WINE WITH 'SPECIAL QUALITIES' SUBJECT TO RIGOROUS TESTING. THE QmP BLANKET DESIGNATION IS BROKEN INTO FIVE SWEETNESS RUNGS, FROM KABINETT TO TROCKENBEERENAUSLESEN plus EISWEIN.

Quady (CENTRAL VALLEY, California) Quirky producer of the wittily named 'Starboard' (hint: you serve it in a decanter), the ORANGE MUSCAT Essencia, (one of the only wines to drink with chocolate), Black Muscat Elysium, and an innovative low alcohol white, Electra. Quady is also notable for being pretty well the only quality wine producer in a hot region otherwise devoted to basic JUG WINE.
**** 1988 Starboard (Batch 88) £9 (ADN, W, VW) **** 1993 Elysium £5.50-£7.50. (VW, HLV, ES, U, MWW, BBR, THP) **** Essencia 1993 £6 (MWW, ES, HLV, THP).

Qualitätswein (Germany) LOOSE 'QUALITY' DEFINITION TO COVER QbA AND QmP WINES, WHOSE LABELS WILL CARRY MORE INFORMATIVE IDENTIFICATION OF THEIR EXACT STATUS.

Quarts de Chaume (LOIRE, France) Luscious but light sweet wines, uncloying, ageing beautifully, from the COTEAUX DU LAYON. 76 83 85 88 89 90 92. **** 1989 Ch. de L'Écharderie £18 (YAP).

Queensland (Australia) The Granite Belt produces Hunter-valley style SHIRAZ and SEMILLON from (relatively) cool vineyards. Not exported.

Côtes de Quenelle (South-west France) Inspired by a comment in last year's Guide, Suzanne Brochet of the Chateau Hareng-Rouge has released the first vintage of the highly distinctive sparkling Chilecon-Carne which was described by Oz Clarke as a spicy 'gobstopper'. Wines take a while to come round but do so very attractively given time; beware though, they're not cheap. *** 1969 Nain Empoisonée £38 (COD).

Quincy (LOIRE, France) Dry SAUVIGNON, lesser-known and sometimes good value alternative to SANCERRE or POUILLY FUME. 93 94. **** 1994 Denis Jaumier £7 (YAP).

Quinta (Portugal) VINEYARD OR ESTATE, PARTICULARLY IN THE DOURO WHERE 'SINGLE QUINTA' VINTAGE PORTS ARE INCREASINGLY BEING TAKEN AS SERIOUSLY AS THE BLENDS TRADITIONALLY SOLD BY THE BIGGER PRODUCERS. FOR A COMPARATIVE TASTING OF SINGLE-QUINTA PORTS, LAY & WHEELER OFFER A RANGE OF HALF A DOZEN. **** 1984 Quinta do Panascal, Fonseca Guimaraens £16 (L&W, WR, BU).

Quinta da Bacalhôa (Portugal) the innovative CABERNET-MERLOT made by PETER BRIGHT at JOAO PIRES.

Quinta da Camarate (Portugal) Attractive CABERNET SAUVIGNON-based red from JM DA FONSECA.

Quinta da Côtto (DOURO, Portugal) Small estate producing so-so port and flavoursome table reds. **** 1994 red £6 (ADN).

Quinta de la Rosa (DOURO, Portugal) Recently established port estate producing (under guidance from David Baverstock, Australian-born former winemaker at DOWS). *** 1992 Quinta de la Rosa £5 (POR, M&V) *** 1988 Quinta de la Rosa Port £12 (M&V).

Quinta do Noval (DOURO, Portugal) Fine and potentially finer estate recently bought by AXA, the insurance company which owns CH PICHON BARON. The ultra-rare Nacional vintage ports are the jewel, made from ungrafted vines. **** 1976 Colheita (half) £11.50 (F&M, SEL) **** 1982 £18 (VW, TH, THP, F&M).

Quintarelli (VENETO, Italy) Wonderful old fashioned RECIOTO-maker producing some of the quirkiest, most sublime (and most expensive) VALPOLICELLA. ***** 1985 Recioto £30 (V&C) **** 1988 Valpolicella Classico Superiore Monte Ca Paletta 'Ripasso' £11 (ADN).

Qupé (Central Coast, California) Run by Bob Lundqvist (with Jim Clendenen, one of the founders of AU BON CLIMAT) this SANTA BARBARA winery is one of the places to find brilliant New World SYRAH. **** 1992 Syrah £10 (M&V).

Racking THE DRAWING OFF OF WINE FROM ITS LEES INTO A CLEAN CASK OR VAT.

Olga Raffault (LOIRE, France) There are several Raffaults in CHINON; Olga's is the best estate – and the best source of some of the richest, ripest examples of this appellation. **** 1990 Chinon Rouge £8 (WSO).

Raïmat (CATALONIA, Spain) Sometime superstar innovative winery founded by fizz giant, CODORNIU, in the newly recognised COSTERS DEL SEGRE region, and notable for being unusual in being allowed to use the irrigation, without which grapes could not be grown in this parched region. Now recovered from a period at the end of the 1980s when it sold inconsistent wines. MERLOT, a CABERNET-Merlot blend called Abadia and TEMPRANILLO are interesting and CHARDONNAY – both still and sparkling – has been good. **** 1990 Tempranillo £6 (DBY, TH, WR, BU) *** 1990 Merlot £6 (DBY, H&D).

Rainwater (MADEIRA) LIGHT, DRY STYLE OF MADEIRA POPULAR IN THE US.

Ch. Ramage-la-Batisse (BORDEAUX, France) Good CRU BOURGEOIS from St Laurent, close to PAUILLAC and benefitting from investment and commitment in the late 1980s. **** 1990 £10 (BOO, DBY, HOU).

Ramitello (Molise, Italy) An intensely spicy-fruity red and a creamy, citric white produced by di Majo Norante in Biferno on the Adriatic coast.

Dom Ramonet (BURGUNDY, France) This CHASSAGNE MONTRACHET grower's cellar is a Mecca for white BURGUNDY lovers the world over who queue to buy wines like the Bienvenue-Batard-Montrachet. Pure class; worth waiting for too. ***** 1993 Chassagne Montrachet £16 (OD).

Ramos Pinto (DOURO, Portugal) Family-run winery recently taken over by ROEDERER CHAMPAGNE. Vintage-dated COLHEITA tawnies are a speciality, but the VINTAGE can be good too. **** Quinta da Urtiga Vintage Character £10 (L&W).

Rancio TERM FOR THE PECULIAR YET PRIZED OXIDISED FLAVOUR OF CERTAIN FORTIFIED WINES, PARTICULARLY IN FRANCE (eg BANYULS) AND SPAIN. **** 1985 Banyuls Tradition, Domaine De Baillaury £9 (RD).

Rapitalà (SICILY, Italy) Estate producing a fresh, peary white wine from a blend of local grapes. **** Rapitalà Gran-Cru Alcano, Tenuta Di Rapitalà £10 (V&C).

Rasteau (Rhône, France) Southern village producing sound, peppery reds with rich berry fruit. The fortified MUSCAT can be good too. 86 88 89 90 91. **** 1993 Côtes du Rhône Villages, Cave de Rasteau £6 (HOL, CNL, OD).

Ch. Rausan Segla (BORDEAUX, France) For a long time an under-performing MARGAUX Second Growth, this property was brought back to life in 1983 when Jacques Théo took over, rejected half the crop and made one of the best Margaux of that vintage. The commitment and investment, not to mention the advice of the great Prof Emile Peynaud have continued to pay off and the 1990 is full of blackberry fruit and oak; one of the best buys in BORDEAUX. 82 83 85 86 88 89 90 91. **** 1988 £16 (F&M).

Raventos i Blanc (CATALONIA, Spain) Josep Raventos's ambition is to produce the best fizz in Spain, adding a small dose of CHARDONNAY to the traditional varieties of the region.

Ch de Rayne-Vigneau (BORDEAUX, France) SAUTERNES estate, located at BOMMES, producing a rich, complex wine. 76 86 90. **** 1990 £37 (NIC).

RD (CHAMPAGNE, FRANCE) RECEMMENT DEGORGEE — A TERM INVENTED BY BOLLINGER TO DESCRIBE THEIR DELICIOUS VINTAGE CHAMPAGNE, WHICH HAS BEEN ALLOWED A LONGER THAN USUAL PERIOD ON ITS LEES. OTHER PRODUCERS MAKE THEIR OWN VERSIONS BUT MAY NOT CALL THEM 'RD'. ***** 1982 Bollinger RD £48 (OD etc).

Recioto (Italy) SWEET OR DRY ALCOHOLIC WINE MADE FROM SEMI-DRIED, RIPE GRAPES. MOST USUALLY ASSOCIATED WITH **VALPOLICELLA** AND **SOAVE**.
**** 1988 Zenato Recioto Della Valpolicella Amarone Classico, Zenato £10 (TH, V&C) *** 1988 Recioto Della Valpolicella, Tedeschi (half) £6 (MWW).

Récoltant-manipulant (RM) (**CHAMPAGNE**, France) INDIVIDUAL WINEGROWER AND BLENDER, IDENTIFIED BY MANDATORY RM NUMBER ON LABEL.

Récolte (France) VINTAGE, LITERALLY 'HARVEST'.

Refosco (**FRIULI-VENEZIA GIULIA**, Italy) Red grape and its **DOC** wine, dry and full-bodied. Benefits from ageing. **** 1991 Giovanni Collavini £6 (V&C, LAV).

Regaleali (**SICILY**, Italy) Big aristocratic estate, using traditional local varieties to produce Sicily's most serious wines. **** 1993 Conte Tasca D'Almerita £6 (V&C).

Régisseur IN **BORDEAUX**, THE PERSON RESPONSIBLE FOR WINE PRODUCTION.

Régnié (**BURGUNDY**, France) Recently created tenth **BEAUJOLAIS CRU** – and a vinous exemplar of the Peter Principal which suggests that employees tend to be promoted beyond their level of competence. The wines of Regnié were perfectly respectable **BEAUJOLAIS VILLAGES**, now they have to compete with **CHIROUBLES**, **CHENAS** and the other Crus, they're generally like decent amateur sportsmen who suddenly have to play with the pros. Fortunately for Regnié, those pros often aren't on great form. 88 89 91 92 93 **** 1993 Regnié, Dom des Buyats, Marc Dudet £6 (C&B).

Reguengos (**ALENTEJO**, Portugal) One of the most important wine regions of **ALENTEJO**, just south of Redondo, next to the Spanish border. *** 1991 Adega Co-op de Reguengos de Monsaraz £4 (MOR).

Reichensteiner Recently developed white grape, popular in England (and Wales). *** 1993 Reichensteiner, Wroxeter Roman Vineyard £5 (TAN).

Reims (**CHAMPAGNE**, France) Capital town of the area and HQ of many **GRANDES MARQUES**, eg **KRUG**, **ROEDERER**.

Schloss Reinhartshausen (**RHEINGAU**, Germany) An innovative estate which has proven unusually successful with **PINOT BLANC** and **CHARDONNAY** (the latter having been introduced following a suggestion by **ROBERT MONDAVI**). The **RIESLINGS** are good too. **** Hattenheimer Hassel Riesling Kabinett 1989 £8 (JN).

Rémélluri (**RIOJA**, Spain) For most modernists, this is the nearest **RIOJA** has got to a top class, small-scale organic estate. Wines are more serious (and tannic) than most, but they're fuller of flavour too and they're built to last. Telmo Rodriguez is a young winemaker to watch. He should be cloned for the benefit of the rest of the Spanish wine industry. Recent bottlings have been slightly less consistent. Adnams has the unfiltered example which is worth seeking out. **** 1991 Reserva £9 (ADN).

Remuage (**CHAMPAGNE**, France) PART OF THE **METHODE CHAMPENOISE**, THE GRADUAL TURNING AND TILTING OF BOTTLES SO THAT THE YEAST DEPOSIT COLLECTS IN THE NECK READY FOR **DEGORGEMENT**.

Reserva (Spain) INDICATES THE WINE HAS BEEN AGED FOR A NUMBER OF YEARS SPECIFIED BY THE RELEVANT **DO**. USUALLY ONE YEAR FOR REDS AND SIX MONTHS FOR REDS AND PINKS.

Réserve (France) LEGALLY MEANINGLESS, AS IN 'RESERVE PERSONELLE', BUT IMPLYING A WINE SELECTED AND GIVEN MORE AGE.

Residual sugar TASTING TERM FOR WINES WHICH HAVE RETAINED NATURAL GRAPE SUGAR NOT CONVERTED TO ALCOHOL BY YEASTS DURING FERMENTATION. IN FRANCE 4 GRAMMES PER LITRE IS THE THRESHOLD. IN THE US, THE FIGURE IS 5 AND MANY SO-CALLED 'DRY' WHITE WINES MADE THERE CONTAIN AS MUCH AS 10. **NEW ZEALAND SAUVIGNONS** ARE RARELY BONE DRY, BUT THEIR ACIDITY IS SUFFICIENT TO BALANCE AND CONCEAL ANY RESIDUAL SUGAR.

Balthasar Ress (RHEINGAU, Germany) Classy producer who blends delicacy with concentration and understands that dry wines need to be made from ripe grapes. Other CHARTA winemakers please copy.

Retsina (Greece) Dry white wine made the way the ancient Greeks used to make it – resinating it with pine to keep it from going off. Today, it's an acquired taste for non-holidaying, non-Greeks, but give the stuff a chance by looking for the freshest examples you can find (yes, I know it's not easy when there's never a vintage indicated on the bottle, but try all the same).
*** Retsina of Attica, D Kourtakis £3.50 (Widely available).

Reuilly (LOIRE, France) (Mostly) white AC for dry SAUVIGNONS, good value, if sometimes rather earthy alternatives to nearby SANCERRE AND POUILLY FUME. Some spicy PINOT ROSE .89 90 91 92 93 *** 1993, Gérard Cordier, £7 (YAP).

Rheingau (Germany) Should produce the finest RIESLINGS of the 11 ANBAUGEBIETE, but has sadly been hijacked by producers who prefer quantity to quality and the CHARTA campaign for dry wine. There are still great things to be found, however. See KUNSTLER. 83 85 88 89 90 91 92 93.
**** 1988 Niersteiner Rehbach Riesling Auslese £7 (OWL) ***** 1992 Kiedricher Wasseros Riesling Eiswein, Robert Weil £70 (HBJ).

Rheinhessen (Germany) Largest of the 11 ANBAUGEBIETE, producing fine wines but better known for LIEBFRAUMILCH and NIERSTEINER. Fewer than one vine in 20 is now RIESLING; throughout the region, easier-to-grow varieties and lazy cooperative wineries prevail. Pick and choose to get the good stuff. 83 85 88 89 90 91 92 93. **** 1993 Niersteiner Pettenthal Riesling Auslese, W.G. Metternich, W.G. Metternich £7 (A).

Rheinpfalz/Pfalz (Germany) Formerly known as the PALATINATE, warm, southerly ANBAUGEBIET noted for riper, spicier RIESLING. 83 85 88 89 90 91 92 93. *** Co-op Spätlese £4 (CWS).

Rhine Riesling/Rheinriesling Widely used – though frowned-on by the EC — name for the noble RIESLING grape.

Rhône (France) Up-and-coming region, packed with the newly sexy GRENACHE, SYRAH and VIOGNIER. See ST JOSEPH, CROZES HERMITAGE, HERMITAGE, CONDRIEU, COTES DU RHONE, CHATEAUNEUF DU PAPE, TAVEL, LIRAC, GIGONDAS, CHATEAU-GRILLET, BEAUMES DE VENISE.

Rias Baixas (Galicia, Spain) The place to find Spain's best examples of spicy, apricotty ALBERINO.

Ribatejo (Portugal) DO area north of Lisbon whose cooperatives are clearly learning how to make highly commercial white and red wine. Traditional GARRAFEIRAS are worth watching out for too, however. 85 86 87 88 89 90.
**** Bright Brothers Fernão Pires-Chardonnay £4 (SAF) **** 1984 'Beira Mar' Garrafeira Reserva, Antonio Bernadino £6 (U).

Ribera del Duero (Spain) Watch out RIOJA; here's a region which will give you a major headache over the next few years. Traditionally known as the source of wines such as VEGA SICILIA and, more recently, PESQUERA, this is increasingly inventive country in which small estates are beginning to flourish. Look out also for BALBAS, Pedrosa and Mauro, a high quality red VINO DE LA TIERRA produced just outside this DO. 82 83 85 86 89 90.
**** 1992 Pago de Carraovejas £9 (LEA) *** 1990 Senorio de Nava Crianza, £6 (CWS, SAF, SPR).

Dom Richeaume (PROVENCE, France) One of the leading lights in the new wave of quality conscious Southern French estates, and a dynamic producer of good, earthy, organic CABERNET and SYRAH. Sadly, as with many smaller organic wineries, quality can be distinctly variable from bottle to bottle. Recommendable, nonetheless. *** 1992 Dom Richeaume Syrah £7 (SAF, VER).

Richebourg (BURGUNDY, France) Top class GRAND CRU just outside VOSNE ROMANEE with a recogniseable floral-plummy style. GROS and JAYER offer good examples, as do the following: **** 1992 Domaine Hudelot-Noellat £64 (HR) **** 1990 Domaine Romanée-Conti £p.o.a (C&B).

Max Ferd Richter (MOSEL-SAAR-RUWER, Germany) Excellent producer of fine, elegant Mosel Rieslings sourced from extremely high quality vineyards. **** 1990 Brauneberger Juffer-Sonnenuhr Riesling Spätlese £10 (SUM) *** 1992 Cuvée Constantin £5 (MWW).

Ridge Vineyards (SANTA CRUZ, California) Paul Draper is a philosopher who thinks his wines through. While his neighbours were importing French oak, he was experimenting with ways of getting better American wood – presaging their interest in it by 25 years. His Chardonnay has become a stunner and his approachable reds are to traditional DUCKHORN wines what Mozart is to Stockhausen. His fidelity to ZINFANDEL and PETITE SIRAH when both were as fashionable as starched petticoats set him firmly apart from the herd. Perhaps most importantly, Draper, and Ridge's hilltop Santa Cruz and SONOMA vineyards are living proof that the NAPA Valley does not even begin to have a monopoly on top quality California wine. *****1992 Geyserville red £17 (F&M,BEN ADN) ***** 1991 Santa Cruz Mountains Cabernet £15.50 (ADN, BEN, MWW, DBY) ***** 1991 Santa Cruz Mountains Chardonnay £15 (OD, BEN).

Riesling The noble grape producing Germany's finest offerings, ranging from light, floral everyday wines to the delights of the BOTRYTIS-affected sweet wines, which still retain their freshness after several years. Also performs well in ALSACE, CALIFORNIA, SOUTH AFRICA and Australia.
***** 1990 Piesporter Goldtröpfchen Riesling Auslese, Reichsgraf Von Kesselstatt £10 (DBY) **** 1994 Tim Knappstein Clare Valley Riesling £5 (OD) **** 1988 Niederhauser Hermannshöle Riesling, St Weinbaudomanen Schloss-Bockelheim £8.50 (VW).

Riesling Italico See ITALIAN RIESLING

Rioja (Alavesa/Alta/Baja), (Spain) Spain's best-known (though not necessarily finest) wine region and the first to get its DOC qualification, is split into three parts. The Alta produces the best wines, followed by the Alavesa, while the Baja is by far the largest. Most Riojas are blends from two or three of the regions – and of local grapes (TEMPRANILLO and the lesser quality GARNACHA for reds) and are made by large BODEGAS. Small BORDEAUX and BURGUNDY-style estates are rare, thanks to restrictive Spanish rules which require wineries to store unnecessarily large quantities of wine if they are to market it as 'Reserva' or 'Gran Reserva'. Experimentation is going on in the vineyards, including plantings of (illegal) Cabernet and (equally illegal) irrigation but with less overt enthusiasm than in neighbouring NAVARRA. REMELLURI, CONTINO and BARON DE LEY are worth watching, as is MARTINEZ BUJANDA. These and others demonstrate the unique, gentle appeal of the region's wines at its best.

Dom. Daniel Rion (BURGUNDY, France) Patrice Rion, young head of this family estate produces impeccably made NUITS ST GEORGES and VOSNE ROMANEES. **** 1992 Bourgogne Passetoutgrains £6.50 (M&V) *****1989 Vosne Romanée Premier Cru Les Beaux-Monts £27 (M&V).

Ripasso (Italy) VALPOLICELLA WHICH, HAVING FINISHED ITS FERMENTATION, IS PUMPED INTO FERMENTING VESSELS RECENTLY VACATED BY RECIOTO AND AMARONE, CAUSING A SLIGHT REFERMENTATION. THIS INCREASES THE ALCOHOL AND BODY OF THE WINE. **** 1990 Capitel San Rocco Rosso, Vino di Ripasso, Flli Tedeschi £7(LAV, WIN).

Riquewihr (ALSACE, France) Town and commune noted for RIESLING. **** 1988 Hugel, Riesling £5.50 (OWL).

Riserva (Italy) DOC WINES AGED FOR A SPECIFIED NUMBER OF YEARS – OFTEN AN UNWELCOME TERM ON LABELS OF WINES LIKE BARDOLINO WHICH ARE USUALLY FAR BETTER DRUNK YOUNG. **** 1990 Taurino Salice Salentino Riserva £5.50 (DBY, SMF).

> **Rivaner** Aka the MULLER-THURGAU – a cross between RIESLING AND SYLVANER. *** 1993 St. Ursula Rivaner Scheurebe, Hugh Ryman £3.50 (SAF).

Riverina (Australia) Irrigated NEW SOUTH WALES region which produces basic-to-good wine, much of which ends up in 'South-East Australian' blends. Late harvest SEMILLONS can, however, be spectacular. **** 1994 Kingston Estate Mataro £4 (BOO, TO) *** 1994 Aldridge Estate Semillon/ Chardonnay, Cranswick Estate £4 (OD, CPW).

Riverland (Australia) Generic name for major irrigated winegrowing regions.

Rivesaltes (MIDI, France) Fortified dessert wine of both colours, the white made from MUSCAT is lighter and more lemony than that of BEAUMES DE VENISE, the red made from GRENACHE is almost like liquid Christmas pudding and ages wonderfully. **** 1994 Dom. Brial Muscat de Rivesaltes, £3.50 (SAF).

Château de la Rivière (BORDEAUX, France) Picture-book FRONSAC property producing instantly accessible, MERLOT-dominant red wines. They aren't the classiest of fare, but they give a lot more pleasure than many a duller ST EMILION or more 'serious' (and pricier) wine from the MEDOC. 82 85 86 88 89 90. *** 1990 £8 (THP).

de Roach Vineyards (RIZLA VALLEY, California) Small winery once patronised by Humphrey Bogart, which has developed a cult following in Holland to which Mari and Tio Juana, the joint owners, frequently take trips. Individual offerings include Hashbong Reef and Stoney Hill. Styles vary widely but all are decidedly smoky, grassy and mellow. Hard to obtain in the high street. ****** 1994 Chillum-Chardonnay £78 (OZ, THC).

Robertson (SOUTH AFRICA) Up-and-coming area where the Cape's new wave of CHARDONNAYS and SAUVIGNONS are grabbing the spotlight from the MUSCATS previously the region's pride **** 1993 Danie de Wet Grey Label £5 (JS) **** 1994 Weltevrede Gewürztraminer £6 (DBY).

Rocca delle Macie (TUSCANY, Italy) Reliable if unspectacular CHIANTI producer. *** 1991 Chianti Classico £5 (V&C).

Rockford (SOUTH AUSTRALIA) Robert, 'Rocky' O'Calaghan makes great, intense BAROSSA SHIRAZ using 100-year-old vines and 50-year-old equipment. There's a mouthfilling SEMILLON, a wonderful Black SHIRAZ fizz and a magical ALICANTE BOUSCHET rosé, sadly only to be found at the winery. ***** Rockford Basket Press Shiraz 1990 £10 (ADN, FUL, OD, AUC).

Antonin Rodet (BURGUNDY, France) Good MERCUREY-based NEGOCIANT which now owns – and is improving the wines of – the Jacques Prieur domaine in MEURSAULT. **** 1991 Château de Rully Rouge £9.

Louis Roederer (CHAMPAGNE, France/MENDOCINO, California, US) Family-owned, and still one of the most reliable Champagne houses. No longer involved with the Jansz sparkling wine in TASMANIA but making good fizz – sold as 'Quartet' at the Roederer Estate in Mendocino, California **** Brut Prémière N.V. £20 (widely available) **** 1986 'Cristal' Brut £70 (OD etc) **** Quartet, Roederer Estate £13 (SEL, MWW).

Domaine de la Romanée-Conti (BURGUNDY, France) Small, exclusively GRAND CRU estate, familiarly known as the DRC by BURGUNDY buffs and others who can afford to buy some of the world's priciest red wines. The jewel in the crown is the MONOPOLE Romanée-Conti vineyard itself, though the LA TACHE runs it a close second. Both can be extraordinary, ultra-concentrated spicy wine beyond compare, as can the Romanée-St-Vivant. The RICHEBOURG, ECHEZEAUX and GRANDS ECHEZEAUX and MONTRACHET are comparable to those produced by other estates – and sold for less kingly ransoms. 1990 Romanée-Conti DRC £p.o.a. (C&B).

Romania Traditional source of sweet reds and whites, but trying to develop drier styles from classic European varieties. Flying winemakers are moving in, but progress is still quite slow. *** 1990 Safeway Romanian Special Reserve Pinot Noir £3 (SAF) **** 1994 Carl Reh Chardonnay, £3.50 (JS).

Rongopai (Te Kauwhata, NEW ZEALAND) Estate in a region of the North Island which has fallen out of favour with other producers. The speciality here is BOTRYTIS wines, but the dry SAUVIGNONS are good too. **** 1994 Sauvignon Blanc £8 (CCL).

Rosato (Italy) ROSE.

Rosé de Riceys (CHAMPAGNE, France) Rare and occasionally delicious still rosé from the PINOT NOIR made only in the ripest years by adding whole bunches to a small amount (10%) of trodden grapes and then subjecting it to MACERATION CARBONIQUE. Pricy stuff. **** 1992 Bonnet £13.50 (OD).

Rosé d'Anjou (LOIRE, France) Widely exported, usually dull semi-sweet pink from the MALBEC, GROSLOT and CABERNET FRANC. Jacques Lurton has made an interesting dry version for Safeway.

Rosemount Estate (NEW SOUTH WALES, Australia) The ultra-dynamic company which, 20 years ago, both established the northern Upper HUNTER VALLEY (previously disdained by winemakers in the Lower Hunter) and introduced the outside world to plentiful doses of oaky Hunter CHARDONNAY, including the benchmark Show Reserve. Since then, the overblown Roxburgh Chardonnay and reliably good-value blends of grapes from other areas have followed, including very impressive SYRAHS and most recently, CHARDONNAYs from the newly developed region of ORANGE. Not the Rolls Royce of Aussie wines; more the BMW. **** 1993 Cabernet Sauvignon/Shiraz £5 (JS, TO) ***** 1991 Show Reserve Syrah £8.99 (DBY, CWS) **** 1993 Orange Vineyard Chardonnay £9 (W, JS, M&S).

Rossignol-Trapet (BURGUNDY, France) Once old-fashioned, now highly recommendable, up-to-the-minute estate in GEVREY-CHAMBERTIN. ***** 1991 Chapelle-Chambertin £27 (CT).

Rosso Conero (MARCHES, Italy) Big DOC MONTEPULCIANO AND SANGIOVESE red, with a hint of bitter, herby flavour. Good value characterful stuff. **** 1992 Umani Ronchi £4 (WC, V&C).

Rosso di Montalcino (TUSCANY, Italy) Recently created DO for lighter, earlier-drinking versions of the more famous BRUNELLO DI MONTALCINO, and often better – and better value – than that wine. Good producers include Altesino, Caparzo and Fattoria dei Barbi. **** 1993 Fattoria dei Barbi £8 (V&C).

Rosso di Montepulciano (TUSCANY, Italy) Younger, lighter version of VINO NOBILE DI MONTEPULCIANO. Well-made SANGIOVESE from producers like Poliziano, AVIGNONESI, Boscarelli and Tenuta Trerose. **** Le Casalte 1993 £7 (V&C).

Rene Rostaing (RHONE, France) High-quality producer of serious NORTHERN RHONE reds. *** Côte Rôtie 1991 £20 (L&W).

Rothbury Estate (NEW SOUTH WALES, Australia) Founded by Len Evans, *Eminence Grise*, coach, Svengali, or what you will, of the Australian wine industry, this is an exemplary source of SHIRAZ, SEMILLON and improving CHARDONNAY from the HUNTER VALLEY as well as wines from nearby COWRA and even a little first class SAUVIGNON from the eastern extent of the estate which surfaces in NEW ZEALAND. ***** 1993 Shiraz £6 (L&W, OD) **** 1994 Hunter Valley Chardonnay £6 (DBY, CWS, WCR, FUL).

Alfred Rothschild (CHAMPAGNE, France) Brand name used in France by the huge MARNE & CHAMPAGNE company and nothing to do with the family of the same name. Despite their low prices, wines can be surprisingly good.

Joseph Roty (BURGUNDY, France) Superstar producer of intensely concentrated but unsubtle GEVREY-CHAMBERTIN. **** 1990 Gevrey-Chambertin Les Fontenys £25 (TVW).

Rouge Homme (SOUTH AUSTRALIA) Founded by the linguistically talented Mr Redman but now part of the huge PENFOLDS empire this is one of the most reliable producers in COONAWARRA. Reds are more successful than whites. ***** 1992 Shiraz/Cabernet £5 (FUL, BOO, DBY, AV) *** 1992 Chardonnay £7 (BOO, AV, DIR, VDV).

Georges Roumier (BURGUNDY, France) Blue chip winery with great quality at every level, from village CHAMBOLLE-MUSIGNY to the GRAND CRU, BONNES MARES and (more rarely seen) white CORTON CHARLEMAGNE . **** 1992 Chambolle-Musigny £16 (HR) **** 1991 Bonnes Mares Grand Cru £40 (HR).

Roussanne (Rhône, France) With the MARSANNE, one of the key white grapes of the northern RHONE. Producers argue over their relative merits **** 1989 'Vielles Vignes', Ch. de Beaucastel, P. Perrin £25 (ADN) **** 1994 Domaines Virginie £4 (M&S).

Armand Rousseau (BURGUNDY, France) Long-established GEVREY CHAMBERTIN estate on top form with a range of PREMIERS and GRANDS CRUS. Well-made, long-lasting wines. **** 1986 Chambertin Clos de Beze £30 (OWL) **** Charmes Chambertin 1988 £27 (OD).

Côtes du Roussillon (MIDI, France) Up and coming for red, white and rosé, though not always worthy of its AC. Côtes du Roussillon Villages is better. 85 86 88 89 90 91. *** 1994 Les Vignerons Catalans £3 (SAF) *** 1990 Domaine Gauby £9 (THP).

Rubesco di Torgiano (UMBRIA, Italy) Well made modern red DOCG; more or less the exclusive creation of LUNGAROTTI. 82 83 85 86 87 88 89 90 91. *** Lungarotti 1990 £7 (V&C).

Ruby CHEAPEST, BASIC PORT; YOUNG, BLENDED, SWEETLY FRUITY WINE. *** Asda Fine Ruby Port, Smith Woodhouse, £5.35 (A) *** Safeway Fine Ruby Port, Calem £6 (SAF).

Ruby Cabernet (California, Australia) A cross between CABERNET SAUVIGNON and CARIGNAN producing big, unsubtly fruity wines. **** 1993 Penfolds Rawsons Retreat Ruby Cabernet/Cabernet Sauvignon/Shiraz £4.50 (MTL, DBY, WR, BU).

Rudesheim (RHEINGAU, Germany) Tourist town producing, at their best, rich and powerful RIESLINGS. *** 1993 Rudesheimer Klosterberg Riesling Kabinett, Josef Leitz £9 (ADN).

Rueda (Spain) DO for clean dry pinks, whites from the local VERDEJO and a traditional, FLOR growing sherry-style wine. Progress is being led most particularly by the LURTONS and the MARQUES DE RISCAL. 82 84 85 86. *** Lurton Rueda Sauvignon 1993 £4 (OD) *** 1988 Monasterio Tinto £5 (MOR).

Ruffino (TUSCANY, Italy) Big CHIANTI producer with good top-of-the-range wines, including the reliable Cabreo VINI DA TAVOLA. *** 1988 Ruffino Cabreo Il Borgo Capitolare di Biturica £16 (V&C).

Ruinart (CHAMPAGNE France) Little-known, high quality sister company to MOET & CHANDON with a superlative BLANC DE BLANCS. **** 1986 Champagne Dom. Ruinart Blanc de Blancs £38 (BI).

Rully (BURGUNDY, France) COTE CHALONNAISE commune producing a red which has been called the 'poor man's VOLNAY'. The white mostly used to end up as CREMANT DE BOURGOGNE but today merchants like JADOT and OLIVIER LEFLAIVE use it to great effect. **** 1991 Château de Rully, Rodet £9 (JS) *** 1992 Rully Rouge, Les Villeranges, Faiveley £8 (MWW).

Ruppertsberg (RHEINPFALZ, Germany) Top-ranking village with a number of excellent vineyards making vigorous, fruity RIESLING 83 85 88 89 90 91 92 93. *** 1992 Ruppertsberger Hofstuck Riesling £3 (A).

Russe (BULGARIA) Danube town best known in Britain for its reliable red blends but vaunted – in BULGARIA – as a source of modern whites. *** Sainsbury's Bulgarian Country Red, Cabernet Sauvignon/Cinsault £3 (JS).

Russian Continuous SYSTEM USED BY JM DA FONSECA INTERNACIONAL WHICH PUMPS STILL WINE, YEAST AND SYRUP THROUGH A SERIES OF TANKS SLOWLY ENOUGH FOR THE YEAST BOTH TO CREATE BUBBLES IN THE WINE AND TO SETTLE ON WOODEN RACKS, ALLOWING THE LIQUID WHICH EMERGES FROM THE FINAL TANK TO BE PERFECTLY CLEAR AND FIZZY. AN APPARENTLY ELEGANT ALTERNATIVE TO CUVE CLOSE BUT NOT ONE BY WHICH MOST OTHER FIZZ-MAKERS HAVE BEEN CONVINCED.

Russian River Valley (California) Cool vineyard area north of SONOMA and west of NAPA. Ideal for apples and good fizz, as is proven by the excellent IRON HORSE who also make increasingly impressive table wines.
**** 1986 Iron Horse Sonoma Brut £16 (CEB) ****1992 Lynmar Pinot Noir £13 (OD).

Rust (Austria) Wine centre of BURGENLAND, famous for Ruster AUSBRUCH sweet white wine. *** 1981 Ruster Beerenauslese Weinkellerei Burgenland £6 (half) (SEL).

Rust-en-Vrede (SOUTH AFRICA) One of the Cape's most successful red wine producers and one of the very few to make recommendable SHIRAZ. The Tinta Baroca is good too. **** 1991 Estate Wine £13 (L&W).

Rustenberg (STELLENBOSCH, SOUTH AFRICA) Once a star producer of PINOT NOIR (by South African standards) this old estate is now best known for its CLARET-style 'Gold', its straight CABERNET and richly Burgundian CHARDONNAY. **** 1989, Rustenberg Cabernet Sauvignon £8 (L&W, AV) **** 1990 Rustenberg Gold £10 (AV).

Rutherford (California) Napa region in which some producers believed sufficiently to propose it – and its geological 'bench' – as an appellation. The jury is still out – and the application pending.

Rutherglen (N.E. VICTORIA, Australia) Hot area on the MURRAY RIVER pioneered by gold miners. Today noted for rich, MUSCAT and TOKAY dessert and port-style wines, incredibly tough reds and attempts at CHARDONNAY which are used by cool-region winemakers to demonstrate why port and light dry whites cannot be successful in the same climate.
**** 1992 Campbells Bobbie Burns Shiraz £7.50 (GNW, DIR, CPW)
**** 1991 Morris of Rutherglen Durif, Morris Wines £10 (ADN)
***** Yalumba Museum Show Reserve Rutherglen Muscat £7 (BEN, TO, VW).

Ruwer (MOSEL-SAAR-RUWER, Germany) Tributary of the MOSEL river, alongside which is to be found the ROMERLAY GROSSLAGE and includes Kasel, Eitelsbach and the great MAXIMIN GRUNHAUS estate.

Hugh Ryman Peripatetic Flying Winemaker whose team annually and extraordinarily reliably turns grapes into wine under contract (usually for UK retailers) in BORDEAUX, BURGUNDY, Southern France, Spain, Germany, CHILE, California and HUNGARY. The give-away sign of a Ryman wine is the initials HDR at the foot of the label.

Saar (MOSEL-SAAR-RUWER, Germany) The other tributary of the MOSEL river associated with lean, slatey RIESLING. Villages include Ayl Ockfen, Saarburg, Serrig and WILTINGEN. 83 84 85 86 88 89 90 91 92 93. *** 1991 Von Hövel, Oberemmel Huette Riesling £7 (OWL).

Sablet (RHONE, France) Good COTES DU RHONE village. **** 1991 Sablet La Ramillade, Ch. du Trignon £6 (TH, WR, BU).

St Amour (BURGUNDY, France) One of the 10 BEAUJOLAIS Crus – usually light and delicately fruity. 88 89 91 92 93. *** 1993 Dom. du Clos du Fief, Michel Tête £8 (L&W).

St Aubin (BURGUNDY, France) Underrated COTE D'OR village for (jammily rustic) reds and rich, nutty, rather classier white; affordable alternatives to MEURSAULT. 85 86 88 89 90 92. **** 1992 St Aubin 1er Cru Les Pucelles, Dom. Lamy Pillot £14 (JAR).

St Chinian (South-west, France) Neighbour of FAUGERES and a fellow AC in the COTEAUX DU LANGUEDOC so far producing mid-weight, good-value wines principally using the CARIGNAN. Greater things may come of the RHONE grapes now being planted here. 88 89 90 91 93. *** 1993 Domaine de Tudery £4 (M&S) *** 1992 Berloup Prestige St Chinian, Co-op de Berlou £4 (TH, WR, BU).

St Emilion (BORDEAUX, France) Large commune with very varied soils and wines. At best, sublime MERLOT-dominated CLARET; at worst dull, earthy and fruitless. Supposedly 'lesser' satellite neighbours – LUSSAC, Puisseguin, ST GEORGES etc – often make better value wine. See PAVIE, AUSONE, CANON, FIGEAC, CHEVAL BLANC. 81 82 83 85 86 88 89 90.

St Estèphe (BORDEAUX, France) Northernmost MEDOC Commune with clay soil and wines which are often a shade more rustic than those of neighbouring PAUILLAC and ST JULIEN. Tough when young but potentially very long-lived. See CALON SEGUR, COS D'ESTOURNEL, MONTROSE. 81 82 83 85 86 88 89 90.

St Georges St Emilion (BORDEAUX, France) Satellite of ST EMILION with good, MERLOT-dominant reds. 82 83 85 86 88 89 90. **** 1989 Ch Macquin-St-George £7 (ADN).

St Hallett (SOUTH AUSTRALIA) Superstar BAROSSA winery whose name has been made on wines made from century-old vines. Rich, spicily intense SHIRAZ. Big, buttery CHARDONNAY.***** Old Block Shiraz 1991 £10 (L&W, TO, RD, BOO, DBY)**** Cabernet Sauvignon/Cabernet Franc/Merlot 1992 £7 (JS, AUC, ADN, L&W)**** Chardonnay 1994 £7.50 (WR, AUC,BOO, DBY, ADN, BU).

St Hubert's (VICTORIA, Australia) Improving (since its purchase by ROTHBURY) pioneering YARRA winery with ultra-fruity CABERNET and mouthfilling CHARDONNAY. **** Cabernet Sauvignon 1993 £9 (OD).

Chateau St Jean (SONOMA, California) Named after the founder's wife, this now Japanese-owned showpiece has long been a source of good single-vineyard CHARDONNAYS and late-harvest RIESLINGS.

St Joseph (RHONE, France) Variable but potentially vigorous, fruity SYRAH from the northern RHONE. Whites are more variable still, ranging from flabby to fabulously fragrant MARSANNES. Look for wines from GRIPPAT and TROLLOT. 85 86 88 89 90 91. ***** 1988 Clos de L'Arbalestrier, Dr. Florentin £14 (ADN) **** 1990 A. Ogier Et Fils £7 (MWW).

St Julien (BORDEAUX, France) Aristocratic MEDOC Commune producing classic rich wines, full of cedar and deep, ripe fruit. See LEOVILLE BARTON, LEOVILLE LASCASES, DUCRU-BEAUCAILLOU, BEYCHEVELLE. 82 83 85 86 88 89 90.

St Nicolas de Bourgueil (LOIRE, France) Lightly fruity CABERNET FRANC; needs a warm year to ripen its raspberry fruit. Good producers include Jamet, Mabileau and Vallée. 85 86 87 88 89 90 92. ****1992 Dom. de Chevrette £8 (YAP).

St Péray (RHONE, France) AC near Lyon for full-bodied, still white and METHODE CHAMPENOISE sparkling wine, at risk from encroaching housing development. Often dull; never cheap. 89 90 91. *** St Péray nature £8 (YAP).

Ch St Pierre (BORDEAUX, France) Reliable ST. JULIEN fourth growth under the same ownership as GLORIA. **** 1982 £30 (ADN).

St-Pourçain-sur-Sioule (LOIRE, France) Red and rosé from GAMAY and PINOT NOIR, and the white from a blend of SAUVIGNON, CHARDONNAY and the local Trésallier. *** 1994 Saint Pourçain sur Sioule, La Ficelle £5 (YAP).

St Romain (BURGUNDY, France) High in the hills of the HAUTES COTES DE BEAUNE, a village producing undervalued fine whites and rustic reds 83 85 87 88 89 90 92. *** 1991 Clos Sous Le Chateau, Jean Germain £11 (D).

St-Véran (BURGUNDY, France) Once sold as BEAUJOLAIS BLANC; affordable alternative to POUILLY FUISSE, often as good – and better than most MACONAIS whites 90 91 92 93 **** 1993 Cuvée Prestige, Roger Lasserat £8.50 (OD) *** 1994 J Drouhin £8 (BEN, HAL).

Chateau Sainte Michelle (WASHINGTON STATE, US) Big winery producing increasingly impressive MERLOT, RIESLING AND SAUVIGNON. **** 1989 Chardonnay £10 (TAN).

Sakar (BULGARIA) Long-time source of much of the best CABERNET SAUVIGNON to come from Bulgaria. 86 88 89 90.

Sainte Croix-du-Mont (BORDEAUX, France) Neighbour of SAUTERNES with comparable though less fine wines. 83 85 86 87 88 89 90. **** Ch. des Tours 1990 £8 (ADN).

Saintsbury (California) Superstar CARNEROS producer of CHARDONNAY and – more specially – PINOT NOIR. (Hence the slogan: 'Beaune in the USA'). The Reserve Pinot is a world-beater. Garnet is the good value second label. ***** 1991 Carneros Reserve Chardonnay £17 (ADN, J&B) ***** Pinot Noir 1991 Reserve £20 (ADN, SOM, SEL, J&S).

Salice Salentino (PUGLIA, Italy) Spicily intense red made from the Negroamaro. Great value when mature. **** 1990 Candido £5 (DBY, L&W).

Salon le Mesnil (CHAMPAGNE, France) Small traditional subsidiary of LAURENT PERRIER with cult following for its pure, long-lived CHARDONNAY fizz from LE MESNIL, one of the region's best white grape villages. ***** 1982 £62 (C&B).

Samos (Greece) Aegean island producing sweet, fragrant, golden MUSCAT once called 'the wine of the Gods'. **** 1985 Samos Nectar £7 (GWC, NI).

San Luis Obispo (California) Californian region gaining a reputation for CHARDONNAY and PINOT NOIR. *** 1990 Wild Horse Pinot Noir £8 (OD).

San Pedro (CHILE) Well-established CURICO winery whose wines have been revolutionised by the arrival of Jacques LURTON in 1994 as consultant winemaker.

Sancerre (LOIRE, France) Much exploited AC, but at its best the epitome of elegant, steely dry SAUVIGNON. Quaffable, generally overpriced pale reds and rosés from the PINOT NOIR. Good producers include Jean-Max Roger, Bourgeois, Pierre Dezat, Crochet, Vacheron, Natter and Vatan. 91 92 93 94. **** 1994 Le Croix au Garde, Henri Pellé £8 (OD) **** 1993 Fortnum and Mason Sancerre, Vacheron £10 (F&M) **** 1993 Guy d'Argent, Dom. Serge Laloue £7 (ABY).

Sanford Winery (Southern California) SANTA BARBARA superstar producer of CHARDONNAY and especially distinctive, slightly horseradishy PINOT NOIR. ***** 1992 Sanford Pinot Noir £14 (BH, OD) **** 1991 Sanford Barrel Select Chardonnay £13 (BH).

Sangiovese The tobaccoey-herby-flavoured red grape of CHIANTI and MONTEPULCIANO, now being used increasingly in Vino da Tavola and in CALIFORNIA where it is seen as a lucrative alternative to CABERNET SAUVIGNON. See ANTINORI, ISOLE E OLENA, BONNY DOON. **** Atlas Peak Reserve Napa Sangiovese 1991 £13.50 (LAV, WIN, DBY) ***1994 Cecchi Sangiovese Cecchi £3 (VW, JS).

Sanlúcar de Barrameda (Spain) Coastal town neighbouring JEREZ, and the centre of production for MANZANILLA sherry.

Santa Barbara (California) Increasingly successful southern, cool-climate region for PINOT NOIR and CHARDONNAY. See AU BON CLIMAT and SANFORD, QUPE and OJAI.

Santa Cruz Mountains (California) Region to the south of San Francisco in which RIDGE and BONNY DOON produce some of the most exciting wines in California. **** 1992 Ridge Santa Cruz Mountains Cabernet £16 (ADN, DBY).

Santa Helena (CHILE) Improving second label of SAN PEDRO. *** Seleccion Directorio Oak-aged Chardonnay 1994 £5 (THP, WRW).

Santa Maddalena (ALTO-ADIGE, Italy) Eccentric high-altitude region whose often lederhosen-clad winemakers use grapes including the local Schiava to make refreshingly tangy red wine. *** 1992 i Viticoltori £6 (V&C).

Santa Rita (MAIPO, CHILE) Once almost the only big modern success story in CHILE; now overtaken by some of its competitors, including, ironically, CALITERRA and SANTA CAROLINA, two wineries at which Ignacio Recabarren, Santa Rita's former winemaker now holds sway. **** 1994 Medalla Real Chardonnay £7 (JS, BI, DBY, LAY, WIN) **** 1994 Merlot Reserva £5 (BI, ABY, DBY, F&M, LAY) *** Reserva Cabernet Sauvignon 1993 £5 (SMF, ADN, DIR, DBY).

Santenay (BURGUNDY, France) Village situated at the southern tip of the COTE D'OR, producing pretty whites and good, though occasionally rather rustic reds. 83 85 87 88 89 90 92. **** 1988 Santenay 1er Clos Tavannes £9 (ABY).

Caves São João (Portugal) Small company which produces high quality BAIRRADA.

Sardinia (Italy) Traditionally the source of good, hearty, powerful reds, robust whites and a number of interesting DOC fortified wines including **** 1991 Carignano del Sulcis Rocca Rubia Santadi £9 (SV, W).

Sassicaia (TUSCANY, Italy) World-class Cabernet SUPER TUSCAN which fascinatingly, like most good VINI DA TAVOLA contrives to have more of an Italian than a claret taste. ***** 1989 £55 (V&C).

Saumur (LOIRE, France) White and rosé METHODE CHAMPENOISE sparklers mostly from the CHENIN BLANC. Often dull enough to compete with CAVA. Langlois Chateau and Bouvet Ladubay make reliably clean and appley versions. Reds and pinks made from CABERNET FRANC can be pleasantly light. **** 1992 Saumur Blanc Vieilles Vignes Langlois-Chateau, £10 (MWW)
*** Saumur Mousseux Brut, Bouvet Ladubay, £8 (DBY, ES).

Saumur Champigny (LOIRE, France) Crisp, refreshing CABERNET FRANC red; like BEAUJOLAIS, serve slightly chilled. 85 86 88 89 90 92. **** 1986 Dom. Lavigne, Lavigne Père et Fils, Cuvée Medaille d'Or £7 (SEB).

Sauternes (BORDEAUX, France) Rich, honeyed dessert wines from SAUVIGNON and SEMILLON (and possibly MUSCADELLE) blends. Should be affected by BOTRYTIS but the climate does not always allow this. That's one explanation for disappointing Sauternes; the other: poor winemaking. See BARSAC, YQUEM , RIEUSSEC, CLIMENS, SUDUIRAUT BASTOR-LAMONTAGE.

Sauvignon Blanc White variety grown the world over, but rarely really loved: people find its innate 'grassy', 'catty', 'asparagussy', 'gooseberryish' character too much to handle. In France it has moved beyond its heartland of the LOIRE and BORDEAUX, and proven successful for SKALLI and HUGH RYMAN in VIN DE PAYS D'OC. NEW ZEALAND gets it tremendously right – especially in MARLBOROUGH, though the French hate the tropical fruit style it achieves there. In Australia, despite feeble early efforts by others, producers like KNAPPSTEIN, CULLENS, STAFFORD RIDGE, AMBERLEY and SHAW & SMITH are also right on target. California has been a relative disaster, as wineries have either banged the Sauvignon on the head with oak (as in the MONDAVI FUME BLANC) or made it sweet (as in KENDALL JACKSON). Ironically, E&J GALLO used to make a better version than most (theirs is sweet now too) and the flag is only being flown by wineries like MONTEVINA, Quivira, Dry Creek, SIMI and – in SEMILLON blends – from Guenoc and CARMENET. CHILE is making better versions every year, despite starting out with Sauvignon vines which proved to be a lesser variety. See CALITERRA, JOSE CANEPA Y CIA, VILLIARD. In South Africa, THELEMA and MULDERBOSCH are the star players, with NEIL ELLIS whose ELGIN wines are impressive too.

Sauvignon de St Bris (BURGUNDY, France) Burgundy's only VDQS, an affordable alternative to SANCERRE from the CHABLIS region. 89 90 91 92. *** 1993 Tricon, A Sorin £5 (TO, W).

Etienne Sauzet (BURGUNDY, France) Absolutely first rank white wine estate whose wines are almost unfindable outside collectors' cellars and the kind of Michelin-starred restaurants whose wine-loving guests take as much notice of prices as British royalty does of the cost of dogfood. 1993 Puligny-Montrachet £11 (THP).

Savagnin white JURA variety used for VIN JAUNE and blended with CHARDONNAY for ARBOIS. Also, confusingly, the Swiss name for the GEWURZTRAMINER. **** 1961 Château Chalon £41 (CEB).

Savennières (LOIRE, France) Fine, rarely seen, vigorous and characterful CHENIN BLANC whites, very long-lived. Coulée de Serrant and La Roche aux Moines are the top names. 82 83 84 85 86 88 89 90 92. *** 1991 La Roche aux Moines £11 (YAP) **** 1990 Coulée de Serrant £28 (YAP).

Savigny-lès-Beaune (BURGUNDY, France) Rarely seen whites and delicious plummy/raspberry reds. When at their best they can compare with the wines of neighbouring BEAUNE. 83 85 87 88 89 90 92. **** 1992 Drouhin £11 (OD) *** 1992 Domaine de la Perriere £13 (CWI).

Savoie (East, France) Mountainous region best known for crisp, floral whites such as Abymes, **APREMONT**, **SEYSSEL** and Crépy. **** Varichon et Clerc Carte Blanche £7 (L&W, D, C&B, J&B).

Scharffenberger (**MENDOCINO**, California) **POMMERY**-owned, independently-run producer of top class, top value fizz. **** Brut £9 (A).

Scharzhofberg (**MOSEL-SAAR-RUWER**, Germany) Top-class **SAAR** vineyard, producing quintessential **RIESLING**. *** 1993, Riesling Kabinett Rudolf Müller £5 (SMF).

Schaumwein (Germany) LOW-PRICED SPARKLING WINE.

> **Scheurebe** White grape, **RIESLING** x **SYLVANER** cross, grown in Germany and in England. Recogniseably grapefruity. *** 1994 Scheurebe Dienheimer Tafelstein Kabinett Dr. Becker £6.50 (SAF) **** 1987 Alois Kracher Scheurebe £20 (NY).

Schilfwein (Austria) LUSCIOUS 'REED WINE' — AUSTRIAN **VIN DE PAILLE** PIONEERED BY **WILLI OPITZ**. ***** 1992 Weisser Schilfmandl, Muskat Vin Paille, Willi Opitz £35 (half) (T&W).

Schloss (Germany) LITERALLY 'CASTLE', OFTEN (AS IN **CHATEAU**) DESIGNATING A VINEYARD OR ESTATE.

Schlossbockelheim (NAHE, Germany) Village which gives its name to a large NAHE BEREICH, and produces elegant, balanced **RIESLING**. Best vineyard: Kupfergrübe. **** 1993 Schlossböckelheimer Kupfergrübe Riesling Kabinett £9 (L&W).

Schloss Saarstein (**MOSEL-SAAR-RUWER**, Germany) High quality **RIESLING** specialist in Serrig. **** 1992 Serriger Riesling Kabinett £8 (SUM).

Schloss Vollrads (**RHEINGAU**, Germany) Well-thought-of (in Germany) Charta pioneer with a devout belief in German dry wines and the way they go with food. Sadly, the estate's own wines are rarely good enough to prove this case; ironically, the later harvest examples are more recommendable. **** 1989 Riesling Auslese White Gold £30 (EP).

Schlumberger (**ALSACE**, France) Great estate owner whose wines can rival those of the somewhat more showy **ZIND HUMBRECHT**. ***** 1989 Gewürztraminer Grand Cru Kessler £8 (half) (JN).

Scholl & Hillebrand (**RHEINGAU**, Germany) Reliable merchant belonging to Bernhard Breuer who markets his estate wines under the Georg **BREUER** label. A sensible **CHARTA** producer.

Scholz Hermanos (**MALAGA**, Spain) The most serious **MALAGA** producer. ***** Solera 1885 £8 (L&S) ***** Moscatel Palido £7 (L&S).

Schramsberg The winery responsible for putting Californian sparkling wine back on the quality trail, reviving classic grape varieties and techniques culled from France. Until recently, wines tended to be over-ripe and too big for their boots, possibly because too many of the grapes were from warm vineyards in **NAPA**. The J Schram is aimed at **DOM PERIGNON** and gets pretty close to the target. **** 1989. J Schram £22 (L&W).

> **Sciacarello** (**CORSICA**, French) Red grape variety, making smooth, aromatic, **RHONE**-style wine. 88 89 90 91 92.

Seaview (**SOUTH AUSTRALIA**) In the UK, the name of a clichéd boarding house and a sparkling wine brand belonging to **PENFOLDS**; in Australia a name to follow for well-made reds. Generally excellent value for money. **** Brut £6 (OD, MTL, BOO).

Sebastiani (**SONOMA**, California) Despite the **SONOMA** address, the main activity here lies in producing inexpensive, unexceptional wine from **CENTRAL VALLEY** grapes. Quality is improving however. The **ZINFANDEL** is the strongest suit. *** 1993 Cabernet Sauvignon, Sebastiani Vineyard £4.50 (MTL, NUR) *** 1993 Vendange Red £4 (MTL).

Sec/secco/seco (France/Italy/Spain) DRY.

Second Label (BORDEAUX, FRANCE) WINE MADE FROM A BORDEAUX CHATEAU'S LESSER VINEYARDS AND/OR YOUNGER VINES AND/OR LESSER CUVEES OF WINE. ESPECIALLY WORTH BUYING IN GOOD VINTAGES. See LES FORTS DE LATOUR.

Seifried Estate (South Island, NEW ZEALAND) Sold as Seifried Estate in NZ, the export label is REDWOOD VALLEY ESTATE. Hermann Seifried makes superb RIESLING especially LATE HARVEST style, and creditable SAUVIGNON and CHARDONNAY. With NEUDORF, demonstrates the potential of NELSON as one of New Zealand's best regions. **** 1994 Redwood Valley Sauvignon £38 (F&M, EP, MG) **** 1994 Redwood Valley Chardonnay £9 (EP, MG).

Sekt (Germany) Very basic sparkling wine best won in rifle booths at carnivals. Watch out for anything that does not state that it is made from RIESLING – other grape varieties almost invariably make highly unpleasant wines. Only the prefix 'Deutscher' guarantees German origin. *** Deutscher Sekt Privat £7 (WSC).

Selaks (AUCKLAND, NEW ZEALAND) A large (by NEW ZEALAND standards) and successful company based in Kumeu near AUCKLAND, best known for the excellent, piercingly fruity SAUVIGNON which was first made a decade ago by a young Aussie-trained Brit called Kevin Judd who went on to produce a little-known wine called CLOUDY BAY. **** 1994 Marlborough Sauvignon Blanc £7 (DBY, ADN).

Selbach-Oster (MOSEL-SAAR-RUWER, Germany) Archetypal MOSEL RIESLING *** 1991 Zeltinger Sonnenuhr Riesling Spätlese £8 (L&W).

Sélection de Grains Nobles (ALSACE, France) EQUIVALENT TO GERMAN BEERENAUSLESEN: RICH, SWEET BOTRYTISED WINE FROM SELECTED GRAPES. **** 1989 Tokay "Furstentum", P. Blanck £22 (half) (ADN).

Selvapiana (TUSCANY, Italy) Estate with 35 ha of vines in the CHIANTI RUFINA DOC which has gradually been modernised. A benchmark CHIANTI, an excellent VIN SANTO, & a terrific olive oil. **** 1992 Chianti Rufina £7 (EWC).

Sémillon Peachy grape blended with SAUVIGNON in BORDEAUX to give fullness in both dry and sweet wines, notably SAUTERNES and, vinified separately to great effect in Australia, though rarely as successful in other New World countries where many versions taste more like SAUVIGNON. CARMENET and GEYSER. See ROTHBURY, MCWILLIAMS, MOSS WOOD.
*** 1993 Leasingham Domaine Semillon, BRL Hardy Wine Co £6 (HBR, DBY, CWS) **** 1994, Neudorf Moutere Semillon £10 (ADN, SEL, SOM)
*** 1994 Fairview Semillon Chardonnay £5 (JS).

Seppelt (SOUTH AUSTRALIA) Old Australian firm now under the control of PENFOLDS. Pioneers of the GREAT WESTERN region of VICTORIA where they have made huge quantities of generally good sparkling wine though the Wannabe-CHAMPAGNE, Salinger, seems to be less good than it used to be. I'd rather spend my money on one of Seppelt's undeniable successes – the wonderful sparkling SHIRAZ (look for old 'Show Reserve' bottlings) and the rich Drumborg bubble-free version. **** 1985 Show Sparkling Shiraz £12 (OD).

Servir frais (France) SERVE CHILLED.

Setúbal Peninsula (Portugal) Home of the SETUBAL DOC, but now equally notable for the rise of two new wine regions, Arrabida and Palmela, where J M FONSECA SUCCS and J P VINHOS are making some excellent wines from local and international grape types. **** Moscatel Do Setubal 20 Yr Old, José Maria Da Fonseca Succs £12 (TAN).

Sèvre-et-Maine (MUSCADET de) (LOIRE, France) Demarcated area supposedly producing a cut above plain MUSCADET. (Actually, it is worth noting that this 'higher quality' region produces the vast majority of each MUSCADET harvest.) *** 1993 Ch du Cleray, Sauvion Et Fils, £7 (LNR, DBY).

Seyssel (SAVOIE, France) AC region near Geneva producing light white wines that are usually enjoyed in *apres-ski* mood when no-one is overly concerned about value for money. *** La Taconnière 1992 £6 (WSO).

> **Seyval blanc** Hybrid grape – a cross between French and US vines – unpopular with **EC** authorities but successful in eastern US, Canada and England, especially at **BREAKY BOTTOM**.

Shaw & Smith (**ADELAIDE HILLS**, Australia) Recently founded winery producing one of Australia's best **SAUVIGNONS** and an increasingly Burgundian **CHARDONNAY**. *** 1993 Chardonnay Reserve £12 (BOO, EWC) *** 1994 Sauvignon Blanc £10 (DBY, OD).

Sherry (Spain) The fortified wine made around **JEREZ**. Similar-style wines made elsewhere should not use this name. See **LUSTAU**, **GONZALEZ BYASS**, **HIDALGO**, **BARBADILLO**, **ALMECENISTA**, **FINO**, **ALMONTILLADO**, **MANZANILLA**, **CREAM SHERRY** and **SOLERA**.

> **Shiraz** The **SYRAH** grape in Australia and **SOUTH AFRICA**. See **WOLF BLASS**, **PENFOLDS**, **ROTHBURY**, **ST HALLETT**, **ROCKFORD**, **PLANTAGENET** etc.

Sicily (Italy) Best known for **MARSALA** and sturdy 'southern' table wine, but there is also an array of unusual fortified wines and a growing range of new wave reds and whites, many of which are made from grapes grown nowhere else. Watch this space. See **CORVO**, **DE BARTOLI**, **REGALEALI**, **TERRE DI GINESTRA**. **** 1993 Passito Di Pantelleria Pellegrino £10 (W, WSO, BH, W).

Siglo (**RIOJA**, Spain) Good brand of modern red and old-fashioned whites. *** 1991 Saco Red Rioja Bodegas Age £5 (MTL, DBY).

Silex (France) TERM DESCRIBING FLINTY SOIL, USED BY DIDIER **DAGUENEAU** FOR HIS OAK-FERMENTED **POUILLY FUMÉ**. ***** 1993 Pouilly Fumé Silex, Didier Dagueneau £23 (ABY).

Silver Oaks Cellars (**NAPA** California) Specialist **CABERNET** producers favouring fruitily accessible wines which benefit from long ageing in (American oak) barrels and bottle before release. **** 1989 Alexander Valley Cabernet £20 (T&W) **** 1989 Napa Valley Cabernet £22 T&W).

Simi Winery (**SONOMA**, California) **MOËT & CHANDON** subsidiary whose (ex-**MONDAVI**) boss Zelma Long is deservedly respected for her complex, long-lived Burgundian **CHARDONNAY**, archetypical **SAUVIGNON** and lovely blackcurranty **ALEXANDER VALLEY CABERNET**. In a properly ordered world, Simi would be one of the best-known wineries in California. **** 1990 Chardonnay £12 (C&B).

Bert Simon (**MOSEL-SAAR-RUWER**, Germany) Newish Estate in the **SAAR** river valley with super-soft rieslings and elegant **WEISSBURGUNDER**. **** 1985 Serringer Herrenberg Riesling Spätlese £6 (VW).

Simon Whitlam (**HUNTER VALLEY**, Australia) One of **ARROWFIELD**'s labels, used for their top of the range wines. Classy **CHARDONNAYS**. **** 1993 Show Reserve.

Ch Siran (**BORDEAUX**, France) Good, quite affordable **MARGAUX CRU BOURGEOIS**. **** 1989 £12 (THP).

Sin crianza (Spain) NOT AGED IN WOOD. 1994 Navajas Rioja £4 (MOR).

Skin contact THE LONGER THE SKINS OF BLACK GRAPES ARE LEFT IN WITH THE JUICE AFTER THE GRAPES HAVE BEEN CRUSHED, THE GREATER THE TANNINS AND THE DEEPER THE COLOUR. SOME NON-AROMATIC WHITE VARIETIES (**CHARDONNAY** AND **SEMILLON** IN PARTICULAR) CAN ALSO BENEFIT FROM EXTENDED SKIN CONTACT (USUALLY BETWEEN SIX AND TWENTY-FOUR HOURS) WHICH INCREASES FLAVOUR.

Slovakia Up-and-coming source of wines from grapes little seen elsewhere, such as the Muscatty **IRSAY OLIVER**. *** 1993 Grüner Veltliner Reh Group, £3 (W).

Smith Woodhouse (**DOURO**, Portugal) Part of the same empire as Dows, Grahams and Warres but often overlooked. Vintage ports can be good, as is the house speciality: traditional Late Bottled Vintage Port. Otherwise, the reliable supplier of most of British supermarkets' own-label ports. **** LBV £8 (OD).

Soave (VENETO, Italy) For the most part, dull white wine; Soave CLASSICO is better; single vineyard versions are best. Sweet RECIOTO di Soave is delicious. PIEROPAN and ANSELMI are almost uniformly excellent. 91 92 93. **★★★★** Soave Classico 1993 Tedeschi £4 (L&W, ADN, MWW) **★★★** 1994 Soave Campagnola £3 (HLV, W).

Ch Sociando-Mallet (BORDEAUX, France) A CRU BOURGEOIS which consistently produces carefully oaked, fruity red wines way above its status. 82 85 88 89 90 91.**★★★★** 1989 £16 (J&B).

Sogrape (Portugal) Big producer of Mateus Rosé and (relatively) modern DAO, DOURO and BAIRRADA. Wines to look out for include the Duque de Viseu, one of the most interesting of all Portuguese reds. **★★★** 1994 Mateus Signature White £4 (SEL) **★★★** 1991 Terra Franca Red £4 (GI, D).

Solaia (TUSCANY, Italy) The ANTINORI family have been making wine in Tuscany since 1365, and were instrumental in creating the SUPER TUSCAN Phenomenon. Solaia is a blend of CABERNET SAUVIGNON and FRANC, with a little SANGIOVESE. **★★★★★** Antinori 1987 £39 (V&C).

Solera AGEING SYSTEM WHICH INVOLVES A SERIES OF BUTTS CONTAINING WINE OF ASCENDING AGE, THE OLDER WINE BEING CONTINUALLY 'REFRESHED' BY THE YOUNGER. **★★★** Solera Manzanilla Pasada, Antonio Barbadillo £7 (WSO, HAR, C&B).

Felix Solís (VALDEPEÑAS, Spain) By far the biggest winery in VALDEPEÑAS, the most go-ahead, and, at the top of the range, perhaps also the best. **★★★** 1988 Safeway Oak Aged Valdepeñas £4 (SAF) **★★★** 1984 Vina Albali Tinto Gran Reserva £5 (SMF).

Somlo (HUNGARY) Ancient wine district, now source of top-class whites. See FURMINT.

Somontano (Spain) DO Region in the foothills of the Pyrénées in Aragon now experimenting with international grape varieties. **★★★★** 1992 Enate Crianza £6 (L&W, MWW).

Sonoma Valley (California) Despite the NAPA hype, this lesser known region not only contains some of the state's top wineries; it is also home to E&J GALLO's super-premium vineyard. The region is subdivided into the SONOMA, ALEXANDER and RUSSIAN RIVER Valleys and Dry Creek. Visibly very different to the NAPA; like the GRAVES and ST EMILION, this is a very easy place in which to get lost, looking for wineries like SIMI, CLOS DU BOIS, IRON HORSE, MATANZAS CREEK, SONOMA CUTRER, JORDAN, LAUREL GLEN, KISTLER, DUXOUP, Ravenswood, KENWOOD, QUIVIRA, Dry Creek, GUNDLACH BUNDSCHU, Adler Fels, ARROWOOD and CARMENET.

Sonoma-Cutrer (SONOMA, California) Single-Vineyard CHARDONNAY producer of the highest order. The Les Pierres Vineyard in particular frequently turns out wines that rank among the best in the world. **★★★★** 1990 Russian River Ranches Chardonnay £11 (WRW).

Marc Sorrel (RHONE, France) Long-established DOMAINE with two good red HERMITAGES (Le Gréal is the top cuvée) and an attractively floral white, **★★★★** 1990 Hermitage Blanc "Les Rocoules" £19 (ADN).

South Africa Oldest winemaking country in the New World (300 years), and increasingly the focus of interest today. Defining styles is tricky. Traditional reds which used to be left to dry out in big old casks are fast being supplanted by winemaking as modern as anywhere on earth. Unfortunately, there is still a tendency to pick grapes too early and consequently to produce wine with a recognisable unripe green flavour. First-class simple dry CHENINS and surprisingly good PINOTAGES; otherwise very patchy in quality.**★★★★** 1991 Kanonkop 'Paul Sauer' £11 (OD) **★★★★** Wildekrans Pinotage 1993, £7 (BI).

South Australia Home of almost all the biggest wine companies and still producing over 50% of Australia's wine, including most of the best known reds. The BAROSSA VALLEY is one of the country's oldest wine producing regions, but like its neighbours CLARE and McLAREN VALE, it increasingly faces competition from cooler areas like the ADELAIDE HILLS, PADTHAWAY and COONAWARRA.

South-East Australia A relatively meaningless regional description increasingly to be found on labels of (usually) lower price wines. Technically, it comprises NEW SOUTH WALES, VICTORIA and SOUTH AUSTRALIA and only omits TASMANIA and WESTERN AUSTRALIA.

> **Spanna** (Italy) The Piedmontese name for the NEBBIOLO grape and the more humble wines made from it. *** 1991 Spanna Del Piemonte, Agostino Brugo & Co £3 (OD).

Spätlese (Germany) SECOND STEP IN THE QMP SCALE, LATE-HARVESTED GRAPES MAKING WINE A NOTCH DRIER THAN AUSLESE.

Spritz/ig SLIGHT SPARKLE OR FIZZ. ALSO PETILLANCE.

Spumante (Italy) SPARKLING.

Staatsweingut (Germany) A State wine estate or domaine e.g. Staatsweingut ELTVILLE (RHEINGAU), a major cellar in the town of ELTVILLE.

Stafford Ridge (ADELAIDE HILLS, Australia) Fine CHARDONNAY and especially SAUVIGNON from LENSWOOD by the former chief winemaker of HARDYS. **** Lenswood Chardonnay 1993 £10 (OD).

Stag's Leap District (NAPA, CALIFORNIA) A long-established district of the NAPA Valley specialising in CABERNET SAUVIGNON. See Shafer, CLOS DU VAL, STAGS LEAP.

Stag's Leap Wine Cellars (NAPA, California) Pioneering supporter of the STAG'S LEAP appellation, and one of the winners of the 1973 Bordeaux v California tasting. Today, the best wines are the Faye Vineyard, SLV and Cask 23 Cabernets; others are sometimes disapointing. **** 1986 Stag's Leap Vineyard Napa Merlot £16.50 (CEB).

Stalky or stemmy FLAVOUR OF THE STEM RATHER THAN OF THE JUICE.

Steely REFERS TO YOUNG WINE WITH EVIDENT ACIDITY. A COMPLIMENT WHEN PAID TO CHABLIS AND DRY SAUVIGNONS.

> **Steen** (South Africa) Local name for (and possibly odd CLONE of) CHENIN BLANC Widely planted (over 30% of the vineyard area) but producing few wines of distinction.

Steiermark (AUSTRIA) An Austrian wine region more commonly known in England as Styria. Generally expensive dry whites in a lean austere style. Chardonnay is confusingly sold here as Morillon.

Georg Steigelmar (AUSTRIA) Producer of extremely expensive, but highly acclaimed dry whites from CHARDONNAY and PINOT BLANC and reds from PINOT NOIR and St Laurent. **** 1989 Chardonnay £14 (SEL).

Stellenbosch (SOUTH AFRICA) Very much the centre of the Cape wine industry; a beautiful university town full of delightful Cape Dutch architecture and flanked by craggy mountains. Many of the most famous traditional estates are to be found within fifteen miles of the centre of town and the bigger companies are sited here. See MEERLUST.

Sterling Vineyards (NAPA, California) Founded by British-born Peter Newton (now at NEWTON vineyards) and once the plaything of Coca Cola, this showcase NAPA estate today belongs to Canadian liquor giant Seagram, owners of MUMM and Oddbins. PINOT NOIR shows promise, there have been some good CABERNETS but there is work to be done on the quality here. At least prices are more realistic than is usual for NAPA. **** Sterling Vineyards Chardonnay, Napa Valley £6 (OD).

Stoneleigh (MARLBOROUGH, NEW ZEALAND) Reliable label owned by COOKS-CORBANS. **** 1993 Stoneleigh Chardonnay Corbans £7 (MTL, DBY, WR, BU).

Stoniers (VICTORIA, Australia) Small MORNINGTON winery proving remarkably successful with PINOT NOIR CHARDONNAY and MERLOT. (Previously known as Stoniers-Merrick). ***** 1993 Pinot Noir £8 (WAW, HOL, OD).

Structure THE 'STRUCTURAL' COMPONENTS OF A WINE INCLUDE TANNIN, ACIDITY AND ALCOHOL. THEY PROVIDE THE SKELETON OR BACKBONE THAT SUPPORTS THE 'FLESH' OF THE FRUIT. A YOUNG WINE WITH STRUCTURE SHOULD AGE WELL

Chateau de Suduiraut (BORDEAUX, France) SAUTERNES, consistently good, occasionally exceptional and promising greater things since its purchase by insurance-to-wine giant AXA. 85 86 88 90. ***** 1985 £20 (L&W).

Suhindol (BULGARIA) One of BULGARIA's best-known regions, the source of reasonable reds, particularly Reserve CABERNET SAUVIGNON. 88 89 90 91. **** 1990 Special Reserve Cabernet Sauvignon £4 (SV, JS, SAF).

Sulfites AMERICAN TERM NOW FEATURING AS A LABELLING REQUIREMENT ALERTING THOSE SUFFERING FROM AN (EXTREMELY RARE) ALLERGY TO THE PRESENCE OF SULPHUR DIOXIDE. CURIOUSLY, NO SUCH REQUIREMENT IS MADE OF CANS OF BAKED BEANS, BOTTLES OF KETCHUP OR JUST ABOUT EVERYTHING ELSE IN THE LARDER.

Sulphur Dioxide/SO2 ANTISEPTIC ROUTINELY USED BY FOOD PACKAGERS AND WINEMAKERS TO PROTECT THEIR PRODUCE FROM BACTERIA AND OXIDATION. NEW WORLD WINEMAKERS HAVE INCREASINGLY MASTERED THE ART OF REDUCING THE DOSES; SUPPOSEDLY TOP CLASS WHITE WINE PRODUCERS IN EUROPE, ESPECIALLY IN GERMANY, THE LOIRE AND BORDEAUX FREQUENTLY – AND UNFORGIVABLY – USE OBSCENE AMOUNTS, OFTEN SPOILING WHAT MIGHT OTHERWISE BE GREAT WINE. SULPHUR ABUSE IS RECOGNISABLE BY THE COUGH-INDUCING SMELL OF 'FREE' SO2 AND A HARD SHORT FINISH. IN WORSE CASES, CARELESSLY MADE WINES CAN SUFFER FROM COMBINED SULPHUR – H2S, OR HYDROGEN SULPHIDE – WHICH WILL MAKE THEM UNPALATABLY EGGY. A COPPER COIN CAN HAVE AN AMAZING EFFECT ON 'CLEANING UP' WINES WITH THIS FAULT.

Suntory (Japan) Japanese drinks conglomerate with substantial interests in various wineries around the world, e.g. FIRESTONE in California; Chateau La Grange in St Julien and Dr Weil in Germany.

Supérieur/Superiore (France/Italy) TECHNICALLY MEANINGLESS IN TERMS OF DISCERNIBLE QUALITY; DENOTES WINE THAT HAS BEEN MADE FROM RIPER GRAPES.

Sur lie THE AGEING 'ON ITS LEES' – OR DEAD YEASTS – MOST COMMONLY ASSOCIATED WITH MUSCADET, BUT NOW BEING INTRODUCED TO OTHER STYLES IN SOUTHERN FRANCE AND IN THE NEW WORLD. THE EFFECT IS TO MAKE WINE FRESHER AND RICHER AND POSSIBLY SLIGHTLY SPARKLING. *** 1994 Louis Chatel Blanc Sur Lie Domaines Listel, £3 (MWW, HAL, WMK).

Super Second ONE OF A SMALL GANG OF MEDOC SECOND GROWTHS: PICHON LALANDE, PICHON BARON, LEOVILLE LASCASES, DUCRU BEAUCAILLOU, COS D'ESTOURNEL; WHOSE WINES ARE THOUGHT TO RIVAL – AND COST NEARLY AS MUCH AS – THE FIRST GROWTHS. LIKE ANY OTHER CLIQUE, THE ORIGINAL MEMBERSHIP LIST LOOKS RATHER DATED NOW THAT CHATEAUX LIKE PICHON LONGUEVILLE and RAUSAN SEGLA HAVE TIDIED UP THEIR ACT. LEOVILLE BARTON ISN'T GREEDY ENOUGH IN ITS PRICING TO BE A SUPER SECOND, BUT THE WINE DESERVES TO BE CONSIDERED AS ONE – AS, IN THEIR WAYS DO LYNCH BAGES, PALMER, LA LAGUNE, MONTROSE AND BRANAIRE DUCRU.

Super Tuscan NEW WAVE VINO DA TAVOLA WINES PIONEERED BY PRODUCERS LIKE ANTINORI WHICH STAND OUTSIDE THE DOC RULES. GENERALLY BORDEAUX-STYLE BLENDS OR SANGIOVESE OR A MIXTURE OF BOTH.

Süssreserve (Germany) UNFERMENTED GRAPE JUICE USED TO BOLSTER SWEETNESS AND FRUIT IN GERMAN AND ENGLISH WINES.

Sutter Home Winery (NAPA, California) Home of robust red ZINFANDEL in the 1970's, and responsible for the invention of sweet 'white' (or as the non colour blind might say, pink) ZINFANDEL which has become such a phenomenal success in California and has incidentally helped to save this variety from the extinction it seemed to face a few years ago. *** 1989 Sutter Home Amador County Reserve Zinfandel £8 (MTL, DBY).

Swan Valley (WESTERN AUSTRALIA, Australia) Well-established, hot and generally unexciting vineyard area in which ports, sherries and port-like wines used to be made. Today, however, HOUGHTON use fruit from this region for their 'white Burgundy' and produce cooler-climate wines in the microclimate of MOONDAH BROOK.

Switzerland Produces, in general, enjoyable but expensive light, floral wines for early drinking. See DOLE, FENDANT, CHABLAIS.

Sylvaner/Silvaner White, relatively non-aromatic grape, originally from Austria but adopted by other European areas, particularly ALSACE and FRANKEN, as a prolific yielder of young, dry wine which can taste unrefreshingly earthy.**** 1993 Sylvaner, Zind Humbrecht £6 (ABY).

Syrah The red RHONE grape, an exotic mix of ripe fruit and spicy, smoky, gamey, leathery flavours. Skilfully adopted by Australia, where it is called SHIRAZ or HERMITAGE, and in southern France for VIN DE PAYS D'OC.

La Tâche (BURGUNDY, France) Wine from the La Tâche vineyard, exclusively owned by the DOMAINE DE LA ROMANEE CONTI. Frequently as good as the rarer and more expensive 'La Romanée Conti'.***** 1991 Domaine de la Romanée Conti p.o.a. (C&B).

Tafelwein (Germany) TABLE WINE. ONLY PREFIX 'DEUTSCHER' GUARANTEES GERMAN ORIGIN.

Chateau Tahbilk (VICTORIA, Australia) Defender of the faith of old-fashioned winemaking and wines in the GOULBOURN VALLEY. Great long-lived SHIRAZ from 100-year-old vines, surprisingly good, quite old fashioned Chardonnay and lemony MARSANNE which needs a decade. In particular, look out for the bargain second wine, Dalfarras.**** 1994 Marsanne £5.49 (OD)***** 1992 Chardonnay £6.49 (DBY, OD).

Taittinger (CHAMPAGNE France) Producer of reliable non-vintage and superlative Comtes de Champagne Blancs de Blancs. There are also special vintage offerings which come mummified in plastic with designs by modern artists and look no better than this description might lead you to expect.

Ch. Talbot (BORDEAUX France) Richly reliable if sometimes slightly jammy Fourth growth. The second wine, Connetable Talbot is a worthwhile buy. **** 1983 £21 (CEB).

Taltarni (VICTORIA, Australia) Run by Dominique Portet whose brother Bernard runs CLOS DU VAL in California. Rich and spicy, though – by Australian standards – understated SHIRAZ and, unsurprisingly, European-style CABERNETS. The sparkling wines are impressive too.
**** Brut Taché, £8 (ES, ADN, C&B)**** 1992 Merlot £9 (DBY).

Tannat Rustic French grape variety traditionally widely used in the blend of CAHORS and in South America, principally Uruguay.
*** 1991 Castel Pujol Cabernet/Tannat £5 (NI, JS).

Tannin ASTRINGENT COMPONENT OF RED WINE WHICH COMES FROM THE SKINS, PIPS AND STALKS AND HELPS THE WINE TO AGE.

Tardy & Ange (RHONE, France) Partnership of Charles Tardy and Mrs Bernard Ange producing top class wine in CROZES HERMITAGE at the Domaine de Entrefaux.**** 1993 Crozes Hermitage, Domaine des Entrefaux £6 (ABY).

Tarragona (CATALONIA, Spain) DO region of Spain south of PENEDES and home to many co-operatives. Contains the rather better quality separate DO region of TERRA ALTA.

Tarrawarra (YARRA VALLEY, VICTORIA, Australia) Pioneer of PINOT NOIR in the cool climate regions of the YARRA VALLEY. Well regarded but could do better. Second label is Tunnel Hill.*** 1994 Tunnel Hill Pinot Noir £8 (DBY).

Tarry RED WINES FROM HOT COUNTRIES OFTEN HAVE AN AROMA AND FLAVOUR REMINISCENT OF TAR. THE SYRAH GRAPE IN PARTICULAR EXHIBITS THIS CHARACTERISTIC.

Tartrates HARMLESS WHITE CRYSTALS OFTEN DEPOSITED BY WHITE WINES IN THE BOTTLE. IN GERMANY, THESE ARE CALLED 'DIAMONDS'.

Tasmania (Australia) Up-and-coming island vineyards (which are similar in climate to those of NEW ZEALAND), showing great potential, and producing increasingly impressive sparkling wine, CHARDONNAY, RIESLING, PINOT NOIR and even (somewhat herbaceous) CABERNET SAUVIGNON. Questions remain, however, over which are the best parts of the island for growing vines. (Look out for HEEMSKERK, Moorilla, PIPER'S BROOK and Freycinet).

Tastevin THE SILVER BURGUNDY TASTING CUP PROUDLY USED AS AN INSIGNIA BY VINOUS BROTHERHOODS (CONFRERIES), BADGE OF OFFICE BY SOMMELIERS AND AS ASHTRAYS BY WINE BUFFS. THE CHEVALIERS DE TASTEVIN ORGANISE AN ANNUAL TASTING OF BURGUNDIES, THE SUCCESSFUL WINES FROM WHICH ARE RECOGNISEABLE BY AN UGLY TASTEVINAGE LABEL. CHEVALIERS DE TASTEVIN OF A 'CONFRERIE' ATTEND BANQUETS, OFTEN IN MOCK-MEDIAEVAL CLOTHES. MEMBERSHIP DOES NOT INDICATE VINOUS EXPERTISE; MERELY THAT A BURGUNDY MERCHANT THOUGHT IT WORTH SHELLING OUT FOR AN INVITATION TO A BANQUET, AN INITIATION AND A NATTY OUTFIT.

Taurasi (CAMPANIA, Italy) Big, old-fashioned red from the AGLIANICO grape, needs years to soften and develop a characteristic cherryish taste. 83 85 88 89 90. **** 1987 Antonio Masteroberadino £13 (V&C).

Tavel (RHONE, France) Dry rosé, usually (wrongly) said to age well. Often very disappointing. Seek out young versions and avoid the bronze colour revered by traditionalists. 92 93 94. *** 1994 Domaine Mejan Louis Mousset £7 (U).

Tawny (Port) EITHER RUBY PORT THAT HAS BEEN BARREL-MATURED TO MELLOW AND FADE OR A CHEAP BLEND OF RUBY AND WHITE PORT. EXAMPLES WITH AN INDICATION OF THEIR AGE (eg 10-YEAR-OLD) ARE THE REAL THING. See DOWS, NIEPOORT, RAMOS PINTO, CALEM.

Taylor (Fladgate & Yeatman) (Oporto, Portugal) With DOWS, one of the 'First Growths' of the DOURO. Outstanding VINTAGE PORT for the last 40 years and – less creditably – creators of 'modern' LATE BOTTLED VINTAGE. They also own FONSECA and GUIMARAENS and produce the excellent Quinta de Vargellas SINGLE-QUINTA port. *** 1983 Vintage Port £20 (ES, ABY).

Te Mata (HAWKES BAY, NEW ZEALAND) Pioneer John Buck was not only one of the first to prove what NEW ZEALAND could do with CHARDONNAY (in the Elston Vineyard); but also how good its reds could be (his Coleraine). **** 1993 Elston Chardonnay £13 (DBY, ES, NY).

Tedeschi (VENETO, Italy) Two brothers based in VALPOLICELLA, crafting some rich and concentrated VALPOLICELLAS. Their AMARONES are particularly impressive. **** Tedeschi Valpolicella Classico Superiore 1991 £4 (L&W, MWW).

Domaine Tempier (BANDOL, France) Provence superstar estate, producing impressive single vineyard Bandols which support the claim of the Mourvèdre (from which they are largely made) to age.

Tempranillo (Spain) The red grape of RIOJA – and just about everywhere else in Spain, thanks to the way in which its strawberry fruit suits the vanilla/oak flavours of barrel-ageing. Until recently, its name rarely featured on labels, but new wave and FLYING WINEMAKERS are frequently anouncing its presence. In Ribera del Duero, incidentally, it is known as Tinto Fino, in the Penedes as Ull de Llebre in Toro as Tinto de Toro and in Portugal – where it is used for port – as Tinto Roriz. *** 1994 Rueda Hermanos Lurton £4 (TH, WR, BU).

Tenuta (Italy) ESTATE OR VINEYARD.

Terlano/Terlaner (TRENTINO-ALTO-ADIGE, Italy) Northern Italian village and its wine: usually fresh, crisp and carrying the name of the grape from which it was made. *** 1985 Cabernet Riserva Lageder £10 (EWC).

Teroldego (TRENTINO-ALTO-ADIGE, Italy) Dry reds, quite full-bodied with lean, slightly bitter berry flavours which make them better accompaniments to food. *** 1991 Teroldego Rotaliano Vigneto Pini Zeni £7 (DBY, ADN, DIR).

Terra Alta (CATALONIA, Spain) Small DO within the larger TARRAGONA DO, but producing wines of higher quality due to the difficult climate and resulting low yields.

Terre di Ginestra (SICILY, Italy) New wave Sicilian wine with plenty of easy-going fruit. *** 1994 £5 (V&C).

Terret (France) Suddenly fashionable white grape which, like MALBEC, used to be used in blends. Whether its lean, grassy style is as convincing when flying solo is less certain. *** 1994 Jacques Lurton £3 (SMF).

Tête de Cuvée (France) An old expression still used by traditionalists to describe their finest wine. *** Vouvray Tête de Cuvée Brut, Cave de Viticulture de Vouvray £8 (U).

Ch du Tertre (BORDEAUX, France) MARGAUX Fifth Growth recently restored to former glory by the owners of Calon Segur. **** 1993 £7 (NIC).

Thames Valley Vineyard (Reading, England) Home winery of Australian-born roving *enfant terrible* John Worontschak, FLYING WINEMAKER for Tesco and consultant to The Harvest Group, which is consistently at the cutting edge of English Wine production. *** 1994 Safeway Stanlake White £4 (SAF).

Dr H Thanisch (MOSEL-SAAR-RUWER, Germany) With WEGELER-DEINHARD, part-owner of the great Bernkasteler Doctor vineyard, the wines from which are sadly almost impossible to find. As an alternative, try the **** 1989 Bernkasteler Badstube Riesling Spätlese £10 (J&B).

Thelema (STELLENBOSCH, South Africa) One of the very best wineries in South Africa, thanks to Gyles Webb's skill as a winemaker and to a set of stunningly situated hillside vineyards. Chardonnay and Sauvignon are the strong suits.

Ch. Thieuley (BORDEAUX, France) Reliable ENTRE-DEUX-MERS producing quite concentrated SAUVIGNON-based, well-oaked whites, and a rather silky red. **** 1993 Ch Thieuley Cuvée Francis Courselle £9 (ES).

Vin de Thouarsais (LOIRE, France) VDQS for a soft, light red from the CABERNET FRANC; whites from the CHENIN BLANC. *** 1993 M. Gigon £6 (YAP).

Three Choirs (Gloucestershire, England) Named for the three cathedrals of Gloucester, Hereford and Worcester, this is one of England's leading estates – and one of the few to understand the value of marketing, with innovative ideas such as the launch of an annual English 'Nouveau' entitled 'New Release'. *** 1993 Three Choirs Estate Premium Dry £4 (W, SAF).

Tiefenbrunner (ALTO-ADIGE, Italy) Consistent producer of good varietal whites, most particularly CHARDONNAY and GEWURZTRAMINER. One of a small band of ALTO-ADIGE producers who are living up to some of the early promise shown by this region. **** 1992 Gewürztraminer £7 (ADN).

Tignanello (TUSCANY, Italy) ANTINORI's 80% Sangiovese, 20% Cabernet SUPER-TUSCAN, the partner to the BORDEAUX lookalike, SOLAIA, and a consistently good example of how happily the SANGIOVESE grape can work with new oak and CABERNET SAUVIGNON. Unlike most CHIANTI, well worth keeping – it should last for at last a decade. **** 1991 £21 (SV, C&B, HAR, WR).

Tinta Negra Mole Versatile and widely used MADEIRA grape traditionally found in cheaper blends instead of one of the four 'noble' varieties. Said to be a distant cousin of the PINOT NOIR.

Tocai (Italy) Lightly herby Venetian white grape, confusingly unrelated to others of similar name. Drink young. *** 1994 Tocai Via Nova £3 (V&C).

Tokay d'Alsace See PINOT GRIS.

Tokay/Tokaji (HUNGARY) Not to be confused with Australian Liqueur Tokay, Tocai Friulano or Tokay d'Alsace, Tokay Aszu is a dessert wine made in a specific region of Eastern Hungary (and a tiny corner of Slovakia) since the 17th century by adding measured amounts (Puttonyos) of ESZENCIA (a paste made from individually picked, over-ripe and/or nobly rotten grapes) to dry wine made from the local FURMINT and Harslevelu grapes. Sweetness levels, which depend on the amount of Eszencia added, range from 1-6 puttonyos, anything beyond which is labelled Aszu Eszencia. Not surprisingly, this last is often confused with the pure syrup which is sold – at vast prices – as ESZENCIA. The heavy investment (principally by French companies such as AXA and by VEGA SICILIA of Spain) has raised quality, international interest, and local controversy over the way Tokay is supposed to taste. Traditionalists like it OXIDISED like sherry. The newcomers and some locals disagree. Names to look for include the Royal Tokay Wine Co and DISZNOKO. **** 1990 Tokaji Aszu 5 Puttonyos The Royal Tokaji Wine Co. £16 (SV, RD).

Tollot-Beaut (BURGUNDY, France) Wonderful BURGUNDY domaine matching modern techniques and plenty of new wood with lots of rich fruit flavour. **** 1987 Corton Bressandes £24 (ABY).

Torcolato see MACULAN.

Torgiano (UMBRIA, Italy) Zone in UMBRIA and modern red wine made famous by LUNGAROTTI. See RUBESCO.

Toro (Spain) Region on the Portuguese border lying on the DOURO producing up-and-coming wines from the TEMPRANILLO. *** 1990 Tesco Toro Bodegas Farinas £4 (TO).

Torre de Gall (PENEDES, Spain) MOET & CHANDON's Spanish fizz. About as good as you can get using traditional CAVA varieties. But why use traditional CAVA varieties? Watch out for innovations, as Richard Geoffroy, MOET & CHANDON'S winemaker, is determined to get it right. **** 1990 Brut £8 (VW).

Torres Acclaimed, family-owned bodega based in PENEDES which, under Miguel Torres Junior, revolutionised Spain's table-wine production with reliable commercial labels like Vina Sol, Gran Vina Sol, Gran Sangre De Toro, Esmeralda and Gran Coronas, before attempting to perform the same trick in CHILE. Sadly, while Torres is still a leading light in Spain with wines like the Milmanda Chardonnay and Mas Borras (the new name for the old 'Black Label' Cabernet Sauvignon), in CHILE, where they were the first to introduce modern methods, they are now far from the front of the grid. Unlike in California where Miguel's sister Marimar is knocking everyone dead with her Pinot Noir and Chardonnay. ***** 1989 Gran Sangre de Toro £5.50 (MTL, CWS, WR, BU) **** 1990 Gran Coronas £7 (CWS, ES, BU).

Toscana (Italy) See TUSCANY.

Touraine (LOIRE, France) Area encompassing the ACs CHINON, VOUVRAY and BOURGUEIL. Also an increasing source of quaffable VARIETAL wines – SAUVIGNON, GAMAY DE TOURAINE etc. *** 1994 Touraine Sauvignon Domaine Joel Delaunay £5 (BBR).

Touriga (Nacional/Francesa) (Portugal) Red port grape, also (though rarely) seen in the New World.

Traminer Alternative name for the GEWURZTRAMINER grape, particularly in Italy and Australia. **** 1990 Alois Kracher Neusiedler See £10 (NY).

Trapet (BURGUNDY, France) See ROSSIGNOL TRAPET.

Trapiche (MENDOZA, ARGENTINA) Big, go-ahead producer with noteworthy barrel-fermented CHARDONNAY and CABERNET-MALBEC. **** 1993 Trapiche Medalla Tinto £9 (GI, M&S).

Tras-os-Montes (Portugal) Wine region of the Upper DOURO, right up by the Spanish border, source of BARCA VELHA.

Trebbiano (Italy) Ubiquitous white grape in Italy; less vaunted in France, where it is called UGNI BLANC. *** 1993 Riva Trebbiano di Romagna £3 (OD).

Trebbiano d'Abruzzo (Italy) a DOC region within Italy where they grow a clone of TREBBIANO, confusingly called Trebbiano di Toscana, and use it to make generally unexceptional dry whites. *** 1994 della Marche £4 (V&C).

Trentino-Alto Adige (Italy) Northern wine region combining the two DOC areas TRENTINO and ALTO ADIGE. TRENTINO specialities include crunchy red MARZEMINO, nutty white Nosiola and excellent VIN SANTO. **** 1994 Traminer Aromatico La Vis £4 (V&C).

Coteaux du Tricastin (RHONE, France) Southern RHONE Appellation, emerging as a source of good value, soft, peppery/blackcurranty reds. *** 1993 Cuvée Tradition Domaine de Grangeneuve £5 (OD).

F E Trimbach (ALSACE, France) Distinguished grower and merchant. **** 1989 Riesling Cuvée Frederic Emile £17 (MTL, DBY, BBR).

Trittenheim (MOSEL-SAAR-RUWER, Germany) Village whose vineyards are said to have been the first in Germany planted with RIESLING, making soft, honeyed wine. 76 79 83 85 86 88 89 90 91 92. *** 1992 Trittenheimer Altarchen Riesling Kabinett Weingut Grans-Fassian £6 (MWW).

Trocken (Germany) DRY, OFTEN AGGRESSIVELY SO. AVOID TROCKEN KABINETT FROM SUCH NORTHERN AREAS AS THE MOSEL, RHEINGAU AND RHEINHESSEN. QBA (CHAPTALISED) AND SPATLESE TROCKEN WINES (MADE, BY DEFINITION, FROM RIPER GRAPES) ARE BETTER. SEE ALSO HALBTROCKEN. *** 1993 Grans Fassian Riesling Trocken £5.50 (TO).

Trockenbeerenauslese (AUSTRIA/Germany) FIFTH RUNG OF THE QMP LADDER, WINE FROM SELECTED DRIED GRAPES WHICH ARE USUALLY BOTRYTIS-AFFECTED AND FULL OF CONCENTRATED NATURAL SUGAR. ONLY MADE IN THE BEST YEARS, RARE AND EXPENSIVE, THOUGH LESS SO IN AUSTRIA THAN GERMANY. *** 1991 Weinkellerei Burgenland Trockenbeerenauslese £8 (CWS, ADN, U).

Trollinger (Germany) The German name for the Black Hamburg grape, used in WURTTEMBERG to make light red wines.

Troncais (France) FOREST PRODUCING SOME OF THE BEST OAK FOR WINE BARRELS.

Tunisia Best known for dessert MUSCAT wines.

Cave Vinicole de Turckheim (ALSACE, France) First class cooperative whose top wines rival those of the best estates. **** Mayerling Brut Crémant d'Alsace, Cave de Turckheim £8 (BOO, DBY, U).

Vin de Tursan (South-West, France) VDQS whose big, country reds are now beginning to be seen in the UK. *** 1992 Ch de Bachen £9 (C&B).

Tuscany (Italy) Major region, the famous home of CHIANTI and reds such as BRUNELLO DI MONTALCINO and the New Wave of SUPER TUSCAN VINI DA TAVOLA. **** 1990 Altesino Palazzo Altesi Rosso £15 (DBY).

Tyrrell's (NEW SOUTH WALES, Australia) CHARDONNAY (sold as Pinot Chardonnay) pioneer in the HUNTER VALLEY, and producer of old-fashioned SHIRAZ and SEMILLON and even older-fashioned PINOT NOIR which tastes like BURGUNDY from the days when France still owned ALGERIA. *** 1990 Tyrrells Vineyards Private Bin Vat 1 Semillon £10 (AV).

> **Ugni Blanc** Undistinguished white grape in France which needs modern
> winemaking to produce anything better than basic fare. Curiously, in Italy,
> where it is known as the **TREBBIANO** it takes on a mantle of (spurious)
> nobility. For reasonable examples try **VIN DE PAYS DES COTES DE GASCOGNE**.

Ull de Llebre (Spain) Literally 'hare's eye'. See **TEMPRANILLO**

Ullage SPACE BETWEEN SURFACE OF WINE AND TOP OF CASK OR, IN BOTTLE, CORK.
THE WIDER THE GAP, THE GREATER THE DANGER OF **OXIDATION**. OLDER WINES
ALMOST ALWAYS HAVE SOME DEGREE OF ULLAGE, THE LESS THE BETTER.

Umbria (Italy) Central wine region, best known for white **ORVIETO** AND
TORGIANO. 88 89 90 91 92. ******* 1994 Orvieto Secco Bigi £4.50 (OD, V&C).

Umathum (**FAUENKIRCHNER, AUSTRIA**) Producer of unusually good red wines
including a brilliant St Laurent. ******* 1992 Von Stein St Laurent £17 (T&W).

Undurraga (**CENTRAL VALLEY, CHILE**) Founded in 1882, greatly improved,
independent family-owned estate. ******** 1994 Undurraga Chardonnay £5 (DBY).

Urzig (**MOSEL-SAAR-RUWER**, Germany) Village on the **MOSEL** with steeply
sloping vineyards and some of the very best producers, including Monchof
and **DR LOOSEN**. ******* 1993 Urziger Schwarzlay Riesling Kabinett £5 (L&W).

Utiel-Requeña (Spain) **DO** of **VALENCIA**, producing heavy red and good fresh
rosé from the Bobal grape.

Vacheron (**LOIRE**, France) Reliable, if unspectacular producer of **SANCERRE** –
including a better than customary red version made from the **PINOT NOIR**.
**** 1993 Sancerre Rouge Les Cailliers £10 (DBY, RD).

Vacqueyras (**RHONE**, France) **COTES DU RHONE** Village producing fine, full-
bodied, peppery reds which can compete with (pricier) **GIGONDAS**. 85 88 89
90 91. ******* 1992 Cave de Vacqueyras £6 (DBY, CWS).

Vajra (**PIEDMONT**, Italy) Producer of serious reds, including rich, complex
BAROLO. ******* 1989 Barbera D'Alba, Bricco delle Viole £8 (EWC).

Valençay (**LOIRE**, France) **AC** within **TOURAINE**, Near **CHEVERNY**, making
comparable whites: light, clean if rather sharp.

Vignerons du Val d'Orbieu (France) The face of the future. An association of
over 200 co-ops and growers in Southern France which competes with **SKALLI**
for the prize of most innovative source in the south of France. Not a name to
seek out in large print on labels, but one which may appear (via the initials
VVO on those of many retailers' better own-label wines) – and which now
features alongside that of **PENFOLDS** on a pair of blends called Laperouse on
which the French and Australians cooperated. ******** 1993 La Cuvée Mythique £6
(SAF, VW, JN) ******** 1994 Laperouse red & white £4.50 (SMF, W, SAF).

Val d'Aosta (Italy) Small, spectacularly beautiful area between **PIEDMONT** and
the French/Swiss border. Great for tourism; less so for wine-lovers.

Valais (Switzerland) Vineyard area on the upper **RHONE**, making good
FENDANT (**CHASSELAS**) which, for some, are the exceptions to prove the
innate dullness of that grape. There are also some reasonable – in all but
price – light reds. ******* 1994 Fendant du Valais £8.50 (C&B).

Valdeorras (Spain) a barren and mountainous **DO** in Galicia beginning to
replant with high quality native grapes. ******* 1993 Montenovo Tinto, Bodegas
Señorío £5 (ADN).

Valdepeñas (Spain) La Mancha DO striving to refine its rather hefty,
alcoholic reds and whites. Progress is being made, however, with
producers like los Llanos and **FELIX SOLIS**, particularly with reds. White
wine lovers will have to await the replacement of the locally widespread
AIREN. 89 90 91 92. ******* 1994 Casa de la Vina Cencibel £3 (DBY, SAF, FUL, U).

Valdespino (**JEREZ**, Spain) Old-fashioned sherry company that still uses
wooden casks to ferment most of their wines. Makes a classic **FINO**
Innocente and an excellent **PEDRO XIMENEZ**. ******* Waitrose Cream, £4.50 (W).

Valencia (Spain) Produces quite alcoholic red wines and also deliciously
sweet, grapey Moscatel de Valencia. ******** Safeway Moscatel de Valencia
Gandia £3.50 (SAF) .

Valpolicella (VENETO, Italy) Over commercialised light red wine which should – with rare exceptions – be drunk young to catch its interestingly bitter-cherryish flavour. Bottles labelled CLASSICO are better; best are RIPASSO versions, made by refermenting the wine on the LEES of an earlier vat. MASI make serious versions, as do ALLEGRINI, Boscaini, TEDESCHI, Le Ragose, Serego Alighieri GUERRIERI-RIZARDI and QUINTARELLI. BOLLA's run-of-the-mill Valpolicella is well, run-of-the-mill, but their JAGO is good. For a different experience, though, it really is worth paying more for a bottle of AMARONE or RECIOTO. 78 79 81 83 85 86 88 89 90.

Valréas (RHONE, France) Peppery, inexpensive red COTES DU RHONE village. 85 86 88 89 90 91. ******** 1993 Domaine de La Grande Bellane Jean Couston £8 (VER).

Valtellina (LOMBARDY, Italy) Red DOC from the NEBBIOLO grape, of variable quality. Improves with age. *** Valtellina Nino Negro 1988/9 £6 (V&C).

Varietal A WINE MADE FROM AND NAMED AFTER A SINGLE GRAPE VARIETY, eg CALIFORNIA CHARDONNAY. THE FRENCH AUTHORITIES WOULD LIKE TO OUTLAW SUCH REFERENCES FROM THE LABELS OF MOST OF THEIR APPELLATION CONTROLEE WINES. HOWEVER THE WORLD HAS LEFT THEM LITTLE ALTERNATIVE BUT TO COMPLY.

Vasse Felix (WESTERN AUSTRALIA) Classy MARGARET RIVER winery belonging to the widow of millionaire Rupert Holmes à Court and specialising in high quality reds. *** 1993 Margaret River Cabernet Sauvignon £12 (DBY, WIN).

Vaucluse (RHONE, France) COTES DU RHONE region producing good VIN DE PAYS and peppery reds and rosés from villages such as Vacqueyras. *** 1994 Vin de Pays de Vaucluse Blanc Cellier Du Marranon £3 (SAF).

Vaud (Switzerland) Swiss wine area on the shores of Lake Geneva, famous for unusually tangy CHASSELAS.

Vaudésir (BURGUNDY, France) Possibly best of the seven CHABLIS GRAND CRUS. *** 1992 Dom. des Malandes £15 (ES).

Vavasour (MARLBOROUGH, NEW ZEALAND) Pioneers of the Awatere Valley sub-region of MARLBOROUGH hitting high standards with BORDEAUX-style reds, powerful SAUVIGNONS and impressive CHARDONNAYS. Dashwood is the second label. **** 1994 Chardonnay £11 (DBY).

VDQS (France) VIN DELIMITEE DE QUALITE SUPERIEUR; OFFICIAL DESIGNATION FOR WINES BETTER THAN VIN DE PAYS BUT NOT FINE ENOUGH FOR AN AC. ENJOYING A STRANGE HALF-LIFE (AMID CONSTANT RUMOURS OF ITS IMMINENT ABOLITION) THIS NEITHER-FISH-NOR-FOWL CAN BE A SOURCE OF MUCH GOOD VALUE WINE – INCLUDING SUCH ODDITIES AS SAUVIGNON DE ST BRIS.

Vecchio (Italy) OLD.

Vecchio Samperi (Italy) Best MARSALA estate, belonging to DE BARTOLI. Although not DOC, a dry aperitif not too dissimilar to an AMONTILLADO sherry. *** 1990 Marco de Bartoli £8 (V&C).

Vega Sicilia (RIBERA DEL DUERO, Spain) Great reputation as Spain's top wine with prices to match. Wines are improving as the period of time spent in barrel is being reduced from what was often as long as a decade (excessive OXIDATION was often a problem for non-Spaniards) and it is easier to appreciate the intense flavour of the TEMPRANILLO-BORDEAUX blend. For a cheaper, slightly fresher taste of the Vega Sicilia style try the supposedly lesser Valbuena. **** 1984 Valbuena 5th year £31 (TAN).

Vegetal OFTEN USED OF SAUVIGNON BLANC AND CABERNET FRANC: LIKE 'GRASSY' CAN BE COMPLIMENTARY – THOUGH RARELY IN CALIFORNIA OR AUSTRALIA WHERE IT IS USED AS A SYNONYM FOR 'UNRIPE'.

Caves Velhas (Portugal) Large, traditional merchants who blend wine from all over the country to sell under their own label. Almost single-handedly saved the BUCELAS DO from extinction. *** 1980 Garrafeira £6 (SMF).

Velho/velhas (Portugal) OLD, AS OF RED WINE.

Velletri (Lazio, Italy) One of the many towns in the Alban hills (Colli Albani), producing mainly TREBBIANO and MALVASIA-based whites, similar to FRASCATI.

Veltliner See GRUNER VELTLINER.

Vendange (France) HARVEST OR VINTAGE.
Vendange Tardive (France) PARTICULARLY IN ALSACE, WINE FROM LATE HARVESTED GRAPES, USUALLY LUSCIOUSLY SWEET. ***** 1989 Gewürztraminer Goldert Dom Zind Humbrecht £30 (DBY, ABY).
Vendemmia (Italy) HARVEST OR VINTAGE.
Vendimia (Spain) HARVEST OR VINTAGE.
Venegazzú (VENETO, Italy) Good, quite understated claret-like VINO DA TAVOLA from the CABERNET SAUVIGNON; a sort of 'Super-Veneto' to compete with those SUPER TUSCANS. Needs five years. Look out too for the rather pricier black label. **** 1991 £9 (CWS, V&C, EWC).
Veneto (Italy) North-eastern wine region, the home of SOAVE, VALPOLICELLA and BARDOLINO. *** Girelli Vino da Tavola del Veneto Merlot £3 (CWS, W).
Côtes du Ventoux (RHONE, France) Improving source of everyday, country reds. 90 91 92 93 93. *** 1994 La Mission £3 (TH, WR, BU).

Verdejo (Spain) Interestingly herby white grape; confusingly not the VERDELHO of MADEIRA and Australia, but the variety used for RUEDA.

Verdelho White grape used for MADEIRA and white PORT and for tastily limey table wine in Australia. **** 1994 Moondah Brook Verdelho £5 (MTL) **** Cossart & Gordon 10 Year Old Verdelho, £14 (BOO, TH, WR, BU).

Verdicchio (MARCHES, Italy) Spicy white grape seen in a number of DOCs in its own right, the best of which – when made by Bucci – is VERDICCHIO DEI CASTELLI DI JESI. In UMBRIA, a major component of ORVIETO. 88 89 90 91. *** 1994 Verdicchio San Nicolo Brunori £6 (BI) .

Verdicchio dei Castelli di Jesi (MARCHES, Italy) DOC concentrating on the VERDICCHIO grape and aiming to make light, clean and crisp wines to drink with seafood. *** Le Vaglie Dei Castelli Di Jesi, Santa Barbera £8 (SAS).

Verduzzo (FRIULI-VENEZIA GIULIA, Italy) White grape making a dry and a fine AMABILE style wine in the Colli Orientali. *** 1990 Verduzzo di Ramandolo Dri (half) £15 (V&C).

Vermentino (Liguria, Italy) The spicy, dry white wine of the Adriatic and, increasingly, in Southern French VINS DE TABLE. *** 1993 Dolianova £4 (V&C).

Vernaccia White grape making the Tuscan DOCG VERNACCIA DI SAN GIMIGNANO (where it's helped by a dash of CHARDONNAY) and Sardinian Vernaccia di Oristano. At best with a distinctive nut 'n spice flavour. 90 91 92 93. *** 1994 Vernaccia de San Gimignano, Teruzzi & Puthod £8 (V&C).

Georges Vernay (RHONE, France) The great master of CONDRIEU who can do things with VIOGNIER that few others seem able to match. **** 1992 Condrieu, Coteau de Vernon £25 (YAP).
Veuve Cliquot (CHAMPAGNE, France) The distinctive orange label is back on form after a few years of producing a rather green non-vintage brut. The prestige cuvée is called Grand Dame after the famous Widow Cliquot. ***** 1985 Vintage Reserve £28 (TH, OD, L&W) *** Yellow Label Brut £21 (OD etc).
Victoria (Australia) Huge variety of wines from the liqueur MUSCATS of RUTHERGLEN to the peppery SHIRAZES of BENDIGO and the elegant CHARDONNAYS and PINOT NOIRS of the YARRA VALLEY. See these, plus MURRAY RIVER, MORNINGTON, GOULBURN VALLEY, GEELONG and PYRENEES.

Vidal (HAWKES BAY, NEW ZEALAND) One of NEW ZEALAND's top four red wine producers. *** 1992 Hawkes Bay Reserve Cabernet Sauvignon/Merlot £10 (VW, MTL) **** 1994 Sauvignon Blanc £7 (VW, MTL).

Vidal-Fleury (RHONE, France) RHONE grower and shipper, bought recently by GUIGAL. **** 1990 Côtes du Rhône Villages £7 (MWW).

VIDE (Italy) A MARKETING SYNDICATE SUPPOSEDLY DENOTING FINER ESTATE WINES.

Vieilles Vignes (France) WINE MADE FROM A PRODUCER'S OLDEST AND BEST VINES.

Domaine du Vieux-Télégraphe (RHONE, France) Modern CHATEAUNEUF-DU-PAPE domaine. **** 1992 £10 (L&W, ADN, TAN).

Ch Vieux Chateau-Certan (BORDEAUX, France) Ultra-classy, small POMEROL property producing reliable, concentrated, complex wine. **** 1985 £33 (BI).

Vignoble (France) VINEYARD; VINEYARD AREA.

Villa Banfi (TUSCANY, Italy) US-owned producer with a range of improving BRUNELLO and VINI DA TAVOLA. **** 1993 Rosso di Montalcino £6 (MWW).

Villa Maria (AUCKLAND, NEW ZEALAND) Beginning to produce some really world class reds under the guidance of KYM MILNE. **** 1994 Villa Maria Private Bin Sauvignon Blanc, Villa Maria Estate £6 (DBY, W, TO, W).

Villa Sachsen (RHEINHESSEN, Germany) Low yielding vineyards in BINGEN. *** 1993 Binger Scharlachberg Riesling Kabinett Halbtrocken £6 (TO).

Villages (France) THE SUFFIX 'VILLAGES' e.g. COTES DU RHONE OR MACON GENERALLY – LIKE CLASSICO ON ITALY – INDICATES A SLIGHTLY SUPERIOR WINE FROM A SMALLER DELIMITED AREA ENCOMPASSING CERTAIN VILLAGE VINEYARDS.

Villany (HUNGARY) Warm area of HUNGARY with a promising future for soft young drinking reds. *** 1994 Safeway Hungarian Cabernet £3.50 (SAF).

Vin de Corse (CORSICA, France) Apellation within CORSICA.

Vin de garde (France) WINE TO KEEP.

Vin de l'Orléanais (LOIRE, France) Small AC in the CENTRAL VINEYARDS of the LOIRE. See ORLEANNAIS. *** 1992 Vin d'Orléanais, Covifruit £5 (rouge & blanc) (YAP).

Vin de Paille (JURA, France) REGIONAL SPECIALITY; SWEET GOLDEN WINE FROM GRAPES DRIED ON STRAW MATS. *** 1990 Vin de Paille, Bourdy £20 (WSO).

Vin de pays (France) LOWEST/BROADEST GEOGRAPHICAL DESIGNATION; SIMPLE COUNTRY WINES WITH CERTAIN REGIONAL CHARACTERISTICS. SEE COTES DE GASCOGNE AND VIN DE PAYS D'OC.

Vin de Savoie See Savoie.

Vin de table (France) TABLE WINE FROM NO PARTICULAR AREA.

Vin doux naturel (France) FORTIFIED DESSERT WINES, BEST KNOWN AS THE SWEET, LIQUOROUS MUSCATS OF THE SOUTH, eg BEAUMES DE VENISE. **** 1991 Domaine de Coyeux Muscat de Beaunes de Venise £6 (WR, BU).

Vin du Bugey (SAVOIE, France) Formerly thin astringent whites of little merit, but becoming rather trendy in France as a source of fresh crisp CHARDONNAY. *** 1993 Chardonnay, Vin de Bugey, VDQS £6 (WSO).

Vin gris (France) CHIEFLY FROM ALSACE AND THE JURA, PALE ROSE FROM RED GRAPES PRESSED BEFORE, NOT AFTER, FERMENTATION.

Vin jaune (JURA, France) A speciality of ARBOIS, golden yellow, slightly oxidised wine, like a dry SHERRY. **** 1987 Ch. Chalon Bourdy £25 (WSO).

Vin Santo (Italy) Powerful white dessert wine from grapes dried after picking by hanging the bunches in airy barns for up to six years, especially in TUSCANY and TRENTINO. Best drunk with sweet almond biscuits. 85 87 88 89 90 91 92. **** 1988 Selvapiana £13.50 (50cl) (DBY).

Vin vert (France) Light, refreshing, acidic white wine, found in ROUSSILLON.

Vina de Meso (Spain) Spanish for house wine. Yllera Tinto 1989 £7 (WR).

Viña Pedrosa (RIBERA DEL DUERO, Spain) Modern wine showing what the TEMPRANILLO can do when blended with BORDEAUX varieties. The Spanish equivalent of a SUPER-TUSCAN.

Vina Pomal (RIOJA, Spain) Dull, unexceptionable RIOJA.

Vinho Verde (Portugal) Young, literally 'green' wine, confusingly red or pale white often tinged with green. At best delicious, refreshing, slightly fizzy 92. *** Asda Vinho Verde, Aveleda £3 (A) *** 1993 Trajadura £4 (TO).

JP Vinhos (Portugal) Excellent modern wine company that employs PETER BRIGHT as winemaker and makes a wide range of wines from all over Portugal. **** 1990 Tinto Da Anfora, J P Vinhos £5 (OD, W, SAF).

Vinícola Navarra (NAVARRA, Spain) Ultra-modern winemaking facilities and newly planted vineyards beginning to come on stream. Owned by the BODEGAS Y BEBIDAS group. *** 1991 Crianza Las Campanas Navarra £4 (OD)

Vinifera PROPERLY VITIS VINIFERA, THE SPECIES NAME FOR ALL EUROPEAN VINES.

Vino da Tavola (Italy) TABLE WINE, BUT THE DOC QUALITY DESIGNATION NET IS SO RIDDLED WITH HOLES THAT PRODUCERS OF MANY SUPERB – AND PRICEY – WINES CONTENT THEMSELVES WITH THIS 'MODEST' APPELLATION. **** 1992 Le Volte, Tenuta Dell'Ornellaia £8 (TH, WR, BU).

Vino Nobile di Montepulciano (TUSCANY, Italy) CHIANTI in long trousers; potentially truly noble (though often far from it), and made from the same grapes. Can age well to produce a traditional full red. Rosso di Montepulciano is the lighter more accessible version. The Montepulciano of the title is the Tuscan town, not the grape variety. 83 85 86 88 89 90 91. **** 1991 Vino Nobile di Montepulciano, Le Casalte £10.50 (EWC)

Vino novello (Italy) NEW WINE FROM THIS YEAR'S HARVEST, EQUIVALENT TO FRENCH NOUVEAU.

Vinos de Madrid (Spain) Wine area that gained DO status in 1990.

Vintage Champagne A WINE FROM A SINGLE, GOOD 'DECLARED' YEAR.

Vintage character (port) SUPPOSEDLY INEXPENSIVE ALTERNATIVE TO VINTAGE, BUT REALLY AN UP-MARKET RUBY MADE BY BLENDING VARIOUS YEARS' WINES. *** Sainsburys Vintage Character Port, Taylor Fladgate & Yeatman £6 (JS) **** Churchill's Finest Vintage Character Port £9 (SV, DBY, LEA).

Vintage (PORT) (DOURO, Portugal) ONLY PRODUCED IN 'DECLARED' YEARS, AGED IN WOOD THEN IN BOTTLE FOR MANY YEARS. IN 'OFF' YEARS, PORT HOUSES RELEASE WINES FROM THEIR TOP ESTATES AS SINGLE QUINTA PORTS. MUST BE DECANTED. 1991 LOOKS PROMISING. 70 75 77 80 83 85 91. See WARRE'S, DOW'S TAYLOR'S etc.

Viré (BURGUNDY, France) Village of MÂCON famous for whites. *** 1993 Cave De Viré £5 (TO). **** 1991 Macon Viré, Dom de Roailly, Henri Goyard £10 (THP).

Viticulteur (-Propriétaire) (France) VINE GROWER/VINEYARD OWNER.

Viura (Spain) White grape of the RIOJA region and elsewhere. *** D'Avalos Viura, Rioja 1993 £3 (WSO).

Côtes du Vivarais (PROVENCE, France) Light southern RHÔNE-like reds, a great deal of fruity rosé and occasional fragrant, light whites. *** 1992 Dom. du Belvezet, VDQS £4 (L&W)

Dom. Michel Voarick (BURGUNDY, France) Slow maturing old fashioned wines that avoid the use of new oak. The CORTON CHARLEMAGNE is particularly spectacular and hard to find.

Dom. Robert Vocoret (BURGUNDY, France) Classy producer of CHABLIS that is known for its ageability. **** 1991 Chablis 'Blanchot' £15 (MWW).

Volatile Acidity (VA) VINEGARY CHARACTER FOUND IN WINES WHICH HAVE BEEN SPOILED BY BACTERIA – AND ALSO IN SUBTLER, AND MORE ACCEPTABLE MEASURE IN MANY ITALIAN REDS, PENFOLDS GRANGE, PINOT NOIRS AND EISWEINS. ANYONE WHO HAS TASTED THE DIFFERENCE BETWEEN REALLY GOOD BALSAMIC VINEGAR AND THE STUFF MOST OF US PUT ON OUR CHIPS WILL APPRECIATE THE DISTINCTION.

Volnay (BURGUNDY, France) Red wine village in the CÔTE DE BEAUNE (the Caillerets vineyard was once ranked equal to le CHAMBERTIN). This is the home of fascinating plummy-violetty reds. Top producers include DE MONTILLE, POUSSE D'OR and LAFARGE. 85 86 87 88 89 90.

Volnay-Santenots (BURGUNDY, France) Once the equivalent of a GRAND CRU, now first among its peers as a PREMIER. A great vineyard under whose name can be sold some red wine from MEURSAULT. **** 1992 Volnay 1er Cru Santenots, Dom. Comtes Lafon £27 (L&W).

Vosges (France) FOREST WHICH IS THE SOURCE OF FINE OAK; LESS AROMATIC THAN ALLIER. GOOD FOR WHITE WINE.

Vosne Romanée (BURGUNDY, France) COTE DE NUITS red wine village with ROMANÉE-CONTI among its many grand names, and many other potentially gorgeous, plummy-rich wines, from producers like JAYER, Hudelot-Noellat and JEAN GROS. 85 86 87 88 89 90. **** 1991 1er Cru Les Suchots, Dom. Hudelot-Noellat £16 (HR) ***** 1989 Dom. Jean Gros £21 (WR, BU).

Vougeot (BURGUNDY, France) COTE DE NUITS Commune comprising the famous GRAND CRU CLOS DE VOUGEOT and a great number of growers of varying skill. 78 80 82 83 85 87 88 89 90 92. **** 1987 Clos Vougeot 'Musigni' Gros Frères £28 (J&B).

Vouvray (LOIRE, France) White wines from the CHENIN BLANC, ranging from clean, dry whites and refreshing sparklers to DEMI SECS and astonishingly honeyed, long-lived, sweet – MOELLEUX – wines. What a pity so many producers spoil it all with massive doses of SULPHUR DIOXIDE. See HUET. 69 71 75 76 83 85 88 89 90 92. **** 1990 Viticulteurs Du Vouvray £10 (U).

Wachau (Austria) Major wine region producing some superlative RIESLING from steep, terraced vineyards. **** 1993 Riesling Smaragd Durnsteiner Kellerberg, Freie Weingartner Wachau £8.21 (OD).

Wachenheim (RHEINPFALZ, Germany) Superior MITTELHAARDT village which should produce full, rich, unctuous RIESLING. 75 76 79 83 85 86 88 89 90 91 92 93. *** 1990 Bohlig Riesling Auslese Dr Bürklin-Wolf £17 (BBR).

Wairau River (MARLBOROUGH, NEW ZEALAND) Classic Kiwi white wines with piercing fruit character. *** 1993 Chardonnay, Marlborough £10 (TH, BU, WR) *** 1993 Sauvignon Blanc £8 (TH, WR, BU).

Walker Bay (SOUTH AFRICA) Promising region for PINOT NOIR and CHARDONNAY as more new wineries (like Wildekrans) begin to spring up. Established vineyards include HAMILTON RUSSELL and Bouchard Finlayson. **** 1992 Hamilton Russell Pinot Noir £8 (AV, CWS).

Warre (OPORTO, Portugal) One of the big seven PORT houses and the oldest of them all; this stablemate to DOWS, GRAHAMS and SMITH WOODHOUSE makes traditional PORT which is both rather sweeter and more tannic than most. The old fashioned LATE BOTTLED VINTAGE is worth seeking out too. ***** Warre's Vintage Port 1983 £18 (widely available).

Warwick (SOUTH AFRICA) Norma Ratcliffe manages to cram an amazing amount of fruit flavour and concentration into her improving red wines – making one each from CABERNET SAUVIGNON, MERLOT and CABERNET FRANC, and Trilogy, a blend of all three. **** 1991 Trilogy £9 (TH, WR, BU, RW).

Washington State (US) Underrated (especially in the US) state whose dusty, irrigated vineyards produce RIESLING, SAUVIGNON and MERLOT to make a NAPA VALLEY winemaker wince. **** 1988 Columbia Merlot, Columbia Winery £9.50 (F&M) *** 1993 Kiona, Late-Picked Reisling £6 (OD).

Wegeler Deinhard (RHEINGAU, Germany) One of the largest producers with estates all over Germany; they have taken the innovative step of leaving out the vineyard name from most of their labels. A large range of acceptable dry RIESLINGS and some of the best German sparkling wine. **** 1990 Wegeler Deinhard Rhinegau Riesling Spätlese £13 (JEH).

Wehlen (MOSEL-SAAR-RUWER, Germany) MITTELMOSEL village making fresh, sweet, honeyed wines; look for the Sonnenuhr vineyard and wines from the great DR LOOSEN, PRUM or WEGELER DEINHARD. 75 76 79 83 85 86 88 89 90 91 92 93. **** 1993 Dr Loosen Wehlener Sonnenuhr Riesling Spätlese £11 (ADN) **** 1983 Wehlener Sonnenuhr Riesling Auslese, Dr F. Weins-Prum Erben £9 (THP).

Dr R Weil (Kiedrich, Germany) Property now owned by SUNTORY whose investment is allowing it to produce stunning late harvest wines. ***** 1991 Kiedricher Grapenberg Riesling Beerenauslese £30 (BAR).

Weingut Germany) WINE ESTATE.

Weinkellerei (Germany) CELLAR OR WINERY.

Weissburgunder The PINOT BLANC in Germany and Austria. Relatively rare, so often made with care. *** 1990 Deinhard Pinot Blanc dry £4 (TH).

> **Welschriesling** Aka Riesling Italico, Ljutomer, Olasz, Lazki Rizling. A dull grape unrelated to the Rhine RIESLING, this variety comes into its own when Austrians have allowed it to be affected by BOTRYTIS.
> ***** 1990 Kracher Welschriesling £19 (NY).

Domdechant Werner'sches Weingut (RHEINGAU, Germany) Excellent vineyard sites at HOCHHEIM and RIESLING produce a number of traditional wines that age beautifully. *** 1985 Hocheimer Domdechaney Riesling Spätlese £8 (VW).

Western Australia (Australia) Varied state whose climates range from the baking SWAN VALLEY to the far cooler MOUNT BARKER and MARGARET RIVER. *** 1993 Tesco Western Australian Chenin Blanc, Moondah Brook £5 (TO) **** 1992 Plantagenet Mount Barker Cabernet Sauvignon £9.95 (WSO).

White port (DOURO, Portugal) Made from white grapes, an increasingly popular dry or semi-dry aperitif, though it's hard to say why, when vermouth's fresher and cheaper. Port producers tend to drink it with tonic water and ice. *** Delaforce Special White Port £9 (SEL).

Willamette Valley (OREGON, USA) The heart of OREGON's PINOT NOIR vineyards.

Wiltingen (MOSEL-SAAR-RUWER, Germany) Distinguished SAAR village, making elegant, slatey wines. Well-known for the SCHARZHOFBERG vineyard. 83 85 86 88 89 90 91 92 93.

Winkel (RHEINGAU, Germany) Village with an established reputation for complex, delicious wine, housing the famous SCHLOSS VOLRADS estate. 85 86 88 89 90 91 92 93.

Winzerverein/Winzergenossenschaft (Germany) COOPERATIVE.

Wirra Wirra McLAREN Vale winery making first class RIESLING, and CABERNET which in best vintages is sold as the Angelus. **** 1993 The Angelus £10 (OD).

Wolff-Metternich (Germany) Good rich RIESLING from the granite slopes of BADEN. *** 1992 Niersteiner Rosenberg Riesling Kabinett £7 (VW).

Wootton (England) Successful vineyard, noted for its SCHONBERGER but recently entering the commercial arena in a very un-English way with the highly marketable 'Trinity'. *** Trinity, Wootton Vineyard £4 (JS).

Wurttemburg (Germany) ANBAUGEBIET surrounding the Neckar region, producing more red than any other. Little seen in the UK.

Wyndham Estate (HUNTER VALLEY, Australia) Ultra-commercial winery which now belongs to Pernod Ricard. Quite what that firm's French customers would think of these jammy blockbusters is anybody's guess. *** 1992 Wyndham Estate Bin 444 Cabernet Sauvignon £6 (DBY) *** 1992 Wyndham Estate Oak Cask Chardonnay £6 (MWW).

David Wynn (South Australia) See MOUNTADAM.

Wynns (SOUTH AUSTRALIA) Subsidiary of PENFOLDS and top class producer of COONAWARRA CABERNETS (especially the John Riddoch) and buttery CHARDONNAY. The Ovens Valley SHIRAZ is another rich, spicy gem. ***** 1991 John Riddoch Cabernet Sauvignon £16 (VW, OD, BOO, DBY). **** 1991 Cabernet Sauvignon £7.50 (BOO, DBY, VW, OD).

> **Xarel-Lo** Fairly basic grape exclusive to Catalonia. Usually employed in the manufacture of CAVA, but successful in the hands of Jaume Serra. *** 1993 Xarel-lo Blanco, Jaume Serra £4 (BI).

"Y" d' Yquem (BORDEAUX, France) Hideously expensive dry wine of CH. D'YQUEM which, like other such efforts by SAUTERNES CHATEAUX is of greater academic than hedonistic interest. 85 88 90. **** 1988 £45 (J&B).

Yakima Valley (WASHINGTON STATE, US) Principal region of WASHINGTON STATE. Good for MERLOT, RIESLING and SAUVIGNON. COLUMBIA CREST, COLUMBIA WINERY, Ch. Ste Michelle. **** 1988 Columbia Winery Merlot £7.50 (BHJ, F&M, SEL).

Yalumba (SOUTH AUSTRALIA) Associated with HILL-SMITH, and the producer of good dry and sweet whites, serious reds and some of Australia's most appealing fizz, including Angas Brut, the brilliant Cuvée One Pinot Noir Chardonnay ***** £8 (TH, W, U etc) and the CHAMPAGNE-like Yalumba D. ***** 1991 The Menzies Cabernet Sauvignon £7 (LAV, WIN, JN, OD, JS). **** 1991 Family Reserve Botrytis Semillon £7.50 (LAV, WIN, JN) **** Museum Show Reserve Rutherglen Muscat £7 (TH, TO, VW, BEN, SOM).

Yarra Valley (VICTORIA, Australia) The fact that this historic wine district is the focus for 'boutiques' making top class BURGUNDY-like PINOT NOIR and CHARDONNAY for COLDSTREAM HILLS and TARRAWARRA shouldn't overshadow the fact that it has also produced some first class BORDEAUX-style reds and, at YARRA YERING, a brilliant SHIRAZ. *** 1991 Mount Mary Quintet £25 (AUC).

Yarra Yering (YARRA VALLEY, VICTORIA, Australia) Proving that this is not just a region for BURGUNDY varieties (though he does make an off-beat Pinot), Bailey Carrodus produces an ultra-rich, complex CABERNET blend including a little PETIT VERDOT ('Dry Red No 1) and a SHIRAZ (Dry Red No 2) in which he puts a bit of VIOGNIER. Underhill is the second label. **** 1992 Underhill Shiraz £12.50 (OD).

Yeasts NATURALLY PRESENT IN THE 'BLOOM' ON GRAPES, OR ADDED IN CULTURED FORM BY (USUALLY NEW WORLD) WINEMAKERS, THEY CONVERT SUGAR TO ALCOHOL, OR, IN SPARKLING WINES, CREATE CARBON DIOXIDE. SOME WINES, eg CHAMPAGNE AND MUSCADET — BENEFIT FROM AGEING IN CONTACT WITH THEIR YEASTS — OR SUR LIE. CHARDONNAY PRODUCERS INCREASINGLY LIKE TO INCREASE THE BISCUITY EFFECT OF THE YEAST ON THEIR WINES BY STIRRING THEIR BARRELS.

Yecla (Spain) DO region of Spain near VALENCIA producing mostly rough alcoholic reds. *** 1993 Viña Las Gruesas, Bodegas Castáno £4 (ADN).

Yonne (BURGUNDY, France) Wine department, home of CHABLIS. See under various CHABLIS growers' entries.

Chateau d' Yquem (BORDEAUX, France) Sublime SAUTERNES, not produced every year. 85 86 88 90. ***** 1986 £155 + (FAR etc).

Zell (MOSEL-SAAR-RUWER, Germany) Bereich of lower MOSEL and village, making pleasant, flowery RIESLING. Famous for the Schwarze Katz (black cat) Grosslage. 76 79 83 85 86 88 89 90 91 92.

Zentralkellerei (Germany) Massive, central cellars for groups of cooperatives in six of the ANBAUGEBIET — the MOSEL-SAAR-RUWER Zentralkellerei is Europe's largest Co-operative.

Zimbabwe The industry here started during the days of sanctions and involved growing grapes in ex-tobacco fields – now the quality is improving to a level of international adequacy. *** 1992 Mukuyo Flirt Rosé £4 (VER).

Zind-Humbrecht (ALSACE, France) Great perfumed, ultra-concentrated single-vineyard wines and good varietals. ***** 1992 Gewürztraminer Heimbourg £12 (ABY) **** 1991 Tokay Rotenburg Selection de Grain Nobles £50 (ABY).

Zinfandel (California) Versatile red grape producing everything from dark, jammy, leathery reds to pale pink, spicy 'BLUSH' wines. Also grown by CAPE MENTELLE in MARGARET RIVER, Australia. **** 1991 Fetzer Barrel Select Zinfandel £7.90 (LAV, WIN) **** 1991 Frog's Leap Zinfandel £10.65 (L&W, M&V, BOO) *** Tesco Californian White Zinfandel, Stratford Winery £4.29 (TO) ***** 1991 Ridge Vineyards 'Lytton Springs' Sonoma £15 (ADN).

Zweigelt Distinctive, berryish red wine grape more or less restricted to Austria. *** 1992 'Classique' Josef Pöckl £7 (NY).

COUNTRY CODES INDEX

Throughout The Merchants section and my Personal Selection of wines (p 23-29), the following abbreviations have been used to denote the countries of origin of the listed wines:

ARG	ARGENTINA
AUS	AUSTRALIA
A	AUSTRIA
BRA	BRAZIL
BUL	BULGARIA
CAN	CANADA
CHI	CHILE
CHN	CHINA
CZE	CZECH REPUBLIC
ENG	ENGLAND
FR	FRANCE
GER	GERMANY
GRE	GREECE
HUN	HUNGARY
IND	INDIA
IS	ISRAEL
IT	ITALY
LEB	LEBANON
MAD	MADEIRA
MAL	MALTA
MEX	MEXICO
MOL	MOLDAVIA
MOR	MOROCCO
NZ	NEW ZEALAND
POR	PORTUGAL
ROM	ROMANIA
RUS	RUSSIA
SA	SOUTH AFRICA
SLO	SLOVAKIA
SP	SPAIN
SWI	SWITZERLAND
US	OTHER USA

An invitation to join Robert Joseph on a journey of
epicurean delights.

WINE ON FILM:

THE GREAT AUSTRALIAN WINE VIDEO

PRESENTED BY ROBERT JOSEPH

During the 1994 harvest, Robert Joseph travelled throughout the
major winegrowing regions of Australia to produce the first truly
impartial, in-depth and wide-ranging video on Australian wine.

The 90 minute film, distilled from over 70 hours of footage,
includes interviews with over 50 of the most significant figures in
Australian wine and tastings by Robert Joseph of wines
representing the unique styles of particular regions and producers.

While the film is packed with information – including advice
from four of Australia's top chefs on what to eat with Australian
wines – it is also as down-to-earth and entertaining as anyone who
has met almost any Australian winemaker would expect.

Sunday Telegraph Good Wine Guide Reader Offer

£19.99
(including postage and packing)

Please send me ....copy(ies) of **The Great Australian Wine Video**
Name..
Address...
....
....Tel. ....

Please return to:
Paddy Mark, Vintage to Vintage Productions,
933 Fulham Road, London SW6 5JD. Tel/Fax (0171) 371 8019